TEXTBOOK OF INDUSTRIAL PHARMACY

TEXTBOOK OF INDUSTRIAL PHARMACY

DRUG DELIVERY SYSTEMS, AND COSMETIC AND HERBAL DRUG TECHNOLOGY

Edited by

Shobha Rani R Hiremath
M Pharm PhD
Professor of Pharmacy Practice and Pharmaceutics
Head, Department of Pharmacy Practice
Al-Ameen College of Pharmacy, Bangalore
(affiliated to RGUHS)

Universities Press

Textbook of Industrial Pharmacy

UNIVERSITIES PRESS (INDIA) PRIVATE LIMITED

Registered Office
3-6-747/1/A and 3-6-754/1, Himayatnagar
Hyderabad 500 029 (Telangana), India
e-mail: info@universitiespress.com

Distributed by
Orient Blackswan Private Limited

Registered Office
3-6-752, Himayatnagar, Hyderabad 500 029 (Telangana), India

Other Offices
Bangalore / Bhopal / Bhubaneshwar / Chennai
Ernakulam / Guwahati / Hyderabad / Jaipur / Kolkata
Lucknow / Mumbai / New Delhi / Noida / Patna

First published by Orient Blackswan Private Limited 2008
Reprinted and reissued by Universities Press 2008
Reprinted 2010, 2014

ISBN : 978 81 7371 639 3

Laser typeset at
Trinity Designers & Typesetters
Chennai 600 041

Printed in India at
Baba Barkha Nath Printers
Bahadurgarh, Haryana

Published by
Universities Press (India) Private Limited
1/24 Asaf Ali Road, New Delhi 110 002

Preface

The Indian pharmaceutical industry is one of the most successful among the science-based industries, with wide-ranging capabilities in drug manufacture and technology. It is currently involved in the manufacture of a variety of medicinal products, dosage forms, herbal formulations and cosmetics.

This book was conceived to reflect this branching of the pharmaceutical industry. *Textbook of Industrial Pharmacy* is divided into three sections: drug delivery systems, cosmetic technology and herbal drug technology. The contents of this book are an integral part of the syllabi prescribed by Indian universities and is aimed at undergraduates and postgraduates as well as PhD scholars, academicians and researchers.

Traditionally, pharmaceutics has consisted of conventional dosage forms such as tablets, capsules, liquid orals and parenterals. During the last three decades, however, formulations that control the rate and period of drug delivery and which target specific areas of the body have become increasingly common and complex. The pharmaceutical industry is now exploring the advantages of these **novel drug delivery systems** and knowledge about the same is the need of the day. Therefore drug delivery systems are a part of the present undergraduate and postgraduate curricula of industrial pharmacy in the country. This book covers important drug delivery systems, both traditional and new, and also methods of enhancing bioavailability and other optimisation techniques. Topics such as pilot plant scale-up, pollution control and effluent treatment which are of particular interest from an industrial perspective are also included.

A similar scientific approach has been followed for **cosmetic technology**. Several important concepts and information such as the raw materials used in cosmetics, concept of cosmeceuticals, formulation aspects of some important cosmetics, herbal cosmetics, quality control, stability, safety and regulatory aspects of cosmetics are explained in this book.

Worldwide there has been a resurgence in the use of traditional herbal drugs and, concurrently, a growing interest in the scientific investigation of their clinical efficacy and safety. Products based on the proven therapeutic utility of medicinal plants used in Ayurvedic medicine are being developed and approved as prescription drugs, over-the-counter preparations and even as nutraceuticals. Pharmacognosy plays an integral role in this process, ensuring the authenticity, purity and consistency of the materials being used and investigated.

Existing books on herbal drugs provide detailed information about theories and methodologies. These may not be applicable in the Indian context. Also, undergraduate students often experience difficulty in finding information and learning about herbal drug technology because of their complexity. To address these problems, this book only discusses relevant information and has been written in simple, straightforward language.

The main motivation behind this book was to cover all the important disciplines of industrial pharmacy under one umbrella at an affordable price to encourage students to read and learn. This has not been attempted previously and this book is thus unique in this respect.

Several authors have contributed to this book. I take this opportunity to thank them for their co-operation. I sincerely hope that this book will be useful to students and I request the readers to give their views and suggestions, if any, for future editions of this book.

Shobha Rani R Hiremath

Editor

Contributors

Mueen Ahmed KK, *M Pharm, PhD*
Assistant Professor
Department of Pharmacognosy
Al-Ameen College of Pharmacy
Bangalore

S Bharath, *M Pharm, PhD*
Professor
Department of Pharmaceutics
MS Ramaiah College of Pharmacy
Bangalore

Amit S Bhat, *M Pharm*
Assistant Professor
Bharat Institute of Technology (Pharmacy)
Hyderabad

Amit Kumar Das, *M Pharm*
Executive, Regulatory Affairs
PharmaLeaf India Pvt Ltd
Bangalore

N Sree Harsha, *MPharm, PhD*
Assistant Professor
CNK Reddy College of Pharmacy
Bangalore

Shobha Rani R Hiremath, *M Pharm, PhD*
Professor and Head
Department of Pharmacy Practice
Al-Ameen College of Pharmacy
Bangalore

K Vanaja
Senior Research Fellow
Indian Council of Medical Research (ICMR)
Department of Pharmacy Practice
Al-Ameen College of Pharmacy
Bangalore

Arun Kumar HS, *DBA, DVM, MVSc, PhD*
Centre for Research in Vascular Biology (CRVB)
Department of Medicine (Cardiovascular Sciences)
Bioscience Institute, University College, Cork
Ireland

S Narasimha Murthy, *M Pharm, PhD*
Assistant Professor
Department of Pharmaceutics
University of Mississippi
USA

KLK Paranjothy
Professor
Dept of Pharmaceutics
Al-Ameen College of Pharmacy
Bangalore

Praveen Saligram, *M Pharm, PhD*
Formulation R&D
Jubilant Organosys Ltd
Noida

HN Shivakumar, *M Pharm, PhD*
Professor
Department of Pharma Technology
KLE Society's College of Pharmacy
Bangalore

Contents

Section I: Drug Delivery and Industrial Pharmacy

SECTION III: HERBAL DRUG TECHNOLOGY

Dedication

This book is dedicated to my late father
Sri K Narasimha Murthy Rao, who made me what I am

SECTION I: DRUG DELIVERY AND INDUSTRIAL PHARMACY

1

Introduction to Novel Drug Delivery Systems

SHOBHA RANI R HIREMATH AND S BHARATH

Learning Objectives

At the end of this chapter, you will be able to:

- Define novel drug delivery systems
- List the advantages of novel drug delivery systems
- Describe the types of novel drug delivery systems

Introduction

For many decades, the treatment of an acute disease or a chronic illness has been mostly accomplished by the delivery of drugs to patients using various pharmaceutical dosage forms such as tablets, capsules, pills, suppositories, creams, ointments, liquids, aerosols and injectables. Even today, these conventional drug delivery systems are the primary pharmaceutical products commonly seen in prescriptions and which are available as over-the-counter medicines. These types of dosage forms are known to provide prompt release of drugs. Therefore, to achieve as well as to maintain the drug concentration within the therapeutically effective range needed for treatment, it is often necessary to take these dosage forms several times a day. This, however, results in a significant fluctuation in drug levels in the body.

The method by which a drug is delivered can have a significant effect on its efficacy. The slow progress in the treatment of certain diseases has suggested a growing need for a multidisciplinary approach to the delivery of drugs to their target sites.

Recently, several technical advancements have resulted in the development of new techniques for drug delivery. These techniques are capable of controlling the rate of drug delivery, sustaining the duration of therapeutic activity and/or targeting the delivery of drug to a tissue. These are referred to as novel drug delivery systems and they have revolutionised the method of medication, providing a number of therapeutic benefits. These drug delivery systems are based on an interdisciplinary approach that combines polymer science, pharmaceutics, bioconjugate chemistry and molecular biology.

Advantages of Novel Drug Delivery Systems

Novel drug delivery systems:

- Improve therapy by increasing the duration of action and reducing the side effects
- Increase patient compliance through decreased dosing frequency and convenient routes of administration
- Achieve targeting of drugs to a specific site to reduce unwanted side effects and obtain maximum efficacy
- Lead to reduction in dose and thus reduction in side effects of drugs

Types of Novel Drug Delivery Systems

Sustained/Controlled Delivery Systems

The term 'sustained release' is known to have existed in medical and pharmaceutical literature for many decades. It is used to describe a pharmaceutical dosage form formulated to retard the release of a therapeutic agent so that its appearance in systemic circulation is delayed and/or prolonged and its plasma profile is sustained in duration. The onset of its pharmacological action is often delayed, and the duration of its therapeutic effect is sustained.

The meaning of the term 'controlled release' on the other hand goes beyond the scope of sustained drug action. It implies a predictability and reproducibility in drug release kinetics, which means that the release of a drug takes place in a controlled fashion.

Drug release involves polymers that release the drug at a controlled rate by a process of diffusion out of the polymer or by degradation of the polymer over time. Controlled/Sustained release is achieved by using drug-carrying polymers that respond to specific stimuli such as exposure to light and changes in pH or temperature.

Controlled/Sustained release systems provide effective concentration for a long period of time. They lead to reduction in dosing frequency and thus improve patient compliance.

Some of these novel drug delivery systems are discussed below.

Hydrogels are three-dimensional, hydrophilic, polymeric networks capable of absorbing large amounts of water or biological fluids. The networks are composed of homopolymers or copolymers and are insoluble because of the presence of chemical or physical crosslinks (tie-points, junctions) such as entanglements or crystallites. Hydrogels exhibit thermodynamic compatibility with water, which allows them to swell in aqueous media. They are used to regulate drug release in reservoir-based controlled release systems or as carriers in swellable and swelling controlled release devices.

Approaches to the design of pharmaceutical products that improve the bioavailability of drugs with high first pass metabolism or significant gastrointestinal degradation are gaining interest. Design of innovative dosage forms to protect the drug from chemical or enzymatic degradation in the gastrointestinal tract is the need of the day.

Colloidal drug carrier systems, such as micellar solutions, vesicle and liquid crystal dispersions, microspheres, microparticle as well as nanoparticle dispersions consisting of small particles 10–400 nm in diameter, show great promise as drug delivery systems. When developing these formulations, the goal is to obtain systems with optimised drug loading and release properties, long shelf life and low toxicity.

Micelles, formed by the self-assembly of amphiphilic block copolymers (5–50 nm in diameter) in aqueous solutions, are generating great interest in drug delivery applications. The drugs can be physically entrapped in the core of block copolymer micelles and transported at concentrations that can exceed their intrinsic water solubility.

Microspheres are delivery systems that contain a matrix of the polymer in which the drug in micron size is uniformly dispersed. Microcapsules are those where the drug is coated with the polymers. Microcapsules and microspheres prolong drug release whereas microspheres are used for drug targeting in addition.

Liposomes are a form of vesicles that consist of many, few or just one phospholipid bilayer. The polar character of the liposomal core enables polar drug molecules to be encapsulated. Amphiphilic and lipophilic molecules are solubilised within the phospholipid bilayer according to their affinity towards phospholipids. Presence of nonionic surfactants instead of phospholipids in the formation of bilayers results in the formation of **niosomes.**

Nanoparticles (including nanospheres and nanocapsules of size 10–200 nm) can adsorb and/or encapsulate a drug, thus protecting it from chemical and enzymatic degradation. Nanocapsules are vesicular systems in which the drug is confined to a cavity surrounded by a unique polymer membrane, while nanospheres are matrix systems in which the drug is physically and uniformly dispersed. Nanoparticles as drug carriers can be formed from both biodegradable and non-biodegradable polymers.

Nanoparticles provide massive advantages regarding drug targeting, delivery and release and, with their additional potential to combine diagnosis and therapy, have emerged as one of the major tools in nanomedicine.

Mucoadhesives are synthetic or natural polymers that interact with the mucus layer covering the mucosal epithelial surface and mucin molecules. They can adhere to the gastric mucosa or the buccal mucosa. The concept of mucoadhesives has alerted many investigators to the possibility that these polymers can be used to overcome physiological barriers in long-term drug delivery. They render treatment more effective and safe, not only for topical disorders, but also for systemic problems.

Transdermal drug delivery is the administration of drugs across the skin. If the skin is the site of action then high concentration of drugs can be localised at the skin, thereby reducing the systemic drug levels and also cutting down the systemic side effects. Transdermal drug delivery is also an alternative route for the delivery of systemically acting drugs. This drug delivery route can have several advantages when compared with oral drug administration. For example, the liver is bypassed using this route, thereby enabling the dose to be reduced and the side effects minimised.

The field of **ocular** drug delivery is one of the most interesting and challenging endeavours facing the pharmaceutical scientist. This field has improved significantly over the past 10–20 years. These improvements have largely focussed on maintaining the drug in the eyes for an extended period of time unlike conventional eye drops.

The **nasal** route appears to be an alternative to parenterals for administering drugs intended for systemic effect in view of the rich vascularity of the nasal membranes, highly permeable structure for absorption and the ease of intranasal administration. Besides avoiding hepatic first pass elimination, the rate and extent of absorption and the plasma concentration versus time profile of the nasal route are comparable to that obtained by IV medication. Proteins such as insulin are reported to have fast and sustained action when administered through the nasal route.

Further research in the use of novel drug delivery systems for the delivery of biotechnology products and genes is underway.

Future Opportunities and Challenges

All of the abovementioned drug delivery systems have been successfully prepared and proved to have several advantages over the conventional dosage forms. However, there are many technological challenges to be met in developing novel drug delivery systems:

- Drug delivery systems that deliver large but highly localised quantities of drugs to specific areas to be released in controlled ways
- Controllable release profiles, especially for sensitive drugs
- Availability of materials for drug delivery systems that are biocompatible and biodegradable
- Advanced polymeric carriers for the delivery of therapeutic peptides/proteins (biopharmaceutics)
- Universal formulation schemes that can be used as intravenous, intramuscular or peroral drugs
- Cell and gene targeting systems
- User-friendly, lab-on-a-chip devices for point-of-care and disease prevention and control at home
- Better disease markers in terms of sensitivity

Key Messages

- Novel drug delivery systems are those that modify drug release, sustain the release or target the delivery of drug to the site of action.
- Sustained release of a drug involves polymers that release the drug at a controlled rate by diffusion out of the polymer or by degradation of the polymer over time.
- Controlled release delivery systems provide effective concentrations for a long period of time.
- Controlled/Sustained release systems lead to reduction in dosing frequency and thus improve patient compliance.
- The other novel drug delivery systems include microspheres, nanoparticles, micelles, liposomes, mucoadhesives, and transdermal, nasal and ocular systems.

Questions

1. What are novel drug delivery systems and what are their advantages over conventional dosage forms?
2. Name the different types of drug delivery systems.
3. What are the technological challenges to be considered during the development of novel drug delivery systems?

2

Controlled Drug Delivery Systems

SHOBHA RANI R HIREMATH AND S NARASIMHA MURTHY

Learning Objectives

At the end of this chapter, you will be able to:

- Describe the theory, advantages and disadvantages of controlled release dosage forms (CRDF)
- List the factors that determine the suitability of a drug for CRDF
- Explain the kinetics of drug release in different types of CRDF
- Describe the mechanistic principle behind the various controlled release (CR), oral and parenteral dosage forms
- Describe the design approach towards CR of drugs
- Provide an insight towards modern formulations/technologies of formulation of CRDF

Introduction

The optimal design of controlled release systems (CRSs) necessitates a thorough understanding of the pharmacokinetics and pharmacodynamics of drugs. The basic rationale behind controlled drug delivery (CDD) is the modification of the pharmacokinetics and pharmacodynamics of drugs by using novel drug delivery systems or by modifying the molecular structure of drugs and/or the physiological parameters inherent in a selected route of administration. The primary objectives of CDD are to ensure safety and improve the efficacy of drugs as well as patient compliance through better control of plasma drug levels and less frequent dosing.

Controlled Release Systems

'Controlled release systems' attempt to control the concentration of a drug in the target tissue (including plasma) or cells. 'Prolonged or sustained release systems' only prolong the therapeutic blood or tissue levels of the drug for an extended period of time.

Figure 2.1 shows the comparative blood drug level profiles obtained by administering drugs in the conventional, controlled and prolonged release dosage forms. A conventional tablet or capsule provides only one transient burst of the drug. As long as the concentration of the drug is above the minimum effective level, a pharmacological response will be observed. Problems occur when the therapeutic range is very narrow or when the peak is greater than the upper limit of this range. Indeed, one of the main purposes of CR is to improve safety and minimise the side effects of the drug by reducing fluctuations in drug level. Prolonged release dosage forms also reduce fluctuations in plasma drug levels by releasing the drug at a slower rate, thereby slowing down the absorption rate of the drug. In many cases, this is achieved by intermittently releasing a small burst of the drug over a prolonged period of time as in the case of repeat action dosage forms. All these terms—'controlled', 'prolonged, 'sustained'— are used interchangeably in textbooks as the technologies behind the formulation design of these types of dosage forms are similar in many respects. In this chapter, the term 'controlled release' has been used to represent different extended release dosage forms.

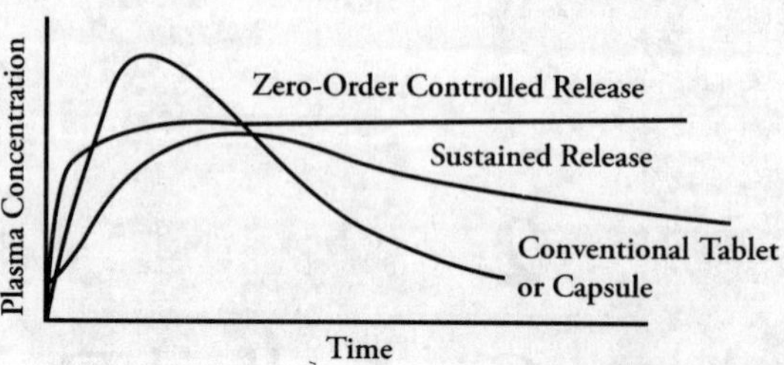

Figure 2.1: The hypothetical plasma drug concentrations resulting from different dosage forms

Figure 2.2 shows the hypothetical in vitro release pattern of drugs in different types of delivery systems.

To maintain a constant drug level in either plasma or target tissue, the release rate from the CRS should be equal to the elimination rate from the plasma or target tissue. The most conventional method used to achieve a constant plasma level is intravenous infusion (Fig. 2.3).

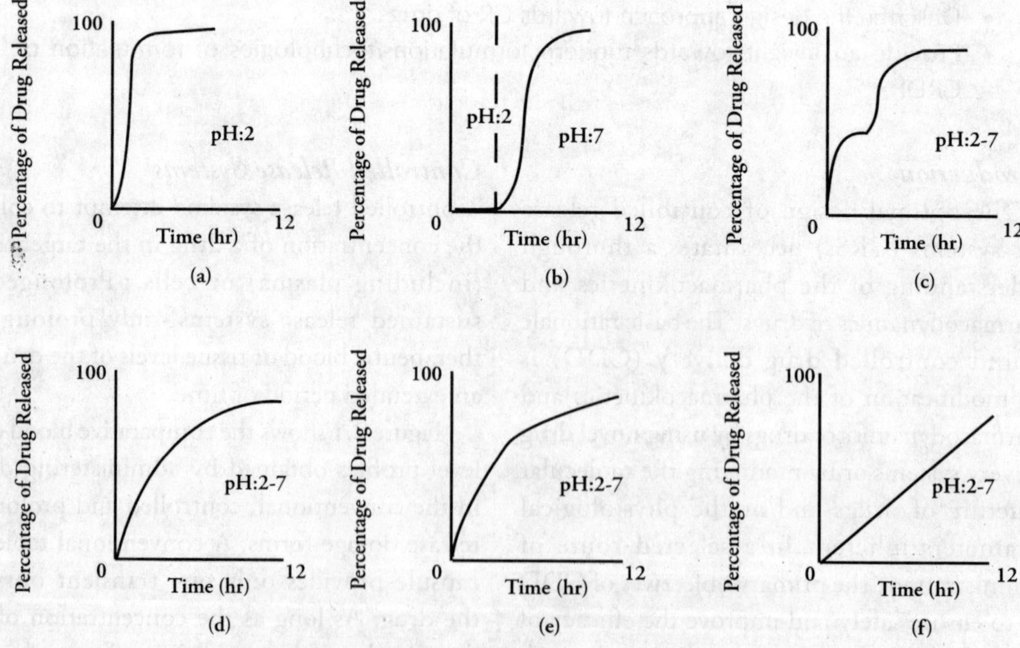

Figure 2.2: In vitro release pattern of (a) conventional, (b) delayed release, (c) repeated action, (d) prolonged action, (e) sustained release and (f) controlled release forms

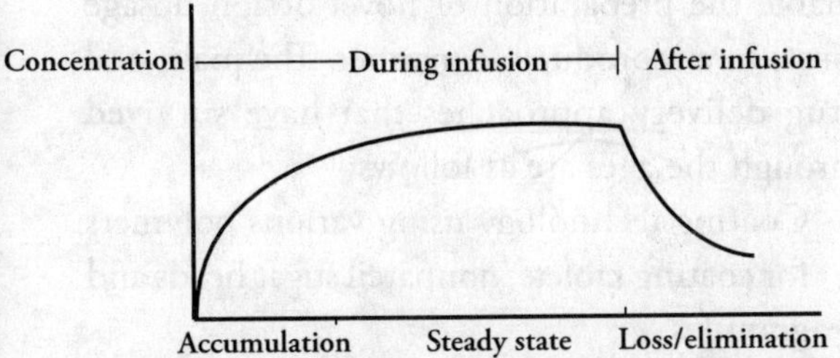

Figure 2.3: Different phases of plasma drug concentration time profile during IV infusion

Advantages of CRS

The CRS controls the release rate of the drug and prolongs activity, thereby reducing the frequency of administration. In addition, a smaller drug dose than that used in conventional systems is administered, thus avoiding accumulation of the drug beyond the minimum effective concentration. Therefore, the severity of the side effects is also proportionately less in CRS. Patient compliance is also better than in conventional systems because of the relative ease of use and reduced frequency of administration.

Disadvantages of CRS

- The CR dosage forms are often more expensive than the conventional dosage forms because of the use of polymers, biomaterials and special manufacturing techniques.
- In case of failure of the dosage form, the risk of dose dumping is present.
- There is reduced potential for dose adjustments.
- In case of oral CR systems, the drug release period is influenced and limited by the gastrointestinal (GI) residence time.

Selection of Drug Candidates for CRDF

Several factors determine the suitability of a drug for CRDF. Drugs that fulfil the following criteria are unsuitable for CRDF:

- Drugs with an elimination half life of <2 hours
- Drugs with an elimination half life of >8 hours (these drugs are sufficiently sustained in the body from conventional dosage forms and design of CR is generally not necessary)
- Drugs that are administered in large doses
- Highly potent drugs (they may prove risky in case of dose dumping as they have a narrow therapeutic window)

Drugs that satisfy the following criteria are considered as good candidates:

- Drugs with a dose of <100 mg
- Drugs with a half life of 3–6 hours and specifically defined minimum therapeutic levels
- Drugs with low protein binding properties
- Drugs that have a large therapeutic index
- Drugs with efficient GI absorption

Pharmacokinetic Requirements for CRS

The most common approach to achieving and maintaining therapeutic levels of drugs in the blood is to combine an initial, rapidly releasing drug fraction with a fraction released in zero order profile. Provided absorption is not rate limiting, the most rational approach to establishing relatively constant plasma drug levels is through zero order release of the drug to the absorption site, or through a combination of this release pattern with an initial, rapidly released fraction.

If the release of the drug from a maintenance dose fraction is zero order, the resultant blood level time course equation is unique for the estimation of the dose. The desired steady state blood level of the drug, $\bar{C}p_{ss}$, will be a function of the absorption rate constant, volume of distribution and elimination rate constant.

$$Cp_{ss} = k_0/(V \times k_{el}) \quad (1)$$

In other words, maintenance of a constant therapeutic drug level in the blood, Cp_{ss}, requires a release rate from the maintenance dose fraction, given by:

$$k_0 = Cp_{ss} \times V \times k_{el} \quad (2)$$

When the dosage form is designed to release the drug in zero order fashion over 'n' hours, the maintenance dose (MD) is given by:

$$MD = k_0$$

$$\text{'n'} = Cp_{ss} \times V \times k_{el} \times n \quad (3)$$

So ideally, if the release kinetics is zero order, the plasma concentration should increase linearly with the increase in the rate of release of the drug from the CRS.

Depending on the intent of the dosage form, the size of the immediate release dosage fraction may vary. If the desired steady state blood level must never be exceeded, then

$$LD = V\,Cp_{ss} \quad (4)$$

Controlled release drug delivery systems are designed for administration of the drug through various routes. In this chapter, the oral and parenteral drug delivery systems are discussed.

Oral Controlled Release Drug Delivery Systems

Controlled release technology evolved from matrix technology. Several articles in the 1950s and 60s reported the development of simple matrix tablets and monolithic granules. In 1952, SmithKline & French introduced the 'spansule', a timed release formulation that launched a widespread search for other applications in the design of dosage forms. Advances in oral controlled release technology have been attributed to the development of novel biocompatible polymers and machineries that enable the preparation of novel design dosage forms in a reproducible manner. The main oral drug delivery approaches that have survived through the ages are as follows:

- Coating technology using various polymers for coating tablets, nonpareil sugar beads and granules
- Matrix systems made of swellable or non-swellable polymers
- Slowly eroding devices
- Osmotically controlled devices

Physiological Limitations

Physiological factors influence the physicochemical nature and stability of the drug and its residence time in the various regions of the GIT as well. Some of the physiological factors that may limit the application of CR are as follows:

- Variable GI transit (food, activity, etc.)
- Rate limitation; absorption rate should exceed release rate
- Site limited absorption (active transport)
- Site dependent intestinal metabolism
- Concentration dependent first pass metabolism

Classification of Oral Controlled Release Drug Delivery Systems

The design and fabrication of oral systems can be classified based on the mechanism of drug release as:

- Dissolution controlled release
- Diffusion controlled release
- Diffusion and dissolution controlled release
- Ion exchange resins
- pH dependent formulations
- Osmotically controlled release
- Altered density formulations/Buoyant systems

Each of these oral systems is now discussed in detail.

Dissolution Controlled Release

A drug with a slow dissolution rate is inherently sustained. Good examples of such drugs are digoxin and griseofulvin. For drugs with high water solubility and, therefore, high dissolution rate, the solubility could be decreased through appropriate salt or derivative formation. However, the rate of drug dissolution may not meet the criteria for controlled release. Drugs with a high dissolution rate need to be *coated with polymers* at varying levels of thickness or be dispersed in the *polymeric matrix*. The rate of dissolution of the polymer determines the time of drug release in the case of the former. The rate of permeation of water into the matrix and rate of dissolution of the polymer in the fluid permeated into the dosage form determine the rate of drug release in the case of the latter.

The rate of dissolution of a solid in a solvent was described by Noyes and Whitney using the following relationship:

$$\frac{dM}{dt} = \frac{DS\,(C_s - C)}{h} \quad (5)$$

where dM/dt is the rate of drug dissolution, C_s is the solubility of the solid and C is the concentration of solid in the solvent at time t. 'D' is the diffusion coefficient of the solute in a solution, 'S' is the surface area of the exposed solid, and 'h' is the thickness of the diffusion layer.

This equation presumes the diffusion coefficient (D), the path length of diffusion (h) and surface area of the drug particle to be constant. However, as dissolution proceeds, all these parameters may change due to changes to the surface area of the particle.

For a drug powder that consists of uniformly sized particles, the rate of dissolution could be expressed by cube root law or using the Hixson–Crowell equation as:

$$M_0^{1/3} - M^{1/3} = \kappa t \quad (6)$$

or

$$dM/dt = \kappa \quad (7)$$

where M_0 is the original mass and M is the mass at time t. κ is called the cube root dissolution constant or Hixson–Crowell constant and dM/dt is the rate of dissolution of the particle.

Dissolution controlled CR dosages can be designed in the following forms:

1. ***Core Coat System:*** The drug particles, granules or tablets are coated with a polymer. The release of the drug is controlled by the dissolution rate of the polymeric coat. The particles may be coated to different levels of thickness, as the time required for the dissolution of the coat is a function of its thickness and the aqueous solubility of the polymer. The thickness of the barrier is regulated by the number of applied coatings to obtain the release characteristics.

   Some formulations are made by coating the drug onto a nonpareil seed or inert granule which is then coated with a polymer as shown in Fig. 2.4.

   A unit of this type contains hundreds of colour-coated pellets divided into 3–4 groups, differing in the thickness of the time delay coating. A typical mix consists of uncoated pellets, generally one-fourth to one-third of the beads, for a non-sustained form or for immediate release. The remaining three-fourths or two-thirds of the pellets are divided into groups of varying coating thickness to provide for sustained effect over the desired time period. Coated granules or drug particles can be placed in a capsule. Compressing the coated granules into a tablet involves the risk of fracture of the coat and interference of excipients with the release.

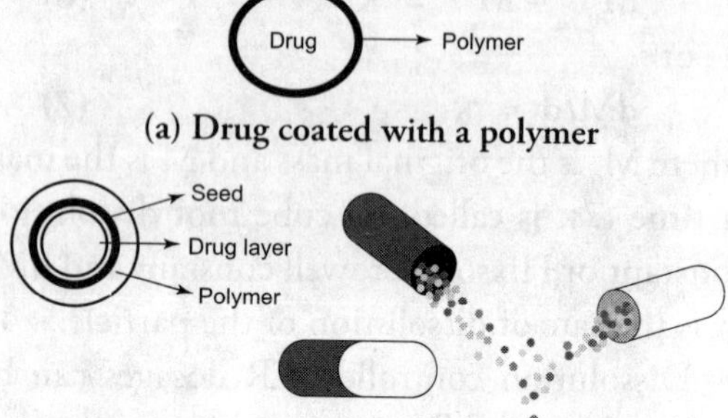

(a) Drug coated with a polymer

(b) Drug coated on an inert bead is coated with a polymer

Figure 2.4: Dissolution controlled drug delivery systems

2. *Embedded or Matrix Systems:* Here, the approach is to compress the drug with a slowly dissolving carrier into a tablet. The rate of availability of the drug is controlled by the rate of penetration of the fluid into the matrix. This in turn depends on the porosity of the tablet matrix, presence of hydrophilic/hydrophobic additives and wettability of the granule surface.
   a. *Wax matrix:* The drug is dispersed in the wax mixture by melting the wax. The wax-drug particles can be prepared by spraying the molten mixture into water (aqueous dispersion and congealing) or by using the congealing and sieving method. The release rate from these systems depends on the process, compression parameters and size of the particles formed.
   b. *Polymer matrix:* High viscosity hydrophilic polymers are blended with the drugs and are either granulated and/or directly compressed into a tablet. The tablet, when placed in the solvent medium, absorbs water and forms a viscous gel, which erodes, slowly exposing the drug to the surrounding medium. Sodium alginate, chitosan and cross-linked gelatin are used for fabricating erosion controlled systems. The surface area cannot be constant during erosion in the absolute sense, since the dosage form will become smaller on erosion; however, the tablets are designed to approach a constant value as closely as possible, Therefore the geometric shape of the dosage form is cylindrical, with a large diameter–height ratio as that would present a constant surface as the tablet dissolves, provided the diameter remains relatively constant (Fig. 2.5).

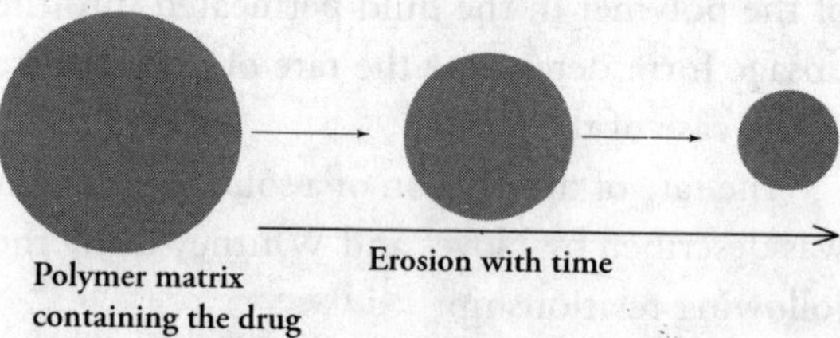

Figure 2.5: Erosion controlled drug release systems

Diffusion Controlled Release Systems

The rate controlling step that determines the release of drug in these systems is diffusion. The driving force that governs the rate of release of drug is the concentration gradient of drug between the dosage form and the bulk of the GI medium. There are basically two types of diffusion controlled drug delivery systems: reservoir and matrix.

Reservoir Devices

The core of the drug is encapsulated within a water insoluble polymeric material.

The permeability of the membrane depends on the nature of the polymer and the thickness of the coat/concentration of the coating solution. The drug will partition into the membrane and diffuse into the fluid surrounding the particle or tablet. Additional drugs will enter into the membrane, diffuse to the periphery and exchange with the surrounding media.

The rate of drug release from reservoir systems can be explained by Fick's Laws of Diffusion.

$$\frac{dM}{dt} = \frac{DSK\,(\Delta C)}{l} \qquad (8)$$

where S is the active diffusion area, D is the diffusion coefficient of the drug across the coating membrane, l is the diffusional path length (thickness of the polymer coat) and ΔC is the concentration difference across l. K is the partition coefficient of the drug between the polymer and the external medium.

To achieve a zero order release constant, all these factors need to be maintained at a constant value. However, in practice, due to variations in one or the other factors, a deviation from the zero order release pattern is observed.

Matrix Devices

In this system, a solid drug is dispersed in an insoluble matrix. The rate of drug release is controlled by the rate of diffusion of the drug and not by the rate of solid dissolution. Higuchi's equation explains the release from matrix devices:

$$\frac{dQ}{dt} = \left(\frac{DAC_S}{2t}\right)^{1/2} \qquad (9)$$

where 'A' is the total amount of the drug in the device, 'D' is the diffusion coefficient of the drug in the polymer, 'C_S' is the solubility of the drug in the polymer and 't' is time.

This equation is simplified to:

$$Q = kt^{1/2} \qquad (10)$$

A graph of the amount of drug released (Q) versus the square root of time would be linear if drug release from the matrix is diffusion controlled. A zero order release is not commonly achieved in vivo using these systems, because of the changing diffusion path lengths.

Matrix granules and tablets can be formulated with hydrophilic polymers such as hydroxypropylmethyl cellulose (HPMC), carboxymethyl cellulose (CMC) and xanthan gum, which swell and form a high viscosity gel around the bead/tablet surface. These polymers can form network structures either by chemical cross-linking or by physical interactions such as electrostatic interactions or hydrogen bonding. These materials absorb large amounts of water, but still maintain a distinct three-dimensional structure, leading to the formation of hydrogels. Because of their high water content, many of these materials have excellent biocompatibility. They also provide a protein-friendly environment—increasingly vital as proteins become more important in pharmaceutical technology.

The matrix system may be incorporated with channelising agents to increase the permeability of the system to water that allows the formation of aqueous channels for diffusion of the drug. The channelising agents form a porous matrix and hence, Higuchi's equation is modified to account for the porosity and tortuosity of the matrix (ε).

$$\frac{dM}{dt} = \frac{D\varepsilon}{\tau}\,(2A - \varepsilon\, C_s)\, C_s t \qquad (11)$$

where ε is the total porosity of the matrix and is often calculated by (ε = A/ρ). A is the total concentration of the drug (amount/unit volume) dissolved and undissolved in the matrix. ρ is the density of the drug.

The reservoir and matrix systems can contain the immediate release dosage of the drug or the loading dose of the drug in a separate, rapidly dissolving coating or layer. This layer dissolves rapidly and releases the loading dose of the drug to the site of absorption. The reservoir or matrix controlled release layer thus releases the drug in a controlled fashion.

Diffusion and Dissolution Controlled Systems

In diffusion and dissolution controlled systems, both dissolution and diffusion from the delivery system significantly affect the net release of the drug.

Partially Soluble Membrane System: The drug is encapsulated in a partially soluble polymer (a polymer that has domains that dissolve with time). The drug diffuses through the pores in the polymer coat (Fig. 2.6).

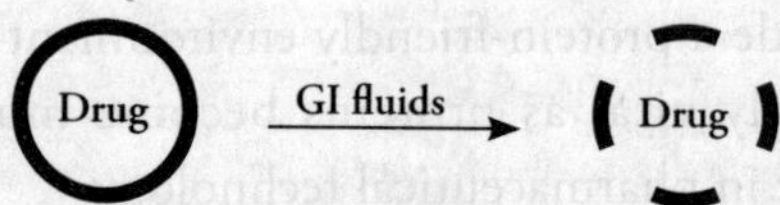

Figure 2.6: Partially soluble membrane system

For example, a cellulose acetate and HPMC (low viscosity) mixture is coated onto the drug particles. HPMC being water-soluble dissolves and creates a microporous cellulose acetate membrane through which the drug diffuses. Here, the drug release is controlled by the rate of dissolution of HPMC as well as the diffusion rate of the drug across the porous cellulose acetate membrane.

Matrix Systems

Matrix systems encapsulate the drug in a membrane coating, where the dissolution of the drug in the fluid that penetrates into the core and diffusion of the drug from the core across the polymer membrane makes for a diffusion and dissolution controlled system. The drug is sparingly soluble in this case, so the release rate is slow and has significant influence on the diffusion of drug across the membrane.

Burst Release

In many of the controlled release formulations, immediately upon placement in the release medium, an initial large bolus of drug is released before the release rate reaches a stable profile. This phenomenon is typically referred to as 'burst release'. As shown in Fig. 2.7, the burst release leads to higher initial drug delivery and also reduces the effective lifetime of the device. The burst release takes place in a very short period of time when compared to the entire release process.

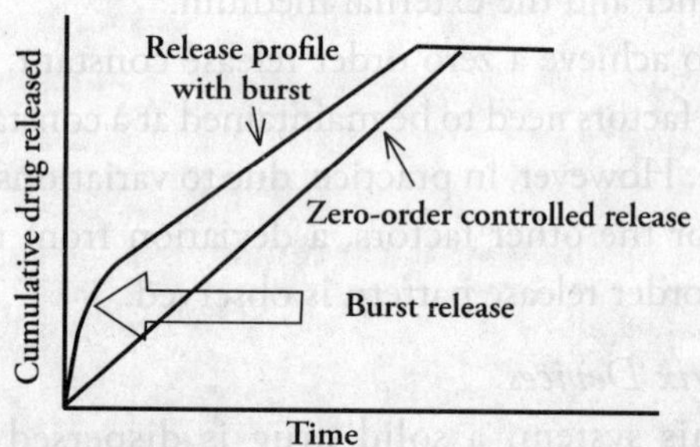

Figure 2.7: Release profile from controlled release formulations showing the burst release effect

The burst release has been attributed to a variety of physical, chemical and processing parameters. For many applications, small burst quantities may be acceptable as long as the burst release is predictable. However, research is focussed on preventing unfavourable or unpredictable burst release of drugs.

Ion Exchange Resins

The ion exchange principles involve the administration of salts of drugs with an ion exchange polymer. There are two major classes of ion exchange polymers: cation exchangers whose functional groups can undergo reactions with cations of the surrounding solution and anionic exchangers whose functional groups can undergo reactions with the anions of a surrounding solution. The drugs that are suitable for resinate preparations include those with acidic or basic proper groups in their chemical structure and those that could be absorbed in all regions of the GI tract.

Anionic exchange resins involve basic functional groups (usually a polyamine) capable of removing anions from acidic solutions. Cation exchange resins contain acidic functional groups. Although their exact composition may vary, they usually contain polystyrene polymers with sulfonic, carboxylic or phenolic groups.

The use of ion exchange resins to prolong the effect of drugs is based on the principle that positively or negatively charged therapeutic molecules combined with appropriate resins yield insoluble poly salt resonates.

$$R\text{-}NH_3^+OH^- + B\text{-}COOH \text{ --- } R\text{-}NH_3^+ \, B\text{-}COO^- + H_2O$$

(1) (2) (3)

where, (1) represents the resin with an anion exchange group and (2) is an anionic drug. The drug is complexed with the resin by the anion exchange process (3).

The drug-resin complexes administered orally are likely to spend about 2 hours in the stomach and about 6 hours in the intestine. They release the drug in the GI fluids at a controlled rate that is determined by the rate of exchange of the common ion with the drug.

In the stomach

$$R\text{-}NH_3^+ \, B\text{-}COO^- + HCl \text{ ---- } R\text{-}NH_3^+ \, Cl^- + B\text{-}COOH$$

In the intestine

$$R\text{-}NH_3^+ \, B\text{-}COO^- + NaCl \text{ --- } R\text{-}NH_3^+ \, Cl^- + B\text{-}COONa$$

The ion exchange and release rate of the drug is in turn determined by factors such as particle size and form, porosity and swelling, cross-linkage, available capacity and acid base strength.

Since ions are required to start this process, ion-free sustained release liquid formulations can be prepared. This simple principle has been used to formulate 12-hour oral, liquid, drug delivery systems for antitussives and decongestants.

The drug-resin complex granules are further treated with an impregnating agent, for example, PEG 4000, to retard the rate of swelling in water and are then coated by an air suspension technique with a water permeable polymer membrane such as ethyl cellulose, to act as a rate controlling barrier to regulate the release of the drug from the system. It is well-known that the ionic strength of the GI fluid is normally maintained at a relatively constant level. In the GI tract, ions diffuse through the ethyl cellulose membrane and react with the drug-resin complex to activate the release of the drug ions. The released drug from the drug-resin complex diffuses into the GI fluid through the coating membrane for GI absorption. The advantage of this type of system is that the rate of drug release is not dependent on the pH conditions and enzyme activities, temperature or volume of the GI tract. The system could also be formulated as a stable liquid suspension–type pharmaceutical dosage form. By combining different ratios of polymer-coated and uncoated granules in the formulation, a range of dissolution profiles and blood levels can be achieved.

Osmotically Controlled Drug Delivery Systems

Osmotic pressure arises from the fundamental law that the chemical potential of a solvent in a solution and a pure liquid must be the same if they are in contact through a semipermeable membrane at the same pressure. In other words, the solute lowers the chemical potential on the solution side of the membrane and results in water moving across the membrane to the solution side. This continues until equilibrium is reached. At equilibrium, the hydrostatic pressure, $gh\rho$, is equal to the osmotic pressure (π).

The elementary osmotic pump, the simplest possible form of an osmotic pump, consists of an osmotic core containing the drug, which is coated with a semipermeable membrane usually cellulose acetate with a delivery orifice. The core may or may not contain an osmotic agent, depending on the osmotic activity of the drug. When exposed to aqueous environments, the core imbibes water osmotically at a controlled rate through the semipermeable membrane, forming a saturated drug solution inside the system. Since the membrane is non-extensible, the interval volume of the pump remains constant. The system delivers, through the orifice, at any time interval, a volume of saturated solution of drug equal to the volume of water uptake. This process continues at a constant rate until all solid drugs inside the tablet have been dissolved and only a solution-filled shell remains. The residual dissolved drug continues to be delivered at a declining rate, until the osmotic pressure inside and outside the pump is equal. The osmotic pumps are ideal for moderately soluble drugs (Fig. 2.8).

The delivery rate of the drug is dependent on the membrane permeability, osmotic pressure of the core formulation and solubility of the drug in question. The volume flux of water (dv/dt) across the semipermeable membrane is given by:

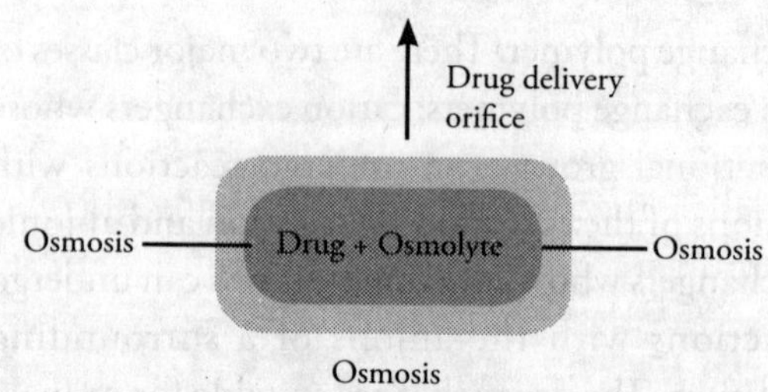

Figure 2.8: Elementary osmotic pump

$$dV/dt = \frac{A}{l} L_p (\sigma\Delta\pi - \Delta P) \quad (12)$$

where $\Delta\pi$ and ΔP are, respectively, the osmotic and hydrostatic pressure differences across the membrane, Lp is the membrane mechanical permeability coefficient, σ is the reflection coefficient and A and l are the membrane area and thickness, respectively. The rate of release of the drug is explained in a simplified form of the abovementioned equation.

$$dM/dt = (dV/dt)\ C \quad (13)$$

where C is the concentration of the active agent in the solution pumped out of the orifice.

Elementary osmotic pumps are suitable for water soluble or sparingly soluble drugs. However, they are not suitable for water insoluble or nonpolar drugs because of the possibility of the orifice being blocked by powder particles.

A push–pull osmotic pump is a modified osmotic pump through which it is possible to deliver both poorly and highly water soluble drugs at a constant rate. The system consists of two layers; one layer contains the drug, osmotic agent and other excipients while the other consists of a polymer, which is an osmotic agent and has the ability to imbibe water and swell. Both the layers are encapsulated in a semipermeable membrane. After the coating has been applied, a small orifice is drilled through the membrane by a laser or mechanical drill on the drug layer side of the capsule.

When the system is placed in an aqueous environment, water is attracted into the tablet by an osmotic pressure gradient across the membrane. The gradient develops because of the high affinity of the osmotic agent to water and low water activity in the drug tablet core. The osmotic agent in the drug layer pulls water into that compartment to form an in situ suspension of the drug. The osmotic agent in the non-drug layer simultaneously attracts water into that compartment, causing it to expand volumetrically. Since the membrane is insoluble and rigid in nature, it maintains a constant shape and volume while the expansion of the non-drug layer pushes the drug suspension out of the delivery orifice, which is large enough to eliminate the built-up pressure within the system and yet not large enough to permit uncontrolled leaching of the drug from the orifice (Fig. 2.9).

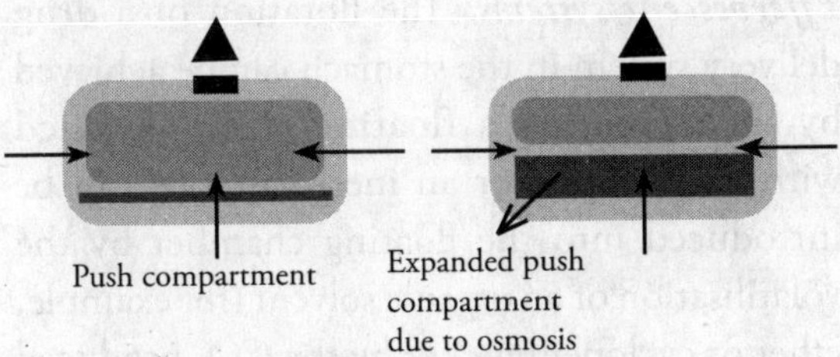

Figure 2.9: Push–Pull osmotic pump

To meet the challenge of poor bioavailability of poorly soluble drug candidates, ALZA Corporation developed the L-OROS™ system, a delivery system adapted for liquid drug formulations. The L-OROS™ systems are said to increase the bioavailability of water insoluble drugs. The L-OROS™ HARDCAP™ system (Fig. 2.10) is similar in design to that of the push–pull pump.

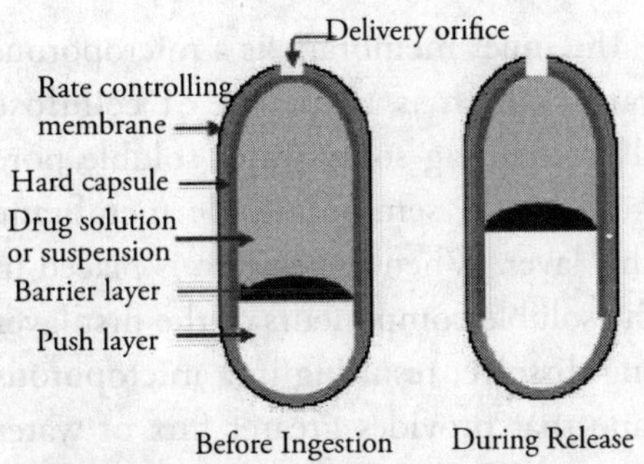

Figure 2.10: L-OROS™ HARDCAP™ system

In the L-OROS™ SOFTCAP™ system (Fig. 2.11), the liquid drug formulation is encased in a soft gelatin capsule surrounded, in order, by a barrier layer, an osmotic engine and a semipermeable membrane. The barrier layer separates the soft gelatin capsule from the osmotic engine, minimising hydration of the soft capsule to prevent its mixing with the drug layer. The delivery orifice in the L-OROS™ SOFTCAP™ system is drilled through the semipermeable membrane, osmotic engine and barrier layer. When the osmotic engine expands, it compresses the soft gelatin capsule, pushing the drug formulation out through the delivery orifice.

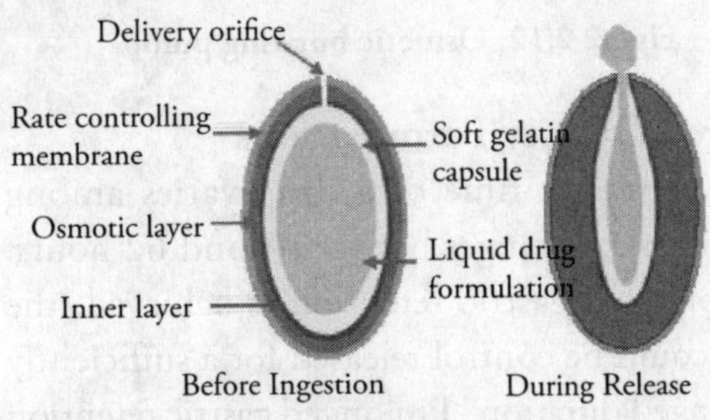

Figure 2.11: L-OROS™ SOFTCAP™ system

Controlled Porosity Osmotic Pumps

To increase the water permeability of the membrane and maintain its semipermeable nature, two layers of membranes are applied on pumps. The inner membrane is a microporous membrane, which is made up of cellulose materials containing some water soluble pore forming agents. A semipermeable membrane covers this layer. When the system is placed in water, the soluble components of the first layer of coating dissolve, resulting in a microporous membrane that provides greater flux of water into the system.

Osmotic Bursting Pumps

These pumps are smaller in size and lack a delivery orifice. The water imbibed into the system builds up the hydraulic pressure, the wall ruptures and the contents are released into the environment. Varying degrees of thickness as well as the area of the semipermeable membrane can control the release of the drug. The system provides pulsated release of the drug (Fig. 2.12).

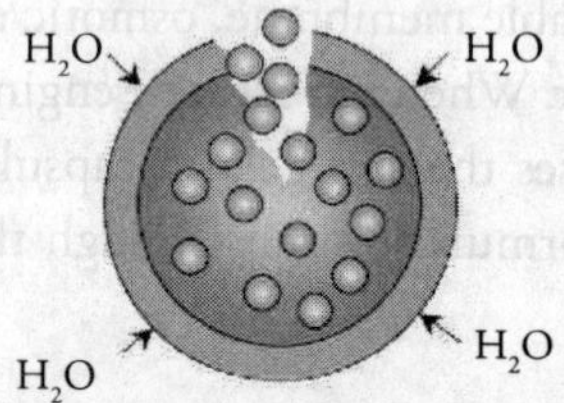

Figure 2.12: Osmotic bursting pump

Altered Density Formulations

The GI transit time of a drug varies among individuals. It ranges between 8 and 62 hours. If prolonged gastric retention is achieved, the drug could be control released for a sufficiently prolonged duration. Prolonged gastric retention can be achieved by using floating, swelling, bioadhesive or high-density systems. The dosage forms that can be retained in the stomach are called *gastro retentive drug delivery systems* (GRDDS) (Fig. 2.13).

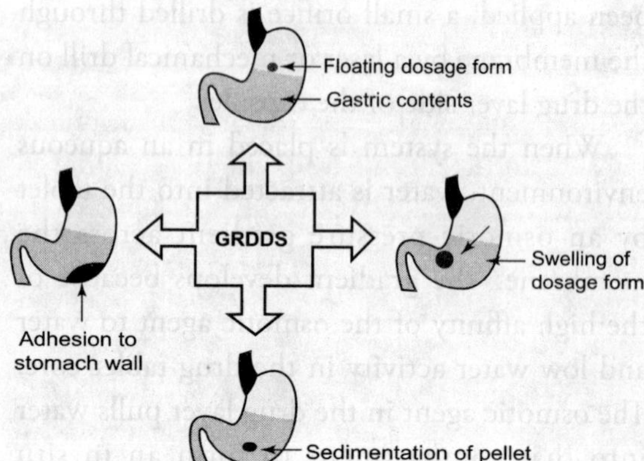

Figure 2.13: The principle behind different gastric retentive systems

Floating Systems

Floating systems have sufficient buoyancy to float over the gastric contents and remain in the stomach for a prolonged period. While the system floats over the gastric contents, the drug is released slowly at the desired rate, which reduces fluctuation in plasma drug concentration. Floating systems can be classified as *effervescent* and *noneffervescent* systems.

Effervescent systems: The flotation of a drug delivery system in the stomach can be achieved by incorporating a floating chamber filled with vacuum, air or an inert gas. Gas can be introduced into the floating chamber by the volatilisation of an organic solvent (for example, ether or cyclopentane) or by the CO_2 produced as a result of an effervescent reaction. These devices contain a hollow deformable unit that converts from a collapsed to an expanded position and returns to the collapsed position after a predetermined amount of time to permit the spontaneous ejection of the inflatable system from the stomach.

Noneffervescent systems: Noneffervescent systems incorporate a high level (20–75%

w/w) of one or more gel-forming, highly swellable, cellulosic hydrocolloids (for example, hydroxyethyl cellulose, hydroxypropyl cellulose, HPMC and sodium carboxymethyl cellulose), polysaccharides or matrix-forming polymers (for example, polycarbophils, polyacrylates and polystyrene) into tablets or capsules. Upon coming in contact with gastric fluid, these polymers hydrate and form a colloidal gel barrier that controls the rate of fluid penetration into the device and the consequent drug release. As the exterior surface of the dosage form dissolves, the gel layer is maintained by the hydration of the adjacent hydrocolloid layer. The air trapped by the swollen polymer lowers the density of and confers buoyancy to the dosage form.

Bioadhesive/Mucoadhesive Systems

Bioadhesive/Mucoadhesive systems bind to the gastric epithelial cell surface, or mucin, and extend the gastric retention time by increasing the intimacy and duration of contact between the dosage form and the biological membrane. This concept is based on the self-protecting mechanism of the GI tract. The mucus secreted continuously by the specialised goblet cells located throughout the GI tract plays a cytoprotective role. Mucus is a viscoelastic, gel-like slime composed mainly of glycoproteins. The thickness of the mucus layer decreases from the membrane surface to the GI lumen. The primary function of mucus is to protect the surface mucosal cells from acid and peptidases. In addition, it serves as a lubricant for the passage of solids and as a barrier to antigens, bacteria and viruses.

The epithelial adhesive properties of mucin are well-known and have been applied to the development of gastric retentive systems through the use of mucoadhesive polymers. The adherence of the delivery system to the gastric wall increases residence time at a particular site, thereby improving bioavailability. A mucoadhesive substance is a natural or synthetic polymer capable of adhering to a biological membrane (bioadhesive polymer) or the mucus lining of the GI tract (mucoadhesive polymer). The characteristics of these polymers are molecular flexibility and hydrophilic functional groups, and specific molecular weight, chain length and conformation. Furthermore, they must be nontoxic and nonabsorbable, form noncovalent bonds with the mucin–epithelial surfaces, have quick adherence to moist surfaces, easily incorporate the drug, offer no hindrance to drug release, have a specific site of attachment and be economical.

Swelling Systems

After being swallowed, these dosage forms swell to a size that prevents their passage through the pylorus. As a result, the dosage form is retained in the stomach for a long period of time. These systems are sometimes referred to as *plug type systems* because they tend to remain lodged at the pyloric sphincter. These polymeric matrices remain in the gastric cavity for several hours even in the fed state. Sustained and controlled drug release may be achieved by selecting a polymer with the proper molecular weight and swelling properties. Upon coming in contact with gastric fluid, the polymer imbibes water and swells. The extensive swelling of these polymers is a result of the presence of physical–chemical cross-links in the hydrophilic polymer network. These cross-links prevent the dissolution of the polymer and thus maintain the physical integrity of the dosage form. A balance between the extent and duration of swelling is maintained by the degree of cross-linking between the polymeric chains. A high degree of cross-linking retards the swelling ability of the system and maintains its physical integrity for a prolonged period. On the other hand, a low degree of cross-linking results in extensive swelling followed by the rapid dissolution of the polymer. An optimum amount of cross-linking is required to maintain a balance between swelling and dissolution. The swollen system will eventually lose its integrity because of a loss of mechanical strength caused by abrasion or erosion, or will burst into small fragments when the membrane ruptures because of continuous expansion. These systems may also erode in the presence of gastric juices so that after a predetermined time, the device can no longer attain or retain the expanded configuration.

High-density Systems

These systems, which have a density of ~3 g/cm^3, are retained in the rugae of the stomach and are capable of withstanding its peristaltic movements. Diluents such as barium sulphate (density = 4.9 g/cm^3), zinc oxide, titanium dioxide and iron powder must be used to manufacture such high-density formulations.

Parenteral Controlled Release Systems

While oral drug delivery continues to be the primary route of administration, the parenteral route does have a significant role to play in fulfilling certain specific objectives. These drug delivery systems are injected or implanted into the muscle or subcutaneous tissue and release the incorporated drug in a controlled manner over extended periods of time, ranging from several days up to one year. The release can be either continuous or pulsatile, depending on the structure of the device and the characteristics of the polymer.

Need for Parenteral CR

Controlled release parenteral dosage is usually selected when there are problems associated with oral delivery (for example, gastric irritation, first pass effects or poor absorption) and a need for extended release and/or targeted delivery (for example, rapid clearance and toxic side effects of drugs). Examples of applications for CR parenteral delivery include fertility treatment, hormone therapy, protein therapy, infection treatments (antibiotics and antifungals), cancer therapy, orthopedic surgery and postoperative pain treatment, chronic pain treatment, vaccination/immunisation, treatment of CNS disorders and immunosupression.

Controlled release parenteral drug delivery systems include suspensions, emulsions, gels, liposomes, microspheres and implants. They are generally used to improve the therapeutic response by providing appropriate dosing strategies (constant or pulsatile release). Such systems can be considered safer than conventional parenteral dosage forms since a smaller amount of the drug is required and since the drug may be targeted to the in vivo site, high systemic levels are avoided. Due to the lower dosing frequency and simpler dosage regimes, patient compliance can be improved with these dosage forms. For example, microspheres and larger implantable devices can be used to modify release over a time period of months to years. Liposomes may achieve targeted delivery both by passive and active means following intravenous administration and are utilised to target toxic drugs such as anti-cancer agents to avoid systemic side effects.

However, injection site residues and tissue irritation are common concerns to be dealt with in case of parenteral CR systems. Controlled release injectable formulations also pose problems with product stability, especially in the case of oily suspensions and emulsions.

CR Parenteral Suspensions

Suspensions are dissolution controlled drug delivery systems. The drug release kinetics can be explained by the Noyes–Whitney or Hixson–Crowell equations. Drugs that are relatively lipophilic have a slow dissolution rate in tissue fluids and are therefore suitable for formulation as controlled release aqueous suspensions. Drugs that are hydrophilic and have a high dissolution rate are often suspended in oily vehicles such as sesame oil, peanut oil and cotton seed oil to provide dissolution controlled release systems. The hydrophilic drug solubilises slowly in the oil phase and diffuses into the external fluid medium from the injected site. Incorporation of viscosifying agents further provides diffusion control of drugs from the injected site. However, diffusion of low molecular weight drugs, that is, drugs with a molecular weight up to about 750 Da are not impeded significantly by aqueous viscous solutions.

For example, Penicillin G procaine in vegetable oil is a depot that sustains the therapeutic blood level of penicillin for 24–48 hours. Gelation of this oil suspension with 2% aluminum monostearate further prolongs the therapeutic blood level of penicillin to 96 hours.

Drugs with greater dissolution rates are often converted to forms that provide slow dissolution to release the parent moiety. This could be achieved by salt, ester or complex formation. Injectable suspensions of insulin have been accepted in the treatment of diabetes to provide long duration control of blood glucose in humans and animals. Prolonged release systems are based on slowly dissolving amorphous or crystalline suspensions of zinc and protamine insulins. The insulin–zinc complex is a good example of the former. The insulin molecule reacts with the Zn ion and precipitates as a water insoluble Zn–insulin complex. Depending on the pH of the solution, it may precipitate as an amorphous or a crystalline solid. Insulin crystals (10–40 μm with high zinc content) can be precipitated from acetate buffer at pH of 5–6. This crystalline zinc-insulin complex is absorbed very slowly and displays a prolonged normoglycemic activity. After subcutaneous injection of this Zn–insulin crystal suspension in the buffer (pH 7.3), the insulin is slowly released/absorbed (4–8 hours to the onset of action) and retains its activity for more than 36 hours. This preparation is called 'ultralente'.

On the other hand, the amorphous Zn–insulin complex is precipitated at a higher pH (pH 6–8). This amorphous insulin has low zinc content, is absorbed more readily and achieves a duration of action shorter than that of ultralente. When administered subcutaneously, the amorphous Zn–insulin suspension (with particles <2 μm) is quickly released and absorbed (1 hour) and displays a shorter duration of normoglycemic activity (12–16 hours). However, this preparation, called 'semilente' insulin, produces longer duration activity than the regular insulin injection USP.

Complexes

Complexation is carried out to form a product with slow dissolution characteristics (dissolution controlled system) or a complex that has slow dissociation kinetics. Complexation between small molecules such as theophylline and caffeine with acetaminophen forms a poorly soluble complex, which, on being injected into the tissue, acts as dissolution controlled delivery system similar to that used by parenteral suspensions.

Forming a dissociable complex of the drug with a macromolecule such as semisynthetic celluloses, PVP or albumin and administering the complex by intramuscular injection could enable the sustained release of the drug. Generally, due to the size of the complex, the absorption of the drug in the complex form is limited. Therefore, the absorption of the drug may be presumed to be proportional to the concentration of the free or undissociated drug present at the site of absorption. The rate of appearance of the free drug at the absorption site depends on the rate of dissociation of the complex.

Milder complexes could also be formed by inclusion complexation with hydrophobic cyclodextrins. Adsorption and desorption mediated release controlled systems have been used for vaccines. For example, the vaccine adsorbed onto aluminum hydroxide gel sustains its release and hence prolongs the duration of stimulation of antibody formation.

Emulsions

Aqueous solutions of drugs are emulsified to provide retarded delivery. Assuming that the drug release proceeds through diffusion rather than by breaking the emulsion, and that the body fluid acts as a perfect sink, the rate of disappearance of the drug from the aqueous phase in the two-dimensional diffusion model can be described by:

$$dc/dt = -kC_0 e^{(-K_p \cdot t)} \quad (14)$$

where C_0 is the initial concentration in the aqueous phase, and k is the rate constant of disappearance of the drug from the aqueous phase and is given by $k = (ADK_p)/VL$, where A is the surface area of the droplet, D is the diffusion coefficient of the drug, K_p is the partition coefficient of the drug between oil and water, V is the volume of the aqueous phase and L is the effective thickness of the oil phase. For a given drug, a faster rate of release is favoured by a large K_p with small droplets and the phase volume ratio favouring the oil phase. The in vivo release rate of drugs depends on the apparent oil/water partition coefficients. The rate of attainment of equilibrium between the oil and aqueous phases is also linearly related to the apparent partition coefficients. Hence, compounds with a high apparent partition coefficient are released at a relatively slower rate.

Drugs that are lipid soluble can be administered as oil-in-water emulsions. Since the continuous phase in these systems is aqueous, they should be absorbed rapidly at the injection site to leave a depot of drug dissolved in small oil droplets.

In Situ Forming Systems

These systems are fluid on injection and rely on a change in the local environment to produce a high viscosity or solid depot at the injection site. Changes that cause solidification following injection include increase in temperature to 37° C, loss of organic solvent from the injected material by diffusion and hydration with water from the injection site. The rheological properties of these systems must remain consistent with injections prior to and during the injection process to be acceptable.

Sucrose acetate isobutyrate (SAIB) and similar materials have been used in the parenteral depot forms. They are liquid formulations that form a viscous system after being injected into the tissue. These systems are yet to be evaluated in a clinical setting.

Microparticles

Microparticles are usually defined as spherical devices with a size range of 1–1000 μm. For injection purposes, microparticles in the range of 10–100 μm are preferred. Microparticles in a general sense can be further divided into microcapsules, that is, microparticles containing the drug in a central core, surrounded by a polymeric membrane, and microspheres, that is, microparticles containing the drug in a polymeric matrix.

The microsphere systems have been applied to narcotic antagonists and antineoplastic agents. The method consists of suspending the drug in a biodegradable/bioerodible polymer, followed by reducing the mixture to particles of the desired size range. The biodegradation and bioerosion could be caused by the hydrolysis or oxidation of the polymers. Generally, polymers that undergo hydrolysis are preferred because of the formation of relatively safer byproducts. Some examples of biodegradable/bioerodible polymers used in parenteral delivery are polyglactin, poly isobutyl cyanoacrylate, poly 2-hydroxyethyl-L-glutamine and poly lactic acid.

Microcapsules have been used for various drugs including vaccine, hormones, hemoglobin, enzymes and proteins. The charge carried on the surface of the particles and the size of the particles influence the release of drug from the microcapsules. Controlled release could be brought about by use of one or more of the mechanisms discussed above.

The Prolease® delivery system/technology is a novel technology specifically used for the controlled delivery of protein formulations. The schematic representation of the technology is shown in Fig 2.14.

The lyophilised formulation of proteins is stable at ambient temperatures for extended periods; therefore, ProLease® technology takes advantage of the superior stability of lyophilised protein formulations by encapsulating the protein in the solid state. In this technology, the water content retained in the formulation is minimal and hence, the protein stability

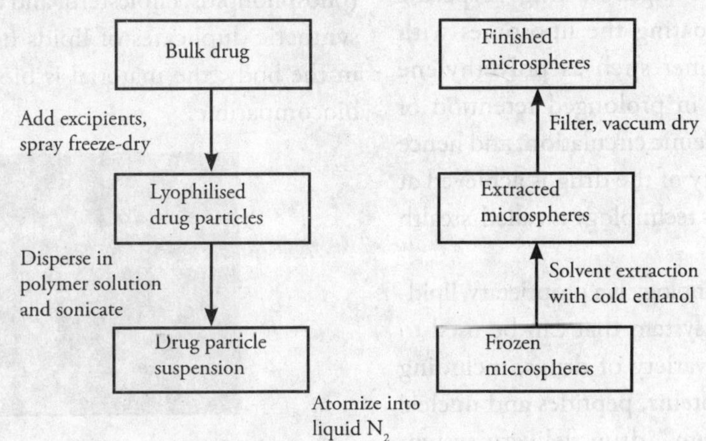

Figure 2.14: The schematic representation of Prolease® technology

is more due to reduced molecular mobility. The kinetics of degradative reactions is retarded significantly in this process. Additionally, there is the opportunity to add excipients to enhance the stability of the protein during the lyophilisation process and for storage stability.

The liquid formulation of proteins containing the stabilising additives or excipient is fed into an atomising nozzle and sprayed into liquid nitrogen. The droplets freeze instantaneously when they come into contact with liquid nitrogen. The frozen droplets are then lyophilised to produce a friable lyophilised powder. This spray-freeze-drying process is used rather than conventional bulk lyophilisation because it provides the ability to control the morphology and friability of the lyophilised powder.

Just before administration, microsphere powder is dispersed in a viscous aqueous diluent and delivered with a hypodermic needle. The release mechanism is determined by the solubility/degradative characteristics of the drug and the polymer.

Lipid-based Drug Delivery

Liposomes are used to target the drugs at specific tissues. However, coating the liposomes with a hydrophilic polymer such as polyethylene glycol (PEG) helps in prolonged retention of the liposomes in systemic circulation, and hence greater bioavailability of the drug is achieved at the target tissue. This technology is called 'stealth technology'.

DepoFoam™ technology is a proprietary, lipid-based drug delivery system that can be used to encapsulate a wide variety of drugs, including small molecules, proteins, peptides and nucleic acids. The DepoFoam™ drug delivery system consists of microscopic, spherical particles composed of hundreds of non-concentric aqueous chambers encapsulating the drug to be delivered. The individual chambers are separated by bilayer lipid membranes made up of synthetic analogues of naturally occurring lipids, resulting in a delivery vehicle that is both biocompatible and biodegradable. The rate of drug release from a DepoFoam™ formulation is controlled by modifying the lipid components, aqueous excipients and manufacturing parameters used in producing the formulation. The DepoFoam™ system provides either local site or systemic delivery, and can be administered by a number of routes such as under the skin, within muscle tissue and into spinal fluid, joints and the abdominal cavity. Typically, a DepoFoam™ particle consists of <10% lipid and 90% aqueous drug solution, giving it a high drug 'loading' factor.

DepoFoam™ particles have a unique multivesicular structure (Fig. 2.15). Sustained release is achieved without a burst effect, since all of the active drug is encapsulated within the multiple chambers of individual particles. Because the components of DepoFoam™ (phospholipids, cholesterol and triglycerides) are synthetic duplicates of lipids normally present in the body, the material is biodegradable and biocompatible.

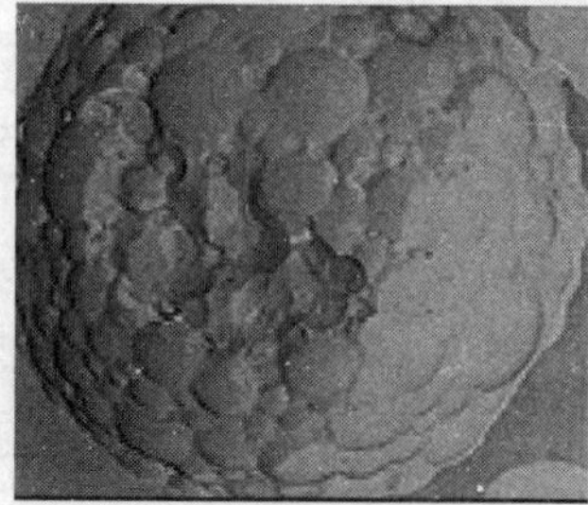

Figure 2.15: Composite electron micrograph of freeze fracture replicas of DepoFoam™ particle

Prodrugs

Prodrugs are inactive forms of drugs that liberate the active drug moiety after undergoing a split or cleavage in the physiological fluid. For example, esterification of drugs to form water insoluble but oil soluble prodrugs could be used for sustained release of the drug. For example, testosterone is readily absorbed orally by such administration. However, it undergoes presystemic metabolism by the liver before reaching the systemic circulation. Testosterone has a short biological half life after parenteral administration in an oleaginous solution, and hence, the androgenic effect is small. The androgenic activity of testosterone is enhanced and prolonged by esterification with β-cyclopentylpropionate ester.

Evaluation of CRDF and Regulatory Aspects of CR Formulations

In the 1980s, the Food and Drug Administration (FDA) in the US introduced rigorous regulations governing bioequivalence and in vitro–in vivo correlations for controlled release products. The mandatory pharmacokinetic evaluations involve:

- Relative bioavailability following a single dose
- Relative bioavailability following multiple administrations
- Effect of food on drug absorption from CR formulation
- Dose proportionality
- Unit dosage strength proportionality
- Single dose bioequivalence study (experimental versus marketed formulations at various strengths)
- In vitro–in vivo correlation
- Pharmacokinetic/Pharmacodynamic (PK/PD) relationship

In general, for drugs in which the exposure–response relationship has not been established or is unknown, applications for changing the formulation from immediate release to controlled release requires demonstration of the safety and efficacy of the product in the target patient population.

In most cases, the drugs available as sustained release oral products are also available as traditional dosage forms. The claims are based not on the therapeutic entity but on the drug delivery system. This raises the question of whether a normal dosage form or a CRDF should be used. Other questions such as 'Does the drug delivery system sustain plasma levels?' and 'Do sustained plasma levels have a clinical advantage?' have also been raised.

These questions should be answered with in vitro release data and preclinical and clinical/pharmacokinetic and dynamic study results. The in vitro dissolution test apparatus USP is used to study the release pattern of the drug from the dosage forms particularly in oral and transdermal formulations. USP dissolution apparatus provide different accessories to suit different dosage forms and conditions. However, for parenteral forms, there are a lot of unanswered questions regarding the suitable in vitro release study method. Paavola et al suggest using the two-compartment in vitro method to study the release from parenteral depot formulation.

The most obvious measure of sustained release is the duration of the drug in the blood. The formulation is designed to produce constant blood levels and the level of success can be determined directly from blood or urine assays as a function of time.

Selection of a suitable animal model is critical for the preclinical evaluation of drug delivery devices. Oral CR formulations in rodents, rabbits and dogs have been used for pharmacokinetic and pharmacodynamics evaluation. Selection of a suitable animal model should be based on their similarity to humans in terms of the transport process/mechanism, gastric emptying time, comparable fluid flow and the composition of the secreted fluids in the gut. For instance, if rodents are chosen for a preclinical pharmacokinetic study of a sparingly soluble drug, the drug is poorly absorbed because of a short GI transit time. Another important consideration is the volume of blood sample required for analytical purposes to extract measurable quantities of the drug. Rodents and small animals may not be suitable for multiple sample withdrawals and for drugs that attain low concentrations in the plasma. Beagle dogs are often employed due to the ease of administration of intact tablets and capsules and also because of the large volume of blood samples that can be withdrawn for analytical purposes.

In Vitro–In Vivo Correlation of CRDF

Traditionally, the in vitro–in vivo correlation (IVIVC) has served as a means of modelling humans and of gaining a better understanding of drug absorption and its dependence on in vitro release processes. However, the chief application of IVIVC is its use in in vitro studies for quality control procedures and as an alternative to in vivo bioequivalence studies. In addition, IVIVC is a beneficial tool for developing a dosage form with the desired in vivo performance with the fewest possible human trials. IVIVC has been described in USP as 'the establishment of a relationship between a biological property or a parameter derived from a biological property produced by a dosage form, and a physicochemical characteristic of the same dosage form.' The FDA, in turn, describes IVIVC as a process used 'to show the relationship

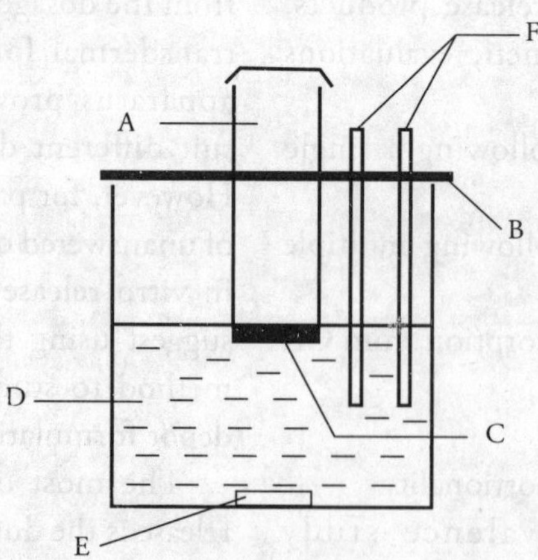

Figure 2.16: Experimental system for the in vitro drug release measurement. A. Glass cylinder (donor compartment); B. Plexiglass cover; C. Membrane; D. Sink solution (acceptor compartment); E. Stirring bar; F. Sampling port.

between two parameters. Typically, a relationship is sought between the in vitro dissolution rate and in vivo input rate. This initial relationship may be expanded to critical formulation parameters and the in vivo input rate'.

Various levels of correlation can be determined from these definitions.

Level A. In a Level A correlation, a one-to-one relationship exists between the in vitro dissolution rate and the in vivo input rate. In this case, IVIVC alone is sufficient to determine the biopharmaceutical performance of a dosage form. Because Level A correlation is based on a full-time profile, it demonstrates the best fit between in vitro release and in vivo dosage form performance.

Level B. Level B indicates a correlation of statistical moments determined in vitro and after administration in vivo. It involves a comparison of the mean in vitro dissolution time (MDT) and either the mean in vivo residence or dissolution time.

Level C. In Level C, a point-to-point relationship exists between a dissolution parameter and a pharmacokinetic parameter. The relationship involves the comparison of a single point measure of dissolution or release rate (such as MDT or time required for a 50% release) and a single point measure of the extent of absorption in vivo (such as the area under the curve).

Key Messages

- Controlled delivery systems provide more uniform plasma drug levels and less frequent dosing, leading to better patient compliance.
- Design of controlled release systems requires a thorough understanding of the pharmacokinetics and pharmacodynamics of drugs.
- Oral controlled release drug delivery systems can be classified based on the mechanism of drug release such as dissolution control, diffusion control, ion exchange resins, pH-dependent, osmotically controlled and buoyant systems.
- The parenteral route has also been used for controlled release in the form of suspensions complexes, emulsions, in-situ gel forming systems and implants.
- Microparticles (microspheres and microcapsules), lipid-based systems (liposomes) and prodrugs are the other controlled delivery systems.

Questions

1. What is the rationale for the formulation of CR dosage forms?
2. What are the advantages and disadvantages of CRDF over conventional dosage forms?
3. Give the criteria for selection of drug candidate for CR formulation.
4. What is the principle behind dissolution controlled drug delivery systems?
5. What is burst release?
6. Explain how ion exchange resins could be utilised in the formulation of CRDF.
7. What is the principle of the working of an elementary osmotic pump?

8. What are the different principles of achieving prolonged gastric retention of dosage form?
9. What is Prolease® technology?
10. Write a note on in vitro-in vivo correlation of CRDF.
11. Discuss parenteral controlled release formulations.

3

Transdermal Drug Delivery Systems

S Narasimha Murthy and Shobha Rani R Hiremath

Learning Objectives

At the end of this chapter, you will be able to:

- Explain the significance, mechanism, advantages and limitations of transdermal drug delivery (TDD)
- Describe the various physicochemical and biological factors that influence transdermal drug absorption
- Describe the various designs and components of the transdermal drug delivery system (TDDS) and release kinetics
- List the evaluation methods of transdermal drug devices
- State the theory and describe the mechanism of physical techniques of transdermal drug permeation enhancement

Introduction

Transdermal drug delivery (TDD) is the delivery of drugs through the skin to elicit a systemic effect. This aspect makes it different from topical formulations, where the drug is expected to display only local activity. The inclusion of local anesthetic transdermal devices has redefined TDD as one that delivers drugs through the skin to elicit 'regional' or 'systemic' effects.

Structure of the Skin

The skin has two major layers: the epidermis and the dermis. The different layers of the skin are shown in the Fig. 3.1. The top layer is called the epidermis. The stratum corneum (SC) or horny layer is the outermost layer of the epidermis, which is responsible for the barrier property of the skin. The SC layer comprises multiple layers of flattened epithelial cells. More than 90% of all cells in the SC are corneocytes. These cells are keratinised and the cells are terminally differentiated and tightly packed in stacks that run perpendicular to the skin surface. The average number of corneocytes per unit area of SC is ~2×10^6 cm^{-2}. The intercellular space in the SC is occupied by lipids. SC lipids are generally nonpolar and enriched with ceramides, free sterols and free fatty acids, with smaller quantities of glycolipids, sterol esters and triglycerides; cholesterol sulfate and hydrocarbons are present as well. The lipids are arranged in the form of lamellar stacks with the polar head groups of the lipids gathered in layers while the nonpolar chains point in opposite directions.

The cells beneath the SC form the viable epidermis. This is physicochemically similar to other living tissues. The cells have thin membranes that encapsulate cytoplasm and are held together by tonofibrils. The density of this region is not very different from that of water (~1g/cm^3). The dendritic cells present in this region are involved in the epidermal immune system. They engulf the foreign matter that invades the epidermis and migrate out of the skin to stimulate an immune response. Melanocytes, which are not very abundant, are the cells in the epidermis that produce the pigment melanin. Melanin absorbs harmful ultraviolet (UV) light before UV radiation can reach the nucleus.

Just beneath the viable epidermis is the dermis or corium. The dermis consists mostly of connective tissue and is much thicker than the epidermis. It is responsible for the skin's pliability and mechanical resistance and is also involved in the regulation of body temperature. The dermis supplies the avascular epidermis with nutrients by means of its vascular network. It contains the sense organs for touch, pressure, pain and temperature (Meissner's corpuscles, Pacinian corpuscles, free nerve endings), as well as blood vessels, nerve fibres, sebaceous and sweat glands and hair follicles. The dermis has a dense network of capillaries and is thus considered to be the primary site of material exchange between the skin and blood.

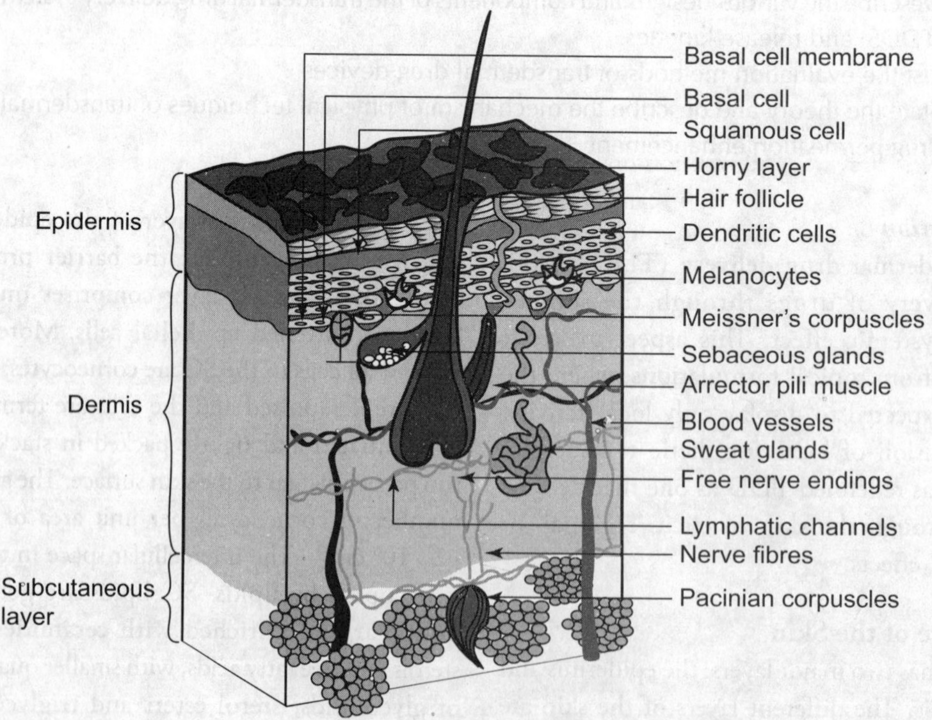

Figure 3.1: The different layers of the skin

Pathways of Drug Absorption

Hydrophilic drugs and ions undergo absorption through the polar pathway of the skin. This polar or porous pathway includes the deformities in the lipid bilayers and appendegial pathways or shunt pathway. The polar pathway is likely to differentiate between the positively charged and negatively charged molecules because the skin is negatively charged at physiological pH. As a result, positively charged molecules may diffuse more readily across the skin than negatively charged molecules. The permeability coefficient obtained for a hydrophilic solute such as sucrose is approximately 1 x 10^{-6} cm/h in human skin.

For most lipophilic molecules with a molecular weight <500 Da, the predominant absorption pathway is via the lipid domains. The drug needs to partition through the lipid region of the intercellular space or the transcellular lipids to diffuse across the SC.

Advantages of TDDS

The TDDS is the most successful non-oral systemic drug delivery system. The non-invasiveness of TDDS makes it a very patient-compliant system. The TDDS obviates specific problems associated with drugs such as gastrointestinal irritation, low absorption and decomposition due to hepatic first pass effect. The side effects of drugs are significantly reduced when administered by the transdermal route. For example, in the case of oral administration of estradiol, the byproducts formed in the liver could cause severe side effects. Here, TDDS has been proved to be relatively more acceptable to patients. The other major advantage of TDDS is its ability to provide constant and prolonged steady state release of drugs, obviating the need for frequent dosing of drugs with a short half life.

An example is nitroglycerin, used in angina pectoris patients as a vasodilator. About 90% of orally administered nitroglycerin undergoes first pass metabolism. Its sublingual use was to abort an attack after it had occurred, whereas it is now used as a transdermal patch to prevent angina pectoris attacks.

Limitations of TDDS

The poor permeability of the human skin limits the daily dose of the drug delivered. Similarly, TDDS is not a means to achieve rapid bolus-type drug inputs; rather, it is usually designed to offer slow, sustained drug delivery over substantial periods of time. Nevertheless, there remains a large pool of drugs for which TDD is desirable but presently unfeasible.

In addition to its use as a physical barrier, the human skin functions as a chemical barrier as well. The activity of the lytic enzyme is the most interesting from a drug transport angle. The skin surface has a population of micro-organisms that can contribute to skin enzymology. Their diversity and abundance can vary considerably among individuals and body sites.

The enzymology of the skin could be a disadvantage if the drug undergoes significant degradation in the skin. On the other hand, the same fact is used as an advantage in formulating prodrugs for significant absorption that undergoes hydrolysis and liberates the active parent molecule after being absorbed.

Skin irritation and contact dermatitis of excipients and enhancers of the drug used to increase percutaneous absorption is another major limitation. The development of a TDD formulation for optimal delivery of drugs is a relatively challenging and expensive task.

Individual variations with clinical results have been shown to be significant.

Transdermal Absorption Flux

The rate of drug delivery is determined by the skin permeability coefficient of the drug and its equilibrium solubility in the SC. The permeability coefficient at steady state (P_{ss}) of the skin tissue to the drug is defined by

$$P_{ss} = K_s D_{ss} / h_s \quad (1)$$

where K_s is the partition coefficient for the interfacial partitioning of the penetrant molecule from a transdermal therapeutic system into the SC, D_{ss} is the apparent diffusivity for the steady state diffusion of the penetrant molecule through skin tissue and h_s is the overall thickness of the skin tissue.

In its simplest form, at steady state, when the amount of drug entering the tissue is equal to the amount leaving the tissue, the flux (J_{ss}), is given by

$$J_{ss} = P_{ss} \times C_{veh} \quad (2)$$

where J_{ss} is the steady state flux (mg/cm²/hr) and C_{veh} is the drug concentration (mg/cm²) in the vehicle/formulation. According to this relationship, transcutaneous fluxes could be improved by increasing solute diffusivity and partitioning in the SC, and by increasing solute concentration in the applied formulation.

Graph 3.1 shows a typical transdermal drug absorption pattern (in vitro). The absorption is non-linear initially, until equilibrium is attained, and then becomes linear after the lag time, indicating steady state diffusion. The slope of the linear portion of the curve gives the rate of drug delivery. The rate expressed per unit area gives the transdermal absorption flux of drugs.

Careful consideration of physicochemical and biological factors of the drug and the formulation design helps to optimise the transdermal flux of drugs.

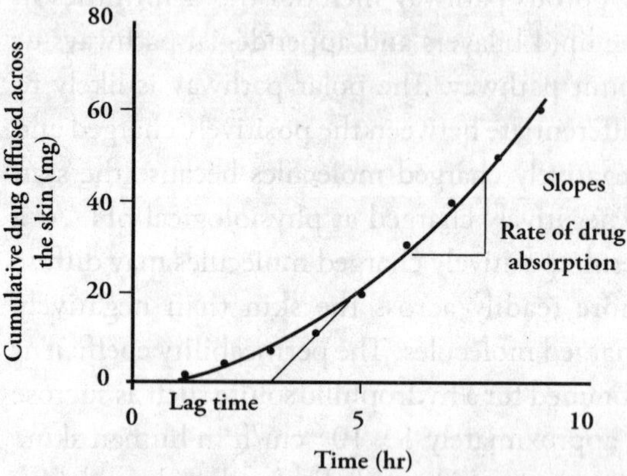

Graph 3.1: Typical in vitro transdermal absorption profile of drugs

Factors that Influence TDD

Skin-related factors such as the region of application of the patch, hydration state of the skin, presence of pigments and lesions and pathological conditions are known to influence the transdermal absorption of drugs. Environmental factors such as the temperature and exposure to air and light significantly affect drug absorption. However, from the formulation perspective, the drug-related factors are more important.

Drug-related Factors

To undergo effective transdermal absorption and elicit regional and systemic pharmacological effects, a drug should possess some physicochemical properties and meet certain biological criteria. During the past three decades, several research groups have investigated the basic physicochemical properties that influence transdermal drug absorption. Properties such as solubility of the drug in the formulation, molecular size, lipophilicity of the drug and drug ionisation and melting point have been found to correlate well with transdermal absorption flux.

Physicochemical Factors

Solubility: The driving force for drug diffusion through the skin is the chemical potential gradient. The solubility of the drug in the formulation influences both the drug concentration gradient and its partition coefficient between the formulation and the skin. Higuchi postulated that, provided the vehicle containing the permeating chemical does not affect the membrane, the drug flux (J) for an idealised system could be expressed in terms of the thermodynamic activity of the penetrating agent in the vehicle by the following equation.

$$J = \frac{\alpha D A}{\gamma L} \qquad (3)$$

where α represents the thermodynamic activity of the drug in the vehicle, γ is the effective activity coefficient of the drug in the membrane, D is the diffusivity, A is the cross-sectional area and L is the thickness of the membrane.

In order to obtain a maximum rate of penetration, the highest thermodynamic activity possible for the penetrating substances should be maintained. Higuchi's postulate assumes that all vehicles that consist of saturated solutions of a particular drug will produce the same rate of penetration because they are at a maximum thermodynamic activity of 1. Any higher activity would then represent supersaturation, with a corresponding increase in penetration rate. However, the main problem encountered with supersaturated systems is their physical instability. Being thermodynamically unstable, the drug crystallises out and, in the process, the flux decreases.

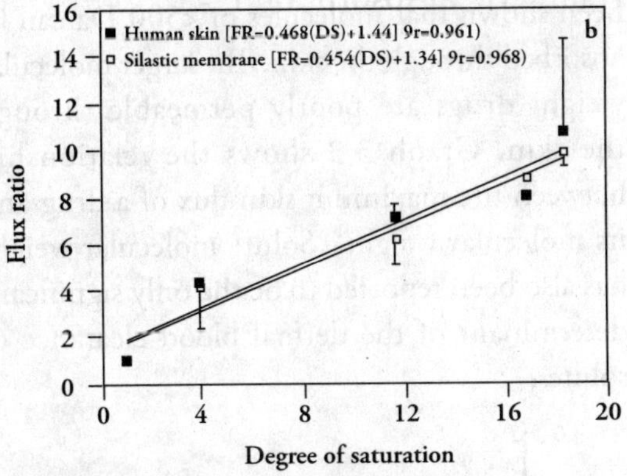

Graph 3.2: Flux ratio

Graph 3.2 shows the flux ratio from supersaturated solutions of different concentrations of estradiol across the human epidermal and Silastic membrane.

The absolute concentration found in the different strata of the skin is also in direct proportion to the degree of saturation of the drug in the formulation. It is important since it is the ratio of the concentration of the drug at the site of application to the concentration in the skin tissue that needs to be as high as possible for optimal bioavailability.

The vehicles in the formulation should provide sufficient solubility of the drug to ensure administration of the desired dose and at the same time enhance the thermodynamic activity of the drug. Enhancement of drug solubility alone may not be useful. For example, if the solubility of the drug in a vehicle is increased by the addition of a cosolvent, then its partition coefficient towards the skin is reduced (presuming that the cosolvent does not affect the barrier properties of the skin).

Molecular size: Molecular weight/size is one of the important factors that determine the skin permeability of drugs. Generally, it has been shown that molecules of <500 Da can be absorbed through the skin. The larger molecular weight drugs are poorly permeable through the skin. Graph 3.3 shows the relationship between the maximum skin flux of a drug and its molecular weight. Solute molecular weight has also been reported to be the only significant determinant of the dermal blood clearance of solutes.

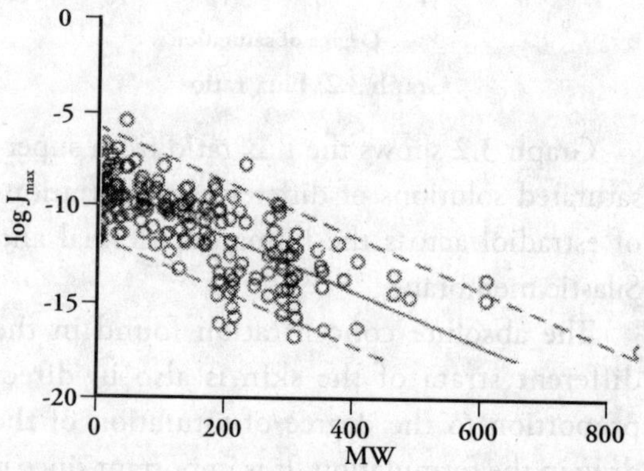

Graph 3.3: The J_{max} data for aqueous solutions and the molecular weight of the penetrant across full- and split-thickness skin.

Lipophilicity: The predominant pathway of passive drug absorption across the skin is the intercellular lipid lamellae in the SC. Ideally, the drug should partition into the SC lipids and equilibrate quickly with the underlying layers to be taken up by the circulation. Therefore, drugs that have a balanced lipophilic/hydrophilic character and a drug with a log $K_{Oct/water}$ value of ≤2 are considered as potential candidates for transdermal delivery. $K_{Oct/water}$ is the partition coefficient of drug between the octanol and water phase at equilibrium. The hydrophilic molecules with low log $K_{Oct/water}$ (-1 and 0) cannot appreciate partitioning into the SC in significant amounts. Highly lipophilic molecules with log $K_{Oct/water}$ >2 may form a drug reservoir in the SC and suffer poor partitioning into the viable cell layers of the epidermis and dermis. This could pose potential problems in establishing steady state concentration in a reasonable timespan.

An empirical formula proposed by Guy and Potts explains the relationship between the lipophilicity, size and skin permeability of molecules:

$$\text{Log } P_{ss} = -6.3 + 0.71 \times \log K_{Oct/water} - 0.061 \times MW \quad (4)$$

Use of appropriate *prodrug* form of the active molecule, which possesses relatively favourable physicochemical characteristics for effective penetration into SC, is a good approach. For example, the penetration of acetonide of triamcinolone is about 1000 times that of the parent steroid because of its favourable lipid solubility.

Ionisation of the drug: Many drugs are weak acids or bases and their pKa influences transdermal absorption. Where the pKa differs considerably from physiological pH, ionisation of the drug occurs and limits absorption. Moreover, anionic drugs are known to be relatively less permeable than cationic and nonionic drugs. It has been established that the skin's isoelectric point is about 4. This implies that at physiological pH, the likelihood that the skin will carry a net fixed negative charge that results from a greater number of protein amino acid and fatty acid residues carrying negative charges (carboxylic acid groups) as opposed to positive charges (amine moieties) is present. This property is most likely responsible for the charge discrimination behaviour of the skin. This charge discrimination property of the skin as well as poor partitioning of the ionic drug could be overcome by the formation of a lipophilic ion pair, which could enable partition into SC lipids, ionisation in the aqueous viable epidermis and absorption into systemic circulation. The ion pair mechanism can be chosen when the desired enhancement is ~ 2–7-fold. However, the extent of enhancement depends on the lipophilicity of the counter ion (13). For example, the pKa of lignocaine is 7.6; therefore, a greater fraction of the drug exists in its un-ionised form at pH 8.3, which favours partitioning into SC lipids. Lignocaine absorption through the human epidermis enhances by 2.4-fold when paired with counter ions such as nitrate, mesylate and bromide.

Melting point: Permeant melting point is inversely proportional to lipophilicity and, therefore, the transdermal flux. There is a reasonably linear correlation in Graph 3.4, indicating that the lower the melting point, the better the penetration.

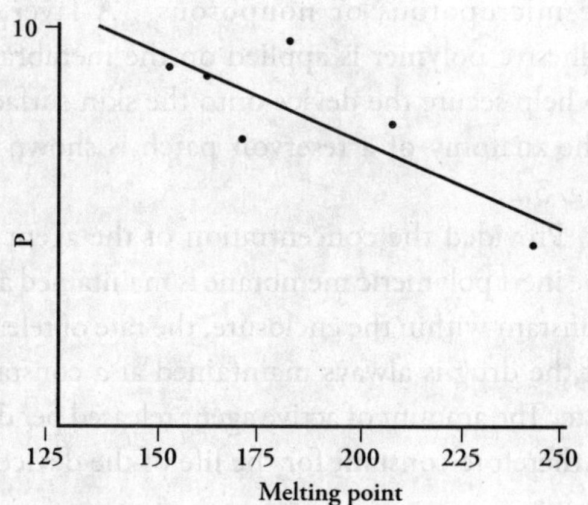

Graph 3.4: The linear relationship between the permeability coefficient (P) and the melting points ($r = 0.8120$, $p < 0.05$) of some antiemetic drugs

Reduction in the melting point of a permeant will have a direct effect on its solubility in skin lipids and so increase transdermal permeation. It follows that if the melting point of a drug can be reduced without causing unfavourable changes to other physicochemical parameters, this should enhance the transdermal flux. A binary eutectic is a mixture of two components that do not interact to form a new chemical compound but which, at certain ratios, inhibit the crystallisation process of the other, resulting in a system with a lower melting point than either of the components. For example, terpenes reduce the melting point of ibuprofen and improve its transcutaneous absorption flux. The formation of *eutectic binary mixtures* appears to work well with local anesthetic agents for topical use. A topical local anesthetic, eutectic mixture of local anesthetics (EMLA) is a binary eutectic mixture of prilocaine and lidocaine cream and was first used to reduce the pain of circumcision in infants. Recently, amethocaine gel (Ametop.®) has been shown to reduce pain during venepuncture. The efficacy of gel as a topical local anesthetic is based on the unique drug phase change system, in which a solid drug base undergoes a phase change in the presence of water at skin temperature, forming penetrative lipophilic oil.

Biological Factors

Biological factors such as the dose of the drug, cutaneous side effects, elimination half life of the drug and stability of the drug in the skin tissue are important factors to be assessed before selection of a drug for transdermal delivery.

Due to limitations of the area of the delivery system that can be applied on the surface of the skin, the drugs to be administered by the transdermal route need to have their dosage in the range of a few mg. Drugs such as nitroglycerin, which penetrate the skin relatively rapidly, do so at fluxes in the range of 10–15 mg/cm^2/h from a saturated aqueous solution. Hence, the total nitroglycerin that can be delivered across the skin from a 50 cm^2 system in a day is approximately only 15 mg. Therefore, drugs with a daily dose of ≤20 mg are preferred for transdermal delivery.

Ideally, the drug should not irritate the skin. However, if a pharmacologically active material is to be presented to the skin under an occlusive patch system, over an extended period, the likelihood of an irritant or allergic response is significant. Limits will have to be determined for acceptability of this undesirable effect. Allergic contact dermatitis reactions to glyceryl trinitrate have been reported on numerous occasions. Despite this, glyceryl trinitrate is one of the most common drugs administered by the transdermal route.

The pharmacokinetic parameters of the drug should be favourable for controlled release over long periods of time. If a drug with a long half life (~1 day) is administered using a transdermal therapeutic system, plasma levels build up slowly over a longer period than desired. On multiple applications of the system, cumulative drug concentration may prove toxic. Therefore, drugs with a relatively short half life (2–6 hours) are preferred for controlled transdermal delivery.

Metabolic inactivation of pharmacologically active compounds in the skin may be the reason for some of the ineffective topical and transcutaneous treatments. Therefore, the drug should be stable in the skin.

Transdermal Therapeutic Systems

The design of transdermal patch formulations available commercially can be categorised into a few types based on their anatomy and release kinetics.

A. Membrane-controlled transdermal drug delivery systems/Reservoir-type systems

The drug reservoir is encapsulated in a shallow compartment moulded from a drug-impermeable metallic plastic laminate and a rate-controlling polymeric membrane. In the drug reservoir compartment, the drug solids are dispersed in the solid polymeric matrix or suspended in an unleachable, viscous liquid medium to form a paste-like suspension. The rate of drug release is determined by the permeability of the rate-controlling membrane, which can be microporous or nonporous. A layer of adhesive polymer is applied on the membrane to help secure the device onto the skin surface. The anatomy of a reservoir patch is shown in Fig. 3.2.

Provided the concentration of the agent in the inert polymeric membrane is maintained at a constant within the enclosure, the rate of release of the drug is always maintained at a constant rate. The amount of active agent released per day is therefore constant for the life of the device:

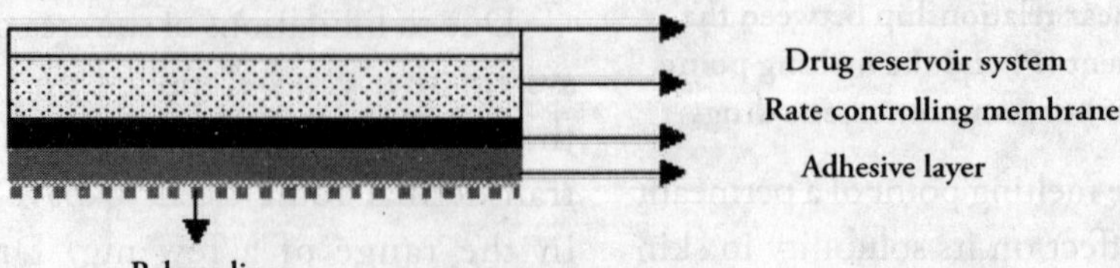

Figure 3.2: Different layers of the membrane-controlled transdermal drug delivery system (Reservoir system)

$$dQ/dt = kt \quad (5)$$

where k is a release rate constant. The above mentioned formula applies to all geometries of the device and the type of release is zero order.

The intrinsic rate of drug release from this type of drug delivery system is defined by

$$dQ/dt = \frac{C_r}{1/P_m + 1/P_a} \quad (6)$$

where C_r is the drug concentration in the reservoir compartment, P_a and P_m are the permeability coefficients of the adhesive layer and the rate-controlling membrane, respectively. For a microporous membrane, P_m is approximately the sum of permeability coefficients across the pores and the polymeric material. P_m and P_a are defined as follows:

$$P_m = K_{m/r} \times D_m / h_m \text{ and} \quad (7)$$

$$P_a = K_{a/m} \times D_a / h_a \quad (8)$$

where $K_{m/r}$ and $K_{a/m}$ are the partition coefficients for the interfacial partitioning of drug from the reservoir to the membrane and from the membrane to the adhesive, respectively; D_m and D_a are the diffusion coefficients in the rate-controlling membrane and adhesive layer, respectively; h_m and h_a are the thickness of the rate-controlling membrane and adhesive layer, respectively. In microporous membranes, the porosity and tortuosity factors of the membrane should be taken into account while calculating the coefficients.

B. Adhesive diffusion-controlled transdermal delivery systems

The drug reservoir is formulated by directly dispersing the drug in an adhesive polymer and then spreading the medicated adhesive by solvent casting onto a flat sheet of drug-impermeable metallic-plastic backing to form a thin drug reservoir layer. On the top of the drug reservoir layer, layers of non-medicated, rate-controlling adhesive polymers of constant thickness are spread to produce an adhesive diffusion-controlled drug delivery system. The anatomy of an adhesive diffusion controlled transdermal delivery system is shown in Fig. 3.3. The rate of drug release is defined by

$$dQ/dt = \frac{K_{a/r} \times D_a \times C_r}{h_a} \quad (9)$$

where $K_{a/r}$ is the partition coefficient for the interfacial partitioning of drug from the reservoir layer to the adhesive layer.

C. Matrix-type and single layer drug in adhesive-type TDDS

Figures 3.4 (a) and 3.4 (b) represent the construction of a matrix-type and single layer drug in adhesive-type transdermal systems, respectively.

In the matrix-type, the drug reservoir is formed by homogeneously dissolving or dispersing the drug in a hydrophilic or lipophilic polymer matrix, and the medicated polymer

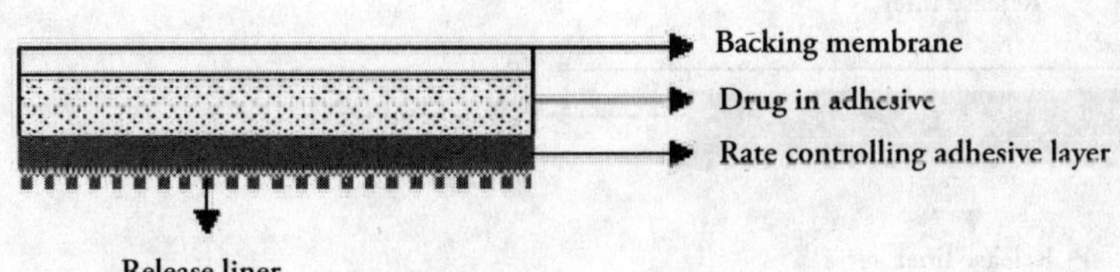

Figure 3.3: Different layers of adhesive diffusion-controlled transdermal drug delivery system

is then moulded into a medicated disc with a defined surface area and controlled thickness. This drug reservoir containing a polymer disc is then glued onto an occlusive base plate in a compartment fabricated from a drug-impermeable plastic backing. Instead of spreading the adhesive polymer onto the surface of the medicated disc, the adhesive polymer is applied along the circumferences to form a strip of adhesive rim around the medicated disc.

In adhesive-type devices, the drug is dissolved/dispersed in a pressure-sensitive adhesive itself, which is glued onto the occlusive base plate in an impermeable plastic backing. This does not require additional adhesive on the circumference.

If the drug in the polymer matrix or adhesive is dissolved homogeneously, the amount of drug released from these systems will be proportional to $t^{1/2}$ until about 60% of the active agent is released. The release rate thereafter is related exponentially to time, that is,

$$dM_t/dt = k_1 e^{-k_2 t} \quad (10)$$

Thus the rate of release above 60%, drops exponentially. This type of release, which is called first order, is also observed in reservoir systems in which the solution of the active agent within the enclosure is less than saturation.

If the drug is dispersed/suspended in the polymer matrix or adhesive, the amount released is proportionate to $t^{1/2}$ as along as the concentration of the active agent present (dispersed and dissolved) is higher than the solubility of the agent in the matrix. Thus, the dispersed systems are similar to the dissolved systems, except that, instead of decreased release rate after 60% of the chemical has been emitted, the relationship holds almost over the complete release curve.

The rate of drug release from the polymer matrix or adhesive layer that contains the drug in the dispersed form is defined by

$$dA/dt = (AC_p D_p / 2t)^{1/2} \quad (11)$$

where A is the initial drug-loading dose dispersed in the polymer matrix; C_p and D_p are the solubility and diffusivity, respectively, of the drug in the polymer.

D. Multilayer drug in adhesive systems

The multilayer drug in adhesive is similar to the single layer drug in adhesive in that the drug is incorporated directly into the adhesive. However, the multilayer encompasses either the addition of a membrane between two distinct

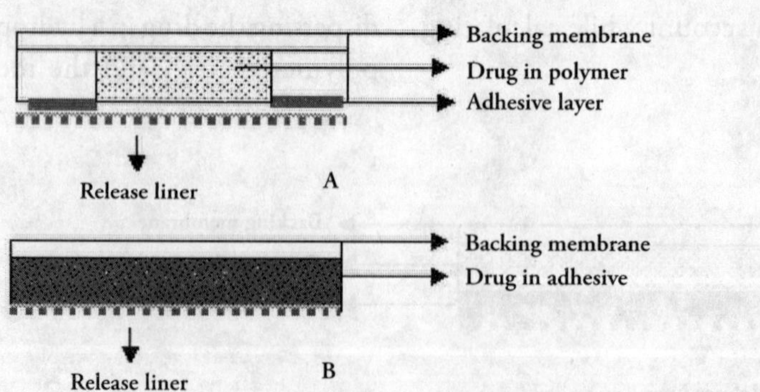

Figure 3.4: A. Matrix-type transdermal systems B. Single layer drug in adhesive-type transdermal systems

drugs in the adhesive layers or the addition of multiple drugs in adhesive layers under a single backing film.

The upper drug in the adhesive layer may serve as a reservoir for prolonged release or enhanced rate of drug release, while the lower drug in the adhesive layer may provide an initial burst of drug delivery immediately after applying to the skin and adhering the system to the skin (Fig. 3.5).

E. Microreservoir-type transdermal drug delivery systems

In this system, the drug reservoir is formed by suspending the solids in an aqueous solution of water-soluble liquid polymer. The drug suspension is then dispersed homogeneously in a lipophilic polymer, by high-shear mechanical force, to form thousands of unleachable, microscopic spheres of drug reservoirs. This thermodynamically unstable dispersion is stabilised by immediately cross-lining the polymer chains in situ, which produces a medicated polymer disc with a constant surface area and a fixed thickness. A TDDS is thus formed with the medicated disc positioned at the centre and surrounded by an adhesive rim. The structure of a typical microreservoir system is shown in Fig. 3.6.

F. Microstructured transdermal systems

Microneedles are a relatively new delivery technique, first appearing in the literature around 5 years ago, and were designed to create a physical pathway through the upper epidermis to increase skin permeability. Individual silicon needles measuring approximately 150 μm in length with a base diameter of 80 μm are fabricated on to arrays of approximately 3 x 3 mm (approximately 400 needles) as shown in Fig. 3.7. Needles with hollow centres have also been produced, each containing a

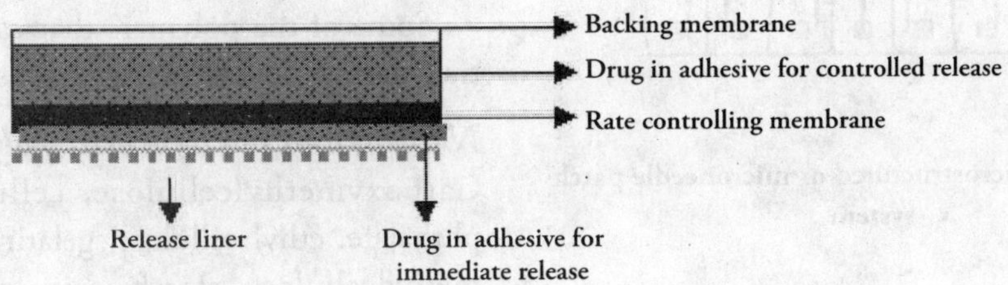

Figure 3.5: The different layers in multilayer drug adhesive system

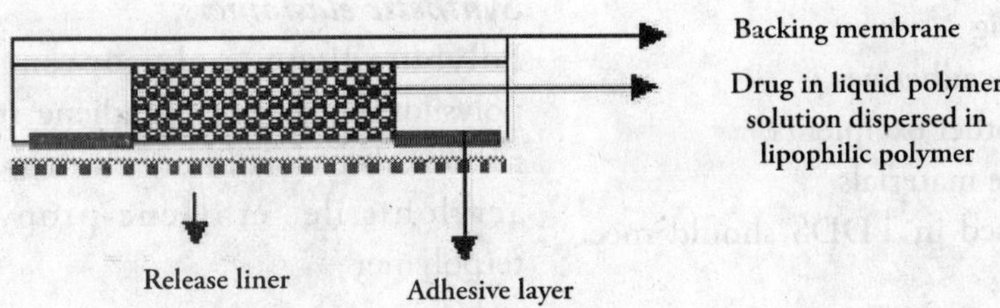

Figure 3.6: A typical microreservoir system

bore 5–70 μm in length (depending on the required design), through which drugs can be administered. Microneedle arrays are applied to the skin surface so that they pierce the upper epidermis (which contains no nerves) far enough to increase skin permeability and allow drug delivery, but too short to cause any pain to the receptors in the dermis. This system enables the disruption of the outermost layer of the skin, the SC, without causing pain. Several successful development milestones have been achieved with the microstructured transdermal system (MTS). The MTS expands the range of drugs that can be delivered transdermally and potentially reduces variation in TDD caused by different skin types and application sites. It is suitable for vaccines and protein- or peptide-based drugs.

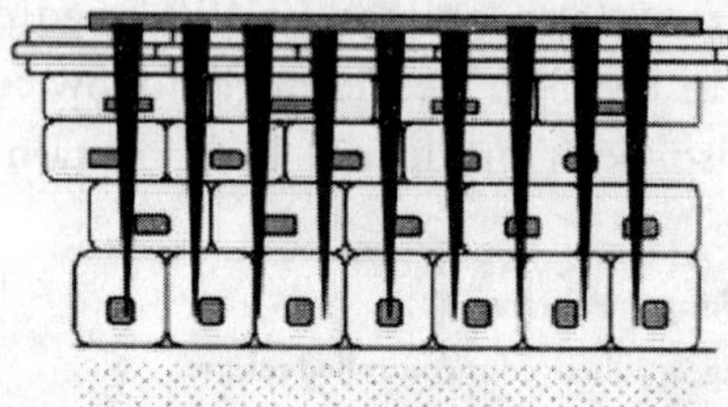

Figure 3.7: Microstructured or microneedle patch system

Components of TDDS

The components of TDDS include:

- Polymer matrix or matrices that regulate the release of the drug
- Pressure-sensitive adhesives
- Enhancers and other excipients
- Other supportive materials

The materials used in TDDS should meet certain basic criteria:

a. They should be non-irritating and non-sensitising to the skin.
b. They should be chemically inert and must particularly not react with the drug.
c. The component or its degradation products must be nontoxic.
d. They should be stable at the conditions of handling.
e. The cost should not be prohibitive.

Polymer Matrix or Polymeric Membrane

The polymer used in the transdermal therapeutic system (TTS) is formulated either as a matrix/reservoir to hold the drug or as a rate-controlling membrane. In addition to the basic characteristics, the molecular weight, glass transition temperature and chemical functionality of the polymer must allow the proper diffusion and release of the specific drug. The polymer must be easily manufactured and fabricated into the desired product. It should allow incorporation of large amounts of active agent without experiencing excessive deterioration of its mechanical properties.

Some of the polymers that can be used for transdermal devices are as follows:

Natural and semisynthetic polymers: Carboxymethylcellulose, cellulose acetate phthalate, ethyl cellulose, gelatin, gum arabic, methylcellulose, starch, zein, nitrocellulose, propylhydroxylcellulose, shellac, waxes, paraffin, proteins, natural rubber, succinylated gelatin

Synthetic elastomers: Polybutadiene, polyisoprene, neoprene, polysiloxane styrene-butadiene rubber, hydrin rubber, butyl rubber, chloroprene, nitrile acrylonitrile, ethylene-propylene-diene-terpolymer

Synthetic polymers: Polyvinyl alcohol, polyethylene, polypropylene, polystyrene polyester, epoxy, ethylene vinyl acetate, polyester, polyacrylamide

Pressure-sensitive Adhesives

Some polymers used in the formulation of TDDS possess pressure-sensitive adhesion properties. However, to impart good adherence characteristics to the device, some specific pressure-sensitive adhesives need to be incorporated in the system.

Pressure-sensitive adhesives (PSAs) help secure the transdermal device on the skin over long periods of time. PSAs must leave no residue when peeled off from either the release liner or the skin. Furthermore, the TDDS must be easy to remove from the release liner and from the skin, without causing pain that might discourage patients from using these products. The characteristics described above are strongly dependent on the mechanical properties of PSAs.

The major classes of PSA polymers are acrylics, silicones and polyisobutylenes. Acrylic PSAs have several desirable features such as resistance to oxidation and thermal degradation and moderate cost. They are permeable to water vapour and oxygen and generally exhibit good tackiness. In addition, their properties can be easily modified by incorporating different monomers during polymerisation.

The properties of the PSA layer in a TDDS depend on the incorporated drug, the components of the TDDS (for example, backing film), the excipients (for example, penetration enhancers, solubilisers) and the chemical composition of the PSA.

PIB-based Adhesives

Polyisobutylenes (PIBs) are elastomeric polymers that are commonly used in PSAs, both as primary base polymers and as tackifiers. They are homopolymers of isobutylene and feature a regular structure of a carbon–hydrogen backbone with only terminal unsaturation (Fig. 3.8). This molecular structure leads to chemical inertness and good resistance to weathering, ageing, heat and chemicals. Their stability, inertness and broad acceptance in applications regulated by the Food and Drug Administration (FDA) means that PIBs are a good candidate adhesive for use in TDD devices.

$$\underset{\text{Isobutylene}}{CH_3-\overset{CH_3}{\underset{}{C}}=CH_2} \longrightarrow \underset{\text{Polyisobutylene}}{\left[-\overset{CH_3}{\underset{CH_3}{C}}-CH_2-\right]_n}$$

Figure 3.8: Polymerisation of isobutylene to polyisobutylene

Because of their highly paraffinic and nonpolar nature, PIBs are soluble in typical aliphatic and aromatic hydrocarbon solvents, but not in common alcohols, esters, ketones and other oxygenated solvents. The structure of close and unstrained molecular packing leads to low air, moisture and gas permeability. The higher the molecular weight of the PIB, the lower its permeability. Polyisobutylenes are, therefore, preferred for use with drugs with a low solubility parameter and low polarity.

The amorphous characteristics and low glass transition temperature (T_g,–62°C) of PIBs impart high flexibility and permanent tack. Despite the favourable tack property, adhesion of PIBs to many surfaces is weak because of their low polarity. This problem is overcome by the addition of tackifiers (such as rosin ester resins) and other materials that impart some polar properties to the formulation.

PIBs are produced over a wide range of molecular weights. Low molecular weight PIBs are very viscous, soft and tacky semi-liquids, whereas the high molecular weight grades are tough and elastic rubbery solids. The low molecular weight polymers are primarily used as tackifiers to provide tack to the high molecular weight PIBs or other adhesive polymers. The high molecular weight PIBs are used to impart internal strength and flow resistance to PSAs.

Because of their favourable stability over a wide range of temperatures, humidity and electromagnetic radiation (UVA, UVB and UVC lights), PIBs do not normally contain stabilisers. If necessary, antioxidants or stabilisers can be added to significantly extend the resistance to extreme conditions.

Acrylic Adhesives

The main advantage of acrylic adhesives is the range of copolymers that can be synthesised, with the corresponding versatility of physicochemical properties that can be attained. They are produced through the copolymerisation of acrylic esters with acrylic acid and other functional monomers (Fig. 3.9). This is a particularly interesting set of PSAs for use as matrix adhesives, given the wide range of drugs that need to be delivered. Clearly, the acrylic family dominates the medical PSA market.

Since the acrylics are saturated polymers, they are highly resistant to oxidation and do not require the addition of stabilisers. They are moderately polar because of their ester structure and thus, have a degree of moisture permeability.

Acrylic polymers have a low T_g (–55 to –15 °C) and are inherently tacky, and therefore, in general, they do not require low molecular weight tackifiers and plasticisers to provide tack and softness.

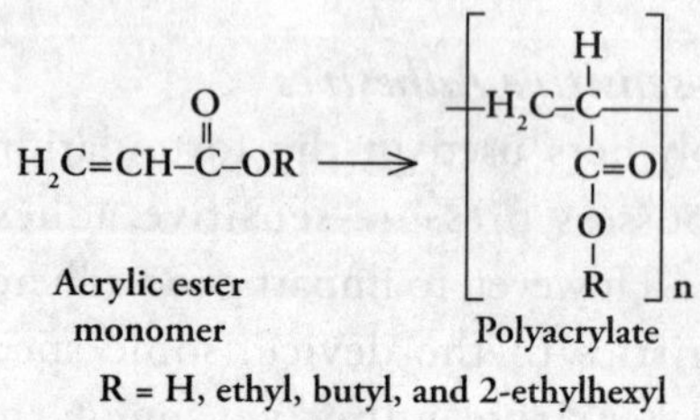

$$H_2C{=}CH{-}\overset{O}{\overset{\|}{C}}{-}OR \longrightarrow \left[{-}H_2C{-}\underset{\underset{\underset{\underset{R}{|}}{O}}{|}}{\underset{C=O}{\overset{H}{\overset{|}{C}}}}{-} \right]_n$$

Acrylic ester monomer — Polyacrylate

R = H, ethyl, butyl, and 2-ethylhexyl

Figure 3.9: Polymerisation of acrylic ester monomers

Silicone-based PSAs

Silicone PSAs are composed of a long-chain polymer (poly dimethyl siloxane (PDMS)) and a benzene-soluble silicate resin. The ratio of resin to PDMS determines the nature of the final product; in general, the higher this ratio, the harder the final silicone. The polymer is a high molecular weight PDMS that contains residual silanol functionality (SiOH) on the ends of the polymer chains. The low T_g of –127 °C and the unique semi-organic structure give silicone a highly flexible and extremely open macromolecular architecture with a high void volume. The resin is a three-dimensional trimethylsiloxy and hydroxyl end-blocked silicate structure (Fig. 3.10). The silicone polymer and silicate resin are dissolved together in a nonpolar hydrocarbon solvent (such as xylene and hexane).

Silicone adhesives have high permeability to moisture and oxygen, which helps reduce the degree of occlusion. This may also be indicative of high permeability of drugs, which is an important factor to be considered for TDDSs in which the drug-releasing surface is covered with adhesive.

They possess excellent chemical stability, low toxicity and skin compatibility.

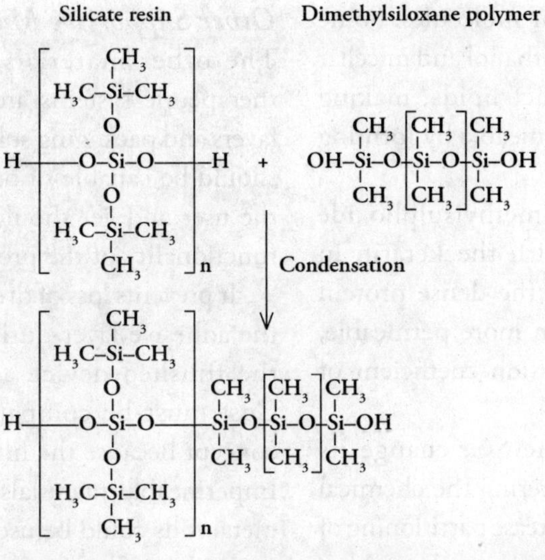

Silicate resin

Dimethylsiloxane polymer

Condensation

Figure 3.10: The chemistry of silicone pressure-sensitive adhesives (PSAs)

The first few generations of silicone adhesives were sensitive to amine drugs because of the presence of silanol groups. Subsequent generations of silicones were developed to be amine resistant and can be used in a wide range of transdermal systems. End-capping the silanol groups with alkyl groups brings about resistance to amine.

Chemical Permeation Enhancers

Substances that temporarily diminish the barrier property of the skin, known as accelerants or sorption promoters, can enhance drug flux. They would ideally work rapidly, and the activity and duration of effect should be both predictable and reproducible. They should have no pharmacological activity. The penetration enhancers should work unidirectionally, that is, they should allow therapeutic agents into the body while preventing the loss of endogenous material from the body. When these accelerants or sorption promoters are removed from the skin, the barrier properties should return both rapidly and fully. However, no such material that possesses all these ideal properties has yet been discovered, although some chemicals demonstrate several of these attributes.

Penetration enhancers act through three possible mechanisms:

1. The enhancer disrupts SC lipid organisation, making it permeable. The essential action increases the drug's diffusion coefficient (D in Equation 1). The accelerant molecules increase the free volume available for drug diffusion. Without enhancers, the free volume fraction is lowest (and D lowest) near the bilayer interface. Even a slight increase in free volume fraction, as enhancer molecules congregate there, dramatically increases D. Azone, terpenes, fatty acids, dimethylsulphoxide (DMSO) and alcohols are the enhancers that operate mainly in this manner. However, oleic acid and terpenes, at high loadings, pool within lipid domains; that is, they phase-separate. Permeable 'pores' form, which allow easier access to the

viable epidermis for polar molecules. Some solvents such as DMSO, ethanol and micellar solutions may also extract lipids, making the horny layer more permeable by forming aqueous channels.

2. Ionic surfactants, decylmethylsulphoxide and DMSO interact with the keratin in corneocytes to open up the dense protein structure and make them more permeable, thus increasing the diffusion coefficient of the permeant.
3. Many solvents enter the SC, change its solution properties by altering the chemical environment and thus increase partitioning of a second molecule into the horny layer (that is, raise Ks in Equation 1). This molecule may be a drug, a coenhancer or a cosolvent (including water). For example, ethanol increases the penetration of nitroglycerine and estradiol. Propylene glycol is also widely employed, particularly to provide synergistic mixtures with molecules such as azone, oleic acid and terpenes to raise the horny layer concentration of these enhancers.

In theory, nonsolvent enhancers that raise drug diffusivity using the mechanisms discussed above (lipid action) should also increase the partition coefficient for lipid drugs. By disordering the lipid interfacial domain, they increase free volume and make a larger fraction of the bilayer available for solute partitioning.

Many chemical enhancers use a combination of these three mechanisms. Thus, high concentrations of DMSO (above 60%) disturb intercellular organisation, extract lipids, interact with keratin and facilitate lipid drug partitioning.

Table 3.1 lists the different classes of enhancers and provides corresponding examples along with their mechanism of action.

Other Supportive Materials

The other materials used in transdermal therapeutic systems are release liners, backing layers and packaging substrates. The release liner should be capable of being easily peeled off by the user and yet should not interfere with the functionality of the product.

It prevents loss of drug that has migrated into the adhesive layer during storage and protects the finished device against contamination. Cost must be compatible with a disposable concept because the liner will be thrown away. Impermeable materials such as polyesters and metal foils could be used as release liners.

Backing films must be flexible and provide a good bond to the drug reservoir—thereby preventing the drug from leaving the dosage form through the top—and accept printing. They are usually impermeable to water vapour. Polyester-polyethylene coextruded films could be used as backing membranes.

Most patches used in a TDDS are packaged as unit doses in sealed pouches. The pouching material is therefore critical to the stability and integrity of the product. This packaging component compensates for the stability or instability of the system. Protecting the product from external factors (light, oxygen, and so on), together with the product characteristics and the reactivity and adsorption phenomena of the active ingredients, dictate the structure and construction of the pouch film, which in most cases will be composite.

Testing of Transdermal Therapeutic Systems

The TTSs are subjected to several physical, chemical and biological tests at the preclinical level to establish the adherence, safety, stability

Table 3.1: Different classes of enhancers and their mechanism of action		
	Example	*Mechanism*
Hydrating substances	Water and occlusive preparations	Hydrates the SC Increases fluidity or disorder of intercellular bilayers
Keratolytics	Urea	Hydrates the SC Keratolysis
Organic solvents	Alcohols	Cotransports with the drug through the lipid layers, partially extracts lipids
	Polyols: Polyethylene glycol (PEG), Propylene glycol	Replaces bound water in the intercellular spaces, enhances penetration of lipophilic drugs
	Sulfoxides (for example, DMSO)	Partitions into the corneocytes, binds keratin, increases lipid fluidity
	Pyrrolidones	Interacts with both the keratin and lipid component of the SC
Fatty acids	Oleic acid	Increases fluidity of the intercellular lipids, shorter chain (C10-12) and branched or unsaturated chain fatty acids are more effective than longer chain saturated fatty acids
Terpenes	Ascaridole	Disrupts intercellular lipid order
	1,8-Cineole	Opens up polar pathway
	L-Menthol	
	D-Limonene	
Surfactants	Polysorbates (Tweens)	Penetrates into skin, micellar solubilisation of SC lipids
	Polyoxyethylene alkylphenols (Brij)	
	(Cationic)-Dodecyltrimethyl ammonium bromide	Penetrates into skin, extracts lipid from SC
	Anionic surfactants (for example, sodium lauryl sulfate (SLS)	Binds to intracellular keratin in corneocytes, removes some of the intercellular lipid
Azone®	1-Dodecylhexahydro-2H-azepine-2on2 and certain derivatives	Disrupts the skin lipids in both the head group and tail regions
Phospholipids	Phosphotidylcholine,	Diffuses into SC, perturbs intercellular lipid, enhances drug partitioning into skin
Cyclodextrins	Methyl, hydroxypropylmethyl, Beta-CD	Increases drug concentration at the interface of skin and formulation, extracts SC lipids

and performance characteristics of the formulation.

In Vitro Evaluation of TDDS

The Franz diffusion cell is probably the most widely used diffusion cell and has been commercially available for many years (Fig. 3.11 (a)). The cell consists of two chambers; the bottom one holds the buffer or the receiver medium and the upper chamber or the donor holds the formulation. The barrier is sandwiched between the two half cells and clamped. The receiver compartment solution may be withdrawn at different time intervals to measure the drug diffused.

The receptor volume varies with the diameter of the opening for the skin specimen. The Franz cell receptor volumes are 3.8 ml for a 7 mm cell and 5.4 ml for a 9 mm cell. Physiological temperature should be maintained during the diffusion experiments. The receptor fluid should be mixed properly with magnetic stirring bars to prevent the formation of stagnant diffusion layers as well as to ensure uniform mixing of the diffused content.

Horizontal diffusion cells are also two-chamber systems. However, in this case, the skin is sandwiched vertically and there is provision for stirring of both the compartments (Fig. 3.11 (b)).

Flow-through diffusion cells:

The advantage of flow-through diffusion cells is that they can be used when the drug has lower solubility in the receptor compartment. In addition, these cells can be fully automated and connected directly to a high performance liquid chromatography (HPLC) instrument. They have a large capacity donor chamber

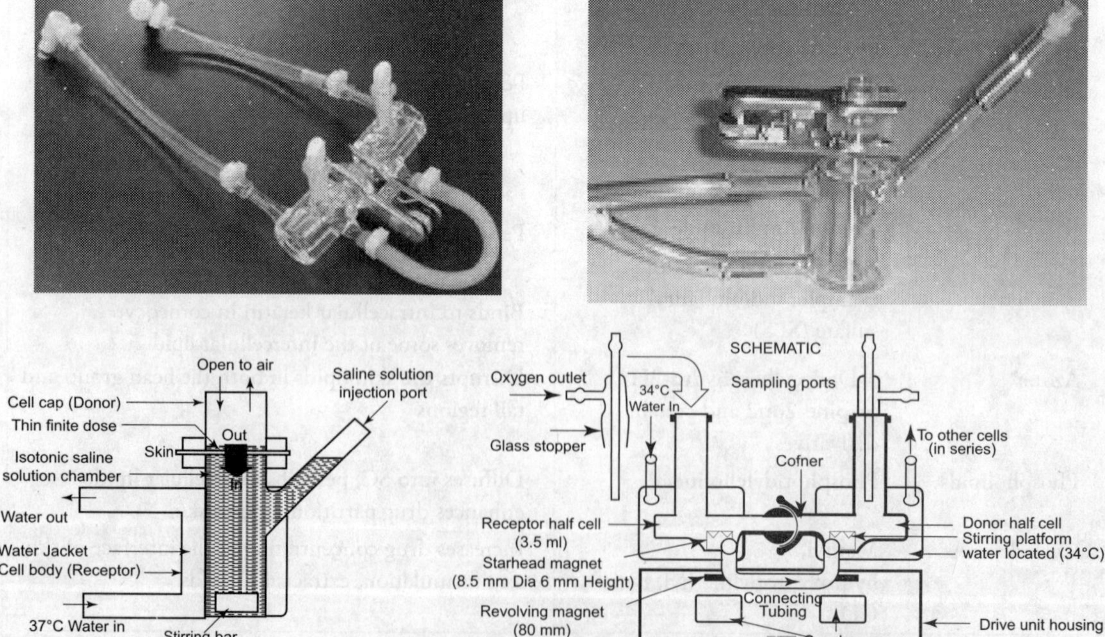

Figure 3.11: Vertical (a) and horizontal (b) diffusion cells and their anatomy

to allow appropriate loading of the applied compound and a low volume (0.3 ml) receiving chamber that ensures rapid removal of the penetrant at relatively low (1.5 ml/h or less) pumping rates. Furthermore, variously sized support disks allow skin pieces as small as 4 mm in diameter to be used.

Preclinical In Vivo Evaluation

The ideal way to determine the transdermal delivery potential of a compound in human beings is to perform a clinical study. Mechanisms and parameters of transdermal delivery elucidated with human skin are most relevant to the clinical situation. However, it is not practically feasible to test the formulation directly on human volunteers without confirming their ability and safety in preclinical studies. Compared to absorption in humans, absorption in common laboratory animals, rats and rabbits is high. The other animal models used are dogs, monkeys and pigs. However, the data gathered thus far suggests that the animal models most predictive of percutaneous absorption for transdermal delivery in humans are the pig and monkey. Rodents are considered as poor models for transdermal permeation studies because of significant differences in skin texture and structure and due to the presence of numerous hair follicles. Absorption in the pig and monkey (squirrel and rhesus) appears more predictive of in vivo data in humans.

Typically, the TDDs formulation is applied on a predetermined shaved surface of the skin and blood samples are obtained at different time intervals to measure the concentration of the drug. The most critically observed parameters include plasma maximum and minimum concentrations, lag time and elimination half life of the drug.

Physical Permeation Enhancement Techniques or Active TTS

Rationale for use of physical permeation enhancement techniques

Physical permeation enhancement techniques are considered superior in efficiency to chemical enhancers. However, use of these techniques increases the cost of the treatment. Choice of physical permeation enhancement technique should be based on suitable therapeutic rationale. Some of the techniques discussed in this section are at the stage of preclinical or early clinical evaluation.

Delivery of Peptide and Protein Drugs

For protein and peptide drugs, the transdermal route has the potential to be an extremely efficient delivery site as it is associated with relatively low proteolytic activity. Insulin, cyclosporin, luteinising hormone-releasing hormone (gonadotrophin-releasing hormone) and thyrotropin-releasing hormone are a few examples. Unfortunately, they are larger molecules (>500 Da) and their permeability through the skin is poor and enhanced minimally by chemical penetration enhancers. Permeation of such larger molecules (>500 Da) is possible only by compromising the barrier properties of the SC by creating larger transport pathways and also by providing a driving force to the diffusing molecules.

Delivery of Vaccines

The function of the skin extends well beyond its obvious barrier properties. In particular, the skin contains associated lymphoid tissue and is home to a large number of professional antigen presenting cells (APCs), such as Langerhans cells (parabasal layer of the viable epidermis), recirculating T cells and dendrocytes (dermis).

The skin, therefore, hosts a highly active immune system and is capable of responding to foreign antigens and channeling activated APCs to the lymph nodes for antigen presentation to CD8+, CD4+ and T helper cells for further processing. The viable epidermis also contains a higher population of APCs than the dermis and is therefore, actually a more desirable biological target for immunisation therapies. The recent surge in biotechnology research has resulted in the development of a significant number of other potentially therapeutic recombinant DNA, monoclonal antibodies, peptides, proteins, carbohydrates, oligonucleotides and other gene-based compounds. Therefore, in recent years, there has been a lot of emphasis on the development of safe and efficient physical techniques for the transdermal delivery of drugs.

Iontophoresis

An iontophoretic device comprises a power source and two electrode compartments. The drug formulation (D^+A^-) containing the ionised molecule (D^+) is placed in the electrode compartment bearing the same charge; for example, a positively charged drug such as lidocaine would be placed in the anodal compartment. The indifferent electrode compartment is placed at a distal site on the skin. Although there are many types of electrodes, the the Ag/AgCl couple is the one best suited for iontophoresis as it avoids the sharp decreases in pH that are seen with, for example, Pt-metal electrodes. The electrochemistry of Ag/AgCl electrodes occurs at voltages lower than those necessary for the electrolysis of water, which is not desirable for two reasons:

- The protons created at the anode compete to carry charge, and because of their small size and high mobility, they may significantly reduce drug delivery efficiency.
- The low pH produced in the anodal compartment can lead to acid-induced skin burns and may have an adverse effect on drug stability.

Once the current is applied, the electric field imposes directionality on the movements of the ions present—positive charges in the anodal compartment move towards the cathode whereas anions move in the opposite direction. The transport across the skin is believed to occur through the appendages of the skin.

The anodal compartment contains an ionisable drug D^+ with its counter-ions A^- and Na^+Cl^-. Application of an electric potential causes a current to flow through the circuit. At the electrode solution interface, Ag^+ and Cl^- react to form insoluble AgCl, which is deposited on the electrode surface. Electromigration transports the cations, including the drug molecule, from the anodal compartment and into the skin. At the same time, endogenous anions, primarily Cl^-, move into the anodal compartment. In the cathodal chamber, Cl^- ions are released from the electrode, and electroneutrality requires that either an anion is lost from the cathodal chamber or that a cation enters the chamber from the skin. The events that occur at the electrodes are represented in Fig. 3.12.

Factors such as the concentration of the penetrant and current strength influence the transport of the penetrant linearly up to a point of saturation due to the transport number of the drug ion. The pH of the drug-containing solution in contact with the skin may have an impact on iontophoretic transport through two distinct mechanisms. It will obviously have an effect on

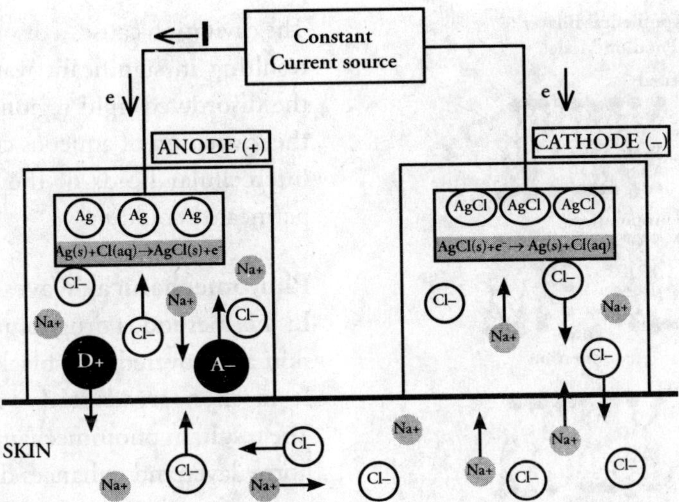

Figure 3.12: Iontophoresis using an Ag/AgCl electrode system

the degree of ionisation of the drug molecule; for weak bases, increasing pH will reduce the ionised fraction of the molecule and result in a decreased electromigratory contribution to iontophoretic transport. However, pH of the medium will also have an effect on the skin, which has an isoelectric point (pI) of 4–4.5. Above this pH, the carboxylic acid groups of the skin lipids are ionised; therefore, at higher pH values, the skin behaves like a permselective membrane, which, in turn, gives rise to the electro-osmotic solvent flow in the anode-to-cathode direction and hence introduces a second iontophoretic transport mechanism. Electro-osmosis is the convective transport of water across the membrane. Therefore, increasing the pH to above that of the pI can affect the iontophoretic delivery of weakly basic molecules in two opposing ways; as the pK_a of the drug is approached, the contribution of electromigration to transport will be reduced. However, at pH>pI, electro-osmosis will begin to contribute to the transport of both ionised and un-ionised permeant moieties. The relative impact and net effect of these opposing trends will depend on the physicochemical properties of the molecule.

Electroporation

Electroporation or electropermeabilisation is the transitory structural perturbation of lipid bilayer membranes by the application of high voltage pulses. The SC contains approximately 100 bilayer membranes in series, and electrical breakdown associated with dramatic increase in transport has been observed for transdermal voltages of 30–100 V (100–1500 V applied voltages). New aqueous pathways would then be created within the SC due to electroporation of its lipid bilayers. The hypothetical mechanism of electroporation is shown in Fig. 3.13. Molecular transport through the skin occurs through different mechanisms, mainly due to electrophoresis and permeabilisation of the stratum corneum. Electroporation could be used for a rapid and pulsed delivery of drugs and therapeutic macromolecules.

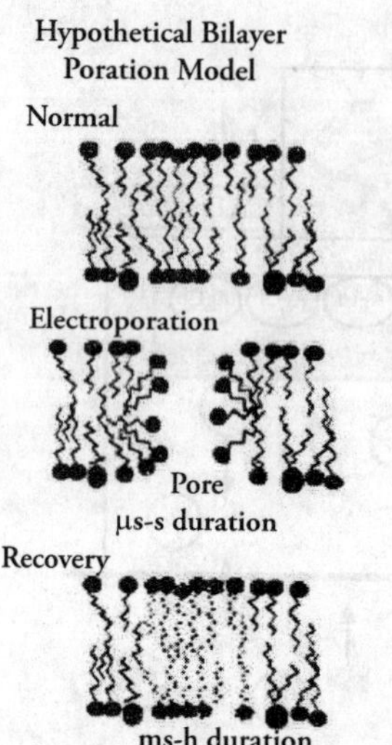

Figure 3.13: Hypothetical model for bilayer poration on application of high voltage short electrical pulses. (h, hour; s, second; ms millisecond; μs microsecond)

Sonophoresis

Ultrasound is defined as sound that has a frequency <18 kHz. Most modern ultrasound devices are based on the piezoelectric effect. Ultrasound over a wide frequency range has been used in medicine in the past century. Therapeutic ultrasound was the most commonly used frequency in early trials for TDD. Later, low frequency ultrasound was found to be more promising.

The ultrasound wave is longitudinal in nature (that is, the direction of propagation is the same as the direction of oscillation). Longitudinal sound waves cause compression and expansion of the medium at a distance of half a wavelength, leading to pressure variations in the medium, including cavitation, thermal effects, generation of convective velocities and mechanical effects. Transdermal transport during the application of low frequency ultrasound occurs across keratinocytes rather than hair follicles. The cavitation causes a disorder of the SC lipids, resulting in significant water penetration into the disordered lipid region. This may result in the formation of aqueous channels through the intercellular lipids of the SC through which permeants could move.

Photomechanical Waves

In this method, a drug solution is placed on the skin and covered by a black polystyrene target. It is then irradiated with a laser pulse. The resultant photomechanical wave stresses the horny layer and enhances drug delivery.

Magnetophoresis

Magnetophoresis is a novel approach to enhance TDD by allowing magnetic fields to move diamagnetic materials through the skin.

Drug diffusion is influenced by magnetic field strength and increases with greater applied field strength. The associated mechanism facilitating drug absorption is magnetohydrokinesis, which is the transport of water across the skin under the influence of a magnetic field. This approach to TDD is still in the early stages of development.

Future Trends

Today, the use of the skin as a route of drug delivery is well established and research into the development of devices for optimum drug delivery is underway. Currently, a few transdermal patches do exist for drugs such as scopolamine, nitroglycerin, nicotine, clonidine, fentanyl, estradiol, testosterone, lidocaine and oxybutinin. Depending on the drug, the time of duration of delivery is generally 1 to 7 days. Patches have been used to enable new therapies and reduce first pass effects. Transdermal clonidine, nitroglycerin and fentanyl patches exhibit fewer adverse effects than conventional oral dosage forms. The value of nicotine patches in preventing smoking and prolonging life has been of particular note.

Various approaches such as chemical enhancers, electricity, ultrasound and microneedles are being explored for the delivery of macromolecules. Iontophoresis has been the primary electrical approach studied and has been shown to provide enhanced transport for some low molecular weight molecules such as pain medications and decapeptides. Electroporation, which involves higher voltage pulses for shorter time periods, has been used to create reversible pores in the skin and has allowed the delivery of even larger molecules such as heparin and oligonucleotides through human cadaver skin. Ultrasound, particularly at low frequencies, has been shown to greatly enhance the flux of large molecular weight substances through the skin; fluxes that are over five thousand times the normal have been achieved for molecules the size of insulin or larger.

Further research will undoubtedly be aimed at better transdermal device design, development of novel methods and techniques and the assessment of the safety and efficacy of existing technologies for delivering a wide variety of molecules.

Key Messages

- Delivery of drugs through the skin has many advantages such as increased patient acceptability, GIT bypass and reduced first pass effects.
- Stratum corneum is the major barrier for transdermal delivery of drugs. However, molecules with favourable characteristics can transport therapeutically relevant quantities. The delivery of hydrophilic molecules requires alteration of the barrier properties of the skin using enhancers.
- Several physicochemical and biological factors influence transdermal drug absorption. It is inferred that for successful transdermal delivery:

a. The daily systemic dose of the drug should be ≤ 20 mg.
b. The daily systemic dose of the drug should have a molecular size ≤ 500 Da.
c. The log $K_{Oct/water}$ should be 1–2.
d. The melting point should be < 200 °C.
e. The drug should not be an irritant or immunogenic in the skin.

- Selection of suitable components and design of transdermal therapeutic system is crucial in determining the kinetics of drug delivery.
- Rate-controlling membrane devices are selected when the rate of drug delivery needs to be controlled by the device and not by the skin. On the other hand, matrix or reservoir devices without a rate controlling membrane should be selected when the drug delivery rate needs to be controlled by the permeability of the SC.
- Chemical permeation enhancers work well for smaller molecular weight hydrophilic drugs and they can easily be incorporated into transdermal therapeutic systems.

- Chemical permeation enhancers act either by increasing the diffusion coefficient or by increasing the partitioning of drugs in the SC.
- Delivery of hydrophilic/polar drugs over 500 Da in molecular size could be facilitated by physical permeation enhancement techniques, which are relatively more efficient as they are capable of creating larger as well as more number of transport pathways in the skin than chemical enhancers. Therefore, they are used to deliver peptides and proteins such as insulin and vaccines.

QUESTIONS

1. What are the possible pathways of drug absorption through the skin?
2. What are the advantages of transdermal drug delivery over oral delivery?
3. What physicochemical factors are assessed while selecting a drug for transdermal delivery?
4. What are the different possible designs of transdermal therapeutic systems?
5. How does the design of a transdermal therapeutic system influence the drug release kinetics?
6. What are the mechanisms of chemical permeation enhancement?
7. How are transdermal systems tested in vitro for drug delivery and absorption?
8. Why is the skin considered a potential route for antigen delivery?
9. What is the principle behind the iontophoresis technique?
10. What is the hypothesis of electroporation?

4

Ocular Drug Delivery Systems

S Narasimha Murthy

Learning Objectives

At the end of this chapter, you will be able to:

- List the factors attributed to poor ocular bioavailability of drugs
- Describe the pathways of corneal absorption
- Evaluate the critical factors influencing transcorneal drug absorption
- Assess the various formulation approaches
- Describe the novel ocular drug delivery systems

Introduction

Ocular medications are administered for the treatment of local infections such as conjunctivitis and keratitis sicca or intraocular problems such as uveitis and glaucoma. Eye drops are the most commonly available dosage form and are easy to formulate. One of the major problems encountered with the topical delivery of ophthalmic drugs using eye drops is the rapid and extensive precorneal loss caused by drainage and high tear fluid turnover. The usual ocular bioavailability with eye drops is estimated to be 1–5% of the applied drug. This necessitates frequent administration of the formulation.

Drugs can often be delivered to the posterior segment by injecting it through the pars plana, as is the case, for example, with ganciclovir, foscarnet and cidofovir. However, depending on the rate of clearance of particular medications from the vitreous humor, large boluses and frequent administrations may be required to ensure therapeutic levels over an extended period of time. In clinical practice frequent injections may not be practical for chronic diseases that can sometimes require multiple weekly administrations over months or years. In addition, multiple intraocular injections may lead to an increased likelihood of complications such as vitreous hemorrhage, retinal detachment and endophthalmitis.

Therefore, attempts are being made to formulate novel ophthalmic dosage forms to overcome the limitations of conventional ocular dosage forms and to facilitate corneal drug absorption. Designing new effective topical ophthalmic drug delivery approaches requires a thorough understanding of the physiological and biochemical basis of the protective mechanism of the eye that limits the absorption of a topically applied dose.

Physiological Limitations of Ocular Drug Delivery

Figure 4.1 provides an overview of the different causative factors of poor corneal absorption of drugs. All liquid dosage forms are rapidly drained from the conjunctival sac to the nasolacrimal duct. This drainage rate becomes even higher when the formulation is perceived to be irritating. Although the protein content of tears is much less than that of blood, the possibility of drug binding, resulting in a reduction in the free drug concentration for ocular absorption, exists.

Though lysozyme is the most important enzyme found in tears, other enzymes including lactate dehydrogenase, pyruvate kinase, malate dehydrogenase, amylase and esterase can also be found in the tear fluid as well as in other ocular tissues.

Corneal permeability: The cornea consists of three membranes: the epithelium, endothelium and inner stroma, which are the main absorptive barriers. The epithelium facing the tears with lipophilic cellular layers acts as a barrier to ion transport. The tight junctions of the corneal epithelium serve as a selective barrier for small molecules and prevent the diffusion of macromolecules through the paracellular route. The stroma beneath the epithelium is a highly hydrophilic layer making up 90% of the cornea. The corneal endothelium is responsible for maintaining normal corneal hydration.

Conjuctival absorption: The conjunctiva is a thin, visualised mucus membrane that lines the inner surface of the eyelids and covers the anterior part of the sclera up to the cornea. Owing to the relative leakiness of the membrane, rich blood flow and large surface area, conjuctival uptake of a topically applied drug from tear fluid is typically an order of greater magnitude than the amount of corneal uptake. This is not desirable not only because of the loss of active ingredients into systemic circulation, but also because of the possible side effects; for instance, the effects on the heart when β-blockers are administered for the treatment of wide-angle glaucoma.

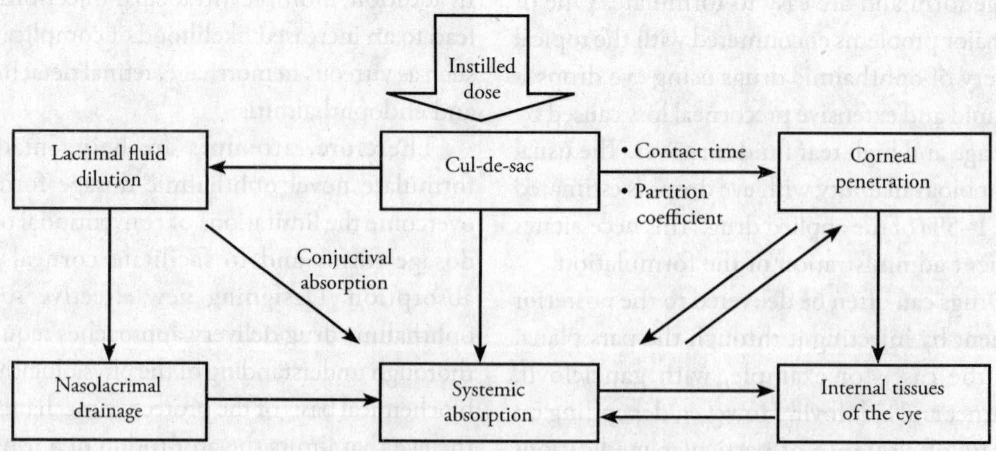

Figure 4.1: Factors contributing to poor bioavailability of drugs administered in the eye

Physicochemical Factors influencing Corneal Absorption of Drugs

The absorption of drugs across the corneal epithelium is generally dictated by its physicochemical properties. The primary physicochemical properties that influence ocular absorption of drugs include lipophilicity, molecular size, pKa and charge on the drug molecule.

Partition coefficient: As with other biological barriers, lipophilic drugs are absorbed better than hydrophilic drugs across the cornea. The more hydrophilic the drug, the more resistant is the epithelium to penetration, whereas the stroma and endothelium are limited in their resistance. Examples of drugs of varying lipophilicity and their transcorneal permeation are given in Table 4.1. Two major pathways are used for the movement of compounds through epithelial tissue: transcellular drug movement, that is a partition-controlled process; and diffusion of molecules through the intercellular pathway. Partitioning is especially important for hydrophobic molecules, which allow rapid movement into the lipid portions of the epithelial membrane. Optimum solubility for absorption is found in drugs with a $K_{Oct/buffer}$ distribution coefficient in the range 100–1000.

Schoenwald and Huang derived an equation about the relationship between the distribution coefficient and the permeability of various β-blockers.

$$\text{Log } P = 0.623 \log (K_{Oct/buffer}) - 0.108 (\log K_{Oct/buffer})^2 - 5.0268$$

where P is the permeability coefficient and $K_{Oct/buffer}$ is the distribution coefficient.

However, low molecular weight water-soluble compounds (mannitol, glycerol, water, methanol and butanol) do not correlate well with this equation and they are absorbed across the cornea. This suggests that these molecules undergo absorption through pores and not by the route associated with the partition coefficient (or distribution coefficient).

Table 4.1: Examples of drugs of different lipophilicity and their transcorneal permeation

Drug	*Log $K_{Oct/buffer}$*	*Apparent Permeability Coefficient ($\times 10^{-6}$ cm/sec)*
Acetazolamide	–1.9	0.95
Sulfacetamide	–1.0	1.02
Guanethidine	–0.3	<0.3
Cimetidine	0.4	0.7
Prednisolone	1.2	4.5
Bunolol	2.4	29.0
Flurbiprofen	4.3	21.0
Flurbiprofen amide	3.2	22.0

Molecular size: Cellular pores and intercellular spaces may be important for the transportation of hydrophilic compounds. An intact, full-thickness cornea is permeable to mannitol (molecular weight 182) but not to insulin and dextran, which are larger in size.

Charge: The corneal epithelial barrier is highly selective for the absorption of positively charged solutes. This is believed to be due to the coulombic attraction between the negatively charged corneal epithelial surface and the positively charged drug molecules.

pKa of the drug: Due to extensive dilution by lacrimal fluid, the pH of the vehicle becomes more or less equal to the lacrimal fluid. Hence, it is only the pKa of the drug that determines its ocular penetrability. Some reports support the pH partition hypothesis; however, some others suggest that ionised compounds are more readily sequestered in the cornea, which serves as a drug depot for prolonged drug delivery and activity.

Approaches to Ocular Drug Delivery Systems

The novel ocular drug delivery systems have been formulated with two main objectives: bioavailability and controlled release.

Viscous eye drops: Several strategies have been adopted to increase the precorneal residence time and reduce the quantity of drug lost to lacrimal drainage. Some simple modifications to eye drops such as incorporation of viscosifying and bioadhesive agents have proved to be very effective. The viscosity enhancers are often hydrophilic polymers, such as celluloses, polyvinyl alcohol and polyacrylic acid.

Gels: Besides providing effective contact between the formulation and the corneal surface, gels also help sustain the rate of release of the drug. The main problem associated with gel formulations has been the difficulty in proper administration due to high viscosity, blurred vision and matted eyelids, which substantially reduce patient acceptability. Despite this, gels are prescribed for their relatively long duration of action, reduced frequency and simplicity of administration and for their intermediate cost.

Polymeric gels are classified into two distinct groups: preformed gels and in situ forming gels, both of which improve bioavailability and decrease the side effects induced by the systemic absorption of topically applied ophthalmic drugs.

In situ gel-forming systems are viscous liquids that, upon exposure to physiological conditions, shift to a gel phase. The principal advantage of this formulation is the possibility of administering accurate and reproducible quantities in contrast to already gelled formulations and promoting precorneal retention. Different methods have been employed to cause phase transitions in the eye surface; change in viscosity triggered by a change in temperature, pH and electrolyte composition or the movement of eyelids. Poloxamers are polyols with thermal gelling properties whose solution viscosity increases when the temperature is raised to physiological temperature (33–34 °C, the surface temperature of the eye) from a critical temperature (16 °C). Cellulose acetate phthalate is a polymer with potentially useful properties for sustained drug delivery to the eye, since latex is a free-running solution at a pH of 4.4, which undergoes coagulation when the pH is raised by the tear fluid to 7.4. The gellan gum is known to form a clear gel in the presence of mono or divalent cations present in the lacrimal fluid.

Bioadhesive polymers have generated considerable interest in recent years as a way of substantially improving the performance of controlled delivery systems. The reasons for this interest are that these polymers can improve drug delivery through optimum contact with the absorbing surface to prolong residence time and reduce dosing frequency. Bioadhesive polymers are capable of forming strong non-covalent bonds with the mucin-coating biological membranes and remain in place as long as the mucin is present. Most of the bioadhesives used for drug delivery systems are composed of synthetic mucoadhesives. These include water-soluble polymers that are linear chains and water-insoluble polymers that are swellable networks joined by cross-linking agents. Typically, these polymers have a high molecular weight, which cannot cross biological membranes and include cellulosic components such as carboxymethyl cellulose and polyanion bioadhesives such as polyacrylic acid. Bioadhesive polymers may be used in small quantities as viscosifying or gel-forming agents in ocular formulations.

Prodrugs: The principle of prodrugs is to enhance corneal drug permeability through modifications to the hydrophilicity (or lipophilicity) of the drug. Several ophthalmic drugs have been investigated for prodrug derivatisation using, in most cases, the esterase properties found in tears and in the anterior chamber. Dipivefin, a prodrug of epinephrine, was found to possess better corneal penetration properties.

Penetration enhancers: Incorporation of penetration enhancers such as chelating agents, preservatives, surfactants and bile salts was found to improve the permeability of the corneal membrane. However, concerns about damage to the corneal membrane on chronic administration of such agents are yet to be clarified. Hydroxypropyl cyclodextrin has revealed favourable toxicological properties after ocular administration as an enhancer. Sulfobutyl ether β-cyclodextrin increases the ocular absorption of drugs. Chitosan has been found to be suitable for the formulation of ocular drug solutions and gels due to its bioadhesive and permeability enhancing properties.

Liposomes: The mechanism of enhancement activity results from the preferential capture of positively charged liposomes on the negatively charged corneal surface. Overall, the liposomal formulations have been found to be more effective for lipophilic drugs than for hydrophilic drugs because of the rapid leakage of the latter from the vesicles. Incorporation of bioadhesive polymers such as carbopol in the vesicular wall may provide bioadhesivity and enhance bioavailability of drugs.

Microemulsions: The main advantage of microemulsions is the increase in the solubilisation of drugs such as indomethacin, chloramphenicol and sodium diclofenac which thus enhance the bioavailability. In vivo studies in rabbits have shown a delay in the effect of the drugs incorporated in microemulsions, which improves their bioavailability. The proposed mechanism of delayed action is based on the adsorption of nanodroplets on the cornea, which are not eliminated by lacrimal drainage and act as reservoirs of the drugs.

Particulates and implants: Retentive systems such as implants and nanoparticles appear to have an advantage over most of the formulation types discussed. They are intended for long-term

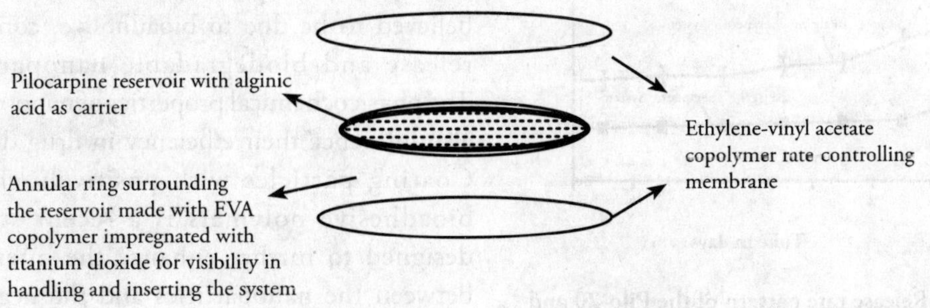

Figure 4.2: Schematic representation of Ocusert®

use and they provide relatively more consistent drug levels. Ocusert® (Alza Corporation) is an insoluble ophthalmic insert that consists of a central reservoir of pilocarpine enclosed between two semipermeable membranes, which allows the drug to diffuse from the reservoir at a constant rate for a period of 7 days (Fig. 4.2). Pilocarpine is a water-soluble oil that has a molecular weight of 280. It is a parasympathomimetic agent, which acts directly on target organs in the iris, ciliary body and trabecular meshwork, increasing the outflow of aqueous humor and decreasing intraocular pressure. Prolonged reduction in intraocular pressure was achieved with a single Ocusert®.

Graph 4.1 illustrates the release pattern of pilocarpine from two Ocusert® systems, Pilo-20 and Pilo-40, which release the pilocarpine at 20 μg/h and 40 μg/h, respectively. Both systems display a 'burst' effect, in which about three times the basal rate of pilocarpine is released during the first day of use. The Pilo-40 system contains Di (2-ethylhexyl) phthalate (DEHP) which enhances the rate of pilocarpine diffusion

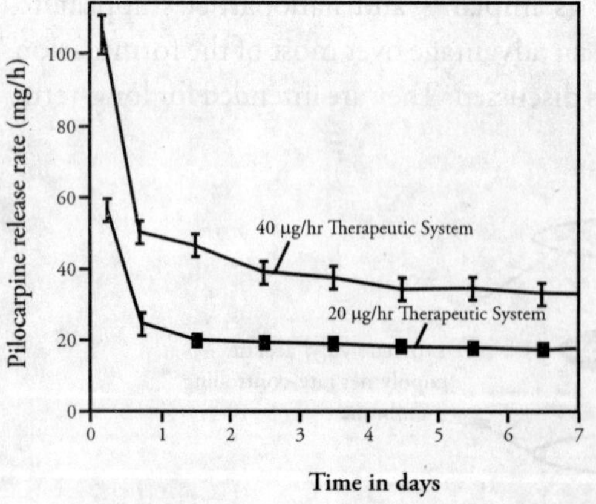

Graph 4.1: Release rate pattern of the Pilo-20 and Pilo-40 Ocusert

across the polymer membrane.

A ***collagen shield*** is a soluble insert that offers the advantage of being entirely soluble so that it does not need to be removed from its site of application, thus limiting intervention to insertion only. They are fabricated from porcine scleral tissue, which has a collagen composition similar to that of the human cornea. Typically, the drug is loaded into the collagen shield simply by soaking it in the drug solution for a period of time prior to application. The shields are hydrated by the tear fluid and then softened to form a clear, pliable, thin film (100 μm thick), which dissolves slowly within a maximum of 72 hours. They have been found to be suitable for the administration of amphotericin B and tobramycin and for the delivery of pilocarpine.

Nanospheres (matricial spheres with the drug incorporated in the matrix or adsorbed on the surface) and nanocapsules (central oily cavity surrounded by a polymeric membrane) have been revealed to be efficient as ocular drug delivery systems by prolonging the duration of action of the drugs. Polyacrylamide, polymethylmethacrylate, polylactic-co-glycolic acid and poly-Є-caprolactone are used to fabricate nanoparticles. The penetration of nanoparticles into eye tissue is limited to the precorneal area. Therefore, the enhanced therapeutic activity of drugs such as pilocarpine and antibiotics is believed to be due to bioadhesive, controlled release and biodegradable nanoparticles. The physicochemical properties of nanoparticles also influence their efficiency in drug delivery. Coating particles with positively charged bioadhesive polymers is a recent strategy designed to further enhance the interaction between the nanoparticles and the negatively charged corneal surface.

Research is underway for the formulation of intravitreal implants (Fig. 4.3). They have been found to have a profound impact on the treatment of cytomegalovirus retinitis. The development of sustained release ganciclovir implants has enabled local delivery of the drug without the need for multiple injections. The ganciclovir implant is produced by coating a compressed pellet of ganciclovir with ethylene vinyl acetate and polyvinyl alcohol. This implant releases the drug at a rate of 1 μg/h and leads to intravitreal drug levels that are much higher than those achieved with maintenance intravenous therapy. Similarly, intravitreal cyclosporin implants for the treatment of uveitis and corticosteroid implants for the management of ocular inflammatory disease have been formulated.

Evaluation of Ocular Drug Delivery Systems

Demonstration of safety and efficacy of the ocular delivery dosage forms at the preclinical in vitro and in vivo levels determines their further progression into clinical investigations. Choosing the appropriate animal tissue model, apparatus and procedures is very important in the evaluation of ocular drug delivery formulations.

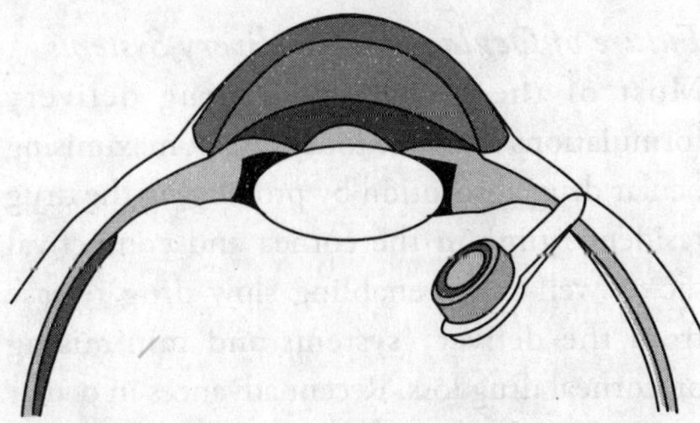

Figure 4.3: Schematic representation of intravitreal implant fixed to the sclera at the pars plana

In vitro diffusion

There are several basic designs for the corneal perfusion chamber. In the Ussing-type chamber, the corneal tissue is clamped in the vertical plane between two perfusion baths. Drugs are added to one bath (usually the corneal epithelial side of the chamber) and corneal penetration is assessed by measuring drug concentration in the other bath (usually on the corneal endothelial side of the chamber).

The perfusion chamber, described by Thiel et al, is constructed from polycarbonate and consists of the main body, a clamping sleeve and a fixation ring as shown in Fig. 4.4.

The central cavity of the main body has a diameter of 12 mm and is 3 mm deep and, together with the mounted cornea, forms the artificial 'anterior chamber'. The main body contains channels for inflow and outflow perfusion lines and an additional drainage channel that connects with a channel in the clamping sleeve. This channel allows the removal of excess fluid after topical application, mimicking lacrimal drainage. Corneoscleral

Figure 4.4: Corneal perfusion chamber. The clamping sleeve sits on top of the main body. The fixation ring that screws onto the main body is shown on the left.

preparations are placed over the central cavity of the main body and secured with the clamping sleeve, which covers both the sclera and the peripheral cornea. The sleeve has two stainless steel guide pins to direct its vertical movement without twisting, minimising sheer stress and edge damage to the cornea. The fixation ring secures the sleeve and the underlying cornea to the main chamber, creating a tight seal. The fixation ring has a 1 mm pitch thread that allows precise adjustment of the clamp.

The corneoscleral discs isolated from an animal are generally used for in vitro evaluation of the formulations. The cornea is mounted in the perfusion chamber and the inflow tube is attached to a peristaltic pump. The cornea is perfused with a continuous flow of buffer. The perfusate from the outflow tube is collected in a reservoir and re-circulated back into the chamber. The reservoir needs to be kept at about 25 cm above the level of the clamped cornea to create a positive pressure of 18 mm Hg inside the artificial anterior chamber, simulating physiological conditions. The perfusion chamber is surrounded by a heat exchange block through which warm water is circulated to maintain the temperature at approximately 35 °C. A construction plan of the cell is shown in Fig. 4.5.

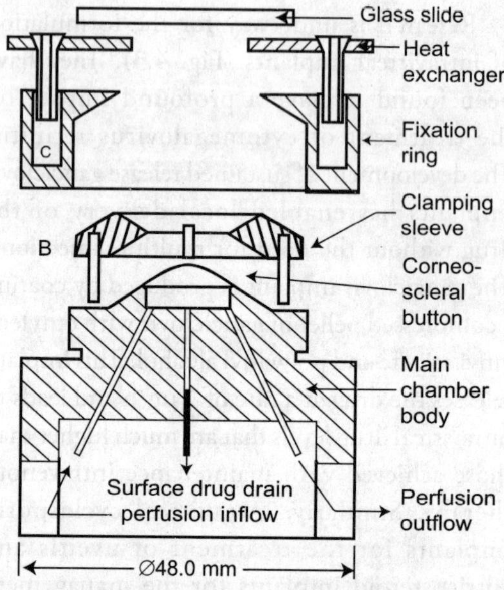

Figure 4.5: Chamber design: A–main body, B–clamping sleeve, C–fixation ring. The cornea is clamped between the main body and the clamping sleeve.

In vivo evaluation

One of the main disadvantages in assessing ocular delivery systems is that it is virtually impossible to carry out in vivo studies on an intact animal, partly because it is difficult to sample fluids and tissues in the quantities necessary for drug measurement. The rabbit has been the common animal model used for ocular drug delivery evaluation. The formulations are administered directly onto the corneas of both eyes, or placed in the cul-de-sac. Animals are then sacrificed at different time intervals post instillation. The corneal surface is washed and dried. Samples of aqueous humor are then removed from the anterior chamber using a 1 ml tuberculin syringe fitted with a 27-gauge needle.

Future of Ocular Drug Delivery Systems

Most of the novel ocular drug delivery formulations available today aim at maximising ocular drug absorption by prolonging the drug residence time in the cornea and conjuctival sac as well as by enabling slow drug release from the delivery systems and minimising precorneal drug loss. Recent advances in ocular technology have made it possible to deliver a wide range of medications for predictable periods of time. A few such products have been commercialised. Though some formulations are easy to manufacture and perform well, patient acceptability is limited because of the discomfort experienced during use. Experimental and clinical trials that are underway are expected to further refine the benefits and limitations of these new ocular drug delivery technologies.

Key Messages

- Formulation retention in the cul-de-sac is a critical factor in determining ocular bioavailability of drugs. Most formulation approaches incorporate this factor along with other aspects.
- Novel drug delivery systems such as Ocusert® have proved to be clinical and commercial successes. However, they suffer a marked 'lack of acceptance' from the patients.
- Conventional ocular dosage forms which have added characteristics to overcome the typical disadvantages have better patient acceptability. They are also less expensive and involve fewer procedures during formulation, and can be scaled up with less difficulty.

Questions

1. What are the physiological factors attributed to poor bioavailability of drugs administered to the eye?
2. What is the importance of the pH of the formulation in facilitating transcorneal partitioning of drugs?
3. What are the advantages of viscous, polymer-based formulations over conventional ophthalmic dosage forms?
4. What are in situ forming gels? Explain with examples.
5. What are the various approaches used to enhance the bioavailability of drugs by increasing the retention time of the formulation?
6. What are ocular implants?
7. What is the principle behind the in vitro evaluation of ocular drug delivery systems?

5

Nasal Drug Delivery Systems

S Narasimha Murthy

Learning Objectives

At the end of this chapter, you will be able to:

- List the advantages of nasal delivery
- Describe the structure of the nasal cavity
- Describe the nasal absorption pathways
- List the factors that influence nasal absorption
- List and describe the various nasal drug delivery formulations
- Describe the experimental setup for the evaluation of nasal drug delivery systems

Introduction

Conventionally, the nasal route has been used for the local delivery of drugs for the treatment of nasal allergies and infections. In recent years, research has established that the nasal route is a safe and acceptable alternative to the parenteral administration of drugs. The nasal route has also been found to be useful in targeting drugs to the central nervous system (CNS).

The major advantages of nasal delivery are:

- Rapid absorption and onset of action of drugs
- Elicitation of local immune response in respiratory infections such as influenza
- Ability to overcome hepatogastrointestinal 'first pass' metabolism associated with oral administration of drugs

Anatomy of the Nasal Cavity

The nasal cavity is divided into two separate cavities by a septum as shown in Fig. 5.1. Each cavity consists of three regions: the vestibule, which consists of the region just inside the nostrils (~0.6 cm^2), the olfactory region, which is situated in the roof of the nasal cavity (15 cm^2) and the respiratory region, which constitutes the remainder of the cavity (135 cm^2).

The respiratory region contains three nasal turbinates: the superior, middle and inferior, which project from the lateral wall of each half of the nasal cavity. The presence of these turbinates creates a turbulent airflow through the nasal passages, which ensures better contact between the inhaled air and the mucosal surface.

The nasal vestibule is covered with stratified squamous epithelium. This gradually changes in

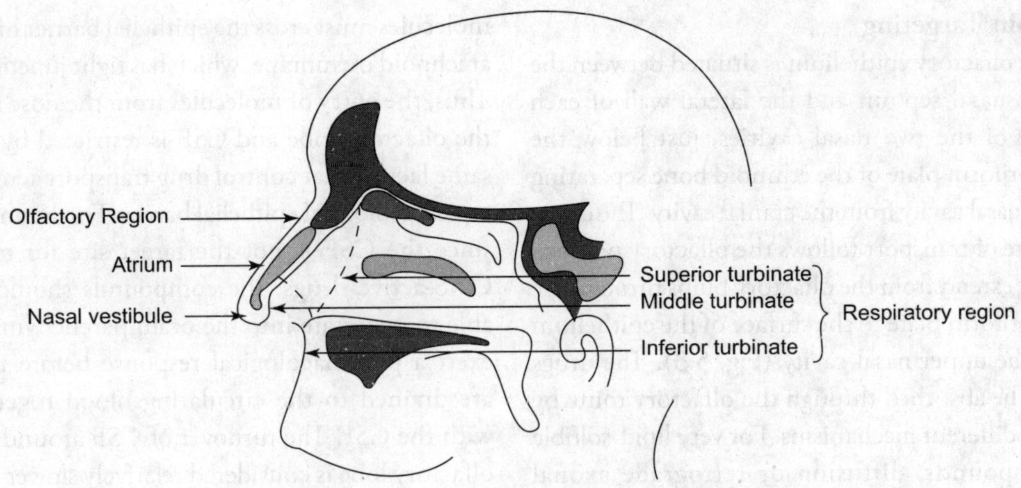

Figure 5.1: Schematic anatomy of the nasal cavity

the posterior into a pseudostratified columnar epithelium that covers the respiratory epithelium. The respiratory epithelial cells are covered with cilia and microvilli, which increase the surface area available for the absorption of drugs. The surface layer of the nasal cavity is composed of mucus, which is renewed every 15–20 minutes.

Absorption Pathways

The nasal absorption of drugs is thought to take place mainly in the respiratory region comprising the turbinates and part of the nasal septum. The drugs pass through the transcellular (across the cell) and paracellular (between the cells) pathways. Lipophilic drugs are transported transcellularly by concentration gradient diffusion while polar drugs are believed to pass through the epithelium through the pores between the cells. A diagrammatic representation of different pathways of drug absorption is shown in Fig. 5.2.

Although tight junctions are dynamic structures that can open and close to a certain extent, the size of these channels is <10 A°. Hence, the paracellular route is less efficient for large molecules and is dependent on the molecular weight of the drug, with a general molecular size cut-off of ~1000 Da. The larger peptides and proteins have been shown to be able to pass the nasal membrane using an endocytotic transport process but only in low amounts.

Carrier mediated transportation across the nasal mucosa has been demonstrated for some of the tyrosine-linked model compounds.

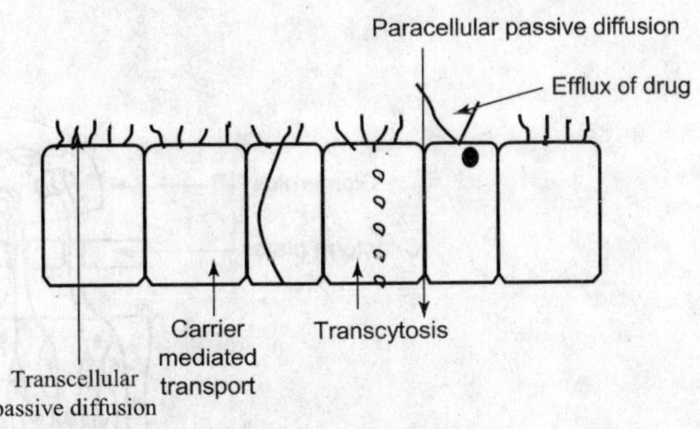

Figure 5.2: A schematic representation of different absorption pathways across the nasal mucosa

Brain Targeting

The olfactory epithelium is situated between the transnasal septum and the lateral wall of each side of the two nasal cavities, just below the cribriform plate of the ethmoid bone separating the nasal cavity from the cranial cavity. The direct route of transport follows the olfactory neurons that extend from the olfactory bulbs through the cribriform plate to the surface of the epithelium in the upper nasal cavity (Fig. 5.3). The drugs can be absorbed through the olfactory route by two different mechanisms. For very lipid-soluble compounds, diffusion or retrograde axonal transport within the neuron can lead to targeting of the olfactory bulbs followed by diffusion to the rest of the brain. This route of transportation is relatively slow and is probably not relevant in terms of drug administration. The second route of transportation is through the subarachnoid space, which extends along the olfactory nerves to the basolateral side of the olfactory epithelium. This route enables relatively quick absorption of hydrophilic and semi-lipophilic substances by the cerebrospinal fluid (CSF). However for molecules to enter the CSF following entry into the submucous spaces of the nose, the molecules must cross the epithelial barrier of the arachnoid membrane, which has tight junctions. Thus, the entry of molecules from the nose into the olfactory lobe and CSF is restricted by the same factors that control drug transport across a typical biological epithelial barrier. Furthermore, since the CSF is not the target site for most CNS-active drugs, the compounds should be able to penetrate into the brain parenchyma to exert a pharmacological response before they are drained to the circulating blood together with the CSF. The turnover of CSF around the olfactory lobe is considered relatively slower due to the more restricted flow.

Absorption by this pathway is determined mainly by the physicochemical properties of the drug. According to Bagger et al, the potential of brain targeting of hydrophilic compounds is limited. Sakane et al studied the transport of sulfonamides to the CSF directly from the nasal cavity. Figure 5.4 represents the relationship between the concentration of drugs in the CSF and their partition coefficients.

Figure 5.5 refers to the various absorption, distribution and elimination pathways of drugs on intranasal administration.

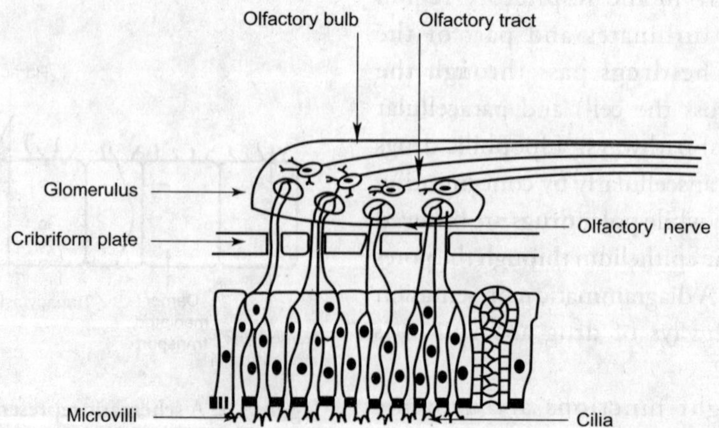

Figure 5.3: The schematic anatomy of nasal mucosa and the olfactory lobe

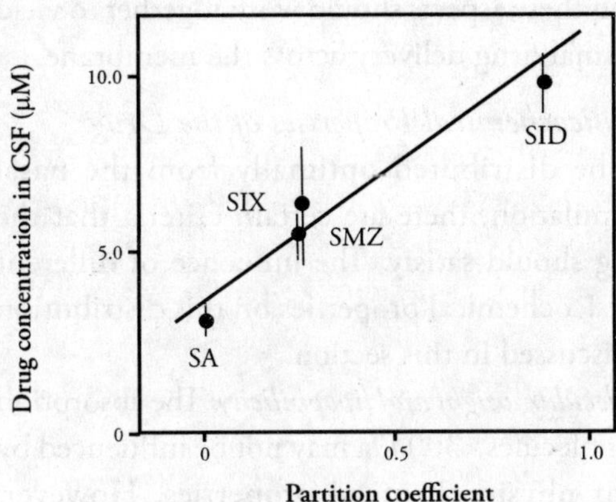

Figure 5.4: The relationship between the concentration in CSF to the partition coefficient for sulfonamides: Sulfisoxazole (SIX), Sulfamethizole (SMZ), Sulfisomidine (SID) and Sulfanilic acid (SA)

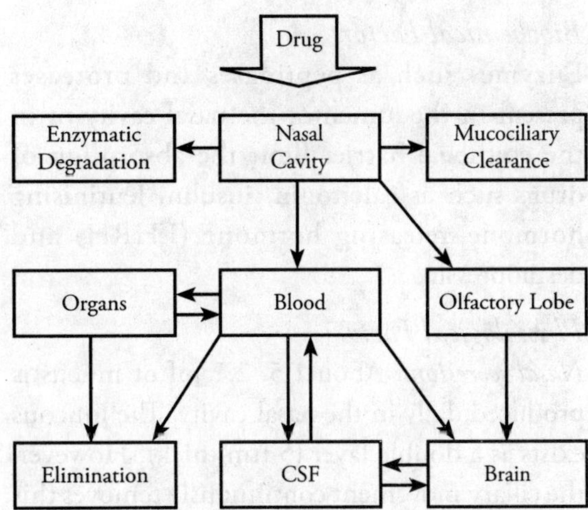

Figure 5.5: The various absorption, distribution and elimination pathways of drugs on intranasal administration

Nasal Delivery of Vaccines

The nasal passages are rich in lymphoid tissues, and the target site for nasally administered vaccines in humans is the nasal-associated lymphoid tissue (NALT), which is situated mainly in the pharynx as a ring of lymphoid tissue named Waldeyer's ring.

The chitosan nasal delivery system has been tested with three different vaccines—influenza, antipertussis and diphtheria—in various animal models and in humans. It has been shown that chitosan significantly enhances the immune response obtained from the influenza vaccine when it is given nasally to mice, with IgG levels similar to those obtained after subcutaneous injections of alum formulation.

Factors influencing Nasal Absorption

The factors that affect the permeability of a drug through the nasal mucosa can be broadly classified as biological, formulation and device-related factors.

1. Biological Factors

The barriers created by cellular arrangement, enzyme milieu and the physiological status of the mucus membranes greatly influence drug absorption. Some of these factors are discussed in this section.

Structural Features

Nasal absorption shows regional variation because different types of cells constitute the nasal epithelium and because of other factors such as the presence of microvilli, cell density and surface area and the number of cells. The respiratory region is richly supplied with blood, has a large surface area and receives the maximum amount of nasal secretions, rendering it most suitable for the permeation of compounds. Ultrastructural studies have shown fragmentation and discontinuity in tight junctions around filled goblet cells, and this discontinuity could be of relevance to the absorption of aerosol drugs deposited on the airway epithelium.

Biochemical Factors

Enzymes such as peptidases and proteases present in the lumen of the nasal cavity or in the epithelial barrier limit the absorption of drugs such as calcitonin, insulin, leutinising hormone–releasing hormone (LHRH) and desmopressin.

Physiological Factors

Nasal secretions: About1.5–2.1 ml of mucus is produced daily in the nasal cavity. The mucous exists as a double layer (5 μm thick). However, the ciliary movement continuously removes this mucous layer. Mucociliary clearance, viscosity of the nasal secretion, solubility of drugs in the nasal secretions and pH of the nasal secretions are the factors that significantly influence the nasal absorption of drugs.

Blood supply and neuronal regulation: Nasal cycles of congestion (increased blood supply resulting from parasympathetic stimulation) and relaxation (decreased supply resulting from sympathetic stimulation) regulate the rise and fall in the amounts of drug permeated, respectively.

Pathological conditions: Diseases such as the common cold, rhinitis, atropic rhinitis and nasal polyposis are usually associated with mucociliary dysfunctioning, hypo or hypersecretions and irritation of the nasal mucosa, which can influence drug permeation.

Environmental conditions: A linear increase in ciliary beat frequency occurs with increase in temperature, which in turn influences the properties of the mucous membrane.

2. Formulation Factors

The bioavailability of drugs from nasal formulations depends on the physicochemical properties of the drug and the formulation. Both these aspects should work together to yield optimal drug delivery across the membrane.

Physicochemical Properties of the Drug

To be distributed optimally from the nasal formulation, there are certain criteria that the drug should satisfy. The influence of different physicochemical properties on this distribution is discussed in this section.

Molecular weight and lipophilicity: The absorption of molecules <300 Da may not be influenced by their physicochemical properties. However, the diffusion of peptides and proteins >1 kDa are affected by their molecular weight. The bioavailability of such macromolecules was found to vary from 0.5 to 5%. Lipophilic drugs have been found to be relatively more permeable across the nasal epithelium.

Solubility: As nasal secretions are more watery in nature, a drug should have appropriate aqueous solubility for increased dissolution. Prodrugs such as testosterone 17 β-N, N-dimethylglycinate hydrochloride have been synthesised to overcome this poor solubility problem.

Partition coefficient and pKa: The pH of nasal secretions is about 5.5–6.5. The pKa of the drug determines the fraction of the drug in the un-ionised form under these conditions. The greater the un-ionised fraction, the higher the partitioning into the nasal epithelium and the better the absorption. However, when the absorption of benzoic acid was studied at a pH of 7.19 (99.9% of the drug existed in the ionised form), it was found that >10% of the drug was absorbed, indicating that the ionised species also permeates through the nasal mucosa. However, the un-ionised species is absorbed four times faster than the ionised species.

In the same study, with different barbiturates, the bioavailability increased with increasing lipophilicity of the drug (Table 5.1). The study was conducted at a pH of 6.0, at which barbiturates exist almost entirely in their unionised form.

Table 5.1: Comparison of the extent of nasal absorption in rats, of barbiturates (in 60 minutes) at a pH of 6 and partition coefficient ($K_{Chloroform/water}$) of the undissociated drug

Barbiturate	$K_{Chloroform/Water}$	*Percentage of Nasal Absorption*
Barbital	0.7	5.0 ± 3.0
Phenobarbital	4.8	10.6 ± 3.88
Pentobarbital	28.0	20.3 ± 4.65
Secobarbital	50.7	23.9 ± 3.38

Physicochemical Properties of the Formulation

The physicochemical parameters of the formulation affect the properties of the drug and the permeability status of the membrane. Therefore it is a challenging task to arrive at the best formulation parameters to achieve therapeutically effective levels of drug delivery.

pH and mucosal irritancy: The pH of the formulation, as well as that of the nasal surface, can affect a drug's permeation. To avoid nasal irritation, the pH of the nasal formulation should be adjusted to 4.5–6.5. In addition to avoiding irritation, it prevents the growth of bacteria.

Osmolarity: Drug absorption can be affected by the tonicity of the formulation. Shrinkage of epithelial cells has been observed in the presence of hypertonic solutions. Hypertonic saline solutions also inhibit or terminate ciliary activity, thus reducing the mucociliary clearance. However, chronic administration of such solutions may have pathological implications. Therefore, isotonic solutions are usually preferred for nasal administration.

Viscosity: Higher formulation viscosity increases the contact time between the drug and the nasal mucosa. It also reduces ciliary beating, thus bringing down the mucociliary clearance of the drugs. For example, incorporation of 2% methyl cellulose in a nasal formulation was shown to enhance the relative bioavailability of metoprolol by ~40% in rats.

Dosage form: Nasal drops are the simplest and most convenient dosage forms but the exact amount that can be delivered cannot be easily quantified and this often leads to overdosage. Moreover, rapid nasal drainage is a problem with drops. Solution and suspension sprays are preferred over powder sprays because powder may cause mucosal irritation. Recently, metered-dose gel devices have been developed that accurately deliver drugs. Gels reduce postnasal drip and anterior leakage, and localise the formulation in the mucosa. Specialised systems such as lipid emulsions, microspheres, liposomes, proliposomes, films and niosomes have been developed for nasal delivery. These offer better permeation for the drugs as they provide intimate and prolonged contact between the drug and the mucosal membrane.

3. Device-related Factors

The size of the droplet or particles delivered and the type of surface distribution influence the absorption of drugs. The site and pattern of deposition is affected by the formulation composition, physical form of the formulation (liquid, viscous, semisolid, solid), device used, design of actuators and adapters and administration technique.

Nasal Drug Delivery Formulations

The typical nasal formulations range from solutions to suspensions and gels. The novel formulations are designed to overcome the disadvantages of the conventional nasal dosage forms and to suit a particular treatment mode.

Nasal Drops

Nasal drops are one of the most simple and convenient systems developed for nasal delivery. Nasal drops contain therapeutically active ingredients dissolved in solutions or mixtures of excipients (for example, preservatives, viscosity modifiers, emulsifiers and buffering agents). Usually, they are administered through a dropper. The main disadvantage of this system is the lack of dose precision.

Nasal Sprays

Both solution and suspension formulations can be formulated into nasal sprays. The dose can be metered by a spray pump or it may have been premetered during manufacture. A nasal spray unit can be designed for unit dosing or to discharge up to several hundred metered sprays of formulation containing the drug substance. The particle size and morphology (for suspensions) of the drug and viscosity of the formulation determine the choice of pump-and-actuator assembly.

Nasal Gels

Nasal gels are highly viscous, thickened solutions or suspensions. The advantages of a nasal gel include the reduction of postnasal drip due to high viscosity, lowering of the taste impact due to reduced swallowing, less anterior leakage of the formulation, reduced irritation by using soothing/emollient excipients and target delivery to the mucosa for better absorption.

Nasal Powders

This dosage form may be developed if the drug lacks stability in the solution and suspension dosage forms. The other advantages of the nasal powder dosage form are the absence of preservatives and superior stability of the formulation. However, the suitability of the powder formulation is dependent on the solubility, particle size, aerodynamic properties and nasal irritancy of the active drug and/or excipients. An intranasal powder form of glucagon was reported to have improved the metabolic status and fatty liver in patients with pancreatectomy.

Microemulsions

This is a thermodynamically stable, isotropically clear product that has a droplet size <0.15 μm. It consists of an oil phase, surfactant, cosurfactant and aqueous phase. Oil in water (o/w) microemulsions represent a promising prospect for the development of formulations suitable for the incorporation of poorly water-soluble drugs because of high solubilisation capacity, as well as the potential for enhanced absorption by the CSF.

Mucoadhesives

Mucoadhesive formulations using polymers such as carbopol, chitosan and polaxomers have been developed to prolong the duration of contact between the nasal mucosa and the formulation.

Formulation Considerations

Nasal formulations are generally administered in small volumes in the range 25–200 μL, with 100 μL being the most common dose volume. This factor limits the administration of drugs that are required in large doses. Excipients should be carefully selected so as to avoid damage to the mucoepithelial layers and to sustain normal physiological ciliary movement. It has been reported that particle sizes >10 μm are deposited in the nasal cavity. Particles that are 2–10 μm in size can be retained in the lungs while particles <1 μm are exhaled.

Buffers

The lysozyme in nasal secretions is responsible for destroying certain bacteria at acidic pH. In alkaline conditions, the lysozyme is inactivated and the nasal tissue is hence susceptible to microbial infection. It is therefore advisable to maintain the formulation at a pH of 4.5–6.5 bearing in mind the physicochemical properties of the drug, as drugs are absorbed in the un-ionised form.

Due to the small volume of administration, nasal secretions may alter the pH of the formulation. This can affect the concentration of the un-ionised drug available for absorption. Therefore, an adequate formulation buffer capacity is required to maintain the pH in situ. Some of the commonly employed buffers include isotonic potassium phosphate buffer, citrate and acetate buffer.

Osmotic Agents

The osmolarity of the formulation may be adjusted using sodium chloride. In some cases, sodium sulfite or sodium acid phosphate is used.

Gelling/Viscosifying Agents or Gel-forming Carriers

Increasing the viscosity of the solution may prolong the therapeutic effect of nasal preparations. The use of a combination of carriers is often recommended from a safety (nasal irritancy) point of view. Common materials that also serve as bioadhesive excipients in the formulation are carbopol, cellulose agents, starch, dextran and chitosan.

Solubilisers

Conventional solvents or cosolvents such as glycols, small quantities of alcohol, transcutol (diethylene glycol monoethyl ether), medium chain glycerides and labrasol (saturated polyglycolyzed C_8–C_{10} glyceride) can be used to enhance the solubility of drugs. Other options include the use of surfactants or cyclodextrins such as HP–ß-cyclodextrin that serve as biocompatible solubilisers and stabilisers in combination with lipophilic absorption enhancers. In such cases, their impact on nasal irritancy should be considered.

Preservatives

Depending on the drug and/or formulation characteristics, sterility may be accomplished by aseptic filling processes, terminal sterilisation or both. Sterility must also be maintained throughout a product's shelf life. Unit dose delivery systems or specialised multidose delivery systems may be used to ensure continued product sterility. Alternatively, preservatives may be added to prevent bacterial growth. Parabens, benzalkonium chloride, phenyl ethyl alcohol and benzoyl alcohol are some of the commonly used preservatives in nasal formulations. Mercury-containing preservatives have a fast and irreversible effect on ciliary movement and should not be used in nasal systems.

Antioxidants

Commonly used antioxidants in nasal formulations are sodium metabisulfite, sodium bisulfite, butylated hydroxytoluene and tocopherol. Usually, antioxidants do not affect drug absorption or cause nasal irritation. Chemical/Physical interaction of antioxidants and preservatives with drugs, excipients, manufacturing equipment and packaging components should be considered during formulation development.

Humectants

To prevent dehydration, adequate intranasal moisture is required. Therefore, humectants can be added, especially in gel-based nasal products. Humectants help to prevent nasal irritation and are not likely to affect drug absorption. Common examples include glycerin, sorbitol and mannitol.

Absorption Enhancers

Along with the common excipients added to maintain drug solubility, stability and ideal formulation characteristics, the formulation may require nasal absorption enhancers when the drug is polar or a macromolecule. The main limiting factor associated with the addition of enhancers to a nasal formulation is the potential toxicity of the nasal mucosa. Nasal absorption enhancers are required to be non-irritating, non-toxic and non-allergenic or at least to have immediately reversible effects. Moreover, they should be systemically inert in the concentrations used.

A large number of absorption enhancers used in combination with drugs increase the permeation of compounds by increasing the fluidity of the membrane, decreasing the viscosity of the mucosal layer, inhibiting the proteolytic enzymes, disrupting the tight junctions, increasing paracellular or transcellular transportation, increasing blood flow, dissociating protein aggregation or initiating pore formation, or by a combination of these factors. Apart from this, mucoadhesive dosage forms have also been shown to increase the permeation of compounds.

Surfactants

Surfactants such as bile salts were the first to be tested, and several other promoters have been investigated subsequently. Non-ionic and anionic surfactants including bile salts were found to enhance the nasal absorption of drugs (for example, human granulocyte colony stimulating factor, rhG-CSF) by multiple mechanisms such as alteration of the mucous layer, opening of the tight junctions between the epithelial cells, reversed micelle formation in the membrane, extraction of membrane components by comicellisation and inhibitory effects on protelytic enzymes.

Chitosan

Recently published Phase I clinical trial data has demonstrated that a nasal solution formulation of morphine containing chitosan enables rapid absorption of the drug, with peak plasma concentration within 15 minutes, and the absorption increases about sixfold to provide a bioavailability of 60% when compared with intravenous injections. The mechanism of action of chitosan in improving the transportation of polar drugs across the epithelial membrane is believed to be a combination of bioadhesion and the transient opening of the tight junctions in the cell membrane to enable the passage of polar molecules.

Cyclodextrins
Cyclodextrins are used in nasal formulations mainly as a means of providing drug solubilisation. However, some reports have demonstrated the permeability enhancement effect of cyclodextrins on nasal mucosa. They are believed to act by increasing drug availability at the formulation–barrier interface.

Complexing Agents
The integrity of tight junctions, which may be seen as barriers to the paracellular diffusion of molecules, is dependent on extracellular Ca^{2+}. It is believed that the mechanism of action of ethylene diamine tetraacetic acid (EDTA) includes depletion of Ca^{2+} from the tight junctional areas, thus allowing the junctions to open.

Co-administration of protease inhibitors has been one of the strategies adopted to prevent the metabolism of the drug in the nasal lumen. Often, combinations of permeation enhancers prove synergistic. Abe et al studied the pharmacokinetics of the LHRH agonist buserelin on nasal administration in rats. Oleic acid and hydroxypropyl β-cyclodextrin provided better drug solubility and stability, thus enhancing absorption significantly. The area under the plasma concentration time curve (2 hours) was 33.2±5.5 ng/ml/h when buserelin acetate (0.1 mg/kg) was administered intranasally. The same was 109±11.4 ng/ml/h when administered with oleic acid. The presence of hydroxypropyl β-cyclodextrin along with oleic acid enhanced the bioavailability of buserelin acetate to 144.3 ± 26.9 ng/ml/h.

Experimental Setup for Evaluation of Nasal Drug Delivery Systems

The in vitro experimental apparatus is based on a three-compartment model. The basic components include two half chambers separated by a semipermeable membrane, a heating block or reservoir used to control the temperature and mixing or stirring equipment. Electrodes for electrophysiological measurements are also often included.

One of the commonly employed diffusion chambers for transepithelial transport measurements is the 'Ussing chamber' (named after the inventor Hans Ussing).

The schematic diagram of the Ussing circulating chamber is shown in Fig. 5.6.

This chamber consists of a U-shaped tubing system, usually made of glass, that is filled with the experimental solution. The tubing can be heated if required and is filled either with air or with different gases such as CO_2, O_2 or N_2. The gassing serves two purposes: first, to oxygenate the liquid contents and second, to stir the liquid to ensure complete convection (termed 'bubble lift'). The lumen of the tubes is connected to the chambers. The U-shaped tube secures an equal hydrostatic pressure on both sides of the chamber and thus, avoids damage caused by bending of the tissue.

Either phosphate buffered saline or Kreb's bicarbonate Ringer's solution at a pH of 7.4 has been used in most studies. The barrier used to simulate the human nasal mucoepithelium is mostly excised nasal mucosa from rats or rabbits. The cultured tissues of nasal mucosa were reported in few studies. The drug solution is introduced into the mucosal side of the chamber and samples of the receiver compartment

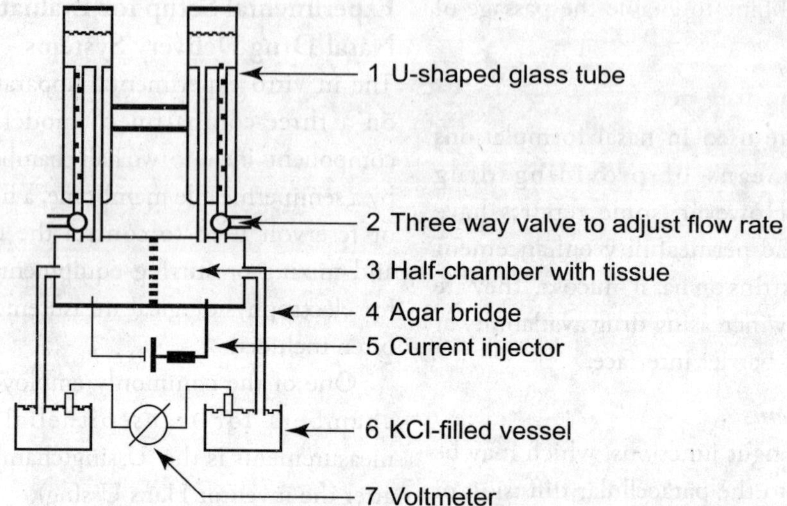

Figure 5.6: Schematic drawing of an Ussing circulating chamber

(serosal side) buffer or ringer are withdrawn for measurement of the amount of drug transported across the nasal mucosal barrier which is sandwiched between the two chambers.

In Situ Nasal Perfusion Method

The in situ model, reported by Hirai et al, is a nasal perfusion method used in anesthetised rats (Fig. 5.7). The trachea of the rat is cannulated and another tube, which serves to introduce the perfusing solution into the nasal cavity through the esophagus to the posterior part of the nasal cavity, is inserted. The nasopalatine is closed with an adhesive agent to prevent drainage of the drug solution from the nasal cavity into the mouth.

The drug solution in the beaker, maintained at 37 °C, is circulated through the nasal cavity of the rat by means of a peristaltic pump. The perfusing solution passes out from the nostrils through the funnel and into the beaker again. The extent of drug absorption is determined in the perfusate collected.

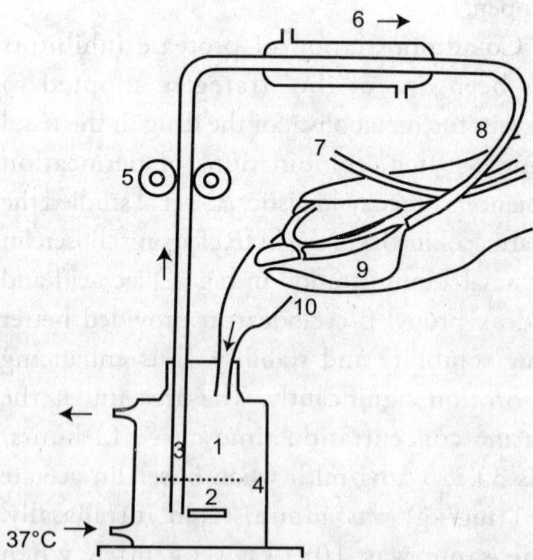

Figure 5.7: Experimental setup for the in situ nasal perfusion experiment (1) Drug reservoir (2) Magnetic stirring bar (3) Tygon tube (4) Water-jacketted beaker (5) Peristaltic pump (6) Water bath (7) Trachea cannulation (8) Esophagus cannulation (9) Nasal cavity (10) Funnel

The In Vivo Model

The rat is commonly used in the in vivo model for nasal drug delivery research. Ease of handling, cannulation and low volume of distribution of the body compartment make rats a suitable model.

The in vivo dog model for nasal absorption studies in beagle dogs has been described by Hussain et al. Male beagle dogs are anesthetised or maintained in the conscious state depending on the characteristics of the drug and the purpose of the study. A positive pressure pump provides ventilation through a cuffed endotracheal tube and a heating pad keeps the body temperature at 37–38 ºC. Blood samples are collected periodically from the jugular vein.

The estimation of drug concentration in the blood/serum may not be feasible sometimes due to the low doses and lesser extent of absorption. In such cases, adopting a pharmacodynamic model may help in evaluating the dosage form.

However, this method may be quantitatively appropriate when the pharmacological response is proportional to the dose of the drug administered.

Ohwaki et al studied the nasal absorption of secretin in rats by measuring the pancreatic juice secreted through the artificial pancreatic duct (created by cannulating the end of the common bile duct nearer the pancreas with a polyethylene tube). After administering a secretin preparation, the pancreatic juice secreted through the artificial pancreatic duct was collected in a glass tube with divisions in microlitres. The volume was noted at 15-minute intervals.

A study was carried out by Wang et al to evaluate the potential of aminated gelatin as a nasal absorption enhancer for peptide drugs. The absorption-enhancing effect was investigated in rats using insulin. The absorption of insulin was estimated by measuring the changes in plasma glucose levels following intranasal administration. The hypoglycemic effect after intranasal administration of insulin with aminated gelatin significantly increased when compared with that after intranasal administration of insulin in phosphate buffered saline, indicating that aminated gelatin effectively enhanced the nasal absorption of insulin. In contrast, neither kind of native gelatin (isoelectric point = 5.0 and 9.0) showed any absorption-enhancing effect. The pH of the formulations and the concentration of aminated gelatin were found to affect the hypoglycemic effect.

Future Trends in Nasal Drug Delivery

Intranasal drug delivery systems can be considered as a potential alternative to the parenteral administration of drugs. The intranasal route appears to be suitable for the delivery of drugs for crisis treatment such as acute pain, panic attacks, sleep induction, nausea and heart attacks. Targeting the brain through intranasal administration is another emerging area of application in the treatment of CNS-related problems such as Parkinson's disease. The delivery of vaccines, especially those against respiratory diseases, provides better protection against infection.

From the formulation scientist's perspective, a better understanding of the pathway of drug absorption, the factors influencing drug absorption and safety and stability of the drug on intranasal administration need to be established prior to the design of a nasal drug delivery system. The selection of suitable excipients is crucial in exploiting the maximum therapeutic activity of a drug and preserving the safety of the formulation.

Key Messages

- Intranasal drug administration results in rapid uptake of drugs and the pharmacokinetics of the drug is more or less similar to that of IV administration.
- Nose-to-brain pathway through the olfactory bulb is utilised for delivering drugs to the CNS, bypassing the blood brain barrier.
- Lipophilic drugs are generally absorbed by the transcellular pathway and hydrophilic drugs by the paracellular pathway.
- Formulation and device-related factors significantly influence the bioavailability of drugs from nasal formulations.

QUESTIONS

1. What are the specific attributes of nasal drug delivery over the other routes of drug delivery?
2. What are the anatomical regions of the nasal cavity that are responsible for drug absorption?
3. What are the various absorption pathways of drugs across the nasal mucosa?
4. What is the hypothesis of brain targeting of drugs through nasal delivery?
5. What are the physiological factors limiting nasal absorption of drugs?
6. How does the pKa and partition coefficient of drugs influence drug absorption across the nasal mucosa?
7. What are the excipients to be incorporated to enhance stability of nasal formulations?
8. What are the mechanisms underlying different transnasal drug absorption enhancers?

6

Buccal Drug Delivery Systems

S Narasimha Murthy

Learning Objectives

At the end of this chapter, you will be able to:

- Explain the need for alternative oral drug delivery systems
- List the advantages and disadvantages of buccal drug delivery
- Describe the structure of mucosa and pathways of drug absorption
- List the various factors to be considered while formulating buccal drug delivery systems
- Describe the different buccal drug delivery formulations, mucoadhesive polymers and drug penetration enhancers

Introduction

Within the oral mucosal cavity, the buccal region offers an attractive route of administration for controlled systemic drug delivery. Buccal delivery is the administration of drugs through the mucosal membrane lining the cheeks. Although the sublingual mucosa is known to be more permeable than the buccal mucosa, the latter is the preferred route for systemic transmucosal drug delivery. This is because the buccal mucosa has an expanse of smooth muscle and relatively immobile mucosa, which makes it a more desirable region for retentive systems. Thus, the buccal mucosa is more appropriate for sustained delivery applications and the delivery of less permeable molecules and peptide drugs.

Advantages and Disadvantages of Buccal Drug Delivery

The advantages of buccal delivery are that the direct entry of the drug into systemic circulation obviates first pass hepatic metabolism and that the formulation can be easily administered and, if necessary, removed from the site of application.

The drawbacks of buccal delivery include the need for the device to maintain its position for many hours against buccal motion and salivary flow, the latter also being responsible for dissolving important parts of the drug, thus reducing mucosal absorption. Another disadvantage is the smaller area of tissue available for drug administration, when compared to the skin, intestinal or lung epithelium.

Both low tissue permeability and the small area limit the dose of drug that can be delivered. In addition, the small area of the buccal mucosa requires the dosage form to be optimal, with respect to the thermodynamic and adhesion properties.

Buccal Mucosa and Pathways of Drug Absorption

The buccal mucosal tissues consist of a multilayered, stratified squamous epithelium covered with mucus (Fig. 6.1). The epithelium of the buccal mucosa is about 40–50 cell layers thick, while that of the sublingual mucosa contains somewhat fewer layers. The epithelial cells increase in size and become flatter as they travel from the basal layers to the superficial layers. The basal lamina connects the epithelium to a connective tissue layer, the lamina propria. The thickness of the buccal mucosa is about 500–800 µm. The buccal epithelium is not keratinised and has small amounts of ceramide, neutral but polar lipids and cholesterol sulfate in the intercellular lipid region. Buccal epithelia have been found to be considerably more permeable to water than keratinised epithelia present in other regions of the oral mucosa. Apart from the intercellular lipids, the basement membrane may present some resistance to permeation as well. The basic drug transport mechanism for the buccal epithelium is the same as that for other epithelia in the body. Two major routes are involved: transcellular (intracellular) and paracellular (intercellular).

The transcellular route may involve permeation across the apical cell membrane, intracellular space and basolateral membrane either by passive transport (diffusion, pH partition) or by active transport (facilitated and carrier-mediated diffusion, endocytosis). The transcellular permeability of a drug is a complex function of various physicochemical properties including size, lipophilicity, hydrogen bond potential, charge and conformation. Transportation through aqueous pores in the cell membranes of the epithelium is also possible for substances with low molar volume (80 cm^3/mol).

The second route, available to substances with a wide range of molar volumes, is the intercellular route (paracellular route). Within the intercellular space, hydrophobic molecules penetrate through the lipidic bilayer, while the hydrophilic molecules pass through the narrow aqueous regions adjacent to the polar head groups of the lipids.

Factors influencing Buccal Absorption of Drugs

Various physicochemical, physiological and formulation factors influence drug absorption through the buccal route. Some of the primary factors are discussed in the following sections.

Physicochemical

Human buccal absorption data demonstrates that the absorption of drugs from the oral cavity obeys the pH partition hypothesis, which implies a passive diffusion mechanism. Therefore, the absorption rate is directly proportional to the concentration of drug molecules in the free form. The octanol-water partition coefficient has been used to predict the mucosal permeability of drugs.

Molecular weight and size influence the diffusivity of the drug through the epithelial layer. Therefore, small molecules (~100 Da) cross the buccal mucosa rapidly, and permeability falls off markedly as the molecular size increases.

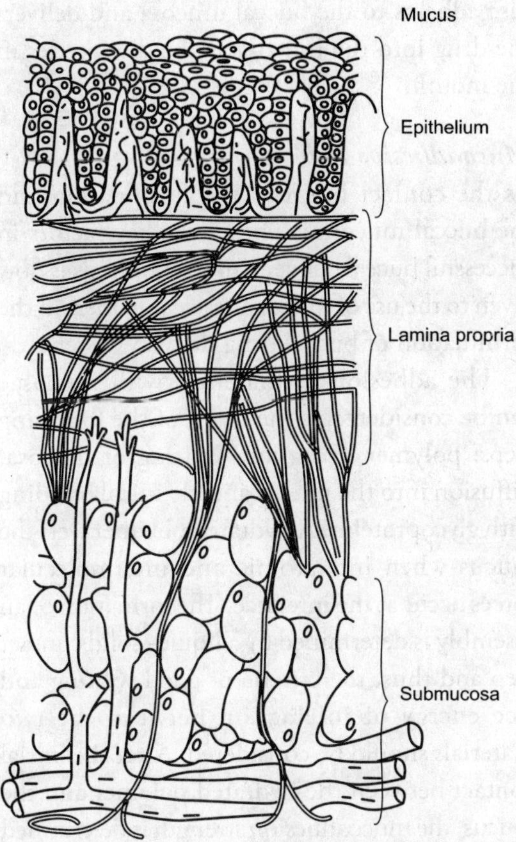

Figure 6.1: Structure of buccal mucosa

The charge discriminating effect of the epithelia is believed to have a significant negative impact on the absorption of anionic drugs. The effect of charge density can be modified to promote drug absorption by changing the pH of the medium and thus, the degree of ionisation of the permeant. Terminal charges on zwitterionic molecules have a negative effect on membrane permeability even though the effective partition coefficient is relatively high.

Buccal Environment

Mucus can form a strongly cohesive gel structure that binds to the epithelial cell surface as a gelatinous layer, reducing penetration of drugs. The negative surface charge of the mucus layer affects absorption of anionic drugs. The mucus turnover clears a significant amount of the drug, thus reducing its bioavailability. Aminopeptidases represent a major metabolic barrier to the buccal delivery of peptide drugs. The drug may also bind to the salivary proteins or be subject to degradation by the salivary enzymes. All these factors need to be considered while designing a buccal drug delivery system.

Formulation Factors

The surface area of the formulation and its drug load and adhesivity on the buccal mucosal layer are the key factors pertaining to the buccal dosage form, which influences the absorption of drugs across the buccal mucosa.

Buccal Drug Delivery Systems

Hydrogels are hydrophilic polymeric matrices that are capable of swelling when placed in aqueous media. These include natural gums and cellulose derivatives. They swell infinitely and the component molecules dissolve from the surface of the matrix. Drug release then occurs through the spaces or channels within the network as well as through the dissolution and/or disintegration of the matrix. Often, hydrogels are cross-linked so that they do not dissolve in the medium and only absorb water.

Multilayered tablets are one of the commonly employed dosage forms. They can circumvent the relatively short residence time of oral gels on the mucosa, which are easily washed and removed by saliva. Unlike conventional tablets, they lack a disintegrating agent and tend to remain intact during the drug release period. Generally, the buccal tablets have a drug-incorporated polymeric matrix with a backing impermeable membrane. The drug-releasing surface is placed on the mucosal surface and the backing membrane faces the oral cavity. The rate of release from such systems is usually diffusion controlled. Buccal tablets are considered relatively bulky when compared to buccal films.

Striant® is a monoconvex, tablet-like, mucoadhesive buccal system recently approved by the United States Food and Drug Administration (FDA). Striant® adheres to the gum tissue above the incisors, with the flat surface facing the cheek mucosa. The active ingredient in Striant® is testosterone. Insertion of Striant® twice a day, in the morning and in the evening, provides continuous systemic delivery of testosterone. Other pharmacologically inactive ingredients in Striant® are anhydrous lactose NF, carbomer 934P, hypromellose USP, magnesium stearate NF, lactose monohydrate NF, polycarbophil USP, colloidal silicon dioxide NF, starch NF and talc USP.

Buccal films are preferred to adhesive tablets because of their flexibility and comfort. Moreover, they are also suitable for protecting wound surfaces, thus reducing pain and increasing the effectiveness of treatment. Buccal films or patches are designed either as matrix-controlled or membrane-controlled devices. Some biodegradable or erodible formulations for the timed release of drugs are being investigated.

Atrix Laboratories, Colorado, USA has developed Bioerodible Mucoadhesive (BEMA™) technology, which is designed to deliver either local or systemic levels of drugs across mucosal tissues. The BEMA™ system consists of a small disc with bioerodible layers that can deliver drugs rapidly at specified time intervals. The BEMA™ disc adheres to the buccal mucosa and delivers the drug into the mucosa as the disc erodes in the mouth.

Mucoadhesive Polymers

As the contact between the formulation and the buccal mucosa is one of the key factors in successful buccal delivery, more emphasis is now given to the use of mucoadhesive polymers in the formulation of buccal drug delivery systems.

The adhesion of materials with mucosae can be considered as the result of the following steps: polymer hydration, wetting of mucosa, diffusion into the mucus and chemical bonding with glycoproteins. A hydrated polymer wets the mucus when interatomic and intermolecular forces occur at the interface. The formation of an assembly is determined by a liquid–solid contact step and thus, the criteria of good wetting and free energy of interaction between the two materials should be considered. After the initial contact between the hydrated polymer and the mucus, the mucoadhesion strength is determined by the formation of secondary chemical bonds due to polymer chain/mucin interpenetration, which is affected by polymer flexibility and mobility. Hence, the ideal bioadhesive polymer should have satisfactory surface energy and chain flexibility favouring its spread and diffusion into the mucus and functional groups forming secondary chemical bonds (for example, ionic and hydrogen bonds).

Appropriate materials for bioadhesion are mostly hydrogel-forming polymers that are cellulose derivatives such as sodium carboxymethyl cellulose, hydroxypropylcellulose, methylcellulose, methylethylcellulose and hydroxyethyl cellulose. Natural gums such as karaya and pectin and other polymers such as starch, sodium alginate and poly vinyl pyrrolidone can also be used. The high molecular weights of polyethylene oxide (PEO) and polyethylene glycol (PEG) show good mucoadhesive characteristics because of their linear flexible molecular structure and ability to form physical bonds entangling the mucus.

Penetration Enhancers in Buccal Drug Delivery

Substances that help to promote drug permeation through the buccal epithelium are referred to as penetration enhancers, permeation promoters or absorption enhancers. The chemicals used as penetration enhancers should ideally be safe and non-toxic, pharmacologically and chemically inert, non-irritant and non-allergenic. In addition, the tissue should revert to its normal integrity and barrier properties on removal of the chemical.

Surfactants, anions such as sodium laurate and sodium lauryl sulfate, cations such as cetylpyridinium chloride and nonions such as poloxamers, brij, span, myrj and tween are known to disrupt the intercellular lipid domain and protein domain integrity, thus enhancing the penetration of hydrophilic molecules. Bile salts are believed to act by the extraction of membrane protein or lipids, membrane fluidisation and reverse micellisation in the membrane, creating aqueous channels.

Fatty acids such as oleic acid and carpylic acid increase the fluidity of phospholipids in the intercellular lipid domain. Cyclodextrins act as drug penetration enhancers by including membrane components. Cationic polymers such as chitosan and poly-L-arginine are known to act by neutralising the charge of the mucosal surface and by opening the tight junctions.

Because of the similarities between buccal mucosa and the skin, chemical enhancers and vehicles that increase transdermal delivery have also been used on the buccal mucosa. Ethanol at different concentrations (5% and 30%), propylene glycol, n-methylpyrrolidone and dimethylsulfoxide have been used as penetration enhancers in buccal dosage forms.

Protease inhibitors such as aprotinin, bestatin, puromycin and bile salts, which have been tested and shown to stabilise peptides against buccal mucosal enzymes have also been used.

Evaluation of Buccal Drug Delivery Systems

The most meaningful method to assess the absorption of drugs from a buccal drug delivery system is by performing a permeation experiment. A suitably excised and preserved buccal mucosa is used for diffusion studies in the Ussing chamber or similar standard diffusion cells. Various kinds of diffusion cells, including continuous flow perfusion chambers, Ussing chambers and Franz cells, in which buccal mucosa are mounted have been used.

Different species feature different epithelial tissues. This largely depends on the functional use of the oral epithelium. For example, the buccal mucosa of hamsters is quite different from that in humans because rodents use their cheeks for the storage of food and therefore, the tissue is keratinised for increased mechanical strength. All of the common laboratory rodents have keratinised oral epithelium on all regions of their oral mucosa, and are, therefore, not suitable models for the study of human mucosal permeability. The pig is probably the most suitable model for studies of buccal permeability because there are essentially no differences between human and pig buccal mucosa in terms of lipid content and composition, membrane morphology and permeability barrier function. Other suitable animals are the dog and the monkey.

The mucoadhesive performance of buccal formulations has been assessed by employing various techniques and parameters. The time taken for the formulation to detach from the porcine buccal tissue in a well-stirred beaker is one of them. The fresh-cut animal buccal tissue is fixed on the side of the beaker with glue. Before adding the buffer, the formulation is attached to the buccal tissue surface by applying a force of ~0.5 N. The beaker is then filled with 800 ml of phosphate buffer and maintained at 37 °C. A stirring rate of 150 rpm is used to simulate buccal and salivary movement. The time taken for the disk to detach from the porcine buccal tissue is recorded as the mucoadhesion time.

The other technique includes two cylindrical metallic supports (2.5 cm in diameter) attached to the load cells of the tensile tester to perform the study. The formulation is stuck to the upper support, and the mucosal tissue to the lower support by using an adhesive. The surface of the formulation is made wet with 50 µl of phosphate buffer at a pH of 6.4. When the formulation and the substrate make contact, a force (0.5 N) is applied for a predetermined time. This is followed by an extension stage until total separation of the components is achieved. The force required to detach the system is then measured.

Future Trends

Buccal delivery has many advantages, such as the avoidance of hepatic first pass metabolism and the fact that the membrane is robust and readily accessible and has high patient compliance. However, the buccal mucosa has limitations with respect to delivery area and permeability. A number of physicochemical factors influence the absorption of drugs from the buccal mucosa. In addition, environmental factors such as the presence of saliva and its pH, movements of the buccal tissues and enzymatic activity on and in the mucosa also determine the bioavailability of drugs. Permeation enhancers could be used to enhance drug absorption across the buccal mucosa. However, there is not enough data to demonstrate the safety of long-term use of these agents.

Therefore the future trends in buccal drug delivery will be towards developing formulations containing safer and more effective penetration enhancers to improve drug absorption and formulations that are fabricated with polymers that provide relatively better adhesivity/interaction with the buccal mucosa.

Key Messages

- Buccal drug absorption is mostly passive and follows one of two pathways: paracellular or transcellular.
- Establishing good contact between the formulation and the mucosal surface is critical for absorption. This is achieved by using natural gums and semisynthetic and synthetic polymers in the formulation.
- The buccal mucosal permeation enhancers act by perturbing barrier integrity. Ideally,

a permeation enhancer that enhances drug permeation with minimal and reversible loss to the integrity of the mucosa should be selected.

- The appropriate animal mucosal model must be selected for proper evaluation of buccal drug delivery. Rodents are considered poor models whereas porcine, monkey and dog buccal mucosa are reported to be more appropriate.

QUESTIONS

1. What are the advantages of buccal drug delivery systems over oral drug delivery systems?
2. What are the different pathways of drug absorption across the buccal mucosa?
3. What are the factors influencing absorption of drugs across the buccal mucosa?
4. What are mucoadhesive polymers and what is the mechanism of mucoadhesivity?
5. What are the different types of buccal drug delivery formulations?
6. What are the ideal characteristics of a mucosal drug penetration enhancer?
7. Why is the porcine model considered better than rodent models for buccal mucosa evaluation?

7

Implant Drug Delivery Systems

S Narasimha Murthy

Learning Objectives

At the end of this chapter, you will be able to:

- Explain the importance of local, prolonged and constant rate drug delivery
- Describe the various approaches of implant drug delivery system (IDDS) design
- Compare the different polymer materials used in the formulation of IDDSs
- Explain the advances in the field of IDDSs

Introduction

The effectiveness of a pharmacological agent can be altered by the route or type of dosage form administered. The more selective a drug is to its site of action, the lesser the dose of the drug to be administered. Site-specific targeted drug delivery lowers the dose to be administered, thereby minimising the side effects. Greater therapeutic efficacy of the drug can also be achieved by such delivery systems when compared to conventional oral or IV formulations. Other potential benefits of this type of delivery system are protection of drugs from rapid in vivo metabolism and immediate termination of drug therapy in case of emergencies or toxicity.

One of the main objectives of designing implant drug delivery systems is to localise the effects of drugs to a particular tissue. Implants are controlled release devices that can provide a larger depot of the therapeutic agent. They are intended for the controlled release of the therapeutic agent over relatively longer periods of time—several days to years. Implants are typically administered by an invasive procedure. Three-dimensional implants may be as small as a few millimeters or a few centimeters. The geometry of the structure (the shape, size and porosity) can be tailored to the application site.

Types of Implant Drug Delivery Systems

Implant drug delivery systems (IDDSs) can be classified into three main categories: biodegradable and non-biodegradable polymeric implants, implantable pump systems and atypical class of implants. Each of these categories is discussed in detail.

Biodegradable and Non-biodegradable Polymeric Implants

Biodegradable and non-biodegradable implants

are available as monolithic/matrix systems or reservoir systems.

a. Non-biodegradable implant systems:

The release kinetics of drugs from non-biodegradable implant systems depends on both the solubility and diffusion coefficient of the drug in the polymer and the drug load. A disadvantage of this system is that a minor surgery is required for the removal of the delivery system from the body.

In the polymeric matrix system, the drug is dispersed homogeneously inside the matrix material. Slow diffusion of the drug through the polymeric matrix material provides sustained drug release from the delivery system. Polymethylmethacrylate (PMMA) has been commonly used for the formulation of matrix systems. Septopal® (Biomet, UK) is a gentamicin implant formulated as chains and minichains and is mainly used in the treatment of osteomyelitis and osteitis (Fig. 7.1).

The magnetically controlled release system is a matrix implant system that contains small magnetic beads that are uniformly dispersed within the polymer. When the unit is exposed to a biological system, normal diffusion of drug due to a concentration gradient is seen. However, on exposure to an external oscillating magnetic field, larger quantities of the drug can be released quickly. The release rate of the drug can be manipulated using the external magnet.

Figure 7.1: Septopal®, a gentamicin implant, used for the treatment of osteomyelitis and osteitis

The reservoir-type system, on the other hand, consists of a compact drug core surrounded by a permeable non-biodegradable membrane, whose thickness and permeability can control the diffusion of the drug into the body. If the concentration of the drug within the reservoir is in constant equilibrium with the inner surface of the enclosed membrane, the driving force for diffusional release of the agent is constant and zero order release kinetics of the drug from the delivery system is obtained.

The Norplant® system has a hormone, levanogesterol, encapsulated in a silicone membrane and implanted intradermally on the inside of the upper arm to provide contraception in women by the sustained release of levanogesterol for up to 5 years.

In reservoir-type systems, the possibility that membrane rupture may potentially lead to 'drug dumping' during therapy exists. Depending on the type of drug involved in the reservoir, drug dumping may result in untoward toxic side effects from drug plasma concentrations that exceed maximum safety levels.

b. Biodegradable systems:

Biodegradable polymers are highly desirable for drug delivery applications because the device will disappear over time, thereby eliminating the need for a second surgical procedure to retrieve the device. During the last decade, the use of biodegradable polymers in the controlled release field as carriers of drug molecules has increased considerably. Biodegradable polymers have been used to develop drug delivery systems for musculoskeletal pathologies to carry proteins and growth factors for bone regeneration, antibiotics to treat osteomyelitis and antiresorptive and antineoplastic drugs. In addition, multifunctional devices that combine mechanical functions and drug delivery have been studied to improve bone tissue regeneration, fixation and augmentation.

The release kinetics of drugs predominantly depends on the in vivo degradation rate of the polymer along with the solubility and diffusion coefficient of the drug in the polymer and the drug load. Many factors such as molecular weight, crystallinity, porosity and the site of implantation determine the rate of polymer degradation. The change in size (surface area) and shape of the system during in vivo degradation and the influence of alterations in pH and temperature on the degradation kinetics of the polymer need to be taken into account during formulation design.

The ZOLADEX® implant is a sterile, biodegradable product containing goserelin acetate equivalent to 10.8 mg of goserelin. ZOLADEX® is designed for subcutaneous implantation with continuous release over a 12-week period. Goserelin acetate is dispersed in a matrix of D, L-lactic and glycolic acids copolymer (12.82–14.76 mg/dose) containing <2% acetic acid and up to 10% goserelin-related substances, and presented as a sterile, white-to-cream–coloured, 1.5-mm diameter cylinder, preloaded in a special single use syringe (SafeSystem™ Syringe).

This is a bioerodible system, designed in the shape of flattened slabs that have no edge. The erosion of the system approximates a zero order release kinetic profile most closely. They may also be formulated as reservoir or matrix systems. A reservoir system is similar in structure to that of the non-biodegradable reservoir-type described earlier. The mechanism of drug release from both systems is quite similar. However, reservoir-type bioerodible systems, in contrast, contain an exterior polymeric membrane that degrades at a slower rate than the expected rate of drug diffusion through the membrane. Therefore, the membrane remains intact while the drug is released completely. Eventually, the exterior polymeric membrane is degraded in vivo and eliminated. The second type of bioerodible system consists of drugs dispersed in a polymer, monolithic type, which is slowly eroded in vivo by biological processes at a controlled rate.

The degradable polymers currently available are limited because of the stringent requirements of biocompatibility and the necessity to be free from degradation-related toxic products (for example, monomers, stabilisers, polymerisation initiators, emulsifiers). Few polymers, such as aliphatic polyesters including polylactic acid (PLA), polyglycolic acid (PGA) and polydioxanone (PDS), which are already used routinely for producing drug delivery devices, have been approved by the Food and Drug Administration (FDA). These polyesters, with poly caprolactone (PCL), polyanhydrides and polyphosphazenes (POPs), substituted with amino acid esters are the most extensively investigated polymers, essentially because of their good hydrolysability and biocompatibility.

Figures 7.2 and 7.3 explain the possible mechanisms of drug release from biodegradable and non-biodegradable implant systems.

The rate of drug release from the matrix implant system depends on the diffusion coefficient and solubility of the drug in the polymer and the drug load. Additionally, the drug release depends on the degradation rate of the polymer in biodegradable systems.

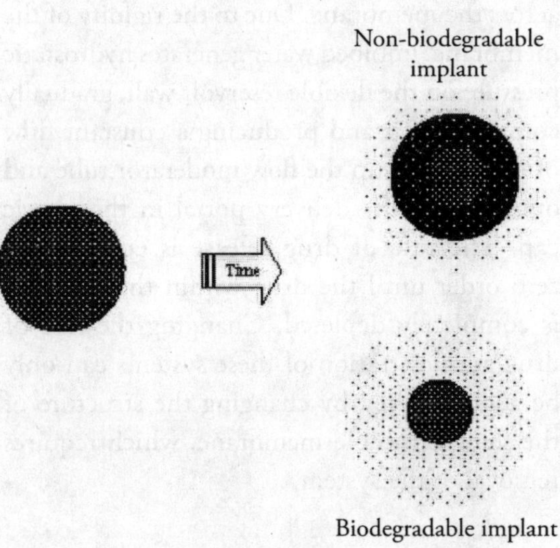

Figure 7.2: Matrix implant system

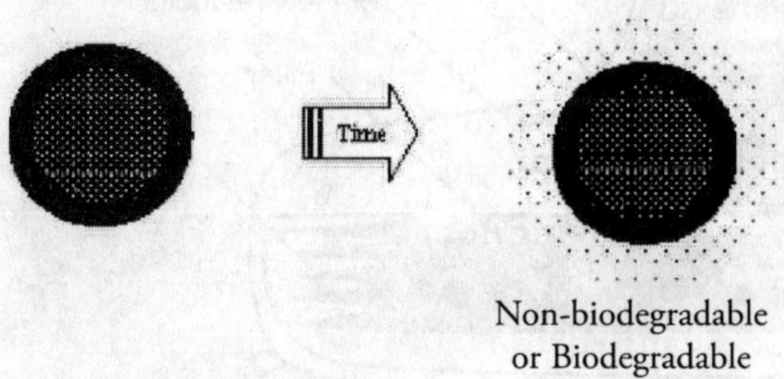

Figure 7.3: Reservoir implant system

The skeleton of non-biodegradable systems remains intact after drug depletion, whereas the drug is released due to surface degradation or erosion in biodegradable implants. In the reservoir system, the drug release rate is mainly controlled by the polymer coat around the drug reservoir. If the implant system is biodegradable, coat thickness decreases with time. However, the exterior polymeric membrane degrades at a slower rate than the expected rate of drug diffusion through the membrane.

Implantable Pump Systems

Pump systems provide external control of delivery rate and volume. Controlled release of drug from an implantable pump is generally achieved by utilising the microtechnology of electronic systems and remote-controlled flow rate manipulation by maintaining a constant pressure difference.

Infusion pumps were first developed for the continuous delivery of pain medication and insulin. The pump consists of a disc-shaped canister made of lightweight biocompatible titanium, which contains a collapsible welded bellow. The bellow separates the canister interior into two separate chambers. The first chamber contains the fluorocarbon propellant and the second the insulin formulation (Fig. 7.4). The gas pushes the drug through a filter and a flow regulator that provides a constant rate of drug release at a given temperature. The delivery rate is adjusted by changing the drug concentration in the pump reservoir. The advantage of this system is that no external energy source is needed to drive the pump action. When the pump reservoir needs to be refilled, an injection of the drug is administered

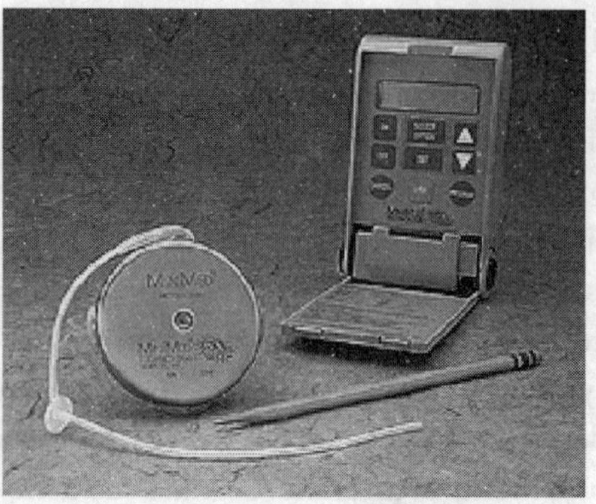

Figure 7.4: Infusaid® infusion pump for constant delivery of insulin (Minimed Technologies, CA)

through a membrane consisting of a self-sealing silicone rubber and Teflon septum. The force of the injection recompresses the fluorocarbon propellant, thereby recharging the system. The cross-sectional view of a similar propellant-based infusion pump is shown in Fig. 7.5.

The **osmotic pump** has a drug reservoir surrounded by a chemically inert and impermeable flexible wall. Outside the reservoir wall is the osmotic sleeve, a cylinder containing a high concentration of sodium chloride. It is the difference in osmotic pressure between the compartment and the aqueous environment in which the pump is placed that drives the delivery of the test solution. Water enters the sleeve along the osmotic gradient and, in doing so, displaces the test solution from the reservoir of the pump. Consequently, the delivery profile of the pump is independent of the drug formulation dispensed. Drugs of various molecular configurations, including ionised drugs and macromolecules, can be dispensed in a variety of vehicles at zero order release rates. The rate at which water enters the osmotic sleeve is regulated by the osmotic permeability of the semipermeable membrane, its dimensions and the osmotic pressure difference across the membrane. Due to the rigidity of the membrane, imbibed water generates hydrostatic pressure on the flexible reservoir wall, gradually compressing it and producing a constant flow of its contents up the flow moderator tube and out through the delivery portal in the plastic cap. The rate of drug release is constant or zero order until the drug within the reservoir is completely depleted. Changing the rate of drug administration of these systems can only be accomplished by changing the structure of the semipermeable membrane, which requires removal of the system.

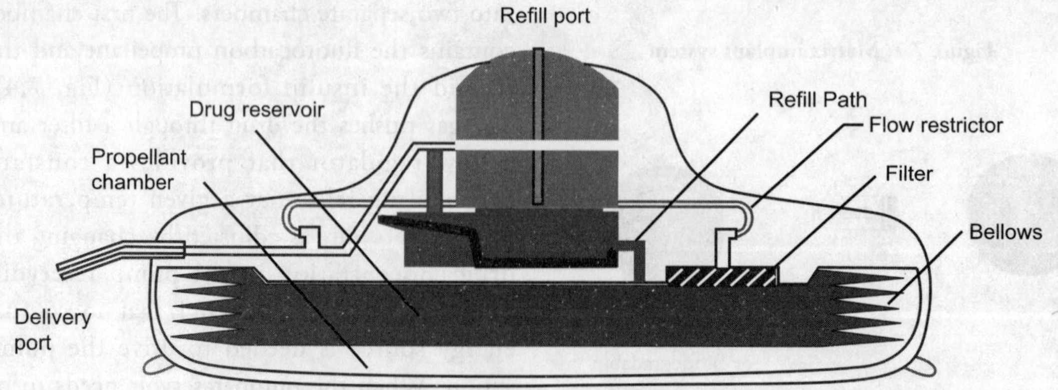

Figure 7.5: Cross-section of a propellant-based infusion implant system

The constant or zero order mass delivery rate from the system (Z) is given by the equation

$$Z = dV/dt \cdot Cd \quad (1)$$

where Cd is the concentration of drug in the reservoir and dV/dt is the volume imbibition of rate of water into the osmotic sleeve compartment. With Πe as the osmotic pressure of the pump environment, the volume delivery rate from the system can be written as

$$dV/dt = K \cdot A/h \cdot (\Pi o - \Pi e) \quad (2)$$

In this equation, A and h are the membrane area and thickness, respectively, and K is the osmotic permeability coefficient of the membrane. Πo is the osmotic pressure of the tissue fluid in contact with the device.

Alzet® was the earliest osmotic pump in the market. Generally, Alzet® pumps (Fig. 7.6) are implanted subcutaneously or intraperitoneally.

The DUROS® implant is a miniature cylinder made from a titanium alloy, which protects and stabilises the drug inside, using ALZA's proprietary formulation technology (Fig. 7.7). Water enters into one end of the cylinder through a semipermeable membrane; the drug is delivered from a port at the other end of the cylinder at a controlled rate appropriate to the specific therapeutic agent. This non-biodegradable, osmotically driven system is intended to enable delivery of small drugs, peptides, proteins, DNA and other bioactive macromolecules for systemic or tissue-specific therapy.

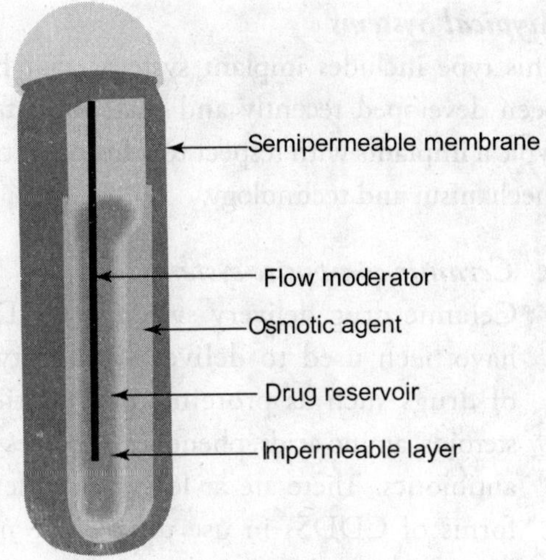

Figure 7.6: Alzet® miniosmotic pump

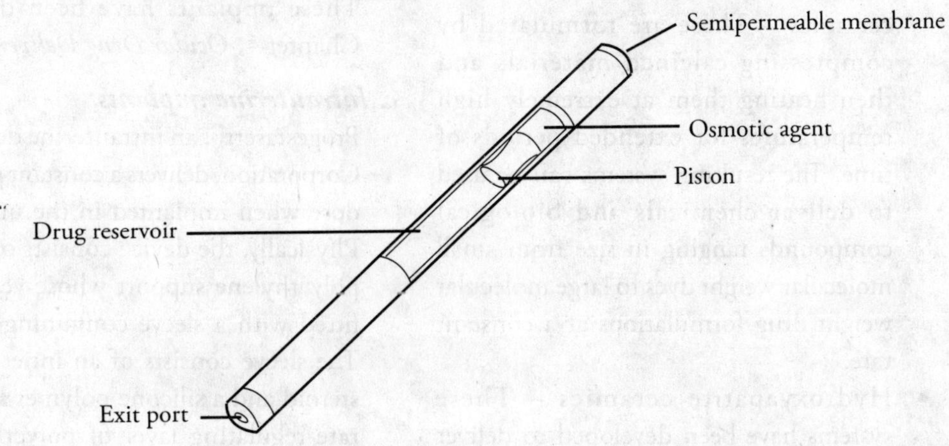

Figure 7.7: Duros® osmotic pump

Atypical Systems

This type includes implant systems that have been developed recently and that differ from typical implants with respect to administration, mechanism and technology.

a. ***Ceramic composite systems:***

Ceramic drug delivery systems (CDDSs) have been used to deliver various types of drugs such as proteins, polypeptides, steroids, amino acids, phenolics, vaccines and antibiotics. There are at least five different forms of CDDSs in use today. The most commonly used ceramic systems consist of the following:

- Inorganic bone meal or osseograft – These contain fragmented pieces of bone from various parts of the body and are used to form bone autografts. Since these grafts are structured from the patient's own bone system, they are biocompatible and readily accessible, which makes them ideal for use. These autografts are used to promote lattice formation and provide rapid regeneration of new bones.
- Alumino calcium phosphorous oxide ceramics – These are formulated by compressing calcined materials and then heating them at extremely high temperatures for extended periods of time. The resulting systems can be used to deliver chemicals and biological compounds ranging in size from small molecular weight dyes to large molecular weight drug formulations at a constant rate.
- Hydroxyapatite ceramics – These systems have been developed to deliver drugs to skeletal tissue at therapeutic concentrations. The hydroxyapatite cement formulations are loaded with antibiotics such as cephalexin or norfloxacin and then placed directly at the site of infection or fracture. Studies have indicated a constant therapeutic release of antibiotics to the site of infection and a reduced recovery time in bone regeneration. Hydroxyapatite systems have also been used to deliver testosterone directly to the site of bone fractures.
- Tricalcium phosphate ceramics – These can be directly bonded to the bone by natural mechanisms, thus allowing for utilisation to stabilise traumatised bone fractures. When loaded with antibiotics, such systems can also release the drug at therapeutic concentrations directly to the infected area. Tricalcium phosphate amino acid antibiotic composite systems are tricalcium phosphates containing cysteine or lysine composites, loaded with erythromycin or penicillin, developed for the treatment of bone infections.

b. ***Intraocular implants:***

These implants have been discussed in Chapter 4, *Ocular Drug Delivery Systems*.

c. ***Intrauterine implants:***

Progestasert®, an intrauterine device by Alza Corporation, delivers a constant progesterone dose when implanted in the uterine cavity. Physically, the device consists of a T-shaped polyethylene support whose vertical arm is fitted with a sleeve containing the steroid. The sleeve consists of an inner reservoir of steroid and a silicone polymer and an outer rate-regulating layer of polyethylene-vinyl acetate. Since the steroid is more soluble in the silicone polymer in the interior of the device than in its outer membrane of polyethylene vinyl acetate, the outer membrane is constantly exposed to a nearly saturated solution of steroid in silicone. The steroid thus has at all times a constant diffusion distance from the saturated solution to the exterior of the device.

d. Transurethral systems:

One form of this type of system is known as Muse and has recently been developed for the treatment of impotence. This system consists of a drug called alprostadil, which is prostaglandin E1, a naturally occurring acidic lipid that is synthesised from fatty acid precursors by many different mammalian tissues. This system is designed to deliver alprostadil directly to the urethral lining for transfer, through the corpus spongiosum, to the corpora cavernosa. After implanting into the urethra, the dispersion of the medicated pellet permits alprostadil to be absorbed by the urethral mucosa. Alprostadil causes direct vasodilatation of the surrounding area.

e. In situ gel-forming formulations:

Liquid formulations that generate a (semi-) solid depot after subcutaneous injection, also designated as implants, are an attractive delivery system for parenteral application for a number of reasons. Firstly, the application is less invasive and painful than implants, which require local anesthesia and surgical intervention. Secondly, localised or systemic drug delivery can be achieved for prolonged periods of time, typically ranging from one day to several months. Thirdly, various therapeutic agents can be incorporated by simple mixing.

In the past few years, an increasing number of in situ–forming systems have been reported in the literature for various biomedical applications including drug delivery, cell encapsulation and tissue repair. When they are used to fill a cavity or a defect, their flowing nature enables a good fit. In situ implant formation can occur as a result of either a physical or a chemical change in the system. Several mechanisms lead to in situ implant formation:

- *Solvent exchange or polymer precipitation* – The solvent exchange approach consists of dissolving a water insoluble polymer in a water miscible, biocompatible solvent. On contact with body fluids, the solvent diffuses out of the polymer while water permeates the liquid polymer matrix. Due to its insolubility in water, the polymer precipitates, resulting in the formation of a solid polymeric implant.

  The Atrigel® drug delivery system consists of biodegradable polymers dissolved in biocompatible carriers. Pharmaceuticals may be blended into this liquid delivery system at the time of manufacturing or, depending on the product, may be added later by the physician at the time of use. When the liquid product is injected into the subcutaneous space using a small gauge needle or placed into accessible tissue sites through a cannula, water in the tissue fluids causes the polymer to precipitate and trap the drug in a solid implant. The drug encapsulated within the implant is then released in a controlled manner as the polymer matrix biodegrades with time. Atrigel® is currently used for the delivery of Eligard® (leuprolide acetate), a treatment for prostate cancer developed by QLT USA, Inc.

- *Thermally induced gelling* – This approach utilises polymeric systems that exhibit thermorheological properties. The polymer in the solution remains liquid at room temperature and converts to a thick gel at body temperature. For example ReGel® (MacroMed, USA) is a thermosensitive, biodegradable triblock copolymer (23% (w/w) ABA-triblock copolymer (PLGA–PEG–PLGA) in phosphate-buffered saline (pH 7.4)) comprising biocompatible components poly lactide-co-glycolide (PLGA) and polyethylene glycol (PEG). Immediately upon injection and in response to body temperature, an insoluble gel depot is formed. This gel depot does not discharge from the needle track but remains in place for six weeks.

  OncoGel® is an injectable, controlled release formulation of paclitaxel, a well-characterised, anti-neoplastic agent that inhibits cell proliferation. Continuous long-term infusion of paclitaxel has been found to be more effective than conventional systemic paclitaxel therapy. Once injected, OncoGel® maintains a high, long-term intratumoural concentration of paclitaxel. OncoGel® therapy may be effective in paclitaxel-resistant tumours and tumours where cell division cycles are prolonged. Over time, the polymer degradation products are eliminated through the Krebs cycle and renal excretion.

- *Thermoplastic pastes* – These are semi-solid polymers that can be injected as a melt and form a depot upon cooling to body temperature. The requirements for such a polymer include low melting or glass transition temperatures in the range 25–65 °C and an intrinsic viscosity in the range 0.05–0.8 dl/g. At injection temperatures >37 °C but <65 °C, these polymers behave like viscous fluids, which solidify to highly viscous depots. Drugs are incorporated into the molten polymer by mixing without the application of solvents. Thermoplastic pastes allow local drug delivery at sites of surgical intervention for the delivery of antibiotic or cytotoxic agents. Alternatively, they can be used to generate a subcutaneous drug reservoir from which diffusion occurs into systemic circulation; for example, intratumoural injection of paclitaxel.
- *Polymer cross-linked gel* – In situ, cross-linking implants have been a challenging objective, as polymers containing double bonds and free radical initiation are required. These two factors are detrimental to living tissue and to the encapsulated drug. Thus, the bioactive agents must be protected during the cross-linking reaction. Biodegradable hydrogels produced from the macromer PEG-oligo-glycolyl-acrylate using a photo-initiator such as eosin and visible light are used for the controlled release of proteins over a period of several days. These hydrogels are restricted to surgical sites accessible to a light source.

f. ***Responsive drug delivery implants:***

An effective approach to individualised therapy involves ascertaining a marker molecule indicative of a disease state and subsequently delivering the type and dose of drug most appropriate for treatment. Chemical biosensors that determine the levels of important marker molecules may serve to guide therapeutic regimens, thereby improving drug safety and efficacy. A responsive drug delivery system located inside the patient's body could continuously detect the early onset of a crisis and respond immediately with the appropriate countermeasure with minimal disruption to the patient's daily life.

An additional advantage of an implantable responsive delivery device is that it continuously monitors a set of parameters and disease markers in patients with known risk factors. Physicians can closely follow the changes in the patient's health by examining the data obtained by the sensing device. The sensors can also serve to alert the physician about the onset of a disease state, such as angina or stroke, or a recurrence of cancer. Closed loop systems that sense the marker and accordingly deliver the appropriate dose of the drug are being investigated. Alternatively, 'smart' polymers or devices that are responsive to the patient's therapeutic requirements and deliver a certain amount of a drug in response to a biological stimulus can be developed. A responsive delivery system that detects *Staphylococcus aureus* through increased thrombin activity and releases an appropriate amount of antibiotic has also been developed. Specifically, the antibiotic gentamicin is bound on a poly vinyl alcohol hydrogel through a peptide linker, Gly-(D)-Phe-Pro-Arg-Gly-Phe-Pro-Ala-Gly-Gly, which contains the Arg-Gly thrombin recognition site. Thrombin's presence releases the biologically inactive antibiotic linker conjugate that is converted to the biologically active free gentamicin by leucine aminopeptidase, which is present at high levels in wound fluid. The rate of gentamicin release thus depends on the concentration of thrombin.

Several self-regulating insulin delivery devices have been coupled with insulin release to construct artificial pancreatic systems. One of the approaches followed is based on immobilising glucose oxidase (GOx) in a pH-sensitive hydrogel, which is used as the insulin release controller. GOx catalyses the oxidation of glucose to gluconic acid. This reaction generates a localised pH change, which causes, because of a volume change in the pH-sensitive hydrogel, the release of the entrapped insulin. GOx has been immobilised in a wide variety of polymers and hydrogels. Because the sensing is based on an oxidase, the pH change of the GOx-based hydrogel is limited by the oxygen level. Therefore, to improve the hydrogel's performance, a catalase has been incorporated into the polymer matrix along with GOx. This enzyme regenerates oxygen from hydrogen peroxide while at the same time reducing the levels of toxic hydrogen peroxide.

g. ***Bioartificial muscle (BAM) implants:***

These are retrievable drug delivery devices used for the long-term delivery of therapeutic proteins. In this technology, muscle precursor cells, myoblasts, are genetically engineered to secrete pharmacological levels of therapeutic proteins. The cells are then fabricated into three-dimensional muscle-like structures that can be implanted using minimally invasive techniques below the skin or at specific sites in the body. When implanted in vivo, the BAM devices can secrete therapeutic levels of proteins, either locally or systemically, for extended periods of time. Research is currently underway on these systems.

Key Messages

- Implants are one of the dosage forms used to achieve effective drug concentrations for extended periods of time.
- Biocompatibility of the materials used in IDDSs is a key factor to be determined during preformulation studies. Biodegradable and non-biodegradable polymers are often utilised as a base material in formulations.
- The main application of IDDS is the interstitial targeting of antibiotics and anti-cancerous drugs, constant delivery of pain medications, delivery of factors responsible for tissue regeneration and delivery of hormones such as insulin.
- A constant systemic or local concentration maintained using IDDSs has resulted in better therapeutic efficacy of drugs. It is very effective in intratumoural delivery of drugs. IDDSs are used when drug delivery is desired over several months or years, for example, contraceptive hormones.
- Osmotic drug delivery systems have been used for delivering different types of drugs, therapeutic proteins and hormones at different rates for prolonged durations.
- Smart systems designed for crisis management would be useful in early detection and control of disorders.
- Several IDDSs have proven success in the market. Some of the atypical systems such as BAM and responsive drug delivery devices are undergoing clinical trials.

QUESTIONS

1. What are the advantages of IDDSs over the other sustained release drug delivery systems?
2. What are the factors determining the release rate of drugs from reservoir and matrix systems?
3. Which are the biodegradable polymers used in IDDSs?
4. What are infusion pumps?
5. What is the principle of the working of an osmotic pump?
6. What are the mechanisms of in situ gel formation exploited in IDDSs?
7. What is the hypothesis of responsive drug delivery systems?
8. What are bioartificial muscle implants?

8

Targeted Drug Delivery Systems

SHOBHA RANI R HIREMATH AND N SREE HARSHA

Learning Objectives

At the end of this chapter, you will be able to:

- Describe the concept of drug targeting
- Explain the rationale behind targeted drug delivery
- State the requirements for targeted drug delivery
- Describe the various approaches to drug targeting
- Describe the drug–carrier delivery system for drug targeting

Introduction

It has been almost 200 years since Dr Paul Ehrlich first put forward the idea of drug targeting. Dr Ehrlich had watched a performance of the opera *Der Freischütz* in which Zauberkugeln (magic bullets) play a major role. In the opera, these magic bullets could be fired in any direction and still reach their goal. Thinking along similar lines, Dr Ehrlich imagined that tiny, drug-loaded, magic bullets could be introduced into the human body to target the required site of action, while non-target sites would be largely exempted from the effect of the drug. Dr Ehrlich's inspired idea led to the development of targeted drug delivery as we know it today.

Rationale for Targeted Drug Delivery

Most of the drugs introduced to clinical medicine produce their effects by interacting with cell and cell membrane–related structures and function through concentration-dependent, reversible interactions at specific receptor sites. Obviously, to obtain a desirable therapeutic response, the correct amount of drug should be transported and delivered to the site of action with subsequent control of the drug input rate. The efficacy of many drugs is often limited by their potential to reach their therapeutic site of action. In most cases, only a small amount of the administered dose of the drug actually reaches this site, while most of the drug is distributed to the rest of the body, depending on the physicochemical and biochemical properties of the drug.

Most drugs, when administered in conventional or controlled release dosage forms, freely travel throughout the body, leading to uptake by cells, tissues or organs other than those that contain their pharmacological receptors. This distribution of the drug to other tissues is unnecessary, wasteful and a potential cause of toxicity. This lack of target specificity can be attributed to the formidable barriers that the body presents to a drug. A drug taken orally must withstand large fluctuations in pH as well as the action of enzymes before it gets absorbed. Moreover, it needs to survive inactivation by the hepatic first pass effect. To produce a therapeutic effect, the drug must selectively access and interact with its pharmacological receptors, and the concentration of the drug at the active site must be adequate.

When the drug is administered by the parenteral route, the problems associated with the gastrointestinal tract (GIT) are avoided. However, deactivation and metabolisation of the drug and dose-related toxicity is frequently observed. Furthermore, there is no certainty that the drug will reach its desired destination in adequate concentrations. There are many diseases such as cancer, rheumatoid arthritis and certain bacterial and fungal parasitic infections that are inadequately accessible to drugs. The treatment of these diseases often entails high frequent dosing of drugs, which can lead to toxic manifestations, inappropriate pharmacodisposition and untoward metabolism.

In contrast, site-specific delivery would not only increase the amount of drug reaching the site but also simultaneously decrease the amount being distributed to other parts of the body. Thus, a target-oriented drug delivery system supplies the drug selectively to its site(s) of action(s) in a manner that provides maximum therapeutic activity (through controlled and predetermined drug release kinetics), prevents degradation or inactivation during transit to the target sites and protects the body from adverse reactions because of inappropriate disposition. For drugs that have a low therapeutic index, targeted drug delivery provides effective treatment at a relatively low drug concentration.

Targeted Drug Delivery Requirements

- The delivery system should be biochemically inert, non-immunogenic and physically and chemically stable in vivo and in vitro.
- The carrier must be biodegradable or readily eliminated without any problems.
- The delivery system must be reproducible, cost-effective and simple.

Different Approaches to Drug Targeting

There are three approaches to drug targeting. The first approach involves the use of biologically active agents that are both potent and selective to a particular site in the body. The second approach involves the preparation of pharmacologically inert forms of active drugs that, on reaching the active sites, become activated by a chemical or enzymatic reaction (prodrug approach). Although these approaches are very successful in some cases, most of the time it is not feasible to synthesise new site-specific drugs for ailments because of the formidable cost and time taken for drug discovery.

For this reason, the third approach—the delivery of the original drug by specially designed drug delivery systems—is the best and only feasible solution thus far. This approach utilises a biologically inert macromolecular carrier system that directs a drug to a specific site in the body where it accumulates and produces a response.

Regardless of the approach followed, the therapeutic efficacy of a targeted drug delivery system depends on the timely availability of the drug in its active form at the target site(s) and its intrinsic pharmacological activity.

The intrinsic pharmacokinetic properties of the free drug should be the same, irrespective of whether or not it is introduced into the body attached to a carrier.

Drug–Carrier Delivery Systems for Drug Targeting

The basic rationale behind using particulate carriers in intravenous applications is that the drugs included in the system get distributed according to the properties of the carrier. Therefore, the carrier is expected to 'seek out' the preferred site and, consequently, the drug is directed to the intended site of action. For this to happen, the particulate carrier must have access to the intended site of drug action and be able to avoid interactions with other sites within the body. Depending on the specific indication, an ideal particulate delivery system should facilitate some of the following properties of drugs:

- Prolong the drug effect by ensuring a longer circulation time than in free drugs
- Increase the drug concentration at the required site of action by preferential sequestering of the particles by the tissue of the site
- Reduce drug toxicity in the tissue
- Protect the drug from metabolism and immune system recognition until it reaches the desired target site
- Confine the drug delivery system to the chosen anatomical compartment by selecting an appropriate particle size
- Interact selectively with the cells of the target site if equipped with specific, biologically recognised structural units
- Retain the drug within the particle while 'in transit' and release the drug at the target site at the appropriate rate
- Deliver drugs to the appropriate phagocytic cells by participating in adsorptive endocytosis

Drug–carrier delivery systems employ biologically inert macromolecules (polymers) to direct a drug to its target site in the body. Depending on the carrier system, the drug can be either molecularly entrapped within the carrier matrix or covalently linked to the carrier molecules. The major advantage of drug–carrier delivery systems is that the distribution of drugs in the body depends on the physicochemical properties of the carrier and not of the drugs. This implies that targeting can be manipulated by choosing an appropriate carrier or by altering the physicochemical properties of the carrier.

The various mechanisms used by the drug–carrier delivery system to vector the drug to the target site can be broadly classified as:

- Passive targeting
- Inverse targeting
- Active targeting
- Double targeting

Passive Targeting

Here, targeting occurs because of the body's natural response to the physicochemical characteristics of the drug or drug–carrier system. It is a passive process that utilises the natural course (attributed to inherent characteristics) of biodistribution of the carrier system, through which it eventually accumulates in the organs of the body. The ability of some colloids to be taken up by the reticuloendothelial system (RES) especially in the liver and spleen has made them ideal vectors for passive hepatic targeting of drugs to these compartments. Passive capture of colloidal carriers by macrophages offers therapeutic opportunities for the delivery of anti-infectives for disease conditions that involve the macrophage cells of the RES.

Inverse Targeting

Inverse targetting is the reversion of the biodistribution trend of the carrier. The method essentially circumvents and avoids passive uptake of colloidal carriers by the RES. This effectively leads to the reversion of the biodistribution trend of the carrier and hence the process is referred to as inverse targeting. One strategy used to achieve inverse targeting is to suppress the function of the RES by preinjecting a large amount of blank, colloidal carriers or macromolecules such as dextran sulfate. This approach leads to RES blockade and results in impairment of the host defense system. Alternative strategies include modification of the size, surface charge, composition, surface rigidity and hydrophilicity of carriers for a desirable biofate.

Active Targeting

Active targeting exploits the modification or manipulation of drug carriers to redefine their biofate. The natural distribution pattern of the drug carrier composite is enhanced using chemical, biological and physical means so that it approaches and is identified by particular biosites. Facilitation of the binding of the drug carrier to target cells by using ligands or engineered homing devices to increase receptor-mediated localisation and target-specific delivery of the drug is referred to as active targeting.

Active targeting can be further classified into ligand-mediated and physical targeting.

Ligand-mediated active targeting

The targeting components that have been studied thus far are bioconjugates, which are anchored as ligands onto some delivery vehicle. These can be specifically functionalised using biologically relevant molecular ligands including antibodies, polypeptides, oligosaccharides and viral proteins. The ligands display specific affinity to drug carriers. The engineered 'carrier constructs' selectively deliver the drug to the cell or groups of cells generally referred to as the target. The cascade of events involved in ligand-negotiated, specific drug delivery is termed ligand-driven, receptor-mediated targeting.

Ligand-mediated active targeting can be achieved by using specific uptake mechanisms such as receptor-dependent uptake of natural, low-density lipoprotein (LDL) particles and synthetic lipid microemulsions of partially reconstituted LDL particles coated with apoproteins. The apoprotein coat serves as a ligand for the LDL receptors expressed in the body.

Physical targeting (triggered release)

Selective drug delivery that is programmed and monitored at the external level (ex vivo) with the help of physical means is referred to as physical targeting. In this mode of targeting, some characteristics of the bioenvironment are used either to direct the carrier to a particular location or to cause the selective release of its contents. The first such approach was the temperature-sensitive liposomes. The release of a drug from temperature-sensitive liposomes in the vicinity of a tumour (temperature status higher than or equal to the phase transition temperature of constitutive lipids) is brought about by serum components, mostly lipoproteins, which, at phase transition, induce the release of the entrapped drug. Alternatively, the application of an external magnetic field has been suggested for localisation of magnoresponsive liposomes and microspheres within a preselected capillary bed.

Double Targeting

In the future, drug targeting may be combined with a methodology other than passive and active targeting for drug delivery systems: the combination of spatial control and temporal control of drug delivery. The temporal control of drug delivery has been developed in terms of controlled drug release (sustained release/stimuli responsive release/self-regulating release). Spatial control has been developed in terms of drug targeting (active/passive). This approach may bring about improvements to the therapeutic index by a combination of a spatially selective delivery and a preferable release pattern for a drug, such as zero order release. When these two methodologies are combined, it is called double targeting.

A large number of drug–carrier delivery systems have been conceived and developed with the purpose of drug targeting. Among these systems, colloidal drug delivery systems hold great promise for reaching the goal of drug targeting. Because of their small size (<1 micron), colloidal drug carriers come close to Dr Ehrlich's idea of magic bullets.

The type of targeting used can be selected based on the drug, the need and the disease in question.

Advances in drug delivery systems such as targeted delivery systems are expected to offer a host of other advantages such as ease of administration, increased patient compliance, decreased side effects and reduced cost of production. Thus, it can be concluded that innovative targeted delivery of drugs would not only increase the safety and efficacy levels of drugs but also improve the overall performance of the drug.

Key Messages

- A targeted drug delivery system increases the amount of drug reaching the site of action and simultaneously decreases the amount being distributed to other parts of the body.
- The different approaches to drug targeting include the use of biologically active agents that are both potent and selective to a particular site in the body, prodrug approach and delivery of the drug by specially designed drug delivery systems.
- Drug–carrier systems appear to be promising for targeted drug delivery as the drugs included in the system are distributed according to the properties of the carrier.
- The various methods of delivering the drug to the target site by the drug–carrier delivery systems are passive targeting, inverse targeting, active targeting and double targeting.

Questions

1. What are the advantages of targeted drug delivery systems over conventional and controlled delivery systems?
2. Briefly explain the various approaches to targeted drug release and state which is the most feasible.
3. What are the various mechanisms by which the drug–carrier delivery system can be used for targeted delivery of drugs?

9
Liposomes

SHOBHA RANI R HIREMATH AND VANAJA K

Learning Objectives

At the end of this chapter, you will be able to:

- Describe the structural features of liposomes
- Describe the morphology and nomenclature of liposomes
- List the methods of preparation of liposomes
- Explain the characterisation techniques of liposomes
- List the applications of liposomes

Introduction

Phospholipid vesicles (liposomes) were first discovered decades ago by Bangham. The hydration of a dry lipid film was found to lead to the formation of enclosed spherical vesicles or liposomes that resemble miniature cellular organelles with lipid bilayers. The potential use of liposomes as biodegradable or biocompatible drug carriers to enhance the potency and reduce the toxicity of therapeutics was then recognised. These vesicles, composed of one or more phospholipid bilayer membranes, can carry aqueous or lipid drugs, depending on the nature of the drugs. Because lipids are amphiphathic (both hydrophobic and hydrophilic) in aqueous media, their thermodynamic phase properties and self-assembling characteristics evoke entropically driven sequestration of their hydrophobic regions into spherical bilayers. These layers are referred to as lamellae.

The structural features shared by liposome bilayers and biological membranes have led to their widespread early use as membrane models for investigating the structural and functional relationships of natural cell membranes and their components. Their potential use as carriers for drugs, cosmetics and many other types of active agents has excited a much greater volume of interest and led to their eventual commercialisation. The applications of liposomes are dependent on the fact that they are sealed structures and so, water soluble substances dissolved in the internal aqucous phasc arc entrapped and isolated from the external environment. Many nonpolar compounds, as well as other amphiphiles, can also be included. The liposomes themselves can be constructed with widely different physical structures, lipid composition and surface properties, thus enabling a great deal of control over the fate of their contents. The basic aspects of liposomal drug delivery are summarised below:

- *Protection*: Both the active material and the host are protected by virtue of the membrane barrier function and the possibility of co-encapsulation of protective agents.
- *Sustained release*: This release is dependent on the ability to vary the permeability characteristics of the membrane by controlling bilayer composition and lamellarity.
- *Controlled release*: Drug release is enabled by exploiting lipid phase transitions in response to external triggers such as changes in temperature or pH.
- *Targeted delivery*: Passive delivery to body organs depends on liposome size and surface charge or the incorporation of antibodies or other ligands to aid delivery to specific cell types.
- *Topical delivery*: Liposomes are similar to the epidermis with respect to their lipid composition, which enables them to penetrate the skin epidermal barrier to a greater extent than other dosage forms.

In the ensuing years, great strides are expected to be made towards understanding the way in which liposomes interact with the biological milieu at the molecular and cellular levels. Various ways have been found to improve liposomal stability in biological fluids so that drugs do not leak significantly. In addition, enhancements have been made to ensure that the presence of vesicles in the circulation is extended and alternative sites are targeted. Important advances in liposome technology have provided indications that many of the problems associated with liposomes can be overcome.

Basic Components of Liposomes

Liposomes or lipid vesicles are colloidal particles with (phospho) lipid molecules as the main constituent in the enclosed lipid bilayers or lipid drug sheet–disk complexes. Most liposome formulations approved for human use contain phosphotidyl choline (neutral charge), with fatty acyl chains of varying lengths and degrees of saturation as a major membrane building block. A fraction of cholesterol is often included in the lipid formulation to modulate rigidity and to reduce serum-induced instability caused by the binding of serum protein to the liposome membrane.

Phospholipids

The general chemical structure of phospholipids shows a glycerol backbone. At position number 3 of the glycerol molecule, the hydroxyl is esterified to phosphoric acid. The hydroxyl groups at positions 1 and 2 of the glycerol are usually esterified with long-chain fatty acids. The lipid nature of the phospholipids can be attributed to these long-chain fatty acids. One of the remaining oxygen groups of phosphoric acid may be further esterified to a variety of organic molecules including glycerol, choline, ethanolamine, serine and inositol. The phosphate moiety along with the attached alcohol represents the head group of phospholipids. The most abundant phosphatides in plants and animals are phosphatidyl choline (also known as lecithin) and phosphatidyl ethanolamine. These two components constitute the major structural part of most biological membranes.

The fatty acid part of a phospholipid molecule is important and differences in this fatty acid part can change the characteristics of the phospholipids. Fatty acids differ in the number of carbon atoms in the chain and the degree of unsaturation. A number of synthetic phospholipids are available and are utilised in the preparation of liposomes. The tissue distribution and clearance kinetics of drug-containing liposomes are known to be affected by lipid composition and surface charge.

Steroids

Cholesterol has a steroid backbone, and its derivatives are included in liposome preparation. It has been used in the preparation of liposomes to improve their bilayer characteristics. It improves the rigidity of the bilayer membrane, reduces the permeability of water soluble molecules through the membrane and improves the stability of the bilayer membrane in the presence of biological fluids such as blood and plasma. The cholesterol molecule orients itself among the phospholipid molecules with its hydroxyl group facing towards the water phase and the tricyclic ring sandwiched between the first few carbons of fatty acyl chains into the hydrocarbon core of the bilayer.

Morphology and Nomenclature of Liposomes

Lamellar-forming lipids exist in a densely packed, crystalline form in the dry state. Below a certain characteristic temperature, the nonpolar hydrocarbon chains are fully extended and rigid, but above this temperature, thermal excitation increases and the chains enter a more disordered, liquid-like state. If water is added to the lipids when they are above this transition temperature (T_c), the polar head groups at the surface of the exposed amphiphile become hydrated and start to reorganise into the lamellar form. The water diffuses through this surface bilayer causing the underlying lipid to undergo a similar rearrangement, and the process is repeated until all the lipids are organised into a series of parallel lamella, each separated from the next by a layer of water. Once this liquid crystalline lipid is fully swollen and is in equilibrium with excess water, mild agitation allows portions of the closely-packed, multilamellar lipids to break away. The resulting large spherical liposomes, each consisting of numerous concentric bilayers in close apposition, alternating with layers, are known as multilamellar vesicles (MLVs). These are heterogeneous in size, varying from a few hundred nanometers in diameter to around 10 μm—in the latter case representing MLVs that are hundreds of lamellae thick.

When the lipid is allowed to hydrate undisturbed and is then gently swirled, individual lamellae are able to detach to form large unilamellar vesicles (LUVs). LUVs vary in size from around 100 nm to tens of micrometers in diameter.

The lower limit of liposome size is fixed by the maximum curvature that the lipid bilayer is able to achieve—around 21 nm in the case of unsaturated, natural phospholipids such as egg and soya lecithin. These single-layered liposomes are known as small unilamellar vesicles (SUVs), and their maximum size is 100 nm.

SUVs together with MLVs and LUVs are the three main morphological categories of liposomes; these may be subdivided further. Oligolamellar vesicles have intermediate lamellarity between LUVs and MLVs, and their formation is favoured under certain conditions.

Preparation of Liposomes

The preparation of various types of lamellar vesicles is now discussed in detail.

Multilamellar Vesicles (MLVs)

MLVs form spontaneously when an excess volume of aqueous buffer is added to dry lipids. When the molecular mixture of lipids is prepared in an organic solvent and subsequently removed by rotary evaporation in a round-bottomed flask under vacuum, the lipids are deposited as a thin film on the flask. The time allowed for the hydration of the lipid layer with the aqueous buffer/drug solution determines the amount of drug entrapped in the vesicles. The presence of negatively charged lipids such as phosphatidyl serine (PS) and phosphatidyl inositol (PI) and positively charged adjuvants such as stearyl amine is likely to increase the interlamellar distance between successive bilayers and thus provide greater encapsulation efficiency. The presence of charged moiety in lipid formulation also reduces the probability of vesicular aggregation following the formation of MLVs.

MLVs can also be produced by hydrating a dry lipid mixture in the presence of organic solvents. A two-phase system consisting of equal volumes of ether dissolved lipids and an aqueous phase are vigorously mixed and the organic phase is removed by passing a stream of nitrogen. As the ether is removed, MLVs are formed in the aqueous media. In a similar method, diethyl ether is used instead of petroleum ether and the two phases are mixed by sonication instead of vortex mixing to prepare MLVs.

Small Unilamellar Vesicles (SUVs)

Dispersions of phospholipids in water are mixed by sonication, either with a bath-type sonicator or a probe sonicator, in an inert atmosphere such as one made up of nitrogen or argon. Probe sonication leads to rapid size reduction with the disadvantage of shedding of metal particles from the probe tip. In comparison, a bath sonicator has the advantage of temperature control of the product during the process by enabling control of the water bath temperature. The product can then be processed aseptically in a sealed container.

Dispersions of MLVs can be converted to SUVs by passing them through a small orifice under high pressure. A French pressure cell is used for this purpose, where the MLV dispersion is placed in the French press and extruded at about 20,000 psi at 4 °C. One pass through the cell produces a heterogeneous population of vesicles ranging from several micrometers in diameter to SUV size. Multiple extrusions result in a progressive decrease in the mean particle diameter. Higher throughput methods using various types of reciprocating piston homogenisers are also used to produce SUVs.

Large Unilamellar Vesicles (LUVs)

This type of vesicle can be produced by reverse phase evaporation and by the detergent removal technique.

Reverse Phase Evaporation

A water-in-oil emulsion is prepared, consisting of a lipid phase and an aqueous phase with excess organic phase. The two phases are emulsified by mechanical methods or by sonication. When the organic phase is removed by rotary evaporation, there is just enough lipid material left to form a monolayer around each of the microdroplets of the aqueous phase. At this stage, emulsion inversion takes place. This involves the collapse of a proportion of these inverted micelles so that their aqueous contents form the new continuous phase, while the lipid components form an outer leaflet around the remaining structures, thus converting them from inverted micelles to a vesicular form. High encapsulation efficiency of up to 65% can be achieved using hydrophilic solutes. The drawback of this method is that the drug is exposed to organic solvents and to mechanical agitation.

Detergent Removal Technique

Removal of detergent molecules from aqueous dispersions of phospholipid-/detergent-mixed micelles represents a different approach. As the detergent is removed, the micelles become progressively rich with phospholipids and finally coalesce to form closed, single-bilayered vesicles. The detergent is then removed using a diffusion-based process such as dialysis or gel chromatography. Ionic detergents such as cholate and deoxycholate or non-ionic detergents such as Triton-X 100 and octylglucoside are used. This approach has the considerable advantage of allowing close control of the final size of the liposomes, which have a homogeneous size range. The main disadvantages are that encapsulation efficiency is lower than with most other methods of LUV preparation and detergent removal by ordinary dialysis techniques is a time-consuming process that can take several days to reduce the residual detergent to a negligible level.

Solvent Injection Methods

Ether infusion, fluorocarbon injection and ethanol injection are the three solvent injection methods used to prepare liposomes.

Ether Infusion

Liposomes are prepared by slowly introducing a solution of lipids dissolved in diethyl ether (ether/methanol mixtures) into warm water. The lipid mixture is injected into an aqueous solution of the material to be encapsulated using a syringe-type infusion pump at 55–65 °C or under reduced pressure. Vapourisation of the ether leads to the formation of single-layer vesicles with diameters ranging 50–200 nm.

Fluorocarbon Injection

To overcome the hazards associated with diethyl ether, a fluorocarbon solvent has been identified for injection. Freon 21 was found to be an excellent solvent for phospholipids; it is immiscible in water and boils at 9 °C (at atmospheric pressure). Large unilamellar and oligolamellar liposomes are formed when the Freon 21 lipid mixture is injected into an aqueous medium at 37 °C. The fluorocarbon boils off at almost the same rate as it is introduced, leaving the lipid behind to hydrate and form liposomes.

Ethanol Injection

Lipids dissolved in ethanol are rapidly injected into an excess of buffer solution. The procedure is simple, rapid and gentle to both lipids and the material to be entrapped. The final concentration of ethanol cannot exceed 10–20% by volume as the SUVs either will not form or will grow in size soon after formation. Another disadvantage is that certain biologically active macromolecules tend to be inactivated in the presence of very small amounts of ethanol.

Characterisation of Liposomes

Liposomes have to be characterised after preparation and on storage for adequate quality control of the product. The characterisation methods have to be reproducible, precise and rapid in the context of their use in the industrial setting.

Physicochemical Characterisation

The methods appropriate for investigation and

characterisation of liposomes are frequently used in the development of drugs in pharmaceutical laboratories. Both macroscopic and microscopic techniques are used.

Particle size determination by laser light scattering

Particle size is an important parameter in in-process control and quality assurance because the physical stability of vesicle dispersions depends on particle size and particle size distribution. Laser light diffraction is applied for particles >1 μm in size and refers to the proportionality between the intensity of diffraction and the square of the particle diameter according to the diffraction theory of Fraunhofer. For particles <200 nm, Rayleigh's theory, which considers the scattering intensity to be proportional to the sixth potency of the particle diameter, holds true. Most colloidal dispersions such as liposomes consist of particles <200 nm to 1 μm in size. Therefore, photon correlation spectroscopy based on laser scattering is an appropriate method of investigation.

Transmission electron microscopy (TEM)

The microstructure of colloidal systems can be visualised with the high magnification power of the electron microscope. However, aqueous samples do not survive the high vacuum of an electron microscope and water loss occurs, leading to microstructure changes. Therefore, special techniques of sample preparation are required prior to electron microscopy. Freeze fracture has proven to be successful at overcoming these problems. Fluid vesicle dispersions can be characterised using cryo-TEM. Sufficient contrast can be given to a thin film of the frozen sample by using osmium tetroxide. This allows the sample to be viewed directly in the TEM (at a temperature of –196 °C). The adjustment of the temperature to –196 °C leads to a very low vapour pressure, especially of water, so that it is possible to examine the sample while preserving the microstructure despite the high vacuum. A disadvantage of cryo-TEM is the difficulty in establishing the size classification of vesicles.

X-ray scattering

A typical interference pattern arises from specific repeat distances of the associated interlayer spacing *d*. According to Bragg's equation, *d* can be calculated as:

$$d = n\lambda/2 \sin\gamma$$

where λ is the wavelength of the x-ray, n is an integer and nominates the order of the interference and γ is the angle under which the interference occurs.

Small angle x-ray diffraction (SAXD) is the most appropriate technique for the exact determination of the distances of interlayer spacing of liquid crystalline systems. This is especially useful for colloidal dispersions because information about the size and shape of the particles can be obtained at the same time.

Differential scanning colourimetry (DSC)

Phase transitions are accompanied by free energy changes and are caused by an alteration in enthalpy (ΔH) or entropy (ΔS) of the system. Enthalpy changes result in either endothermic or exothermic signals, depending on whether the transition is due to the consumption of energy, such as melting of a solid, or a release of energy, such as recrystallisation of an isotropic melt.

Crystalline to liquid crystalline and liquid crystalline to amorphous transitions as well as changes between different liquid crystalline phases, all consume low amounts of energy. Care has to be taken to ensure that the measuring device is sensitive enough to give a sufficiently low detection limit.

Rheology
Colloidal vesicular carriers exhibit different rheological properties. With increased organisation of the liquid crystal microstructure, viscosity increases. The coefficient of dynamic viscosity η describes the viscosity of ideal flow behaviour (Newtonian system) and is rather high for cubic and hexagonal liquid crystals but fairly low for lamellar systems. The flow characteristics exhibited by this system are plastic and pseudoplastic.

The high viscosity of lyotropic liquid crystals such as cubic and hexagonal mesophases is due to their three-dimensional and two-dimensional orders, respectively. Lamellar mesophases with a one-dimensional, long-range order have a fairly low viscosity. Due to their gel character, cubic and hexagonal mesophases exhibit a yield value after which flow occurs.

Mechanical oscillation measurement is the method of choice for determining liquid crystalline gel elasticity. Since shear strain is not applied, the viscoelastic properties of such systems may be studied without a change in network microstructure. The oscillation experiments enable determination of the viscoelastic character of cubic, hexagonal and lamellar mesophases, in addition to highly contracted vesicle dispersions displaying viscoelastic behaviour.

Per Cent Drug Encapsulation

The quantity of drug entrapped in a liposome vesicle can be determined by column chromatography or other methods. Liposome preparations are a mixture of encapsulated and unencapsulated drug fractions. The unencapsulated drug fraction is also referred to as a 'free' drug. The first step is to separate free and encapsulated drug concentrations to assess the per cent drug encapsulation. Then, the encapsulated fraction of the drug is treated with the detergent to lyse the liposomes and completely discharge the drug from the liposomes into the surrounding aqueous media.

Per cent entrapment
Various methods are employed to separate the free drug from the entrapped material. In general, mini-column centrifugation is most commonly used. In this method, a hydrated gel (Sephadex G) is filled in the barrel of the syringe without a plunger and the syringe is plugged with a Whatman GF/B filter pad. This barrel is placed in a centrifuge tube, which is spun at 2000–3000 rpm for a few minutes to remove the excess saline solution from the gel. The eluted saline is removed from the collection tube. Liposome suspension is applied drop by drop to the top of the gel bed, and the column is spun at 2000 rpm for three minutes to expel the void volume containing the liposomes into the centrifuge tube. The elute is then removed and set aside for the assay.

Another method is the protamine aggregate method, which may be used for liposomes of any composition but with a negative charge. Here, liposome suspension in normal saline is placed in a conical glass centrifuge tube; 0.1 ml of the protamine solution is added and mixed and allowed to stand for three minutes. Saline is added and the tube is then spun for 20 minutes at 2000 x g at room temperature. The supernatant is removed and assayed for free, unentrapped compounds by standard methods. The liposomal pellet is resuspended in Triton X-100 to disrupt the liposomes. The amount of material entrapped is analysed by various analytical methods.

Entrapped volume

The per cent drug encapsulated in liposomes can also be determined by entrapped volume per lipid weight which varies for MLVs and SUVs. The trapped volume is determined by dispersing lipids in an aqueous medium containing a radioactive solute that does not readily permeate across bilayers. Carboxyfluorescein is also used as a marker to determine the volume of entrapped water per mole of phospholipid.

Release Kinetics of Encapsulated Drugs from Liposomes

Interaction between liposomes and blood components

The lipid composition of liposomes is a critical factor in determining the release property of encapsulated drugs. The rigid membranes retain aqueous phase markers for a longer period in blood circulation. The addition of cholesterol to egg phosphotidyl choline (PC) and the replacement of PC by distearoylphosphatidyl choline (DSPC) can reduce the release rate of encapsulated carboxyfluorescein (CF) both in vitro and in vivo.

High density lipoprotein (HDL) was shown to remove phospholipid molecules from liposomes, and encapsulated drugs were released at rates that depend on the extent of liposomal damage. The complement system also plays an important role in the degradation and opsonisation of liposomes. Although the exact mechanism of activation pathway is inconsistent, a negative charge, saturated acyl chains and the size of liposomes are important factors in the activation of the complement system.

Hydrophilic compounds

The rate and extent of release of encapsulated drugs from liposomes has been measured both in vitro and in vivo. Quantitative evaluation of the release process of liposomally entrapped drugs in vivo is more complete than in vitro, because the blood concentration of liposomes changes due to uptake by the reticuloendothelial system (RES). [^{3}H] inulin is a suitable marker to evaluate the release process from liposomes in vivo, because it is injected only into extracellular space and is rapidly excreted from the kidneys by glomerular filtration. The release process of [^{3}H] inulin from liposomes is estimated by the fitting of the time course of [^{3}H] inulin excreted into urine, based on the pharmacokinetic model of free [^{3}H] inulin linked with the first-order degradation rate constant (k_d) of the marker from liposomes and the disappearance curves of liposomally encapsulated [^{3}H] inulin.

Lipophilic compounds

The transmembrane pH-gradient method is an efficient method for encapsulating weak bases such as doxorubicin or vincristine. Weak bases are concentrated in the acidic compartment according to the pH partition theory, in addition to its partitioning to the lipid membrane. Almost 100% of these drugs can be loaded into liposomes with different kinds of lipid composition.

Surface Charge

Depending on the head group composition of the lipid and pH forms, liposomes may bear a negative, neutral or positive charge on their surface. The nature and density of charge on the surface of the liposomes influences the stability, kinetics and extent of biodistribution, as well as the interaction with and uptake of liposomes by target cells.

Surface charge is normally characterised in terms of a voltage at the particle surface—the surface potential (zeta potential)—rather than a charge density. The zeta potential occurs at a distance from the surface and is measured by the Doppler shift of light scattered from moving particles in an electric field. The zeta potential normally lies within the range of ±100 mV for most systems immersed in aqueous media. A zeta potential value of –40 to –50 mV has been found to be sufficient to provide good stability and a shelf life of at least two years for colloidal pharmaceutical formulations.

Phospholipid Determination

Lipids can be measured by standard analytical methods such as wet chemistry, HPLC, thin layer chromatography and gas chromatography. Because lipid formulations may have several components and the formulation may have an overall aggregate structure, it is usually necessary to develop strategies for isolation and detection of lipid ingredients. Dissociation of the individual components using temperature, solvents, detergents, reducing or oxidising agents or mechanical disruption prior to analysis may be necessary. Further separation or extraction of the components before analysis is required if interference is encountered. With lipid solvent extraction, there is a greater likelihood of loss of material. More often than not, a combination of techniques will be required for validation of the product. There are worldwide compendial procedures for the analysis of various lipids by wet chemistry procedures to determine concentration, end group analysis, acid value, hydroxyl value, iodine value and saponification value.

Analysis of nonpolar lipids by HPLC is best carried out using normal phase columns. However, for mixed phases with polar drugs or drugs within an aqueous phase, some compromise may be necessary. Good separation of polar and neutral lipids with a C8 column and a four-solvent mobile phase has been reported. Elution of neutral lipids such as triglycerides from C18 columns is slow; however, good resolution can be achieved. Mobile phase development is usually necessary to affect a high degree of separation and for resolution of similarly eluting components. Heated columns are beneficial for increasing the temperature above the phase transition temperature of the lipid, thus minimising clogging. Lipids with predominantly saturated chain lengths will have poor ultraviolet (UV) absorption even at lower wavelengths (190 nm). Alternative detectors may then have to be considered.

Thin layer chromatography

One- and two-dimensional, thin layer, silica gel chromatography remains a cornerstone of lipid analysis. Sensitivity by this method is typically as low as 2 μg/spot. Lipid visualisation can be achieved by many methods, including iodine vapour or charring of plates following exposure to sulfur dichromic acid, cupric reagents, phospray or α-naphthol. Other useful reagents include stains and dyes such as fluorescamine, rhodamine 6G, bromothymol blue, molybdenum blue, phosphomolybdic acid and silver nitrate, which may be impregnated into the silica. Validation of lipid purity and quantification is performed using gel or plate scanners.

Gas chromatography (GC)

Capillary and packed GC columns are of value in the analysis of complex mixtures of lipids.

The best capillary column length will depend on the complexity of the material injected; however, 30 m columns are often used. In packed columns, many types of stationary phases are available for lipid separation, and these include silicone and alkylated or cyanogenated derivatives, polyesters, polyglycols and carboranes. It is also common to derivatise fatty-acid side chains to the corresponding methyl esters by reaction in methanol prior to chromatographic analysis to achieve more distinct and uniform separation.

Residual Solvent Analysis

Residual solvents in pharmaceuticals are volatile organic chemicals that are used in and/or produced during the synthesis or production of drug substances or formulations. Many of these residual solvents generally cannot be completely removed by standard manufacturing processes/techniques and are left behind, mostly at low levels. The pharmaceutical industry gives special importance to residual solvent testing as it affects the physicochemical properties of the drug substances/formulations and because high levels of these solvents represent a potential risk to human health due to their toxicity.

Chloroform is used as a solvent for egg phosphotidyl glycerol and egg phosphotidyl choline to protect the lipids from oxidation during storage and to facilitate good molecular dispersion of various lipids during the process. Although chloroform is a good solvent for the dispersion of lipids, its complete removal from the lipid mixture is imperative when the liposomes are intended for human use. Carbon tetrachloride, a contaminant of chloroform, is known to be a carcinogenic material. A process involving chloroform as a solvent should include a test method.

Liposomal Stability

Changes in the structural characteristics of liposomes on storage can be monitored by one or more of the techniques mentioned. While designing the lipid composition of liposomes for the entrapment of a drug within their aqueous phase, monitoring of the stability of the bilayers must be ensured. One of the easiest and most effective methods is the use of calcein or carboxyfluorescein as marker solutes. Calcein and carboxyfluorescein self-quench at high concentrations but acquire a green, fluorescent colour on excessive dilution. Suspended liposomes containing quenched dye appear brown or orange in colour. Drug leakage on storage can be monitored by techniques that separate the entrapped from the leaked drug. This can be achieved by ultracentrifugation, dialysis, molecular size chromatography or ion exchange chromatography.

Novel Liposomes

Transferosomes

These are bi or multicomponent aggregates capable of crossing semipermeable barriers and transferring material between the application and the destination sites on either side of the barrier. They are liquid droplets that can be deformed to penetrate pores much smaller than their own size. An elastic bilayer energy to the order of thermal energy or less is required for penetration. This high deformability allows them to deliver drugs across barriers such as the skin.

Archaeosomes

Membranes of archaeobacteria contain lipids that are chemically distinct from the eukaryotic and prokaryotic species. The saturated, branched

C-20, C-25 and C-40 phytanyl chains can form liposomes with unique properties with respect to physical and chemical stability and uptake. They are less sensitive to oxidative stress, high temperature, alkalinc pH, phospholipases and bile salts.

Proteosomes

These vesicles are mainly of bacterial origin. They are prepared by solubilisation of bacterial outer membranes, followed by ammonium sulphate precipitation and dialysis against a detergent-containing buffer. Electron micrographs reveal liposomal vesicles at a size of about 100 nm, but the protein–lipid ratio is higher than can be achieved with purified protein incorporated in liposomes. Proteins and peptides can be noncovalently complexed to the proteosomes, making them highly immunogenic.

Virosomes

Liposomes attach to the cell membrane and are taken up into cells by phagacytosis or endocytosis. Most of the macromolecules in liposomes are degraded in lysosomes before they reach the cytoplasm. Introduction of molecules directly into the cytoplasm has been attempted. Virosomes are membranous vesicles that carry viral fusion proteins in their membrane. For influenza virosomes, influenza HA is anchored in the virosomal membrane.

Ethosomes

Ethosomes arc tailored vesicles composed mainly of phospholipids and ethanol or isopropyl alcohol in relatively high concentration, sometimes along with glycols and water. The high concentration of ethanol makes the ethosomes unique, as ethanol causes disturbance of skin lipid bilayer organisation. Therefore, when integrated into a vesicle membrane, it gives the vesicle the ability to penetrate the stratum corneum. Because of their high ethanol concentration, the lipid membrane is packed less tightly than conventional vesicles but has equivalent stability, allowing a more malleable structure that gives it more freedom and the ability to squeeze through small spaces such as openings created while disturbing the stratum corneum lipids.

Stealth Liposomes

Liposomes that are formulated to escape from being recognised by the RES can remain in circulation for prolonged periods and may serve as microreservoir systems. They may also minimise the problems associated with conventional liposomes. Liposomes that possess this evasive property are commonly referred to as stealth lipids. They consist of bilayer-compatible polymers such as polyethylene glycols, gangliosides and glycolipids. They can be used for controlled release within the vasculature by manipulating the phospholipid composition of bilayers.

Applications of Liposomes

Vaccine adjuvants

Liposomes have been firmly established as immunoadjuvants (enhancers of immunological response), that increase the potential of both cell-mediated and humoral immunity. Liposomal immunoadjuvants act by slowly releasing encapsulated antigens on intramuscular injection and also by passively accumulating within regional lymph nodes. Strategies that enhance the targeting of liposomes to regional lymph nodes, for example, the use of phosphatidylserine liposomes, may thus improve adjuvanticity. Liposomal vaccines are prepared by associating microbes, soluble antigens, cytokines or deoxyribonucleic acid (DNA) with liposomes, the latter stimulating an immune response on expression of the antigenic protein. Liposomes encapsulating antigens that are subsequently encapsulated within alginate lysine microcapsules to control antigen release improve the antibody response. Liposomal vaccines may also be stored dried at refrigeration temperatures for up to 12 months and still retain their adjuvanticity.

Liposome formulation provides an excellent way to enhance antigen delivery and presentation for both humoral and cellular immune stimulation of vaccines. A liposome-based hepatitis A (Epaxal®) vaccine was developed by Swiss Serum and tested by the Vaccine Institute. This vaccine contains formalin-inactivated hepatitis A virus particles attached to phospholipid vesicles together with influenza virus hemaglutinin. The advantage of such a vaccine is that not only does it induce antibody reactions to hepatitis A antigens but it also provokes the expression of the influenza virus proteins on the liposomal surface.

Cancer

Liposomes have been used for the treatment of cancer because of their tumour-targeting potential. A variety of cytotoxic drugs encapsulated in liposomes have been administered through various routes to a range of animal tumour models. Daunosome™ consists of daunorubicin incorporated into an SUV with a diameter of 40–50 nm and composed of DSPC and cholesterol and is supplied as a ready-to-use aqueous liposome suspension. This composition forms a rigid bilayer that inhibits opsonisation by the plasma lipoproteins. This, together with their small size, results in an extended circulation time of 24 hours in the blood. A substantial portion of the extravasated liposomes are taken up intact by the tumour, where they then release their contents over a prolonged period of time to produce sustained drug action.

Antimicrobial agents

Liposomes have been widely investigated as delivery systems for the treatment of bacterial, fungal, viral and parasitic diseases. Liposomes can be used for passive delivery of immunomodulators to macrophages, which brings about nonspecific resistance to infections in general.

Ambisome™ is a liposomal form that consists of SUVs composed of hydrogenated soya PC, distearoyl phosphatidyl glycerol and cholesterol, stored as a lyophilised powder. Molecules of the drug are believed to align in parallel lines to form cylindrical structures, two of which fit end to end to form a bilayer-spanning pore across which ions and other solutes can pass. These pores can be inserted into the fungal cell membrane, allowing rapid loss of cell contents. In vitro studies have shown binding of Ambisome liposomes to fungal cells, followed by liposome disintegration and subsequent cell disruption.

Ophthalmic therapy

The efficacy of liposomes in ophthalmic therapy depends on the drug encapsulation efficiency, size and charge of the vesicles, distribution of the drug in liposomes, stability of the liposomes after instillation, residence time of the liposomes in the conjunctival sac and affinity of the liposomes to the cornea. The use of liposomes has been demonstrated by animal studies, which report that entrapping idoxuridine in liposomes was more effective than the free drug in the treatment of acute and chronic herpetic keratitis. Studying the corneal uptake of penicillin G and indoxole with different types of liposomes showed that corneal uptake of drugs was largely increased with positively charged liposomes.

Oral drug delivery

The use of liposomes in oral drug delivery has been studied. However, the three major destabilising factors are pH, bile salt and pancreatic enzymes in the gastrointestincal (GI) tract. Several membrane surface polymerisation chemistry methods have been developed to shield liposomes and their contents from the hostile environment of the GI tract; however, incomplete polymerisation and toxicity of residual reagents and derivatives remain a concern. An oral liposome antigen formulation may be used to stimulate mucosal immune response, enhancing delivery of antigens to antigen-presenting cells that actively take up particles in the GI tract. The advantages of using liposomes for such applications include biocompatibility, flexibility in design, protection of antigens, targeting of antigens to antigen-presenting cells and ineffective stimulation of immune responses by oral delivery of soluble antigens.

Gene delivery

Human genome characterisation and recombinant DNA technology have created opportunities for gene therapy that did not previously exist. Target diseases for such technology include certain cancers, arteriosclerosis, cystic fibrosis, hemophilia, sickle cell anemia and other genetic diseases. In addition, genes encoding for various antigens may be administered as vaccines.

The knowledge gained in the development of anti-cancer liposomes, such as the prolongation of liposome circulation using polyoxyethylene lipids, may be applied in the development of gene delivery liposomes to produce efficient carriers. This strategy should aid liposome targeting in gene delivery. Thus far, targeting efforts with cationic liposomal gene formulations have been few and far between. A rare example is the targeting of cationic liposome DNA complexes coated with chylomicron remnants to mouse hepatocytes by portal vein administration. Such liposomes are specifically taken up by the apolipoprotein receptor. However, these chylomicron remnant coated liposomes were not targeted at the hepatocytes on tail vein administration.

Although clinical trials with liposomal gene delivery in cystic fibrosis patients have concentrated on administration through non-parenteral routes, for the obvious reason that the disease manifests itself in the alveolar epithelium, it may be possible to treat this condition by the intravenous administration of the replacement gene–liposome complex. This is because such a strategy results in gene expression in distal regions of the alveolar epithelium. Liposomal DNA is superior to free DNA in the treatment of experimental tumours. A cationic liposome formulation of the human interleukin 2 (IL-2) gene was found to improve the tumouricidal activity of IL-2 in experimental xenografts. Cell kill in this case is mediated by the expression of the IL-2 cytokine, which stimulates natural killer (NK) cell activity. Efficient arterial gene transfer may be beneficial for the treatment of arteriosclerosis, and gene transfer into porcine arteries, through catheters, is enhanced by complexing the gene with liposomes.

Additionally, IV injection into tumour-bearing mice of the gene for diphtheria toxin A-chain complexed with cationic liposomes significantly reduces tumour volume when compared with untreated animals. DNA vaccines administered as liposomal complexes also provoke better antibody responses than those seen with free DNA. Cell-and humoral-mediated immunity after intramuscular administration of plasmids encoding for the S region of hepatitis B are enhanced by liposomal complexation. Cationic liposomes, by virtue of being able to transfer DNA more efficiently into cells than can be achieved with naked DNA alone, should lead to an increase in the level of antigen expression and hence, an increase in the immune response to the antigen.

Topical drug delivery

Topically applied liposomal formulations, mainly prepared from lipid mixtures of compositions similar to the stratum corneum, are an effective delivery system for the treatment of skin diseases. Liposomal formulations provide sustained, enhanced levels in the deeper strata of the skin; they also have the capacity to meter a sufficient quantity of drug into deeper tissue to treat various skin conditions. Such a delivery system also reduces the incidence of undesirable side effects arising from systemic administration or enhanced systemic absorption of drugs after topical administration with vehicles that disrupt the stratum corneum bilayer structure.

Key Messages

- Liposomes are vesicles composed of one or more phospholipid bilayer membranes (multilamellar or unilamellar) that can carry aqueous or lipid drugs, depending on the nature of the drugs.
- Liposomes are colloidal particles composed of mainly phospholipids and cholesterol.
- Liposomes are prepared by various techniques such as reverse phase evaporation, thin film hydration, detergent removal techniques and solvent injection methods.
- Characterisation of liposomes includes physicochemical characterisation, drug entrapment, drug release, determination of surface charge, phospholipid determination, residual solvent analysis and liposomal stability.
- The technology of liposomes has been applied in various fields such as vaccine adjuvants, antimicrobial agents, ophthalmic therapy, gene delivery and oral and topical drug delivery.

Questions

1. What are liposomes? Classify them and list their advantages.
2. Explain briefly the various methods used to prepare liposomes.
3. How do you determine drug entrapment?
4. What is the importance of carrying out residual solvent analysis?
5. Describe the various physicochemical characterisation techniques used to characterise liposomes.
6. Give a few applications of liposomes.

10

Niosomes

SHOBHA RANI R HIREMATH AND VANAJA K

Learning Objectives

At the end of this chapter, you will be able to:

- Define niosomes
- Describe the components of niosomes
- Describe the preparation of niosomes
- Explain the characterisation of niosomes
- List the applications of niosomes

Introduction

Niosomes (non-ionic, surfactant-based vesicles) are formed from the self-assembly of non-ionic amphiphiles in aqueous media, resulting in closed bilayer structures. The assembly into closed bilayers is rarely spontaneous and usually involves the input of energy such as physical agitation or heat. The result is an assembly in which the hydrophobic parts of the molecule are shielded from the aqueous solvent and the hydrophilic head groups have maximum contact with the same. These structures are analogous to phospholipid vesicles (liposomes) and can encapsulate aqueous solutes, thereby serving as drug carriers. The main advantages such as low cost of production, greater stability and resultant ease of storage of non-ionic surfactants have made these vesicles good alternatives to phospholipids.

Components of Niosomes

Niosomes have been prepared from several classes of non-ionic surfactants such as polyglycerol alkylethers, glucosyl dialkylethers, crown ethers and polyoxyethylene alkyl ethers and esters. Often, a charged surfactant is intercalated in the bilayers to introduce electrostatic repulsion between the vesicles, thereby increasing their stability.

The formation of niosomes depends on

- Surfactants
- Membrane additives
- Formation of vesicles
- Surfactant/Lipid levels
- Gel-liquid transitions

Surfactants

Niosome formation requires the presence of a particular class of amphiphile and an aqueous solvent. Cholesterol, in certain cases, is required in the formulation, and vesicle aggregation can be prevented by including molecules that stabilise the system against the formation of aggregates by repulsive steric or electrostatic effects. Various types of non-ionic surfactants are known to form vesicles. These amphiphiles possess a hydrophilic head group and a hydrophobic tail. The hydrophobic moiety consists of one or two alkyl or perfluoroalkyl groups or, in certain cases, a single steroidal group. The alkyl group chain length is usually C_{12}–C_{18}. Molecules may possess one or three alkyl chains. It has been reported that some of the members of the dialkyl polyoxyethylene surfactant series have been used to form vesicles. Vesicular systems are formed when a mixture of cholesterol and a non-ionic surfactant are hydrated. Ether surfactants consisting of either a mono or a dialkylether chain have also been used. Various surfactants are used to prepare niosomes, but the vesicle-forming properties of each surfactant have to be optimised.

Membrane Additives

Considering the geometry of models for the possible structures of micelles, the interfacial area 'A' per surfactant molecule plays an important role. It is postulated that the hydrocarbon interior is a continuum. This implies that the shortest distance between the centre of the micelle and the interface should be smaller or equal to the maximally attainable length, 'l_c', of the hydrocarbon tail. With 'Vc' being the hydrocarbon volume, simple geometric conditions can be derived for the formation of micelles and vesicles. Self-assembly of surfactants into vesicles can be determined by a critical packing parameter, which is defined as:

$$CPP = v / l_c a_o$$

where v represents the hydrophobic group volume, l_c is the critical hydrophobic group length and a_o is the area of the hydrophilic head group. A CPP of between 0.5 and 1 indicates that the surfactant is likely to form vesicles. A CPP of <0.5 (indicating a large contribution from the hydrophilic head group area) is said to produce spherical micelles, while a CPP of >1 (indicating a large contribution from the hydrophobic group volume) should produce inverted micelles, the latter presumably only in an oil phase as precipitation would occur otherwise. Various additives must be included in the formulation to prepare stable niosomes. The most common additive found in niosomal systems is cholesterol. Thus, in cases where a mixture of surfactants or cholesterol is used to prepare niosomes, the operational CPP values will be those of all the components.

Niosomes can also be stabilised by the addition of a charged molecule such as dicetyl phosphate to the bilayer as it is reported to prevent aggregation.

Formation of Vesicles

The ability of surfactants to form vesicles has been studied by freeze fracture electron microscopy and polarisation microscopy. Using polarisation microscopy, large multilamellar vesicles (MLVs) can be identified. Studies of C_nEO_m (polyoxyethylene alkyl ether surfactants) have revealed that surfactants with a small head group such as C_nEO_3 are able to form vesicles, but when using surfactants from a gel state bilayer ($C_{16}EO_3$ and $C_{18}EO_3$) at room temperature, only aggregates of vesicles are found most of the time.

This could be attributed to the nature of the bilayers: gel state bilayers of uncharged vesicles are known to destabilise the suspension. The gel-liquid transition of hydrated $C_{16}EO_3$ and $C_{18}EO_3$ surfactants takes place at a temperature of 40–48 °C and 50–58 °C, respectively.

Vesicles can also be formed from single-chain surfactants with a bulky head group by adding cholesterol, which possesses only a hydroxyl group as a hydrophilic moiety. Cholesterol compensates for the large hydrophilic head groups of the surfactants. Therefore, it is possible to prepare vesicles from C_nEO_m with relatively large head groups such as $C_{10}EO_5$, $C_{12}EO_5$ and $C_{12}EO_7$. On the other hand, cholesterol decreases the chain order below T_c. The reason for this behaviour becomes apparent after cholesterol is added to the solution of vesicles prepared from $C_{16}EO_3$ and $C_{18}EO_3$. It is observed that cholesterol increases the membrane undulations of lecithin liposomes, resulting in larger repulsion forces between the vesicles. Using C_nEO_m and cholesterol in a molar ratio of 3:2, vesicles can be prepared from the whole series of C_nEO_m surfactants. However, when using single-chain surfactants that are capable of forming micelles, it should be kept in mind that the addition of cholesterol could still lead to the formation of micelles.

Surfactant/Lipid Levels

The level of surfactant/lipid used to make niosomal dispersions is generally 10–30 mM (1–25% w/w). Altering the surfactant:water ratio during the hydration step could affect the system's microstructure and hence the system's properties. However, increasing the surfactant/lipid level also results in an increase in the total amount of drug encapsulated.

Gel–liquid transitions

The fluidity of bilayers studied using fluorometry, shows that it was strongly dependent on the hydrophilic head group, alkyl chain length and cholesterol content. With this method, the fluidity may be characterised by the dynamic parameter D_u, which reflects the mobility of the hydrocarbon chains, and the static parameter θ_c. This parameter also accounts for the orientational degree of the chains.

It has also been reported that cholesterol is known to abolish the gel-to-liquid phase transition of niosomal systems, resulting in niosomes that are less leaky. Span 60 niosomes prepared without cholesterol form a gel, and only on the addition of cholesterol are homogeneous niosome dispersions obtained. Cholesterol is therefore included in a 1:1 molar ratio in most formulations.

Preparation of Niosomes

Preparation methods are chosen depending on the use of niosomes as they influence the number of bilayers, size, size distribution, entrapment efficiency and membrane permeability of vesicles.

The various methods used to prepare niosomes are similar to those used to prepare liposomes. In brief, they are the:

1. *Ether injection method:*
   The surfactant/cholesterol mixture is dissolved in diethyl ether and injected slowly through a needle into the aqueous phase at 60 °C. Large unilamellar vesicles (LUVs) are formed during the evaporation of the ether. The main disadvantage of this method is that a small amount of ether is often present in the vesicle suspension and is very difficult to remove.

2. *Hand shaking (film) method:*
   A surfactant/lipid film is formed by the evaporation of an organic solution of surfactants/lipids. This film is then hydrated with a solution of the drug.

3. *Sonication:*
   An aqueous phase is added to the surfactant/cholesterol mixture in a glass vial. The mixture is then probe-sonicated for a certain time period. Small unilamellar vesicles (SUVs) are then formed.

4. *Reverse phase evaporation:*
   An oil-in-water (o/w) emulsion is formed from an aqueous solution of the drug. The organic solvent is then evaporated to leave niosomes dispersed in the aqueous phase. In certain cases, the resulting gel has to be further hydrated to yield niosomes.

The size and number of bilayers of vesicles consisting of polyoxyethylene alkyl ethers and cholesterol can be changed by increasing the temperature to more than 60 °C; this transforms SUVs into unilamellar vesicles. The transformation from unilamellar to MLVs at higher temperatures may be characteristic of the polyoxyethylene alkylether (ester) surfactants, since it is known that polyethylene glycol (PEG) and water mix at a higher temperature because of a breakdown of hydrogen bonds between the water and PEG moieties.

Characterisation of Niosomes

Size, Shape and Morphology

The structure of surfactant-based vesicles can be visualised by freeze fracture electron microscopy, while photon correlation spectroscopy can be successfully used to determine the mean diameter of the vesicles. Morphological studies can be carried out using electron microscopy. Laser light scattering techniques are used to determine the size distribution of niosomes.

Entrapment Efficiency

Hydration of surfactant/lipid mixtures rarely leads to the entire drug being encapsulated. The unentrapped drug has to be separated to determine the entrapment efficiency. The methods used for the removal of unentrapped materials are dialysis, gel filtration and ultracentrifugation.

Entrapment efficiency may also be determined by using markers such as carboxyfluorescein (CF). A concentration of 200 mM of CF is used for hydration within the vesicles. At this concentration in vesicles, CF is self-quenched and does not produce any fluorescence. Vesicles are disrupted using hydrophilic surfactants such as Triton X-100 or 50% propranalol, which increases the fluorescence by releasing the entrapped CF. The ratios of CF before and after the disruption of vesicles is calculated to determine entrapment efficiency, and it is expressed as a millilitre of CF per mole of surfactant.

Osmotic Activity

The osmotic activity of niosomal dispersions is estimated by a change in the size of the niosome when it is dispersed in a hyper or hypotonic medium. Osmotic activity may not be observed in some systems because initial aggregation of the vesicles can be seen as the ions in the disperse phase shield the electrostatic charge on the vesicle surface. The incorporation of steric stabilisers such as polyoxyethylene compounds in the vesicle membrane prevents this aggregation and enables the study of the osmotic activity of niosomes.

Vesicle Surface Charge

The presence of surface charge in vesicular dispersions is important as it has been found that aggregation of vesicles in isotonic saline solution occurs when the vesicles are prepared with charged molecules included in the bilayer. Surface charge is normally characterised in terms of a voltage at the particle surface, the surface potential (zeta potential), rather than a charge density. The zeta potential occurs at a distance from the surface and is measured by the Doppler shift of light scattered by moving particles in an electric field.

Toxicity Studies

Surfactants have enormous toxicity; however, the literature about niosome toxicity is limited. A toxological profile is fundamental to any regulatory agency.

The toxicity of C_nEO_m was studied with different models. As a toxicity model for the topical application of niosomes, the cell proliferation of keratinocytes was measured after it was incubated for three days with niosomes. Ester and ether-type surfactants were compared, and it was observed that ester-linked surfactants were significantly less toxic than ether-linked surfactants, probably because of the degradation of the ester bond by enzymes.

Specialised drug delivery systems mostly aim to modulate drug toxicity, and this has been achieved with certain niosomal formulations. The encapsulation of vincristine within niosomes has been shown to reduce the neurological toxicity, diarrhea and alopecia associated with the intravenous administration of vincristine alone.

Applications of Niosomes

The success achieved with liposomal systems stimulated the search for other vesicle-forming amphiphiles. Non-ionic surfactants were among the first alternative materials studied and a large number of surfactants have since been found to self-assemble into closed bilayer vesicles, which may be used for drug delivery.

Anti-cancer niosomes: Anti-cancer niosomes, if suitably designed, are expected to accumulate within tumours in a similar manner to that of liposomes. The niosomal encapsulation of methotrexate and doxorubicin increases drug delivery to the tumour and enables enhanced tumouricidal activity. Unlike non-stealth liposomes, 800 nm doxorubicin niosomes that possess a triglycerol or 200 nm doxorubicin niosomes that possess a muramic acid surface are not taken up significantly by the liver. As such, these triglycerol niosomes accumulate in the tumour. It is obvious that, as with liposomes and presumably any parenterally administered colloidal particulates, body disposition may be controlled by alterations to particulate surface chemistry.

The accumulation of certain niosomes within the liver may however be exploited. Doxorubicin polymer conjugates are prepared by conjugating the anti-cancer drug to a polymeric backbone through an enzymatically cleavable spacer. The encapsulation of these polymeric prodrugs within 200 nm niosomes provides a depot system within the liver from which the free drug is gradually cleaved off, and the liver levels of the drug are seen to rise over a 24-hour period. This technology may prove advantageous for the treatment of hepatic neoplasms. The activity of other anti-cancer drugs such as vincristine, bleomycin and plumbagin, a plant-derived anti-cancer agent, are also improved on niosomal encapsulation.

Niosomes and other drugs: Uptake by the liver and spleen make niosomes ideal for targeting diseases that manifest in these organs. One such condition is leishmaniasis, and a number of studies have shown that niosomal formulations of sodium stilbogluconate improve parasite suppression in the liver, spleen and bone marrow. Niosomes may also be used as depot systems for short-acting peptide drugs on intramuscular administration.

Niosomes as vaccine adjuvants: Niosomal antigens are potent stimulators of cellular and humoral immune response. The formulation of antigens as a niosome in a water-in-oil emulsion further increases the activity of antigens. The controlled release property of the emulsion formulation is responsible for enhancing immunological response.

Niosomes as topical delivery: Niosomes are also used for the topical delivery of drugs because of certain advantages such as higher chemical stability, intrinsic skin penetration enhancing properties and lower cost of production. Various drugs are reported to be loaded into niosomes as the presence of non-ionic surfactants improves skin penetration and increases its accumulation in the superficial skin strata.

Key Messages

- Niosomes are vesicles prepared with non-ionic surfactants.
- Niosomes can be prepared from several classes of non-ionic surfactants such as polyglycerol alkylethers, glucosyl dialkylethers, crown ethers and polyoxyethylene alkyl ethers and esters.
- The methods of preparation of niosomes are similar to those used to prepare liposomes.
- Niosomes are characterised by their size, shape, drug entrapment and osmotic activity.
- Niosomes have several applications, namely, as targeted drug delivery systems in the treatment of cancer, as vaccine adjuvants and also for topical drug delivery.

Questions

1. Define niosomes and describe the components of niosomes.
2. Explain the different methods of preparing niosomes.
3. Give the differences between liposomes and niosomes.
4. What are the applications of niosomes?

11
Microspheres

Shobha Rani R Hiremath and N Sree Harsha

Learning Objectives

At the end of this chapter, you will be able to:

- Describe the technology, applications and advantages of microspheres
- Explain the importance of the size of microspheres
- Describe the methods used to prepare microspheres
- List the various characteristics of microspheres
- Describe the pathway of in vivo microspheres

Introduction

Microspheres are solid, approximately spherical particles ranging 1–1000 µm in size. They are made up of polymeric substances, in which the drug is dispersed throughout the microsphere matrix. Microcapsules are small particles that contain an active agent or core material surrounded by a shell or coating of polymers.

The substances used in the formulation are biodegradable synthetic polymers and natural products such as starches, gums, proteins, fats and waxes. The natural polymers of choice are albumin and gelatin, the synthetic ones being polylactic acid and polyglycolic acid. The polymers used to manufacture microspheres are chosen according to their solublity, stability profile, process safety and economic suitability.

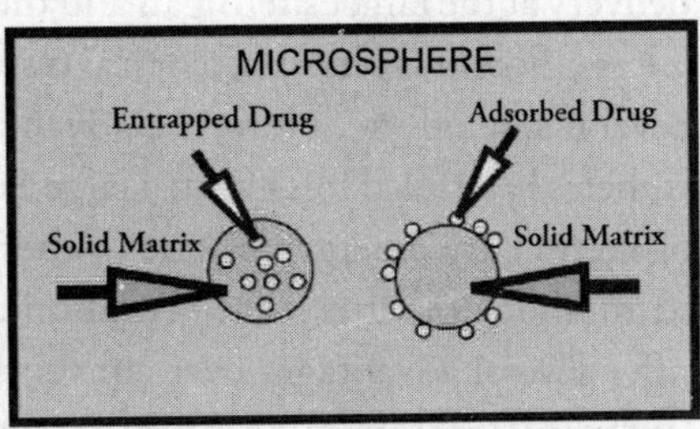

Figure 11.1: Schematic representation of microspheres

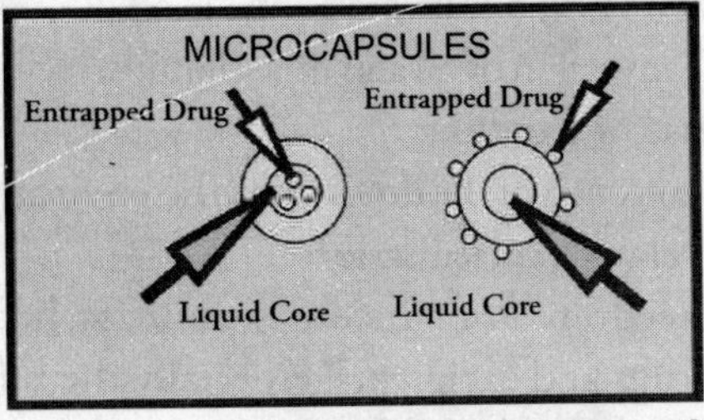

Figure 11.2: Schematic representation of microcapsules

Microspheres: Contextual Perspective

The concept of packaging microscopic quantities of materials within microspheres dates back to the 1930s and the work of Bungenberg de Jong and his colleagues on the entrapment of substances within coacervates. The first commercial application of encapsulation was undertaken by the National Cash Register Company for the manufacture of carbonless copying paper. The technology and applications have advanced over the past several decades. The agricultural, food, household products, medical, graphics and cosmetics industries all use this technology. The potential use of microspheres in the pharmaceutical industry has been considered since the 1960s.

The conventional drug delivery systems in use, in many cases, fail to meet the need of efficient drug delivery at the target site/organ and thereby elicit a less efficacious pharmacological response with several side effects. However, advances in microspheres have filled this gap to a large extent. Microspheres have emerged as one of the most desired methods of drug administration since they offer several advantages over conventional drug administration. The administration parameters that can be satisfactorily controlled are as follows:

- Taste and odour masking
- Conversion of oil and other liquids, facilitating ease of handling
- Protection of the drugs from the environment
- Delay of volatilisation
- Freedom from incompatibilities between drugs and excipients, especially the buffers
- Improvement of flow properties
- Safe handling of toxic substances
- Dispersion of water insoluble substances in aqueous media
- Production of sustained release, controlled release and targeted medications

Advantages of Microspheres

- ➢ They facilitate accurate delivery of small quantities of potent drugs and reduced concentration of the drug at sites other than the target organ or tissue.
- ➢ They provide protection for unstable drugs before and after administration, prior to their availability at the site of action.
- ➢ They provide the ability to manipulate the in vivo action of the drug, pharmacokinetic profile, tissue distribution and cellular interactions of the drug.
- ➢ They enable controlled release of drugs.

Examples of drugs that are formulated as microspheres include antineoplastic drugs, narcotic antagonists, steroid hormones, leutinising hormone analogs, antibiotics and other macromolecules.

Preparation of Microspheres

The physicochemical parameters to be considered during the preparation of microspheres include:

- Particle size distribution
- Ratio of drug to polymer
- Entrapment/Encapsulation efficiency

The manufacturing process must consider the abovementioned parameters to produce an efficient drug delivery system. The various methods used to prepare microspheres include:

- Wax coating and hot melt
- Spray coating and pan coating

- Coacervation
- Spray drying
- Solvent evaporation
- Precipitation
- Freeze drying
- Formation of water-in-oil emulsions

Wax Coating and Hot Melt

An aqueous drug solution is dispersed in molten wax to form a water-in-oil emulsion, which is then emulsified in a heated external aqueous phase to form a water-in-oil in water emulsion. The system is cooled and the microcapsules collected. For highly aqueous soluble drugs, a non-aqueous phase can be used to prevent loss of drug to the external phase. Wax-coated microcapsules are inexpensive and often used, and they release the drug more rapidly than polymeric microcapsules. Carnauba wax and beeswax can be used as coating materials and mixed to achieve the desired characteristics.

Spray Coating and Pan Coating

Spray coating and pan coating employ heat-jacketed coating pans in which the solid drug core particles are rotated and the coating material is sprayed. The core particles are in the size range of micrometers up to a few millimeters. The coating material is usually sprayed at an angle from the side into the pan. The process is continued until an even coating is achieved. Coating a large number of small particles may provide a safer and more consistent release pattern than coated tablets. In addition, several batches of microspheres can be prepared with different coating thicknesses and mixed to achieve specific controlled release patterns.

The Würster process, a variation of the basic pan coating method, is an adaptation of the fluid-bed granulator. The solid core particles are fluidised by air pressure and a spray of dissolved wall material is applied from the perforated bottom of the fluidisation chamber parallel to the air stream and onto the solid core particles. The fluid-bed technique produces a more uniform coating thickness than the pan coating method. However, the main disadvantage of this method is that problems can arise with inflammable organic solvents because of the high risk of explosion in the enclosed fluidiser chamber.

Coacervation

The coacervation technique is one in which solid particles are entrapped in coacervate systems. On phase separation by simple or complex methods, tiny coacervate droplets are formed, which sediment or coalesce to form a separate coacervate phase. The coacervate forms around any core material that may be present, such as drug particles. Agitation of the coacervate system can prevent coalescence and sedimentation of the droplets, which can be cross-linked to form stable microcapsules by adding an agent such as glutaraldehyde or by applying heat. Cross-linking of the coacervate is done to stabilise coacervate emulsion droplets and hence form microcapsules.

Although many successful coacervate micro-encapsulation systems have been prepared, they have a number of limitations:

- They can be produced only at specific pH values
- They require stabilisation by cross-linking agents or heat
- The retention of the encapsulant depends on the extent of cross-linking

The pH limitation can be overcome to some extent by adding water soluble non-ionic polymers, such as polyethylene oxide or polyethylene glycol. The presence of a small amount of these polymers allows microencapsulation to occur over an expanded pH range.

Spray Drying

Spray drying is a single-step, closed-system process applicable to a wide variety of materials, including thermolabile materials. This process is often used commercially as a closed system; it is ideal for good manufacturing practice and the production of sterile materials. The drug and the polymer coating materials are dissolved in a suitable solvent (aqueous or non-aqueous) or the drug may be present as a suspension in the polymer solution. Alternatively, it may be dissolved or suspended within an emulsion or coacervate system. The size of the microsphere is controlled by the rate of spraying, feed rate of the polymer drug solution, nozzle size, temperature in the drying and collecting chamber and the size of these chambers.

Solvent Evaporation

This is one of the earliest methods of microsphere manufacture. The polymer and the drug must be soluble in an organic solvent. The solution containing the polymer and the drug may be dispersed in an aqueous phase to form droplets. Continuous mixing and elevated temperatures may be employed to evaporate the more volatile organic solvent and leave the solid polymer–drug particles suspended in an aqueous medium. The particles are finally filtered from the suspension.

One disadvantage of this method is that continuous mixing and elevated temperatures might denature the thermolabile drugs or the polymers employed in the preparation process.

Precipitation

Precipitation is a variation of the evaporation method. Here, the emulsion consists of polar droplets dispersed in a nonpolar medium. The solvent may be removed from the droplets by using a cosolvent. The resulting increase in polymer drug concentration causes precipitation, forming a suspension of microspheres.

Emulsion Polymerisation

Emulsion polymerisation involves the dispersion of the monomer units in an aqueous phase to form droplets. Surfactants, in a concentration higher than their critical micelle concentration, are present in the aqueous phase. Excess surfactant molecules form micelles whose hydrophobic interiors take up part of the available monomer, causing them to swell. Initiator radicals diffuse into these swollen micelles and begin the polymerisation process. As the monomer is consumed, it is replaced by progressive diffusion of the remaining monomer from its location in the emulsified droplets to the interior of the micelles. The micelles continue to swell in size as polymerisation proceeds. The enlarging surfaces compete for the available surfactant, thus influencing the number of available micelles that can participate in polymer formation. This method yields particles of very small size and predictable number at low temperatures.

Micelle polymerisation differs from emulsion polymerisation in that all of the monomer and the drug are contained within micelles composed of surfactant. Diffusion of the monomer from the micelles is prevented by the nonsolvent properties of the outer phase. Therefore, the increase in particle size is negligible as polymerisation proceeds.

Characterisation of Microspheres

The parameters and methods used to characterise microspheres are listed in Table 11.1.

Microsphere Recovery/Yield

Microsphere recovery studies can be referred to as microsphere yield, since these studies account for the amount of microspheres obtained at the end of preparation, and the polymer and the drug that went into its preparation. It is calculated using the following equation:

$$\text{Percentage Yield} = \left(\frac{\text{Practical Yield}}{\text{Theoretical Yield}}\right) \times 100$$

$$\text{Practical Yield of Microspheres} = \frac{\text{Amount of encapsulated drug}}{\text{Amount of added drug}}$$

Drug Entrapment Efficiency

Entrapment efficiency is measured by calculating the amount of drug that is entrapped in the microsphere and the drug, which is adsorbed on the surface or the interior of the polymer. This measure is of vital importance in surface studies since it is indicative of the amount of drug that is used to form the microsphere, present in an adsorbed state on the surface of the polymer or as free drug and as a fraction that is found entrapped within the polymeric matrix.

The experimental method devised to quantify the entrapment efficiency of a microsphere should take into account the free adsorbed and entrapped portions of the drug. Experimental plans should

Table 11.1: Microsphere characterisation – parameters and methods

Sl #	*Parameters*	*Characterisation Method(s)*
1	Yield/Microsphere recovery	Chemical assay employing suitable ultraviolet(UV)/
2	Drug incorporation efficiency	high performance liquid chromatography (HPLC)/ gas chromatography (GC) methods
3	Surface morphology	Scanning electron microscopy Transmission electron microscopy Scanning tunneling microscopy Laser defractrometry Fourier transform Raman spectroscopy X-ray photoelectron spectroscopy (XPS)
4	Particle size and size distribution	
5	Residual solvent analysis	XPS or GC
6	In vitro release study	Dialysis
7	Physicochemical status of the drug in the microsphere/glass transition temperature (Tg)	Differential scanning calorimetry (DSC) analysis
8	Crystallography characterisation	X-ray diffraction analysis (XRD)
9	Drug stability	As per International Conference on Harmonisation (ICH) Tripartite guidelines
7	Targeting potential	In vivo tissue distribution in an animal model
8	In vivo pharmacokinetics of microsphere	Modelling the data (compartment model) or non-compartmental analysis

be devised in such a way that the total drug content of the microspheres should quantify all three portions of the drug—free, adsorbed and entrapped—and they should be capable of being determined separately. This determination is an indication of the efficacy of the microspheres produced in terms of its active ingredients.

Determination of Free Drug in Microspheres (Unentrapped Drug)

Accurately weighed microspheres are taken in a beaker, saline (0.9% weight/volume [w/v]) is added to the mixture and shaken well to liberate the free drug present in the polymeric matrix. The free drug is quantified by a suitable analytical method.

Adsorbed Drug in Microspheres

The amount of drug present at the surface is measured by digesting the microsphere with saline (0.9% w/v) at room temperature, sonicating the solution in an ultrasonic bath for 5 minutes and centrifuging it at 3000 rpm for 2 minutes. The supernatant is filtered through a 0.45 μm filter (millipore) and the drug is quantified by a suitable analytical method.

Entrapped Drug in Microspheres

The residue left over from the extraction of the free and adsorbed drug is mixed with 5 ml of glacial acetic acid 0.1 M. The sample is centrifuged at 5000 rpm for 10 minutes. The supernatant is filtered through a 0.45 μm filter (millipore) and the amount of drug entrapped is quantified by a suitable analytical method.

The free drug in the microsphere can be determined using the formula:

$$L = \frac{Q_m}{W_m} \times 100$$

where L is the percentage loading of microspheres and Q_m is the quantity of free drug present in W_m grams of the microsphere.

The adsorbed drug in the microsphere can be determined using the formula:

$$L = \frac{Q_m}{W_m} \times 100$$

where L is the percentage loading of microspheres and Q_m is the quantity of drug present in W_m grams of the microsphere.

The amount of drug entrapped in the microsphere is determined using the formula:

$$E = \frac{Q_p}{W_t} \times 100$$

where E is the percentage of the encapsulated drug, Q_p is the quantity of drug encapsulated in the microsphere in grams and W_t is the quantity of the drug added for encapsulation in grams.

Surface Morphology

An examination of the surface of a polymeric drug delivery system can provide vital information about the porosity and microstructure of these systems. The distribution and morphology of the surface and the encapsulated matrix can also be directly observed.

The most common technique used to characterise the surface morphology of drug delivery systems is scanning electron microscopy (SEM). This method offers several advantages because of its versatility of method, simplicity of sample preparation and ease of operation. The sample sizes range from nanometers to micrometers to centimeters. This method can also use unlimited amounts of samples, offering innumerable viewpoints by means of its translational, tilting and rotary axis, over a high range of resolving powers of the instrument.

The sample prepared for this method should be sufficiently dehydrated since a vacuum field is necessary for image generation in SEM. Prior to loading the samples for taking the photomicrograph, they are coated (20–30 nm in thickness) with electron-dense coating materials such as gold, palladium or a combination of both. This is done to enhance the signal emitted by the sample by providing heavy metal atoms with an incident beam of electrons and to conduct the accumulated sample charge and heat to the sample holder. The coating process is either carried through sputter coating or thermal vacuum evaporation.

Particle Size Analysis

The particle size characterisation of microspheres is an important study to ensure that the particle size of the formulation lies in the optimal range. This is the crucial factor since the activity, as intended in any study, depends exclusively on the particle size of the microspheres produced.

A wide variety of methods have been developed to measure the particle size. These methods use different physical principles for the determination of size. Because of this, there is no single method of sizing that can be used for all types and sizes of microspheres. The method chosen will depend on several factors such as the type of equipment available and the size and material from which the microspheres are prepared. None of the methods is a truly direct method. Although the microscope allows the observer to view the actual particles, the results obtained are probably more 'direct' than those from other methods, since only two of the three particle dimensions are ordinarily seen. The commonly used methods are described below.

The earliest methods were based on various types of microscopic techniques; recently, laboratory automation has become more common, and automated instruments are now being used to size microspheres. Here, calibration is important for automated sizing equipment. The European Community Bureau of Reference (BCR) brought out a range of crushed quartz reference standards in 1980 for particle sizing instrument calibration. Calibration is done by primary methods in which the standard particle size can be derived using these methods. These standard particles can be used to calibrate automated equipment. A primary method is defined as one in which the dimensions of length and weight are directly traceable to international standards and do not depend on second order effects such as diffraction patterns, turbidity, Brownian motion or computer modelling. The five primary methods are (a) gravitational sedimentation, (b) centrifugal sedimentation, (c) electroformed sieve analysis, (d) optical microscopy and (e) electrical sensing zone (Coulter).

Sizing Methods

A Manual
- a) Optical microscopy
- b) Electron microscopy
  - 1 Transmission electron microscopy
  - 2 Scanning electron microscopy
- c) Sieving
- d) Sedimentation (Andreasen pipette method)

B Automated
- a) Particle counters
  1. Optical particle counting
  2. The Coulter principle
  3. Permeability
  4. Impaction and inertial techniques
- b) Light scattering
  1. Dynamic (or quasielectric) light scattering
  2. Enhance laser diffraction
- c) Flow cytometry
- d) Field flow fractionation

In Vitro Release Studies

In vitro release profiles aid in understanding the behaviour of these systems in terms of drug release and their efficacy. The initial release is characterised by a 'burst release' due to the release of the weakly bound drug at the particle surface of the microspheres. These are bound by adsorption and do not involve any chemical bonding with the polymer. When such microspheres are briefly washed in a sink condition, the drug particles are washed—the drug bound to the surface of the microspheres is rapidly washed—and lead the way to a rapid release of the drug in the early stages. However, this phenomenon holds good for only a brief period with maximum drug release. After this time window, the release pattern is more uniform as time progresses.

Since microspheres are heterogeneous systems, the drug release from the polymer faction of the microsphere takes place through a diffusion process in an in vitro environment. As a result, the drug and the polymer matrix are phase separated into two distinct domains—a biphasic system—and the release of the drug is determined by the extent of degradation of polymeric microspheres.

The entrapped drug, which separates into a biphasic system upon liberation from the polymeric matrix and through a diffusion process, is released from the microspheres through the process of diffusion. Several models of release have been suggested based on variants such as diffusion, nature of the polymer, concentration of the drug and the extent of cross-linking of the polymer. The drug release patterns in an in vivo environment are numerous. Various release patterns have been suggested by a number of researchers (Nevin, 1996; Guyot, 1998; Lacoulonche, 1999) taking into account all the variants mentioned above. The loading of the drug into the polymer matrix also plays a significant role in the release profile of the drug. A point of domain separation is reached and the drug particles come in contact with one another, and the drug diffuses out of the matrix leaving the solvent-filled channels open. Through this void channel, the drug is preferentially released, paving the way for a controlled drug delivery state, coupled with the size of the microspheres.

The in vitro release experiments can be performed using the dialysis method. In this method, a weighed quantity of the microsphere is placed in a dialysis bag, which is immersed in a larger volume of continuous phase acceptor fluid. The compartment is stirred and the drug which diffuses out of the microspheres into the continuous phase is periodically sampled and assayed.

In Vitro Release Kinetics

To quantify the drug release pattern, the drug depletion from microspheres can be explained by means of regression. This is a statistical concept used to investigate:

- How the response variable (drug release pattern) changes as a particular predictor (dependent variable such as time) changes
- What the value of the response variable for any value of the predictor variable or a combination of values of predictor variables will be, thereby predicting the drug release pattern

Since the response and predictor responses in this case may not follow a linear pattern (due to formulatory and experimental variants) a non-linear approach is adopted where the release data is attempted to fit in a pattern, thereby predicting the release rate. The regression equation is an algebraic representation of the regression line and is used to describe the relationship between the response and predictor variables. Several workers have adopted different approaches to curve fit; this study has used the prominent regression models to study drug release and the mode of release. These models are as follows:

- First order release
- Higuchi model
- Hixon–Crowell model
- Peppas model
- Baker–Lonsdale model

The best model of fit is determined by the R^2 and adjusted R values. They represent the proportion of variation in the response data explained by the predictor factors. R^2 describes the amount of variation in the observed response values that is explained by the predictor. The higher the R^2 value, the better the fit offered by the equation/model.

The fitted line in the plot is a regression line, which examines the relationship between the response variable (y – % drug release) and the predictor variable (x – time of release). The method used to draw the line using a 95% confidence interval and around 3σ values is used to attain precision in replicate runs.

Differential Scanning Calorimetry (DSC) Analysis

The DSC technique can provide qualitative and quantitative information about the physicochemical status of the drug in the microsphere. This involves an endothermic or exothermic process, and the related thermal transitions include melting, recrystallisation, decomposition, out-gassing or a change in the heat capacity of the tested material. DSC is used to monitor different samples of the same material to assess their similarities or differences, or the effects of additives on the thermal properties of a material. Using the DSC analysis of the drug, polymer materials and microspheres produced, the nature of the drug inside the polymer matrix can be assessed, which may emerge in solid solution, metastable molecular dispersion or crystallisation and may display relevant properties during in vitro release. Hence, this can be utilised as a characterisation tool. There is no detectable melting endotherm if the drug presents in a molecular dispersion or a solid solution state as in the case of polymeric microspheres loaded with enough amount of the drug. This is because the melting point of the drug, when present in this mixture, disappears in the drug-loaded microspheres, and the endothermic polymer undergoes a 'glass transition', T_g, and shifts the peak to a lower temperature with respect to the unloaded microsphere (the ones without drugs). This is indicative of the fact that preparations lead to a formation of amorphous dispersions of the drug inside the polymer matrix formation, even if the drug loading is of higher levels, as in this case.

Chemical interactions are indicated by the appearance of new peaks, whereas second order transitions produce changes in the baseline. Such observations may also be indicative of the production of eutectic or solid solution-type melts.

The advantages of DSC over more traditional, routine compatibility screening methods such as thin layer chromatography (TLC) are that neither long-term storage of the mixture prior to evaluation nor any inappropriate thermal stress is required to accelerate the interactions.

Residual Solvent Analysis

Residual solvents in pharmaceuticals are volatile organic chemicals that are used in and/or produced during the synthesis/production of drug substances/formulations. Many of these residual solvents generally cannot be completely removed by standard manufacturing processes/techniques and are left behind, mostly at low levels.

Presently, in the pharmaceutical industry, special importance is given to residual solvent testing as they affect the physicochemical properties of the drug substances/formulations and because high levels of these solvents represent a potential risk to human health due to their carcinogenicity and toxicity.

Residual solvent testing is carried out by a number of analytical techniques, the most important of which is the GC technique, used to determine the concentration of the organic solvent in microsphere formulations.

Stability Studies

The stability study of a pharmaceutical product is done to provide assurance that the product intended to be used is of adequate quality and has the safety characteristics intended for a specific use. This may be defined as the capability of a particular formulation in a specific container to remain within its physical, chemical, microbiological, therapeutic and toxicological specifications.

Deciding on the stability testing protocol for a particular product can be challenging because of the complexity and diversity of modern pharmaceutical products such as microspheres.

The de facto guideline for the stability testing procedure is the ICH guideline titled '*Stability testing of new drug substances and products*', which describes the stability test requirements for drug formulations and new drug substances.

This guideline provides generic directives to study the stability of a drug product on a real-time basis since that provides more realistic data. The storage conditions described in the guideline are based on worldwide storage temperatures (mean kinetic temperature or MKT) and the per cent of relative humidity (RH) conditions. The countries of the world are segregated into four zones depending on their climatic conditions, namely, Zones I, II, III and IV. India is designated as Zone III/IV for its tropical climate and high levels of ambient temperature and humidity levels. The minimum time period to be covered by the stability analysis is at least 12 months for long-term conditions and at least 6 months for accelerated conditions.

At least two containers are required to be sampled during the stability study.

The parameter used to evaluate the drawn samples generally varies with the type of dosage form. As per the ICH guideline '*Specifications: Test procedures and acceptance criteria for new drug substances and new drug products (Q6A)*', the organoleptic, physical, chemical, biological and microbiological quality characteristics of the product, which are susceptible to change during storage should be considered, in addition to drug assay and analysis of degradation products, thus covering the whole gamut of quality issues in terms of efficacy and elegance.

The stability protocols are designed based on the ICH 'Q1AR' and 'Q6A' guidelines.

The microsphere formulations are stored at 25 ± 2 °C and 60 ± 5% RH for a period of 6 months and at 5 ± 3 °C for a period of 12 months, which is the accelerated storage temperature and long-term storage temperature, respectively, for products intended to be refrigerated. The decision to refrigerate was taken because of the thermosensitivity and thermolability of the polymers chosen. The stored samples are tested for their drug content, particle size distribution and for any physical change.

In Vivo Tissue Distribution Studies

In vivo studies are a key component of any study since they provide tangible evidence of the efficacy of microspheres, and because the properties exhibited by microspheres are crucial for understanding the functional characteristics of formulations in a biological system.

To examine the appropriate properties of the formulations in vivo, adult albino mice weighing between 20±2 g can be used. A calculated dose of the drug is administered to each animal as a dispersion in saline with 1% of tween 80. At predetermined time intervals, the animals are injected with the microspheres through the tail route vein and are sacrificed by cervical dislocation. The organs that are studied for target action, namely, the lungs, liver, kidneys, heart and spleen, are extracted. The tissue samples are stored for 24 hours at -20°C. Then the concentrations of drug localised in each organ are determined quantitatively using the HPLC method.

In vivo tissue distribution studies in animal models are carried out to prove the hypothesis of targeting of microsphere/formulations to the organs and compare them with conventional dosage forms of the drug.

In Vivo Pharmacokinetics of Microspheres

Pharmacokinetics, in simple terms, describes how drugs move in the body and how quickly or at what rate the movement occurs.

It is concerned with the study and characterisation of the time course of drug absorption, distribution, metabolism and excretion as well as their relationship to the time-course of therapeutic and adverse effects of drugs. Pharmacokinetics is also described as ADME processes—adsorption, distribution, metabolism and excretion. Once the drug is absorbed, it is distributed throughout the body depending on the physicochemical properties of the drug and the physiological properties of the body membranes and fluids. The drug then interacts with receptors and causes therapeutic or/and toxic responses. The distribution characteristics of the drug can be described by a multicompartment model, such as a two-compartment model.

Data obtained from the blood analysis studies of all the experiments can be fitted to multiexponential equations using a computer-assisted non-linear curve-fitting program, and several pharmacokinetic parameters can be calculated.

Key Messages

- Microspheres are spherical particles made up of polymeric substances, in which the drug is generally dispersed.
- Microcapsules are small particles that contain an active agent or core material surrounded by a shell or coating of polymers.
- They are simple to prepare, industrially feasible and easy to characterise, and hence are promising delivery systems for a wide variety of drugs.
- They have several advantages including controlled and site-specific delivery.
- Microspheres can be prepared by several methods such as wax coating and hot melt, spray coating and pan coating, coacervation, spray drying, solvent evaporation, precipitation, freeze drying and formation of water-in-oil emulsion.
- Microspheres can be characterised by yield, drug incorporation efficiency, surface morphology, particle size and size distribution, in vitro release studies, stability and in vivo pharmacokinetics.

Questions

1. Define microspheres.
2. What is the difference between microspheres and microcapsules?
3. What are the advantages of microspheres?
4. List the applications of microspheres.
5. Explain the different methods used to prepare microspheres and list their advantages.
6. What are the different methods used to characterise microspheres?
7. What is SEM and what is its importance?
8. Why does particle size play an important role in the preparation of microspheres?
9. What are the different methods used to analyse particle size?
10. Why are in vitro release studies carried out for microspheres?
11. Explain how the DSC technique can provide qualitative and quantitative information about the physicochemical status of the drug in the microspheres.
12. Why is XRD used as a characterisation tool?
13. What is the importance of residual solvents in formulations?
14. Why do we carry out stability studies for any formulation?

12

Nanoparticles

Shobha Rani R Hiremath and Praveen Saligram

Learning Objectives

At the end of this chapter, you will be able to:

- Define nanoparticles and explain the types of nanoparticles
- Explain the history and manufacture of nanoparticles
- Describe the various methods used to prepare nanoparticles
- Explain the pharmaceutical aspects of nanoparticles
- List the characterisation parameters of nanoparticles
- Describe the methods used to obtain an in vitro profile of nanoparticles
- List the therapeutic applications of nanoparticles

Introduction

Nanoparticles are solid, colloidal particles ranging 10–1000 nm (1 μm) in size. They consist of macromolecular materials in which the active ingredient (drug or biologically active material) is dissolved, entrapped or encapsulated, and/or adsorbed or attached.

Depending on the process used for their preparation, two types of nanoparticles can be obtained: nanospheres and nanocapsules.

Nanospheres have a matrix-type structure in which a drug is dispersed, whereas nanocapsules exhibit a membrane-wall structure with an oily core containing the drug (Fig. 12.1). As nanoparticulate systems have a very high surface area, drugs may also be adsorbed on their surface. Nanoparticles are made of artificial or natural polymers. The use of these polymers is often restricted by their bioacceptability.

In addition to the properties of the carrier material, that is, the polymer and the auxiliary substances, bioacceptability is also influenced by particle size. Reduction in the particle size enables intravenous injection. The diameter of the

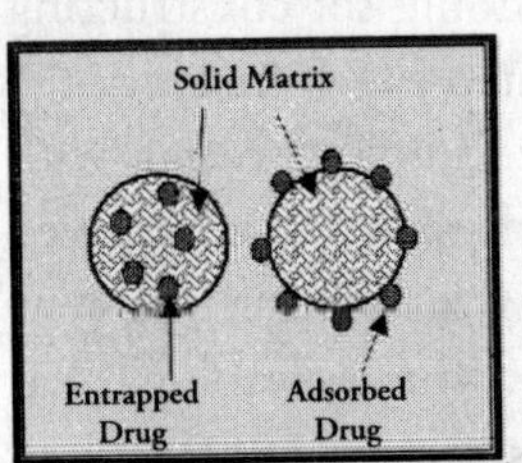

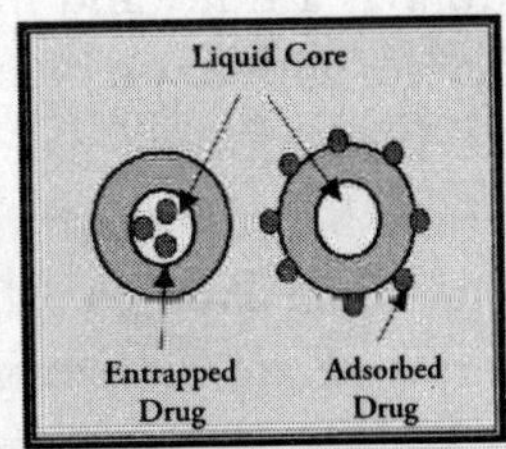

NANOSPHERES NANOCAPSULES

Figure 12.1: Structure of nanospheres and nanocapsules

smallest blood capillaries is 4 μm; consequently, solid particles must have a smaller diameter to be able to traverse the capillaries. A small particle size is also desirable for intramuscular and subcutaneous administration. It has also been demonstrated that a reduction in particle size of polymeric particles minimises possible irritant reactions at the injection site.

The final choice of the appropriate polymer, particle size and manufacturing method will depend firstly on the bioacceptability of the polymer, secondly on the physicochemical properties of the drug and thirdly on the therapeutic goal to be achieved.

Advent of Nanotechnology (Nanoparticles)

The word nanotechnology comes from the Greek prefix *nano* (symbol **n**) in the SI system of units, denoting a factor of 10^{-9}. In modern scientific parlance, one nanometer is one-billionth of a meter. To provide a comparison, the diameter of a single atom is one-fourth of a nanometer, and the diameter of a human hair is 10,000 nanometers. The smallest devices on commercially available chips are about 200 nanometers. The nanoscale refers to dimensions ranging from a fraction of a nanometer to hundreds of nanometers. Nanotechnology is about building things one atom at a time, and in doing so, constructing devices with unprecedented capabilities.

The history of nanotechnology began with Erwin Schrödinger, a physicist who received the Nobel Prize in 1933 for discovering new forms of atomic energy. The technology was subsequently hypothesised in 1959, when Richard Feynman, the brilliant Nobel Laureate physicist, delivered his now-famous lecture, 'There is Plenty of Room at the Bottom'. He stimulated his audience at the California Institute of Technology with the expectation of new discoveries facilitated by materials and devices at the atomic level. He observed that the principles of physics do not deny the possibility of manipulating things atom by atom. These discoveries, Feynman pointed out, require a new class of miniaturised instrumentation to manipulate and measure the properties of structures—nanostructures.

In the next few decades, chemists and biologists focused on deciphering the molecular structures that constitute materiality from the 'bottom up', while physicists and electrical engineers attempted to build ever smaller machines from the 'top down'. Both efforts resulted in powerful technologies. Molecular science produced revolutionary medicines as well as the synthetic materials that permeate the modern world—nylon, teflon and superglue. Micromachinists, after creating the first transistor in 1948, learned to build logic and computation machines with micron-scale components, thereby starting a global industry second only to agriculture in terms of revenue.

In recent years, attempts have been made to bring these two monumental efforts together in a new scientific era. While top-down engineers such as computer chip designers build a fairly small number of complex machines as minutely as possible, chemists and other bottom-up technologists build relatively simple but atomically precise machines by the billions. The revolution they seek is 'nanotechnology', which rises out of this confluence and aims at building complex, atomically precise machines by the trillions.

In 1981, the invention of the scanning tunnelling microscope (STM), by Gerd Binnig and Heinrich Rohrer at IBM's Zurich Research Labs, and the atomic force microscope (AFM) five years later, made it possible to not only take photos of individual atoms, but also to actually move a single atom. Soon after, John Foster of IBM's Almaden labs was able to spell out I-B-M using 35 xenon atoms on a nickel surface by utilising an STM to push the atoms into place. It had taken 27 years to prove Richard Feynman's 1959 hypothesis beyond any doubt.

Nanotechnology as it is understood now is the brainchild of Feynman's one-time student Eric Drexler. Drexler presented his key ideas in a paper on molecular engineering published in 1981, and expanded these themes in a general interest book entitled 'Engines of Creation'. Drexler received a unique doctorate degree in the field of nanotechnology in 1991, under the supervision of Marvin Minsky, the world-renowned artificial intelligence pioneer. The following year he published a more technical book, 'Nanosystems: Molecular Machinery, Manufacturing and Computation', which describes the principles and mechanisms of molecular nanotechnology.

Nanoscience, as it is popularly called today, broadly encompasses both nanotechnology and nanomedicine. Nanomedicine is the application of nanotechnology for the prevention and treatment of disease in humans. This science is still in its infancy, in the theoretical phase; however, once the practical applications of this science are realised, it has the potential to change the course of medical history in the years to come. In the future, people may not suffer from many of the ailments of today because they will have in them tiny soldiers (nanoparticles) guarding, fighting and evading most of the infections of the human body.

Nanoparticles are thus the 'precursors' of the next technological revolution of the twenty-first century—**nanotechnology**.

Manufacture of Nanoparticles

Many methods are used to manufacture nanoparticles. All of them allow extensive modulation of their structure, composition and physicochemical properties. The choice of the manufacturing method essentially depends on the raw materials intended to be used and on the solubility characteristics of the drug to be associated with the particles.

Historically, the first methods used to produce nanoparticles were derived from the field of latex engineering, developed by polymer chemists. These methods were based on the in situ polymerisation of a monomer in various media. Despite many technological advances in this field, polymerisation-based methods still have several drawbacks and limitations:

- Nanoparticles produced by polymerisation have inadequate biodegradability properties precluding their use for regular therapeutic administration.
- Due to the multicomponent nature of polymerisation media, it is generally very difficult to predict the molecular weight of the resulting polymerised material.
- Possible inhibition of drug activity due to interactions with activated monomers or with the numerous H^+ ions present in the anionic polymerisation process.
- Presence of toxic residues, namely, the unreacted monomer, initiator and surfactant molecules whose elimination requires time-consuming and not always efficient procedures.

In order to circumvent these limitations and extend the manufacturing possibilities to achieve biodegradable, well-characterised and nontoxic nanoparticles, new methods based on the dispersion of well-characterised, preformed polymers (natural macromolecules such as biopolymers and synthetic polymers) have been proposed, thus enlarging the field of possibilities for nanoparticulate formulation. These new techniques allow the production of both nanospherical and nanocapsular systems.

Using natural macromolecules such as biopolymers as preformed polymers for the preparation of nanoparticles has some disadvantages. When compared to the polymerisation methods, these are superior; however, the use of high volumes of organic solvents or oils and toxic chemical cross-linking agents coupled with uncertainty over the source and purity of natural macromolecules and potential antigenicity of these agents restricts their use.

Considering all these limitations of nanoparticles obtained from polymerisation techniques and from natural preformed polymers (as these nanoparticles are most often designed for parenteral administration), the focus today is on employing only synthetic preformed polymers of the polyester class as carriers because of their biocompatibility, biodegradation and bioresorbable characteristics.

The most important milestones in the development of nanoparticulate systems are summarised in Table 12.1.

Table 12.1: Milestones in the development of nanoparticles

Year	*Milestones*
	Nanoparticles formed by polymerisation
1976	Polyacrylamide nanospheres
1976	Poly (methyl methacrylate) nanospheres
1979	Poly (alkyl cyanoacrylate) nanospheres
1986	Poly (alkyl cyanoacrylate) nanocapsules
	Nanoparticles obtained using preformed polymers
1972	Albumin nanospheres by heat denaturation
1978	Gelatin nanospheres by desolvation
1979	Albumin nanospheres by cross-linking
1981	Poly (lactic acid) nanospheres by emulsification-solvent evaporation
1986	Poly (lactic-acid) nanospheres by direct precipitation
1987	Poly (lactic-acid) nanocapsules by interfacial deposition
1988	Poly (lactic-acid) nanospheres by salting-out process
1995	Poly (lactic-acid) nanospheres by emulsification-diffusion

Nanoparticle Preparation from Synthetic Preformed Polymers

Among the numerous synthetic polymers available for the preparation of nanoparticles, the most commonly used are poly D, L-lactide -co-glycolide (PLGA) and poly D, L-lactide (PLA), which belong to the family of polyesters. These polymers are known to exhibit adequate biodegradability and biocompatibility in addition to their bioresorbability characteristics. They are said to be bioresorbable because the degradation products of PLA and PLGA, namely, glycolic acid and lactic acid, are physiological substances easily eliminated through the Krebs cycle.

The preparation methods that use synthetic preformed polymers are classified into:

- Solvent emulsification evaporation
- Salting out
- Emulsification diffusion
- Spontaneous emulsification, solvent diffusion
- Solvent displacement

Solvent Emulsification Evaporation

This is a well-established method based on the classical procedure patented by Vanderhoff et al.

In this technique, the preformed polymer and the drug are dissolved in a water-immiscible organic solvent, which is emulsified in an aqueous solution containing a stabiliser. This crude emulsion is then exposed to a high-energy source such as an ultrasonic sonicator or passed through homogenisers, colloid mills or microfluidisers to reduce the globule size. The subsequent removal of the organic solvent by heat and vacuum results in the formation of a fine aqueous dispersion of nanoparticles (Fig. 12.2).

Formation of Nanoparticles (Mechanism)

The homogenisation step is the key factor in obtaining submicronic particles. The emulsification of oil and water by mechanical shear produces, in most cases, a droplet of size 2–5 μm. On the other hand, the diffusional motion of water-immiscible solvents into the aqueous phase is slow and once the limiting concentration for polymer precipitation is reached, phase separation occurs from the interface. Thus, each emulsion droplet forms one polymer particle when the solvent is removed. In general, good emulsion homogenisation such as in ultrasonication produces droplets with a diameter <0.5 microns and thus, a similar size is yielded for nanoparticles.

Advantages and Disadvantages

Though ultrasonication is a convenient homogenisation procedure, it presents some drawbacks such as induction of chemical reactions or degradation and difficult scaling up in an industrial setup. Therefore, to overcome these problems, the use of high-pressure homogenisers or microfluidisers is advocated. Another problem is the use of chlorinated solvents, such as chloroform and dichloromethane, which are best

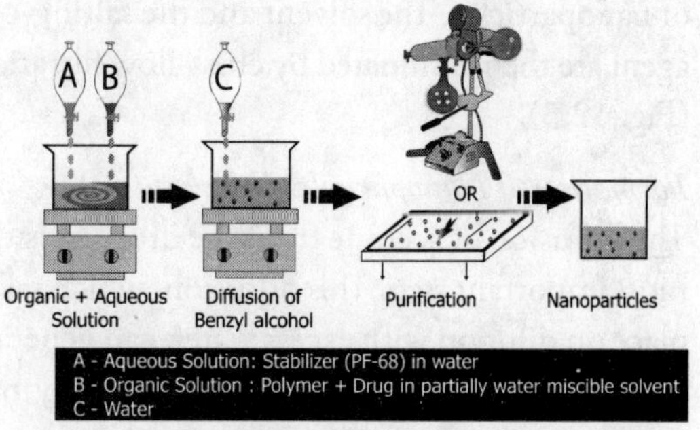

Figure 12.2: Schematic representation of solvent emulsification evaporation method

avoided and, if used, have to be <600 ppm as per the International Conference on Harmonisation (ICH) guidelines. Other water insoluble solvents such as ethyl acetate or a mixture of chlorinated and polar solvents such as acetone/methanol have been used lately.

Salting Out

In 1988, Bindschaedler et al patented a new procedure to prepare pseudolatexes. This method was subsequently adapted and optimised by Allemann and Leroux for drug-loaded nanoparticles. This method is based on the separation of a water-miscible solvent from aqueous solutions through a salting-out effect.

Acetone is generally chosen as the water-miscible solvent because of its solubilising properties and its well-known separation from aqueous solutions by salting out with electrolytes. The preformed polymer and the drug are dissolved in acetone and this solution is emulsified under vigorous magnetic stirring in an aqueous gel containing the salting-out agent (electrolytes such as magnesium acetate or magnesium chloride) and a colloidal stabiliser. The resulting emulsion is then diluted with a sufficient volume of water to enhance the diffusion of acetone into the aqueous phase, thus inducing the formation of nanoparticles. The solvent and the salting-out agent are then eliminated by cross-flow filtration (Fig. 12.3).

Formation of Nanoparticles (Mechanism)

The diffusion of acetone from the droplets is the most important step. This diffusion, which takes place on dilution with excess water, can generate interfacial turbulence leading to polymer aggregation in the form of nanoparticles.

Advantages and Disadvantages

The major advantages of this technique are the possible incorporation of high amounts of polymer and drug, excellent yields and the easy scaling up of the process in an industrial setup. On the other hand, this technique is limited to lipophilic drugs, salting-out agents that enable phase separation without precipitation and soluble stabilisers that are compatible with saturated aqueous solutions and do not coacervate in the presence of the solvent. The salting agents for acetone are magnesium chloride, sodium chloride and magnesium acetate and one non-electrolyte, sucrose. With regard to stabilisers, only poly vinyl alcohol (PVA) has been successfully used; nevertheless, PVA has the disadvantage of not being accepted for parenteral administration by the US Pharmacopeia. Also, the process requires

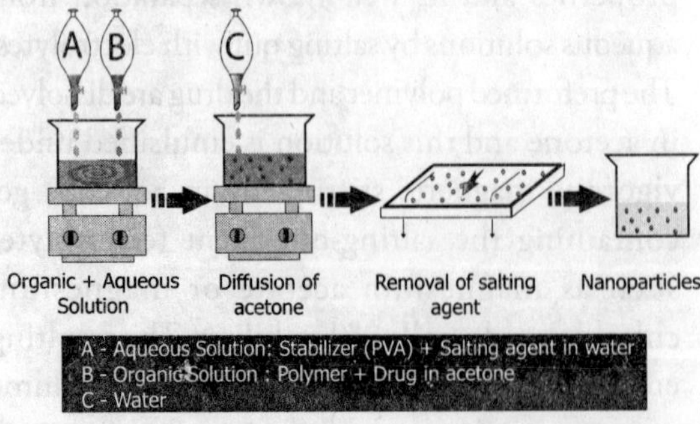

Figure 12.3: Schematic representation of the salting-out method

intense purification to ensure complete removal of the electrolytes.

Emulsification Diffusion

This method is considered to be a modification of the salting-out procedure, avoiding the use of salts and hence the intensive purification steps. It involves the use of a partially water-soluble solvent, which is previously saturated in water to ensure the initial thermodynamic equilibrium of both liquids.

The preformed polymer is dissolved in the water-saturated solvent, and this organic phase is emulsified under vigorous agitation in an aqueous solution containing a stabiliser. The subsequent addition of water to the system causes the solvent to diffuse into the external phase, resulting in the formation of nanoparticles. Depending on the boiling point of the solvent, this can be eliminated by distillation or cross-flow filtration (Fig. 12.4).

Formation of Nanoparticles (Mechanism)

Each emulsion droplet produces several nanoparticles, and these are formed by interfacial phenomena during solvent diffusion. However, these phenomena cannot be entirely explained by the convection effects caused by interfacial turbulence. Therefore, it is suggested that nanoparticles are also formed because of a physichochemical instability produced by solvent transport. The diffusion of the solvent from the globules carries molecules into the aqueous phase, forming local regions of supersaturation from which new globules or polymer aggregates (not totally desolvated) are formed. The stabilisation of these 'protonanoparticles' is then carried out by the stabiliser that is present at the liquid–liquid interface, forming nanoparticles after complete diffusion of the solvent.

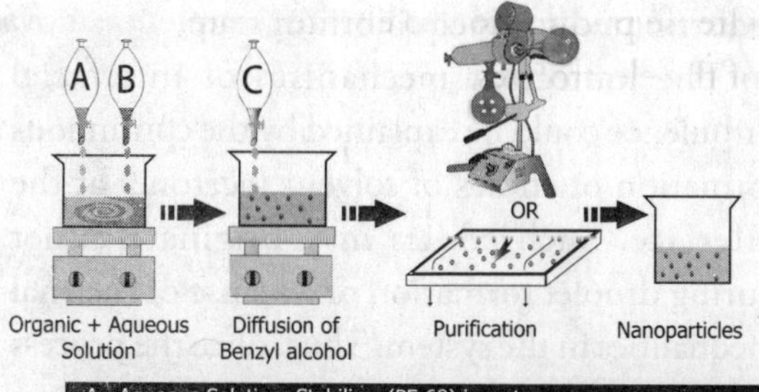

Figure 12.4: Schematic representation of emulsification diffusion method

Advantages and Disadvantages

The biggest advantage of this technique is the absence of homogenisation steps (sonication), thus making it possible to be scaled up in an industrial setup. It also provides high yields and high batch-to-batch reproducibility. The drawback of this method is the high volume of water that has to be eliminated from the suspension. In addition, nanoparticles obtained using this process cannot be freeze-dried because of the presence of residual benzyl alcohol.

Spontaneous Emulsification Solvent Diffusion

This method was first reported by Niwa et al. In this method, nanoparticles are obtained by pouring the polymeric organic solution into an aqueous phase with moderate magnetic stirring. One technical characteristic of this method is the use of a binary mixture of a water-miscible organic solvent and a water-immiscible solvent for the polymeric solution, and the particles are formed by emulsification and subsequent solvent evaporation (Fig. 12.5).

Formation of Nanoparticles (Mechanism)

Here, the preformed polymer is dissolved in an organic solvent mixture consisting of dichloromethane and acetone, which are water-immiscible and water-miscible solvents, respectively. This polymeric solution is then slowly poured into the aqueous solution containing a stabiliser and agitated with a magnetic stirrer. When the polymeric solution is added, emulsion droplets are formed in the aqueous phase; acetone quickly diffuses out from each emulsion droplet, drastically reducing the size. Consequent solvent evaporation removes dichloromethane, solidifying the droplets to form polymeric nanoparticles.

Advantages and Disadvantages

As the technique does not require the use of homogenisation (sonication), it can be easily scaled up in an industrial setup. However, due to a considerable amount of residual dichloromethane, the particles are likely to aggregate during the solvent evaporation process, when a larger payload of polymer is used. To overcome this, a mixture of acetone and alcohol has sometimes been used instead of dichloromethane.

Solvent Displacement

This technique was first described and patented by Fessi et al. In this process, the polymer, the drug and optionally a lipophilic stabiliser

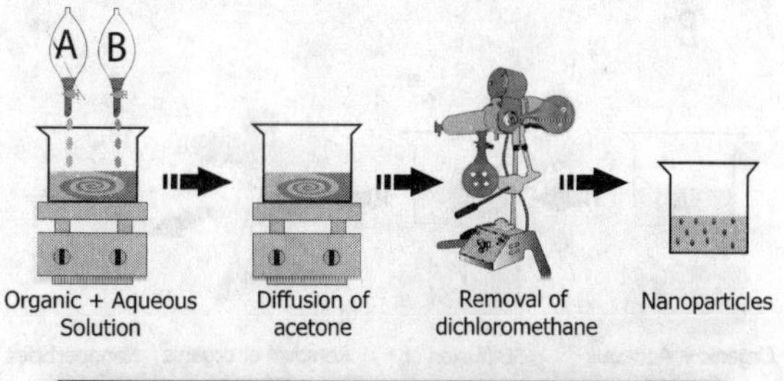

Figure 12.5: Schematic representation of spontaneous emulsification solvent diffusion method

(phospholipids) are dissolved in a semipolar water-miscible solvent such as acetone or ethanol. This solution is poured or injected into an aqueous solution containing a stabiliser (poloxamer-188) under magnetic stirring. Nanoparticles are formed instantaneously by rapid solvent diffusion, which is then eliminated from the suspension by heating under reduced pressure (Fig. 12.6).

Formation of Nanoparticles (Mechanism)

The formation of nanoparticles by this technique is explained by the interfacial turbulence generated during the solvent displacement phase. Subsequently, a violent spreading is observed because of mutual miscibility between the solvents. Droplets of solvent, probably of nanometric size, are torn from the interface. These droplets are rapidly stabilised by the stabilising agent, until diffusion of the solvent is complete and polymer aggregation has occurred. It is suggested that the interfacial turbulence is caused by localised lowering of the interfacial tension where the oil phase undergoes rapid and erratic pulsations or 'kicks', each of which is quickly damped out by viscous drag. The energy required for these jerky movements comes from the free energy released as the solvent is redistributed to its equilibrium state.

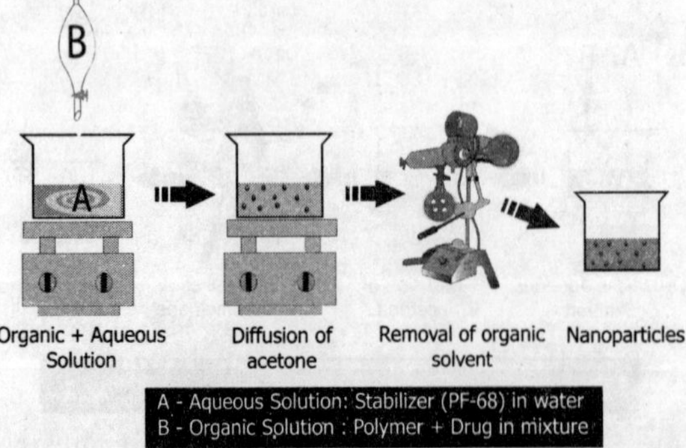

Figure 12.6: Schematic representation of solvent displacement method

The molecular mechanism of interfacial turbulence could be explained by the continuous formation of eddies of solvent (acetone) at the interface. Such eddies may originate either during droplet formation or because of thermal inequalities in the system. Thus, once the process has started, movements associated with previous kicks change the pressure inside the solvent by increasing the surface pressure or decreasing the interfacial tension. Thus, if the solvent droplets formed contain polymer, these would tend to aggregate and form nanoparticles because of the continuous diffusion of solvent and the presence of a nonsolvent medium. This process is also termed nanoprecipitation.

Advantages and Disadvantages

This technique is very simple, does not involve the use of homogenisers (sonication) and can hence be scaled up easily in an industrial setup. A major drawback of this technique is the difficulty in choosing the drug/polymer/solvent/nonsolvent system in which nanoparticles would be formed and the drug efficiently entrapped.

Pharmaceutical Aspects of Nanoparticles

Nanoparticles are intended to be used as pharmaceutical dosage forms in humans and therefore they have to be free from any potentially toxic impurities, should be easy to store and administer and, above all, sterile, as most of them are meant for parenteral use. Accordingly, three important processes are performed:

- Purification
- Freeze-drying
- Sterilisation

Purification of Nanoparticles

Depending on the preparation method used,

various potentially toxic impurities can be found in the nanoparticulate suspensions including organic solvents, electrolytes, surfactants, stabilisers and large polymer aggregates. Simple filtration will only remove polymer aggregates, while other impurities require more sophisticated procedures.

The most commonly reported procedures are gel filtration, dialysis and ultracentrifugation. However, these methods are not entirely satisfactory because they are restricted to the lab scale or are incapable of eliminating molecules with high molecular weights.

The necessity of finding an efficient purification technique that can be scaled up from an industrial standpoint led to the development of the cross-flow filtration method. In this method, the nanoparticle suspension is filtered through membranes, with the direction of the fluid being tangential to the surface of the membranes. The suspension is submitted to several filtration cycles while the filtrate containing components smaller than the pores of the membrane as well as soluble impurities is discarded. Most importantly, this technique can be scaled up by enlarging the filtering surface.

Freeze-drying of Nanoparticles

If nanoparticles are stored as aqueous suspensions, degradation and/or solubilisation of the polymer, drug leakage, drug desorption and/or drug degradation may occur. Freeze-drying or lyophilisation is one of the methodologies used to ensure the long-term conservation of polymeric nanoparticles.

This technique involves the freezing of the suspension and the subsequent elimination of its water content by sublimation under reduced pressure. After complete desiccation, nanoparticles are obtained in the form of a dry, free-flowing powder that is easy to handle and store. Freeze-dried nanoparticles are usually readily redispersible in water without modifications to their physicochemical properties because of the presence of stabilisers such as poloxamer-188.

However, in some cases, full redispersion of the system may be difficult to achieve because of the composition of the nanoparticulate polymeric matrix. Lyophilising these systems in the presence of appropriate lyoprotective agents such as glucose, trehalose or sucrose can circumvent this problem. It has been suggested that during freeze-drying, sugars may interact with the solute of interest through hydrogen bonding. As a result, the solute might be maintained in a 'pseudo-hydrated' state during the dehydrating step of freeze-drying and therefore protected from damage during dehydration and subsequent rehydration.

Sterilisation of Nanoparticles

Nanoparticles intended to be used parenterally are required to be sterile and apyrogenic. Some of the well-established methods of sterilisation such as filtration through 0.22 μm filters are not adequate for nanoparticle suspensions because microorganisms and nanoparticles are generally similar in size (0.3–1 μm).

Therefore, sterilisation of nanoparticles is best achieved by using aseptic techniques throughout their processing and preparation. However, this is not a totally foolproof method and therefore, a terminal sterilisation step is required to ensure the microbiological safety of the final product.

Autoclaving (moist heat sterilisation) and γ-irradiation are the techniques that can be applied for terminal sterilisation. However, these techniques may have an impact on the physicochemical properties of the particles. Thus, it is apparent that sterilisation of nanoparticulate formulations is a critical step that should be systematically investigated to arrive at suitable techniques.

Characterisation of Nanoparticles

Nanoparticles are generally characterised by size, density, electrophoretic mobility, angle of contact and specific surface area, recovery and drug incorporation efficiency.

Size and Morphology

The particle size is one of the most important parameters of nanoparticles. Two techniques are used to determine the particle size distribution of nanoparticles: photon correlation spectroscopy (PCS) and electron microscopy (EM). The latter includes SEM, transmission electron microscopy (TEM) and freeze-fracture techniques. The size evaluation of nanoparticle dispersion demonstrates better results, with freeze-fracturing microscopy and photon correlation spectroscopy as quantitative methods.

EM, however, could be adopted as an alternative option that measures individual particles for size and distribution. It is relatively less time consuming. Additionally, the freeze fracturing of particles allows for morphological determination of their inner structure. In combination with freeze-fracture procedures, TEM permits differentiation among nanocapsules, nanoparticles and emulsion droplets. Similarly, SEM is much less time consuming. However, since particles are based on organic and non-conductive materials, they require gold coating. The thickness of the gold coat may be 30–50 nm. Thus, the determined size should be denoted as a gold-coated particle size rather than as the particle size.

AFM is an advanced nanoscopic technique applied for the characterisation of PLA nanospheres and solid lipid nanoparticles. AFM images can be obtained in an aqueous medium, and for this reason, it is an effective means of investigating nanoparticle behaviour in a biological environment. Mercury porositometry is an equally suitable technique for the sizing of nanoparticulates. The freeze-dried nanoparticles are filled in a dilatometer under vacuum and then measured with the help of a mercury pressure porositometer. This method largely measures particulate agglomerates as mercury fails to penetrate to a greater extent within the primary particles.

Specific Surface

The specific surface area of freeze-dried nanoparticles is generally determined with the help of a sorptometer. The equation given below can be used to calculate specific surface area:

$$A = 6 / \rho.d$$

where **A** is the specific surface area, ρ is the density and **d** is the diameter of the particle. In most cases, the measured and calculated specific surface areas fairly compare while in some cases, the residual surfactant could produce a deviation in the measured values. The surfactant coating reduces the specific surface area.

Surface Charge and Electrophoretic Mobility

The nature and intensity of the surface charge of nanoparticles is very important as it determines their interaction with the biological environment as well as their electrostatic interaction with bioactive compounds. The surface charge of colloidal particles in general and nanoparticles in particular can be determined by measuring the particle velocity in an electric field. Laser light scattering techniques such as laser Doppler anemometry or velocimetry are used as fast and high-resolution techniques for determining nanoparticle velocities.

The surface charge of colloidal particles can also be measured as electrophoretic mobility. The charge composition critically decides the biodistribution of drug-carrying nanoparticles. Generally, the electrophoretic mobility of nanoparticles is determined in a phosphate saline buffer and human serum. The phosphate saline buffer (pH 7.4) reduces the absolute charge value due to ionic interaction of buffer components with the charged surface of nanoparticles. The zeta potential can be obtained by measuring the electrophoretic mobility by applying the Helmholtz–Smoluchowski equation.

Surface Hydrophobicity

The surface hydrophobicity of nanoparticles influences the interaction of colloidal particles with the biological environment. Hydrophobicity and hydrophilicity collectively determine the biofate of nanoparticles and their contents. Hydrophobicity regulates the extent and type of hydrophobic interactions of nanoparticulates with blood components. Several methods including hydrophobic interaction chromatography, two-phase partition, adsorption of hydrophobic fluorescent or radiolabelled probes, and contact angle measurements have been adopted to evaluate surface hydrophobicity. Recently, several sophisticated methods of surface chemistry analysis have been used.

Density

In addition to surface SEM, TEM following freeze fracturing could successfully be used in the morphological investigation of nanoparticles. The interiors are continuous or some structural imperfections exist that provide an indication about the density distribution across the matrix. Some polymeric nanoparticles, especially polycyanoacrylate and poly methyl methacrylate, seem to have porous interiors and also exhibit more irregular and rough surfaces. The density of nanoparticles is determined with helium or air using a gas pycnometer. The value obtained with air and with helium is much more pronounced due to the specific surface area and porosity of the structure.

Molecular Weight Measurements

The molecular weight of the polymer and its distribution in the matrix can be evaluated by gel permeation chromatography (GPC) using a refractive index detector. Using GPC, it was shown that polyalkylcyanoacrylate (PACA) nanoparticles are built by an entanglement of numerous small oligomeric subunits rather than by the rolling up of one or a few long polymer chains.

Nanoparticle Recovery and Drug Incorporation Efficiency

Nanoparticle recovery, also referred to as nanoparticle yield, can be calculated using the following equation:

$$\text{Nanoparticle Recovery (\%)} = \frac{\text{Concentration of drug in nanoparticles}}{\text{Concentration of nanoparticles recovered}} \times 100$$

Drug incorporation efficiency has been expressed both as drug content (%w/w), also referred to as drug loading, and drug entrapment (%) represented by the following equation:

$$\text{Drug incorporation efficiency in nanoparticles} = \frac{\text{Amount of drug entrapped in nanoparticles}}{\text{Total amount of added drug}}$$

In Vitro Release

The in vitro release profile of nanoparticles can be determined using standard dialysis, diffusion cell or modified ultrafiltration techniques which have been recently introduced and which use phosphate buffer utilising double chamber diffusion cells on a shaker stand. A millipore, hydrophilic, low protein–binding membrane is placed between the two chambers. The donor chamber is filled with nanoparticulate suspension and the receptor chamber with plain buffer. The receptor compartment is assayed at different time intervals for the released drug using standard procedures.

The modified ultrafiltration technique is also used to determine the in vitro release behaviour of nanoparticles. The nanoparticle suspension is added directly into a stirred ultrafiltration cell-containing buffer. At different time intervals, aliquots of the dissolution medium are filtered through the ultrafiltration membrane using <2 bar positive nitrogen pressure and assayed for the released drug using standard procedures.

In Vivo Fate and Biodistribution of Nanoparticles

Following intravenous administration, the colloidal carriers first come into contact with plasma/serum proteins before they reach the target cells. Most notably, the interaction of the colloidal carriers with the phagocytes often requires some serum components and then subsequently, interaction with complement, Fc and sugar/lectin receptors on the macrophage.

The Fc receptor is a protein found on the surface of certain cells, including natural killer cells, macrophages, neutrophils and mast cells, that contributes to the protective functions of the immune system. Its name is derived from its binding specificity for a part of an antibody known as the Fc (Fragment, crystallisable) region. Fc receptors bind to antibodies that are attached to infected cells or invading pathogens. Their activity stimulates phagocytic or cytotoxic cells to destroy microbes or infected cells by antibody-mediated phagocytosis or antibody-dependent cell-mediated cytotoxicity.

It is now recognised that phagocytosis of the particulates by elements of the reticuloendothelial system (RES) is regulated by the presence and balance between two groups of serum components: opsonins, which promote phagocytosis, and dysopsonins, which suppress the process.

The opsonins adsorb on to the surface of the colloidal carriers and render the particles recognisable and more palatable to the RES. Thus, they mediate their phagocytosis by the fixed and circulating macrophages of the RES.

Immunoglobulins and components of complement systems (particularly C3 and C5) are known as classical opsonin molecules. The central dogma in opsonin-driven phagocytosis is the higher protein adsorbability of hydrophobic surfaces relative to hydrophilic surfaces. The same has been related to the enhanced uptake of more hydrophobic particles by phagocytosis in vitro and the rapid removal of hydrophobic particles in vivo.

Thus, it is the macrophages (fixed and circulating) located in the RES that play a crucial role in opsonin-mediated phagocytosis of the injected colloidal particulate systems. It is reported that short circulation half lives were observed for the injected colloidal systems irrespective of their composition, namely, albumin, poly (lactide), poly (lactide-co-glycolide), poly (cyanoacrylate) or polyacryl starch. Therefore, using these polymers, drugs can be targeted to macrophages of RES-rich organs such as the liver, spleen and lungs.

Therapeutic Applications of Nanoparticles

Nanoparticles have been widely employed for different therapeutic applications, some of which are listed below:

- For intracellular targeting of anti-infective drugs to combat the 'difficult to treat' intracellular infections of the human body
- For targeting of cytostatic drugs to reduce toxicity and increase therapeutic activity
- For specific targeting of anti-inflammatory drugs to areas of inflammation, by which the side effects of these drugs can be minimised
- For ocular delivery systems, to deliver pilocarpine and other miotic drugs
- As carriers for radionucleotides for diagnostic purposes in nuclear medicine
- To improve the solubility and bioavailability of poorly soluble drugs
- For skin and hair care in the form of solid lipid nanoparticles (SLN), wherein the oily core contains a wide variety of different cosmetic oils and lipophilic agents
- To deliver drugs across the blood brain barrier (BBB)
- To formulate sustained release preparations
- For the controlled delivery of disinfectants or algaecides into large bodies of water such as insect pest feed on colloidal particles
- For targeted delivery of proteins and peptides
- As adjuvants to render antigens potent enough to be useful for vaccines

Key Messages

- Nanoparticles are solid, colloidal particles ranging 10–1000 nm (1 μm) in size.
- Nanoparticles can be prepared by emulsification-based methods such as solvent emulsification evaporation, salting out, emulsion diffusion and spontaneous emulsification–solvent diffusion. Direct precipitation-based methods such as solvent displacement can also be used.
- Nanoparticles can be purified by gel filtration, dialysis and ultracentrifugation and cross-flow filtration through membranes.
- Nanoparticles are generally freeze-dried or lyophilised for long-term conservation of polymeric nanoparticles.
- Nanoparticles intended to be used parenterally are required to be sterile and apyrogenic. Sterilisation of nanoparticles is best achieved by using aseptic techniques throughout their processing and preparation. Terminal sterilisation can be carried out by autoclaving and γ-irradiation.
- Nanoparticles are generally characterised by size, density, electrophoretic mobility, angle of contact and specific surface area, recovery and drug incorporation efficiency.

- The in vitro release profile of nanoparticles can be determined using standard dialysis, diffusion cell or recently introduced, modified ultrafiltration techniques.
- Following intravenous administration, nanoparticles undergo phagocytosis and the drug is released.
- Nanoparticles have a wide variety of applications such as intracellular targeting of anti-infective drugs, targeting of cytostatic drugs to reduce toxicity and increase therapeutic activity, specific targeting of anti-inflammatory drugs to areas of inflammation, use in ocular delivery systems for pilocarpine and other miotic drugs. It also acts as a carrier for radionucleotides for diagnostic purposes in nuclear medicine and in the targeted delivery of proteins and peptides to improve the solubility and bioavailability of poorly soluble drugs, for skin and hair care in the form of solid lipid nanoparticles (SLN), to deliver drugs across the blood brain barrier (BBB) and for sustained release.

Questions

1. Define nanoparticles. Discuss their applications.
2. Discuss briefly the various methods of preparation of nanoparticles.
3. How are nanoparticles purified?
4. Why are nanoparticles freeze-dried?
5. Write a note on the sterilisation of nanoparticles.
6. Discuss how nanoparticles are characterised.
7. Write a note on the in vitro release of nanoparticles.
8. Explain what happens when nanoparticles are injected intravenously.
9. Explain how the drug particles are targeted to macrophages.

13

Methods of Enhancing Bioavailability of Drugs

SHOBHA RANI R HIREMATH AND HN SHIVAKUMAR

Learning Objectives

At the end of this chapter, you will be able to:

- Define bioavailability and state its importance
- Describe the different methods used to enhance bioavailability

Introduction

Bioavailability is defined as the fraction of the drug administered that reaches systemic circulation. The pharmacological response of a drug is dependent on its bioavailability.

Due to the present emphasis on bioavailability as an indicator of the bioefficacy of drug products, significant efforts are being extended towards augmenting the absorption characteristics of various dosage forms, especially those with known vulnerability to bioavailability problems.

The methods used to enhance bioavailability follow one of two approaches. The first is pharmaceutically dependent and involves improvement of the absorption attributes by increasing the dissolution rate of the drug preparation. This is usually achieved by changing certain ingredients in the formulation, optimising the manufacturing process or by altering the physicochemical properties of the drug substance without altering its molecular structure.

The second approach is pharmacokinetically dependent and deals with resolving specific bioavailability problems that are intrinsic to the drug chemical entity. Methods based on this approach require modification of the pharmacokinetic properties of the drug, which can be achieved only by changing its molecular structure. Pharmacokinetic improvements usually involve the optimisation of drug permeability and/or its aqueous solubility to facilitate its absorption. In certain cases, however, significant enhancement of bioavailability can be obtained by modulating the drug's metabolic fate, distribution characteristics or excretion profile.

Methods to Enhance Bioavailability

When poor bioavailability is caused by dissolution rate–limited absorption, improvements in the dissolution characteristics of the dosage form usually result in an increase in the rate and extent of drug absorption. The major advantage of this approach is its relative accessibility and the fact that, by keeping the molecular structure of the drug intact, no new and expensive clinical studies will have to be conducted. In addition, the risk of solving the absorption problems at the expense of creating another pharmacokinetic disorder or of causing clinically adverse side effects is avoided.

Enhancement of the dissolution rate of a dosage form can be achieved by increasing the effective surface area of the drug either by micronisation or by incorporating surface active agents in the formulation. Another approach involves increasing the aqueous solubility of the drug by using highly soluble metastable polymorphic forms or by altering the pH of the drug's microenvironment. Examples of the latter are in situ salt formation or addition of buffer compounds to the formulation. Also, solute–solvent complexation reactions and solid state solutions have been used successfully to enhance the dissolution rate of drug products.

Each of these methods is now discussed in detail.

Bioavailability: Formulation Effects

Formulation factors such as the kind of dosage form used and its design, and the nature of the excipients and their amount can have a significant effect on the bioavailability of poorly soluble drugs mainly by influencing the dissolution rate. For certain drugs that are known to exhibit pH-dependent solubility/stability or which have their absorption window in specific regions of the gastrointestinal tract (GIT), it is not only how fast the active ingredients are released that is important, but also where they are released. Weakly acidic drugs, which are absorbed extensively from the stomach, need to be dissolved as soon as possible in the gastric juice. The types of diluent, binder, disintegrant and lubricant and their amounts have to be optimised to retain the dosage form in the stomach to enhance their oral bioavailability.

A gastroretentive drug delivery system is highly advisable for drugs such as ofloxacin that are characterised by pH-dependent solubility and are readily soluble in the acidic environment of the stomach. Mahesh Chavanpatil et al have formulated a sustained release effervescent drug delivery system for ofloxacin that could be retained in the stomach for extended periods of time. Improved bioavailability was obtained by utilising a mixture of gelling agents (psyllium husk and hydroxy propyl methyl cellulose [HPMC]), which are known to swell and float in the gastric fluid. The gas generating agent (sodium bicarbonate) was found to render the system more buoyant, thereby ensuring high drug concentrations in the gastric fluid because of enhanced gastric retention time.

Nishimura et al prepared an effervescent enteric-coated tablet of levodopa, which characteristically maintains high drug concentrations in the upper part of the small intestine. Improved bioavailability was achieved by selecting the proper enteric dosage form (using HPMC) to inhibit drug decomposition in the stomach and to ensure high drug concentration at the desired site. The drug is released in large amounts by rapid tablet dissolution caused by the presence of optimum amounts of the effervescent agent. The enhanced bioavailability was attributed to high drug concentration at the target site, which induces temporary saturation of levodopa carboxylase in the intestinal wall, thereby inhibiting possible conversion of the drug to dopamine.

Glyceryl monooleate (GMO), a Food and Drug Administration (FDA)-approved food additive, is a mixture of glycerides of oleic acid and other fatty acids consisting mainly of mono oleate that has the ability to form different types of lyotropic liquid crystals in the presence of water. The cubic liquid crystals of GMO have been investigated to formulate an oral drug delivery system for furosemide with a view to enhancing its oral bioavailability. Furosemide was dispersed in GMO and used to fill hard gelatin capsules that, when exposed to gastric fluid at body temperature, would swell to form a cubic liquid crystal phase. The system developed was known to produce a sustained release formulation with a prolonged gastric residence time because of its bioadhesive nature.

Buffered Tablets

The use of buffered tablets to improve dissolution and bioavailability of poorly soluble drugs such as aspirin was recommended by Levy in the early 1960s. Since then, buffered formulations have been prepared to increase gastrointestinal stability and enhance the bioavailability of certain penicillins.

Particle Size

The use of finely subdivided or micronised particles to enhance bioavailability by increasing the dissolution rate has been highly recommended for water insoluble drugs whose absorption is limited by the dissolution rate. An effective method of increasing the solubility of any drug, whether readily or sparingly soluble in water, is through the comminution of the drug into fine particles. Small, micron-sized particles have higher dissolution rates because of increased surface area. Besides this, particles smaller than 1 micron display higher saturation solubility and better adhesion to the wall of the GIT, which enhances bioavailability. Several attempts have been made to investigate the effect of particle size on the absorption of greseofulvin in humans and animals following oral administration. It was observed that reducing the particle size from 10 microns to 2.7 microns resulted in the doubling of the effective absorption of the drug. A number of techniques such as spray drying have been successfully employed to produce micronised particles.

Surface Active Agents

Various non-ionic, anionic and cationic surfactants have been investigated as potential intestinal permeation enhancers. Surfactants that are too hydrophobic to be water soluble are poor absorption enhancers while those that are very hydrophilic cannot partition into the hydrophobic environment of the lipid bilayer, thereby resulting in an intestinal absorption-promoting effect. The absorption enhancing ability is influenced by the size and shape of the alkyl chain and the polar group. A medium-length alkyl chain surfactant may penetrate the lipid bilayer easily and because of its aqueous solubility have greater monomer and higher critical micellar concentration than a longer alkyl chain surfactant.

Non-ionic surfactants have been used to solve the bioavailability problems of poorly water-soluble drugs. These surfactants are known to accelerate dissolution and improve the bioavailability of these super lipophilic drugs. Solid preparations comprising a mixture of surfactants (tween 80, hydrogenated castor oil and labrasol) have been reported to improve the dissolution and absorption of lansoprazole. The bioavailability of solid preparations was measured in rats and beagle dogs. The bioavailability of the acid labile drug lansoprazole was found to be dependent on the surfactant and adsorbent used. The combination of hydrogenated castor oil and porous silicon dioxide showed the highest bioavailability in rats (28.1%). The drug, when used to fill an enteric capsule and orally administered to dogs, showed a bioavailability of 77.7%. The solid systems consisting of surfactants and adsorbents showed good promise to improve the bioavailability of lansoprazole, which is known to exhibit wide intersubject variation.

Gentamicin is a polarised, water-soluble compound with poor intestinal membrane permeability resulting in low oral bioavailability. Ramprasad et al have conducted in vivo studies of gentamicin formulations containing poly ethylene glycol-8 (PEG-8) caprylic/capric glycerides after using them to fill enteric-coated capsules, in beagle dogs. Oral administration of an aqueous solution of gentamicin in labrasol showed higher values of C_{max} and the area under the curve (AUC). An adsorbent synthetic sponge was used to adsorb the gentamicin solution and was then encapsulated by capsules coated with Eudragit L and Eudragit S.

Solid Dispersions

Solid dispersion systems have been used as formulations to improve the solubility, release and bioavailability of poorly water-soluble drugs. Solid dispersion systems with polymers such as Eudragit, sodium carboxy methyl cellulose (CMC) and HPMC chitosan and ethyl cellulose improved drug solubility but retarded its release. Solid dispersion systems with hydrophilic or amphiphilic polymers such as polyethylene glycol, phospholipids and isopropyl myristate improved the solubility, dissolution and absorption of poorly soluble drugs. The increase in the solubility and dissolution rate could be attributed to factors such as a reduction in the particle size of the drug, solubilising effect of the drug by the water-soluble carriers, enhancement of the wettability and dispersibility of the drug by the carrier material and possible formation of the metastable dispersion that has greater solubility resulting in a faster dissolution rate and improved bioavailability.

Solid dispersion systems of cyclosporine A prepared from sodium lauryl sulphate/dextrin using a spray drying technique has been reported by Eun-Jin Lee et al. The solid dispersions of the drug: sodium lauryl sulphate (SLS): dextrin ratio of 1:3:1 showed maximum drug concentration when compared to that of the drug alone. This means SLS and dextrin improve drug absorption.

Solid dispersions of tetrahydrocannabinol with inulin and oligosaccharide as carriers using the lyophilisation technique have been reported by van Drooge et al. The inulin matrix was found to enhance the stability and dissolution rate of the drug from the solid dispersions. Tablets formulated using the solid dispersions, poly vinyl pyrrolidone (PVP) and mannitol, showed great promise for sublingual administration.

Ahmad et al have studied the solid dispersion of the poorly soluble drug halofantrine in polyethylene glycol, PVP and gelucire prepared using the lyophilisation technique.

Ali and Gorashi studied the dispersion and coprecipitation of the poorly water-soluble drug nitrofurantoin in PVP, PEG and mannitol. Comparision between the in vivo absorption of the nitrofurantoin and the solid dispersions was conducted based on the cumulative amount of nitrofurantoin excreted in the urine as a function of time, following oral administration to human volunteers. A significant enhancement of the bioavailability of the solid dispersion was observed over that of the drug alone.

Particulate Drug Delivery

One approach to overcoming the bioavailability problem of poorly water-soluble drugs is to formulate them as nanosuspensions. Nanosuspensions are drug-loaded nanoparticles dispersed in a liquid phase. The drug nanoparticles can be transferred to a dry product by spray drying or lyophilisation. Particulate formulations have previously been proved to be an efficient approach to achieving better pharmacokinetic profiles and even to increasing the oral bioavailability of several drugs. This enhanced bioavailability can be ascribed to increased saturation solubility and dissolution velocity caused by the enlarged surface area. The increased bioavailability can also be attributed to the fact that the particles in the nano size range are efficient at crossing the permeability barrier. The absorption and oral bioavailability of heparin, enalaprilat and tobramycin were demonstrated to be significantly enhanced when administered as nanoparticles, when compared to oral free drugs.

Rajesh Pandey et al reported the preparation of azole antifungal nanoparticles by emulsion solvent evaporation/cation controlled gelification technique using synthetic or natural polymers. The biodistribution and pharmacokinetic data suggested a significant improvement in the relative and absolute bioavailability of each drug.

Amorphous nanoparticle suspensions of poorly water-soluble drugs such as cyclosporine A were produced by evaporative precipitation into the aqueous phase. The rapid evaporation of the heated organic solution of the drug, which is automised into the aqueous solution, resulted in faster nucleation leading to nanoparticle suspension. Hydrophilic stabilisers were introduced in the organic or aqueous phase to limit particle growth and inhibit crystallisation at high drug concentrations. The suspensions can be used as a parenteral formulation to enhance bioavailability or may be dried to produce an oral dosage form with the potential for high dissolution rates due to low crystallinity and small particle size.

Bioadhesive insulin-loaded chitosan nanoparticles were prepared by mild ionotropic gelation procedure. From the biopharmaceutical point of view, chitosan has the special feature of adhering to the mucosal surface and transiently opening the tight junction between the epithelial cells. It has been proved that chitosan enhances insulin absorption across human intestinal epithelial cells (Caco-2) without injuring them.

Self-emulsifying Systems

Oil-in-water emulsion dosage forms can be used to improve the dissolution characteristics of poorly water-soluble drugs. However, emulsions consisting of two immiscible liquids are thermodynamically unstable and therefore the two phases tend to separate. In the absence of water, a mixture of oil and non-ionic surfactants forms a clear, transparent isotropic solution known as a self-emulsifying system (SES) and used as a vehicle for drug delivery. SES systems have recently been used to improve the characteristics of in vitro dissolution and, therefore, to enhance the in vivo absorption of indomethacin. This system was known to form a fine oil-in-water emulsion with gentle agitation when exposed to aqueous media. This property makes SES a good vehicle for the oral delivery of hydrophobic drugs that have adequate oil solubility. Soft, gelatin capsules containing SES readily disperse in the stomach to form a fine emulsion; in this case, gastrointestinal motility can provide the agitation effect required for emulsification. For drugs that display characteristics of dissolution rate–limited absorption, SES could enhance the rate and extent of absorption as well as improve the reproducibility of the plasma-level profiles.

A self-microemulsifying drug delivery system containing structured triglycerides was developed for oral administration of halofantrine. The drug was found to demonstrate better oral absorption and bioavailability from the system.

Cyclodextrins are torus-shaped oligosaccharides produced by enzymatic hydrolysis and cyclisation of starch, containing six (α-CD), seven (β-CD) or eight (γ-CD) α-1, 4–linked D-glucose units, with a hydrophilic hydroxyl group on their outer surface and a relatively hydrophobic cavity. Cyclodextrins have the ability to entirely or at least partially trap drug molecules in their cavities to form noncovalent inclusion complexes. They are also known to improve the solubility, dissolution and bioavailability of poorly water-soluble drugs by forming inclusion complexes. Zingone and Rubessa have reported the preparation of β cyclodextrin inclusion complexes of warfarin. The complexes formed exhibited better solubility and dissolution rates. Sunil Jambhekar et al have reported the preparation and physicochemical characterisation of inclusion complexes of indomethacin with β cyclodextrin and its derivatives. Complexation was found to augment both the solubility and dissolution rates. Bioavailability comparison by analysis of variance (ANOVA) showed a significantly higher AUC for the inclusion complex than in other formulations. Consequently, the effectiveness of complexation in enhancing bioavailability may allow a decrease in the dose with probably fewer side effects. Uekama et al have reported that the formation of complexes of phenytoin with water-soluble cyclodextrin-epichlorhydrin polymers was found to significantly increase the plasma levels of the drug after oral administration in dogs. Similar enhancement results were obtained by other investigators for sulphamethoxazole, spiranolactone and cinnarizine.

Poorly water-soluble drugs reportedly show increased oral bioavailability when incorporated as oil-in-water emulsions. This effect was ascribed to improved dispersion of the lipid phase resulting in more efficient absorption. The emulsion was stabilised by spray drying to obtain directly compressible powder containing stabilised lipid droplets that could be reconstituted before use or on contact with intestinal fluids.

Modification of the Partition Coefficient

It is recognised that in an analogous series, increasing the nonpolar portion of a molecule by extending the length of the chain produces certain characteristic features such as elevated boiling point, decreased aqueous solubility and increased partition coefficient, viscosity and surface activity. Hansch suggested that many biological responses depend to a large extent on the capability of the drug molecule to move through various anatomical and physiological compartments composed of aqueous and lipid vesicles. The drug molecule with the structural features that enable them to move between compartments with minimum change in free energy are the drugs with perfect hydrophilic/ lipophilic balance (HLB) and with the best chance to reach the desired site of action. Hansch recommended the property π to denote the measure of the substituent group contribution to the HLB of the drug molecule:

$$\pi_x = \log P_x - \log P_H$$

where π_x is the contribution of the substituent group and P_x and P_H are the partition coefficients of the substituted derivative and the parent compound between water and nonpolar 1-octanol.

The contribution of different substituent groups to the lipophilicity of the molecule or its partition coefficient is additive, assuming no group interaction is introduced. The Hansch value π is usually taken in conjunction with the Hammett sigma value (σ), which is a measure of the electronic contribution of the substituent group in comparison with hydrogen. Hansch recommended the following equation to correlate the π and σ values to biological activity:

$$\text{Log } 1/c = -k\,\pi + k'\,\pi + \rho\,\sigma + k''$$

where c is the drug concentration required to elicit the desired biological response, k, k' and k" are constants relevant to the specific systems under study and ρ is a reaction constant. The molecular structure of the drug can be manipulated skillfully to increase the partition coefficient, thereby improving the permeability and ability to penetrate the biological lipophilic barriers which, in turn, lead to enhancement of bioavailability. However, for dissolution-limited drug absorption, the increased lipophilic character may be accompanied by decreased aqueous solubility and slowing of the dissolution rate, such that bioavailability suffers. In this case, methods for improving the aqueous solubility of the drug must be utilised to solve the bioavailability problem.

Aqueous Solubility

Improvements to the aqueous solubility of a drug can be achieved in many cases through physical means such as micronisation or complexation and suspension in an inert, water-soluble matrix. Marked improvements, however, can also be achieved by modifying the molecular structure of the drug.

One of the most accessible methods, where applicable, is the formation of salts. In most cases, salts have different solubility and dissolution characteristics from those of the original drug. For insoluble weak acids, sodium and potassium salts are significantly more soluble, while calcium salts are only modestly soluble. Aluminium salts are generally less soluble and dissolve at a much slower rate than the parent drug.

Penicillins provide a good example of the effect of salt formation on the dissolution rate and bioavailability of drugs. The sodium and potassium salts of the popular penicillin G (benzyl penicillin) are commonly employed to achieve high blood level concentrations. Calcium salts are less soluble and subsequently yield lower plasma concentration peaks than sodium and potassium salts. Aluminum salts of penicillin G have also been used because they are insoluble in the gastric pH and are, therefore, less susceptible to inactivation in the stomach. The amine salt of penicillin G, procaine penicillin, is considerably less soluble in water; however, because free penicillin is released gradually, this salt has a longer duration of action than metal salts. Several commercial penicillin products are mixtures of the potassium or sodium salts used to provide the initial high blood level, with procaine penicillin G used to yield the long duration desired.

Barbiturates are also utilised as their soluble sodium salts gain a higher level of bioavailability and faster onset of effect. The antiepileptic drug phenytoin is practically insoluble in water, with a slow dissolution rate; however, its water-soluble sodium salt has much better dissolution characteristics and better bioavailability.

Free sulfonamides are relatively insoluble in water, but they combine with bases to form more soluble salts. The pH of the sodium salts of sulfa drugs (except sulfacetamide) makes them damaging to tissues, so they cannot be used in high concentrations on mucous membranes.

Water insoluble weak bases are mainly used as salts. Their acid salts are usually water soluble and highly ionised. The selection of a specific acid to prepare the salt determines the taste, solubility, rate of absorption and stability of the parent drug. Strong acid salts, such as the hydrochlorides and sulfates, are the most common forms for weak bases. Epinephrine is used as the hydrochloride, borate and bitartrate. Both borate and bitartrate are less acidic and can thus be used for ophthalmic solutions. It is also more stable than the hydrochloride. The tetracyclines are amphoteric compounds and the salt of tetracyclines is most commonly used because of its stability.

Gastointestinal Stability

The molecular structure of drugs can be modified to improve their gastrointestinal stability and thus enhance their bioavailability. For example, penicillin G and methacillin are very unstable in the stomach; however, ampicillin was introduced later with a half life that is about 180 times longer under the same conditions. This dramatic increase in stability was achieved by introducing an electron withdrawing group at the α-carbon atom, which inhibits the hydrolytic cleavage of the β lactum ring. Another approach to increase gastric stability of the penicillins is the formation of insoluble salts. Benzathine penicillin is a diamine salt with two molecules of penicillin available from each molecule of the salt. The compound is quite stable at gastric pH and food intake does not interfere with its absorption because of poor solubility (1/5000).

Another example is the case of the in vivo stability of adrenergic drugs after oral administration. It has been recognised that the α-methyl group in the epinephrine molecule imparts in vivo stability to the drug; thereby making its oral ingestion effective. Similarly, aphetamine is an active oral analeptic drug while β-phenyl ethylamine, which has no methyl group at the α-carbon, is totally inactive if given by mouth due to its degradation in vivo.

Hepatic First Pass Effect

Following oral administration, several drugs undergo appreciable loss in bioavailability due to presystemic metabolism. Although some undergo degradative metabolic reactions in the intestinal wall before absorption, most of the loss in bioavailability is caused by the hepatic first pass effect. One of the methods used to to minimise excessive metabolism in the liver, before reaching systemic circulation, is increasing the oral dosage regimen, which is thought to temporarily saturate the hepatic enzyme involved in the metabolism of the drug in question and hence lower its loss due to the first pass effect. In most cases, however, modification of the molecular structure of a drug to decrease its susceptibility to metabolic attack is necessary.

Improving Bioavailability by Using Prodrugs

A prodrug is an inactive form of the drug that upon metabolism gives rise to the active parent drug. The prodrug may be converted before reaching systemic circulation or rapidly after appearing in the bloodstream. The use of prodrugs is another example of controlled design modifications of the chemical structures of drug entities to introduce new forms with better pharmacokinetic properties and enhanced bioavailability. One of the main reasons for employing prodrugs is to improve in vivo stability and absorption of the original drug. This has been applied successfully in the case of oral penicillins. Ampicillin was introduced as an acid-resistant form of penicillin with a significantly longer half life and better bioavailability. However, its oral absorption was found to be incomplete and erratic. Esters of penicillin were found to have better absorption characteristics and were introduced to improve the bioavailability of ampicillin. However, because a free carboxylic group is essential for antimicrobial activity, these drugs have to be readily hydrolysed to the free drug ampicillin in the body. Therefore, the ester, pivampicillin hydrochloride, was introduced with almost twice the absorption of ampicillin and a half life of 5 minutes before complete conversion to ampicillin.

Hetacillin, another prodrug of ampicillin, was originally synthesised to improve the bioavailability of ampicillin. However, because of its susceptibility to rapid in vivo and in vitro hydrolysis, its methoxy-methyl ester, sarpicillin, was introduced and found to have more rapid absorption as well as faster and higher plasma levels of ampicillin. This was attributed mainly to its better lipophilicity and higher partition coefficient.

Bacampicillin is also a recent prodrug of ampicillin that has been shown to be absorbed more rapidly and to a larger extent than its parent drug. This was based on both AUC and urinary excretion data following peroral ingestion. Again, the improvement in absorption was caused by its increased lipid solubility as its aqueous solubility remained the same as that of ampicillin. A disadvantage of bacampicillin is its bitter taste, which can limit its acceptability for use in the liquid form. To mask the bitter taste, a microencapsulated aqueous suspension of small particles of bacampicillin hydrochloride coated with a thin polymeric film of ethyl cellulose was developed. The thickness of the coat was adjusted so that the dissolution rate of the drug was not inhibited severely and a good bioavailability profile was retained. To optimise the bioavailability of the prepared suspensions, the in vitro dissolution half lives of the microcapsules were used as a relative indicator of absorption for absorption efficiency.

Key Messages

- The efficacy of drugs depends on their bioavailability.
- Formulation factors have a significant influence on the bioavailability of drugs.
- Surface active agents, solid dispersions, particulate drug delivery and self-emulsifying systems are some of the important methods of improving bioavailability.
- Modification of the partition coefficient and solubility, minimising hepatic metabolism, improving gastrointestinal stability and using prodrugs are the other ways of improving bioavailability.

Questions

1. Define bioavailability and explain its importance.
2. Write a note on solid dispersions.
3. How can bioavailabilty of drugs be improved by the prodrug approach?
4. What is the role of particle size and surface active agents in enhancing bioavailability?
5. What are self-emulsifying systems?

14

Pilot Plant and Scale-up

PRAVEEN SALIGRAM

Learning Objectives

At the end of this chapter, you will be able to:

- Explain the need for scaling up drug production
- Define the types of batches
- List the scale-up and post-approval change guidelines
- Describe how scaling up can be done scientifically

Introduction

The pace of drug discovery has been accelerating at an exponential rate. The past two decades in particular have witnessed amazing inventions and innovations in pharmaceutical research, resulting in the ability to produce new drugs faster than ever before.

New drug applications (NDAs) and abbreviated new drug applications (ANDAs) are at an all-time high. Different types of laboratories have been motivated to adopt new processes and technologies in an effort to stay at the forefront of scientific innovation.

Pharmaceutical pilot plants that can quickly form numerous short-run production lines of multiple batches are essential for ensuring success in the clinical testing and bioequivalence study phases. Drug formulation research time targets are met by having a well-designed facility, with the appropriate equipment mix, to quickly move from the laboratory to the pilot plant scale.

To avoid repetition of lengthy and costly tests, it is necessary to gather as much relevant information as possible during properly designed development and process optimisation studies, when scaling up from the laboratory through pilot to the production scale. Such information provides the basis for justifying that scale-up can be achieved without a consequent loss in quality.

Figure 14.1 represents a typical process development cycle. As can be seen, the process development activity begins after the laboratory scale batches have been identified and include the scale-up, pre-exhibit/process qualification and pivotal/exhibit batches. The process development activities are generally carried out in the pilot plant.

Laboratory Scale Batches

Laboratory scale batches are produced at the

Figure 14.1: Flow of a typical drug product development process

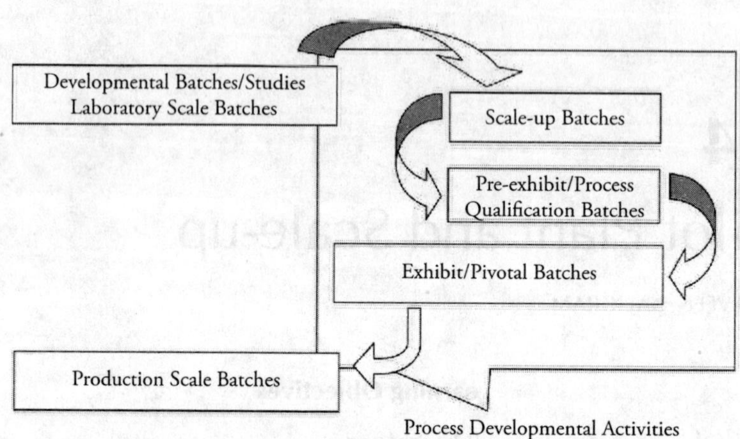

research and early development laboratory stages; they may be of very small size (100–1000 times less than the production scale). These batches may be used for many purposes, for example, to support formulation and packaging development or for preclinical studies. The data derived from these batches assist in the evaluation and definition of critical product performance characteristics, thereby enabling selection of the appropriate manufacturing process.

Scale-up Batches

Scale-up batches are prepared if problems are anticipated in larger size batches, namely, pre-exhibit batches. During the scale-up activity, all the unit operations involved in the manufacturing process are scaled up, resulting in identification of critical parameters.

Pre-exhibit/Process Qualification Batches

The pre-exhibit batch is developed to detect any problem that may arise during the manufacture of exhibit batches, allowing for the resolution of the problem prior to the actual manufacture of the exhibit batch. In these batches, the proposed product specifications are challenged to test the ruggedness/robustness of the process.

It is a full in-house simulation of the pivotal process (sometimes 70% of the size of the pivotal batch) with complete process documentation and fully validated analytical methodologies, including stability indicating assay analysis. These form the basis from which the manufacturing instructions and specifications of the exhibit batch are evolved.

Final optimisation and documentation editing is performed prior to initiating the exhibit batches.

Exhibit/Pivotal Batches

The exhibit batch is the demonstration batch that contains the manufacturing documentation, product specifications and accelerated stability data normally submitted to the Food and Drug Administration (FDA) as part of the regulatory data required for the ANDA filing. Bioequivalence testing against a reference listed drug (RLD) is performed on samples from this batch.

The exhibit batch size should correspond

to at least 10% of the production scale batch. For oral solid dosage forms, this size should be 10% of production scale or 100,000 units, whichever is greater.

The exhibit batch has to be manufactured and packaged under full good manufacturing practice (GMP) conditions using the commercial production equipment and staff under which the proposed future commercial batch lots will be manufactured. In some cases, where there is a dedicated 'process development' laboratory and team, these batches can be manufactured at these locations provided the process development equipment and commercial production equipment are the same in principle but different in capacities.

In summary, the production of exhibit batches should provide a high level of assurance that the product and process will be feasible on an industrial scale.

An exhibit batch is:

- An ANDA submission batch
- A regulatory reference batch
- A bioequivalence batch
- A process qualified batch
- A full GMP batch
- A stability tested batch

Production Scale Batches

These batches are of the size that will be produced during routine marketing of the product. Data on production scale batches may not always be available prior to granting marketing authorisation. Hence, a thorough evaluation and characterisation of the critical process parameters at the exhibit scale are carried out, followed by a formal validation programme on production scale batches, the results of which can subsequently be verified by the supervising authority.

Scale-up and Post-approval Changes (SUPAC)

The joint workshop between the FDA and the American Association of Pharmaceutical Scientists (AAPS) provided the scientific foundation for the scale-up and post-approval changes required for immediate release products. This evolved into guidelines titled Scale-up and Post-approval Changes for Immediate Release (SUPAC-IR).

SUPAC-IR proposed ranges for various classes of drug and excipient levels that could be considered as major or minor formulation changes. These guidelines provide recommendations for post-approval changes in the following:

- Components or composition
- Site of manufacture
- Scale-up of manufacture
- Manufacturing (process and equipment) of an immediate release oral formulation

Thus, SUPAC-IR provides for levels of changes to the scale of manufacture, site of manufacture, manufacturing process, equipment and composition and is used as a guideline in the scale-up of formulations from the laboratory to the plant.

Scientific Scale-up

Scaling up from the laboratory bench to the production plant is best done in incremental steps, with the process being validated for each new scale. As this is a very difficult task, coupled with the time and money constraints of a developmental activity, it is often not carried out.

This is when 'dimensional analysis' (similitude concepts) is applied as a tool to scale up processes scientifically. For similitude concepts to be applied, the equipment (in process development scale and in production scale) should possess geometric,

Table 14.1: Parameters for scaling up a wet, granulated tablet formulation

Stage of Production	*Parameters*
During granulation	Pre-mix time Granulation time Mixing speed Mixing temperatures Addition rate of granulating fluid
During drying in a fluid bed dryer	Inlet air temperature Air volume Product temperature and drying time
During milling with a Co-Mil	Impeller type Impeller speed Screen size Screen type Milling speed
During compression in a tablet press	Compression force Tablet hardness Ejection force Press speed Different press speeds Impact on weight and dosage Effect of incremental differences in hardness on dissolution profile of tablet
During coating	Spray rate Inlet air temperature Inlet air volume Product bed temperature

kinematic and dynamic similarities.

Geometric Similarity

This requires all corresponding dimensions on production scale equipment to have the same ratio as in-process development equipment. These dimensions include parameters such as vessel and impeller diameters and baffle widths and quantity.

Kinematic Similarity

This requires corresponding points in each system to have the same velocity ratio.

Dynamic Similarity

This adds the requirement of equal force ratios at corresponding points in each system. Properties such as gravitation, surface tension, viscosity and inertia are included in balancing force ratios.

Two systems are geometrically similar if they have the same ratio of linear dimensions. Two geometrically similar systems are kinematically similar if they have the same ratio of velocities between corresponding points. Two kinematically similar systems are dynamically similar when they have the same ratio of forces between corresponding points. For any two dynamically similar systems, all the dimensionless numbers necessary to describe the process have the same numerical value. Table 14.1 lists the parameters to be considered for scaling up a wet granulated tablet formulation—the tablet is the most commonly studied dosage form and hence has been selected as an illustrative example.

It is an acknowledged fact that rational scale-up should replace the empirical approach of yesteryears, as in the long run it will save precious resources and time for a pharmaceutical company looking at manufacturing generic products. Dimensional analysis provides a powerful scientific scaling up technique that has been proven by a century of sound engineering principles and applications.

Key Messages

- Drug formulation research time targets are met by having a well-designed facility, with the appropriate equipment mix, to move quickly from the laboratory to the pilot plant scale.
- Developmental batches are produced at the research and early development laboratory stages; they may be of very small size (100–1000 times less than the production scale).
- During the scale-up activity, all the unit operations involved in the manufacturing process are scaled up, resulting in identification of critical parameters.
- Pre-exhibit batches are a full in-house simulation of the pivotal process (sometimes 70% of the size of the pivotal batch) with complete process documentation and fully validated analytical methodologies, including stability indicating assay analysis.
- The exhibit batch is the demonstration batch that contains the manufacturing documentation, product specifications and accelerated stability data normally submitted to the Food and Drug Administration (FDA) as part of the regulatory data required for the ANDA filing.
- SUPAC-IR provides for levels of changes to the scale of manufacture, site of manufacture, manufacturing process, equipment and composition and is used as a guideline in the scale-up of formulations from the laboratory to the plant.
- 'Dimensional analysis' (similitude concepts) is applied as a tool to scale up processes scientifically.

Questions

1. What do you understand by development batches, scale-up batches and pivotal batches?
2. What is dimensional analysis and where is it used?
3. What is the stipulated batch size of a pivotal batch of a solid dosage form?
4. What are the factors to be considered while scaling up a wet granulated tablet formulation?

15

Optimisation Techniques in Pharmaceutical Formulation and Processing

SHOBHA RANI R HIREMATH AND VANAJA K

Learning Objectives

At the end of this chapter, you will be able to:

- Define optimisation
- Explain the design of experiments (DOE) and their advantages
- Describe the types of DOE
- List the applications of DOE

Introduction

Optimisation is the process of finding the best way of using the existing resources while taking into account all of the factors that influence decisions in any experiment. It is a means of finding the best possible value of a dependent variable by changing certain independent variables.

Pharmaceutical formulation is composed of several factors and process variables. Several responses relating to effectiveness, usefulness, stability as well as safety must be optimised simultaneously. Consequently, expertise and experience are required to design acceptable pharmaceutical formulations. The optimisation of pharmaceutical formulations with regard to one or more attributes has always been a subject of importance and attention for those engaged in formulation research. In a typical pharmaceutical formulation experiment, the process variables that most affect the responses must be determined.

The logical step is to optimise, that is, to determine the part of the factors that leads to the best possible response. In addition to the experience of the formulator, techniques that can aid the scientist's choice of formulation components and which will result in the optimisation of one or more product attributes are available.

Theoretically, all the parameters that can affect the physicochemical properties of a final product may be included in experimental design. However, in pharmaceutical manufacturing processes, there may be numerous important parameters because of the large number of ingredients usually required for formulation. If all the variables are included in the experimental design, the process may lead to a prohibitive number of experiments.

Hence, the formulator must first identify the potentially dominant parameters that should be subjected to the screening process in order to limit to a reasonable extent the number of experiments needed. A delicate equilibrium is established between what is worth and what is not worth investigating. The formulator's skill, knowledge and experience play a crucial role in selecting the appropriate variables.

The composition of pharmaceutical formulations is often subject to trial and error. This approach is time-consuming and unreliable. Optimisation by means of an experimental design may be helpful in shortening the experimenting time. Such a design, with its concomitant mathematical models, reveals the effects and interactions of the variables. The independent variables are the different compositions of the mixtures of the chosen ingredients (drug(s) and excipients). The dependent variables are the properties (responses) of the formulation. When all responses of interest have been expressed in models that describe the response as a function of the composition of the mixture, the models can be combined graphically or mathematically to arrive at a composition that satisfies all demands.

Design of Experiments

Design of experiments (DOE) is a structured, organised method used to determine the relationship between the factors (Xs) affecting a process and the output of that process (Ys).

Statistical DOE refers to the process of planning the experiment in such a way that appropriate data can be collected and analysed statistically, resulting in a valid and objective conclusion. This approach is used to draw meaningful conclusions from the experimental data.

Efficiency in the experimental sciences involves judiciously combining modelling and actual experimentation. Laboratory experiments are expensive. Although a few experiments may have to be performed to obtain preliminary estimates of parameters and to check techniques, it is generally inefficient to rush to carry out many experiments. It is far more efficient to formally list hypotheses and the models of possible experiments and then run the experiments on the models of the system.

Advantages of DOE

The advantages of DOE are as follows:

- Aids in handling experimental error.
- Helps to determine the important variables that need to be controlled and find the unimportant variables that need not be controlled.
- Eliminates the confounding of effects whereby the effect of design variables is mixed up.
- Helps to measure interactions, which is very important.
- Allows extrapolation of the data and search for the best possible product within the test variable ranges.
- Allows plotting of graphs to depict how variables are related and what level of variables produces the optimum product. Use of statistical models reveals the interrelationship between variables.

Phases of DOE

The phases of DOE are as follows:

- Identifying factors that may affect the outcome of the experiment and responses that give a measure of the outcome.
- Choosing an appropriate experimental design, either for screening or response surface modelling.
- Generating a design matrix to determine the experiments to be conducted.
- Conducting the experiments.
- Fitting the data and generating plots that describe the trends in the results.
- Drawing conclusions and planning the next step.

The Parsimony principle states that some of the factors are important while others are not. This principle is also known as the Pareto principle or the '80–20' rule. This rule implies that a few variables are responsible for most of the effects on the response while most variables contribute little.

Statistical Designs

A number of statistical designs are available based on the Parsimony principle according to the experimental objectives required, which are as follows:

Comparative objective

If one or several factors are under investigation, but the primary goal of the experiment is to draw a conclusion about one *a-priori* important factor, (in the presence or existence of the other factors), and the question of interest is whether or not that factor is 'significant', then it is a *comparative problem* and a *comparative design* solution is required.

Screening objective

The primary purpose of the experiment is to select or *screen out* the few important effects from the many less important ones. These *screening designs* are also termed main effects designs.

Response surface objective

The experiment is designed to allow estimation of interaction and even quadratic effects, and therefore provide an idea of the (local) shape of the response surface being investigated. For this reason, they are termed *response surface method (RSM) designs.*

Optimising responses when factors are proportions of a mixture objective

If factors are proportions of a mixture and the 'best' proportions of the factors should be determined so as to maximise (or minimise) a response, then a *mixture design* is required.

Types of Experimental Designs

The following are types of experimental designs in common use:

- Completely randomised designs
- Randomised block designs
- Factorial designs
  - Full
  - Fractional
- Response surface (second order) designs
  - Central composite designs
  - Box–Behnken designs
- Adding centre points
- Three-level full factorial designs

Each of these types is now discussed in detail.

Completely Randomised Designs

The experiment compares the values of a response

variable based on different levels of that primary factor. For completely randomised designs, the levels of the primary factor are randomly assigned to the experimental units. In randomisation, the run sequence of the experimental units is determined randomly. For example, if there are 3 levels of the primary factor with each level to be run 2 times, then there are 6 factorial possible run sequences.

Randomised Block Designs

For randomised block designs, there is one factor or variable that is of primary interest. Unimportant factors are those that may affect the measured result but are not of primary interest. To control non-significant factors (nuisance factors), an important technique known as blocking can be used to reduce or eliminate the contribution of these factors to experimental error. The basic concept is to create homogeneous blocks in which the non-significant factors are held constant and the factor of interest is allowed to vary. Within blocks, it is possible to assess the effect of different levels of the factor of interest without having to consider variations caused by changes in the block factors, which are accounted for in the analysis. The general rule is to *block what is possible and randomise what is not possible.*

Factorial Designs

Factorial designs allow the evaluation of multiple factors simultaneously. The factorial designs available fall into two broad categories: full and fractional.

Full Factorial Design

This design is useful when a detailed analysis of higher order interactions among the factors is needed. Runs are made at all possible combinations of factor levels. Because the number of runs required increases rapidly as the number of factors increases, full factorials are usually used when a relatively small set of factors that are known to be important are available or when collecting a large number of observations is feasible.

A common experimental design is one in which the input factors are set at two levels each. These levels are called 'high' and 'low' or '+1' and '−1', respectively. A design with all possible high/low combinations of all the input factors is called a full factorial design in two levels. For example, if there are k factors, each at 2 levels, a full factorial design has 2^k runs (Table 15.1).

Table 15.1: Number of runs for a 2^k full factorial

Number of Factors	*Number of Runs*
2	4
3	8
4	16
5	32
6	64
7	128

When the number of factors is 5 or more, a full factorial design requires a large number of runs and is not very efficient. A fractional factorial design or a Plackett–Burman design is a better choice for 5 or more factors.

A two-level, full factorial design for three factors, namely the 2^3 design, implies eight runs. Graphically, the 2^3 design can be represented by the cube shown in Fig. 15.1. The arrows show the direction of increase of the factors. The numbers '1' through '8' at the corners of the design box reference the 'standard order' of runs.

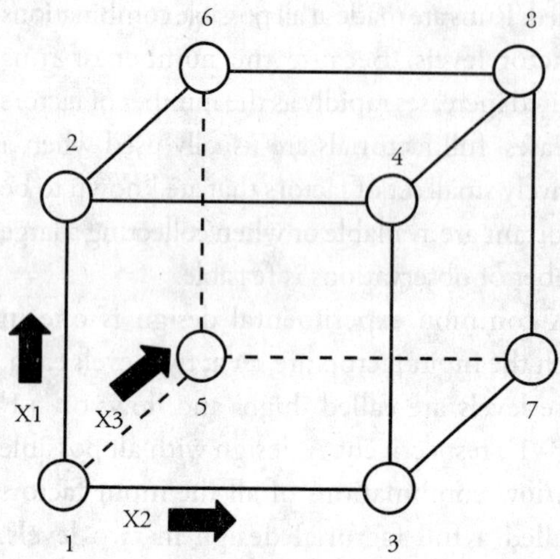

Figure 15.1: A 2^3 two-level, full factorial design; factors X1, X2, X3

Fractional Factorial Design

One difficulty with factorial designs is that the number of combinations increases exponentially with the number of variables that need to be manipulated. Fractional factorial design is used to examine multiple factors efficiently with fewer runs than the corresponding full factorial design. It works by assuming that some or all interactions are negligible so that these effects can be confounded with each other.

These methods are useful when a large number of factors need to be screened to identify the important ones for further study or when certain interactions can be ignored and resources for experimentation are limited. At the cost of a somewhat larger design, a fractional factorial design that is much smaller than a full factorial design allows estimation of main effects independent of interactions between pairs of variables. Thus, the basic purpose of a fractional factorial design is to economically investigate cause-and-effect relationships of significance in a given experimental setting.

Broadly speaking, with designs of resolution three, and sometimes four, the aim is to screen out the few important main effects from the many less important ones. For this reason, these designs are often termed main effects or screening designs.

The term 'screening design' refers to an experimental plan that is intended to find the few significant factors from a list of potential ones. Alternatively, a screening design is so called if its primary purpose is to identify significant main effects, rather than interaction effects, the latter being assumed to be less important.

Even when the experimental goal is to eventually perform an RSM analysis, the first experiment should be a screening design when there are multiple factors to consider. In short, screening designs are economical experimental plans that focus on determining the relative significance of many main effects. On the other hand, designs of resolution five and higher are used for focussing on more than just the main effects in an experimental situation. These designs enable the estimation of interaction effects and such designs are easily augmented to complete a second order design—a design that permits estimation of a full second order (quadratic) model.

The types of fractional factorial designs that can be generated are as follows:

- Homogeneous fractional
- Mixed level fractional
- Box–Hunter
- Plackett–Burman
- Taguchi
- Latin square

Homogeneous fractional

These designs are useful when a large number of factors must be screened efficiently and the higher order interactions are assumed to be negligible. These designs are sometimes used to screen a large set of candidate variables to identify important ones for more detailed study. In these designs, all variables have the same number of levels.

Mixed level fractional

These are useful when a variety of factors need to be evaluated for main effects and higher level interactions can be assumed to be negligible. They are often used to screen a large set of candidate variables to identify the important ones for more detailed study.

Box–Hunter

They are straightforward fractional designs encompassing a wide range of resolutions. Fractional designs with factors of more than two levels can be specified as homogeneous fractional or mixed level fractional designs.

Plackett–Burman

A popular class of screening designs is the Plackett–Burman design (PBD), developed by RL Plackett and JP Burman in 1946. They described the construction of economical designs with the run number as a multiple of four (rather than a power of 2). Plackett–Burman designs are very efficient screening designs when only the main effects are of interest. These designs are useful for detecting large main effects economically, assuming all interactions are negligible when compared with the few important main effects.

PBDs are used to investigate n–1 variables in *n* experiments, proposing experimental designs for more than seven factors and especially for n x 4 experiments, that is, 8, 12, 16, 20, etc. that are suitable for studying up to 7, 11, 15, 19, etc. factors, respectively. Such designs are known as saturated designs.

Taguchi

Similar to the PBDs, they allow estimation of main effects while minimising variance. For most of these designs, accurate results depend on the absence of any interaction. It also allows for some degree of heterogeneity in factors.

Latin square

They are a special case of fractional factorial design where there is one treatment factor of interest and two or more blocking (or nuisance) factors. These designs enable the isolation of the real effect from the nuisance effects by counterbalancing the levels of the real factor across levels of the nuisance factors.

Response Surface (Second Order) Designs

Sometimes, simple, linear and interaction models are not adequate; for example, if defects and yield are the outputs, and the goal is to minimise defects and maximise yield. As these optimal points are in the interior of the region in which the experiment is to be conducted, a mathematical model that can represent curvature having optimum response is necessary. This model has the quadratic form

$$\gamma = \beta_0+\beta_1X_1+\beta_2X_2+\beta_{12}X_1X_2+\beta_{11}X_1^2+\beta_{22}X_2^2$$

containing linear terms for all factors, squared terms for all factors and products of all pairs of factors.

Designs for fitting these types of models are known as response surface designs. One such design is the full factorial design having three values for each input. Although the Statistics Toolbox is capable of generating this design, it is not really satisfactory in most cases because it uses many more runs than are necessary to fit the model.

Introduced during the 1950s, the two most common designs generally used in response surface modelling are central composite designs and Box–Behnken designs.

Box–Wilson Central Composite Design

Commonly called 'a central composite design,' this type contains an embedded factorial or fractional factorial design with centre points that is augmented with a group of 'star points' that allow estimation of curvature. If the distance from the centre of the design space to a factorial point is ±1 unit for each factor, the distance from the centre of the design space to a star point is $\pm\alpha$ with $|\alpha| > 1$. The precise value of α depends on certain properties desired for the design and on the number of factors involved.

Similarly, the number of centre point runs the design is to contain also depends on certain properties required for the design. A central composite design always contains twice as many star points as there are factors in the design. The star points represent new extreme values (low and high) for each factor in the design. To picture a central composite design, it must be imagined that there are several factors that can vary between low and high values, say from −1 to +1. One central composite design consists of cube points at the corners of a unit cube that is the product of the intervals [−1,1], star points along the axes at or outside the cube and centre points at the origin.

Central composite designs are of three types. Circumscribed (CCC) designs are as described above. Inscribed (CCI) designs are as described above but scaled so the star points take the values −1 and +1 and the cube points lie in the interior of the cube. Faced (CCF) designs have the star points on the faces of the cube. Faced designs have three levels per factor, in contrast with the other types, which have five levels per factor. Figure 15.2 shows these three types of designs for three factors.

Box–Behnken Design

Like central composite designs, Box–Behnken designs are response surface designs that can fit a full quadratic model. They are independent quadratic designs in that they do not contain an embedded factorial or fractional factorial design. Unlike most central composite designs, Box–Behnken designs use just three levels of each factor. This makes them appealing when the factors are quantitative but the set of achievable values is small.

Central composite faced (CCF) designs also use just three factor levels. However, they are not rotatable as Box–Behnken designs are. On the other hand, Box–Behnken designs can be expected to have poorer prediction ability in the corners of the cube that encloses the design, because unlike CCF designs, they do not include points at the corners of that cube.

Figure 15.3 shows a Box–Behnken design for three factors, with the circled point appearing at the origin and possibly repeated for several runs. A repeated centre point makes it possible to compute an estimate of the error term that does not depend on the fitted model. For this design, all points except the centre point appear at a distance $\sqrt{2}$ from the origin. That does not hold true for Box–Behnken designs with different numbers of factors.

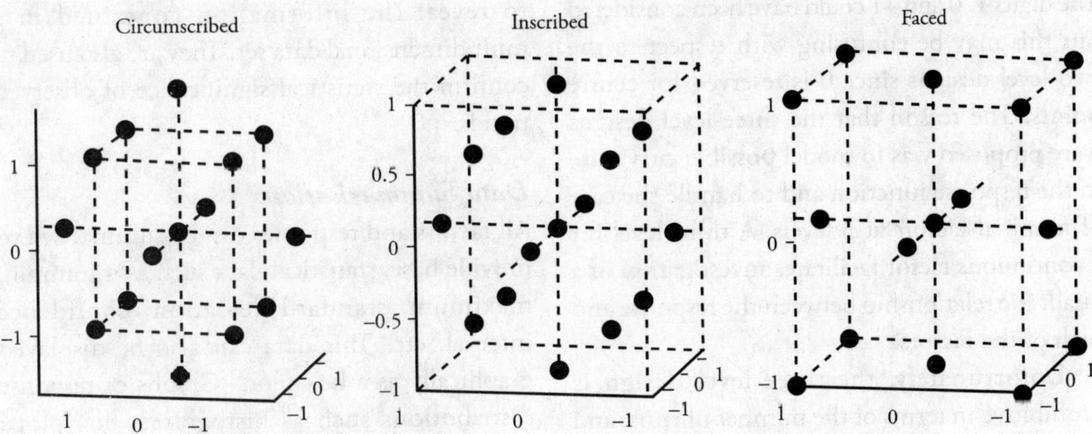

Figure 15.2: Circumscribed, inscribed and faced centre point designs

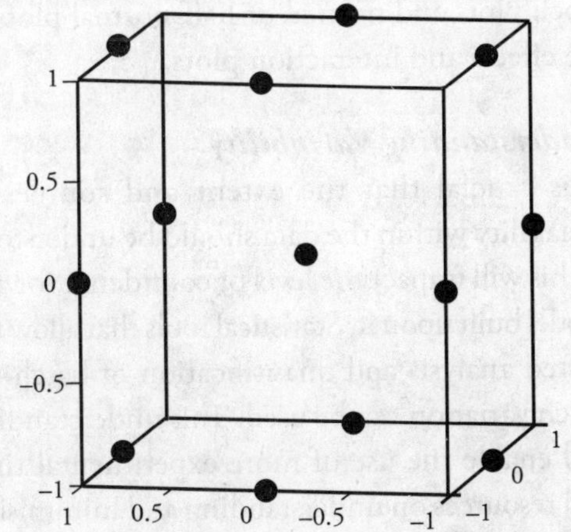

Figure 15.3: Box–Behnken design for three factors

In this design, the treatment combinations are at the midpoints of edges of the process space and at the centre. These designs are rotatable (or near rotatable) and require 3 levels of each factor. The designs have limited capability for orthogonal blocking compared to the central composite designs.

Adding Centre Points

Centre points that run interspersed among the experimental setting runs are added for two purposes:

- To provide a measure of process stability and inherent variability
- To check for curvature

The centre point runs should begin and end the experiment, and should be dispersed as evenly as possible throughout the design matrix. These runs are not randomised. There would be no reason to randomise them as they act as guardians against process instability, and the best way to find instability is to sample the process on a regular basis.

As a rough guide, approximately 3–5 centre point runs should be added to a full or fractional factorial design.

Three-level Full Factorial Designs

The three-level design is written as a 3^k factorial design. It means that k factors are considered, each at 3 levels. These are (usually) referred to as low, intermediate and high levels. These levels are numerically expressed as 0, 1 and 2.

The digits 1, 0 and +1 could have been considered but this may be confusing with respect to the two-level designs since 0 is reserved for centre points. The reason that the three-level designs were proposed was to model possible curvature in the response function and to handle the case of nominal factors at 3 levels. A third level for a continuous factor facilitates investigation of a quadratic relationship between the response and each of the factors.

Unfortunately, the three-level design is prohibitive in terms of the number of runs, and thus in terms of cost and effort. For example, a two-level design with centre points is much less expensive while it still is a very good (and simple) way to establish the presence or absence of curvature. This is a design that consists of three factors, each at three levels. It can be expressed as a 3 x 3 x 3 = 3^3 design. The model for such an experiment is as follows:

$$Y_{\mu k} = \mu + A_i + B_j + AB_{ij} + C_k + AC_{jk} + BC_{jk} + ABC_{jk} + E_{ijk}$$

where each factor is included as a nominal factor rather than as a continuous variable. In such cases, main effects have two degrees of freedom: two-factor interactions have 2^2 = 4 degrees of freedom and k-factor interactions have 2^k degrees of freedom. The model contains 2 + 2 + 2 + 4 + 4 + 4 + 8 = 26 degrees of freedom. Note that if there is no replication, the fit is exact and there is no error term (the epsilon term) in the model. In such cases, if it can be assumed that there are no three-factor interactions, then these 8 degrees of freedom can be used for error estimation.

In this model, i = 1, 2, 3 and similarly for j and k, resulting in 27 treatments.

Statistical Analysis of Data

Robust statistical techniques are often required to reveal the information contained in a multidimensional data set. They are also used to confirm the statistical significance of observed trends.

Data Summarisation

All factors and responses can be summarised to provide basic statistical data such as minimum, maximum, standard deviation, confidence interval, etc. This data can also be displayed graphically as a box plot. Graphs of response distributions such as histograms, box plots, responses versus time order scatter plot and responses versus factor levels can be plotted. Typical DOE plots are main effects mean plots, block plots and normal or half-normal plots of the effects and interaction plots.

Understanding Variability

It is crucial that the extent and sources of variability within the data should be understood as this will impact the level of confidence for any model built upon it. Statistical tools that allow the nested analysis and quantification of batch-to-batch variation can be used. This understanding will enable the use of more experimental time and resources on understanding and minimising the major sources of variability.

Numerical Models and Trends

For a given block of data, numerical models can be built and trends analysed. A numerical model allows the determination of the optimum conditions and response. It also predicts results for areas where there is no experimental data. These numerical models are analysed statistically against known variability to provide confidence and avoid over-fitting. Techniques used include:

- Multiple linear regression (MLR)

- Partial least squares (PLS)

Regression Coefficients and Analysis of Variance

After collection of all the runs and calculated responses, calculation of regression coefficients is initiated. After the estimation of the factor regression coefficients, the determination of significant factors affecting the dependent variables of interest (responses) is followed by an analysis of variance.

Analysis of variance (ANOVA) presents the sum of squares (SS) used to estimate the factor main effects, the F-ratios (F) as the ratio of the respective mean-square effect (MS) and the mean-square error, where 'P' probability values indicate the significant factors affecting the response.

Assuming that a starting model has been selected for which the experimental data needs to be fitted and the experiment was designed correctly for the objective, most DOE software packages will analyse the DOE data. (for example, Design Expert).

Applications of DOE

The applications of DOE are in the following areas:

- Formulation development
- Dissolution testing
- Tablet coating
- Excipient–drug interaction in solid dosage form

Formulation Development

In the pharmaceutical industry, the most concentrated use of screening designs is found in the product and process development functions, including analytical method development, because of increasing complexity in the optimisation of formulation and validation of analytical methods. In the evolving environment of research, experimental screening designs continue to gain acceptance as a valuable development tool. A screening design helps in isolating and understanding the most significant factors affecting the desired response. Hence, DOE has a wide range of applications in various areas of formulation development of many novel drug delivery systems such as transdermal drug delivery, osmotic drug delivery, liposomal drug delivery, nanoparticles, microspheres, etc.

Dissolution Testing

The dissolution test has emerged in the pharmaceutical field as a very important tool used to characterise drug product performance. Statistical experimental design methodologies have been evaluated to study the influence of critical dissolution test variables on release of drugs from the dosage form. The pH, volume of dissolution medium and stirring speed can be kept as the factor variables and dissolution efficiency as the response variable.

Tablet Coating

Critical processing variables for coating onto tablets can be identified through statistically designed experiments. The different process variables that can be investigated are inlet airflow, pan speed, inlet air temperature, coating time, atomisation pressure and fan pressure. The potential of these variables to significantly affect content uniformity, and per cent drug loading can be examined using screening designs.

Excipient–Drug Interaction in Solid Dosage Form

Identification of the stabilising and destabilising effects of excipient–drug interactions in solid dosage forms can be carried out. A compatibility screening procedure is reported to efficiently detect positive and negative excipient–drug interactions.

Key Messages

- The (statistical) design of experiments (DOE) is an efficient procedure for setting up a detailed experimental plan prior to doing any experiments. Well-chosen designs maximise the amount of information that can be obtained for a given amount of experimental effort.
- A complete DOE procedure will involve factorial designs for screening and central composite designs for optimisation.
- Optimisation through design of experiments has been applied in many functional areas, one being research to quantify interrelationships between variables and to screen a large number of variables to identify important ones.
- Another area is product development, where it is used to improve products through reformulation and development of new products.
- Design of experiments is based on sound and logical statistical principles. All principles are based on statistics that is a proven and reliable method, backed by trial and error.
- A formula for a successful product starts with the experimenter's knowledge of the product, continues with good test design and ends with statistical modelling.

QUESTIONS

1. Define optimisation.
2. What do you understand by design of experiments?
3. Classify the different types of statistical designs.
4. What are the different types of factorial designs?
5. Explain the different phases in design of experiments.
6. What are the various steps in analysis of DOE?
7. Explain the importance of adding a centre point.
8. Give a few applications of DOE.

16

Process Validation

PRAVEEN SALIGRAM

Learning Objectives

At the end of this chapter, you will be able to:

- Define process validation
- Define quality assurance and state its principles
- Explain the role of process validation in quality assurance
- Describe the elements of process validation

Introduction

Process validation is a requirement of the current Good Manufacturing Practice (GMP) Regulations for Finished Pharmaceuticals, 21 CFR Parts 210 and 211, and of the Good Manufacturing Practice Regulations for Medical Devices, 21 CFR Part 820. Therefore, process validation is applicable to the manufacture of pharmaceuticals and medical devices.

Definitions of Process Validation Terms

Installation qualification

Establishing confidence that process equipment and ancillary systems are capable of consistently operating within established limits and tolerances.

Process performance qualification

Establishing confidence that the process is effective and reproducible.

Product performance qualification

Establishing confidence through appropriate testing that the finished product produced by a specified process meets all release requirements for functionality and safety.

Prospective validation

Validation conducted prior to the distribution of either a new product or a product made under a revised manufacturing process, where the revisions may affect the product's characteristics.

Retrospective validation

Validation of a process for a product already in distribution based on accumulated production, testing and control data.

Validation

Establishing documented evidence that provides a high degree of assurance that a specific process will consistently produce a product meeting its predetermined specifications and quality attributes.

Validation protocol

A written plan stating how validation will be conducted, including test parameters, product characteristics, production equipment and decision points on what constitutes acceptable test results.

Worst case

A set of conditions encompassing upper and lower processing limits and circumstances, including those within standard operating procedures, that pose the greatest chance of process or product failure when compared to ideal conditions. Such conditions do not necessarily induce product or process failure.

Quality Assurance

Assurance of product quality is derived from paying careful attention to a number of factors including selection of quality parts and materials, adequate product and process design and control of the process, in-process and end-product testing. Due to the complexity of today's medical products, routine end-product testing alone is often insufficient to assure product quality for several reasons:

- Some end-product tests have limited sensitivity.
- In some cases, destructive testing would be required to show that the manufacturing process was adequate.
- In other situations, end-product testing may not reveal all possible variations that may occur in the product and which may have an adverse impact on its safety and effectiveness.

Principles of Quality Assurance

The goal of the basic principles of quality assurance is the production of articles that are fit for their intended use. These principles may be stated as follows:

- Quality, safety and effectiveness must be designed and built into the product.
- Quality cannot be inspected or tested or inserted into the final product.
- Each step of the manufacturing process must be controlled to maximise the probability that the finished product meets all quality and design specifications.

Role of Process Validation in Quality Assurance

Process validation is a key element in ensuring that the quality assurance goals are met. It is through the careful design and validation of both the process and the process controls that a manufacturer can establish a high degree of confidence that all manufactured units from successive lots will be acceptable. Successfully validating a process may reduce the dependence on intensive in-process and finished product testing. It should be noted that in most cases, end-product testing plays a major role in ensuring that quality assurance goals are met, that is, validation and end-product testing are not mutually exclusive.

The Food and Drug Administration (FDA) defines process validation as follows:

Process validation is establishing documented evidence that provides a high degree of assurance that a specific process will consistently produce a product meeting its predetermined specifications and quality characteristics.

It is important that the manufacturer prepares a written validation protocol that specifies the procedures (and tests) to be conducted and the data to be collected. The purpose for which data should be collected must be clear; the data must reflect facts and be collected carefully and accurately. The protocol should specify a sufficient number of replicate process runs to demonstrate reproducibility and provide an accurate measure of variability among successive runs.

The test conditions for these runs should encompass upper and lower processing limits and circumstances, including those within standard operating procedures, which pose the greatest chance of process or product failure compared to ideal conditions. Such conditions have become widely known as 'worst case' scenarios. Validation documentation should include evidence of the suitability of materials and the performance and reliability of equipment and systems.

Key process variables should be monitored and documented. Analysis of the data collected from process monitoring will establish the variability of process parameters for individual runs and also whether or not the equipment and process controls in place can provide assurance that product specifications are met.

Finished product and in-process test data can be of value in process validation, particularly in situations where quality attributes and variabilities can be readily measured. Where finished (or in-process) testing cannot adequately measure certain attributes, process validation should be derived primarily from the qualification of each system used in production and from the consideration of the interaction of the various systems.

Process Validation Considerations

A manufacturer should evaluate all the factors that affect product quality when designing and undertaking a process validation study. These factors may vary considerably among different products and manufacturing technologies and could include, for example, component specifications, air and water handling systems, environmental controls, equipment functions and process control operations. No single approach to process validation will be appropriate and complete in all cases; however, the following quality activities should be undertaken in most situations.

During the research and development (R & D) phase, the desired product should be carefully defined in terms of its characteristics, such as physical and chemical characteristics and in terms of its performance. It is important to translate the product characteristics into specifications as a basis for description and control of the product.

The product's end use should be a determining factor in the development of its characteristics and specifications. All pertinent aspects of the product that may have an impact on its safety and effectiveness should be considered. These aspects include performance, reliability and stability. Acceptable ranges or limits should be established for each characteristic to set up allowable variations. These ranges should be expressed in readily measurable terms.

The validity of acceptance specifications should be verified through testing and by challenging the product on a sound scientific basis during the initial development and production phase.

Elements of Process Validation

Process validation comprises prospective process validation and retrospective process validation. These two elements of process validation are explained below.

Prospective Process Validation

Prospective validation includes those considerations that should be made before a new product is introduced by a firm or when there is a change in the manufacturing process that may affect the product's characteristics, such as uniformity and identity. The following are considered as key elements of prospective validation:

Equipment and Process

The equipment and process should be designed and/or selected so that the product specifications are consistently achieved. This should be done with the participation of all the appropriate groups concerned with assuring a quality product, for example, engineering design, production operation and quality assurance personnel.

Equipment: Installation Qualification. Installation qualification studies establish confidence that the process equipment and ancillary systems are capable of consistently operating within established limits and tolerance levels. After process equipment is designed or selected, it should be evaluated and tested to verify that it is capable of operating satisfactorily within the operating limits required by the process. This phase of validation includes examination of equipment design, determination of calibration, maintenance and adjustment requirements and identifying critical equipment features that could affect the process and product. Information obtained from these studies should be used to establish written procedures covering equipment calibration, maintenance, monitoring and control.

In assessing the suitability of a given piece of equipment, it is usually insufficient to rely solely on the representations of the equipment supplier or on the experience acquired while producing some other product. Sound theoretical and practical engineering principles and considerations are a first step in the assessment of equipment.

It is important that equipment qualifications simulate actual production conditions, including those that are 'worst case' situations. Tests and challenges should be repeated enough number of times to assure reliable and meaningful results. All acceptance criteria must be met during the test or challenge. If any test or challenge shows that the equipment does not perform within its specifications, an evaluation should be performed to identify the cause of the failure.

Corrections should be made and additional test runs performed, as needed, to verify that the equipment performs within specifications. The observed variability of the equipment between and within runs can be used as a basis for determining the total number of trials required for subsequent performance qualification studies of the process.

Once the equipment configuration and performance characteristics are established and qualified, they should be documented. The installation qualification should include a review of pertinent maintenance procedures, repair parts lists and calibration methods for each piece of equipment. The objective is to assure that all repairs can be performed in such a way that it will not affect the characteristics of the material processed after the repair. In addition, special postrepair cleaning and calibration requirements should be developed to prevent inadvertent manufacture of non-conforming products. Planning during the qualification phase can prevent confusion during emergency repairs that could lead to the use of the wrong replacement part.

Process: Performance Qualification. The purpose of performance qualification is to provide rigorous testing to demonstrate the effectiveness and reproducibility of the process. In entering the performance qualification phase of validation, it is understood that the process specifications have been established and essentially proved acceptable through laboratory or other trial methods and that the equipment has been judged acceptable on the basis of suitable installation studies.

Each process should be defined and described with sufficient specificity so that employees understand what is required. Parts of the process that may vary so as to affect product quality should be challenged. In challenging a process to assess its adequacy, it is important that challenge conditions simulate those that will be encountered during actual production, including 'worst case' conditions. The challenges should be repeated enough number of times to ensure that the results are meaningful and consistent.

Each specific manufacturing process should be appropriately qualified and validated. There is an inherent danger in relying on what are perceived to be similarities between products, processes and equipment without appropriate challenges.

Product: Performance Qualification. Before reaching the conclusion that a process has been successfully validated, it is necessary to demonstrate that the specified process has not adversely affected the finished product. Where possible, product performance qualification testing should include performance testing under conditions that simulate actual use. Product performance qualification testing should be conducted using products manufactured from the same type of production equipment, methods and procedures that will be used for routine production. Otherwise, the qualified product may not be representative of production units and cannot be used as evidence that the manufacturing process will produce a product that meets the predetermined specifications and quality attributes.

Timely Revalidation

The quality assurance system followed must require revalidation whenever there are changes in packaging, formulation, equipment or processes, which could have an impact on product effectiveness or product characteristics, and whenever there are changes in product characteristics.

Furthermore, when the raw material supplier is changed, the manufacturer should consider the subtle, potentially adverse differences in the raw material characteristics. A determination of adverse differences in raw material indicates a need to revalidate the process.

One way of detecting the type of changes that should initiate revalidation is the use of tests and methods of analysis that are capable of measuring characteristics that may vary. Such tests and methods usually yield specific results that go beyond the mere pass/fail basis, thereby enabling detection of variations within product and process specifications and allowing determination of whether or not a process is slipping out of control.

The quality assurance procedures should establish the circumstances under which revalidation is required. These may be based on the equipment, process and product performance observed during the initial validation challenge studies.

The extent of revalidation will depend on the nature of the changes and how they affect different aspects of production that had previously been validated. It may not be necessary to revalidate a process from scratch merely because a given circumstance has changed. However, it is important to carefully assess the nature of the change to determine potential ripple effects and what needs to be considered as part of revalidation.

Documentation

It is essential that the validation program is documented and that the documentation is properly maintained. Approval and release of the process for use in routine manufacturing should be based on a review of all the validation documentation, including data from the equipment qualification, process performance qualification and product/package testing to ensure compatibility with the process.

For routine production, it is important to adequately record process details (for example, time, temperature, equipment used) and to record any changes that have occurred. A maintenance log may be useful in performing failure investigations concerning a specific manufacturing lot. Validation data (along with specific test data) may also determine expected variance in product or equipment characteristics.

Retrospective Process Validation

In some cases, a product may have been on the market without sufficient process validation. In such cases, it may be possible to validate, in some measure, the adequacy of the process by examining accumulated test data on the product and records of the manufacturing procedures used.

Retrospective validation can also be used to augment the initial prospective validation of new products or changed processes. In such cases, preliminary prospective validation should have been sufficient to warrant product marketing. As additional data is gathered on production lots, such data can be used to build confidence in the adequacy of the process. Conversely, such data may indicate a declining confidence in the process and a commensurate need for corrective changes.

Test data may be useful only if the methods and results are adequately specific. As with prospective validation, they may be insufficient to assess the process solely on the basis of lot-by-lot conformance to specifications if test results are expressed merely in terms of pass/fail. Specific results, on the other hand, can be statistically analysed and a determination made of what variance in data can be expected.

It is important to maintain records that describe the operating characteristics of the process, for example, time, temperature, humidity and equipment settings. Whenever test data is used to demonstrate conformance to specifications, it is important that the test methodology be qualified to ensure that test results are objective and accurate.

Final Report

At the conclusion of validation activities, a final report should be prepared. This report should summarise and reference all protocols and results. It should also derive conclusions regarding the validation status of the process. The final report should be reviewed and approved by the validation team and appropriate management.

Key Messages

- Process validation is a requirement of the current good manufacturing practices (GMP).
- Process performance establishes confidence that the process is effective and reproducible.
- Prospective validation, timely revalidation and documentation are the essential components of process validation.
- Quality, safety and effectiveness must be designed and built into the product. It cannot be inserted into a final product.
- Each step of the manufacturing process must be controlled to maximise the probability that the finished product meets all quality and design specifications.
- Process validation is a key element in ensuring that the quality assurance goals are met.
- A manufacturer should evaluate all the factors that affect product quality when designing and undertaking a process validation study.
- All pertinent aspects of the product that may have an impact on its safety and effectiveness should be considered for process validation.
- Process validation activity culminates with a final report referencing all the relevant protocols and conclusions to be drawn regarding the validation status of the process.

QUESTIONS

1. Define validation, prospective validation, retrospective validation, installation qualification and performance qualification.
2. Give the FDA definition of process validation.
3. What are the three principles of quality assurance achieved by process validation?
4. What are the preliminary requirements that need to be considered before the process validation activity can be initiated?
5. Enlist and explain the different elements of process validation.

17

Pollution Control and Effluent Treatment in Pharmaceutical Industries

KLK Paranjothy

Learning Objectives

At the end of this chapter, you will be able to:

- Define environmental pollution
- List some of the key environment protection legislations applicable to the pharmaceutical industry
- Describe the steps and processes involved in treating effluents using an effluent treatment plant (ETP)
- List the pollution control guidelines applicable to pharmaceutical companies

Introduction

The earth, with its rich diversity of flora and fauna, took millions of years to evolve. However, a century of industrialisation has caused irreversible damage to the environment. As this damage results in the disruption of the delicate ecological balance, it is imperative that conservation of the environment be taken seriously so that future generations can enjoy a habitable planet.

Forward-looking, progressive pharmaceutical companies, while introducing current good manufacturing practices (cGMPs) to qualify their facilities and validate their processes, should give equal importance to pollution control, effluent treatment and environment-friendly methodologies in the entire plant.

The environment comprises water, air and land and the interrelationship that exists between these three elements and human beings and other living creatures such as plants, animals, microorganisms, etc.

Environmental pollution refers to the presence in the environment of any solid, liquid or gaseous substance in such concentrations as may be, or tend to be, injurious to the environment. While the legislators at the national and international levels are trying to work towards a clearer and greener environment, the Government of India has taken steps to protect the environment through various legislations:

- The Water (Prevention and Control of Pollution) Act, 1974
- The Air (Prevention and Control of Pollution) Act, 1981
- The Environment (Protection) Act, 1986

Pharmaceutical Manufacturing Processes

Pharmaceutical plants can be categorised into those that manufacture bulk drugs or which include active pharmaceutical ingredients (APIs) and those that manufacture formulations produced as tablets, capsules, syrups, ointments, creams and injectables. To understand the treatment of the waste water that emerges from these factories, it is very important to have a thorough knowledge of their composition, which, in turn, depends on the products manufactured. The treatment control technologies will then depend on the nature of the waste water and pollutants that emerge from these factories.

Effluent Treatment Plants

Effluent treatment plants (ETPs) process the effluents produced by factories and render them harmless to human beings before releasing them into the environment. Both bulk drug units and formulation units have their own ETPs. The steps involved in the treatment of effluents from formulation units are similar to those for bulk drug plants. However, the former is simpler in structure as the effluents mostly consist of the wash water that is used to clean containers and closures in the plant. In addition, the QC and R&D labs produce small quantities of solvents and chemicals, which are also treated along with the wash water.

For a bulk drug plant, the following steps are usually applicable in the treatment of waste water effluents (Fig. 17.1):

- ***Oil and grease trap:*** The raw effluent from the process may contain oil and grease. As their presence interferes with biological action in the aeration tanks to which the effluent is directed, it is advisable that they are removed using an oil and grease trap. This trap is provided with a baffle arrangement, which enables the lighter oil particles to float on top. These oil particles can thereafter be manually removed for further disposal.
- ***Equalisation tanks:*** The effluent is collected from the end pipe and stored in the equalisation tanks where it is stirred constantly to homogenise the contents for further treatment. Sometimes, two tanks are also used for equalisation.
- ***pH correction:*** A solution of 5% sulfuric acid or 5% sodium hydroxide is used to adjust the pH level of the effluent to between 7 and 8.
- ***Nutrient addition:*** Nutrients such as di-ammonium phosphate (DAP) or urea (0.25 kg of DAP/batch) are added, mixed thoroughly and stirred well in equalisation tanks, prior to further disposal.
- ***First stage aeration:*** The aeration tank is the primary tank for biological processes—aeration induces air (oxygen) into the effluent to hasten the biodegradability of the waste. As the waste water flows into the tank, an equal quantity flows into the next unit. The tanks are operated continuously, round the clock, with heavy-duty motor pumps. The mixed liquor suspended solid (MLSS) concentration is fixed at 4000 mg/litre of the effluent.
- ***First stage settling tank:*** The overflow from the first stage aeration tank is directed to

the first stage settling tank through an inlet pipe and funnel arrangement. Here, the sludge settles at the bottom. As the tank is provided with a hopper bottom, the sludge can be easily removed from below through a pipe because of the hydraulic pressure acting on it. At periodic intervals, the sludge outlet valve has to be opened to let out the sludge into the sludge sump.

- *Second aeration tank:* The overflow from the first stage settling tank enters into the second stage aeration tank. This additional aeration further reduces the biological oxidation demand (BOD) to acceptable levels before final discharge. Here, the MLSS concentration is fixed at 2500 mg/litre.
- *Second stage settling tank:* The overflow from the second stage aeration tank is led into the second stage settling tank, wherein the sludge settles at the bottom and is periodically removed by operating the corresponding valve. The overflow from the second stage settling tank is the treated effluent.
- *Treatment by extended aeration:* Sometimes, extended aeration is done so that the microorganisms in the aeration tanks are kept alive and allowed to proliferate. This is automatically ensured when an active biological mass is continuously supplied with oxygen and food, that is, organic waste water (sewage) and, if necessary, nutrients. Oxygen supply is assured when waste water is aerated with the help of surface aerators that absorb oxygen from the atmosphere.
- *Sludge drying beds:* The sludge is diverted to sludge drying beds, where it takes 2–3 weeks or more to dry, depending on the weather and other factors. The cake can thereafter be scraped and disposed off as manure for plants.
- *Treated effluent channel:* The overflow from the second stage settling tank passes through this channel, where a flow indicator/V-notch arrangement is provided to monitor the flow in the system.
- *Treated effluent sump:* This is a reservoir for the treated effluents. After passing through the treated effluent channel, the water is collected in this sump. This treated effluent is tested for effluent parameters and allowed to pass only if the treatment is efficient.

Guidelines for the Pharmaceutical Industry

Although the prevention and control of pollution is a matter that comes within the purview of the Government of India, the state governments enforce them in their respective states. For example, in Karnataka, the Karnataka State Pollution Control Board provides the guidelines for the industries in Karnataka.

In general, pharmaceutical companies are required to follow the guidelines given below in order to prevent pollution:

- The factory should segregate the waste streams as biodegradable, non-biodegradable and inorganic based on their characteristics and adopt appropriate methods for their treatment and disposal.
- A state-of-the-art effluent treatment plant should be installed to treat the effluents to the standards stipulated. The treatment should ensure that the effluents are free from toxic and hazardous substances.
- Transport of toxic effluents from one stage to another, for the sake of disposal by dilution, is prohibited.
- The discharge of effluents into streams, rivers or surface water bodies is strictly prohibited.

Figure 17.1: Effluent treatment plant (ETP) flow chart

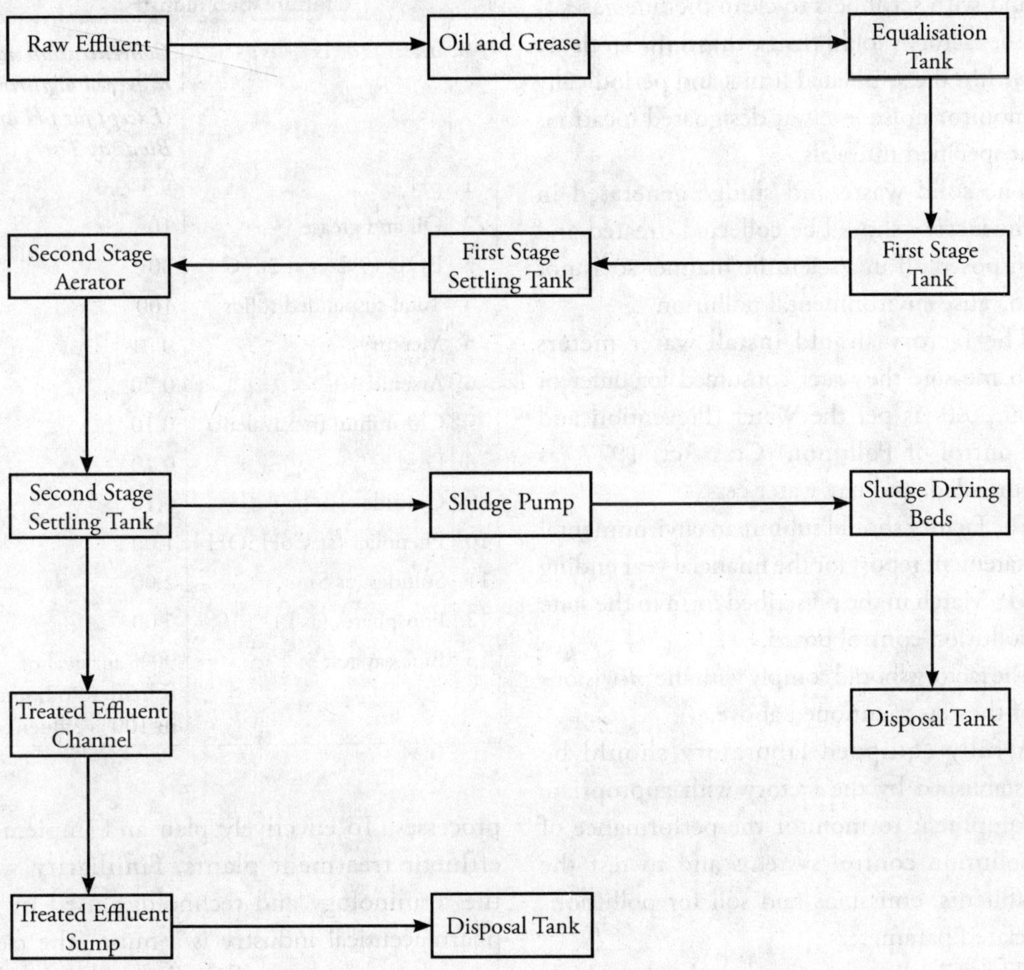

- The treated effluent conforming to stipulated standards should be used on land for agriculture. The factory should own/acquire sufficient area of land for this purpose.
- Boilers, diesel generating sets, etc. should be provided with chimneys of the prescribed height.
- The general exhaust from different sections should be collected and scrubbed to control the emissions of different gases/vapours.
- All solvent tanks located above ground level should be blanketed with nitrogen, thereby preventing any solvent evaporation and consequently minimising odourous emissions.
- A state-of-the-art incinerator should be provided wherever feasible to incinerate all combustible effluents, solids, gases, toxic

substances, etc. The incinerator should be fitted with a chimney of the prescribed height and with scrubbers to clean the flue gases.

- The factory should ensure that noise levels are within the stipulated limits and periodically monitor noise levels at designated locations at specified intervals.
- The solid waste and sludge generated in the factory should be collected, treated and disposed off in a scientific manner so as not to cause environmental pollution.
- The factory should install water meters to measure the water consumed for different purposes as per the Water (Prevention and Control of Pollution) Cess Act, 1977, as amended, and pay water cess.
- The factory should submit an environmental statement report for the financial year ending 31st March in the prescribed form to the state pollution control board.
- The factory should comply with the provisions of the acts mentioned above.
- A fully equipped laboratory should be established by the factory with appropriate equipment to monitor the performance of pollution control systems and to test the effluents, emissions and soil for pollution-related parameters.

Table 17.1 lists the standards that have been set for various effluent parameters.

Pharmaceutical manufacturing has become a complex activity involving many high technological processes. To effectively plan and implement effluent treatment plants, familiarity with the terminology and technology used in the pharmaceutical industry is a must. The trend towards environment-friendly approaches has compelled manufacturers to adhere to the stipulated standards so that the quality of life is improved.

Table 17.1: Standards for effluents discharged from pharmaceutical manufacturing and formulation industry

No.	*Tests*	*Concentration not to exceed mg/litre (Except for pH and Bioassay Test)*
1	pH	5.5–9.0
2	Oil and grease	10
3	BOD (5 days at 20 °C)	30
4	Total suspended solids	100
5	Mercury	0.01
6	Arsenic	0.20
7	Chromium (hexavalent)	0.10
8	Lead	0.10
9	Cyanide	0.10
10	Phenolics (as C6H5OH)	1.00
11	Sulfides (as S)	2.00
12	Phosphates (as P)	5.00
13	Bioassay test	90% survival of fish after 96 hours in 100% effluent

Key Messages

- Pharmaceutical companies need to give importance to pollution control, effluent treatment and environment-friendly methodologies in the entire plant.
- The Government of India has taken steps to protect the environment through various legislations.
- The industries can be classified as factories manufacturing bulk drugs (APIs) and those that manufacture formulations.
- The treatment control technologies used depend on the nature of the waste water or pollutants that emerge from the factories.
- The quality of life can be improved if pharmaceutical companies implement the guidelines specified for pollution control and effluent treatment.

Questions

1. Write briefly about the guidelines to be followed for implementing pollution control measures in pharmaceutical companies.
2. What is an effluent treatment plant (ETP)? What are the stages in the treatment of effluents? Write briefly about how formulation units treat their effluents before letting them into the fields for irrigation purposes.
3. Briefly write about the specifications and limits of the treated effluents.
4. What is the function of aerators in an ETP plant? How do they help in effluent treatment?
5. What is the function of the equalisation tank? Why is pH adjustment required in the effluent treatment process?

SECTION II: COSMETIC TECHNOLOGY

18

Raw Materials Used in Cosmetics

SHOBHA RANI R HIREMATH AND AMIT BHAT

Learning Objectives

At the end of this chapter, you will be able to:

- List the raw materials used in the formulation of cosmetics
- Explain the importance and functions of these raw materials

Introduction

A raw material is defined as a basic material from which a product is made. Various ingredients are required for the manufacture of different cosmetics that are stable and acceptable to the consumer. The various classes of raw materials used in the manufacture of cosmetic products are as follows:

- Bases
- Solvents
- Surface active agents
- Humectants
- Preservatives
- Antioxidants
- Emulsifying agents
- Emollient materials
- Colourants
- Perfumes
- Flavours
- Opacifiers
- Detergents
- Binders
- Antiseptics
- Absorbents
- Abrasives

Each of these classes is now discussed in detail.

Bases

Waxes and hydrocarbon oils are used as bases in the preparation of cosmetics. A base is an oily or waxy medium into which all the active ingredients are incorporated. Bases are required to obtain a semisolid preparation (for example, creams) or a solid preparation (for example, lipsticks) into which colours, fragrances, preservatives, etc. are blended. Waxes are esters of an alcohol other than glycerol (long chain alcohol, sterol, hydroxycarotenoids, Vitamin A) and a long chain acid (wax esters) while hydrocarbon oils are oils such as liquid paraffin which are derived from hydrocarbons. Waxes and hydrocarbon oils make good bases in cosmetics as they produce products of good consistency, stability and texture.

The commonly used waxes and hydrocarbon oils are as follows:

Paraffins: Paraffins are colourless or white, somewhat translucent, hard waxes consisting of a mixture of solid, straight-chain hydrocarbons with a melting point of 48–66 °C (120–150 °F). Paraffin wax is obtained from petroleum by dewaxing light, lubricating oil stocks. They may be hard or soft, and are used as bases for creams and other cosmetic preparations.

Beeswax: This is a raw material of natural origin. It is an important ingredient that determines the quality of the cosmetic product. Nearly 80% is composed of myricyl palmitate and the remainder is a mixture of hydrocarbons. Its colour ranges from light yellow to dark brown, and it is easily bleached either by sunlight or by chemicals.

Carnuba wax: This wax is available in several grades of which the yellow No. 1 has a melting point of 85 °C. Purified and bleached, this wax is recommended, particularly for its high melting point. It forms a film that is water repellent.

Spermacity wax: It is a pearly-white, fatty substance obtained from the cavities of the head of the cachalot (sperm) whale, *Physeter macrocephalus*, by hot water treatment.

Ozokerite: This is a mineral wax. Most ozokerites consist of hydrocarbons (C20–C32) and their melting point is about 90 °C. It is used to make lubricants, lipsticks, deodorants, etc. It is used to stiffen the cream and prevent bleeding of oils when the oil content is high.

Lanolin (wool wax): This material is secreted by the sebaceous glands of sheep and collected from crude wool by dilute alkali or detergent washing. Lanolin contains fatty esters (14–24%), sterols and triterpene alcohol esters (45–65%), free alcohols (6–20%), sterols (cholesterol, lanosterol) and terpenes (4–5%). Hydroxylated fatty acids (mainly hydroxy palmitate) are found either free or esterified. As with beeswax, lanolin has been used since ancient times in the fields of cosmetics and dermatology.

Synthetic waxes and esters: As natural waxes are versatile, they suffer inherent variability in quality and availability; therefore, cosmetic products increasingly include synthetic waxes. These waxes are made of ethylene glycol diesters or triesters of long-chain fatty acids (C18–C36). Their melting points have a range of 60–75 °C and can be used to confer rigidity to sticks and to modify the product's crystallinity. While having the structure of waxes, esters of alcohols and fatty acids either with a straight or branched chain, but shorter than for waxes, are manufactured for cosmetic applications.

Depending on the chain length and structural arrangement of the two materials from which they are manufctured, esters are tailored to display different physical properties and types of emollience. Straight chain esters, such as cetyl palmitate and cetostearyl stearate, which are solid at room temperature, are used to increase the viscosity of emulsions. Liquid branched chain esters, such as isopropyl myristate or cetostearyl ethylhexanoate, provide products with good spreading properties. Furthermore, the choice of the ester influences both the solubility and spreadability of creams and their ability to penetrate the skin.

Mineral oils: This is a hydrocarbon that is stable, inexpensive, not subject to rancidity and is odourless. Although all viscosity ranges of mineral oils are used in cosmetic creams, the most suitable ones for cleansing creams are the light- and medium-viscosity grades.

Vegetable oils: These oils are obtained from plants by placing the relevant part of the plant under pressure and extracting the oil. Vegetable oils, if used, should be in a formula in which at least half of the total oil content is replaced by a light-viscosity mineral oil. Otherwise, the cream is apt to be sticky and of poor lustre. Examples of vegetable oils include arachis oil, olive oil, coconut oil and almond oil.

Solvents

These are the vehicles used to dissolve the ingredients used in the formulation of cosmetics. The most common solvents are water, acetone esters such as amyl acetate, butyl acetate; ethyl acetate and isopropyl myristate; oils such as castor oil, arachis oil, coconut oil and olive oil; alcohols such as ethanol and butyl alcohol and glycols such as polyethylene glycol and propylene glycol.

Surface Active Agents

The term surfactant is used to refer to a surface active agent. Surfactants are usually organic compounds that are amphipathic—they contain both hydrophobic groups (their 'tails') and hydrophilic groups (their 'heads'). Therefore, they are typically sparingly soluble in both organic solvents and water. Surfactants reduce the surface tension of water by adsorbing at the air–water interface. They also reduce the interfacial tension between oil and water by adsorbing at the liquid–liquid interface.

A surfactant can be classified by the presence of charged groups at the head portion. A non-ionic surfactant has no charge groups at its head. The head of an ionic surfactant carries a net charge. If the charge is negative, the surfactant is called anionic; if the charge is positive, it is called cationic. If a surfactant contains a head with two oppositely charged groups, it is termed zwitterionic. Some commonly encountered surfactants of each type include:

Ionic

- Anionic (based on sulfate, sulfonate or carboxylate anions)
  - o Sodium lauryl sulphate, sodium dodecyl sulfate (SDS), ammonium lauryl sulfate and other alkyl sulfate salts
  - o Sodium laureth sulfate, also known as sodium lauryl ether sulfate (SLES)
  - o Alkyl benzene sulfonate
  - o Soaps or fatty acid salts (see acid salts)
- Cationic (based on quaternary ammonium cations)
  - o Cetyl trimethylammonium bromide (CTAB), hexadecyl trimethyl ammonium bromide and other alkyl trimethyl ammonium salts
  - o Cetyl pyridinium chloride
  - o Benzalkonium chloride
- Zwitterionic (amphoteric)
  - o Dodecyl betaine
  - o Dodecyl dimethylamine oxide
  - o Alkyl amino propionates

Non-ionic

- Alkyl poly (ethylene oxide)
- Fatty alcohols
  - o Cetyl alcohol
  - o Oleyl alcohol

Surfactants play an important role in the preparation of many cosmetic formulations as detergents, emulsifiers, wetting agents, foaming agents and solubilisers. Quaternary ammonium compounds such as cetalkonium chloride, myristalkonium chloride and cetrimide are used as preservatives in emulsions and gels in cosmetics.

Humectants

Humectants are hygroscopic materials that can absorb water vapour from the moist air. Humectants (or moisturisers) are important cosmetic ingredients that prevent loss of moisture, thereby enabling the skin to retain its natural moisture. Some compounds also have the ability to actively attract moisture. Humectants are key ingredients in most skin care products but are also often used in hair care products to volumise the hair by attracting moisture, which expands the hair shaft. There is a large variety of very different compounds providing moisturising effects including proteins, acids, polysaccharides and various small molecules (for example, glycerine, sorbitol, urea and aloe vera).

Humectants are added to cosmetics to:

- Keep the cosmetic product from drying out on exposure to air (particularly in oil-in-water cosmetics)
- Improve the texture and condition of the skin, a consequence of the hygroscopic properties of the film of humectant, which remains on the skin on application of the product

There are three classes of humectants:

Inorganic humectants

These are efficient but may be corrosive and incompatible with the other chemicals and are hence not used much in cosmetics. For example, calcium chloride.

Organic humectants – metallic

Both lactic acid and lactates are very effective humectants. Lactic acid and glycerin have an equal water-holding capacity, while sodium lactate has double the capacity of glycerin. Its disadvantages include incompatibility with some raw materials and a corrosive nature. However, it is widely used in skin creams, particularly because lactates occur naturally in the body and there is no risk of toxicity or dermatitis. Sodium lactate is an example of an organic metallic humectant.

Organic humectants

These are the most widely used type of humectant. They are usually polyhydric alcohols, their esters and ethers. The most common of them all are glycerol and sorbitol. The other compounds used are ethylene glycol, propylene glycol, glycerol and poly ethylene glycol.

Preservatives

The most important factor in the preparation of any cosmetic product is its safety. Cosmetic products are easily contaminated with microbes. Containing water, oils, peptides and carbohydrates, cosmetics are a very good medium for the growth of microbes. All these factors contribute to the fact that cosmetic products need very good preservation to prevent microbial growth and spoiling of the product and also infections of the skin. To control microbial growth and stabilise any cosmetic product, some form of preservative must be used. Preservatives are used in cosmetics to protect them against microbial growth, both to protect consumers and to maintain product integrity.

Preservatives are active ingredients that can prevent the growth of bacteria, fungi and viruses. They have potent antimicrobial properties that protect personal care and makeup products from spoiling, thereby substantially prolonging their shelf life.

Some ingredients used as preservatives can cause allergies in susceptible people, including dermatitis and other side effects. Therefore, preparations should include just enough of the preservative to control microbial growth.

Preservatives can be classified as follows:

- *Alcohols:* Ethyl alcohol and isopropyl alcohol (15–20%) provide a broad spectrum of activity.
- *Quaternary ammonium compounds:* Cetrimide may be used as an active agent in products such as deodorants.
- *Acids:* Benzoic, sorbic and dehydro acetic acids are active against fungi.
- *Formaldehyde:* This provides a broad spectrum of activity.
- *Parabens:* Methylparaben and propylparaben are very active against fungi and gram-positive bacteria.
- *Organic mercurials:* Phenyl mercuric salts offer a broad spectrum of activity.
- *Phenolics:* Phenol and cresol are disinfectants.

Parabens are the most widely used preservatives in cosmetic products. Chemically, parabens are esters of p-hydroxybenzoic acid. The most common parabens used in cosmetic products are methylparaben, propylparaben and butylparaben. Typically, more than one paraben is used in a product, and they are often used in combination with other types of preservatives to provide protection against a broad range of microorganisms. The use of mixtures of parabens allows the use of lower levels while increasing the preservative activity. Cosmetics that may contain parabens include makeup, moisturisers, hair care products and shaving products, among others.

The Cosmetic Ingredient Review (CIR) reviewed the safety of methylparaben, propylparaben and butylparaben in 1984 and concluded that they were safe for use in cosmetic products at levels of up to 25%. Typically, parabens are used at levels of 0.01–0.3%.

Other commonly used preservatives in skin care products and cosmetics are methyl chloroisothiazolinone and methyl isothiazolinone. They have a broad spectrum of activity and are compatible with most cosmetic formulations. Thimerosal is a preservative used in cosmetics and topical medicaments. Thimerosal is effective against both bacteria and fungi. Although it is not commonly used in skin care products, it is often found in mascara. Formaldehyde and formaldehyde-releasing preservatives are some of the most effective preservatives. They are especially effective in preventing growth of gram-negative bacteria. Formaldehyde releasers are a diverse group of chemicals that can be recognised by a small, easily detachable formaldehyde moiety. The five most commonly used chemicals in this category are quaternium-15, dimethyl-dimethyl (DMDM) hydantoin, imidazolidinyl urea, diazolidinyl urea and 2-bromo-2-nitropropane-1,3-diol (bronopol).

Quaternium-15 displays activity against bacteria, fungi and moulds, and is especially effective against the *Pseudomonas* species. Quaternium-15 is a water-soluble preservative that can preserve cosmetics for as long as two years. DMDM hydantoin, another formaldehyde releaser, is one of the most commonly used preservatives in cosmetics today. It is water soluble and is found most commonly in shampoos and cosmetics. The formaldehyde releaser imidazolidinyl urea is commonly used as a preservative in personal care products (for example, cosmetics and many over-the-counter medicaments). It is active against bacteria, especially the *Pseudomonas* species, but is less effective against fungi. To provide more broad spectrum activity against gram-positive and gram-negative bacteria and fungi, imidazolidinyl urea is often combined with another preservative such as parabens. Imidazolidinyl urea is widely used because it is not a strong irritant and is generally well tolerated. Diazolidinyl urea is quite similar to imidazolidinyl urea. 2-bromo-2-nitropropane-1,3-diol (bronopol) is a formaldehyde-releasing preservative found in cosmetics and topical medicaments. It has a broad spectrum of activity against bacteria and fungi.

Antioxidants

The ability of oxygen to oxidise fats, fatty acids and other organic materials present in cosmetics leads to complete spoilage of the same. An **antioxidant** is an ingredient that keeps oils and fats from turning rancid. The optimum concentration of antioxidants is 0.02–0.1%. The ideal antioxidant should be stable and effective over a wide pH range.

Generally, antioxidants interrupt oxidation reactions and prevent the effects of oxygen radicals (for example, peroxides), both processes known to damage the integrity and function of various natural substances. Antioxidants are useful in two ways. On the one hand they prevent degradation of natural ingredients (proteins, sugars, lipids) in the cosmetic product. On the other, they protect the skin cells from being damaged and slow down the ageing process. Antioxidants have been shown to boost the skin's radiance and minimise age spots, sun spots and fine lines. Some examples of antioxidants are given below:

Phenolic antioxidants

- Nordihydro guaiaretic acid
- Tocopherols
- Gallates: Methyl, ethyl, propyl octyl, dodecyl gallates
- Butyrated hydroxy anisole (BHA) is seldom used alone. It has synergistic effects with gallate esters.
- Butylated hydroxy-toluene (BHT) is widely used. It neutralises free oxygen radicals and prevents auto-oxidation of organic materials (prevents rancidity of fats and oils), extends the product shelf life and stabilises the colourants of cosmetics. It is added to the fat phase in a concentration of 0.01–0.1%, and is best used in combination with ethylene diamine tetra acetic acid (EDTA). It is also used to preserve and stabilise cosmetics such as creams, lotions, shampoos, makeup and sunscreen products.

Non-phenolic antioxidants

Many non-phenolic antoxidants are chelating agents.

- Lecithin is an effective synergist for many phenolic antioxidants. Many of the antioxidants used in cosmetics are derived from certain vitamins, mainly A, C and E, which form part of the body's natural defence and balance system.
- Ascorbic acid is a potent antioxidant that protects the skin from the oxidative damage caused by ultraviolet rays. It also has anti-ageing (improves skin elasticity by enhanced collagen production, avoids hyperpigmentation including age spots), anti-inflammatory and soothing effects. The antioxidant effect can be increased by

combining L-ascorbic acid with L-ascorbyl palmitate and/or Vitamin E. Used in concentrations of 0.2–4%, ascorbic acid should be formulated at a pH of <3.5 for best results. It is used in lotions, creams, sun protection and after sun products, shampoos and makeup (for example, lipsticks).

- Vitamin E (d-alpha-tocopherol) is a natural antioxidant (protects from damages by reactive oxygen radicals and UV rays) that increases the sun protection factor (SPF), moisturises and produces an anti-ageing effect, soothes and provides anti-inflammatory properties, promotes epithelisation and enzyme activity and stabilises oils and fats (prevents rancidity). Used in concentrations of 1–10%, it is used in skin care, sun protection, makeup, and hair treatment preparations.
- Coenzyme Q10 is a ubiquinone, ubidecarenone, vitamin-like molecule obtained from plant material. Q10 is encapsulated in liposomes (phospholipid nanoemulsion with Vitamin E) to maintain activity and enhance skin penetration, potency and water solubility. It can be added in concentrations of 2–6%. It is a potent antioxidant with effective anti-ageing and anti-wrinkle properties. It can be added to formulas at a concentration of 2–6%. It is added in anti-ageing and anti-wrinkle products, pre/after sun lotions, hydrating/rejuvenating and moisturising skin care products and eye wrinkle treatments.

Emulsifying Agents

Emulsifiers are used in creams and lotions to keep the water and oil phases together. Since water and oil do not mix but stay separated, an additional agent (emulsifier) is required to form a homogeneous mixture that keeps the water and oil together. There are two types of emulsifiers. Oil-in-water (o/w) emulsifiers keep oil drops packed in water, while water-in-oil (w/o) emulsifiers keep water drops packed in oil. Water-in-oil emulsifiers are used in night and sun protection creams, whereas oil-in-water emulsifiers are used more in moisturising products (for example, body lotions, day creams).

Emulsifiers can be classified as follows:

Anionic Emulsifiers: They are based on soap formulations within the emulsion from alkaline materials in the aqueous phase and fatty acids in the oil phase. Alkalis include sodium, potassium and ammonium hydroxide, diethanolamine, triethanolamine, isopropanolamine, amino glycol and borax.

The fatty acids are 'triple pressed' stearic, oleic, palmitic and lauric acids. Emollient creams based on these soap emulsifiers are always slightly alkaline (pH of about 7.5–9.5). Amine soaps comprise triethanolamine stearate oleate and triethanolamine stearate.

Alkyl sulphates are esters of fatty alcohols and sulphuric acid, for example, sodium lauryl sulphate and sodium ceto stearyl sulphate.

O/W emulsions of the anionic type may be prepared with alkali soaps and/or alkyl sulphates. W/O emulsions of the anionic type may be prepared with divalent soaps formed from calcium or magnesium hydroxide and fatty acids. A beeswax–borax combination with sodium cerotate as soap emulsifier is a classic emulsifying agent.

Cationic Emulsifiers: They are based on the quaternary ammonium, morpholinium, pyridinium and imidazolinium salts. Cetrimide is one of the commonly used emulgents.

Quaternary ammonium compounds comprise the most important group in this class. Both o/w and w/o preparations may be made with cationic emulsifiers.

Non-ionic Emulsifiers: These include the following:

- Glycol and glycerol esters
- Sorbitan esters
- Polysorbates
- Macrogol esters
- Macrogol ethers
- Poloxalkols
- Poly vinyl alcohols
- Higher fatty alcohols

Glycol and glycerol esters include glyceryl mono stearates, propylene glycol monostearate and other polyhydric alcohol esters of fatty acids.

Sorbitan esters where sorbitans are mixtures of mono or di anhydrides derived from sorbitol by the elimination of one or two molecules of water. For example, sorbitan monolaurate, mono oleate and mono stearate and mono palmitate. They produce w/o emulsions. They are known as spans and a number is used to identify the different types: Spans 20, 60 and 80 are sorbitan mono laurate, mono stearate and mono oleate, respectively.

Polysorbates are poly ethylene glycol derivatives of sorbitan esters. They are popularly known as tweens. For example, polysorbate 20/ tween 20 or polyoxyethylene sorbitan mono laurate, polysorbate 60 or polyoxyethylene sorbitan mono stearate and polysorbate 80 or polyoxyethylene sorbitan mono oleate. These yield o/w emulsions.

Macrogol esters are polymers of ethylene oxide and therefore contain many hydrophilic (oxyethylene) groups, for example, poly oxyl stearates such as poly oxyl 8 stearate/macrogol stearate 400. Macrogol esters are generally used to prepare o/w emulsions.

Macrogol ethers are condensation products of poly ethylene glycol and fatty alcohols, for example, cetyl or ceto stearyl alcohols. Ceto macrogol 1000 is the most widely used macrogol.

Poloxalkols are poly oxy ethylene derivatives of poly oxy propylene. They are used as o/w emulgents.

Poly vinyl alcohols are used in concentrations of 1% to stabilise emulsions in which the emulsifying agent is soap.

Higher fatty alcohols are w/o emulgents as well as stabilisers of o/w emulsions, for example, cetyl alcohol, stearyl alcohol ceto stearyl alcohol and oleyl alcohol.

Emollient Materials

These are substances added to cosmetic products to soften and smoothen the skin. Emollient substances can be classified into two groups: water soluble and oil soluble.

The water-soluble, polyhydric alcohols—glycerol, propylene glycol, sorbitol, polyoxyethylene sorbitol, polyethylene glycols—are considered to act as emollients by keeping the skin soft and smooth. The oil-soluble emollients comprise a long list of materials that fall into several chemical groups:

- Wax esters: Lanolin, spermaceti, beeswax
- Steroid alcohols: Cholestrol and other lanolin alcohols
- Fatty alcohols: Lauryl, cetyl, oleyl, and stearyl alcohols
- Triglyceride esters: Animal and vegetable fats and oils

- Phospholipids: Lecithin and cephalin
- Polyhydric alcohol esters: Mono- and di-fatty acid esters of ethylene glycol, diethylene glycol, polyethylene glycols, propylene glycol, glycerol, sorbitol, sorbitan (Spans, Arlacels), mannitol, pentaerythritol, polyoxyethylene sorbitol, and polyoxyethylene sorbitol (Tweens)
- Fatty alcohol ethers: Cetyl, stearyl, or oleyl ether of ethylene oxide polymers
- Alkyl fatty esters: Methyl, isopropyl, and butyl esters of fatty acids
- Hydrocarbon oils and waxes: Mineral oils, petrolatum and paraffin
- Hydrocarbon lanolin derivatives: Polyoxyethylene sorbital lanolin and polyoxyethylene lanolin derivatives
- Hydrophilic beeswax derivatives: Polyoxyethylene sorbitol beeswax
- Silicon oils

Colourants

These are substances added to cosmetic products to colour the product and/or to impart colour to the skin and/or its appendages.

Organic colours (lakes and dyes) are synthetic, chemically very complex molecules divided into various groups including indigoids, xanthenes, azos, nitros and others. Organic colours are available in a larger variety of shades than inorganic colours. Since most organic pigments are soluble (either water or oil soluble), they can be utilised not only in solid makeup products (for example, lipsticks), but also in aqueous products (for example, nail lacquer, liquid makeup). As certain organic pigments can irritate the mucous membranes, all organic pigments must be approved and certified by the Food and Drug Administration (FDA). There are three types of colour certifications:

- Food, Drug & Cosmetics (FD&C)-certifiable colours that are used in food, drugs and cosmetics
- Drug & Cosmetics (D&C)-certifiable colours that are used in drugs and cosmetics including those in contact with mucous membranes
- External D&C-certifiable colours that are used in drugs and cosmetics that do not come in contact with mucous membranes

Colourants are of three types: staining dyes, lake colours and pigments.

Staining Dyes

The most widely used staining dyes are water-soluble eosin and other halogenated derivatives of fluorescein, which are referred to collectively as 'bromoacids', a term originally applied to acid eosin and tetrabromofluorescein. Eosin, also known as D&C Red No. 21, is an insoluble orange compound that changes to an intense red salt when the pH is above 4. Similarly, D&C Red No. 27 (tetrachlorotetrabromofluorescein) produces a brilliant bluish-red stain while D&C Orange No.5 (dibromofluorescein) a yellow red, which is often used in conjunction with D&C Red No. 21 and D&C Orange No. 10 (di-iodofluorescein).

The FD&C colours are widely used in food, drug coatings and cosmetic products and are approved by the FDA. Table 18.1 lists the commonly used FD&C colours and their corresponding common names and hues.

Lake Colours

Lake colours are water insoluble and ideal for colouring products that contain fats and oils or items lacking sufficient moisture to dissolve dyes. Lake colours are a combination of dyes

Table 18.1: FD&C colours, their common names and hues		
FD&C Colors	*Common Name*	*Hue*
FD&C Yellow 5	Tartrazine	Lemon Yellow
FD&C Yellow 6	Sunset Yellow	Orange
FD&C Blue 1	Brilliant Blue FCF	Bright Blue
FD&C Blue 2	Indigotine	Royal Blue
FD&C Red 3	Erythrosine	Cherry Red
FD&C Red 40	Allura Red	Orange Red

and insoluble materials. They are dispersible in vegetable oil and can be mixed with oils, fats, etc.

Generally, lake colours are more stable than dyes. They are typically used in cosmetics. Table 18.2 lists the lakes that are used in cosmetic and personal care products such as in lotions, creams, powders, lipsticks, eyeliners and eye shadows, toothpastes and tooth powders.

The following lakes are considered to be the most useful lipstick colourants:

- Calcium lakes of D&C Reds Nos 7, 31 and 34
- Barium lakes of D&C Red No. 9 and D&C Orange No. 17
- Aluminum lakes of D&C Reds Nos 2, 3 and 19 and FD&C Yellow Nos. 5 and 6

Table 18.2: Lakes used in cosmetics
Lake Quinoline Yellow
Lake Tartrazine
Lake Sunset Yellow FCF
Lake Erythrosine
Lake Ponceau 4R
Lake Allura Red
Lake Carmoisine
Lake Amaranth
Lake Chocolate Brown HT
Lake Brilliant Blue FCF
Lake Indigo Carmine

Pigments

Both inorganic and organic pigments and metallic lakes are used to impart intensity and variation of colour. When selecting lakes, the possibility of a reaction with the base, for example, soap formation with free fatty acid, must be kept in mind.

Inorganic colours (pigments) are composed of insoluble metallic compounds that are derived from natural sources (for example, china clay, carbon deposits) or are synthesised. Based on their composition, pigments are divided into iron oxides, zinc oxides, carbon blacks, chromium oxide greens and ultramarines. As inorganic pigments are not considered to be irritants to mucous membranes, they do not require certification as organic pigments do. Because inorganic pigments are not water soluble, they are utilised preferentially in solid makeup products such as lipsticks, lip glosses, powders and eyeliners. Inorganic colours are not available in a wide range of shades and this limits their range of applications. Nevertheless, they are the colours of choice for eye shadows, mascara and other products used in close proximity to the eye.

Titanium dioxide, often used at levels of up to 4%, is the most effective white pigment for obtaining pink shades and providing opacity. Two D&C colors, D&C Red No. 36 and D&C Orange No. 17, are so insoluble in both water and oil that they may be considered as pigments, although they are not in the form of metallic lakes. Lakes of many of the D&C colours with metals such as aluminium, barium, calcium and strontium are potential pigments.

Perfumes

These are components of cosmetics that impart fragrance to the products. Most perfume oils are a blend of natural oils and specific aroma chemicals. The fragrances can be used in a wide variety of products, from bath salts and skin lotions, to face creams, body sprays, shampoos and aromatic moisturisers. The level of fragrance required varies according to the product type. A face cream may contain only 0.01% fragrance by weight, while a soap bar might contain 0.5–3.0% of the fragrance. The various ingredients that can impart fragrance are as follows:

- Cinnamic alcohol
- Cinnamic aldehyde
- Di propylene glycol
- Diethyl phthalate
- Dimethyl phthalate
- Essential oils
- Ethyl benzoate
- Hexyl cinnamic aldehyde
- Iso propyl alcohol
- Methyl benzoate
- Octanal
- Phenyl ethyl acetate
- Phenyl ethyl alcohol
- Triethyl citrate
- Amyl cinnamic aldehyde
- Benzaldehyde
- Benzophenone
- Benzyl acetate
- Benzyl benzoate
- Benzyl salicylate

Flavours

These are added to improve the value of the product in terms of consumer acceptability. Examples of flavours are mint, peppermint, citrus, spearmint, clove, wintergreen and eucalyptus.

Opacifiers

These are substances that are added to transparent or translucent cosmetic products to render them opaque. Examples of opacifiers are hydrous lanolin, titanium dioxide, zinc oxide zinc stearate and polyethylene glycol 400.

Detergents

These are used in shampoos and toothpastes to obtain detergency. A detergent should be able to bring about wetting, foaming, emulsifying and ultimately removal of dirt. Detergents are surfactants. Examples of detergents include monoethanolamine, diethyl sodium lauryl sulphosuccinate, coconut diethanolamine, sodium alkyl benzene sulphonates and sodium lauryl sarcosinate.

Binders

These are substances that are added to solid cosmetic mixtures to provide cohesion. Examples of binders are carboxymethyl cellulose, methyl cellulose, sodium alginate, tragacanth, karya gum and polyvinyl pyrrolidone.

Antiseptics

These are substances added to cosmetic products to kill the microorganisms on the skin or body. Examples of antiseptics are boric acid, camphor, chlorhexidine diacetate, menthol, methyl salicylate, clove oil, formalin and thymol.

Absorbents

Substances that are added to cosmetic products to take up water- and/or oil-soluble substances are called absorbents. Examples of absorbents are bentonite, calcium carbonate, starch (rice, wheat, corn), magnesium carbonate, magnesium oxide and kaolin.

Abrasives

Substances that are added to cosmetic products either to remove materials from various body surfaces or to aid mechanical tooth cleaning or to improve gloss are called abrasives. Some examples of abrasives are calcium carbonate, di calcium phosphate and tri calcium phosphate.

The specific uses of these raw materials in various cosmetic products will be discussed in subsequent chapters.

Key Messages

- Various raw materials are required for the manufacture of cosmetics that are stable and acceptable to the consumer. Waxes and hydrocarbons are used as bases.
- The most commonly used solvents are water, esters, oils, ethanol and butyl alcohol and glycols such as polyethylene glycol and propylene glycol.
- Surfactants have multiple functions as detergents, emulsifiers, wetting agents, foaming agents and solubilisers. Quaternary ammonium compounds are used as preservatives in emulsions and gels are used in cosmetics.
- Humectants (or moisturisers) are important cosmetic ingredients that prevent loss of moisture, thereby enabling the skin to retain its natural moisture.
- As cosmetic products contain water, oils, peptides and carbohydrates, they are a very good medium for the growth of microbes and hence preservatives are needed.
- As oxygen can oxidise fats, fatty acids and other organic materials present in cosmetics leading to rancidity, antioxidants are added in cosmetic formulations.
- Emulsifiers are important ingredients used in creams and lotions to keep the water and oil phases together. These are substances added to cosmetic products to soften and smoothen the skin.
- Colourants are used to colour cosmetic preparations. They are of three types: staining dyes, lake colours and pigments.
- Perfumes are an important class of ingredients that impart fragrance to products.
- The other ingredients used in cosmetics are flavours, detergents, opacifiers, binders, antiseptics, absorbents and abrasives.

QUESTIONS

1. Enumerate the raw materials used in the preparation of cosmetics with a few examples of each.
2. Write short notes on colourants.
3. Differentiate between dyes and lakes.
4. What are the types of bases used in cosmetics?

19

Cosmeceuticals

SHOBHA RANI R HIREMATH

Learning Objectives

At the end of this chapter, you will be able to:

- Define cosmeceuticals and explain how they are different from cosmetics
- Narrate the history of cosmeceuticals
- List the categories of products included under cosmeceuticals
- Describe the various ingredients used in cosmeceuticals
- Describe the recent developments in cosmeceuticals

Introduction

Historically, 'drugs' have been defined as compounds used in the treatment and prevention of disease, or are intended to affect a physiological structure or function of the body. In contrast, 'cosmetics' have been thought of as inert substances that cleanse or enhance the appearance of the skin without any therapeutic benefit.

The term 'cosmeceuticals' is derived from a combination of 'cosmetics' and 'pharmaceuticals'. Cosmeceuticals can be defined as 'a category of cosmetic products that produce or claim to produce therapeutic benefits'.

They are topical cosmetics, pharmaceutical hybrids intended to enhance the health and beauty of the skin. For example, a shampoo is a cosmetic because its intended use is to cleanse the hair. An anti-dandruff treatment is a drug because its intended use is to treat dandruff. Consequently, an anti-dandruff shampoo is both a cosmetic and a drug. Among other cosmetic/drug combinations are toothpastes that contain fluoride, deodorants that are also antiperspirants and moisturisers and sunscreen preparations. Such products must comply with the requirements of both cosmetics and drugs.

This supplement category was created primarily to classify products that were neither food nor drugs, but which had an effect on the structure/function of the body nonetheless.

Cosmeceuticals are best described as 'functional ingredients'. These products have an effect on the body and by definition cannot be 'cosmetics'. However, they are neither formulated nor regulated as 'over-the-counter (OTC)/drug' products. Some cosmeceuticals are naturally derived while others are synthetic.

Natural cosmeceuticals, if they are to be considered truly natural, must be, as much as possible, free from synthetic ingredients such as fragrances, preservatives, additives, surfactants and emulsifiers, as well as artificial colours and sweeteners, irradiation and animal testing. They must also be minimally processed. The claims made about drugs are subject to high scrutiny by the Food and Drug Administration (FDA) review and approval process. However, cosmetics are not subject to mandatory FDA review. In general, cosmetics and/or their ingredients are tested for safety, but evidence is seldom given that their 'beneficial' claims are truthful. Although a lot of benefits are claimed, because they have not been scrutinised and approved by the FDA, the manufacturers are prohibited from making definitive statements. Some experts are calling for increased regulation of cosmeceuticals that would require proof of safety, which is not mandatory for cosmetics. For now, relatively few components of cosmetic skin care products have been proven to be active in the concentrations at which they are presently used. Regulation of cosmeceuticals has not been harmonised among the USA, Europe, Asia and other regions.

While the Food, Drug and Cosmetic Act does not recognise the term cosmeceuticals, the cosmetics industry has begun to use this word to refer to cosmetic products that have drug-like benefits. In general, vitamins, herbs, various oils and botanical extracts may be used in cosmeceuticals. Cosmeceuticals include:

- Beauty supplements: Dietary supplements such as Vitamins A and E enhance beauty by stopping the free radical chain reaction, thereby preventing faster ageing of the skin.
- Active cosmetics: Products that contain 'active' ingredients that may produce desirable health benefits.
- Performance/Functional cosmetics: Products that imply that they perform some useful task or function beyond the merely cosmetic.
- Phytocosmetics: Products that contain 'herbal' ingredients.
- Dermaceuticals/Skinceuticals: Cosmetics pertaining to skin care.
- Cosmetic drugs: Products that the FDA defines as combinations of cosmetics and drugs. For example, flouride toothpaste and anti-dandruff shampoos.
- Therapeutic cosmetics: Products that may produce therapeutic benefits; for example, wound healing.

History of Cosmeceuticals

The term cosmeceutical was first coined by the American dermatologist Albert Kligman in the late 1970s.The Egyptians were the first to recognise the health-giving properties of cosmetics. The earliest reported cosmeceutical (1600 BC) included a formulation using honey and milk that claimed to help cure skin diseases. The role of cosmetics as a positive healing aid was ignored until its revival in the late 1970s and early '80s. During this period, Kligman developed formulations to improve the appearance of wrinkled skin using retinoic acid. Kligman said that novel cosmetic technology would make it possible to incorporate an unlimited number of active substances from natural sources in skin care products. This includes vitamins, antioxidants, anti-inflammatories, mood-influencing fragrances and hormones.

The cosmetics industry is generally divided into the following subsectors:

- Skin Care – including sun protection

- Hair Care – including shampoos and conditioners
- Body Care – including deodorants and toiletries
- Decorative – including nail care, eye care and colour cosmetics

The majority of cosmeceuticals have been developed for skin care, with special emphasis on the subcategory of sun protection and anti-wrinkle treatments. The next biggest category is hair care. Cosmeceutical body care formulations have been limited, and cosmeceuticals are almost by definition, not found in the decorative cosmetics segment.

Cosmeceutical Agents

Retinoids

Retinoids are possibly the most prevalent cosmeceuticals in the market. Retinoids are Vitamin A derivatives present in all living organisms either as preformed Vitamin A or as carotenoids. Vitamin A (retinol) is the prototype of all other retinoids and is necessary for proper growth, bone development and integrity of mucosal and epithelial surfaces. In Vitamin A deficiency, the eyes and the skin are severely affected. The conjunctiva and the cornea develop metaplasia and keratinisation, leading to night blindness. The skin develops follicular hyperkeratosis or phrynoderma. The hyperkeratotic follicular papules are usually clustered around bony prominences such as the elbows and the knees, but in severe deficiency, the papules can be found throughout the skin surface.

Early civilisations recognised the benefits of Vitamin A in treating and healing night blindness with diets rich in liver. In the 1930s, the clinical manifestations of Vitamin A deficiency were recognised, and the idea of using Vitamin A in the treatment of skin diseases was initiated. The advent of synthetic analogs of Vitamin A in the 1970s brought new interest in their biological activity, especially on the skin. Since then, Vitamin A and its derivatives have been used in the treatment of many skin disorders such as ichthyosis, acne and psoriasis. A great deal of research has concentrated on its use as an anti-ageing compound as well as for other cutaneous disorders; therefore, today, Vitamin A is recognised as comprising a magnitude of biological effects far beyond those on the cornea.

Vitamin A and its derivatives have two main functions: they act as antioxidants and they activate specific genes and proteins. As antioxidants, they protect cells from oxidative damage by scavenging peroxyl radicals, quenching singlet oxygen and using triplet-state sensitisers. Vitamin A also exerts a hormone-like effect on the skin, activating specific genes through nuclear receptors.

Structural changes underlying the cosmetic benefits of Vitamin A include correction of epidermal atrophy, deposition of new collagen, generation of new vessels and enhancement of mitogenesis. This enhanced mitogenesis promotes the shedding of melanin-laden keratinocytes, resulting in bleaching and subsequent depigmentation. The ability of topical tretinoin to improve the appearance of aged and photo-damaged skin by reducing wrinkles, decreasing laxity, bleaching hyperpigmented spots and bringing about a smoother surface have been well documented. Further remedial qualities of retinoids remain to be elucidated.

Retinoic acid (tretinoin) is a naturally occurring form of Vitamin A that may be used topically for the treatment of mild-to-moderate acne and sun-damaged (photo-aged) skin. It is also used for other skin conditions. It is available in several prescription medications but is not allowed in cosmetics. Retinol is chemically similar to tretinoin, but is less effective (and less irritating) and is allowed in cosmetic products. After topical administration, tretinoin appears to increase the rate of cell division and turnover. The number of cell layers in the outer portion of the skin decreases. When pimples are present, they are more rapidly resolved. Topical tretinoin is effective in reducing fine wrinkling, mottled hyperpigmentation and roughness associated with overexposure to the sun. The results of treatment are not immediate. Darkened spots usually begin to fade at 6–8 weeks, and there is a decrease in fine lines and wrinkles in 3–6 months. Discontinuation of treatment usually results in loss of tretinoin's effects. Exposure to the sun's ultraviolet (UV) radiation increases the amount of several protease enzymes in the skin that cause the degradation of collagen. Pretreatment of the skin with tretinoin decreases the activity of these enzymes. Products that cause drying of the skin, such as alcohol and benzoyl peroxide used to treat acne, or salicylic, lactic acid or buffing pads used for skin exfoliation increase the effects of tretinoin and can cause severe irritation. These products should not be used simultaneously.

Hydroxy Acids

Hydroxy acids are the second most commonly available cosmeceutical and, in low concentrations, found in mass-marketed cosmetic formulations. Hydroxy acids are organic carboxylic acids classified into alpha hydroxy acids (AHAs) and beta hydroxy acids (BHAs) according to their molecular structure.

Alpha hydroxy acids (AHAs)

AHAs range from simple aliphatic compounds to complex molecules. Many are derived from natural sources and are often referred to as fruit acids. The different AHAs include glycolic acid, lactic acid, citric acid, mandelic acid, malic acid and tartaric acid. AHAs have been shown to decrease the signs of ageing. The skin appears smoother and more uniform. The likely cause of these changes is the property of AHAs to enhance epidermal shedding. Some claim that AHAs increase the synthesis of glyco-saminoglycans (GAGs), improve the quality of elastic fibres and increase the density of collagen. Scientific evidence to support such claims is still incomplete and controversial. Although some researchers have concluded that AHAs cause increased skin thickness, improvement in skin elasticity and increased collagen content, other researchers are concerned about the end result of constant low-grade irritation and the potential to produce reactive free radicals that are capable of damaging collagen and elastic fibres. The most common AHAs used in cosmeceutical formulations are glycolic acid and lactic acid. They weaken the linkage of cells in the outer layers of dry skin, allowing normal shedding to occur. They also increase the flexibility of the outer layer of the skin and the barrier function.At high concentrations, irritation and peeling occur as a result of damage or death of certain skin cells. Under medical supervision, a certain degree of pain and peeling may be tolerated to receive the beneficial treatment of certain skin lesions.

Beta hydroxy acids (BHAs)

BHAs are aromatic compounds. Salicylic acid is the reference BHA; it has dermolytic properties and helps in various xerotic and ichthyotic disorders. Other BHAs include 2-hydroxy-5-octanoyl benzoic acid, also known as beta-lipohydroxyacid (B-LHA), and tropic acid. BHAs have been used for many years in the treatment of dry, scaly skin and warts (at high concentrations). They appear to weaken the linkage of cells in the outer layers of dry skin, allowing the normal shedding process to occur. The effects are less potent than those of AHAs.

Despite their popularity, the exact mechanism of action of hydroxy acids remains unknown and is largely controversial; however, at least one aspect of their biological activities may be attributed to the inherent acid strength of the compounds. Studies show that AHAs may increase sensitivity to UV radiation and that application of sunscreen may be advisable when these products are used.

Minoxidil

It was originally used to treat high blood pressure, but the drug was also found to stimulate hair growth. Minoxidil's once undesirable side effect—hair re-growth—has been exploited in hair care products and is available as a generic OTC medication.

Antioxidants

The skin is exposed to a constant barrage of endogenous and exogenous damaging agents. Agents such as UV radiation, drugs, air pollutants and heat/cold continually challenge the protective character of the skin. In addition to these external insults, the skin also has to cope with endogenous mitogens, most importantly, reactive oxygen species (ROS) and other free radicals. These species are continuously produced during physiological cellular metabolism. To counteract the harmful effects of ROS, the skin is equipped with an antioxidant system to maintain the equilibrium between the pro-oxidants, or damaging agents, and the antioxidants, or protective agents; these antioxidants intervene at different levels in the protective process.

The key antioxidants are now discussed in detail.

Vitamin C

Vitamin C (L-ascorbic acid) is essential for life. The functions of Vitamin C are numerous. It is necessary for the hydroxylation of procollagen, proline and lysine. Deficiency of Vitamin C results in purpura, keratotic follicles and bleeding gums. Vitamin C is a water-soluble antioxidant that clenches free radicals and regenerates Vitamin E. It is an important regulator of collagen expression, stimulating its synthesis. Studies have shown that Vitamin C levels in the skin are severely depleted after UV irradiation and that, histologically, Vitamin C improves and normalises the changes caused by photo damage. Thus far, however, studies on Vitamin C have been few, and information about its in vivo effects is lacking.

Vitamin C has been used effectively to stimulate collagen repair, thus diminishing some of the effects of photo-ageing on the skin. However, it is easily degraded by heat and light, which, along with its high acidity, presents certain challenges for use in a multipurpose skin care formulation. A recently introduced synthetic collagen fraction offers greater stability and compatibility, along with improved efficacy.

Vitamin E

Vitamin E is well-known for its antioxidant effects. Vitamin E (alpha-tocopherol) is a major lipophilic antioxidant in plasma, membranes and tissues. It comprises eight naturally occurring molecules (4 tocopherols and 4 tocotrienols). Its major role is generally considered to be the arrest of chain propagation in lipid peroxidation by scavenging lipid peroxyl radicals, thereby protecting the cell membrane from destruction. Vitamin E topically applied before UV radiation has been shown to reduce erythema, edema, sunburnt cells, immunosuppression caused by sunlight and DNA adduct formation.

Hydroquinone (HQ)

It is used as a reducing agent, an antioxidant, a polymerisation inhibitor and a chemical intermediate. HQ is used in OTC drugs as an ingredient in skin lighteners, and it is a natural ingredient in many plant-derived products, including vegetables, fruits, grains, coffee, tea, beer and wine. The skin pigment lightening properties of HQ appear to be caused by the inhibition of melanocyte tyrosinase.

Adverse effects that are associated with the OTC use of HQ in FDA-regulated products have been limited to a small number of cases of exogenous ochronosis (the potential to cause permanent darkening of certain areas of the skin) though higher incidences of this disorder have been reported with the inappropriate use of unregulated OTC products that contain higher concentrations of HQ. The most serious human health effect related to HQ is pigmentation of the eye and, in a small number of cases, permanent corneal damage. It is reported to have a mutagenic effect.

Kinetin

Kinetin (in Kinerase™), a hormone-like growth factor obtained from plants and yeast, acts as an antioxidant and free radical scavenger. There is evidence that Kinerase's active ingredient kinetin can influence cell growth and maturation in plant and non-plant tissues and may slow down the ageing process. Little is known about its effects on the ageing of human skin.

Grape Seed Extract

This contains powerful antioxidants known as oligomeric proanthocyanidins (OPCs) or procyanidins. Pycnogenol from pinebark extract and constituents of wine, cranberries, green and black teas, black currant, onions and hawthorn are similar to grape seed extract in their active ingredients and medicinal uses. OPCs are reported to possess a broad spectrum of biological, pharmacological and therapeutic activities against free radicals and oxidative stress. In Europe, preparations containing OPCs have been used in the treatment of many conditions including edema associated with surgery, atherosclerosis (hardening of the arteries) and vascular insufficiency, but these effects are controversial and further research is needed for verification.

Topically, grape seed extract has been used in cosmetic preparations for their purported anti-ageing effects. Several European studies have indicated that OPCs inhibit enzymes such as collagenase, elastase and hyaluronidase that are involved in the breakdown of structural components of the skin. These effects need to be proven by clinical trials.

Coenzyme Q10

Coenzyme Q10 (ubiquinone) is a benzoquinone compound synthesised by human and animal tissues. CoQ is found in the membranes of the endoplasmic reticulum, peroxisomes, lysosomes, vesicles and notably the inner membrane of the mitochondrion where it is an important part of the electron transport chain. Because of its ability to transfer electrons, it acts as an antioxidant. Coenzyme Q has become a valued dietary supplement.

Although topical application of ubiquinone may retard some of the processes associated with photo-ageing, clinical experiments are required to prove this effect.

The demand for cosmeceuticals in the US is expected to grow. Skin care products are likely to remain the dominant segment. Some of the popular products include age-defying, sunless tanning, skin depigmenting and acne treatments, sun protection, hair growth products, anti-dandruff treatment, collagen injection and implants, teeth whiteners and lip care.

Panthenol

Panthenol, the alcohol analog of Vitamin B5, is a water-soluble humectant commonly found in various commercial skin creams, lipsticks, lotions and hair preparations. It is stable in the presence of oxygen and light but unstable in the presence of acids, bases and high temperatures. Panthenol is converted in the skin to pantothenic acid, which is an important component of coenzyme A and essential for normal cellular metabolism.

Lipoic Acid

This is a unique free radical protector. It is fat and water soluble. Once lipoic acid crosses the cell membrane, it is broken down into dihydrofolic acid, which is also an antioxidant. Alpha lipoic acid also recycles other key antioxidants such as Vitamin C, Vitamin E and glutathione.

Niacinamide

Niacinamide (nicotinamide) is a basic amide that is a member of the Vitamin B complex. It is used in the prophylaxis and treatment of pellagra. Niacinamide does not induce peripheral flush that accompanies therapy with nicotinic acid. It is one of the newest vitamins in the marketplace. In vitro studies have shown anti-tumour activity on keratinocytes and suppression of UV-B photocarcinogenesis. The main reason for its surge in popularity is its stability. Niacinamide is stable in the presence of oxygen, acids and high temperatures, and it is inexpensive to formulate. Most of its known effects are the result of increased epidermal turnover and exfoliation.

Dimethylaminoethanol (DMAE)

Topical preparations containing DMAE have been touted for their ability to improve skin firmness and to lift sagging skin. DMAE has been used as a dietary supplement and is associated with improved mental function and enhanced physical performance due in part to its ability to increase the neurotransmitter responsible for stimulating muscles. DMAE is able to diminish the cross-linking of proteins that occurs during ageing, probably acting as a free radical scavenger. It also increases the activity of these enzymes in a dose-dependent manner only in the particulate fractions glucose-6-phosphate dehydrogenase and 6-phosphogluconate dehydrogenase.

Melatonin

Melatonin, a hormone secreted by the pineal gland, is known to have antimutagenic and oncostatic actions. This beneficial action has been explained in terms of its ability to scavenge free radicals and to augment the activities of antioxidant enzymes. It has been shown to suppress UV radiation–induced erythema.

Catalase

Catalase, an enzyme present in almost all cells of the human body, catalyses the decomposition of hydrogen peroxide to water and oxygen. High amounts of this enzyme in the skin can impart antioxidative activity.

Glutathione

Glutathione is a tripeptide of glutamic acid, cysteine and glycine. It is found in all active animal tissues. It is fundamentally an antioxidant, and significantly decreased amounts of glutathione are found after UV exposure.

Superoxide Dismutase (SOD)

This is an enzyme that destroys superoxide (a highly ROS). SOD is a large molecule and has difficulty penetrating deep into the skin. In theory, once in the lower epidermis and dermis, SOD should decrease UV erythema and damage and act as an excellent antioxidant.

Glucopyranosides

Resveratrol and polydatins are glucopyranosides found in many fruits and vegetables, the highest concentrations being found in grape skins, which synthesise these compounds in response to exposure to UV-A and UV-B and fungal pathogens. The biological activities of these glucopyranosides include potent free radical scavenging, with cardioprotection, neuroprotection and inhibition of lipid peroxidation similar to that seen with Vitamins C and E.

Polyphenols

Polyphenolic compounds (for example, catechins, flavonols, thioflavins and thearubigins), also known as epicatechins, are antioxidant by nature. These compounds, when tested against human keratinocyte cells stressed by UV-B irradiation showed high antioxidative properties. Many laboratories have shown that topical treatment or oral consumption of polyphenols inhibits chemical or UV radiation–induced skin tumourigenesis in different animal models. It possesses anti-inflammatory activity. One of the major and most chemopreventive constituents responsible for the biochemical or pharmacological effects is epigallocatechin-3-gallate (EGCG), found in green tea. Genistein, the isoflavone found in soybeans, and pycnogenol, an extract of the bark of French maritime pine (Pinus pinaster), have been shown to significantly prolong tumour latency to decrease tumour multiplicity with the potent ability to scavenge free radicals.

Cysteine

Several studies have shown that cysteine derivatives can protect against the negative effects of UV exposure. In particular, N-acetylcysteine (NAC) has been proved to be an effective protector against UV-B–induced immunosuppression, to modulate the expression of some oncogenes and tumour suppressor genes, and to increase the amounts of intracellular glutathione. Glutathione is known to be critical in protecting the body's cells against oxidative stress; however, taking glutathione itself does not raise the levels of glutathione in the blood as effectively as taking its precursor NAC. Current research places NAC at the centre of the measures used to combat the ageing process.

Allantoin

Allantoin promotes cell proliferation, thereby aiding in the healing process. Allantoin has long been known to enhance the effectiveness and desirability of cosmetic creams and lotions by its action as a skin protectant. It has been incorporated into shampoos, lipsticks, shaving creams, suntanning products, bath foams, hair gels, baby powders and various aerosol preparations. It has also been used in topical pharmaceutical markets. Most recently, allantoin has been used in various dental preparations such as toothpastes and mouthwashes. Allantoin has been called a cell proliferant, an epithelisation stimulant and a chemical debrider. It is said to clean away necrotic tissue, hastening the growth of new healthy tissue.

Furfuryladenine

Furfuryladenine (Kinerase) is a natural plant growth factor that retards the ageing process in plants. Cut leaves dipped in a solution that contains furfuryladenine remain green, while untreated leaves turn brown. It is marketed as the natural evolution of anti-ageing treatment with similar effects in vitro on human skin cells, thereby helping to slow and reverse alterations that naturally occur in the cell-ageing process.

Uric Acid

In the past, uric acid was generally looked upon merely as an end product of purine metabolism. More recently, however, uric acid has been recognised as an important biological antioxidant. Scientific studies have demonstrated that uric acid is a potent physiological antioxidant, playing a major role in both extracellular and intracellular defense mechanisms. Although the precise biochemical mechanism has not been completely determined, uric acid appears to have a sparing action in plasma ascorbate, probably by complexing transition metals such as iron and copper.

Carnosine

Carnosine (beta-alanyl-L-histidine) is a physiological dipeptide that can rejuvenate senescent cultured human fibroblasts. It has been shown to be involved in antioxidant, free radical and metal ion–scavenging activities.

Moisturisers

The cutaneous permeability barrier is localised in the stratum corneum interstices and is mediated by the lamellar bilayers enriched in cholesterol, free fatty acids and ceramides. Formulations containing skin-identical lipids have been suggested to facilitate a cascade of physiological events in keratinocytes, normalising damaged skin. When applied to the skin for an extended period, water can cause the excretion of cytokines. These proinflammatory molecules induce edema, vasodilation and frank inflammation; therefore, water alone may alter both the structure and the function of the skin in some conditions. By the same token, moisturisers that make the stratum corneum softer and more pliant by increasing its hydration could be considered as cosmeceuticals.

Depigmenting Agents

Hyperpigmentation is the result of an increased amount of melanin in the epidermis, the dermis or both. This pigmentary change can be divided into two pathophysiological processes: melanocytosis (increased number of melanocytes) and melanosis (increased amount of melanin). Depigmenting agents work best when melanosis or melanocytosis is restricted to the epidermis. Other methods of depigmentation are chemical peels. Depigmenting agents can be divided into several groups:

Phenolic compounds include the following:

- Hydroquinone
- Monobenzylether of hydroquinone
- 4-methoxyphenol
- 4-isopropylcatechol

- 4-hydroxyanisol
- *N*-acetyl-4-S-cysteaminylphenol

Non-phenolic compounds include the following:

- Corticosteroids
- Tretinoin
- Azelaic acid
- *N*-acetylcystein (NAC)
- L-ascorbyl-2-phosphate
- Kojic acid

Combination formulas include the following:

- Kligman's formula
- Pathak's formula
- Westerhof's formula

Some of these depigmenting agents are now discussed in detail.

N-acetyl-4-S-cysteaminylphenol

A phenolic thioether, N-acetyl-4-S-cysteaminylphenol is a new type of depigmenting agent. It claims to be more stable and less irritating to the skin than HQ and is specific to melanin-synthesising cells. A monophenol compound, tert-butyl-4-hydroxyanisol (mequinol), has been studied in the treatment of solar lentigines and related hyperpigmented lesions. The topical combination product containing 2% 4-hydroxyanisole/0.01% tretinoin solution (Solage) is well tolerated and superior to either active component.

Kojic acid (5-hydroxy-2-[hydroxymethyl]-4-pyrone)

A fungal metabolic product, Kojic acid has been increasingly used as a skin depigmenting agent in skin care products marketed in Japan since 1988. Several studies have shown Kojic acid to inhibit tyrosinase activity; this finding has been attributed to its ability to chelate the copper required by tyrosinase.

Arbutin

Arbutin, or hydroquinone-beta-D-glucopyranoside, consists of HQ bound to glucose; arbutin is a naturally occurring beta-D-glucopyranoside derivative of HQ. It can inhibit melanogenesis by affecting the activity of tyrosinase rather than by killing melanocytes and decreasing the synthesis of melanin. Arbutin executes its activity by mimicking the amino acid tyrosine, the usual substrate of tyrosinase.

Azelaic acid (AZA)

This is a dicarboxylic acid originally isolated from Plasmodium ovale. It has been reported to have depigmenting effects, while showing no significant activity on normal skin. AZA is believed to selectively inhibit tyrosinase in hyperactive melanocytes.

Paper-mulberry compound

The compound 5-(3-2,4-[dihydroxy phenyl]propyl)-3,4-bis (3-methyl-2-butenyl)-1,2-benzenediol obtained from the paper-mulberry root bark has been shown to inhibit mushroom tyrosinase, scavenge free radicals and depigment UV-induced hyperpigmentation in guinea pigs. Studies in humans show no irritation or sensitisation.

Tretinoin

This has been successful in the treatment of epidermal pigmentation. Topical 0.1% tretinoin produces a clinical improvement of melasma and lentigines. The proposed mechanism of tretinoin in lightening the skin is by inhibiting melanogenesis, though this is still poorly understood. When combined with HQ, tretinoin has a synergistic effect.

Chemical peeling agents

Chemical peeling has become an established

technique in treating cutaneous hyperpigmentation. Chemical peeling agents include glycolic acid, resorcinol and salicylic acid.

Chemical compounds

Kligman's formula consists of 5% hydroquinone (HQ), 0.1% tretinoin and 0.1% dexamethasone in hydrophilic ointment. Pathak's formula consists of 2% HQ and 0.05-0.1% tretinoin. Westerhof's formula consists of 4.7% N-acetylcysteine (NAC), 2% HQ and 0.1% triamcinolonacetonide.

Other Cosmeceuticals

Botanicals

Because of increased awareness of the environmental damage caused by industrialisation, a new trend has emerged—one that advocates the use of products with natural ingredients. No other ingredient can serve this purpose as well as botanicals. Botanicals are now part of every product in the market, from cosmetics to soft drinks. Avocado, banana, lemon and other botanicals are listed on thousands of labels. They exert their purported effects through the mechanisms of antioxidants, AHAs, BHAs and other properties that are as yet unclear.

Some examples of botanicals include **chamomile**, which inhibits the release of histamine and has anti-inflammatory properties, and **ginseng**, which stimulates the biosynthesis of proteins, RNA and lipids. **Ginkgo biloba** extract was found to locally induce SOD and to catalase enzyme activity in the epidermis after topical application, as well as to systemically increase the activity of both enzymes in the liver, heart and kidneys. **Curcumin** found in curry produces anti-inflammatory activity by inhibiting leukotriene formation and platelet aggregation and stabilising neutrophilic lysosomal membranes. **Glycyrrhizin** found in licorice roots inhibits the proinflammatory activities of prostaglandins and leukotrienes. **Capsaicin** inhibits substance P, a peptide transmitter of the inflammatory process. **Aloe vera** has been shown to accelerate wound healing and to protect and soothe the skin. Some of the other important botanicals are discussed below.

Cassia angustifolia: Contains polysaccharides of the cassia seed that have been extracted and purified. The extract includes 64% mannose, 27% galactose, 2% glucose, 1% xylose and 1% arabinose. The cosmetic properties of this extract perform the following functions:

- Repair rough and dry skin
- Enable the formation of films
- Provide sustained moisturising
- Improve capacity of stratum corneum to hold water

Centella asiatica: It has been widely used in Ayurvedic medicine. It is a new entrant in the cosmetics market. The asiaticosides and triterpenes extracted from the plant have modulating effects on the development and metabolism of connective tissue. It has been found that in poor connective tissue conditions, the triterpenes are able to renew the collagen, in quantity and quality, and restore tissue firmness and skin elasticity, thereby improving skin appearance and comfort. Centella extract (40% standardised asiaticoside) is taken either in the form of 10 mg capsules, 3–9 times a day, or as a topical application with cream at 2–4%.

Echium Oil: This oil contains significant amounts of gamma-linolenic acid, ranging 1.77–5.02% of total seed weight depending on the variety. It also contains 2–12% stearidonic acid. Echium oil has recently been considered an interesting therapeutic cosmetic raw material in sun protection and anti-wrinkle products. The anti-inflammatory properties of echium lipids have been shown to be effective in after-care products following exposure to the sun. Studies on the anti-wrinkle properties have shown that echium oil is effective in reducing skin roughness.

Tamarind: More recently, the polysaccharides of tamarind have been extracted for use in cosmetic products. They are recommended for the stimulation of skin repair, environmental skin protection and for premature ageing. A tri-dimensional polysaccharide from tamarind, known as Xyloglucan, includes 49% glucose, 31% xylose and 18% galactose. The product has been shown to have both immunostimulating effect and anti–free radical activity.

Tea: The growth in green tea consumption as a dietary supplement and functional beverage has been enormous. Green tea extracts are now amongst the fastest growing herbal products. The use of tea extracts in cosmetics has been a more recent phenomenon, although the high level of complex polyphenolic compounds in tea provides the same protective effect for the skin as for internal organs. Further study is being undertaken to assess the benefit of green tea extract to treat or prevent body odour or acne produced by skin bacteria. More than 19% of the content of green tea extract is catechins, which are known to have effective free radical scavenging properties. White tea is claimed to possess far higher levels of polyphenols than green tea, mainly because only the tiny young buds at the very tip of the plant are picked.

Zinc pyrithione (ZPT): This was the first scientifically based organic therapeutic agent to offer alleviation from dandruff. Dandruff is a scalp disorder which manifests itself as the detachment of flakes of scalp skin. Another contemporary of ZPT is the anti-dandruff agent called piroctone olamine (PO).

Red Raspberry: Red raspberries have gained prominence recently for their use in cosmeceutical applications. Ketones present in the raspberry are found to have weight-lowering properties. The fruit extract contains anthocyanin pigments and polyphenolic compounds. Anthocyanins act as antoxidants, providing many health benefits such as retarding the effects of ageing.

Glycosaminoglycans: Hyaluronic acid (HA), or hyaluronan, is the prototype of all other GAGs. Studies have demonstrated that decreased amounts are present in aged skin and that topically applied HA accelerates wound repair. Other studies have noted epidermal regeneration after the application of low molecular weight HA.

Anticellulites

Lipolysis is mediated, in part, by beta-adrenergic receptors, which induce fat breakdown, and alpha2-adrenergic receptors, which inhibit fat breakdown. Agents that bind to these receptors may hypothetically have a therapeutic effect on cellulite. Beta-adrenergic stimulators include theobromine, theophylline, aminophylline, caffeine, isopropylarterenol hydrochloride and epinephrine. Alpha2-adrenergic inhibitors include yohimbine, piperoxan, phentolamine and dihydroergotamine.

Enzymes

Papain: Papain, an enzyme found in the papaya fruit, chemically digests intercellular bonds. It has been studied in the treatment of hypertrophic scars and can be used to exfoliate keratotic skin.

Deoxyribonucleic acid (DNA) repair enzymes: UV-B radiation–induced cyclobutane pyrimidine dimers in the DNA of epidermal cells are detrimental to human health because they cause mutations and immunosuppressive effects that contribute to photocarcinogenesis. Lotions containing bacteria-derived DNA repair enzymes and photolyase-containing liposomes have been shown to reduce the incidence of cancerous and precancerous lesions. When the bacterial DNA repair enzyme T4 endonuclease V is intracellularly delivered, it increases the rate of repair of sunlight-induced DNA damage in human cells. The topical application of a DNA repair enzyme to sun-damaged skin lowered the rate of development of actinic keratoses and basal cell epitheliomas during a year of treatment.

Growth Factors

Epidermal growth factor (EGF): This is found in plasma, sweat, urine, saliva and semen. When the endothelial differentiation gene (EDG) is bound to the epidermal growth factor receptor (EGFR), it stimulates epidermal growth and differentiation. It has been used in the treatment of burns and excision wounds, where it accelerates re-epithelisation.

Transforming growth factor (TGF): This stimulates normal skin growth and cellular growth and repair. TGF exerts positive regulatory effects on the accumulation of the body's extracellular matrix proteins. It is also a mediator of fibrosis (repair tissue formation) and angiogenesis (development of new blood cells), and it promotes the healing of wounds.

Hormones

Hormonal creams claim to be the most effective means to stop or slow the ageing process by reversing the loss in tone and elasticity of the skin. Confirmatory evidence of this claim is yet to be published.

Estrogens: Some studies have shown the anti-ageing effects of estrogens. One investigation found that after 6 months of applying 0.01% estradiol and 0.3% estriol compounds, the elasticity, firmness, wrinkle depth and pore sizes of the skin were markedly improved. On immunohistochemical analysis, significant increases of type III collagen labelling were combined with increased numbers of collagen fibres at the end of the treatment period. Also, no systemic adverse effects were noted. However, more exhaustive studies are needed before these agents are routinely used for their anti-ageing effects.

Progesterone: Progesterone creams are being marketed as formulations that reverse the chemical changes that occur in collagen with ageing and that normalise the immune system. Some manufacturers' claims also state that progesterone creams heal skin conditions such as acne, psoriasis, rosacea, seborrhea and keratoses. Other manufacturers claim that progesterone creams are a topical supplement for women who experience symptoms relating to premenstrual syndrome (PMS), menopause or osteoporosis. None of these claims are supported by well-designed studies.

Testosterone: Topical application is quickly becoming the preferred method of testosterone administration. Theoretically, when topically applied, testosterone bypasses the stomach and the liver and does not cause an undesirable rise in estrogen. Manufacturers claim that testosterone creams have many benefits, such as memory enhancement, antidepressant effects, increased resistance to stress and the ability to treat disorders associated with hypogonadism (for example, increased storage of fat, shrinkage of muscle mass). Recent studies have shown that daily application of testosterone gel to the skin restored blood levels of the hormone in men with hypogonadism.

Growth hormone (GH): GH and its mediator insulin-like growth factor-1 (IGF-1) are responsible for many effects on growth, development, immunity and metabolism. Produced and secreted by the anterior pituitary gland in the brain, GH is released in pulses in response to signals from the hypothalamus. GH exerts anabolic effects throughout the body, favouring the growth of tissues, bones and muscles. Studies have shown that the ageing population has reduced levels of GH in the body, with resultant decreased lean body mass, fat deposits, immunity and overall energy.

Botulinum A exotoxin

This is a neurotoxin produced by the bacterium Clostridium botulinum. This toxin is now being used by cosmetically oriented specialists for the treatment of a large variety of movement-associated wrinkles on the face and neck. As a simple and effective non-surgical procedure, the injection of botulinum toxin A seems to be an effective method of eliminating crow's feet and wrinkle lines that are on the upper third of the face and producing a temporary browlift. This form of temporary chemical denervation compliments the cosmetic practitioner's armamentarium. In addition, the use of botulinum toxin to block sympathetic innervation of eccrine sweat glands is proving to be valuable in treating hyperhidrosis of the axillae, palms and soles.

Antimicrobial Agents

The use of antimicrobial agents in cosmetics and related toiletries has been rampant in recent years. It is increasingly found in baby oils, creams and lotions to help prevent and control impetigo and milia; in deodorants, to inhibit microbial decomposition of perspiration; and in various scalp preparations, to inhibit microorganisms that are associated with seborrheic dermatitis.

Triclosan: This is the latest weapon in the arsenal of antibacterial chemicals and is included in detergents, dish washing fluids, soaps, deodorants, cosmetics, lotions, creams and even toothpaste. Triclosan (2, 4, 4'-trichloro-2'-hydroxydiphenyl ether) is a broad-spectrum antimicrobial agent, routinely used in various personal care products. It is also incorporated into polymers through melt-mixing, with the aim of providing persistent antibacterial action on the surface of the polymer.

Chlorhexidine: This is effective against a wide range of gram-negative and gram-positive vegetative bacteria, yeasts, dermatophyte fungi and lipophilic viruses. It is inactive against bacterial spores except at elevated temperatures.

Povidone iodine: This compound is soluble in water, forming a golden-brown solution. Like iodine, the solution of the iodine complex is bactericidal and fungicidal. However, unlike solutions of iodine, it does not stain. The antiseptic action of povidone-iodine solutions is caused by the available iodine present in the complex.

Para Chloro Meta Xylenol (PCMX): PCMX is effective against both gram-positive and gram-negative bacteria and fungal and yeast microorganisms. PCMX has been tested as safe for use in long-term wound care and is more effective on a broader range of microorganisms than the other antiseptics.

Hydrogen peroxide: In solution, hydrogen peroxide provides mechanical cleansing and some debridement of wounds by its effervescent action; however, it can cause ulceration of newly formed tissue and create granulomas. It is toxic to fibroblasts and, therefore, should never be used as an aftercare solution for wounds.

Anti-dandruff Preparations

Most preparations for the treatment of dandruff largely depend on antimicrobial agents for their therapeutic effect. One leading anti-dandruff lotion is a combination of benzethonium chloride and *N*-trichloroethyl mercapto-4-cyclohexene-1, 2-dicarboximide.

Biphenamine hydrochloride is another active chemical moiety that provides an excellent bacteriostatic, antifungal property and local anesthetic action.

Deodorants

Antimicrobial substances, such as hexachlorophene, aluminum phenolsulfonate and zinc peroxide, as well as various quaternaries such as cetyltrimethylammonium bromide, alkyldimethylbenzylammonium chloride and isobutyl phenoxy ethyl dimethyl benzyl ammonium chloride have been used in antiperspirant and deodorant formulations.

Tyrothricin and neomycin have also been used in deodorant formulations. Studies have shown that neomycin alone or in combination with aluminum chlorhydroxide produces effective odour suppression, along with a significant increase in gram-negative organisms. Its effectiveness as a deodorant is attributed to its exceptional suppression of gram-positive organisms.

Trichlorocarbanilide is a high-duty, wide-spectrum bacteriostatic agent also used in deodorants. It has a lasting, safe and stable bactericidal effect. It also inhibits and kills gram-positive, gram-negative bacteria, fungus, saccharomycetes and viruses.

Other Antimicrobial Preparations

Several diverse chemical substances are used to treat and cure various fungal infections, including fatty acids and their derivatives (for example, zinc, calcium, alkanolamine undecylenates), phenolics (4-halothymols), halogenated quinolines (iodochlorhydroxyquin), quaternary ammonium salts (hexadecamethylenebis-isoquinolinium chloride) and sulfur and sulfur compounds (zinc ethylene bisdithiocarbamate). Phenol and polyphenol derivatives that are used in cosmetic formulations include hexylresorcinol, *p*-chloro-*m*-xylenol, *o*-phenylphenol and chlorothymol. Quaternary ammonium compounds that are used in cosmetic formulations include benzalkonium chloride, benzethonium chloride, cetylpyridinium chloride and cetyltrimethylammonium bromide.

Topical Anesthetics and Antipruritics

Specific local anesthetic agents are often found in a variety of topical drugs and toiletry products such as hand and scalp lotions, foot preparations and aftershave products to relieve local discomfort and to reduce pruritus. Anesthetic agents are also found in formulations designed to be useful in diaper dermatitis, sunburn and acne vulgaris.

Ethyl aminobenzoate: Ethyl aminobenzoate (benzocaine) has perhaps been one of the most widely used local anesthetics; however, the increasing incidence of sensitisation has prompted the introduction of noncaine anesthetics.

Benzyl alcohol: In creams, lotions and ointments, benzyl alcohol at a 2% level provides effective local anesthetic effects and preservative qualities.

Diperodon hydrochloride: Diperodon hydrochloride and monohydrate are piperidine compounds in the class of N-substituted aminobenzenes. At a 1% level, they provide local anesthetic effects and antipruritic actions.

Pramoxine hydrochloride: Pramoxine hydrochloride, which is reportedly more potent than cocaine, is used in topical preparations at concentrations of about 1%; however, the monohydrate salt is often preferred in some applications because it is not alkali sensitive, it is more soluble with various solvents and it may help prevent certain colour changes or darkening in products that contain hydrochloride-sensitive components. Specific local anesthetic agents such as benzocaine, pramoxine and diperodon exert their effects on mucous membranes and abraded, broken or irritated cutaneous membranes. They are not effective on unbroken skin.

Menthol: Menthol and related cooling compounds are widely used in products that range from common cold medications to toothpastes, confectionery, cosmetics and pesticides. Menthol affects the nerve endings to provide a cooling antipruritic action.

Capsaicin: Capsaicin is the active component of chili peppers, which are plants that belong to the genus *Capsicum*. It is an irritant and produces a burning sensation in any tissue that it comes into contact with. Capsaicin and several related compounds are called capsaicinoids. It is primarily used to relieve pain and itching. It is also used in topical creams to relieve the pain of peripheral neuropathy. It may be used in concentrations of between 0.025% and 0.075%.

It may also be used as a cream for the temporary relief of minor aches and pains of muscles and joints associated with arthritis, fibromyalgia, bursitis, simple backache, strains and sprains.

When it is applied to the skin, capsaicin cream has been found to deplete substance P—a neurochemical that transmits pain—which desensitises a person to pain.

Varicose Vein Sclerosing Agents

Sclerosing agents can be divided into different groups depending on their mechanism of action.

Cleaning solutions: These types of sclerosants provoke damage of the endothelium by attacking the lipids of the membrane, thereby causing cell damage and inflammation. Sclerosing agents belonging to this group include polidodecanol (Aethoxysclerol), sodium tetradecyl sulfate (Sotradecol), sodium morrhuate and ethanolamine oleate (Ethamolin). Aethoxysclerol is a local anesthetic and is therefore painless and probably the most effective.

Osmotic solutions: These solutions work by dehydrating the endothelial cell by osmosis, until they are destroyed. Substances that belong to this group include hypertonic saline and sclerodex (10% NaCl, 25% dextrose, 1% phenethyl alcohol).

Hair Removal Agents

Depilatory agents: The standard chemical depilatory agents, available in gels, creams, lotions, aerosols or roll-on forms, are the salts of thioglycolic acid (sodium thioglycolate or calcium thioglycolate) that were patented in the 1930s for de-hairing cattle hides. Thioglycolate depilatories work by hydrolysing and disrupting disulfide bonds of hair keratin, causing the hair to break in half and allowing the hair to separate from the skin.

Eflornithine HCl 13.9% cream: This cream (Vaniqa) is approved by the FDA for the reduction of unwanted facial hair in women. It works by inhibiting the enzyme ornithine decarboxylase (ODC), an enzyme in human skin that stimulates hair growth. When this enzyme is blocked, metabolic activity in the hair follicle decreases and hairs grow in more slowly. Investigators have found that activity increases in rodent skin within 4 hours after hair plucking. In humans, ODC was found where follicles develop, and it is abundant in the proliferating cells of anagen follicles and decreased in the catagen phase, which persists until the next follicular stage. Increased activity of ODC shows prolongation of the anagen phase and decreased activity shows reduction of this phase.

Ketoconazole: This is a potent anti-androgen drug. Ketoconazole works by blocking the production of hormones by the ovaries and the adrenal glands. The intake of ketoconazole may be 200–400 mg/d.

Hair Loss Treatments

There is no cure for hair loss but thinning of the hair can be reduced. Alopecia, the lack of hair, can be distinguished by hair follicles that are destroyed by the male hormone di hydro testosterone (DHT)), the main cause of transitory damage to follicles. This type of hair loss is dominated by pattern baldness, which occurs in as much as 75% of males and 25% of females. Hair loss treatments may help control hair loss.

The different hair loss treatments are discussed below.

Spironolactone: This is an aldosterone antagonist. It works by competitively binding to receptors thereby stopping binding of natural androgens to receptors. Spironolactone is a potent competitive inhibitor of dihydrotestosterone (DHT) at its receptor sites. Therefore, spironolactone effectively prevents DHT from attaching to the receptor sites on the hair follicles. Spironolactone may have potential as a topical application to treat hair loss. Treatment of an animal model revealed that spironolactone was able to penetrate the skin and produce an effect at the site of hair follicle bulbs.

Cyproterone acetate: This permits or promotes androgenetic alopecia-affected hair follicles to become less dystrophic, it allows the ratio of anagen hair to telogen hair follicles to increase and enables a small increase in the diameter of hair shafts.

Flutamide: This has powerful anti-androgen effects that block the androgen receptor. It has also been used to treat female androgenetic alopecia. Results in one study showed that flutamide was significantly superior to spironolactone in treating androgen-dependent conditions in women.

Azelaic acid: This is a saturated dicarboxylic acid found naturally in wheat, rice and barley. Azelaic acid affects the hornification process of the epidermal cells and appears to normalise the keratinisation of cells in the skin and hair. Azelaic acid also appears to act as an anti-androgen by blocking the activity of 5 alpha reductase.

Ketoconazole: This is an antifungal shampoo. It has some anti-androgenic effects, but it is not known whether the amount in the shampoo is absorbed. If it helps with hair loss, it may work in a way other than as an anti-androgen. The combination treatment of minoxidil shampoo with ketoconazole shampoo has shown more synergistic effects than with minoxidil alone.

Areas of Rapid Growth

There are several rapidly growing areas within the natural cosmeceutical category. Some of these products are listed below.

- *Sun protection:* This is an area that, like aromatherapy, also encompasses most personal care areas. Companies are adding botanical ingredients such as green tea and genestein to hair care products, skin care products and many others as skin damage becomes more prevalent.
- *Antioxidants:* Antioxidant protection is necessary to safeguard the skin from the sun's harmful rays, but natural antioxidants such as Vitamin C are finding their way into all kinds of skin care products as stress and pollution become more difficult to avoid in our daily lives.
- *Anti-ageing products:* Some of these ingredients such as white tea address wrinkles, while others such as ursolic acid from the botanical uva ursi deal with lightening skin tone. There are literally countless possible combinations and many ingredients have multiple functional properties.
- *Anti-cellulite:* As obesity becomes more endemic, more products will be created to address the symptoms. Skin firming agents such as bupleurum are becoming more common.
- *Anti-bacterial/Anti-inflammatory:* Natural cosmeceuticals now address skincare problems such as acne and other types of inflammation, including wound healing and rashes along with many others. Ingredients such as avocado, tea tree oil, uva ursi, echinacea and even rosemary have properties dealing with these issues.

Recent Developments

Newer technologies such as transdermal liposomes, soft gels and microsponges are being considered in cosmeceuticals. Microsponge technology enables active ingredients such as retinol and salicylic acid to be trapped in a polymeric material to give controlled release from a formulation into the skin. By using a controlled, pulsed delivery system, high levels of active ingredients can be delivered without the dangers of skin irritation and other side effects. In addition, the use of soft gels in therapeutic cosmetics is ideal for somewhat unstable active ingredients, which formerly could not have been used in skin care.

Cosmeceuticals improve appearance by delivering nutrients necessary for healthy skin. The use of cosmeceuticals has drastically risen in recent years. The rise of this new area can be largely attributed to the trend toward self-treatment, environmental awareness and overall health and wellness. Cosmeceuticals are the fastest-growing segment of the natural personal care industry and will continue to enjoy the same status as long as consumers are interested in maintaining a youthful and healthy appearance. However, the challenge before the cosmetic industry lies in providing evidence of the effectiveness of these compounds.

Key Messages

- Cosmeceuticals are cosmetic products that have drug-like benefits.
- While drugs are subject to an intensive review and approval process by the FDA, cosmetics are not approved by the FDA.
- The Food, Drug and Cosmetic Act does not recognise the term 'cosmeceutical' by law.
- Cosmeceuticals are the fastest growing segment of the personal care industry.
- In general, vitamins, herbs, various oils and botanical extracts are used in cosmeceuticals.
- Cosmeceuticals are topically applied but they contain ingredients that influence the biological function of the skin.

Questions

1. How do cosmeceuticals differ from cosmetics?
2. Name five classes of ingredients that can be used in cosmeceuticals.
3. Give an account of natural ingredients used in cosmeceuticals.
4. List the applications of cosmeceuticals.

20

Formulation of Cosmetics

SHOBHA RANI R HIREMATH

Learning Objectives

At the end of this chapter, you will be able to:

- List the different types of skin creams and describe their formulation
- Define dentifrices and describe their classification
- List the various classes of ingredients used to formulate toothpastes and describe their preparation
- Describe the preparation of a toothpowder
- Define mouthwashes and list the ingredients used in their preparation
- List the shaving preparations and the ingredients used in their formulation and describe the process of manufacturing them
- List the components used in the formulation of lipsticks and describe the process of manufacturing them
- Describe the types of shampoos and list the ingredients used in their formulation
- List the ingredients used in the formulation of face powders and describe the methods of preparing them
- Explain the differences between face powders and compact powders
- Describe the different ingredients used in the formulation of nail lacquers and describe their preparation
- List the various eye cosmetics, and describe the ingredients used in their formulation and their preparation
- Describe hair dyes, list the types of hair dyes and describe the problems associated with them

Skin Creams

Skin creams are solid or semisolid emulsions. If the emulsion has a 'pourable' consistency, it is termed a lotion. Emulsions can be oil in water (o/w) or water in water (w/w). Creams generally contain an aqueous phase and an oily phase. Emulsifying agents stabilise the emulsion. The other ingredients of skin creams are viscosity imparting agents, preservatives and perfumes.

The different types of skin creams are discussed below.

Cleansing Creams

The purpose of cleansing creams is the removal of facial makeup and oil from the face. Cleansing creams dissolve the greasy, binding material on the skin and leave an emollient residual film behind.

A cold cream based on a beeswax–borax combination has the following formula.

Formula

Beeswax—16%
Mineral oil—50%
Borax—0.8%
Water—33%
Perfume—qs
Preservatives—qs

When borax is mixed with molten beeswax, it undergoes hydrolysis and the subsequent reaction of sodium hydroxide with the free acids present in the beeswax form the corresponding soaps (sodium salts of the wax acids). These soaps emulsify the mineral oil in the water. Other components of beeswax such as myricyl alcohol stabilise the emulsion.

The beeswax–borax emulsion represents the most important formulation among cleansing creams. Typically, they are white, lustrous creams of o/w-type emulsion. When the cream is rubbed on the skin, sufficient water evaporates to permit the phase inversion to w/o-type with oil as the external phase; the solvent action of the oil then facilitates cleansing of the skin.

Cleansing Lotions

Cleansing lotions perform the same functions as cleansing creams but can be spread easily and more uniformly.

Formula

Stearic acid—5.33%
Triethanolamine—2.66%
Mineral oil—35%
Beeswax—2%
Water—55%
Perfume—0.5–1%

Triethanolamine stearate, formed by the reaction of stearic acid and triethanolamine, is an effective emulsifier. Beeswax is used to thicken and stabilise the emulsion.

Emollient Creams

Emollient creams are preparations containing emollients, which are used to prevent or provide relief from dryness as well as to protect the skin. These creams are effective in softening and imparting emollience to the dry, scaly stratum corneum.

An emollient cream with a non-ionic, o/w-type emulsion has the following formula.

Formula

Glyceryl mono stearate—4.5%
Lanolin—1.0%
Isopropyl myristate—4.3%
PEG 1000 monostearate—6.0%
Stearic acid—7.2%
Propyl paraben—0.15%
Methyl paraben—0.15%
Propylene glycol—2.5%
Water—74.0%
Perfume—qs

Glyceryl mono stearate, PEG 1000 monostearate, lanolin and propylene glycol are all emollients. Parabens are preservatives. The general method of preparation of creams is as follows.

The lipids and oil-soluble ingredients are heated to 75° in a steam-jacketed kettle. The water-soluble components are dissolved in the aqueous phase and heated to 75°. The internal phase is very slowly added to the external phase, stirring continuously. Perfume is added to the emulsion at 45°; then the mixture is stirred and allowed to cool.

Emollient Lotions

Another method of applying an emollient material is in the form of a lotion. The oils and waxes are identical to those of emollient creams but in lower concentrations. Lotions are preferred for day use. The formulation of emollient lotions is similar to that of emollient creams.

Formula

Cetyl alcohol—0.52%

Lanolin—1.04%

Stearic acid—0.04%

Stearyl alcohol—0.94%

Light mineral oil—26%

Triethanolamine—0.52%

Sodium alginate—0.36%

Methyl paraben—0.15%

Propylene glycol—2.5%

Water—qs to 100%

Perfume—qs

The emollient oils are light mineral oil and lanolin; emollient waxes include stearyl alcohol and stearic acid; poly hydric alcohols such as propylene glycol provide viscosity and stability. Sodium alginate and triethanolamine stearate are the emulsifying agents and methyl paraben is the preservative.

Vanishing Creams

Creams that spread with ease and vanish or disappear on rubbing on the skin are called vanishing creams. They are based on stearic acid, which gives the cream its pearly white appearance.

Formula

Stearic acid—17%

Potassium hydroxide—0.7%

Glycerin—5%

Water—qs to 100%

Perfume and preservatives—qs

In the above formula, potassium hydroxide reacts with stearic acid to form potassium stearate, which acts as an emulsifying agent.

All-purpose Creams

These creams contain stearic acid, humectant and lanolin in addition to the usual ingredients. Stearic acid reduces the oiliness of the cream. Lanolin and humectants such as glycerol are emollients that act as both cleansers and emollients. All-purpose creams are not as oily as cold creams and they leave a thin film when removed from the skin; they can be used as a foundation base.

Formula

Stearic acid—15%

Lanolin—4%

Beeswax—2%

Mineral oil—23%

Polysorbate 85—1%

Sorbitan trioleate—1%

Sorbitol—12%

Water, perfume, preservative—qs

Polysorbate 85 and sorbitan trioleate are the emulsifying agents and stabilisers. The rest of the ingredients (except perfume and preservatives) act as emollients.

Dentifrices

Dentifrices are preparations used for the oral cavity, primarily to clean the teeth, prevent tooth decay, maintain gingival health and prevent bad odours. They can be classified as toothpastes, tooth powders and mouthwashes.

Toothpastes

The main ingredients used in the formulation of toothpastes are as follows:

Abrasives: The main function of abrasives is to clean the surface of the teeth. They remove debris and residual stains from the teeth and polish the surface. Precipitated calcium carbonate or chalk is an efficient cleaning agent but does not make the teeth lustrous. Calcium phosphates such as dicalcium phosphate (DCP), tricalcium phosphate (TCP) and calcium pyrophosphate are also examples of abrasives. DCP is the most commonly used abrasive. DCP dihydrate reverts to the anhydrous form with consequent hardening of the paste. This process is accelerated in the presence of fluorides. DCP is therefore stabilised by the addition of tetrasodium pyrophosphate, calcium sodium pyrophosphate and trimagnesium phosphate. TCP is not commonly used while calcium pyrophosphate is used in toothpastes containing fluorides.

Detergents: Detergents aid cleaning by producing foam; surfactants are used for this purpose. Sodium lauryl sulphate is the most popular detergent and foaming agent used in toothpastes. Sodium N lauroyl sarcosinate, sodium ricinoleate and sodium sulpho ricinoleate are the other surfactants used.

Humectants: These are components added to prevent drying of the toothpaste. Examples of humectants are glycerin, sorbitol and propylene glycol.

Binding agents: These are added to ensure that the solids are suspended uniformly. The various binding agents used are gum tragacanth, carragheen (derived from the seaweed chondrus crispus or Irish moss) and cellulose derivatives—the most commonly used gelling agents (binding agents) for toothpastes. Among these, the widely used ones are carboxy methyl cellulose (CMC), sodium carboxy methyl cellulose (Na CMC), methyl or hydroxyethyl ethers of cellulose, methyl cellulose and hydroxyl ethyl cellulose. Carbopol and sodium alginate are the other gelling agents.

Flavours: Flavours are one of the most important constituents as they enable consumer acceptability. The most commonly used flavours are based on the oil of spearmint and peppermint. Clove, wintergreen, eucalyptus and aniseed are also popular.

Sweetening agents: Sweeteners are required to make the paste more acceptable. Saccharin is the sweetener of choice.

Preservatives: These are added to protect toothpastes from the effects of microorganisms. Formalin sodium benzoate and para hydroxy benzoate are the commonly used preservative agents.

Colouring agents: Colours are added to toothpastes to make them attractive. Even flourides can be added to toothpaste. About 0.2% of sodium fluoride or 0.4% of stannous fluoride (Sn F2) can be included; this corresponds to 1000 PPM of fluorine.

Formula

Calcium carbonate—40%
Sodium carboxy methyl cellulose—1%
Glycerin—10%
Propylene glycol—10%

Saccharin—0.1%
Sodium lauryl sulphate—2%
Methyl paraben—0.1%
Propyl paraben—0.05%
Colour—qs
Flavour—1%
Water—qs to100%

Method I

The binder is wetted with the humectant and dispersed in the liquid portion containing saccharin and preservative and allowed to swell to form a gel. This may be accelerated by heat and agitation. To the gel, the abrasive agent is added slowly, stirring continuously till the entire mass is homogeneous. The flavour and detergent are added last and distributed uniformly.

Method II

The binder is premixed with solid abrasives and introduced simultaneously with an aqueous solution of humectant, preservative and saccharin into a suitable mixer. After mixing to a homogeneous paste, the flavour and detergent are added, and mixing is completed. The binder must be adequately expanded. Heat may be utilised to accelerate the swelling of the binder.

Tooth Powders

Toothpowders are the simplest and cheapest form of dentifrice. Care should be taken while preparing toothpowders as the ingredients should be of fairly uniform size; this prevents separation on shaking. The product should also not become caked on storage.

Formula

Dicalcium phosphate—75%
Precipitated calcium carbonate—20%
Sodium lauryl sulphate—1%
Flavouring agent—qs
Sweetening agent—qs

The powder mixture of abrasive and other solid ingredients are mixed with sweeteners, flavour and a little alcohol if required. This is then mixed with the rest of the powder in a conventional powder mixture.

Mouthwashes

A mouthwash is a product used for oral hygiene. Antiseptic and anti-plaque mouth rinses claim to kill the germs that cause plaque, gingivitis and bad breath. Anti-cavity mouth rinses use fluoride to protect against tooth decay. The use of mouthwashes does not eliminate the need for both brushing and flossing.

Common use involves rinsing the mouth with about 20 ml of mouthwash twice a day, after brushing. The mouthwash is typically swished or gargled for about half a minute and then spat out.

Active ingredients in commercial brands of mouthwash may include thymol, eucalyptol, hexetidine, methyl salicylate, menthol, chlorhexidine gluconate, benzalkonium chloride, cetylpyridinium chloride, methylparaben, hydrogen peroxide, domiphen bromide and sometimes fluoride, enzymes and calcium. Water, sweeteners such as sorbitol and sodium saccharine, and a significant amount of alcohol (around 20%) are also added. Mouthwashes usually contain a preservative such as sodium benzoate to preserve freshness once the container has been opened. Many newer brands are alcohol-free and contain odour-elimination agents such as oxidizers and odour-preventing agents such as zinc ion technology to prevent bad breath.

Formula

Thymol—0.03%
Alcohol—3%
Borax—2%

Glycerine—10%
Flavour—qs
Water—qs to 100%

Shaving Preparations

Shaving preparations help prepare the beard and face for shaving. They also increase speed and comfort during the shave and confer a feeling of well-being afterwards. Shaving preparations can be classified as follows:

- Wet shaving preparations
- Dry shaving preparations
- After-shave preparations

Wet Shaving Preparations

The different types of wet shaving preparations are:

- Beard softening creams
- Lather shaving creams
- Lather shaving sticks
- Aerosol shaving foams
- Brushless or non-lathering creams
- Brushless shaving sticks

Beard Softening Creams

These pre-shave preparations are used to wet and soften the beard and to lubricate the skin. They are helpful for those with easily abraded skin or large-diameter beard hair. These creams contain soaps and synthetic softeners that enable a more complete wetting and softening of the beard and thus ensure a closer and smoother shave. They contain a lime soap–dispersing agent to improve the wetting action in hard water, a soap-compatible antibacterial agent, menthol and a preservative. Triethanolamine stearate, stearyl alcohol, lanolin and surfactants such as tweens and spans are used as ingredients.

Lather Shaving Creams

These are very popular shaving preparations. Lather shaving creams are concentrated dispersions of alkali metal soaps in glycerol and water. Careful control of the manufacturing process is essential to maintain the desired levels of foamability, consistency and product stability. These usually contain 30–50% soaps. Formulations based on stearic acid alone do not produce a sufficiently voluminous lather, so some amount of coconut oil fatty acids are added. Normally about 25% coconut oil with 75% stearic acid is added. A mixture of sodium hydroxide and potassium hydroxide is used to saponify the fatty acids. A 5:1 ratio of potassium hydroxide to sodium hydroxide with 3–5% of free fatty acids will give shaving creams the correct degree of plasticity.

Lather creams made with only potassium soaps tend to be less stable. Therefore, a small amount of sodium soaps must be included in the formulation. However, a high level of sodium soaps makes them thick and stringy.

Humectants such as glycerol are added to prevent premature drying out of the cream and to make the creams softer. They are added in concentrations of up to 15%. Sorbitol and propylene glycol are other examples. Emollients such as lanolin, cetyl alcohol, mineral oil and fatty acid esters should be kept at a low level (around 1%) as higher percentages will interfere with lathering. Other additives such as synthetic surfactants, cooling agents and anti-bacterials may also be added to the cream.

Changes in the texture of lather creams occur with a change in temperature during storage. An increase in temperature causes increase in viscosity or makes the cream gel-like. Decrease in temperature (due to cold weather) makes the cream hard and difficult to apply. These variations can be reduced by adding 0.5% borax.

Corrosion of metallic tubes by the cream can be reduced by adding 1–1.5% sodium silicate.

Lather Shaving Stick

These are prepared from a mixture containing 80% fatty acid soaps, 5–10% glycerol and 8–10% water. The ratio of fatty acids and the ratio of potassium to sodium soaps are similar to those in lather shaving creams. This mixture is then chipped, dried and milled with other components such as perfumes, colours or opacifiers. The soap flakes are then packed to the desired shape using a soap plodder.

Aerosol Shaving Foams

These are oil-in-water emulsions in which a propellant liquefied under pressure forms a substantial part of the oil phase. When the emulsion is discharged into the atmosphere, the dispersed propellant droplets vapourise, producing foam that consists of propellant vapour bubbles surrounded by an aqueous surfactant phase.

Saturated, long-chain fatty acids containing 12–18 carbons at a level of 7–9% are the main components of aerosol shaving foams. The ratio of the fatty acids can be varied to produce foams with different physical properties. High proportion of stearic acid in the fatty acid mixture tends to produce stiffer foams and a reduction in the number of shaves per can. Replacing some of the stearic acid with lauric acid tends to produce softer foams and also improves the expulsion characteristics.

The other ingredients that go into the formulation of aerosol shaving foams are:

Bases: Triethanolamine, potassium hydroxide or a mixture of the two are the preferred bases for the saponification of the fatty acids. Triethanolamine soaps are used to get better foams than potassium soaps.

Surfactants: Anionic and nonionic surfactants are used to improve:

- Emulsion stability (for example, self-emulsifying glycerol monostearate)
- Wetting properties of the foam (for example, sodium lauryl ether sulphate)
- Water dispersability of the foam and shaving debris (for example, polyethoxylated fatty alcohols)
- Foam stability (for example, lauric diethanolamide)
- Emolliency (for example, ethoxylated lanolins)

Humectants: Polyols such as glycerol, sorbitol or propylene glycol are usually added at 3–10%.

Lubricants: Mineral oils, silicone fluids, lanolin or isopropyl myristate are added at a concentration of 1–2% to supplement the effects of the free fatty acids. These lubricants assist the passage of the razor over the face and improve emolliency. Water-soluble polymers such as polyvinyl pyrrolidone, sodium carboxy methylcellulose or polyacrylic acid and its derivatives can also improve lubrication and increase foam stability.

Propellants: These contain 7–10% fluorocarbon propellant or 2.8–3.5% hydrocarbon propellant. The fluorocarbon propellants are usually 40:60 to 60:40 weight ratio blends of dichlorodifluromethane and dichlorotetrafluoroethane. The hydrocarbon propellants are mixtures of n-butane, isobutene and n-propane. The higher the concentration of the propellant, the lower the foam density, the stiffer the foam and the greater the number of shaves obtained.

Perfume: Perfumes are used at a level of 0.15–0.5%.

Cooling agents: Menthol, at concentrations of 0.05–0.2%, is the most frequently used cooling agent.

Colour: D&C or FD&C dyes are used to colour the foams at a very low concentration.

Preservatives: 0.2% of a mixture of methyl and propyl p-hydroxybenzoate may be added to some shaving foams. Antioxidants are sometimes required to avoid rancidity in formulations that contain low levels of unsaturated compounds.

Corrosion inhibitors: These are not normally required with suitably lacquered containers. Borax (0.04%, 10 mol) can be used with tinplate containers and 0.25% of sodium silicate at 35 °C in a solution with aluminum containers.

Bacteriostats: 0.05% trichlorohydroxydiphenyl ether and 0.05% allantoin are used to reduce skin infections and promote healing of cuts.

Pilomotor agents: These agents have the ability to cause the contraction of the hair follicle muscles, thus producing a closer shave. Examples include 2-(2',5'-dimetoxy-4',6'-dimethylbenzyl)-2-imidazoline , 2-amino-imidazolines, morpholines, etc.

Heated Shaving Foams

These were developed as an increase in temperature was known to result in improvements in beard softening. These are obtained either by an exothermic chemical reaction between components which are kept separate within the aerosol container or by bringing the foam into contact with a heat exchanger connected to a hot water supply. Products relying on an exothermic redox reaction require a dual dispensing aerosol valve, the inner compartment containing hydrogen peroxide and the outer compartment containing the soap solution, propellant and a pyrimidine, thiourea, sulphite or thiosulphite. Heated shaving foams are based on aqueous solutions of triethanolamine stearate, superfatted with free stearic acid. Stearic acid has the ability to thicken the foams at elevated temperatures. Propylene glycol or nonionic surfactants produce much richer and more viscous forms at room temperature but tend to have a watery consistency at elevated temperatures. A satisfactory formulation may contain 8–15% triethanolamine stearate, 1% triethanolamine, coconut oil soap and 2/3% stearic acid.

Brushless or Non-lathering Creams

These are oil-in-water emulsions. They are similar to vanishing creams, the only difference being that the concentration of oils and emulsifying agents tends to be higher in the shaving preparation.

A typical oil phase comprises:

- 4–10% lubricant (mineral oil, long-chain fatty acid esters, petrolatum)
- 10–25% stearic acid to provide a superfatting action and to assist the characteristic pearlescent appearance of the cream
- 0–5% emollient (lanolin, cholesterol, cetyl alohol, stearyl alcohol, spermaceti). Spermaceti is widely recommended to prevent the cream from vanishing rapidly.

The aqueous phase contains:

- 1–5% soaps (potassium or triethanolamine stearate)
- 0–5% synthetic surfactant to improve emulsion stability, beard wetting and rinsability (glycerol monostearate,

sulphoanated fatty alcohols, fatty acid amides)
- 0–1% thickening agents which improve emulsion stability (gum tragacanth, sodium alginate, polyvinylpyrrolidone, polyacrylic acid and its derivatives)
- 2–10% humectants to prevent drying out of the cream (glycerol, sorbitol, propylene glycol)

Preservatives (p-hydroxybenzoic acid) are also added. Other additives include perfumes, cooling agents, bacteriostats, etc.

Brushless Shaving Stick

These can be applied directly to the face. The continuous thin smear left on wetted skin provides adequate lubrication for the shaving operation. The stick is composed of fatty or waxy materials to which hydrophilic properties have been imparted by a suitable emulsifier such as soap or a fatty acid ester of polyhydric alcohol, ensuring that the product is readily wetted. Pigment, dyestuff or opacifiers are incorporated to indicate the presence of the composition on the face.

Dry Shaving Preparations

Dry shaving preparations are used before shaving with an electric razor and the different types of the same include:

- Pre-electric shave lotions
- Collapsible foam pre-electric shave lotions
- Pre-electric shave gel sticks
- Pre-electric shave talc sticks
- Pre-electric shave powders

Pre-electric shave lotions may be applied directly to the face by a roll-on type of applicator. Quick-breaking aerosol forms were developed to aid transfer of the pre-electric shave lotion from the hand to the face. The foam is stable and confined to a limited area when dispensed, but breaks to a thin liquid when sheared or warmed by body heat. This is the principle of collapsible foam pre-electric shave lotions.

The foam typically contains 55–70% of an aqueous alcoholic solution, 4–10% of a lubricant, 0.5–5% of a surfactant and 3–10% of a liquefiable propellant. The persistance of the foam when left undisturbed on the hand varies from a few seconds to several minutes depending on the proportion of alcohol, water and propellant and the type and concentration of the surfactant. The foam collapses on shearing as the bubble walls are extremely thin. The surfactants used are nonionic emulsifiable waxes composed of polyethylene glycol ethers of cetyl and stearyl alcohol.

Solid pre-electric shave gel sticks of the cologne type can be created by gelling ethanol with sodium stearate in the presence of glycerol and a suitable lubricant. Talc is used as the main component in pre-electric shave talc stick preparations to absorb perspiration and sebaceous secretions from the skin and to confer the characteristic slip so that the head of the shaver will glide smoothly over the face. Talc can reduce 50% of the frictional force between the skin and the polished steel. Colloidal kaolin is also added to improve the moisture absorbing capacity and adhesion to the skin. Zinc or magnesium stearate is added to enhance both adhesion and slip. Magnesium carbonate or precipitated chalk serves as a carrier for the perfume as well as increasing the absorbent properties. Talc is best applied onto the face in the form of sticks. The sticks can be moulded from an aqueous dispersion of the powders using colloidal magnesium aluminum silicate (Veegum) as the binder.

Pre-electric shave powders consist of loose powders with talc, kaolin, magnesium carbonate, cetyl alcohol, glycerol monostearate, zinc stearate and zinc oxide as the ingredients. To overcome the problems of handling the powder and to avoid spillage, pre-electric shave powders are packed in aerosol containers. A low-pressure propellant mixture and careful selection of actuator are required to produce a soft, dry spray which does not result in excessive 'bounce' of fine particles from the target surface.

After-shave Preparations

These preparations are used to relieve the slight irritation that results from shaving and to confer a pleasant feeling of comfort and well-being after shaving. These preparations produce an effect of a slight coolness, anesthesia, mild astringency or emolliency on the skin. They also have antiseptic properties to help keep the skin free from bacterial infections during the short time it takes to recover from the slight degree of injury inflicted during the shaving operation.

The most important type of after-shave preparation is the after-shave lotion.

After-shave Lotions: An after-shave lotion is a clear, aqueous, ethyl alcohol solution containing a perfume. They contain 50–70% ethyl alcohol by weight. To achieve the required perfume level it is necessary to increase the alcohol content. In a situation where it is undesirable to increase the alcohol content or reduce the fragrance level, a solubiliser is added to obtain a clear lotion. Nonionic surfactants with a hydrophile–lipophile balance number in the range of 15–18 are the most effective solubilisers, although anionic surfactants have also been used. Humectants and emollients are frequently added to after-shave lotions at levels not greater than 5%. Glycerol has the best humectant properties but propylene glycol is often preferred because of its greater solvent power, lower viscosity and higher volatility. Water-soluble lanolin derivatives can be used to provide emolliency and to assist in solubilisation of the perfume oil. Menthol is added in concentrations below 0.1% to give a cooling effect to the skin. Lignocaine at 0.025–0.05% is added to achieve surface anesthesia of the skin. Witch hazel extract, zinc phenolsulphonate, aluminum chlorhydroxide or alcohol-soluble aluminum chloride complexes are added to supplement the mild astringency of alcohol. 0.1% benzalkonium chloride is used as the antibacterial. Cationic surfactants are wide germicides. Anionic surfactants have some activity against gram-positive and yeast organisms. Nonionic surfactants are not considered to be germicidal. Allantoin at 0.1–0.2% is frequently added to after-shave lotions to promote wound healing.

Lipsticks

Lipsticks are dispersions of colouring matter in a base that consists of a mixture of oils, fats and waxes. Lipsticks are used to impart colour to the lips, make them look attractive and enhance the appearance of the person. A good lipstick should have a smooth surface, uniform colour, be stable and safe, both dermatologically and in case of accidental ingestion.

Ingredients

Colouring agents: Colour is the major ingredient in lipsticks. Colouring agents impart colour by staining the skin—this requires a dye in a solution—and by covering the lip with a coloured layer which hides any surface roughness and presents a smooth appearance.

All colour additives in cosmetics must be specifically pre-approved for use by the US Food and Drug Administration (FDA). The official names for colour additives are designated by the FDA; these colours are classified under Food, Drugs & Cosmetics (FD&C) and Drugs & Cosmetics (D&C). The colouring agents used in lipsticks are broadly classified as staining dyes and pigments.

Staining dyes

The most commonly used dyes are eosin, which is water soluble, and halogenated derivatives of fluorescein, collectively known as 'bromoacids'. Eosin (D&C Red No 21) is an insoluble orange compound; when applied to the lips in the acid form, it produces a relatively purple-red stain on the lips.

The other colours are as follows:

D&C Red No 27 (tetrachlorotetrabromofluorescein)—brilliant bluish-red
D&C Orange No 5 (dibromofluorescein)—yellow-red
D&C Red No 24 (tetrachlorofluorescein)
D&C Red No 19—rhodamine
FD&C Red No 40—red

Staining dyes are used at a concentration of 0.5–3%.

Pigments

Pigments are insoluble. They are prepared by converting dyes into an insoluble form. A pigment should be smoothly dispersed in oil to produce a streak of high opacity. D&C Red No 35, D&C Red No 36, D&C Red No 38 and D&C Orange No 17 are insoluble in both water and in oils and can be used as lipstick pigments without being converted to metallic lakes.

Colours made by combining these soluble colours with 'substrates' (sodium, potassium, aluminum, barium, calcium strontium or zirconium) are known as 'lakes' and are named using the same convention, but with the addition of the substrate and the word 'lake'; for example, FD&C Red No 40 Aluminum Lake.

Other examples of pigments:

Calcium lakes of D&C Red No 7
Barium lakes of D&C Red No 9
Calcium lakes of D&C Orange No 17
Aluminium lakes of FD&C Red No 40

Pigments and lakes are commonly used in the range of 8–10%.

Titanium dioxide is the most effective white pigment for obtaining a pink shade and for producing opacity. TiO_2 is generally used at up to 4%. Pigments and lakes are used to give intensity and variation of colour.

Bases

Bases consist of oils, fats and waxes which incorporate colours and disperse them uniformly. Bases give strength to the lipstick, helping it to maintain its shape and not break and making it soft enough to permit easy application.

Oils: Vegetable oils such as olive oil and sesame oil are not used very often as they tend to become rancid. Among vegetable oils, castor oil is used to dissolve bromo acids and because its high viscosity prevents the settling of pigments during the preparation from the molten liquid mass. However, the penetration of the oil into the dry pigment mass is delayed during the mixing operation. Castor oil can be used at a concentration of 25–50%.

Mineral oils such as liquid paraffin oil are poor solvents for colour and do not hold the colour. They are used in small proportions to enhance gloss.

Fatty alcohols: Lauryl, myristyl, stearyl, oleyl or cetyl alcohol can be used according to the consistency required.

Esters: Butyl stearate, propylene glycol monoesters and fatty esters of lower alcohols may be used.

Glycols: Polyethylene glycols and their ethers are used in bases.

Lanolin: This is very useful in assisting dispersion of colours. Lanolin is an emollient and used at concentrations of up to 10%.

Lecithin: This is used in small proportions to improve the smoothness, emolliency and ease of application.

Waxes: Carnuba wax is one of the hardest waxes. Even a small percentage of this wax raises the melting point and the strength of the lipstick. Candelilla wax has a lower melting point than carnuba. Beeswax is the stiffening agent for lipsticks and is used extensively. Ozokerites are hydrocarbon waxes available in a wide range of melting points and textures. Paraffin waxes are not very useful. However, in small quantities, they impart gloss.

Perfumes

A pleasant fragrance is a very important factor for consumer acceptance. Floral, fruity and light spicy odours are the most acceptable.

Antoxidants

Antioxidants such as butylated hydroxy anisole (BHA) and butylated hydroxy toluene (BHT) can be included to prevent rancidity in the proportion of 0.1 to 0.5%

Examples of formulas for lipsticks are given below:

Formula I

Carnuba wax—10%
Beeswax—15%
Lanolin—10%
Cetyl alcohol—10%
Castor oil—25%
Colour—5%
Pigments—8%
Perfume—1%

Formula II

Carnuba wax—10%
Paraffin wax—10%
Beeswax—15%
Cetyl alcohol—5%
Castor oil—25%
Liquid paraffin—10%
Lanolin—10%
Bromo acid—1%
BHT—0.1%
Pigments—5%
Perfume—qs

The colours (bromo acids, pigments and lakes) are blended separately with the appropriate constituents of the base mixture. The objective is to obtain a uniform dispersion of colours. Different mills such as ball, roller and colloid can be used and, if needed, heat can be used to disperse the colours. Soluble dyes are first blended with a solvent, then the pigments are incorporated and dispersed well.

Alternatively, dye blends (pigment dispersion) are added. Pigment dispersion can be accomplished by milling the pigment constituents which wet them, such as lanolin and propylene glycol, and then adding the non-polar bases. The high-melting-point waxes are melted and blended together and then blended with the rest of the mixture.

The mixture should be transferred to a jacketed, closed vessel and stirred gently, applying vacuum to remove the occluded air.

After all the air has been removed, the vacuum is removed and the perfume is added. This mass can be poured into a mould immediately or stored till it is moulded.

If the liquid mass is stored, it is re-melted in a small jacketed pan and agitated slowly over a period of 30 minutes. Moulds made of brass and aluminium are filled to excess to prevent the formation of a depression at the centre of the stick. The excess is scrapped off and the mould is then carefully cooled to allow the mass to set without overcooling so that there is no delay in the removal of the stick from the moulds.

Shampoos

Shampoos are preparations whose primary function is to cleanse the hair. A good shampoo should clean and rinse the hair, impart gloss and leave it in a manageable condition. The ingredients used in the preparation of shampoos are:

- Detergents
- Opacifying agents
- Clarifying agents
- Sequestering agents
- Conditioning agents
- Thickening agents
- Foam boosters
- Activators
- Preservatives
- Special additives

Detergents

As the principle function of shampoos is to clean, detergents are the most important ingredients. Surfactants are used for this purpose.

Surfactants

Anionic: They carry a negative charge when ionised. These are most widely used as they have very good foaming properties, excellent cleaning properties, and are less expensive. They also can be rinsed off easily from the hair. A major disadvantage is that they can be harsh and irritating to the scalp. For example, soaps—metallic or alkanolamine salts of fatty acids obtained by the saponification of vegetable oils. Soaps being alkaline may cause roughening of the hair, giving a dull appearance. This may be overcome by mild acid rinse or using less alkaline alkanolamine salts. Sodium lauryl sulphate produces good foam and foam volume. Another surfactant is alkyl sulphate, especially those derived from lauryl and myristyl alcohols. Lauryl sulphate produces greater volume of lather while myristyl sulphate gives greater richness, so a mixture of these two is a good combination.

Ammonium lauryl sulphate gives good lather and solubility and has greater stability than sodium salt. Alkyl polyethylene glycol sulphates such as polyethoxylated lauryl sulphate and sulphosuccinates such as sodium sulpho succinate are the other anionic surfactants.

Non-ionic surfactants: They carry no charge when ionised. Although they have sufficient cleaning activity, they do not have sufficient foaming power. For example, fatty acid alkanolamides such as mono ethanolamides and isopropanolamide are used with the lauryl sulphates. Sorbitol esters such as poly ethylene sorbitol monoesters (Tweens) are mild compounds and are therefore widely used in shampoos (Tween 20, Tween 80). Polyglyceryl ethers are mild in nature and have great foam generating capacity.

Cationic surfactants: They carry a positive charge when ionised. They do not have very good cleaning and foaming properties. They should not be used at high concentrations. Many of these are irritating to the eyes but are safe when used in small amounts. Some of them may be incompatible with the anionic surfactants. However, newer types have overcome this disadvantage. For example, alkyl trimethyl ammonium salts, stearyl dimethyl benzyl ammonium salts, cetyl pyridinium salts, quartenary ammonium salts such as dicetyl dimethyl ammonium, distearyl dimethyl ammonium and dimethyl ammonium chlorides.

Amphoteric surfactants: They carry both positive and negative charges when ionised. They are used in mild shampoos such as baby shampoos. For example, alkyl amines such as dimethyl palmitamine, alkyl imidazolines such as alkyl hydroxyl ethyl imidazoline and betaines, which are zwitterionic compounds derived from trimethyl glycine, compatible with cationics, anionics and non-ionics.

Opacifying Agents

Opacifiers are added to make the shampoo opaque and give it a pearly look. For example, alkanolamides of higher fatty acids such as stearic acid, glycol mono and distearates, and cetyl and stearyl alcohols.

Clarifying Agents

Clarifying agents are used in clear liquid shampoos. Clarity may be improved and stabilised by the addition of solubilising alcohols such as ethanol, isopropanol and propylene glycol in an amount not exceeding 1%. Clarifying agents can reduce the formation of micelles.

Sequestering Agents

Sequestering agents are used for their ability to form complexes with metallic ions, if the product is made in hard water. When hair is rinsed with hard water, Ca and Mg soaps are deposited on the hair; this makes the hair appear dull. The function of sequestering agents is to bind the Ca and Mg salts, prevent the formation of Ca and Mg soaps and to offset the dulling effects of hard water. For example, EDTA.

Conditioning Agents

Conditioning agents are added to the shampoo to offset the harsh effects of surfactants on the hair. They help make the hair more manageable and lustrous. For example, polymers, cetyl alcohol, cetrimonium bromide, lanolin and mineral oil.

Thickening Agents

Thickening agents are used to increase the viscosity of the shampoos. For example, alkanolamides, alginates, hydroxyethyl, hydroxypropyl, carboxy methyl cellulose and carbopol 934 & 941, 1–4% w/w NaCl.

Foam Boosters

These are added to shampoos to improve the foaming characteristics of the formulation. For example, guar gum, xanthum gum, sarcosinates and lactylates, alkanolamides such as lauramide DEA or cocamide DEA.

Activators

Preservatives

Since preservatives are made from water and organic compounds, the possibility of contamination from bacteria and other microbes exists. Preservatives are added to prevent such growth. Two of the most common preservatives used in shampoos are DMDM hydantoin and methylparaben.

Special Additives

One of the primary factors that influence the purchase of a shampoo is its colour and odour. Perfumes and colour add to the consumer acceptability of the product. Natural materials such as botanical extracts, natural oils, proteins and vitamins all impart special qualities and help sell shampoos. FD&C dyes are used as colouring agents in shampoos. Fragrance oils such as floral, fruity and herbal oils are also added.

Types of Shampoos

Clear liquid shampoos

These shampoos are colourless and transparent.

Formula

Triethanolamine lauryl sulphate 30% solution—40%
Coconut momoethanolamide—2%
Perfume—qs
Colour—qs
Water—qs to100%

TEA lauryl sulphate provides clarity even at low temperatures.

Liquid cream shampoos

These are opaque in nature and hence opacifying agents are used in the formulation.

Formula

Sodium lauryl sulphate 30% solution—25%
Coconut diethanolamide—5%
Magnesium stearate—1%
Polyethylene glycol diestearate—5%
Lanolin—0.5%
Perfume—qs
Colour—qs
Water—qs to 100%

Polyethylene glycol distearate and magnesium stearates are the opacifiers used in the formula.

Cream/Gel shampoos

These shampoos are thick with good consistency.

Formula

Sodium lauryl sulphate—20%
Coconut monoethanolamide—1%
Glycol monstearate—2%
Stearic acid—4%
Sodium hydroxide—1%
Perfume —qs
Colour—qs
Water—qs to100%

Solid cream and gel shampoos

These shampoos are thick enough to stay in a cream form. They are generally made with sodium lauryl sulphate.

Formula

Sodium lauryl sulphate—20%
Coconut monoethanolamide—1%
Propylene glycol monstearate—2%
Stearic acid—5%
Sodium hydroxide—0.75%
Water—qs to100%

Powder shampoos

Formula

Sodium lauryl sulphate—25%
Sodium bicarbonate—15%
Sodium sulphate—60%

Sodium lauryl sulphate is the detergent powder and sodium bicarbonate is the diluent.

Dry shampoos

These consist of powders brushed into and out of the hair. They are, however, not very efficient in cleansing the hair. They consist of a mixture of absorbent materials such as starch, borax and silica.

Formula

Rice starch—30%
Boric acid—5%
Silica, finely divided—20%
Talc—20%
Perfume—qs

Face Powders

A face powder is a cosmetic product that is applied to the face at the end of the makeup process, either directly or over a powder base. A face powder should

- be harmless on application to the skin
- spread evenly
- remove the shine from the face and cover minor imperfections
- give a glow to the face
- be pleasant to wear and perfumed lightly

Ingredients

The following ingredients are used in the formulation of face powder.

Absorbents: These are used to eliminate the shiny look on the face by absorbing sebaceous secretions and perspiration. The absorbents that are commonly used are kaolin, starch, microcrystalline cellulose, precipitated calcium carbonate and magnesium carbonate. Kaolin is widely used in face powders because of its absorbent and soothening properties. It should be used in a concentration of 30%.

Rice starch has got excellent absorptive and good covering properties and is also capable of imparting smoothness but its disadvantage is that it tends to cake in hot humid conditions. Microcrystalline cellulose is also reported to have very good oil absorption properties.

Precipitated calcium carbonate has excellent absorption characteristics. It removes the shine of the talc. However, it affects the slip of the product and imparts an undesirable dry feel. It should not be used in amounts greater than 15%. Magnesium carbonate has high absorbing properties. It imparts fluffiness to face powders. It has a tendency to dry the skin and is therefore used at a concentration of about 5%.

Covering agents: Covering agents are used to cover up various defects of the face such as scars, blemishes, pores, etc. The ingredients used for this purpose are titanium dioxide and zinc oxide. Titanium dioxide has very good covering properties and is better than zinc oxide in this respect. However, it does not blend well with the other ingredients of the powder. Up to 10% of titanium dioxide can be used with zinc oxide. Zinc oxide has good covering, astringent, antiseptic as well as soothening properties. It should be used in the range of 15–25%.

Slip imparting agents: Slip refers to the quality of a powder that helps in easy spread and application to produce a smooth feeling on the skin. Talc is the main ingredient used to impart slip. Metallic soaps such as zinc stearate can also be used. The talc used for face powders should be white, odourless and slip on the skin easily. Very fine–size talc, which is passed through a standard 200 mesh sieve, should be used and it should be free of asbestos. Talc is hydrated magnesium silicate. It can be used at up to 70% or more. It has good 'slip' and 'adhesion' properties.

Adhesion agents: Adhesion is that property of a face powder that determines how well the powder clings to the face. Adhesion can be imparted by inclusion of talc and some water-insoluble metallic soaps such as zinc and magnesium stearate at a concentration of 3–10%. Emollients such as cetyl or stearyl alcohol and glyceryl mono stearate at a concentration of 0.5–1.5% improve the adhesion.

Blooming agents: Bloom is the delicate powdery surface deposit which indicates freshness. The ingredients used to impart bloom are rice starch, calcium carbonate and prepared starch.

Colouring agents: Pigments and lakes can be used to colour face powders. Water-soluble or oil-soluble dyes should be avoided because of the danger of colour bleeding after application, due to solubilisation by sweat and sebaceous secretions. Only colours approved by local regulators should be used.

Dyes are not suitable as they are soluble either in water or in oil. Pigments are insoluble colouring material, which may be inorganic or organic. Many inorganic pigments are salts of heavy metals and some of them can be toxic. Organic pigments are available as lakes in red, pink, orange, etc.

Perfumes: Usually, very light perfumes are used in face powders. A flowery or fruity (lemon) perfume is preferred. Care should be taken to ensure that there are no compatibility problems, as perfumes may not mix well with other ingredients such as talc, chalk, kaolin, etc.

Light Powder

Formula

Talc—80%
Zinc oxide—5%
Zinc stearate—5%
Rice starch—10%
Perfume—qs
Colour—qs

Opaque Powder

Formula

Talc—30%
Zinc oxide—20%
Zinc stearate—10%
Rice starch—40%
Perfume—qs
Colour—qs

Medium Powder

Formula

Talc—60%
Precipitated chalk—15%
Zinc oxide—20%
Zinc sterate—5%
Perfume—qs
Colour—qs

In manufacturing face powder, the materials should be ground to a very fine state of subdivision and then passed through a sieve of at least 100 or 120 mesh and then mixed in a horizontal mixer with a screw agitator.

If water- or alcohol-soluble dyes are used, they are best sprayed on the mix or alternatively on to one of the constituents that possess good absorbency, such as talc, kaolin or magnesium carbonate. This mixture is then dried and mixed into the main bulk

Perfumes can also be added by spraying the liquid perfumes onto the powder. The main bulk is then mixed in a mixer and sieved.

Compact Powders

Compact powders are face powders that are in the form of a cake. They are convenient to use and are very popular.

Methods

There are two methods of preparation: the damp method and the dry method.

In the damp method, the powder is mixed with a suitable binding agent and milled to the requisite plasticity. It is then compressed into suitable containers and dried for the requisite period in a current of warm air. In the dry process, the mass is subjected to compression without being wetted to any appreciable extent. This method is probably the best for manufacturing compacts on a large scale.

The presses available for the manufacture of compact powders may be of the hydraulic or the reciprocating mechanical type, varying in size, operating pressures and output. Compact powders are used with a powder puff and should not crumble or break during handling.

The main difference between loose powders and compact powders lies in their binding properties. Satisfactory binding properties are essential for trouble-free compression and the production of good quality cakes over long manufacturing periods. The powders used should be free flowing so that they do not adhere to punches or dyes during compression.

The composition of compact powders is generally very similar to that of loose powders. Here, colloidal kaolin, zno and metallic stearates are usually present in higher levels than in loose face powders and starch is sometimes incorporated to facilitate compression. If the powders are not significantly binding, they may require a binding agent to improve their cohesion, so that a firm cake is produced on compression. Natural and synthetic gums such as tragacanth and low viscosity carboxy methyl cellulose may be used for binding purposes in amounts of 0.1–3%. Water-insoluble binding agents such as glyceryl monostearate, cetyl and stearyl alcohol, lanolin, oozokerite and paraffin waxes may be used in the form of o/w emulsions so that they are uniformly distributed throughout the product. Emulsifying agents such as triethanolamine stearate and poly oxy ethylene sorbitan esters can be used for this purpose. Materials such as zinc stearate and magnesium stearate can be used as dry binders.

To formulate compact powder, 5 parts of binding solutions must be added to 100 parts of powders.

Formula I

Talc—40%
Kaolin—30%
Cacium carbonate—10%
Magnesium stearate—5%
Zinc stearate—15%
Colour—qs
Perfume—qs

Formula II

Talc—30%
Kaolin—50%
Zinc oxide—5%
Rice starch—15%
Colour—qs
Perfume—qs

The following are the formula for binders.

Formula I

Sodium carboxy methyl cellulose—2%
Water—qs to 100%

Formula II

Stearic acid—35%
Mineral oil—25%
TEA—10%
Water—qs to 100%

All the ingredients are blended in a mixer for an hour. The binding solution is then sprayed to the powder mixture and the mixture is passed through the pulveriser and compressed at 1000 psi.

Nail Lacquer (Nail Varnish/Enamel)

Nail lacquer or polish, also known as nail varnish, is a cosmetic lacquer that is applied on both finger and toenails. Apart from enabling ornamentation, nail polish also protects nails from harmful external agents.

The requirements of a nail lacquer are as follows:

- It should be harmless to the skin and nails.
- It should be convenient and easy to apply.
- It should be stable on storage.

- It should form a satisfactory film on nails.

The characteristics of a satisfactory film are as follows:

- It should have proper viscosity (neither too thick nor too thin) and good wetting and flow properties so that the film formed is even.
- It should have uniform colour, which requires a very finely divided pigment, intimately wetted and grounded by the medium.
- It should have good gloss, which implies a very smooth surface.
- It should have good adhesion to the nail.
- It should have sufficient flexibility so that it does not crack or become brittle.
- It should have a sufficiently hard surface that is resistant to impact and scratches.
- It should have reasonable drying time (1–2 minutes) without developing bloom.
- It should maintain the abovementioned properties for at least 1 week.

Ingredients

The following are the ingredients used in the formulation of nail lacquers:

- Film formers
- Resins
- Plasticisers
- Solvents
- Diluents
- Colours
- Pearlescent pigments
- Suspension agents

Film Formers

The basic film-forming material in nail lacquers is nitrocellulose. Special grades of nitrocellulose are available for nail lacquers; each give sufficiently fluid solutions to allow easy application on the nails. Other film formers include cellulose acetate, cellulose acetate butylate, ethyl cellulose, vinyl polymers and various polymers of methacrylate.

Films produced by nitrocellulose are waterproof, hard, tough and resist abrasion. However, when used alone, nitrocellulose has some drawbacks such as poor gloss, tendency to shrink and become brittle and moderate adhesion. Therefore, modifying resins are used to impart adhesion and gloss, and plasticisers to induce flexibility and reduce shrinkage.

Resins

Resins impart adhesion and improve gloss. Resins of aryl sulphonamide formaldehyde provide good lustre to nail varnish films and improve their resistance in detergent solutions. Santolite MHP and Santolite MS 80% and maleic alkyd resins are examples of commercially available resins.

These resins are moderately stable to light and soluble in the majority of lacquer solvents and diluents usually employed. However, as their solvent release for higher alcohols is slow, the volume of high alcohols used should be kept to a minimum. The use of nylon in amounts of up to 4% of solids has been known to produce an improved film with quick drying properties. Maleic alkyd resins have also been used because of their compatibility with nitrocellulose and their enhancement of light stability, hardness and solvent release.

Plasticisers

Plasticisers produce flexibility and adhesion in films. They ensure that the film that remains on the nails after the solvents have evaporated adheres well, is flexible and does not flake off. By virtue of their high boiling point, plasticisers will remain in the film after the solvents present in the formulation have evaporated and render the film pliable.

A good plasticiser must:

- Be miscible in all proportions with the solvent, nitrocellulose and resin used
- Be dermatologically innocuous and free from any sensitising properties
- Have low volatility
- Improve the flexibility and adhesion of the lacquer
- Not cause any discolouration of the finished product
- Be stable and odourless

There are two groups of plasticisers: solvent and non-solvent. Solvent plasticisers are true plasticisers that are solvents of nitrocellulose. They comprise high-molecular-weight esters, with fairly high boiling points and low volatility. Non-solvent plasticisers are referred to as softeners. They are not solvents for nitrocellulose and are not compatible with it. They must be used in conjunction with solvent plasticisers to hold them in the solution as, in the absence of solvent plasticisers, they will form separate droplets on the film once the solvents have evaporated.

The amount of plasticiser used in nail lacquers varies from about 25–50% based on the dry weight of the nitrocellulose present and on the degree of flexibility required.

A formulation may contain one or more plasticisers. Pthalates, phosphates, pthalyl glycollates, sulphonamides and citrate are the main groups of plasticisers. The most widely used is dibutyl phthalate. Other examples include tributyl phosphate, butyl glycollate, triethyl citrate, castor oil and dibutyl tartrate.

Solvents

The part that evaporates from the nail polish is the solvent. It is also responsible for the strong odour of the nail polish. Once the nail polish has been applied on the nails, the solvent evaporates evenly, leaving behind a hard and smooth coat. It is essential to choose the combination of the solvent properly, failing which the solvent might take too long to evaporate, ruining the coat of the polish. It is because of this that nail polish bottles are kept covered so that the polish does not lose the solvent and become too thick to use.

Solvents are generally classified according to their boiling points as:

- Low boiling solvents (with a boiling point of up to 100 °C); for example, acetone or ethyl acetate
- Medium boiling solvents (100 °C); for example, N-butyl acetate
- High boiling solvents (over 150 °C); for example, cellosolve, cellosolve acetate, butyl cellosolve

Although the boiling point does play a role, it is the evaporation rate at temperatures not much above 30 °C that is the main concern. This will depend on a number of factors such as specific heat, latent heat of evaporation, molecular weight, degree of association, etc.

Diluents

These are organic solvents miscible with nitrocellulose solvents. They are used as solvents for modifying resins used in lacquers, since true nitrocellulose solvents are expensive. They also help to stabilise the viscosity of lacquers.

There are three classes of diluents:

- Alcohols
- Aromatic hydrocarbons
- Aliphatic hydrocarbons

There is a limit to the amount of diluents that can be tolerated by the nitrocellulose solution;

this is called the dilution ratio. Dilution ratio is defined as the maximum diluent-to-solvent ratio that can be tolerated by a nitrocellulose solution without causing the latter to be precipitated.

Also, in the formulation of lacquers, use of a high-boiling-point diluent with a low-boiling-point solvent must be avoided if precipitation of nitrocellulose and blushing of the film are not to occur. In general, when dealing with compositions containing solvent and diluent mixtures, the rate of evaporation of the diluents should be greater than that of the solvent or the solvent mixture employed. Otherwise the diluents–solvent ratio in the film will steadily increase and eventually the tolerance ratio will be exceeded, causing nitrocellulose to precipitate on the film. As a result, instead of the smooth, clear and continuous film expected to be achieved, a harsh, rough and cloudy film will be produced which will lack adhesion.

Alcohols, particularly ethyl, isopropyl ethyl and butyl are very efficient diluents, their tolerance ratio being 9:1. Isopropyl alcohol is widely used because of its low cost and easy availability. Aromatic hydrocarbons such as toluene and xylene are used. Their tolerance ratio is 3:1, which is lower than that obtained with alcohols, and they are not such efficient diluents. They also tend to increase the viscosity of nitrocellulose solutions and tend to impart poor flow properties. This may be overcome by using a mixture of toluene and isopropyl alcohol.

Colours

Insoluble lakes are incorporated in the majority of nail lacquers to produce the suitable shade. Soluble dyestuffs such as erythrosine, carmoisine and rhodamine are no longer used as they stain the surrounding skin.

Requirements for a pigment:

- It should be non-toxic and non-sensitising.
- It should be non-staining.
- It should be substantially insoluble in lacquer solvents.
- It should be free from any tendency to bleed.
- It should be compatible with other lacquer constituents.
- It should be moderately stable to light.
- It should be of very small particle size, free from grit.
- It should have satisfactory dispersing properties.

The most widely employed pigments include D&C Red No 6, D&C Red No 30, D&C Red No 36, D&C Red No 9, D&C Red No 7, FD&C Yellow No 5 and FD&C Yellow No 6. Titanium dioxide has been used to impart opacity and produce pale shades, while iron oxides are used to produce brown and tan shades.

Pearlescent Pigments

Nail lacquers can incorporate iridescent materials such as guanine, a crystalline substance produced by the scales and body of various fish. They give a pearly lustre and brilliance to the nail lacquer. Synthetic pearl pigments like bismuth oxychloride produce high lustre and brilliance at low cost.

Another example is mica coated with titanium dioxide. It is less brilliant and has less covering power but has good suspending properties.

Suspension Agents

Insoluble pigments and iridescent materials have a tendency to settle. The use of suspending agents has shown them to be technically superior and to have enhanced consumer acceptance. Suspending properties have been achieved by developing thixotropic system using pre-treated colloidal clays, for example, benzyl dimethyl hydrogenated tallow, ammonium montmorillonite (Bentone 27) and dimethyl dioctadecyl ammonium bentonite (bentonite 34). These clays increase the viscosity to a great extent and the heavy oxides remain suspended. Being thixotropic, viscosity drops either when the bottle is shaken or when a product is applied with a brush on the nail. The concentration of bentone ranges 0.5–2%. Viscosity can be further enhanced by adding small quantities of polyvalent acid, for example, orthophosphoric acid.

The following is a typical nail lacquer base formula.

Formula

Nitrocellulose—10%
Resin—10%
Plasticiser—5%
Ethyl alcohol—5%
Ethyl acetate—30%
Butyl acetate—10%
Toluene—30%

The manufacturing of nail lacquer is usually carried out by specialised manufacturing firms which are familiar with the hazards of working with nitrocellulose and solvents. The following three steps are involved in the manufacture of nail polish:

1. Grinding of pigments: The pigments are mixed with nitrocellulose and the plasticiser using a 'two-roll' differential speed mill. The goal is to produce fine dispersion of colour. When properly and fully milled, the mixture is removed from the mill in sheet form. This sheet while hot is soft and plastic and can be easily dissolved in the lacquer. On cooling the sheet hardens and can be broken into chips for later use.
2. Manufacture of nail lacquer: Portable or stationary stirrer-type mixers made of aluminum or stainless steel are used. For manufacturing clear lacquers, diluents are first charged into the mixing tank. Nitrocellulose is then added with the stirrer turned on and is wetted thoroughly with diluents. Subsequently, the solvent is added, then the plasticiser is added, followed by the resin. Mixing is continued for several hours until a solution of all the ingredients is obtained. Thus formed, clear lacquer is passed through a filter press or is centrifuged. The clear lacquer is stored in suitable containers until required for use. Filtration or centrifugation is an important step as it removes foreign particles and insoluble particles imparting clarity and brilliance to the lacquer.
3. Mixing of pigments with lacquer: For manufacturing nail enamels, the required amount of clear lacquer is charged into the mixing tank and the stirrer is switched on. To this pigment chips or pigment concentrate are added and mixing is continued. The product is then filled into containers and closed and screw-sealed immediately.

The nail polish is tested throughout the manufacturing process for several important parameters such as drying time, smoothness of flow, gloss, hardness, colour, abrasion resistance, etc. The criteria for evaluating the nail enamel are its colour, application wear, dry time, gloss and hardness.

Eye Cosmetics

Eye cosmetics have been used for thousands of years by women of different cultures. Kohl was used to colour the eyelids black while malachite was used by Egyptians to produce a green tint. Chinese and Japanese women used Peruvian bark as eye makeup and Phoenician women lengthened their eyebrows with a black paste made of gum arabic, musk, ebony and powdered black insects.

Modern eye cosmetics include the following:

- Mascara
- Eye shadow
- Eyeliner
- Eyebrow pencil
- Eye makeup removers

Mascara (Eyelash cosmetic)

Mascara is a black pigmented preparation applied to the eyelash or eyebrows for beautifying the eyes. It has been used to darken the eyelash and to increase their apparent length, thereby enhancing the brightness and expressiveness of the eyes.

Mascaras are available as:

- Cake (Block) mascara
- Cream mascara
- Liquid mascara

A good mascara should possess the following characteristics:

- It should be capable of easy and even application.
- It should not smudge.
- It should not cake as this would cause the eyelashes to stick together.
- It should have good drying properties.
- It should be neither a toxic nor an irritant.

The US FDA has banned the use of coal tar colours in eye preparations. Only natural colours such as vegetable colours, inorganic pigments and lakes (black and dark brown pigments) can be used.

Pure vegetable colours include chlorophyll, except the grade containing copper. Black pigments include black iron oxide (Fe_3O_4). When this is used along with ultramine blue, a blue-black shade results. Umbers (brown ochres), burnt sienna and synthetic brown oxides are used for brown shades. Yellow ochres are used for yellow shades. Soluble blue oil is used to produce a bluish shade, chromium oxide for a green shade and carmine for a red shade. To lighten the shades, white pigments such as titanium dioxide and zinc oxide are used.

Cake (Block) Mascara

Cake mascara is applied with a wet brush. The amount of water mixed with cake mascara varies significantly from person to person and therefore there might be no uniformity in application.

Earlier types of mascara were based on a mixture of soap and carbon black. These were made into a stiff paste using water, and later dried and stamped into cakes. As these formulations contained a water-soluble base, tears and even heavy rain produced black streaks and smudges. Also, a trace of the soap base in the eye could caused extreme irritation.

Modern cakes essentially consist of a soap modified in consistency with oils and waxes, and colour. Unlike the sodium soaps of coconut and palm oil used in earlier mascaras, modern mascaras contain less alkaline and less irritant triethanolamine soaps, for example, triethanolamine stearate.

Formula

Triethanolamine stearate—40%

Paraffin wax—30%

Beeswax—12%

Anhydrous lanolin—5%

Lampblack—13%

The waxy materials are first melted and colour is then added. The mixture is then mixed thoroughly till an even distribution is obtained. This resultant mixture is then cooled and worked in a heated roller mill. It is then re-melted in a pan and cast into cakes.

Cream Mascara

These are preparations containing pigments in a vanishing cream base.

Formula

Triethanolamine stearate—45%

Carnauba wax—15%

Glyceryl monostearate—5%

Anhydrous lanolin—10%

Unbleached beeswax—5%

Lampblack—20%

The coloured pigment may be incorporated into the base immediately after emulsification has been completed and agitated while the product is cooling. Alternatively, a previously prepared base is melted and the pigment is incorporated into the base.

Special Cream Mascara

The development of novel brushes and applicators has led to the development of a special cream mascara. Waterproof mascara is one such example. This is currently very popular.

This is the formula of a typical waterproof mascara.

Formula

Isoparaffins—50%

Ozokerite wax—15%

Carnauba wax—5.5%

Aluminum stearate—2%

Isopropyl myristate—2%

Mineral oil—0.5%

Kaolin—10%

Black iron oxide—5%

Yellow iron oxide—1%

Liquid Mascara

These have been available in the market for many years but did not gain wide consumer acceptance until the development of a special cylindrical container with a small-diameter brush integrated into a screw-on lid. This dispenser makes it convenient to use and to carry in the handbag.

Earlier preparations were prepared by suspending the pigment in mucilage, but these preparations were sticky and tended to smudge. To overcome these drawbacks, modern preparations use an alcoholic solution of a resin in which carbon black is suspended. Examples of such resins include rosin (10% alcohol solution) and ethyl cellulose. A little castor oil is also added.

Formula

Rosin (10% alcohol solution)—3%

Castor oil—3%

Ethyl alcohol—84%

Lampblack—10%

The resin is first dissolved in alcohol by stirring it in. Then carbon black is made into a pourable paste using castor oil and an alcoholic solution of resin. This mixture is then stirred well and poured into dispensers.

Eye Shadow

These are cosmetic creams or powders in various colours that are applied to the eyelids to accentuate the eyes. Eye shadows are applied to produce an attractive moist-looking background for the eyes. They are available in a variety of shades such as brown, green, blue, etc. Bronze powder, gold and silver leaf and aluminum powder are used to produce a glittering effect. Pearlescent pigments such as bismuthoxychloride and mica coated with titanium dioxide may also be used.

The characteristics of a good eye shadow are as follows:

- It should have good skin adhesion.
- It should be easy to apply.
- It should not get smudged by sweat or sebum.
- It should be non-irritant and safe.

Eye shadow preparations are available in various forms:

- Cream eye shadow
- Emulsion-type eye shadow
- Stick eye shadow
- Press-powder eye shadow
- Liquid eye shadow

Cream Eye Shadow: These are eye shadows made with a cream base.

Formula

Cocoa butter—2%

Beeswax—3%

Spermaceti—7.5%

Lanolin—7.5%

Petroleum jelly—50%

Zinc oxide—30%

Cosmetic lake, preservative—qs

Colours are mixed and then blended with petroleum jelly in a roller mill. This mass is then stirred into a blend of melted fatty and waxy constituents. The mixture is then thoroughly agitated and poured into suitable containers when still in liquid form.

Alternatively, the powder pigments may be stirred directly into the molten mass of fats and waxes and then passed through a roller mill to ensure thorough distribution of colours and to remove any lumps. The resultant mixture is again mixed before being poured to the container.

Waterproof cream eye shadows can be prepared by adding silicone complexes.

Emulsion-type Eye Shadow: In this type, pigments are mixed into an emulsion and distributed evenly throughout the base.

Formula

Stearic acid—2%

Glyceryl monostearate—2%

Lanolin—5%

Isopropyl myristate—5%

Triethanolamine—1.25%

Propylene glycol—5%

Ultramine blue—5%

Black iron oxide—1%

Mica coated with titanium dioxide—10%

Water—qs to 100%

These are produced by mixing suitable pigments into an emulsion and distributing them evenly throughout the base. The product is then filled into containers when cold. Special care must be taken when filling these products as problems with stability may be encountered.

Stick Eye Shadow: These contain a fairly high proportion of waxes such as ozokerite or carnauba. These are manufactured in the same way as lipsticks.

Formula

Castor oil—45%

Mineral oil—5%

Carnauba wax—30%

Titanium dioxide—10%

Iron oxide—10%

Pressed-powder Eye Shadow: These are prepared either as loose powder or as compressed powder. They are applied by means of a sponge-tipped plastic rod, although finger-tip application is also popular.

Formula

Talc—80%

Zinc stearate—10%

Ultramine blue—5%

Black iron oxide—0.5%

Chrome hydrate—2%

Base*—4%

*Formula: Beeswax—12%; Lanolin—2%; Mineral oil—86%

Liquid Eye Shadow: These are in the form of a liquid suspension or a liquid dispersion. The liquid suspension is prepared by suspending pigments in a mixture of oils. The liquid dispersion is prepared from dilute solutions of alcohol in water which are thickened with a synthetic gum such as methylcellulose. They are suitably preserved and contain a wetting agent in which the pigments are dispersed. These preparations are however not very popular.

Eyeliner: Eyeliners are preparations for use on eyelids, particularly the upper eyelids. They help increase the expressiveness of the eye. They are available in liquid, cake and pencil forms.

Dry Eyeliner

Formula

Mineral oil—5%

Colour—30%

Titanium dioxide—5%

Talc—60%

Liquid Eyeliner

Formula

Veegum—2.5%

PVP K-30—2%

Water—85.5%

Pigment—10%

Preservative—qs

Liquid eyeliners are prepared by dispersing solids in an emulsion base. The preparation of cake eyeliners is similar to that of a cake eye shadow.

Eyebrow Pencil

Eyebrow pencils are used to accentuate the natural eyebrow line or to modify their outline after plucking. These may be of a wax crayon type or an ordinary lead pencil type in which a crayon type formulation is enclosed in a wooden casing. They are available in shades such as black, brown, blue, etc.

Formula

Hydrogenated castor oil—46%

Hydrogenated cottonseed oil—12%

Cocoa butter (odourless) —8%

Castor oil—8%

Lanolin absorption base—17%

Black iron oxide—9%

An eyebrow pencil is made by dispensing the pigments in a wax base of liquid type. The proportion of beeswax can be increased to produce a firmer pencil.

Eye Makeup Remover

These are low-viscosity fatty materials such as mineral oil, alone or in combination with other oils and/or fatty acid esters. These products are either sold as cotton pads saturated with oil or as tissue oils which are applied around the eye and removed with a tissue paper.

Formula

Light mineral oil—80%

Isopropyl myristate—20%

Hair Dyes

Hair dyes are cosmetic preparations used to colour the hair. The reasons for colouring the hair are as follows:

- To change the natural colour
- To colour the white/grey hairs that begin to appear with age
- To change the colour of the hair temporarily on a particular occasion

An ideal hair dye should colour the hair without impairing its natural texture and gloss. It should be non-irritant and non-toxic as the chemicals used in these preparations have the potential to be mutagenic, teratogenic and carcinogenic.

Hair dyes are of three types: temporary, semi-permanent and permanent.

Temporary Hair Colour

These dyes coat the surface of the hair and usually wash out within two or three sessions of shampooing. These products use colours of high molecular weight. As the pigment molecules in temporary hair colour are large they do not penetrate the cuticle layer, allowing only a coating action that may be removed by shampooing.

Acid dyes are used to coat the surface of hair, since they have a low affinity to hair and can thus be removed by shampooing. Temporary hair colours are available in various product forms including rinses, shampoos, gels and sprays. This type of hair colour is typically used to produce brighter, more vibrant shades or colours such as orange or red; that may be difficult to achieve with semi-permanent and permanent hair colours. This phenomenon is due to the fact that temporary hair colorants do not penetrate the hair shaft itself. Instead, these dyes remain adsorbed to the follicle and can be easily removed.

While the demand for temporary hair colour products is less than that for semi-permanent and permanent agents, they have value in that they can be easily and quickly removed without bleaching or application of a different dye.

Examples of temporary hair dyes are those belonging to the chemical classes azo, anthraquinone, triphenyl methane and xanthine (Table 20.1).

Semi-permanent Hair Colour

Semi-permanent hair colours have smaller molecules than those of temporary hair dyes,

Table 20.1: Chemical classes and the corresponding colours

Chemical Class	*Colour*
Acid dyes	
Azo	Yellow
Red	
Orange	
Brown	
Triphenylmethane	Green 22
Xanthenes	Acid violet
Azine	Nigrosines (violet)
Anthraquinone	Acid violet 43
Basic dyes	
Azo	Yellow 57
Orange	
Triphenylmethane	Basic blue 5
Azine	Red
Disperse dyes	
Azo	Yellow
Anthraquinonone	Orange 11
Metallised dyes	
Azo	Cibane blue

and are therefore able to penetrate the hair shaft. These dyes penetrate into the hair shaft, but not as deeply as permanent dyes. Although semi-permanent dyes do not rinse off with water, they do fade and wash out of the hair after about five to 10 shampoo sessions. The colours used in this case are direct dyes of low molecular weight and have a good affinity to hair keratin.

The majority of these dyes belong to the group of nitro-phenylenediamines, nitroaminophenols and aminoanthraquinones. The shades produced vary from yellow and orange to red. These are available in the form of lotions containing surfactants or shampoos.

Permanent Hair Dyes

These are resistant to shampooing and other external factors such as brushing, friction, light, etc. These are based on the use of oxidation dyes which are colourless and which are transformed into coloured material in situ on the hair as a consequence of chemical reaction. It makes use of two ingredients, namely, oxidation bases and couplers or modifiers.

In the hair, two types of melanin protein are found: eumelanin, which is responsible for hair shades from black to brown, and phaeomelanin, which is responsible for red and yellow-ish colours.

The melanin type and granule size determine the colour of the hair, while the density of distribution of these pigment granules determines how light or dark the hair is. Before any permanent colour can penetrate the hair shaft, the cuticle or outer layer must be opened so that chemicals can get into the natural pigment molecules.

The ingredients that are used in the formulation of permanent hair dyes are as follows:

Bases: These compounds are called oxidation bases or primary intermediates. These are benzene derivatives having electron donor groups such as NH2 and/or OH, which are para or ortho to each other. This confers the property of easy oxidation. For example, p-phenylenediamine, p aminophenol and o-aminophenol.

Couplers or Modifiers: These are aromatic compounds, benzene derivatives having the same groups NH2 and/or OH as the bases but in the meta position to each other. They do not have the property of easy oxidation. For example, m-phenylenedamine, resorcinol, phenyleneaminophenols and m-aminophenol.

Oxidising agent: This is almost always hydrogen peroxide but sometimes urea peroxide may be used. The chemical reactions in the formation of dyes are oxidation reactions and coupling or condensations, effected by alkaline pH (presence of ammonia) by the action of the oxidising agent (hydrogen peroxide or urea peroxide). Examples of colours to be achieved with various couplers and p-phenylediamines are given in Table 20.2.

Permanent hair-colouring products consist of two components that are packaged separately and mixed together immediately before application. One package contains a solution of hydrogen peroxide (usually 6%) in water. The other

Table 20.2

Coupler	*Colour Obtained*
Resorcinol	Green/Brown
m-aminophenol	Magenta/Brown
2,4-diaminoanisole and m-phenylenediamine	Blue
1-naphthol	Puple-blue

package usually contains an ammonia solution of bases and couplers.

The bases develop colour on oxidation. The colour couplers do not oxidise readily but react with the oxidised bases to provide a wider variety of colours. As soon as the ammonia dye solution and the hydrogen peroxide solution are mixed together, they are applied to the hair. The ammonia in the mixture (less than 1% concentration) causes the hair to swell and the cuticle scales to separate a little. After this happens, the dye precursors are able to penetrate the cuticle before they have fully reacted with each other and with the hydrogen peroxide.

Darker shades are obtained by using higher concentrations of bases. Tones can also be adjusted. For example, addition of resorcinol will make a shade more yellow, while adding 4-amino-2-hydroxytoluene will make the shade more red. Sometimes dyes are used along with the oxidation dye intermediates (bases) to add vibrancy to a tone that is not otherwise available. Usually these dyes are used to add intensity to gold or red shades.

The two main problems of para dyes are skin irritation and systemic toxicity. All hair colour products, except for temporary colour, suggest a patch test before application to determine if the client has any skin irritation or reaction. Toxicologcal/Epidemiological studies will be carried out to ascertain systemic toxicity in the long run.

The FDA requires that these preparations be labelled with the statement 'Caution. This product contains ingredients which may cause skin irritation on certain individuals, and a preliminary test according to the accompanying directions should first be made. This product must not be used for dying the eyelashes or eyebrows; to do so may cause blindness.'

Alternatives to Chemical Based Dyes

It has been recorded that ancient civilisations dyed their hair using plant susbstances. Some of these substances are discussed below:

Henna

Henna consists of the dried powdered leaves of Lawsonia alba, Lawsonia spinosa and Lawsonia inemis. It owes its hair-dyeing properties to the presence of 2-hydroxy-1,4-naphthaquinone, often termed lawsone, which is soluble in hot water and is, in acid solutions, a substantive dye for keratin. In dyeing with henna, a part of the powdered henna and hot water, slightly acidified with citric and adipic acids to an optimum pH of about 5.5 is applied to washed hair.

Advantages

- It is neither a primary irritant nor a sensitizer; nor does it possess local or systemic toxicity.
- The colour obtained is relatively stable and is deposited in the hair shaft.

Disadvantages

- Messy to use.
- Range of colours produced is limited to reddish-auburn shades.
- Stains the keratin of the finger nails.
- Repeated dyeing tends to spoil the effect and produce a somewhat hard auburn colour.

Henna Reng

By the addition of other substances to henna different shades can be obtained. For example, a mixture of powdered indigo leaves and henna produces blue-black shades and such mixtures are known as henna rengs.

Chamomile

Anthemis nobilis (Roman chamomile) and Matricaria chamomillae (German chamomile) are used to tint hair. The active ingredient in these flowers is 1, 3, 4-trihydroxyflavone, known as apigenin.

Metallic Hair Dyes

Compounds of lead are the most frequently used. The less frequently used are compounds of copper, silver, iron, nickel, cobalt and bismuth. These dyes deposit a coloured film along the hair shaft, which eventually gives the hair a characteristic dull metallic appearance. However, it also renders the hair brittle and diminishes the efficiency of a subsequent permanent wave.

Lead Dyes

The active ingredient in these dyes is lead acetate along with some precipitated sulphur, glycerin and water. The action of lead dyes is slow and progressive, and the shades produced in grey hair usually pass from yellow through brown to black. The shades depend on the concentration of lead salts in the preparation, number of applications, original colour of hair and duration that the colour has been allowed to develop.

These are relatively non-toxic probably because of the interaction with skin proteins. These preparations can be fatal especially in children if ingested when the lead left behind on the hands contaminates food.

Other non-toxic safer products that do not produce the side-effects of chemical-based dyes are also available. These alternatives generally have fewer chemicals or are plant-based. Some of the most well-known examples of vegetable dyes are henna, indigo, cassia, senna, turmeric and amla. They come as temporary, semi-permanent and permanent options. However, these products typically do not last as long as chemical-based dyes.

Key Messages

- The different types of skin creams are cleansing creams and lotions, emollient creams and lotions and all-purpose creams.
- The purpose of cleansing creams and lotions is the removal of facial makeup and oil secretions and to cleanse the face.
- Cold creams are based on a beeswax–borax combination.
- Emollient creams are preparations containing emollients which are used to prevent or provide relief from dryness as well as to protect the skin.
- All-purpose creams act as both emollients and cleansing creams.
- Dentifrices are preparations used for the oral cavity, primarily to clean the teeth, prevent tooth decay, maintain gingival health and prevent bad odours.
- Dentifrices can be classified as toothpastes, tooth powders and mouthwashes.
- Abrasives, detergents, humectants, binding agents, flavours, sweetening agents, preservatives and colouring agents are used in the manufacture of tooth powders.
- Antibacterials, sweetening agents and flavouring agents in hydroalcoholic medium are used in the preparation of mouthwashes.

- Shaving preparations help prepare the beard and face for shaving, increase speed and comfort during the shave and confer a feeling of well-being after shaving.
- Shaving preparations include wet shaving preparations, dry shaving preparations and after-shave preparations.
- Lipsticks are colour cosmetics used on lips to enhance their attractiveness.
- Lipsticks consist of dispersions of colours in a base of oils, fats and waxes.
- Colouring agents, such as staining dyes, pigments and lakes, are very important components of lipsticks.
- A face powder is a cosmetic product applied to the face at the end of the makeup process, either directly or over a powder base.
- Absorbents, covering agents, slip imparting agents, adhesive agents, blooming agents, colouring agents and perfumes are the ingredients used in the formulation of face powder.
- Compact powders are face powders in the form of a cake. They are convenient to use and are very popular.
- Nail lacquers are used to colour or gloss the nail.
- Film formers, resins, plasticisers, solvents, diluents, colours, pearlescent pigments and suspending agents are used in the formulation of a nail lacquer.
- Eye cosmetics include mascara, eye shadow, eyeliner, eyebrow pencil and eye makeup removers.
- Mascara is a black pigmented preparation applied to the eyelash or eyebrows to beautify the eyes. Mascaras are available as cakes (blocks), creams and liquids.
- Eye shadow preparations are available in the form of creams, emulsion-types, sticks, press-powder and liquids.
- Eyeliners are preparations used on eyelids, particularly the upper eyelids. They help increase the expressiveness of the eyes. They are available as liquids, cakes and pencils.
- Eyebrow pencils are used to accentuate the natural eyebrow line or to modify the outline after plucking. These may be in the form of a wax crayon or an ordinary lead pencil.
- Eye makeup removers are low-viscosity fatty materials such as mineral oils, alone or in combination with other oils and/or fatty acid esters, applied around the eye to remove makeup.
- Hair dyes are cosmetic preparations used to colour the hair.
- Hair dyes can be of three types: temporary, semi-permanent and permanent.
- Aromatic polyhydroxy compounds, vegetable hair dyes (henna, henna rang, chamomile) and metallic hair dyes (lead) are other examples of hair colourants.

Questions

1. Classify the different types of skin creams with a formula for each type.
2. How do cold creams differ from vanishing creams?
3. List the various classes of ingredients used in the formulation of toothpaste with their functions.
4. What are mouthwashes? What are their constituents?
5. Give the formula for tooth powder.
6. Classify the colours used in lipsticks with examples.
7. What are the various classes of ingredients used as bases?
8. Explain how lipsticks are manufactured.

21
Herbal Cosmetics

SHOBHA RANI R HIREMATH AND MUEEN AHMED KK

Learning Objectives

At the end of this chapter, you will be able to:

- Define herbal cosmetics
- Classify herbal cosmetics
- Describe the formulations used in herbal cosmetics
- Describe the nature of human skin and state the requirements of cosmetics for different skin conditions
- List the ingredients used in herbal cosmetics
- Describe the evaluation methods used in herbal cosmetics
- Define essential oils and aromatherapy
- Describe the methods used to extract essential oils
- List the plants from which essential oils are extracted

Introduction

Beauty has been a concern of men and women since time immemorial. The hectic lifestyles of today leave people with much less time for personal grooming than they had before. This has made people turn increasingly to professionals to give them a groomed and 'manicured' look. Moreover, as a larger number of people are concerned about their appearance, the need to appear well-groomed and attractive has assumed greater importance. This factor, combined with the changes wrought in lifestyle by the sharp rise in income, has transformed beauty care (cosmetology) into a multicrore industry.

Cosmetology includes the care and treatment of the skin, hair, face and body and covers diet and exercise as well. Cosmetic products are used all over the world and, although aiming at the same high level of consumer protection, their regulations and requirements are quite different.

In the last two decades, the pharmaceutical industry in general and the cosmetics industry in particular has had a magical metamorphosis with regard to consumer products. In a sense, plants and herbs have always been held to have a powerful magical force. From ancient times, when humans first started searching for medicines to cure illness, or ingredients for cosmetics and products for magical remedies of unconquerable and mostly fatal ailments, plants and herbs have always appeared to possess mysterious properties. While much of this 'mystery' is yet to be unravelled, the scientific quest for herbal therapies has led to experiments with plants and herbs that have considerably improved and enhanced human knowledge.

In recent years, there has been a rapid growth in worldwide demand for plant-based raw materials for the manufacture of food flavours, fragrances, perfumes, cosmetics and related products. Some of them are high-value chemicals and their individual demand may comprise a sizeable chunk of the global market.

At first, the principles underlying these plant or herbal medicines and remedies were far from scientifically defined. The practice of medicine was linked with magical cures, witchcraft, divinity and superstitions. In fact, the origins of most herbal remedies or cosmetic preparations can be traced to sages and mystics, and this has led to their perception as substances that are beneficial to humans.

Definition of a Cosmetic Product

According to the European Commission Directive 93/35/EEC, Article 1:

'A cosmetic product is any substance or preparation intended to be placed in contact with various parts of the human body (epidermis, hair system, nails, lips and external genital organs) or with the teeth and the mucous membranes of the oral cavity with a view exclusively or mainly to cleaning them, perfuming them, changing their appearance and/or correcting body odours and/or protecting them or keeping them in good condition.'

According to the US Federal Food, Drug and Cosmetic Act:

'Cosmetics are defined as (1) articles intended to be rubbed, poured, sprinkled, or sprayed on, introduced into, or otherwise applied to the human body or any part thereof for cleansing, beautifying, promoting attractiveness, or altering the appearance and (2) articles intended for use as a component of any such articles, except that such term shall not include soap.'

Included in both definitions are products such as skin creams, lotions, perfumes, lipsticks, nail polish, eye and facial makeup preparations, shampoos, products used for permanent waves on hair, hair colours, toothpastes and deodorants. Soap products, however, are not considered as cosmetics under this law.

Classification of Herbal Cosmetic Formulations

- Body powders
- Foot powders
- Tooth powders
- Skin cleansers
- Blackhead removers
- Fairness creams
- Face masks
- Skin nourishers
- Hair conditioners
- Skin shampoos
- Bath oils
- Soap bars
- Hair colourants
- Perfumes
- Slimming pills
- Anti-ageing creams

Some of the cosmetic products available for skin care, hair care and general personal care are listed below:

Skin care

- Creams, emulsions, lotions, gels and oils for the skin (face, hands, feet, etc.)
- Face masks (except peeling products)
- Tinted bases (liquids, pastes, powders)
- Makeup powders, after-bath powders, hygienic powders
- Toilet soaps, deodorant soaps
- Perfumes, toilet waters and Eau de Cologne
- Bath and shower preparations (salts, foams, oils, gels)
- Deodorants and anti-perspirants
- Sunbathing products
- Products for tanning without sun
- Skin-whitening products
- Anti-wrinkle products

Hair care

- Depilatories
- Hair care products
  - Hair tints and bleaches
  - Products for waving, straightening and fixing
  - Setting products
  - Cleansing products (lotions, powders, shampoos)
  - Conditioning products (lotions, creams, oils)
  - Hairdressing products (lotions, lacquers, brilliantines)
- Shaving products (creams, foams, lotions)

Miscellaneous

- Products for making up and removing makeup from the face and eyes
- Products intended for application on the lips
- Products for care of the teeth and mouth
- Products for nail care and makeup
- Products for external intimate hygiene

Skin – An Overview

The skin is the largest and one of the most intriguing organs of the body, accounting for 16% of body weight. The skin continually repairs and renews itself. In young people, the main skin complaints are greasy skin and acne. However, as they grow older, the skin becomes dry and the challenge is to counteract this dryness. However, one can have beautiful skin regardless of age, racc or colour.

The skin is composed of cells, sweat pores and sebaceous glands. The surface layer of the skin is covered with a thin sheath of dead cells. These are continually being pushed up to the surface from below. If the dead cells are not removed, they can reduce and even block the skin's effort to breathe and eliminate waste.

For most people, skin care signifies caring for the face. It is true that the face, more than any other part of the body, needs care and attention. The face is constantly exposed to the elements, even in severe winter when the rest of the body is wrapped up. Hence, the face is one of the first parts of the body to show signs of ageing.

The skin has several important functions:

- It provides a protective barrier, defending the body from outside environmental influences, including extremes in temperature and exposure to disease organisms such as harmful bacteria and infections, wind and ultraviolet (UV) rays from sunshine.
- It acts as a thermostat, retaining heat or cooling the body down with sweat.
- It acts as a waste disposal agent. Waste is expelled from the body 24 hours a day through the skin in the form of excess water, toxins and carbon dioxide.

- It is important in body processes such as respiration and metabolism.
- It provides a sense of touch that enables people to communicate with the outside world.
- It responds to sudden changes in emotions.
- The skin is the body's main organ of sexual attraction.

Parts of the Skin

The skin is a complex, engineered covering that has a slightly acidic coating of oil at the surface. This coating protects the skin from some bacteria. Below the surface is a complex of sweat and oil glands, hair follicles, blood vessels, nerves and muscle tissue held together by a tough connective tissue called collagen (Fig. 21.1).

Collagen is very important in determining the health of the skin. The relative health of the collagen determines the contour of the skin, how wrinkled and lined it is. Healthy collagen is often called soluble collagen, because it can absorb and hold moisture.

Below the collagen is a layer of fat and muscle that provides some contour and acts as a cushion and as insulation. The skin has three layers. The innermost layer is known as the **lower dermis**, the middle layer is called the **dermis** and the outer layer is known as the **epidermis.**

Lower Dermis

Various glands such as oil and sweat glands originate in the lower dermis. They rise to the surface of the skin to eliminate waste matter. The lower dermis also acts as a cushion for the rest of the skin. It contains the finely distributed muscles of the skin that regulate body temperature.

Dermis

The dermis is the layer that lies underneath the epidermis and is composed entirely of living cells. It consists of bundles of tough fibres that give the skin its elasticity, firmness and strength.

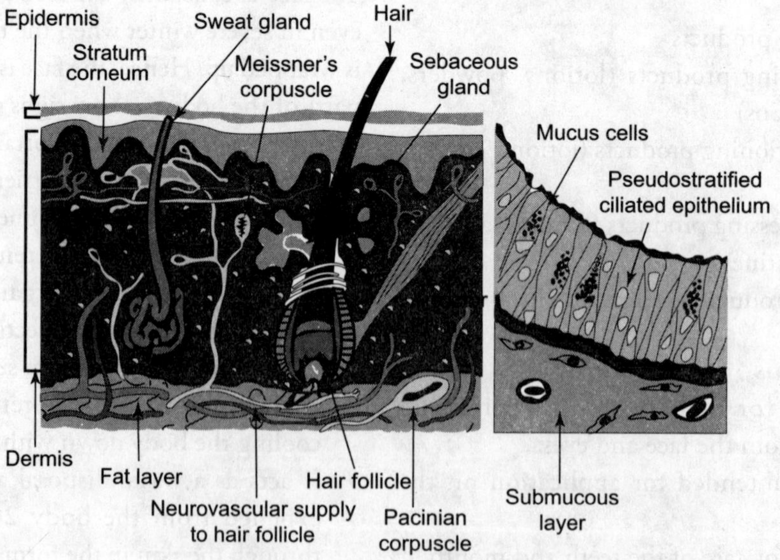

Figure 21.1: Structure of the skin

The dermis also contains blood vessels, which feed vital nutrients to these areas.

The most important function of the dermis is respiration. The countless tiny blood vessels, or capillaries, end here in finely drawn networks, from where they feed the outer skin layer. The dermis also determines the tone of the skin.

Epidermis

This is the topmost layer of skin and is visible. It protects the body from invasion and infection and helps to seal in moisture. It comprises several layers of living cells that are topped by sheets of dead cells. The epidermis grows constantly, with new cells being produced at its base. They quickly die and are pushed up to the surface by the arrival of new cells. These dead cells eventually flake away, which means that every new layer of skin is another chance to have a soft, glowing complexion. The lower levels of living cells are fed by the blood supply from underneath, whereas the upper dead cells only need water to ensure that they are kept plump and smooth. The epidermis is responsible for a person's colouring, as it holds the skin's pigment. It ranges in thickness from $1/20^{th}$ of an inch on the palms and soles, to $1/200^{th}$ of an inch on the face.

The skin contains the following specialised organs:

Sebaceous glands are tiny organs that usually open into hair follicles on the surface of the skin. They produce an oily secretion, called sebum, which is the skin's natural lubricant. The sebaceous glands are most concentrated on the scalp and face, particularly around the nose, cheeks, chin and forehead, due to which, they are usually the most oily areas of the skin.

Sweat glands are present all over the body; there are millions of them and their main function is to regulate body temperature. When sweat evaporates from the skin's surface, the temperature of the skin falls.

Hairs grow from hair follicles. They help keep the body warm by trapping air underneath them. There are no hairs on the soles of the feet and palms of the hands.

Problems of the Skin

The common skin problems are wrinkling (due to age), blemishes or acne, pigmentation, blackening of skin under the eye and blackheads.

Ageing or Wrinkling

Ageing of the skin happens when collagen becomes hard and meshes with neighbouring collagen fibres. This prevents the collagen from holding water and plumping up. Instead, it collapses on itself, binds with other collagen fibres and forms a kind of fishnet below the surface of the skin, which manifests as wrinkles. Oxidation or free radical formation plays a pivotal role in the cross-linking of collagen.

Acne

Acne occurs when oil, called sebum, blocks the pores and hair follicles at the skin's surface, thus preventing the skin from eliminating oil and waste. This causes waste to accumulate in the pores, resulting in pockets of infection that manifest as red sores, boils and pimples, Acne does not occur when the pores remain unblocked.

Skin Pigmentation

The colour of the skin depends on the amount of brown melanin pigment mixed with blue (from reduced hemoglobin), red (from oxyhemoglobin) and yellow (from carotenoids in the diet).

The amount of melanin is determined by constitutional colour (white, brown or black skin) and skin phototype, that is, the result of exposure to UV radiation (tanning).

Blackheads

Blackheads look like black spots; they are actually pores filled with oil deposits and dead skin cells that form plugs. They become coloured because of oxidation of the debris (dead skin cells) that lies on top of them. Because blackheads actually occur below the skin's surface, they need to be purged.

Basic Skin Care

The care given to the skin depends to a large extent on the type of the skin. A daily skin care routine requires no more than ten minutes and consists of only three simple steps every morning and evening:

1. Cleansing
2. Toning
3. Moisturising

Cleansing the Skin

Cleansing the skin is important as it removes the dead cells from the surface of the skin. It also removes the dust and dirt that choke the pores on the skin. If dust is allowed to accumulate, it can block the pores thus blocking the secretions of the glands from coming to the top of the skin and providing it the weapons it needs to fight against infections and toxic agents. It also gives a shine or glow to the surface of the skin.

Soap and Natural Cleansers

Skin experts recommend avoiding soap because of its high pH content. A high pH (alkaline) soap will dry the skin and diminish its life expectancy. The skin's surface is mildly acidic, having a pH of around 5. Most soaps are well over 7, and some are as high as 10. Soaps with a high pH will not only dry the skin but also eliminate its acid mantle (coating on the surface).

Good skin cleansers from natural products can be used. For example, products that contain vegetable oils such as coconut oil and water combine with sebum and allow it to be dissolved and rinsed away. At the same time, water also dissolves dirt.

Effective skin cleansers can contain a number of different vegetable oils, including coconut, sesame or palm oils. These are safe and effective and have a relatively low pH. Stearic acid provides the skin with a pearly firmness.

Facial Scrubs

Facial scrubs help clean the surface of the skin by removing dead cells and dirt mechanically. Abrasives are recommended as facial scrubs. For example, they may contain a very fine, mild base of oatmeal or ground-up almonds. Some products may however contain coarser materials such as silica, fine sand or the shells of almonds, apricots or walnuts.

Toners

Thorough cleansing removes more than makeup, grime and cellular debris. It also strips the skin of its protective shield. Toners, fresheners and astringents restore the pH balance of the acid mantle and remove any remaining makeup that was not cleaned up, oily cleanser or soap film.

After the skin is thoroughly clean, apply a skin toner or rinse that has an astringent effect. This will close the pores, tighten the skin and keep it from being exposed to many of the toxins that are floating in the air or other environmental pollutants.

The common herbs used in toners include witch hazel, geranium, honey, lemon, ivy, sage, nettle and burdock. Witch hazel has a tendency to dry the skin. So this should be balanced with moisturisers such as Vitamin E and honey.

Essential oils are the gentlest way of toning up. Rose water for normal or dry/sensitive skin or witch hazel for oilier skin are ideal bases for fresheners. These can be applied with cotton wool or sprayed on to the face for a more refreshing effect.

Moisturisers

Water is the secret ingredient for dewy-fresh skin. Well-moisturised skin is soft and supple, reflects a healthy glow and ages less quickly. Water prevents the skin from drying and chapping, thus slowing the ageing process. Water moves through the body to the surface in a process called 'transepidermal water loss' leaving the skin pleasingly plump and firm. If the system is deficient in water, the skin's upper layers become dry and brittle. Drinking at least six glasses of water daily and eating fluid-rich fruits and vegetables helps normalise dry or oily conditions and is essential for preventing the body from getting its required moisture at the expense of the skin.

In addition to internal liquid refreshment, the skin also needs external water replenishing. Moisturisers or humectants attract moisture to the skin's surface and hold it there. Younger skin needs only light conditioning whereas older skin needs specific nourishing treatments.

A wide variety of moisturisers are available that range from the inexpensive to the very expensive. Examples are vegetable glycerin, rose water, jojoba oil, Vitamin E oils, sorbitol (derived from plants), honey, aloe vera and iris. Aloe vera is very good for skin care. Since ancient times, it has been used effectively to treat everything from dry skin, burns and insect bites to skin irritations, acne, cuts and abrasions. Mineral oils, used in many skin care products, can dry the skin, block pores and prevent the skin from breathing and eliminating waste.

Masks

Facial masks are some of the oldest known beauty treatments. The ancient Egyptians used mud and clay to remove dead skin cells and heal blemishes. Seventeenth century European women experimented with milk and egg masks. Fresh foods, flowers and herbs were used to cleanse and nourish the skin. A mask softens the skin, unclogs the pores and removes impurities. It also replaces lost moisture and soothes the skin. It is also very relaxing.

Clay and oatmeal are ideal ingredients for any face mask. Fuller's earth is a natural powdered clay that can be mixed into a paste with hot water. It should then be cooled and yogurt should be added for a smoother consistency.

Eye Treatments

The skin around the eyes is much thinner than the skin on the rest of the face. This skin requires extra care to ward off signs of ageing.

Herbal Cosmetics and Formulations

Skin Care

Sunscreen Lotions

Sun filters consist of ingredients that act by penetrating the skin and absorbing the sun's rays so that they do not reach down into the lower layers of the skin and cause damage.

Ingredients

Mulathi—Glycyrrhiza glabra, Aloe vera gel—

Aloe vera, Grape seed oil—Vitis vinifera, Masoor dal extract—Masoorika, Mulberry extract— Morus alba, Base.

Sunscreen Creams

They protect the skin from the harmful rays of the sun and also guard against dust and dirt. Sunscreen creams also protect the skin from sunburns and sun tans.

Ingredients

Genda—Tagetes erecta, Mulathi extract—Glycyrrhiza glabra, Chamomile—Anthemis nobilis, Neem—Melia azadirachta, Gajar—Daucus carota, Aloe—Aloe barbendensis, Tarbuj seed oil—Cytrullus vulgaris, Wheatgerm oil—Triticum sativum, Grape seed oil—Vitis vinifera, Gandhpura oil—Gaultheria procumbans, Puspanzan, Base.

Anti-pigmentation Creams

They are day protection face creams. Anti-pigmentation creams and emulsion creams can be used for all skin types, even sensitive skin. This cream repairs damage caused to DNA by UV light. It has powerful anti-inflammatory properties in sensitive skin and helps to regenerate tissues.

Ingredients

Mulethi—Glycyrrhiza glabra, Lodhra—Symplocos racemosa, Daruhaldi—Berberis aristata, Khus—Vetiveria zizanioides, Sonth—Zingiber officinalis, Alum, Wheatgerm oil—Triticum sativum, Almond oil—Prunus amygdalus, Ghee Kwar, Aloe vera, Base.

Anti-wrinkle Creams

Anti-wrinkle creams reduce the appearance of wrinkles, scarring and signs of ageing by helping the body's natural repair system heal the skin. In a very short space of time, the skin will feel smoother and healthier, be more hydrated and moisture enriched and have a natural glow. Anti-wrinkle creams are also essential for maintaining an already healthy and young-looking skin.

Ingredients

Sweet almond oil—Terminalia catalpa, Grape seed oil—Vitis vinifera, Carrot—Daucus Carota, Vegetable Squalene, Olea europeae (Oil of Europe, a natural oil), Honey, Base.

Face Glow Mask (Herbal Face Packs)

Face packs are a softer and more porous type of face mask. They improve circulation and cleanse the entire face, besides making the skin taut. Because they are soft, they allow the skin to breathe more and are gentler than masks. The juice of fresh fruits and vegetables tone and provide enzymes that help balance and cleanse the skin.

Ingredients

Masoorika ark—Lens esculenta, Jaiphal ark—Myristica fragrans, Majuphal ark—Quercus infectoria, Kukutand powder—Pushpanzan garika, Orange oil—Citrus aurantium, Multani Mitti, Base.

Skin Toners

A natural skin toner improves skin tone by tightening the pores. This helps to reduce the appearance of fine lines and wrinkles; it also increases circulation, giving the face a healthy glow, hydrates the skin and restores the skin's natural pH balance.

Ingredients

Angelica, Arnica, Calendula, Chamomile, Comfrey, Elderflower, Ginger, Ginseng root, Honeysuckle, Hops, Horsetail, Juniper, Lavender,

Lemon balm, Nettle, Pegaga, Peppermint, Rosemary, Sage, St. John's wort, Turmeric, Witch hazel, Yarrow, Aloe vera extract, Vegetable glycerin, French lemon essential oil, Vitamin C, Acetic acid, Grapefruit extract, Vitamin E.

Skin Moisturisers

Moisturisers are designed to reduce water loss from the epidermis. They do not reverse sun damage but they do prevent further dryness. They also can protect the barrier from soot and dirt and there is a temporary feeling of smoothness when they are used. The skin may swell slightly and cause some loss of fine wrinkles. The pores may appear to be smaller because of this swelling. Moisturising is not required for those with oily skin.

Ingredients

Angelica, Arnica, Calendula, Chamomile, Comfrey, Elderflower, Ginger, Ginseng root, Honeysuckle, Hops, Horsetail, Juniper, Lavender, Lemon balm, Nettle, Pegaga, Peppermint, Rosemary, Sage, St. John's wort, Turmeric, Witch hazel, Yarrow, Natural emulsifiers of olive oil, Hibiscus rose extract, Aloe vera extract, Vegetable glycerin, Titanium dioxide, Chamomile extract, Hibiscus rose essential oil, Plant gel (Xanthan gum), Vitamin A, Vitamin C, Acetic acid, Grapefruit extract, Vitamin E.

Night-time Moisturisers

A new kind of anti-ageing moisturiser that works throughout the night, targeted night-time moisturisers rejuvenate and correct the skin to achieve the healthiest look possible.

Ingredients

Angelica, Arnica, Calendula, Chamomile, Comfrey, Elderflower, Ginger, Ginseng root, Honeysuckle, Hops, Horsetail, Juniper, Lavender, Lemon balm, Nettle, Pegaga, Peppermint, Rosemary, Sage, St. John's wort, Turmeric, Witch hazel, Yarrow, Natural emulsifiers of olive oil, Aloe vera extract, Vegetable glycerin, Titanium dioxide, Chamomile extract, Mangosteen extract, Essential oil of orange, Plant gel (Xanthan gum), Vitamin C, Acetic acid, Grapefruit extract, Vitamin A, Vitamin E.

Fairness Creams

They improve the complexion and impart a glow to the skin.

Ingredients

Sandal—Santalum album, Saffron—Crocus sativus, Lemon oil—Citrus limonum, Cucumber extract—Cucumis sativa, Aloe vera gel—Aloe vera

Skin Nourishing Gels

They help to balance the skin's natural oils and nourish the skin with natural extracts of herbs and fruits.

Ingredients

Cucumber extract—Cucumis sativa, Neem extract—Azadirachta indica, Aloe Vera—Aloe vera, Grape seed extract—Vitis vinifera

Skin Nourishing Creams

Skin nourishing creams recreate the vitality of the skin, provide essential nourishment for 24 hours and regenerate and make the skin smooth. In addition to Vitamin E, these creams contain highly effective nourishing agents and herbal oils that soften and soothe the skin. They prevent dehydration and the formation of wrinkles, keeping the skin supple with no oily deposit. Fully absorbed, the nourishing cream is also suitable as a day cream for dry skin.

Ingredients
Wheatgerm oil—Triticum sativum germ, Lavender oil—Lavandula vera, Carrot—Daucus carota, Avocado oil—Persea gratissma, Cucumber extract—Cucumis sativa. Base.

Moisturising Lotions
These are dermatological formulations suitable for dry, sensitive skin. They contain a superior system of extra-strength emollients to soften and smooth the skin and humectants that both bind water to the skin and prevent moisture loss. This superior system results in hydration and improvement in the texture of the skin.

Ingredients
Jasmine—Jasminum arborescens, Gulab—Rosa damascene, Chakramard seed—Cassia tora, Ghee kawar—Aloe barbadensis, Cucumber juice—Cucumis sativus, Neem—Melia azadirachta, Base.

Herbal Foot Creams
Herbal foot creams transform hard heels into smooth ones. They penetrate deep into the skin using botanical oils and peppermint to help rejuvenate the skin on the feet.

Ingredients
Sweet almond oil—Terminalia catalpa, Aloe—Aloe vera, Geranium oil—Pelargonium graveolens, Peppermint oil—Mentha piperita, Lavender oil—Lavandula vera, Tea tree oil—Melaleuca alternifolia, Ylang-Ylang—Cananga odorata, Clary sage—Salvia sclera, Base.

Undereye Gels
They reduce dark circles and puffiness under the eyes. The spinach and cucumber extracts help to soothe tired skin and combat inflammation which leads to dark circles and puffiness. These gels help to reverse the signs that lack of sleep, water retention, stress caused by computer strain and general wear and tear can leave on the skin.

Ingredients
Cucumber extract—Cucumis sativa, Chamomile—Matricaria chamomilla, Spinach extract—Basella alba, Aloe—Aloe vera, Base.

Facial Care

Cleansing Milks
A powerful and rejuvenating cleansing milk helps to remove dirt, dust and makeup from the skin, They also nourish the skin and make it healthy.

Ingredients
Khus—Vetiveria zizaniodus, Fenugreek—Trigonella foenum gracecum, Jojoba oil—Simmondsia chinensis, Tea tree oil—Melaleuca alternifolia, Onion extract—Allium cepa, Base.

Cold Creams
Conventional cold creams, also known as vanishing creams, are non-greasy, and most current commercial brands tend to be made of mineral oil (a petroleum product) and/or stearic acid (a fatty acid from animal or vegetable sources).

Ingredients
Jojoba oil—Simmondsia chinensis, Grape seed oil—Vitis vinifera, Liquorice extract—Glycyrrhiza glabra, Nutmeg extract—Myristica fragrans, Rose extract—Rosa vamascena.

For Normal and Combination Skin

Rosemary Cleansing Milk
Cleansing milk is the ideal night cleanser, helping to strengthen and invigorate while

maintaining moisture. These are gentle, non-lathering, moisturising cleansing creams that have been formulated to cleanse sensitive, dry or normal-to-dry skin types and may also be used for the removal of light facial makeup. Cleansing milk dissolves daily dirt, excess oil and makeup residue.

Ingredients

Angelica, Arnica, Calendula, Chamomile, Comfrey, Elderflower, Ginger, Ginseng root, Honeysuckle, Hops, Horsetail, Juniper, Lavender, Lemon balm, Nettle, Pegaga, Peppermint, Rosemary, Sage, St. John's wort, Turmeric, Witch hazel, Yarrow, Aloe vera extract, Natural emulsifiers of olive oil, Vegetable glycerin, Jojoba oil, Rice bran wax, Wheatgerm oil, Calendula oil, Flaxseed oil (essential fatty acids), Stearic acid, Soybean oil, Essential oil blend of rosemary, Geranium, Ylang-Ylang, Vitamin C, Acetic acid, Plant gel (Xanthan gum), Grapefruit extract, Vitamin A, Vitamin E.

Orange Blossom Skin Toner

Ingredients

Angelica, Arnica, Calendula, Chamomile, Comfrey, Elderflower, Ginger, Ginseng root, Honeysuckle, Hops, Horsetail, Juniper, Lavender, Lemon balm, Nettle, Pegaga, Peppermint, Rosemary, Sage, St. John's wort, Turmeric, Witch hazel, Yarrow, Aloe vera extract, Vegetable glycerin, Essential oil blend of orange blossom, Ylang-Ylang, Petitgrain; Vitamin C, Acetic acid, Grapefruit extract, Vitamin E.

For Dry and Sensitive Skin

Calendula Cleansing Milk

Ingredients

Angelica, Arnica, Calendula, Chamomile, Comfrey, Elderflower, Ginger, Ginseng root, Honeysuckle, Hops, Horsetail, Juniper, Lavender, Lemon balm, Nettle, Pegaga, Peppermint, Rosemary, Sage, St. John's wort, Turmeric, Witch hazel, Yarrow, Natural emulsifiers of olive oil, Aloe vera extract, Calendula oil, Vegetable glycerin, Jojoba oil, Rice bran wax, Flaxseed oil (essential fatty acids), Stearic acid, Soybean oil, Lavender essential oil, Vitamin C, Acetic acid, Plant gel (Xanthan gum), Grapefruit extract, Vitamin A, Vitamin E, Chlorophyll.

Chamomile Skin Toner

Ingredients

Angelica, Arnica, Calendula, Chamomile, Comfrey, Elderflower, Ginger, Ginseng root, Honeysuckle, Hops, Horsetail, Juniper, Lavender, Lemon balm, Nettle, Pegaga, Peppermint, Rosemary, Sage, St. John's wort, Turmeric, Witch hazel, Yarrow, Aloe vera extract, Vegetable glycerin, Chamomile extract, Lavender essential oil, Vitamin C, Acetic acid, Grapefruit extract, Vitamin E.

Aloe and Lavender Day Time Moisturiser

Ingredients

Angelica, Arnica, Calendula, Chamomile, Comfrey, Elderflower, Ginger, Ginseng root, Honeysuckle, Hops, Horsetail, Juniper, Lavender, Lemon balm, Nettle, Pegaga, Peppermint, Rosemary, Sage, St. John's wort, Turmeric, Witch hazel, Yarrow, Aloe vera extract, Natural emulsifiers of olive oil, Vegetable glycerin, Jojoba oil, Titanium dioxide, Rice bran wax, Flaxseed oil (essential fatty acids), Stearic acid, Soybean oil, Vitamin C, Essential oil blend of lavender, Acetic acid, Plant gel (Xanthan gum), Grapefruit extract, Vitamin A, Vitamin E.

For Oily Skin

Alpinia Cleansing Milk

Ingredients

Angelica, Arnica, Calendula, Chamomile, Comfrey, Elderflower, Ginger, Ginseng root, Honeysuckle, Hops, Horsetail, Juniper, Lavender, Lemon balm, Nettle, Pegaga, Peppermint, Rosemary, Sage, St. John's wort, Turmeric, Witch hazel, Yarrow, Aloe vera extract, Alpinia extract, Natural emulsifiers of olive oil, Vegetable glycerin, Rice bran wax, Flaxseed oil (essential fatty acids), Stearic acid, Ylang-Ylang and Geranium essential oils, Vitamin C, Acetic acid, Plant gel (Xanthan gum), Grapefruit extract, Vitamin A, Vitamin E.

Body Care

Body Massage Oils

Body massage oils are used to massage the body, increase blood circulation and relax the body.

Ingredients

Olive oil—Olea europaea, Ground nut oil—Arachis hypogaea, Lavender oil—Anisochilus carnosus, Base.

Body Scrubs

Body scrubs are used to cleanse the body. They contain surfactants, and some natural extracts of herbs and walnut shells, which cleanse the skin with soft lather and also nourish it.

Ingredients

Strawberry extract—Fragaria vesca, Chamomile extract—Matricharia chamoilla, Walnut shells—Juglans regia, Aloe vera gel—Aloe vera, Mulberry root extract—Morus alba, Carrot seed extract, Daucus carota, Base.

Bath and Shower Gels

These gels help to eliminate impurities and neutralise the effects of hard water.

Ingredients

Avocado oil—Persea gratissma, Chamomile extract—Matricharia chamoilla, Tea tree oil—Melaleuca alternifolia, Lavender oil—Lavandula vera, Khus extract—Vetiveria zizaniodes, Base.

Hair Care

Hair Conditioning Shampoos

Hair conditioning shampoos effectively cleanse the hair and scalp and provide essential copper micronutrients. These shampoos also condition the hair while invigorating and stimulating the scalp.

Ingredients

Henna extract—Lawsonia inermis, Jojaba oil —Simmondsia chinensis, Cucumber extract —Cucumis sativa, Lavender oil—Lavandula vera, Carrot seed extract—Daucus carota, Base.

Hair Styling Gels

Hair styling gels are used to keep hair firm in a desired position. They may also make the hair appear shiny.

Ingredients

Cucumber extract—Cucumis sativa, Chamomile extract—Matricharia chamomilla, Ginseng extract —Panax quinguefolia, Aloe vera gel—Aloe vera, Carrot seed extract—Daucus carota, Khus extract—Vetiveria zizaniodes, Base.

Anti-dandruff Shampoos/Hair Cleansers

Anti-dandruff shampoos remove and control dandruff. They are also used to clean and condition the hair.

Ingredients

Tea tree oil—Melaleuca alternifolia, Henna extract—Lawsonia inermis, Lemon oil—Citrus limonum, Fenugreek—Trigonella foenum graecum, Ginger extract—Zingiber officinale, Jojaba oil—Simmondsia chinensis, Base.

Hair Conditioners

They help to make hair more manageable and often impart a smoother and softer texture.

Ingredients

Neem extract—Azadirachta indica, Gotukola—Centella asiatica, Bhrangraj—Eclipta alba, China rose—Hibiscus rosa sinensis, Henna extract—Lawsonia inermis, Jatamansi—Narbostachys Jatamansi, Base.

Herbal Shampoos

Ingredients

Angelica, Arnica, Calendula, Chamomile, Comfrey, Elderflower, Ginger, Ginseng root, Honeysuckle, Hops, Horsetail, Juniper, Lavender, Lemon balm, Nettle, Pegaga, Peppermint, Rosemary, Sage, St. John's wort, Turmeric, Witch hazel, Yarrow, Glycerides from olive oil, Laureth decyl polyglucose, Vegetable glycerine, Jojoba oil, Soybean oil, Alginate sea minerals, Panthenol, Vitamin C, Essential oil blend of rosemary, lavender, geranium and ylang-ylang, Acetic acid, Grapefruit extract, Vitamin E, Carotene.

Jasmine Shampoo

Ingredients

Angelica, Arnica, Calendula, Chamomile, Comfrey, Elderflower, Ginger, Ginseng root, Honeysuckle, Hops, Horsetail, Juniper, Lavender, Lemon balm, Nettle, Pegaga, Peppermint, Rosemary, Sage, St. John's wort, Turmeric, Witch hazel, Yarrow, Glycerides from olive oil, Laureth decyl polyglucose, Vegetable glycerin, Jojoba oil, Soybean oil, Alginate sea minerals, Panthenol, Essential oil blend of jasmine, chamomile and orange, Vitamin C, Acetic acid, Grapefruit extract, Vitamin E.

Walnut Oil Shampoo

Ingredients

Angelica, Arnica, Calendula, Chamomile, Comfrey, Elderflower, Ginger, Ginseng root, Honeysuckle, Hops, Horsetail, Juniper, Lavender, Lemon balm, Nettle, Pegaga, Peppermint, Rosemary, Sage, St. John's wort, Turmeric, Witch hazel, Yarrow, Glycerides from olive oil, Laureth decyl polyglucose, Vegetable glycerin, Jojoba oil, Walnut oil, Soybean oil, Alginate sea minerals, Panthenol, Vitamin C, Acetic acid, Grapefruit extract, Essential oil of bitter almond, Vitamin E, Caramel.

Hair Repair Conditioning Treatment

Ingredients

Angelica, Arnica, Calendula, Chamomile, Comfrey, Elderflower, Ginger, Ginseng root, Honeysuckle, Hops, Horsetail, Juniper, Lavender, Lemon balm, Nettle, Pegaga, Peppermint, Rosemary, Sage, St. John's wort, Turmeric, Witch hazel, Yarrow, Natural emulsifiers from olive oil, Xanthan gum, Vegetable glycerin, Jojoba oil, Soybean oil, Alginate sea minerals, Panthenol (Vitamin B), Essential oil of lemon, Ricinus oil, Vitamin C, Acetic acid, Citric acid, Grapefruit extract, Vitamin E.

Basil Conditioning Scalp Toner

Ingredients

Angelica, Arnica, Calendula, Chamomile, Comfrey, Elderflower, Ginger, Ginseng root,

Honeysuckle, Hops, Horsetail, Juniper, Lavender, Lemon balm, Nettle, Pegaga, Peppermint, Rosemary, Sage, St. John's wort, Turmeric, Witch hazel, Yarrow, Holy basil extract, Aloe vera extract, Vegetable glycerin, Jojoba oil, Soybean oil, Peppermint essential oil, Vitamin C, Acetic acid, Grapefruit extract, Menthol, Sodium benzoate, Vitamin E.

Nutritious Colour Cosmetics

Nutritious Lip Colours, Lip Gloss and Coverup Sticks

Ingredients

Plant waxes, Plant oils, Cetyl alcohol (this is not ethanol alcohol but a natural fatty acid), LevensESSENTIE™ 23 herbal extract (dried pulverised form), Ceramides, Pycnogenol, Vitamin E. May contain: Iron oxides, Carmine, Titanium dioxide (natural colours).

Herbal Colour Mascaras

Ingredients

23 herb extracts, Plant waxes, Natural chalk, Linseed oil, Calendula oil, Carbomer, Chamomile extract, Vegetable glycerin, Vitamin E, Panthenol, Iron oxides: Blue, Black and Brown (natural colours), Vitamins A & C, Acetic acid, Grapefruit extract, Ceramides.

Makeup Remover

Ingredients

Angelica, Arnica, Calendula, Chamomile, Comfrey, Elderflower, Ginger, Ginseng root, Honeysuckle, Hops, Horsetail, Juniper, Lavender, Lemon balm, Nettle, Pegaga, Peppermint, Rosemary, Sage, St. John's wort, Turmeric, Witch hazel, Yarrow, Natural emulsifiers of olive oil, Aloe vera extract, Vegetable glycerin, Jojoba oil, Rice bran wax, Flaxseed oil (essential fatty acids), Stearic acid, Soybean oil, Vitamin C, Acetic acid, Plant gel (Xanthan gum), Grapefruit extract, Vitamin E.

Common Herbs used in Cosmetic Formulations

Aloe vera

Botanical Name: Aloe vera, Aloe barbadensis
Family Name: Liliaceae
Common Name: Aloe, Barbados Aloe, Curacao Aloe, Indian Aloe, Ghikunvar
Parts Used: Flowers, roots
Habitat: South and southwestern India
Other Uses: It is useful for x-ray burns, dermatitis and cutaneous disorders of the skin. The juice is used as a tonic and in jaundice, amenorrhea and piles. Aloe vera gel has the remarkable ability to heal wounds.

Azadirachta indica

Botanical Name: Azadirachta indica
Family Name: Meliaceae
Common Name: Lilac, Margosa tree, Neem, Neem Chal
Parts Used: Leaves, flower, oil, seed
Habitat: It is an evergreen that grows throughout India.
Other Uses: Vermifuge, insecticide, astringent, tonic and antispetic. It possesses anti-diabetic, anti-bacterial and anti-viral properties and has been used successfully for stomach pain, worms and ulcers. The root bark possesses astringent, tonic and anti-periodic properties. It is also useful in malarial fever. The oil is used to make neem-based soaps, shampoos and toothpaste.

Centella asiatica

Botanical Name: Centella asiatica
Family Name: Appiaceae

Common Name: Pennywort, Indian Pennywort, Artayniya-e Hindi, Jal Brahmi
Part Used: Whole plant
Habitat: Grown in waterlogged places throughout India
Other Uses: It is used as a tonic and a diuretic. It is used in the treatment of leprosy and is known to ameliorate the symptoms of the disease and improve the general health of the patient. It is used as a hair tonic to stimulate hair growth.

Emblica officinalis

Botanical Name: Emblica officinalis
Family Name: Euphorbiacae
Common Name: Gooseberry, Phyllanthus Emblica, Emblica, Indian Gooseberry, Amla
Part Used: Fruit
Habitat: Northern and Southwestern India
Other Uses: It is used as an asperient, carminative, diuretic, aphrodisiac, laxative, astringent and refrigerant. It is the richest known source of Vitamin C. It is useful in anemia, jaundice, dyspepsia, hemorrhage disorders, diabetes, asthma and bronchitis. It cures insomnia and helps to keep the hair healthy.

Henna

Botanical Name: Lawsonia inermis
Family Name: Lythracea
Common Name: Henna, Al-Khanna, Al-Henna, Jamaica Mignonette, Mehndi, Mendee, Egyptian Privet, Smooth Lawsonia
Parts Used: Flowers, powdered leaves, fruit
Habitat: Scarce in dry deciduous forests, widely cultivated as a hedge plant
Other Uses: It is used in the treatment of burns, the cracking of nails and in making temporary tattoos.

Juglans regia

Botanical Name: Juglans regia
Family Name: Juglanduceae
Common Name: Walnut, Persian Walnut, European Walnut, Akhrot
Parts Used: Leaves, bark, fruits
Habitat: Cultivated in the Himalayas and the Khasia hills
Other Uses: Leaves are astringent, tonic and anthelmintic. They are useful in herpes, eczema, scrofula and syphilis. Fruits are sweet and emollient, thermogenical and aphrodisiac.

Liquorice

Botanical Name: Glycyrrhiza glabra
Family Name: Papilionaceae
Common Name: Calamus, Mulethi, Sweet Liquorice, Sweetwood
Parts Used: Root
Habitat: Cultivated in Northern and Southern India
Other Uses: It is used as a tonic, diuretic, demulcent, expectorant, emmenagogue and laxative. It is also used to allay coughs and catarrhal infections and is useful in irritable conditions of the mucous membrane of the urinary organs, in sore throat, cough, anorexia and persistent low fever. It can also be used to flavour tobacco, confectionery, beverages, jams and marmalades.

Punica granatum

Botanical Name: Punica granatum
Family Name: Puniacaceae
Common Name: Pomegranate, Anar
Parts Used: Seeds, flowers
Habitat: Commonly cultivated as ornamental and fruit trees

Other Uses: A decoction of seeds is used to treat syphilis. The juice is used to treat jaundice and diarrhea. The juice of the flower is used to treat nose bleeds while the fruit pulp and seed are used as stomachic.

Terminalia arjuna

Botanical Name: Terminalia arjuna
Family Name: Combretaceae
Common Name: Arjuna, Arjuna Herb, Arjuna Root
Parts Used: Bark
Other Uses: The bark is astringent, sweet, acrid and cooling. It is used as an aphrodisiac, cardiotonic, urinary astringent, expectorant and alexiteric and is useful in fractures, ulcers, cirrhosis of the liver, hyperhidrosis, otalgia and hypertension.

Terminalia belerica

Botanical Name: Terminalia belerica
Family Name: Combretaceae
Common Name: Beleric, Bellric Myrobalan, Baehra
Parts Used: Fruit
Habitat: Grown throughout India
Other Uses: It is used as an astringent, tonic, expectorant and laxative. It is used in coughs and sore throat. The pulp is used in dropsy, piles and diarrhea. It is useful in leprosy, fever and hair care. It is also used in oxalic acid and the preparation of ink.

Tinospora cordifolia

Botanical Name: Tinospora cordifolia
Family Name: Meninspermaceae
Common Name: Gulanshe Tinospara, Gulansha Tinospara,Tinospara, Giloy
Parts Used: Stem
Habitat: North and South India.
Other Uses: It is anti-periodic, antipyretic, alterative, diuretic and anti-inflammatory. It is a constituent of several compound preparations. It is used in fever, urinary disorders, dyspepsia, general debility and urinary diseases. It is also used in the treatment of rheumatism and jaundice.

Valeriana wallichi

Botanical Name: Valeriana wallichi
Family Name: Valerianaceae
Common Name: Valerian, Indian Valerian, Valerian Jatamansi, Taggar
Parts Used: Roots
Habitat: Temperate zone of Northwestern Himalayas up to an altitude of 3000 m
Other Uses: It is anti-spasmodic, stimulant, calmative and stomachic. It is useful in diseases of the eye, blood and liver. It is used as a remedy for hysteria, hypochondriasis, nervous unrest and emotional stress. It is also useful in clearing up the voice and acts as a stimulant in advance stages of fever and nervous disorders.

Zingiber officinalis

Botanical Name: Zingiber officinalis
Family Name: Zingiberaceae
Common Name: Calamus, Sweet Ginger, Ginger Root, Sonth (dried)
Parts Used: Fresh and dried fruit
Habitat: Southeast Asia and throughout India
Other Uses: This is clinically proven as a prophylactic of nausea and vomiting associated with motion sickness, sea sickness and pregnancy. It is also known for its gastrointestinal benefits and as an anti-inflammatory and carminative.

Evaluation of Herbal Cosmetics and Finished Products

Cosmetic products are concerned with personal care, hygiene and well-being, with products such as sunscreen lotions with UV filters, decay-fighting toothpastes, anti-dandruff shampoos, deodorants and baby care applications, as well as creativity, with makeup products and perfume. The evaluation of the safety of the finished products is based on knowledge of the ingredients' toxicity, provided supplementary information is available:

- When the vehicle used in the formulation is different from the solvents used in toxicity tests and when there is a likelihood of an increase in skin penetration or skin irritation
- When a new, potentially toxic substance is liable to be created through the combination of ingredients present in the finished product
- When the in-house experience acquired by major cosmetic firms is particularly interesting in the domain of in vitro tests on finished products
- When tests on finished products can be restricted to in vitro tests because of prior knowledge of toxicity data about the ingredients. However, no in vitro alternative tests have as yet been successful in validation studies.

The following are the possible skin reactions:

- Percutaneous absorption
- Phototoxicity/Photoirritation
- Eye irritation
- Skin irritation
- Acute toxicity
- Skin densitisation
- Subchronic toxicity
- Mutagenicity/Genotoxicity
- Photomutagenicity

The most important of these symptoms, skin sensitisation, is now discussed in detail.

Skin Sensitisation

Patch testing for skin allergies

Patch testing is a way of identifying whether a substance that comes in contact with the skin can cause inflammation of the skin (contact dermatitis). There are two types of contact dermatitis: irritant and allergic. Patch testing can help to differentiate between the two. This test involves the application of various test substances to the skin under adhesive tape that is then left in place for 48 hours. The skin is then examined a further 48 hours later for any response.

Patch testing

Patch testing should be done on a skin site where the dermatitis is not apparent. The cosmetic products are mixed with a non-allergic material (base) to a suitable concentration. They are then placed in direct contact with the skin, usually on the upper back, within small aluminium discs. Adhesive tape is used to fix them in place, and the test sites are marked. The patches are left in place for 48 hours, during which time it is important not to wash the area or play vigorous sports because if the adhesive tapes peel off, the process will have to be repeated.

The patches should not be exposed to sunlight or other sources of UV light. After 48 hours, the patches are removed and an initial reading is taken one hour later. The final reading is taken a further 48 hours later. Additional readings beyond 48 hours increase the chance of a positive patch test by 34%. The patient should refrain from washing until the last reading is taken.

Interpretation of results

Any reaction seen is scored according to the International Contact Dermatitis Research Group system, as follows:

+? = doubtful reaction: mild redness only

\+ = weak, positive reaction: red and slightly thickened skin

++ = strong positive reaction: red, swollen skin with individual small water blisters

+++ = extreme positive reaction: intense redness and swelling with coalesced large blisters or spreading reaction

IR = irritant reaction: red skin improves once patch is removed

NT = not tested

The distinction between allergic and irritant reactions is of major importance. An irritant reaction is most prominent immediately after the patch is removed and fades over the next day. An allergic reaction takes a few days to develop and is therefore more prominent on Day 5 than when the patch is removed.

A substance (cosmetic) that causes an irritant reaction may exacerbate any underlying dermatitis such as atopic eczema, but this will not get worse with time and can be prevented by wearing a barrier cream or plenty of moisturiser. A substance that causes an allergic reaction will cause dermatitis and should be avoided completely if possible. The more number of times the skin is exposed to the substance, the worse the allergic reaction can become.

Photo-patch testing

Some chemicals produce an allergic reaction only when exposed to light (usually UVA). Patients who are oversensitive to light and those with a rash that appears on parts of the body normally exposed to light (mostly the face, the 'V' of the neck and the hands) but that does not appear in areas shielded from the light (for example, under the chin and the triangle between the nose and the mouth) should have a photo-patch test.

With photo-patch testing, two identical sets of allergens are applied to the back on Day 1. One of the sets is exposed to UVA light, and the sites are then examined. A positive photo-patch test is recorded when an allergic reaction appears only on the light-exposed site.

Alternatives to Animal Testing

For products used either in cosmetics or in any other type of product, the safe use of chemicals requires a 'base set' of toxicity data. These measures aim to achieve the following objectives:

- To guarantee adequate protection for humans and the environment against the potential risks of cosmetic substances
- To introduce a uniform notification procedure for new chemical substances and provisions on packaging and temporary labelling for dangerous substances
- To introduce an environmental hazard mark
- To reduce as far as possible the number of experiments on animals

Four alternative methods have been accepted to date:

- Phototoxicity testing: 3T3 Mouse Fibroblast Neutral Red Uptake Phototoxicity (NRU-PT)
- Skin corrosion testing: human skin models
- Skin corrosion testing: transcutaneous electrical resistance (TER) assay
- Dermal absorption and percutaneous

penetration: in vitro tests (link), including the local lymph node assay (LLNA) to test for skin sensitisation

Human Skin Models

Scientists have developed non-animal tests for skin corrosion based on commercially available human skin models (reconstructed human skin). A number of artificial human skin models have been shown to represent a valid alternative to animal testing for skin corrosion. These human skin models produce results that are reproducible under defined experimental conditions and have been validated to international standards. Animal tests for skin corrosion are no longer permitted (Fig. 21.2).

3T3 Neutral Red Uptake Phototoxicity Test

Phototoxicity is a light-induced injury of the skin, triggered when the skin is exposed to certain substances under sunlight. 3T3 NRU-PT identifies the phototoxic potential of substances without using laboratory animals.

In Vitro Testing of Dermal Absorption and Percutaneous Penetration of Chemical Substances

Excised pig or human skin (both are comparable with respect to absorption and penetration properties) is used to mimic the in vivo situation and to assess the dermal absorption and percutaneous penetration of chemicals. The test substance, normally in a cosmetic formulation, is applied to the surface of the excised skin, which is positioned between the upper (donor) and lower (receptor fluid) chambers of a 'penetration cell'. The exposure time can be chosen according to the intended use of the product (for example, rinse-off or leave-on). Analysis of the test substance (residue on the skin surface, amounts in different layers of the skin and in the receptor fluid) yields a mass balance of the test substance. This in vitro test mimics the in vivo situation and yields reproducible and reliable results.

Other General Evaluation Methods

Typical measurements include:

- Hardness - for example, in lipstick, lip balm, wax, false nails
- Break strength - for example, in lipstick, eye liner, lip liner
- Consistency - for example, in moisturising cream, paste
- Compaction strength - for example, in eye shadow, face powder
- Container lid opening force
- Actuation force of pump/spray
- Stickiness - nail lacquer
- Curing - nail lacquer

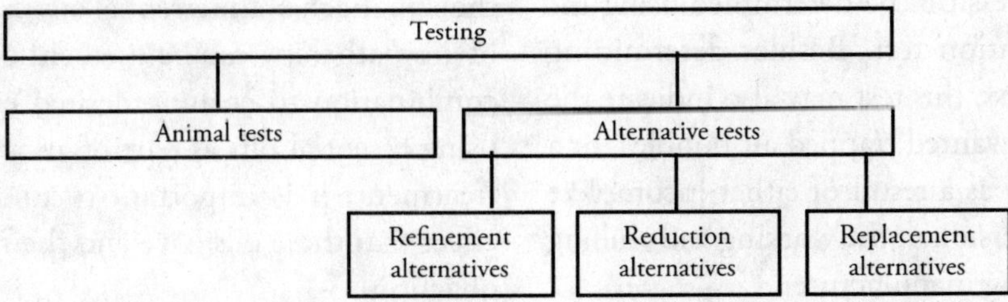

Figure 21.2: Various tests performed for cosmetics

- Hair curl compression
- Tress combing forces

Lipstick Break Strength

This cantilever test provides both imitative and empirical results in one test. Action is provided by a hemispherical edged blade that simulates the bending action caused during application.

Eye Pencil Rig

The test provides the means to quantitatively measure the hardness of pencil tips such as those for eye or lip lining products. Results will assess such process variables as the modification of wax content or product quality as a result of extreme temperature conditions.

Cone/Cylinder/Needle Probe

A standard test using a needle or conical probe provides a means of measuring the firmness or consistency of waxes and is also suitable for assessing the hardness of soap and similar products.

Small Diameter Cylinder Probes

The test can indicate the presence of air pockets beneath the sample surface, which may be undesirable, and the optimal pressing time and weight of eyeshadow and compressed face powders.

Cylinder/Needle Probes

Lipstick hardness can be determined using the needle penetration test. Besides determining lipstick hardness, this test may also indicate the presence of unwanted trapped air bubbles, or a 'grainy' texture as a result of either incomplete colourant dispersion or the working and chilling processes during manufacture.

Future Trends

Recent trends in the way research, discovery and development are being carried out in the cosmetics industry have opened new prospects for incorporating natural products from Nature. Traditional knowledge of herbal cosmetics will serve as a powerful search engine and, more importantly, will greatly facilitate intentional, focussed and safe natural products research to rediscover the applications of various cosmetics.

Essential Oils and Aromatherapy

Essential oils are liquids that are generally distilled (most frequently by steam or water) from the leaves, stems, flowers, bark, roots or other parts of a plant. Essential oils are not really oily at all. Most essential oils are clear, but some such as patchouli, orange and lemongrass are amber or yellow in colour. Essential oils contain the true essence of the plant it was derived from. They are highly concentrated but are not the same as perfumes or fragrance oils. Essential oils are derived from the true plants, whereas perfume oils are artificially created fragrances or contain artificial substances and do not offer the therapeutic benefits that essential oils do. The chemical composition and aroma of essential oils can provide valuable psychological and physical therapeutic benefits. These benefits are usually achieved through methods such as inhalation and application of the diluted oil on the skin. Each of the essential oils that forms part of aromatherapy can be used either alone or in combination to create a desired effect. Before using essential oils as part of an aromatherapy treatment, it is important to understand the effect that these oils have and their mechanism of action.

These oils are extracted from different parts of the plant such as the flowers, twigs, leaves and bark, or from the rind of the fruit. For example, in roses, essential oils are found in the flowers; in basil, they are extracted from the leaves; in sandalwood, from the wood, and so on.

The methods used to extract the oil are time-consuming and expensive and require a high degree of expertise. India is blessed with a wide variety of soils and climatic conditions that support an enormous range of diverse plants. Of the 18,000 native species found in this country, some 1,300 are known to contain aromas. Though these plants possess aromas, only about 65 enjoy a large and consistent demand in world trade and are accordingly grown in different parts of the globe. India, however, produces limited items of commercial value both from its rich natural forest vegetation and through cultivation. There is great scope for commercial cultivation of several aromatic crops in India and there is always a demand for new and specific aroma chemicals for the development of new and exotic flavours and fragrances.

India in the Herbal Global Market

With respect to essential oils, aroma chemicals, natural flavours and fragrances, the projected demand for industrial raw material was valued at US$12 billion in 1994. As per an estimate, the worldwide production of essential oils at raw material level was around Rs 3,200 crores in 1994, of which 55–60% goes to food flavours, 15–20% as fragrances and the remainder is utilised as starting raw material for the isolation of aroma chemicals. However, in terms of market share in production, India (6.1%) is sliding down and now ranks sixth after China (30.7%), Brazil (13.1%), Turkey (10.4%), Morocco (9.1%) and Indonesia (8.7%) and is followed by Egypt (3.1%).

A report from Chemexcil, Mumbai, which overviews exports in this sector, has stated that India exported perfumes, cosmetics, toiletries, toothpastes, soaps and detergents and joss sticks worth Rs 144.8 crores in 1992–93, a figure that rose to 335.4 crores in 1995–96. The export value of essential oils was Rs 51.3 and 60.1 crores, respectively, with 10–12% of the ingredients sourced from plants. India has done fairly well in the export of mint oil (Rs 1,075 lakhs), menthol (Rs 1,310 lakhs) and jasmine concrete (Rs 397 lakhs). There has been a decline in the export of sandalwood oil and lemongrass, which have been our traditional export items.

Many essential oils are also being imported. However, efforts are being made to cultivate these plants in different parts of the country.

Extraction of Essential Oils

Essential oils can be extracted using a variety of methods, although some are not commonly used today. Currently, the most popular method of extraction is steam distillation, but technological advances have led to the development of more efficient and economical methods.

Steam Distillation

To extract the essential oil, the plant material is placed in a still, and pressurised steam is passed through it. The heat from the steam causes globules of oil in the plant to burst and the oil then evaporates. The essential oil vapour and steam then pass out of the top of the still into a water-cooled pipe, where the vapours are condensed back to liquids. At this point, the essential oil separates from the water and floats to the top.

Maceration

Maceration actually creates more of an 'infused oil' rather than an essential oil. The plant matter is soaked in vegetable oil, heated and strained, at which point, it can be used for massaging.

Cold Pressing

Cold pressing is used to extract the essential oils from citrus rinds such as orange, lemon, grapefruit and bergamot. The rinds are separated from the fruit, ground or chopped and then pressed. The result is a watery mixture of essential oil and liquid which will separate given time. It is important to note that oils extracted using this method have a relatively short shelf life, so it is advisable to make or purchase only what will be used within the next six months.

Solvent Extraction

A hydrocarbon solvent is added to the plant material to help dissolve the essential oil. When the solution is filtered and concentrated by distillation, a substance containing resin (resinoid) or a combination of wax and essential oil (known as concrete) remains. From the concentrate, pure alcohol is used to extract the oil. When the alcohol evaporates, the oil is left behind. This is not considered the best method for extraction as the solvents can leave a small amount of residue behind, which could cause allergies and affect the immune system.

CO_2 Extraction

Only recently developed, this method uses carbon dioxide to extract the essential oil from the plant when it is liquefied under pressure. Once the liquid depressurises, the carbon dioxide returns to a gaseous state and only pure essential oil remains.

Essential Oils

- Agarwood
- Ajwain
- Ambrette seed
- Basil
- Betel leaf
- Calamus root
- Cardamom
- Carrot seed
- Cedarwood
- Celery seed
- Cinnamon bark
- Cinnamon leaf
- Citronella java
- Clove bud
- Clove leaf
- Coriander
- Fennel seed
- Nutmeg
- Olibanum
- Palmarosa
- Pepper black
- Rose damascenia
- Sandalwood
- Spearmint
- Sugandh kokila
- Sugandh mantri
- Tagetus erecta
- Tagetus minuta
- Turmeric
- Valerian root
- Vetiver (cultivated)
- Vetiver (wild)

Exotic Oils

- Basil holy
- Chamomile blue
- Costus root
- Cumin seed
- Cyprus scariosus root
- Cyperus rotundus root
- Dill seed
- Eucalyptus citriodora
- Eucalyptus globulus
- Lavender
- Patchouli

Oleoresins

- Capsicum
- Celery seed
- Coriander
- Fenugreek
- Galangal
- Geranium
- Ginger
- Ginger grass
- Green chilli
- Hedychium/Ginger lily
- Jamarosa
- Jatamansi/Spikenard
- Juniper berry
- Keora/Screw pine
- Lemongrass
- Lime cold-pressed
- Lime distilled
- Mace
- Mentha arvensis
- Mentha citrata
- Mentha piperity
- Mentha spicata
- Myrrh
- Pepper black
- Turmeric

The changing scenario of world trade now demands globalisation of the market and open economy. These new developments are certain to provide unlimited export opportunities, especially to a producing country such as India, which is gifted with varying soil and climatic conditions and vast natural resources. However, at the same time, importing countries may place riders by fostering stringent regulatory laws prescribing quality parameters and maximum limits for microbial counts, pesticide residues, heavy metal content and ration activity.

Areas of Opportunity

In future, this sector needs systematic procedures to face new emerging challenges and opportunities. Therefore, India's research and development efforts should be need-based, relevant, and demand and market oriented. Documentation of genetic resources of aromatic plants for utilisation and safe conservation should get high priority. A mission mode approach is needed to introduce important crop varieties and germplasm from abroad, which have high value and can be cultivated in India.

In order to ensure regular supply of uniform quality raw materials, commercial cultivation of aromatic plants is the need of the hour. For this purpose, development of low-cost, environment friendly and economically viable production technology to check the losses during processing, marketing and storage are required.

Innovations made in biotechnology need to be used judiciously for this sector. To enhance exports and achieve leadership, intensive research on value addition, isolation of newer aroma chemicals and development of analytical procedures to identify and estimate adulterants need to be attempted systematically. Herbal cosmetics, aromatherapy and quality seed production are other promising areas that require the attention of researchers, industrialists and new entrepreneurs. To address all these issues, a dedicated and trained human resource is of vital importance.

Plants with Essential Oils

Bergamot

(Source: www.wildflowersofontario.ca)

Effects: Refreshing and uplifting
Aroma: Top note
Scent: Sweet, spicy
Combines well with: Chamomile, geranium, lavender
Properties: Antidepressant, antiseptic, anti-spasmodic
Uses: Abcesses, acne, boils, chicken pox, colds, cold sores, cystitis, flatulence, loss of appetite, mouth infections, sore throat
Contraindications: Bergamot is a photosensitiser (increases the skin's reaction to sunlight, making it more likely to burn) so it should not be used on skin exposed to sunlight or tanning beds. Bergamot has anti-spasmodic properties and should therefore be avoided during pregnancy.

Chamomile

(Source: www.british-wild-flowers.co.uk)

Effects: Soothing, relaxing
Aroma: Middle note
Scent: Sweet, herbal, fruity
Combines well with: Bergamot, geranium, lavender
Properties: Analgesic, antibacterial, antiseptic, digestive, stimulant
Uses: Acne, blisters, boils, colitis, depression, digestive problems, flatulence, gout, headaches, indigestion, irritable bowel syndrome, neuralgia, nervous tension (anxiety, fear), rheumatism, skin conditions (dermatitis, eczema, psoriasis)
Contraindications: Chamomile may cause skin irritation. It should not be used in early pregnancy.

Cedarwood

(Source: www.seedlingrus.com)

Effects: Soothing, strengthening
Aroma: Base note

Scent: Woody
Combines well with: Bergamot, rosemary, sandalwood
Properties: Antifungal, antiseptic, astringent, expectorant, sedative
Uses: Arthritis, bronchitis, cellulite, cystitis, dandruff (blend with rosemary), skin conditions (such as acne, eczema, oily skin)
Contraindications: Cedarwood may cause irritation to sensitive skin. Do not use during pregnancy.

Clove

(Source: www.phototakeout.com)
Effects: Warming
Aroma: Base/Middle note
Scent: Sweet, spicy, fresh
Properties: Analgesic, expectorant, stimulant
Uses: Bronchitis, colds, indigestion, infected wounds, insect repellant, mouth sores, toothache, muscle and nerve tension, room disinfectant,
Contraindications: Clove is highly irritating to the skin and must be diluted to concentrations <1% prior to use.

Eucalyptus

(Source: www.labspec.co.za)
Effects: Balancing, stimulating
Aroma: Top/Middle note
Scent: Camphorous, woody
Combines well with: Juniper, lavender, marjoram
Properties: Analgesic, anti-inflammatory, antiseptic, antiviral, stimulant
Uses: Asthma, bronchitis, burns, cuts, decongestant, flu, headaches, muscle aches, rheumatism, sinusitis, skin ulcers, urinary infections, wounds, air disinfectant, insect repellant
Contraindications: Eucalyptus should not be used in persons who have high blood pressure or epilepsy and can be fatal if ingested.

Fennel

(Source: www.ups.gov)
Effects: Clearing
Aroma: Middle note
Scent: Sweet, earthy
Combines well with: Geranium, lavender, sandalwood
Properties: Antiseptic, anti-spasmodic, diuretic, stimulant
Uses: Digestive disorders, gout (combine with juniper), nervous tension
Contraindications: Fennel should not be used during pregnancy and in persons with epilepsy. Fennel may irritate sensitive skin.

Geranium

(Source: www.ubcbotanicalgarden.org)

Effects: Comforting, healing
Aroma: Middle note
Scent: Floral, sweet, earthy
Combines well with: Chamomile, cypress, juniper
Properties: Antifungal, antiseptic, anti-spasmodic, diuretic
Uses: Burns, eczema, edema, fluid retention, neuralgia, PMS symptoms (including swollen breasts), poor circulation, rheumatism, tonsillitis
Contraindications: Geranium may irritate sensitive skin. Avoid use during pregnancy due to anti-spasmodic properties.

Ginger

(Source: www.garaherbs.com)

Effects: Warming
Aroma: Top note
Scent: Warm, spicy, woody
Combines well with: Cedarwood, citrus oils, eucalyptus
Properties: Analgesic, antidepressant, expectorant, stimulant
Uses: Arthritis, bronchitis, catarrh, colds, colic, constipation, diarrhea, exhaustion, flatulence, flu, indigestion, poor circulation, rheumatism, sinusitis
Contraindications: Ginger may irritate sensitive skin.

Jasmine

(Source: http://gracemagazine.files.wordpress.com)

Effects: Soothing, relaxing
Aroma: Base note
Scent: Warm, floral
Combines well with: Chamomile, citrus oils, rose
Properties: Antidepressant, antiseptic, anti-spasmodic, expectorant
Uses: Anxiety, catarrh, cough, headache, lack of confidence, laryngitis, mental tension, sensitive or dry skin
Contraindications: Jasmine is generally agreeable with most, but some allergic reactions can occur. Jasmine should not be used during pregnancy because of its anti-spasmodic properties.

Lavender

(Source: http://usp.ucsd.edu)

Effects: Calming, therapeutic
Aroma: Middle note
Scent: Floral, sweet, woody, herbal
Combines well with: Clary sage, frankincense, geranium
Properties: Analgesic, anti-inflammatory, antiseptic, diuretic, sedative, insecticide
Uses: Acne, anxiety, bronchitis, burns, catarrh chilbains, circulatory problems, colds, dandruff, eczema, flu, headaches, insect bites, insomnia, muscle aches and pains PMS symptoms, psoriasis, rheumatism, sinusitis, skin problems, sunburn tension, throat infection, wounds and sores
Contraindications: Lavender should not be used during the early stages of pregnancy or in persons with low blood pressure.

Lemongrass

(Source: http://schools.moe.edu.sg)

Effects: Refreshing, toning
Aroma: Top note
Scent: Sweet, citrus
Combines well with: Basil, cedarwood, lavender
Properties: Antidepressant, antiseptic, diuretic
Uses: Colic, fatigue, indigestion, muscle aches and pains, stress, stimulates appetite
Contraindications: Not known

Lemon

(Source: http://upload.wikimedia.org)

Effects: Refreshing, stimulating
Aroma: Top note
Scent: Fresh, sharp citrus
Combines well with: Chamomile, lavender
Properties: Antiseptic, astringent, antiviral, stimulant
Uses: Circulatory problems, cold sores, constipation, corns, gingivitis, headaches, insect bites, migraine, rheumatism, sinusitis, skin tonic, sore throat, tonsillitis, varicose veins
Contraindications: Lemon is a photosensitiser so it should not be used when exposed to sunlight or tanning beds. Lemon should not be directly inhaled.

Peppermint

(Source: www.cas.vanderbilt.edu)

Effects: Refreshing, stimulating
Aroma: Top note
Scent: Stong, fresh, menthol
Combines well with: Eucalyptus, lavender, rosemary
Properties: Analgesic, antiseptic, anti-spasmodic, astringent, decongestant, digestive aid, expectorant
Uses: Asthma, bronchitis, colic, headaches, indigestion, migraine, muscle and joint pain, nausea, sinusitis, sore/tired feet, toothaches, insect repellant
Contraindications: Peppermint has anti-spasmodic properties, therefore use during pregnancy is not advised.

Pine

(Source: www.forestry.ky.gov)

Effects: Refreshing, stimulating
Aroma: Middle note
Scent: Fresh, woody
Combines well with: Eucalyptus, geranium, lavender
Properties: Antiseptic, decongestant, disinfectant, expectorant, tonic
Uses: Bronchitis, cystitis, flu, gout, laryngitis, muscle aches and pains, respiratory problems, rheumatism, sinusitis. disinfectant
Contraindications: Pine may cause irritation in sensitive skin.

Rosemary

(Source: www.lattaplantation.org)

Effects: Refreshing, stimulating
Aroma: Middle note
Scent: Refreshing, woody, herbal
Combines well with: Cedarwood, geranium, juniper
Properties: Analgesic, antidepressant, antirheumatic, antiseptic, anti-spasmodic, decongestant, diuretic, stimulant
Uses: Burns, cellulite, colds, digestive problems, fatigue, flu, gout, liver and gall bladder problems, oily skin, poor circulation, rheumatism, water retention, wounds
Contraindications: Rosemary has anti-spasmodic properties and should not be used during pregnancy or in persons with high blood pressure or epilepsy.

Rose

(Source: www.climb.org.uk)

Effects: Relaxing
Aroma: Base/Middle note
Scent: Warm, deep floral
Combines well with: Bergamot, chamomile, geranium
Properties: Antibacterial, antidepressant, antiseptic, anti-spasmodic, astringent, diuretic, sedative
Uses: Ageing skin, broken veins, depression, dry skin, headache, insomnia, PMS symptoms, sensitive skin, sore throat, stress
Contraindications: Rose has anti-spasmodic properties and should not be used during pregnancy.

Sandalwood

(Source: www.hawaii.edu)

Effects: Warming, relaxing
Aroma: Base note
Scent: Woody, sweet, exotic
Combines well with: Frankincense, geranium, jasmine
Properties: Anti-inflammatory, antiseptic, anti-spasmodic, aphrodisiac, diuretic, sedative
Uses: Anxiety, bronchitis, cystitis, fatigue frigidity, impotence, immune system booster, nervous tension, skin conditions (such as acne, dry skin, eczema), sore throat, stress, urinary infections, water retention
Contraindications: Sandalwood has anti-spasmodic properties and should not be used during pregnancy or in states of depression (may cause an even lowered mood).

Thyme

(Source: www.twofrog.com)

Effects: Refreshing, warming
Aroma: Top note
Scent: Sweet, strong, herbal
Combines well with: Bergamot, cedarwood, chamomile
Properties: Anti-rheumatic, antiseptic, anti-spasmodic, aphrodisiac, diuretic, emmenagogue, expectorant
Uses: Arthritis, colds, cough, depression, fatigue, laryngitis, rheumatism, sore throat, tonsillitis, stress; boosts immune system, enhances memory, raises low blood pressure
Contraindications: Thyme has anti-spasmodic properties and should not be used during pregnancy or in the case of high blood pressure. Avoid prolonged use as toxicity is possible.

Other Herbal Formulations

Herbal teas are the most basic of all natural mediums; they are absorbed by the body as hot liquids. They are the least concentrated of all herbal forms, but many are optimally effective when steeped in boiling water. The hot brewing water releases herbal potency and provides a flushing action that is ideal for removing toxic wastes that have been loosened and dissolved by the herbs. Although teas have milder and more subtle effects than capsules or extracts, they are sometimes the only way for a weakened system to accept therapeutic support, and often work synergistically with stronger medicinal forms to boost their value.

Herbal capsules are generally four times stronger than teas, more concentrated in form, convenient to take and bypass any herbal bitterness. Capsules can make both oil- and water-soluble herbs available through stomach acid and enzyme alteration. Freeze-dried powdered herbs, with all the moisture removed, are also available in capsules and are four times more concentrated than regular ground herbs. As noted with herbal teas, grinding herbs into powders creates facets on the whole herb structure causing potential loss of volatile oils. The effective potency of powdered herbs is 6–12 months.

Herbal extracts are 4–8 times stronger than capsules. They are effective when used as sprays where all the mouth receptors can be brought into play, or as drops held under the tongue, that bypass the digestive system's acid/alkaline breakdown. Their strength and ready availability make extracts reliable emergency measures. Small doses can be used repeatedly over a period of time to help build a strong base for restoring body balance. Holding an extract dose in the mouth for as long as possible, 3–4 times daily, is effective for the first week of acute conditions.

Herbal tinctures are also extractions made using a 25% alcohol and water mixture as the solvent. Tinctures are generally extracted from individual herbs rather than compounds. Commercial tinctures use ethyl alcohol and may even be formed from fluid extracts, but diluted alcohol spirits are suitable for home use; vodka is ideal.

Extracts are more concentrated (10 or 5 units of extract from 1 unit of herbs), while a fluid extract is usually 1:1. Even stronger, a powdered extract has the solvent completely removed. Powdered extracts are at least 4 times as potent as an equal amount of fluid extract, and 40 times as potent as tincture.

Herbal syrups are well accepted by children and can greatly improve the taste of bitter herbal compounds. They are also excellent treatment forms for throat coats and gargles, or bronchial, chest/lung infections. Syrups are simple and quick to make.

Herbal pastes and electuaries are made by grinding or blending herbs in the blender with a little water into a paste. The paste may then be mixed with twice the amount of honey, syrup, butter or cream cheese for palatability and taste. Other electuaries (mediums that mask the bitter taste of medicinal herbs) include fresh bread rolled around a little of the paste or peanut butter.

Herbal lozenges relieve mouth, throat and upper respiratory conditions. They are marshmallow or slippery elm, or a gum, such as tragacanth or acacia. Both powdered herbs and essential herbal oils may be used. Proper mucilage preparation is the key to an effective lozenge.

Herbal baths provide a soothing, gentle way to absorb herbal therapy through the skin instead of the mouth and digestive system. The procedure for taking an effective infusion bath is almost as important as the herbs themselves.

Herbs boiled in water and herbal steam are used to induce sweating. ***Steam baths*** improve peripheral circulation by vasodilatation. This reduces blood pressure. It also helps in the absorption of medicinal particles present in the herbal oil and augments the elimination of impurities in the system through excretory and secretory outlets such as sweat glands, kidneys and liver. Besides, the medicine used for herbal steam baths will help reduce stiffness, pain and swelling.

A complete bath with an application of herbal essences has many curative effects. It has a calming effect, as well as a positive effect on decreasing stress. Fresh herbs can be used but in general dried herbs are used more frequently. Herbal baths can be supplemented with herbal essences added to the bath to promote action and combine bath treatment with aromatherapy. Biologically active constituents of herbs released into the water during brewing include saponins, phenols, polyphenols, alkaloids, peptides and others. Some of these ingredients may exercise a therapeutic effect by acting on the skin receptors, others by being absorbers through the skin and assimilated by the body, just like pharmaceuticals in modern skin patches are slowly absorbed through the skin to induce desirable therapeutic action.

Herbal douches are an effective method of treating simple vaginal infections. The herbs are steeped as for a strong tea, strained off, and the liquid poured into a douche bag. The patient should sit on the toilet, insert the applicator and rinse the vagina with the douche. One full douche bag should be used for each application. Most vaginal conditions need douching three times daily for 3–7 days.

Herbal suppositories and boluses are an effective way to treat rectal and vaginal problems, acting as carriers for the herbal medicine. Herbal compounds for suppositories generally serve one of three purposes: to soothe inflamed mucous membranes and aid the healing process, help reduce swollen membranes and overcome pus-filled discharge and to work as a laxative, stimulating normal peristalsis to overcome chronic constipation.

Herbal ointments and salves are semi-solid preparations that allow absorption of herbal benefits through the skin. They may be made with Vaseline, UN-Petroleum jelly or cocoa butter for a simple compound; or in a more complex technique, with herbal tea, oils and hardening agents such as beeswax, lanolin or lard.

Herbal compress and fomentations draw out waste residue, such as cysts or abscesses through the skin, or release them into the body's elimination channels. Compresses are made by soaking a cotton cloth in a strong herbal tea and applying it as hot as possible to the affected area. The heat enhances the activity of the herbs and opens the pores of the skin for fast assimilation. Alternating hot and cold compresses should be used to stimulate nerves and circulation. The herbs are applied to the hot compress and the cold compress left plain. Cayenne, ginger and lobelia are good choices for the hot compress.

Herbal poultices and plasters are made from either fresh herbs, crushed and blended in a blender with a little olive or wheatgerm oil, or dried, mixed with water, cider vinegar or wheatgerm oil into paste. Either blend may be spread on a piece of clean cloth or gauze and bound directly on the affected area. The whole application is then covered with plastic wrap to keep from soiling clothes or sheets and left on for 24 hours. There is usually a great deal of throbbing pain when the poultice draws out the infection and neutralises the toxic poisons. This stops when the harmful agents are drawn out. A fresh poultice should be applied every 24 hours.

Herbal liniments are used as warming massage mediums to stimulate and relieve sore muscles and ligaments. They are for external use only. Choose heat-inducing herbs and spices such as cayenne, ginger, cloves and myrrh, and drops of heating oils such as eucalyptus, wintergreen and cajeput.

Herbal oils are used externally for massage, skin treatments, healing ointments, dressings for wounds and burns, and occasionally for enemas and douches. The herb is infused in oil instead of water. Olive, safflower or almond oil are good bases for herbal oil.

Future Trends

The future is likely to witness India's strong and dominating position in mint oils and menthol, spice oils and oleoresins and other isolates. The quality of these products is being upgraded and large capacities are being installed to meet local and international demand. Another area where huge potential is forecasted is the processing of minor oils such as basil, jamrosa and palmarosa, not only to isolate major constituents but also other minor constituents; for example, ocimenes from jamrosa and eudesmol from eucalyptus and citronella java oil. Indian Cedarwood oil is one such item with great potential.

Many other aroma chemicals based on turpentine oil and/or other petroleum products will be lucrative to produce for export. No expansion is being undertaken in other developed countries due to environmental constraints. Big players are looking at India with a view to setting up their own bases for many products. The possibility of shortage of aroma chemicals in the next millennium exists and India has the potential to fulfill this increased demand.

Key Messages

- Cosmetics play an important role in the present era. Herbs remain one of the oldest sources of cosmetics.
- Synthetic cosmetics have been known to cause harmful effects to the skin, eyes and other parts of the body. This has led to the exploration of the therapeutic effects of herbs.
- Herbs are considered to be safe and effective; hence, they are used as alternatives to synthetic cosmetics.
- Various herbal preparations and formulations (in combination) increase the aesthetic value of existing cosmetics.
- Various formulations containing herbal ingredients are readily available in the market.
- Essential oils are mainly used in aromatherapy and enjoy a large and consistent demand in world trade.

QUESTIONS

1. What are herbal cosmetics? Classify in detail with examples.
2. Write a note on formulations used in cosmetics with reference to herbs.
3. Discuss the different raw materials and ingredients used in the manufacture of herbal cosmetics.
4. Write a detailed note on evaluation parameters of herbal cosmetics.
5. Define and classify essential oils.
6. Write a short note on aromatherapy.

22

Quality Control of Cosmetics

SHOBHA RANI R HIREMATH AND AMIT KUMAR DAS

Learning Objectives

At the end of this chapter, you will be able to:

- Explain the concept of quality and quality control aspects of cosmetics
- Describe the general and specific quality control tests of cosmetics

Introduction

Quality is the degree of excellence. It is an inherent part of a product. A product is said to be of good quality if it conforms to requirements and is fit for use. It should be understood that the term 'quality' is not used in the sense of a 'quality article', meaning the finest available, but in the competitive sense of being adequate and suitable for an article that fulfils a certain need. It should be understood that quality cannot be inserted into a product but must be built in.

Quality Control

The concept of quality control (QC) in cosmetics refers to the process of striving to produce a perfect cosmetic product by a series of measures requiring an organised effort by the entire company to prevent or eliminate errors at every stage during production. Manufacturers are required to establish a QC unit with the authority to approve or reject raw materials and finished products and also review production records.

QC in cosmetics is essentially a tool that enables the company to:

- Maintain product quality at the desired level and within previously determined limits of acceptability
- Recognise and take advantage of any possibility of narrowing these limits while keeping the average at the desired level
- Recognise and presumably eliminate causes of excessive variation
- Reduce cost of production and inspection
- Foresee impending quality changes and prevent them as far as possible

As the operation of quality control inevitably results in the occasional rejection of lots of raw materials, semifinished and finished products, it is essential that the QC department should operate with complete freedom with respect to production demands. The results of QC work must be reported to the concerned persons.

The manner of reporting is of great importance, and only written reports should be accepted. Verbal reports are sometimes necessary in emergencies, but they should always be confirmed in writing in order to avoid errors and misunderstanding. The records stand as evidence of work done and as a source of information in the future.

If quality is to be controlled, it must be with respect to certain criteria called 'standards'. Adherence to standards should be assured by periodic audits, the objective of which is to determine whether any deviations from approved practice have crept in. If the audit discloses any deviation from standards, the person in charge of QC should take action:

- Direct an immediate return to standard procedure
- Permit the deviation to continue temporarily, pending investigation and further experience
- Authorise an immediate amendment of standards

Evaluation of the raw materials, intermediate and finished products should be carried out by sampling, analytical and other testing procedures. After the testing has been completed, at least a portion of the sample should be preserved in a suitable container, and indexed and filed for future reference. Although non-technical, the standards should include instructions for proper storage of materials before use, especially materials that are adversely affected by heat, light, high humidity, etc.

Apart from hour-to-hour and day-to-day control of products, much useful information for purposes of record may be obtained by shelf testing. Such testing is designed to reveal potential shortcomings of the product and would ordinarily include storage of finished containers under ordinary room conditions, with such periodic examination and analyses as may be required to appraise both the product and its containers. This work should be supplemented by storage under severe conditions, such as at various combinations of high and low temperatures (including freezing), high and low humidity, exposure to direct sunlight, etc. The ultimate objective of such testing is the correlation of the results of accelerated tests with shelf life.

Control of quality during filling of cosmetics is of as much importance as at any other stage of the process. The finished package must be clean, undamaged and otherwise presentable. The closure must be properly applied. Each individual package should bear a code number identifying it as part of a larger unit of stock, and this number should be correlated with bulk manufactured lots and with raw material lots. Checking the net contents of packages from time to time is required to ensure conformance to the declaration of contents and to avoid unnecessarily large overweights.

An 'on-the-market' control is also carried out to check product behaviour. It is done in three ways:

- By sampling the market at selected intervals
- By prompt and intelligent interpretation of complaints
- By scrutiny of returned goods

Statistics is involved in the production and quality control of cosmetics. Statistical quality control is the monitoring of quality by application of statistical methods in all stages of production. The ideal state of statistically controlled process is one in which both the quality level as reflected by averages and the variability remain within the limits as predicted from ordinary variation.

Product Development Protocol for Quality

- **Manufacturing Quality Control Procedures:** Protocols of Good Manufacturing Procedures (GMP) and strict Food and Drug Administration (FDA) guidelines should be followed.
- **Premanufacturing Quarantine:** All raw materials (ingredients) are maintained in quarantine until a sample is tested and evaluated against a preset standard. This assures the highest quality of products and integrity of suppliers.
- **Sampling:** During manufacturing, samples are randomly selected for QC testing and formula verification.
- **Consistency Testing:** Samples from every production batch are run through a battery of tests again to assure stability and to check that characteristics such as pH, viscosity, colour, etc. match the preset standard to ensure that every batch is identical and has a shelf life of at least two years.
- **Microbiological Analysis:** To ensure the safety of the product, a sample from each batch is tested for microbiological analysis to ensure there are no bacteria or other foreign contaminants.
- **Accelerated Stability Studies:** To assure physical stability, the formula must pass various stability tests to validate the consistency of colour, thickness and pH (percentage of acidity and alkalinity). Samples are subjected to at least three freeze and thaw cycles, and to temperature ranges up to 51.11°C (124°F) for as long as 90 days.
- **Microbiological Challenge Tests:** All formulas must pass preservation tests against microbiological spoilage, with products undergoing sterility and double challenge tests. In each challenge test, products are inoculated with one million organisms of each gram-positive bacteria, mould and yeast and allowed to incubate for 56 days. The preservative system is accepted as adequate only if the product demonstrates that it is capable of suppressing the growth of each of the pathogens.
- **Packaging, Design and Labelling:** Attention to accuracy and detail is a top priority when the product's ingredient labelling is created. The product claims and all other product information should be correct.
- **Shipability Studies:** A 6000-mile shipping test is performed on all final packages. Products are filled into actual packaging and shipped from coast to coast and back again using commercial carriers.
- **Retains:** A sample is retained in the laboratory for five years to provide verification of purity and formula stability.

Analytical Methods

Analytical methods are employed to ensure that products conform to standards. Generally, cosmetic products are difficult to analyse because of their heterogenous nature. However, the following are the analytical methods used for the assessment of quality in cosmetic formulations.

Chromatographic techniques are used to identify the presence or absence of components or as a quantitative technique to determine the amount of analyte present in a sample. For example, thin layer chromatography (TLC) has been successfully used to identify semi-permanent and direct dyes used for hair colouring. Gas chromatography (GC) and high-performance liquid chromatography (HPLC) are the most widely used of all instrumental techniques. The other techniques used are UV/

Visible and IR spectrophotometry. For example, the determination of p-aminobenzoic acid (PABA) in cosmetics is done spectrophotometrically.

Obtaining a representative sample of the manufactured product or of a raw material is a critical part of the analytical process. Screening tests such as visual examination are used to obtain information on the uniformity of a particular size. For dried or powdered material, the most rapid test is visual examination followed by microscopic examination; liquid-based/emulsified products can be smeared onto a slide and observed under the microscope.

Spot tests involve the addition of specific chemical reagents to small samples of material on a microscope slide to detect the presence (or absence) of a range of anions and cations, which, from a quality point of view, confirms the presence of additives or indicates the presence of contaminants.

Determination of melting point particularly for lipid-based material is through a rapid, non-destructive and inexpensive test that can be used on many raw materials and manufactured products. Absorptiometry is an instrumental technique that is particularly suited to the screening of raw material. GC techniques are used to analyse fatty acids after extraction and conversion to their methyl esters. HPLC is widely used in the analysis of raw materials, impurities and even cosmetic products.

Examples:

- A rapid, sensitive and selective method involving reversed-phase liquid chromatography (LC) with electrospray ionisation (ESI) mass spectrometry (MS) is employed for determining ceramides in cosmetics for quality control of the product formulation. Using this LC/ESI-MS technique, simultaneous separation and characterisation of ceramides as an impurity is possible.
- The reversed phase (RP)-HPLC method is used for the simultaneous separation of various antimicrobial agents used in cosmetics.
- An isocratic RP-HPLC method is proposed for the practical and reliable determination of triclosan, an antimicrobial agent incorporated into a variety of personal heathcare products.
- An ion-interaction HPLC-diode-array detection method has been developed and optimised for the separation of typical antimicrobial agents used in cosmetics and hygiene products.
- A HPLC method and a capillary zone electrophoresis (CZE) method have been developed for the analysis of methylparaben, ethylparaben, propylparaben and butylparaben in commercial cosmetic products.
- Toothpastes containing fluorides should be analysed to determine available free fluoride and total available fluorine. Fluoride and monoflurophosphate are determined by HPLC.
- Rapid HPLC is carried out for the simultaneous assay of sunscreen agents.
- Ketoconazole, an anti-fungal agent, is often incorporated in shampoos as it is known to be effective against fungal infections on the scalp. The amount of ketoconazole to be incorporated is quantified by the HPLC method. Permethrin, a highly effective insecticide agent, widely used for pest control and the treatment of lice in humans, is added in shampoos. A fast and reliable method for the determination of permethrin is desirable to support formulation screening and quality control. The UV spectroscopic method is

followed for the determination of permethrin in shampoos.

- A GC-MS quantitation procedure is employed for the determination of fragrance in perfumes as they may elicit skin sensitisation reactions.

Acid value, ester value and saponification value are determined in raw materials consisting wholly or largely of fatty esters and products containing such materials. Unsaponifiable matter may form part of the specification of certain raw materials. This method is also useful for determining the fatty alcohols, sterols, etc. in products. The contents of acids and bases, free and combined, should be determined in shampoos, creams, lotions and other products containing acids, bases or a combination of both. Creams and lotions should be analysed for neutral fatty matter and total fatty acids. Thioglycolic acid, hydrogen peroxide or bromate should be determined for hair treatments.

General Techniques

- Raw materials and products should be tested for moisture and total volatile and non-volatile matter by drying. Many skin cleansing products or powders and skin peeling products may contain aflatoxins. These are carcinogenic and can be absorbed through the skin. These should be completely absent from cosmetics. This can be achieved by careful quality control of the raw materials.
- Products such as toothpastes, creams and lotions may have high water content due to which they may foam excessively. Therefore, the water content of these products should be measured.
- Measurement of pH is very important for products and raw materials, aqueous liquids, gels, creams, shampoos, etc. pH meters are used to measure the pH.
- Ash and metal ions should be determined by atomic absorption spectrophotometry for products and raw materials, dried products and powders, paste, gels, creams or water-based solids and water-insoluble solids dispersed in an aqueous base.
- Lipid materials such as fats or oils of animal or vegetable origin, fatty acids, glycerol, lanolin, terpines, steroids and other raw materials soluble in organic solvents should be removed by solvent extraction.

Quality Control Tests

Hair Care Products

Shampoos

The dermatological safety of shampoos is extremely important. They should be safe on the skin and eyes as well as be generally non-toxic.

Prediction of ocular irritancy of shampoos

One of the oldest tests is instilling a few drops of the shampoos in the eyes of a rabbit. Consumers demand and have a right to expect that the products they depend on are safe if used properly. Currently, the only way to guarantee this protection is through knowledge gained from animal testing. Although every possible measure has been taken to limit the number of animals used and to find new testing methods, replacement of animals is impossible at present. The majority of test animals are rodents (primarily mice and rats).

Federal laws require that the public be protected from hazardous commercial products, but specific animal tests are not mandated by law. Related federal regulations do explicitly or implicitly call for animal testing. A number of federal agencies have a significant role in animal testing for regulatory purposes.

The Draize Test: This eye and skin irritancy test is used to determine whether substances that may come into contact with the eye or skin will cause irritation or injury. Since live animals, not test tubes, are used, scientists can also observe the healing process after exposure to an irritant. In the eye test, drops of the test substance are placed in one eye in each of as few as three test animals. Rabbits are commonly used because their eyes are at least as sensitive as the human eye. Affected eyes are observed at regular intervals and results are scored based on the degree of various reactions: corneal clouding, percent of cornea involved, condition of iris, redness, etc.

For the skin irritancy test, the fur of as few as three animals is clipped from a small area and the test substance is placed in contact with the skin. The skin is not abraded. The site is covered for four hours and then the patch is removed to evaluate any irritation for up to three more days.

While the basic Draize procedures are essentially the same as those used since the 1940s, modifications to reduce or eliminate any pain or distress in test animals are now employed. These modifications include using ophthalmic anesthetics whenever possible and using diluted solutions or lower doses of test substances. Generally, the rabbits can move freely and have access to food and water.

Isolated Rabbit Eye (IRE): The isolated rabbit test was first proposed by Burton et al (1981), as a means of screening for severe irritants without using live animals. The IRE confers the advantage that animals are not bred exclusively for the purpose. The method is capable of distinguishing between mild and moderate eye irritants, such as 'baby' and normal 'adult' shampoos.

Bovine Corneal Opacity and Permeability (BCOP) Assay: The BCOP assay was introduced by Gautheron et al (1992) as a method for screening process intermediates for worker safety. BCOP data correctly predicted whether a compound would be irritating or not. Both methods use the metric of corneal opacity, which, in relation to accidental human exposure to an irritant, is arguably the most important parameter, since it provides information on how visual acuity may be impaired by accidental exposure.

Non-animal Alternatives: The scientific community has been successful in reducing the number of animals used in safety testing, as well as in refining test methods to reduce any pain or distress these animals may experience. As useful as 'alternative' methods have proven to be, each has its limitations.

Mathematical models can help to predict an organism's responses to varying levels of exposure to a particular substance. They can also help in improving the design of scientific experiments. These models are, however, no substitute for observation of the effects of a substance in a complex, living system.

Computer data banks allow for the reduction of test duplication. They are also useful in the initial evaluation of chemicals slated for further study; unsuitable chemicals can be eliminated from consideration prior to the institution of animal testing. However, computers can only process and store existing knowledge, much of which has come from animal studies. Animal testing is required to expand that knowledge base.

Cells, tissues, and even whole organs obtained from animals and humans can be used for preliminary screening of chemical compounds. They can help identify substances that are so toxic that there is no purpose in continuing to investigate their potential use. However, in vitro tests cannot reveal the effects of a substance on a complex living organism composed of many different organs and systems. In the end, the validity of such tests must be verified by testing on an appropriate intact, living organism.

Microorganisms and lower invertebrates (single-cell organisms such as protozoa and bacteria) are increasingly useful in early screening for toxic effects. However, because of their simple physiology, they shed little light on complex toxicity questions, and are thus less useful in late stages of testing protocols. Invertebrate animals such as insects and mollusks are also useful in preliminary tests, but the results obtained are often too general to be applied to multiorgan toxicity problems in humans.

The Health Protection Branch (HPB), Canada states that 'new methods can never totally replace testing in an appropriate animal model. For example, in vitro methods cannot show complex interactions of a chemical in a living being. Indeed, the extreme complexity of biochemical systems in living creatures cannot be duplicated by our current knowledge, nor will it be in the foreseeable future'.

For economic and ethical reasons, there is an active commitment to refine existing tests by minimising animal distress, to reduce animal usage, replace whole-animal testing and search for more of these alternatives. However, before any non-animal method can be accepted as an 'alternative', its value as a genuine substitute has to be proven or validated. Industry supports both internal and external efforts to develop and evaluate promising non-animal procedures.

The public may be confused by announcements that some companies do not test their products on laboratory animals, thus providing 'cruelty-free' products. Generally, such claims do not present the full picture. Often, the ingredients in the product have already been animal tested, or the manufacturer may have purchased a product formulation from a supplier that previously conducted these tests. Almost all products or chemical compounds that comprise them will have been previously tested in animals.

Because a given product may not require animal tests is not evidence that testing can be abandoned for all products. New chemicals, new uses of old chemicals and new mixtures of chemicals must be subjected to toxicity testing so that unsafe products will not be marketed inadvertently.

Surfactants

Surfactants are one of the main ingredients in shampoos and the various functions of surfactants are cleansing, foaming, conditioning, viscosity and aesthetic appeal combined with safety and mildness in use. Shampoos are rather concentrated aqueous solutions of mostly anionic surfactants in combination with salts, particularly sodium chloride. In addition to foaming, detergency and mildness to the skin, the rheology of these liquids is of key importance. In use, the consumer expects the liquids to have non–Newtonian flow behaviour, that is, a slow flow from the bottle, indicating a high active content and allowing optimum dosage and easy distribution on the hair.

The characterisation of flow behaviour has been limited mainly to the measurement of flow curves, that is, recording the shear viscosity as a function of the shear rate γ. A typical viscosity profile shows a pronounced pseudoplastic behaviour. The shear rate ranges applicable to actual use are about 5–10 s-1 for flow from the bottle and about 50–100 s-1 for distribution on the hair.

Methods for testing surfactants in shampoos

Generally, there are two methods for surfactant analysis in shampoos: one is qualitative examination and the other is quantitative analysis.

Qualitative examination

- *Behaviour on acidification*: The first step in qualitative examination is to acidify an aqueous solution of the product with hydrochloric acid. If the latter persists, the presence of a surfactant is indicated.
- *Test for elements*: If a surfactant is present, a filtered ethanol extract of the product is tested for sulphur, nitrogen, phosphorus and halogen either by the sodium-fusion method or preferably by the zinc dust–sodium carbonate fusion method.
- *Test with mixed dimidium bromide–disulphine blue dyes*: In the presence of an anionic surfactant, this indicator imparts a pink colour to the chloroform phase. In the presence of cationic matter, the chloroform phase is coloured blue.
- *Paper chromatography*: It permits the identification of a number of different types of active matter, organic bases and a number of additives that may be present.

Quantitative analysis of anionic surfactants

Depending on the different function groups of anionic surfactants, there are different quantitative methods; one of the general methods is volumetric titration. Titration techniques are among the earliest methods developed for the analysis of anionic surfactants. They include:

- Acid base titration
- Single- and two-phase titration with cationic active matter
- Double decomposition reactions

Quantitative analysis of cationic surfactants

Generally, there are small amounts of cationic surfactants in shampoos; about five methods can be used to test them:

- Gravimetric method
- Volumetric method
- Colourimetric method
- Chromatographic techniques
- UV spectroscopic method

A new method namely, flow injection analysis (FIA), is based on the extraction of the cationic surfactant with anionic dyes.

Quality Tests for Hair Dyes

The following tests are carried out to ensure the quality of hair dyes:

- pH of 5% solution in water
- Active matter as paraphenylenediamine (PPD) content, percent by mass. (PPD is a chemical substance that is widely used as a permanent hair dye)
- Calculated active matter (as PPD) in solution after recommended dilution with water, percent by mass

Quality Control for Hair Spray

During the manufacturing process, samples are pulled from the conveyor line and checked to ensure they meet all the specifications. Key properties that are monitored include the fill weight, concentration of active ingredients and pressure of the can. Spray characteristics such as spray rate (the amount of product delivered per second) and spray pattern (the physical size and shape of the spray) are also monitored. Long-term stability testing is conducted to ensure that the cans do not clog when sprayed and that they remain free of internal corrosion.

Quality Control for Lipsticks

Quality control procedures are strict, since the product must meet FDA standards. Lipstick is the only cosmetic ingested, and because of this, strict controls on ingredients as well as the manufacturing processes are imposed. Lipstick is mixed and processed in a controlled environment thereby enabling it to be free of contamination. Incoming material is tested to ensure that it meets required specifications. Samples of every batch produced are saved and stored at room temperature for the life of the product (and often beyond that) to maintain a control on the batch.

As noted above, the appearance of lipstick as a final product is very important. For this reason, everyone involved in its manufacture becomes an inspector, and non-standard products are either reworked or scrapped. Final inspection of every tube is performed by the consumer, and if not satisfactory, will be rejected at the retail level. Since the retailer and manufacturer are often not the same, quality problems at the consumer level have a major impact on the manufacturer.

Colour control of lipstick is critical. The dispersion of the pigment is checked stringently when a new batch is manufactured, and the colour must be carefully controlled when the lipstick mass is reheated. The colour of the lipstick mass will bleed over time, and each time a batch is reheated, the colour may be altered. Colourimetric equipment is used to provide some numerical way to control the shades of lipstick. This equipment gives a numerical reading of the shade, when mixed, so it can match that of previous batches. Matching of reheated batches is done visually, so careful time and environment controls are placed on lipstick mass when it is not immediately used.

There are two special tests used for lipsticks: the heat test and the rupture test. In the heat test, the lipstick is placed in the extended position in a holder and left in an oven at a constant temperature of over 54 °C (130 °F) for 24 hours. There should be no drooping or distortion of the lipstick. In the rupture test, the lipstick is placed in two holders, in the extended position. Weight is added to the holder on the lipstick portion at 30-second intervals until the lipstick ruptures. The pressure required to rupture the lipstick is then checked against the manufacturer's standards. Since there are no industry standards for these tests, each manufacturer sets its own parameters.

Quality Control for Nail Polish

Extreme attention to quality control is essential throughout the manufacturing process. Not only does quality control increase safety in the process, but it is the only way that a manufacturer can be assured of consumer confidence and loyalty. A single bottle of poor quality polish can lose a customer forever.

The nail polish is tested throughout the manufacturing process for several important factors (drying time, smoothness of flow, gloss, hardness, colour, abrasion resistance, etc.). Subjective testing, where the mixture or final product is examined or applied, is ongoing. Objective, laboratory testing of samples, though more time-consuming, is also necessary to ensure a usable product.

Quality Control for Toothpastes

Each batch of ingredients is tested for quality as it is brought into the factory. The testing lab also checks samples of the final product. Formulating dental creams for consumer acceptance requires optimising many physical and chemical attributes. Much work has to be done to develop toothpastes that are not stringy, do not show separation of a liquid phase from the dentifrice and do not increase in viscosity on ageing. Dentifrices must also have an appealing taste for consumers to keep buying the product. Along with consumer tests and sensory evaluations, analytical data on flavour composition and release is usually obtained using GC while new dental creams are being created. These quantitative data can show the interactions between flavour and other dentifrice components and are a very useful tool in the formulation process.

Toothpastes must have certain flow properties to be accepted and liked by the consumer. The formulation should not separate into liquid and solid phases with ageing. The dentifrice must be easy to dispense from a tube and yet have excellent ribbon qualities, which enable it to stand up after it is extruded onto the toothbrush bristles. Furthermore, the ribbon should not exhibit a long string. This is particularly important because stringy toothpastes contribute to messiness around the cap, which the consumer dislikes. To predict these consumer-perceivable attributes, the rheology of the toothpaste has to be studied.

Rheological properties are measured at a constant temperature of 25 °C using a cone and plate viscometer. The plates are 4 cm in diameter with a constant gap distance of 1000 mm. Three types of measurements are conducted with the rheometer. The first involves creating a flow curve in which the shear rate is measured as a function of applied stress. This measurement is used to predict ease of dispensing from a toothpaste tube and the stand-up properties. The flow curves (shear stress versus shear rate) yield information on the strength of the structure at rest (yield stress) and how easily the three-dimensional network will break down (shear thinning) at high applied stresses. An apparent yield stress can be obtained at a very low shear rate (<0.10/s), which approximates conditions at rest.

Studies are performed to monitor changes in strain or structural deformations in response to a constant applied stress over a period of time. The linear portion of creep curves yields the Newtonian viscosity. Measured at high applied stresses (400–500 Pa), Newtonian viscosity can be used to predict ease of squeezing; at low applied stresses (50 Pa), it can be used to predict how runny the toothpaste will be when it is squeezed out of a tube. Dynamic oscillatory experiments are also conducted on toothpastes. An oscillatory stress is imposed on the material, and the resulting shear strain response (degree of deformation) is measured. The stress measurement has two components: one in phase with the displacement (elastic modulus, G') and one 90|SD out of phase (loss modulus, G"). The ratio of G"/G' is known as the tangent delta and is a measure of the relationship between the elastic and viscous natures of the dentifrice. Highly elastic structures (tangent delta <1) are less subject to phase separation during the ageing process. They also recover more quickly after stress is imposed on the toothpaste.

Additionally, dental cream viscosity measurements are conducted to gain information on the overall thickness of the product. The string properties of dental creams may be important not only as a contributor to the messiness of the product but also in how they affect the processing of the product, for example, in the latter stages of tube filling. This attribute can be qualitatively determined in the laboratory by measuring the conductivity of toothpaste sandwiched between two separating plates. The stringiness index is measured on the basis of current versus time curves and is unitless: high stringiness values indicate messy dentifrices.

Flavour is an important constituent of a toothpaste. The extent to which dentifrice flavour interacts with the product's continuous phase and its abrasiveness profoundly affect how the flavour will be perceived by the consumer. The effect of various types of surfactants on dentifrice systems can also be important. It has been reported that volatile flavour components of toothpastes diluted with water can be significantly reduced by surfactants such as alkyl polyglycosides. Flavour release measurements, along with sensory evaluations from flavourists and consumers, constitute another method that the formulation chemist can use to achieve the optimal dentifrice preparation. Headspace GC is often used to measure the flavour release from neat dentifrices as well as from toothpaste slurries diluted with water.

Separation of water-soluble and water-insoluble components and water-insoluble matter in toothpastes should be determined. A need for quality control is recommended to find the total and free fluoride in toothpastes. A parameter called relative effectiveness coefficient (REC) is also used for the qualitative assessment of toothpastes containing active ingredients. REC is the ratio between the concentration of the active component in water eluates obtained after three minutes and adequately prolonged dispersion of the toothpaste in distilled water at a 1:4 ratio. The change in REC during storage as well as during testing of the toothpaste stability at high and low temperatures provides evidence of deviations in its quality.

Quality Control of Eye Cosmetics

All products in the eye cosmetics range have to be developed to avoid all types of sensitive reactions in the eyes such as tears, irritation to the cornea, eye lash etc. with or without contact lenses.

The raw materials used should be ultra-micronised and bioinert. Non-ionic preservatives should be used. Gentle mascara, cream eyeshadow, pencils and ophthalmic mascara should be paraben free. Only water-insoluble mineral pigments should be used. Components such as tocopherol linoleate and γ orizanol fulfill these conditions. Components such as nickel, cobalt, colophane and allergenic fragrance notes that present a potential risk should not be used. Components such as formol, toluene, acetone and formaldehyde resin that are harmful to nails and skin should not be used. Mascaras, eyeliners, pencils, eyeshadows, nail enamels and treatments should be fragrance free.

Systematic tests (toxicological using a substitutive method, bacteriological, physicochemical) and permanent control of product quality should be carried out by a cosmeto-vigilance panel. Raw materials, packaging components and finished products must meet tightly controlled specifications.

Testing includes pH, specific gravity, heavy metals, microbial counts, viscosity and visual appearance. All products are tested like pharmaceuticals, and samples from production batches are kept on file for three years from the date of manufacture. Acute eye irritation tests must be carried out.

Quality Control for Skin Products

- Testing of all incoming raw materials, fragrances, packaging materials and labelling materials is done to assure identity and consistent quality.
- Quality control personnel are responsible for all in-process checks, adjustments and colour matching.
- Quality control tests for all manufactured products using various methods such as pH, viscosity and moisture determination.
- In-house microbiological testing of all products is done prior to filling.
- Assay of active ingredients by various methods including volumetric titrations, UV scanning and HPLC testing

Because many products are intended for topical use, or for use in and around the eyes, consideration for potential skin and eye irritancy is an important aspect of safety evaluation.

Topical Creams

There are many methods used to predict the potential activity of substances to induce irritation or sensitisation in human skin. This applies to skin care products also.

Test for primary irritation: The substance is applied to the intact skin of rabbits and the site of application is examined at intervals. The changes seen are assessed in severity according to the scale of numerical values. The skin of the rabbit is more susceptible to irritation than that of humans. The product may be tested for skin irritation potential in humans using several techniques such as patch test and repeated insult patch test.

Delayed hypersensitivity (contact allergic dermatitis): There are several techniques designed to detect the potential of the substance in induced contact allergic dermatitis in humans. A delayed hypersensitivity test (DHT) is an immune function test measuring the presence of activated T cells that recognise a certain substance. The immune system protects against infection by viruses, bacteria, fungi and parasites. After initial exposure to a foreign substance or antigen, the immune system creates both antibodies and sensitised T cells. Both these immune agents respond when the body is re-exposed to the antigen. Antibodies, which are circulating proteins, respond within minutes to give what is termed an immediate hypersensitivity reaction. T cell responses occur over several days and are thus called delayed hypersensitivity reactions. The cascade of events initiated by the T cells leads to hardening (induration) and redness (erythema) at the injection site.

A small amount of material is injected into the skin. The area is examined 48–72 hours after the injection. In the patch test, 20–30 adhesive patches are usually placed on the upper back. The patches are kept in place and the area is kept dry for 48 hours. The patches are then removed, and the skin is examined 24 hours later and possibly again a day or two following that. Patch testing is usually performed following a patient complaint of skin irritation from an unknown substance.

The test of overall T cell responsiveness is

performed with several injections. Each area injected is circled and marked. Results are read 48 hours after the injection. Patch test areas that become red and irritated indicate reaction to the substance in the patch. The main parameters for the quality control evaluation of creams are consistency and viscosity.

Viscoelastic Evaluation of Topical Creams

Rheological testing of various cream formulations should be performed at ambient temperature using a control stress rheometer.

Dynamic Mechanical Testing

Strain sweep

All test samples can be subjected to constant frequency (10 rad/sec) using an amplitude ramp with 0.2–100% strain at 25 °C. The aim is to investigate the structural properties of the creams under increased strain.

Time sweep

Each sample can be subjected to preshearing (1 minute applied value of 20 1/sec shear rate at 25 °C) to examine the structure recovery after the structure is broken down. The samples are normally subjected to a frequency of 10 rad/sec, with a 1.0% strain as controlled variable for 30 minutes at 25 °C.

Drug release studies from various formulations can be evaluated using United States Pharmacopeial [USP] Type II apparatus and an Enhancer® Cell assembly. Samples are withdrawn at regular intervals and analysed for the drug content by suitable methods of analysis.

Hence, quality control tests should be performed on all cosmetic formulations. They are as essential in the cosmetic industry as they are in the pharmaceutical industry. Maintaining quality ensures the safety of consumers.

Key Messages

- Quality is the degree of excellence and is an inherent part of a product.
- Quality cannot be applied to a product but must be built in.
- The concept of quality control (QC) in cosmetics refers to the process of striving to produce a perfect cosmetic product by a series of measures requiring an organised effort by the entire company.
- Quality is determined by certain criteria called 'standards'.
- Statistical quality control is the monitoring of quality by the application of statistical methods in all stages of production.
- Various chromatographic and spectrophotometric methods are used to assess the quality of cosmetics.

Questions

1. Write briefly about the concept of quality control in cosmetics.
2. List the quality control tests used in cosmetics, with some examples.
3. Describe the quality control tests for shampoos.
4. Explain the importance of QC tests in lipsticks.

23

Safety and Efficacy of Cosmetics

Shobha Rani R Hiremath

Learning Objectives

At the end of this chapter, you will be able to:

- Explain the importance of safety of cosmetics
- Explain the need for safety studies
- Describe the process of safety evaluation
- List the topical and systemic effects of cosmetics
- Describe the general aspects of efficacy testing of cosmetics/cosmeceuticals
- Describe the efficacy testing of some cosmeceuticals

Introduction – Safety of Cosmetics

The safety of cosmetics to its users, consumers and aestheticians (professionals in the industry) is of utmost importance. Cosmetic/Cosmeceutical products have seldom been associated with serious health hazards. However, it does not mean that cosmetics are completely safe, especially when used over a long period of time and when their possible long-term effects are considered. Therefore, it is important that their safety-in-use is evaluated by controlling the ingredient contents and toxicity.

Apart from good manufacturing practice (GMP) and quality control, the toxicological profile of cosmetic ingredients and the finished products must be made a prerequisite. As such, it is important that cosmetic manufacturers conduct toxicological evaluations on raw materials and finished products to substantiate the safety of their products. Where adequate data on the toxicity of the ingredients is available, the final product may not need to be evaluated.

However, when new ingredients and formulations are used, the testing of the ingredients and final products becomes essential. It is, therefore, the responsibility of the manufacturers and suppliers of new products to ensure that adequate information is provided for safety assessment of the finished product.

Need for Safety Studies

All cosmetics can cause allergic reactions. There is no list of ingredients that can be guaranteed not to cause allergic reactions. With the advent of herbal cosmetics, more emphasis has been placed on the use of natural ingredients obtained from plant or animal products but not all of these are safe.

In 1994, the Food and Drug Administration (FDA) received around 200 reports of adverse drug reactions (ADRs) to cosmetics, out of which makeup accounted for 30%. Most ADRs were either skin irritations or allergic reactions. Out of these, 11% were caused by the chemical alpha hydroxy acid (AHA) used in 'skin peelers'. According to a study of cosmetic reactions by the North American Contact Dermatitis Group, fragrances and preservatives are the most common causes of allergic and irritant reactions.

According to the FDA Office of Cosmetics and Colours, hair straighteners and dyes are among the top consumer complaint areas. Consumers complained of hair loss, scalp irritation, discoloured hair and baldness caused by the use of hair straighteners. Some consumers have reported hair loss, burning, redness and irritation from hair dyes. Other allergic reactions to dyes include itching, swelling of the face and even difficulty in breathing. The FDA has also received several reports of injuries from hair dyes accidentally getting into the eyes.

There are reports (from researchers of Brigham and Women's Hospital, Boston) of increased risk of all fatal cancers with the prolonged use of hair dyes. Malignant melanoma is a common adverse effect of topical sunscreens. Considering these factors, it becomes essential to ensure the safety of the products on the market.

Safety Evaluation

The process of safety evaluation consists of two phases:

- Hazard determination—estimate the potential hazard of each ingredient
- Risk assessment—determine the likelihood or risk of any hazard identified in the first phase actually causing harm to the consumer

Hazard Determination

In practice, evaluation of most new products does not involve a full hazard assessment of every ingredient. In most cases, the ingredients will have a long history of safe use and the new product will primarily be a recombination of known ingredients.

Hazard Determination of New Ingredients

It is important to consider a number of possible adverse hazardous effects that could occur from the use of an ingredient. These effects are divided into:

- Topical effects that affect the external parts such as the skin, eyes or mucous membranes
- Systemic effects that may occur should an ingredient enter the body through the skin, by swallowing or by inhalation

Topical Effects

Skin irritation: It is caused by a direct chemical attack on the skin, resulting in dry, flaky or rough skin, inflammation and reddening. Irritation is an effect to which everybody is susceptible. Normally, there is a threshold concentration below which the great majority of consumers will not react. It is important to estimate this threshold concentration for possible risk assessment.

Eye irritation: Damage to the eye is a greater hazard than skin irritation because of possible side effects on vision. Great care must be taken particularly with cosmetics intended for use around the eyes. The same principles of concentration effects and comparative data for risk assessment also apply to eye irritation. It must always be remembered that a mistake or negligence in this area could lead to very serious consequences for the consumer.

Mucous membrane irritation: Cosmetic products may come in contact with mucous membrane areas (around the eye and the genital region) either accidentally or by design. Mucous membranes do not have the protective horny layer and are therefore more susceptible to irritants. Some ingredients may be acceptable for use on the skin but not for use in products that are likely to come in contact with mucous membranes. Again, the principles of concentration limits and comparison with existing ingredients are used in assessing risk of mucous membrane contact.

Skin sensitisation/allergy: All chemicals will sensitise someone, somewhere. Zero reaction is an impossible target. Allergy differs from irritation in the mechanism that produces the reaction; in the case of allergy, the immune system is involved. Chemicals differ in their allergic potential and vary from materials such as poison ivy, which sensitises most people, to chemicals of which only one or two cases of sensitivity have been reported. As with irritation, sensitisation is also concentration dependent. However, in sensitised people, the concentration required to elicit a reaction may be much lower.

Photo irritation/allergy: Some chemicals cause skin irritation or allergy only in the presence of ultraviolet (UV) light. The reactions are of concern only for products applied to skin that is exposed to sunlight. Ingredients that do not absorb UV light are not considered to present a problem. Sunscreen agents are a potential problem for this type of effect and new ingredients should be thoroughly evaluated before use.

Other skin reactions: An urticarial response (nettle rash) is caused by the release of histamines and other mediators of inflammation into the skin. This effect is seen in cosmetics that contain cinammic aldehyde. Some people also suffer a stinging sensation when lactic acid is applied to the skin.

Systemic Effects

Systemic effects comprise harmful effects resulting from a cosmetic ingredient entering the body. A cosmetic ingredient may enter the body through the skin or mucous membranes, by swallowing or by inhalation.

Through the skin and mucous membranes: Almost any chemical that comes in contact with the skin will penetrate it to some extent. The extent of penetration will vary depending on the following:

- Nature of the chemical
- Concentration of the chemical
- Duration and amount of skin exposed
- Nature of the vehicle
- State and site of the skin
- Variations between individuals

Skin penetration plays an important part in risk assessment

By swallowing: Significant quantities may be swallowed during normal use, for example, with oral hygiene products or with lipsticks. The possibility of children obtaining and accidentally swallowing a cosmetic product always exists. Therefore, some information on the effects of swallowing must be provided.

By inhalation: This route of entry is of most significance for aerosols and other spray products.

Systemic Toxicity

Several types of systemic toxicity need to be considered during safety evaluation:

- Carcinogenicity
- Teratogenicity

- Neurotoxicity

More general effects include acute toxicity, with the effect confined to specific organs following a large single dose, and subacute/chronic toxicity, with the effect caused by smaller repeated doses over a prolonged period.

Risk Assessment

Zero risk or absolute safety does not exist. Risk assessment defines whether a risk is acceptable or not. The purpose of risk assessment is to arrive at a conclusion about the likelihood of a hazard manifesting itself during use of a cosmetic product. The process of risk assessment consists of two stages:

- *First stage (risk of ingredients):* Evaluation of the risk of each ingredient
- *Second stage (risk of products):* Evaluation of the risk of the combination of ingredients in the final product.

Of Ingredients

The risk of an ingredient with a known hazard depends on the degree of consumer exposure. To determine exposure, the following factors must be considered:

- Concentration of ingredients in a product
- Frequency and quantity of product used
- Total area of skin contact
- Method of product use—left on the skin, rinsed off, sprayed, etc.
- Number of products containing the ingredients

After making a quantitative estimate of all these factors, the total dose to which a consumer is likely to be exposed can be calculated.

Of Products

The risk presented by a product depends primarily on the risks of the individual ingredients. However, there remains the possibility that combining ingredients in the product may change the risk by some form of interaction. The three main types of interaction are as follows:

- *Chemical interactions:* These comprise interactions among the product ingredients that result in the production of a new chemical whose safety must be considered.
- *Biological interactions:* These are interactions in which two or more ingredients react with a biological system, producing a different effect from that of a single ingredient.
- *Other interactions:* Some ingredients such as surfactants can cause damage to the skin which, although is not a problem by itself, may allow greater penetration of other ingredients and thereby make the cosmetic dangerous. The degree of skin penetration of an ingredient depends on the solvent. Only when a product contains completely new combinations of a potentially hazardous ingredient with other ingredients such as solvents or surfactants is product risk assessment required.

Efficacy Testing

The ultimate parameter that determines a product's value is its efficacy. Although providing proof of efficacy is secondary to safety testing, it is nonetheless an essential aspect of cosmetic formulation. Especially in cosmetics, there are several claims made about products such as 'improves skin elasticity', 'reduces fine lines and wrinkles', 'softens, smoothens and firms skin', 'delays visible signs of ageing', 'makes one fair', etc. which may be used merely to attract consumers.

The need to prove claims for either the legal or the marketing and advertising departments has led to a proliferation of methods of substantiating such claims and of test laboratories able to undertake the necessary testing of the products for efficacy.

General Aspects of Efficacy Testing

Human testing is the ultimate test for any novel product to prove its performance. The first step in human volunteer testing is to set up a panel of test subjects and obtain information about various parameters such as skin and hair type, types of products used on a regular basis and medical history including known allergies. Other information, such as the name, address and telephone number, date of birth and physical characteristics of the subject should also be obtained.

All the subjects should understand the objectives of the test and what is required of them before they agree to take part. The subjects should give their 'informed consent' in writing when they enroll for the study. The subjects must also be reminded that they should not take part if they are allergic to cosmetics or toiletries and that any medical treatment being received during the study should be reported. Female subjects who are pregnant or lactating should not take part in the study.

The adoption of an independent 'ethical committee' is recommended. This committee should consist of scientific, legal and non-technical representatives, who should make an independent evaluation of the new test protocols.

Study Design

Efficacy tests are designed to show that a product performs the function for which it is intended. For example, a moisturiser should moisturise the skin. To establish a frame of reference for the evaluation of product efficacy, it is usual to include both positive and negative controls in a study. Alternatively, the test may be a simple comparison of new versus old, such as a comparison between novel and conventional moisturising agents in a standard moisturising lotion base. The study should be run on a double-blind basis. The code is broken only on completion of the study.

Selection of a Suitable Test Panel

Subjects must demonstrate characteristics that render them suitable for a specific study.

For example, if a moisturiser is to be evaluated, it is necessary to select subjects with visible dry skin. At least 20–30 subjects should be included in each treatment group.

Preconditioning Period

This is required to standardise conditions to some extent at the start of a test. For example, bland inactive shampoos are used for up to 4 weeks prior to testing an anti-dandruff preparation; in the evaluation of antiperspirants, total abstinence from using the product type to be treated is practised.

Baseline Assessment

It is the first assessment of the main trial and will help in the selection of the most suitable volunteers. For example, those with the most dry skin/most greasy hair, etc.

Period of Use of Products

The period of product use varies; for example, a single application monitored over a few days in the case of a nail polish durability test, on the other hand, several weeks' use may be required in the case of an anti-dandruff evaluation.

Questionnaire

A questionnaire is normally completed after the subjects have finished using the products. Questions should be posed with a range of responses between two extremes, from 'excellent' to 'very poor', requiring the volunteer only to choose the appropriate response. Volunteers should be encouraged to make any additional comments they consider relevant, as this may raise points of interest that have been missed in the preparation of the questionnaire and it also gives the volunteer a chance to make a personal contribution.

Post-treatment Period

At the end of the treatment period, it is sometimes of interest to compare the test and control products for any effects observed during treatment. It is a phase often included in the evaluation of anti-dandruff products, as there is a demand for products that are effective for longer periods of time. This involves a period of abstinence from using the active product while monitoring any changes. Many consumers find that anti-dandruff shampoos promote hair greasiness and would prefer to use a more cosmetic shampoo between active treatments.

Product Crossover

This involves a second treatment period in which the test and control groups reverse roles. For example, in the evaluation of deodorants, which involves applying the test sample to one axilla and the control sample to the other. During the first treatment period, half the panel uses the test product on the left axilla and the other half on the right. In the crossover, the two volunteer groups exchange application patterns.

Efficacy Testing of Cosmetics/ Cosmeceuticals

Many models are used to assess the efficacy of sunscreens, moisturisers, anti-ageing products and anti-dandruff products. The models used for each category of products are now discussed in detail.

Sunscreens

Sunscreens are intended to protect the skin from sunburn. As the amount of protection needed varies among individuals, sunscreens offer consumers different levels of protection. These levels are currently expressed as a numerical value, called the sun protection factor (SPF), which is the ratio between the minimal erythema dose (MED) of sunscreen-protected skin and the MED of unprotected skin.

$$SPF = \frac{\text{MED of protected skin}}{\text{MED of unprotected skin}}$$

The MED is the smallest amount of UV light or the shortest exposure time required to produce a minimally perceptible sunburn 16–24 hours after irradiation. For instance, if unprotected skin shows mild sunburn after only 20 minutes of sun exposure and the same skin protected by a sunscreen burns minimally after 60 minutes of exposure, then

$$SPF = 60/20 = 3$$

Clinical Evaluation of Sunscreen Efficacy

The sunscreen test is a three-day procedure. The procedure described here is the method principally used in the United States.

- Subjects
  - Number – 20
  - Inclusion criteria – Should be healthy with no history of abnormal responses to sunlight

such as phototoxicity or photoallergic reactions.

- o Exclusion criteria – Individuals with skin diseases such as eczema, psoriasis and skin cancer, and those who are sensitive to sunscreens or are taking any medications

Source of light

- o The FDA allows the use of either natural sunlight or a solar simulator.
- o The preferred method of irradiation would be a solar simulator as natural sunlight varies in intensity and depends on the time of day, season, altitude, latitude, cloudiness and air pollution.
- o A solar simulator is a light source that produces a spectrum of light which closely matches that produced by the sun.
- o The xenon arc solar simulator is best suited as it satisfies the requirements stipulated by the FDA. It emits a continuous UVB spectrum (290–320 nm).

Procedure

1. The MED of each subject is determined:
   - Each subject receives five times the usual exposure on the untreated, unprotected skin of the back.
   - The exposure sites are usually at least 1 cm wide. Each exposure lasts 25% longer than the previous one.
   - After 24 hours, the test sites of all the subjects are examined for erythema.
   - The site with the smallest perceptible erythema is selected as the MED (preliminary) for that individual.
2. Once the preliminary MED has been established, the MED for the sunscreen-protected skin can be determined as follows (the skin on the back is used for this portion of the test also):
   - Both the test material and the control formula with a known SPF are applied on the test sites.
   - Irradiation is carried out as described previously.
   - About 16–24 hours after irradiation, each test site is examined for erythema, which will give the MED of the protected skin.

- Evaluation
  - o The SPF is calculated according to the formula.
  - o The overall SPF of the product is determined by calculating the arithmetic mean of the individual SPF ratings (NMT ± 5% of the mean).

Moisturisers

Moisturisers are topically applied products that relieve the signs and symptoms of dry skin.

Clinical Evaluation of Moisturiser Efficacy

The most widely used method is the regression method proposed by Kligman.

- Subjects
  - o Number – 20
  - o Inclusion criteria – Individuals who have a history of dry skin of sufficient severity to require routine use of moisturisers during the dry skin season
- Procedure
  1. The 20 subjects are treated twice daily with the appropriate test products on each week day for two weeks.
  2. The applications are made by a technician who applies liberal amounts of the product with moderate hand pressure for a period of 30 seconds. This forms the treatment phase.
  3. During the treatment phase, the test sites

are evaluated on Days 7 and 14.
4. After the treatment phase, follow-up observations are made on a daily basis every week day for the next two weeks; this forms the regression phase.
5. During the regression phase, the application of test products is not carried out.

- Evaluation
  - One approach to grade the clinical expression of dry skin is to utilise a comparative rating scheme using the terms slight, moderate or dramatic to describe the degree of difference.
  - Another approach is to use a scoring scheme that has a sufficient number of grades (6 or more) to allow good resolution between products.
  - A reference set of standardised photos can be used to visually define the grading scheme for the various attributes of dry skin being evaluated.

Anti-ageing Products

Ageing is a biological process associated with certain biochemical and biophysical changes that relate to reduced functional capacity of the individual through time. Among the many theories of ageing, the 'free radical concept' is widely accepted.

Free Radical Concept of Ageing

Free radicals are chemical species that are electronically incomplete, chemically unstable and highly reactive. They tend to react enthusiastically with other molecules, particularly oxygen. Free radicals are usually produced by an initiating force such as UV radiation. Among the constituents of the cell, the unsaturated fatty acid (phospholipid) reacts with a free radical, forming a free radical fatty acid, which in turn reacts with oxygen to form a peroxy radical. The peroxy radical then preys on adjacent fatty acid molecules to satisfy its instability, thus, producing a cascading chain reaction. The net result of all these reactions is a reduction in the functional capacity of the cell/organism—ageing.

Clinical Efficacy of Anti-ageing Products

The most commonly employed method is that of measurement of skin lipid peroxides. The skin surface lipids are prone to attack by oxygen from the atmosphere and from biological oxidation processes, leading to ageing of the skin. The degree of ageing and the amount of lipid peroxides in the skin are proportional. Thus, a measure of lipid peroxides in the skin as a function of age or UV exposure and efficacy of the product can be tested.

- Test Procedure
  1. A glass cylinder measuring 5 cm in diameter is placed on the skin and held snugly.
  2. Two aliquots of pure acetone are used to extract the lipids in 5 ml portions.
  3. The first 5 ml is added to the cylinder and the skin in gently rubbed with a teflon rod for 1 minute.
  4. The acetone is removed with a micropipette and placed in a test tube.
  5. A second 5 ml portion of acetone is added and the procedure repeated again.
  6. The combined portions are then dried under a nitrogen stream.
- Assay Procedure
  1. The lipid residue obtained after drying is emulsified with 0.2 ml of 8% sodium dodecyl sulphate, 1.5 ml of 20% acetic acid and 1.5 ml of 0.5% thiobarbituric acid solution.
  2. Final volume is made up to 4 ml with water.

3. The tube is then heated to 90 °C for 1 hour and cooled to room temperature.
4. The tube is centrifuged and the supernatant is extracted with 4 ml of n-butanol.
5. The absorption is read at 531 nm and the final concentration of peroxides is determined as malonyldialdehyde (MDA) precursors.

- Evaluation
  - o There is a linear relationship between the quantity of peroxides recovered and the subject's age.
  - o This study is used to evaluate products used over time.
  - o As the production of peroxides is influenced by UV light, care must be exercised in long-term studies regarding the exposure of subjects to this agent.

Anti-dandruff Products

In the study of anti-dandruff products, the protocols involve subjective assessment of the degree of scaling.

- Subjects
  - o Number – 30
  - o Inclusion criteria – The subjects must be currently suffering from dandruff
- Preconditioning Period
  - o Most people who suffer from dandruff would have used or be using one of the many commercially available anti-dandruff formulations.
  - o An effective formula can suppress dandruff levels for up to a month, so it is important that the test product is avoided for at least a month.
  - o Normally, a bland shampoo is used by the subject during the 4-week preconditioning/ pretreatment phase.
- Treatment Phase
  - o The objective is to stimulate the normal home-use situation as closely as possible.
  - o The subjects are permitted to wash their hair at home according to the normal pattern of use for at least once a week.
  - o This protocol requires a fairly lengthy treatment period (about 8 weeks).
  - o Intermediate assessments are made at selected intervals during the treatment phase.
  - o A final post-treatment period of bland shampoo use may follow the treatment phase in order to investigate the duration of any observed effects.
- Assessment
  - o Among the various grading systems, the 'ten-point' scale of assessment is commonly used.
  - o According to Kligman et al, scrapings of dandruff at several points on the scalp can be made and a single estimate of the average dandruff grade for the whole head can be given. Table 23.1 shows the scale used to assess dandruff.

Table 23.1: Dandruff Assessment Scale

Score	*Description*
0	No visible dandruff
1, 2	Minimal diffuse scaling
3, 4	Slight scaling
5	Moderate scaling
6	Moderate-heavy scaling
7	Heavy scaling
8, 9, 10	Very heavy scaling, not routinely observed

The advantage of this design is that positive results are likely to reflect a benefit that will be perceptible to the consumer under normal home-use conditions.

Future Trends

Three of the five senses—smell, sight and touch—find expression in cosmetic usage. The instinctive desire of human beings to gratify these senses explains why cosmetic usage dates back to centuries, accounts for their current popularity and is predictive of continued growth. Today's cosmetics consumer is knowledgeable. While an attractive package is still an important factor in product appeal, the user expects a product that is elegant and more than anything 'safe and effective' and which lives up to expectations. Thus, for a successful cosmetic product, the psychological key is an enhanced sense of well-being; the physical key is a product that is effective and safe.

Cosmetic products are safe for consumers to use under normal or reasonably foreseeable conditions of use. Advertising claims relating to product performance are usually supported by valid test data. Safety testing of raw materials may be conducted in vitro, using cell or tissue culture techniques, ex vivo using excised tissue or in vivo, using laboratory animals or (finally) human volunteers. All animal testing purely for cosmetic purposes has been banned in most developed countries. There is a continuing trend for in vitro and human volunteer testing protocols to replace animal tests where possible. Safety testing of formulated products may not always be necessary and can usually be done by patch testing or home-use testing in human volunteers. It is, however, necessary to have a safety assessment performed by a competent scientist on each new product before placing it on the market. Larger companies may have their own safety and evaluation facilities but it is more common to use specialised contract research organisations (CRO), working to international guidelines (good laboratory practice [GLP] or good clinical practice [GCP]) and providing an independent assessment of safety or performance. Failure to ensure the safety of manufacturing staff and consumers can result in costly and damaging litigation.

Substantiation of a wide variety of claims, including skin moisturisation, fine lines, wrinkles and anti-ageing solutions, are often performed using sensitive electronic equipment such as a Novometer, Primos System or a TEWL evaluator. Additionally, microbiological safety, especially in the form of preservative and antimicrobial efficacy and total plate counts, are performed daily.

In addition, claims may be supported by subjective evaluation using sight, touch and other sensory perceptions to identify cosmetic benefits under conditions of normal use. The responsibility that the product is capable of performing as claimed, lies with the product evaluation and consumer testing specialists.

The testing of antiperspirants and sunscreen products has evolved as two major areas for cosmetics testing in recent years, both of which have become rigorously regulated due to safety issues. The basic criteria is that all products should be tested to assure both safety and efficacy and an adequate quality assurance programme established by the individual manufacturer to ensure testing should be developed and adhered to.

The Regulatory Affairs department keeps in touch with current regulatory policies and also ensures an understanding of the

technical issues related to personal care products. This department also provides inputs for market trials, label claims and advertising issues. Their role is to ensure that the product meets all safety and labelling requirements and is in compliance with government regulations.

'Testing of cosmetics is driven by the regulations attached to the products and varies greatly according to the different governmental regulators'.

Key Messages

- Safety of cosmetics/cosmeceuticals is of utmost importance to consumers and professionals in the industry.
- The process of safety evaluation consists of estimation of potential hazards of each ingredient and determination of the risk of the hazard identified to the consumer.
- Cosmetics can cause a number of adverse effects, classified as topical and systemic effects.
- Efficacy tests are designed to show that a product performs the function for which it is intended.
- Human testing for efficacy is the ultimate test for any product.
- A good and successful product should be both effective and safe.

Questions

1. What are the systemic toxicity effects exhibited by cosmetics?
2. Enumerate the topical effects of cosmetics.
3. Why should safety studies be carried out in cosmetics?
4. What general aspects should be considered before carrying out efficacy testing of cosmetics?

24

Stability Testing

SHOBHA RANI R HIREMATH AND VANAJA K

Learning Objectives

At the end of this chapter, you will be able to:

- Describe how stability studies are carried out as per ICH guidelines
- List the parameters to be evaluated during stability studies

Introduction

According to the United States Pharmacopia (USP), stability is 'the extent to which a preparation retains, within specified limits and throughout its period of storage and use, the same properties and characteristics that are possessed at the time of compounding'.

Stability testing is a routine procedure performed on drug substances and products, and it is involved at various stages of product development. The stability of pharmaceutical products is a broad area that encompasses many potential routes of degradation.

Any change that occurs in a pharmaceutical product, subsequent to its preparation, that adversely affects any attribute of the quality of the product in terms of its potency for use is a matter of concern to pharmaceutical scientists and the regulators involved in stability testing. The stability data on any dosage form that comprises selected parameters of each dosage form or drug product is the 'stability profile'. This stability profile forms the basis for specifying storage conditions and assigning shelf life to a pharmaceutical product.

SHELF LIFE

The shelf life of a drug is the duration it is known to stay within acceptable specifications for potency and other important parameters. The expiry date is the date when a given batch reaches the end of its shelf life. After the expiry date, the product does not necessarily become useless, as it may only have reached the potency limit of the active ingredient. However, other physicochemical characteristics (such as pH, dissolution rate of tablets and capsules, particle size in creams and suspensions) may have changed, or toxic degradation products may reach unacceptable levels, and the use of the product may be harmful. When a customer uses a product that is past its expiry date, it may result in a lower dose of the active ingredient than that stated on the label. It may also result in altered bioavailability or patient discomfort or present a safety hazard. Therefore, it is a good practice not to use drugs that are past the expiry date.

Factors Affecting Stability

- *Storage time*: The longer the storage time, the greater the degradation of the drugs and dosage forms.
- *Storage conditions*: Storage temperature and percentage relative humidity at the place of storage may have an adverse effect on the stability of the dosage form.
- *Type of dosage form*: The chemical stability of the drug depends on the type of dosage form. Liquid dosage forms exhibit more drug degradation than semisolid and solid dosage forms.
- *Container and closure system*: Plastic containers and rubber closures are reported to adsorb antioxidants and preservatives from the solutions in contact with them, leading to destabilisation and microbial attack.

Objectives of Stability Testing

- To develop a stable dosage form
- To ensure the efficacy, safety and quality of active drug substances and dosage forms
- To establish the shelf life or expiration period and support label claims
- To study decomposed products
  - To identify the degraded product
  - To determine the modifications to the chemical structure
  - To study its physical and chemical properties
  - To find out its pharmacological action

International Conference on Harmonisation (ICH)

The ICH is a joint initiative that involves regulators and the industry as equal partners in scientific and technical discussions in the testing procedures required to ensure and assess the safety, quality and efficacy of medicines.

The focus of ICH has been on the technical requirements for medicinal products containing new drugs. The vast majority of these new drugs and medicines are developed in western Europe, Japan and the United States and therefore, when ICH was established, it was agreed that its scope would be confined to registration in these three regions.

The ICH comprises six Parties, which are directly involved, as well as three Observers and the International Federation of Pharmaceutical Manufacturers and Associations (IFPMA). The six Parties are the founder members of the ICH and represent regulatory bodies and the research-based industry in the European Union, Japan and the United States. These parties include the EU, European Federation of Pharmaceutical Industries and Associations (EFPIA), Ministry of Health, Labour and Welfare, (MHLW) Japan, Japan Pharmaceutical Manufacturers Association (JPMA), US Food and Drug Administration (FDA) and Pharmaceutical Research and Manufacturers of America (PhRMA).

ICH Observers

Since the ICH was initiated in 1990, Observers have acted as a link with non-ICH countries and regions. These ICH Observers are the World Health Organization (WHO), European Free Trade Association (EFTA) and Health Canada.

Stability Evaluation

Selection of batches

Data from stability studies should be provided on at least three primary batches of the drug substances. The primary batches should be of the same formulation and packaged in the same container closure system as proposed for marketing. The manufacturing process used for the primary batches should simulate the process to be applied to production batches and provide a product of the same quality and meeting the same specifications as that intended for marketing. Two of the three batches should be at least pilot scale batches while the third can be smaller.

Containers and closures

Testing should be conducted using the containers and closures proposed for storage and distribution. The protocol should provide information about the type, size and source of the containers and closures.

Sampling intervals

Long-term studies

Frequency of testing should be sufficient to develop a stability profile for the drug product. For products with a proposed shelf life of at least 12 months, the frequency of testing at long-term storage conditions should be every three months over the first year, every six months over the second year and annually thereafter throughout the proposed shelf life.

Accelerated storage conditions

A minimum of three time points, including the initial and final time points, from a 6-month study is recommended. If a significant change is expected, more tests should be conducted either by adding samples at the final time point or by including a fourth time point in the study design.

Intermediate storage conditions

A minimum of four time points, including the initial and final time points, from a 12-month study must be sampled.

Storage conditions

The design of the formal stability studies for a drug product has to be based on knowledge of the behaviour and properties as well as stability studies of the drug substance and on the experience gained from clinical formulation studies.

Storage conditions are based on worldwide temperature and humidity (% RH) conditions. Haynes divided the countries of the world into four climatic zones, namely, Zone I (temperate), Zone II (subtropical and Mediterranean), Zone III (hot and dry) and Zone IV (hot and humid). At the fortieth meeting of the WHO Expert Committee on Specifications for Pharmaceutical Preparations, in Geneva, in October 2005, Zone IV was split into IV A (hot and humid) and IV B (hot and very humid). The storage conditions for drug products are listed in Table 24.1.

Protocol for Conducting a Stability Study

The protocol for conducting a stability study should extend to the end of the shelf life period and include the following parameters:

- Number of batch(es) per strength and different batch sizes, if applicable
- Relevant physical, chemical, microbiological and biological test methods
- Acceptance criteria
- Reference to test methods
- Description of the container closure system(s)
- Testing intervals (time points)
- Description of the conditions of storage
- Other applicable parameters specific to the pharmaceutical product

Table 24.1: Stability storage conditions for drug products			
Product	*Type of Study*		
	Long-term	*Intermediate*	*Accelerated*
General case	25°C ± 2°C/ 60% RH ± 5% RH or 30°C ± 2°C/ 65% RH ± 5% RH	30°C ± 2°C/ 65% RH ± 5% RH	40°C ± 2°C/ 75% RH ± 5% RH
Drug products packaged in semi-permeable containers	25°C ± 2°C/ 40% RH ± 5% RH or 30°C ± 2°C/ 35% RH ± 5% RH	30°C ± 2°C/ 65% RH ± 5% RH	40°C ± 2°C/ not more than (NMT) 25% RH
Drug products intended for storage in a refrigerator	5°C ± 3°C		25°C ± 2°C/ 60% RH ± 5% RH
Drug products intended for storage in a freezer	–20°C ± 3°C		

Evaluation of Parameters

- Tablets: Dissolution (or disintegration, if justified), water content and hardness/ friability.
- Hard gelatin capsules: Brittleness, dissolution (or disintegration, if justified), water content and level of microbial contamination.
- Soft gelatin capsules: Dissolution (or disintegration, if justified), level of microbial contamination, pH, leakage and pellicle formation.
- Emulsions: Phase separation, pH, viscosity, level of microbial contamination and mean size and distribution of dispersed globules.
- Oral solutions and suspensions: Formation of precipitate, clarity for solutions, pH, viscosity, extractables and level of microbial contamination. Polymorphic conversion may also be examined, if applicable. Additionally for suspensions, redispersibility, rheological properties and mean size and distribution of particles should be evaluated.
- Powders for oral solution or suspension: Water content and reconstitution time. Reconstituted products (solutions and suspensions) should be evaluated as described above for oral solutions and suspensions, after preparation according to the recommended labelling, through the maximum intended use period.
- Metered-dose inhalers and nasal aerosols: Dose content uniformity, labelled number of medication actuations per container meeting dose content uniformity, aerodynamic particle size distribution, microscopic evaluation, water content, leak rate, level of microbial contamination, valve delivery (shot weight) and extractables/leachables from plastic and elastomeric components. Samples should be stored in upright and inverted/ on-the-side orientations. For suspension-type aerosols, the appearance of the valve

components and the container's contents should be evaluated microscopically for large particles and changes in morphology of the drug surface particles, extent of agglomerates, crystal growth, as well as foreign particulate matter. These particles lead to clogged valves or non-reproducible delivery of a dose. Corrosion of the inside of the container or deterioration of the gaskets may adversely affect the performance of the drug product.

- Nasal sprays, solutions and suspensions: Clarity (for solution), level of microbial contamination, pH, particulate matter, unit spray medication content uniformity, number of actuations meeting unit spray content uniformity per container, droplet and/or particle size distribution, weight loss, pump delivery, microscopic evaluation (for suspensions), foreign particulate matter and extractable/bleachable from plastic and elastomeric components of the container, closure and pump.
- Topical ophthalmic and otic preparations: Included in this broad category are ointments, creams, lotions, paste, gel, solutions, eye drops and cutaneous sprays. Topical preparations should be evaluated for clarity, homogeneity, pH, resuspendability (for lotions), consistency, viscosity, particle size distribution (for suspensions, when feasible), level of microbial contamination/sterility and weight loss (when appropriate). Evaluation of ophthalmic or otic products (for example, creams, ointments, solutions and suspensions) should include sterility, particulate matter and extractability. Evaluation of cutaneous sprays should include pressure, weight loss, net weight dispensed, delivery rate, level of microbial contamination, spray pattern, water content and particle size distribution (for suspensions).
- Suppositories: Softening range, dissolution (at 37 °C).
- Small volume parenterals (SVPs): Colour, clarity (for solutions), particulate matter, pH, sterility and endotoxins. Stability studies for powders for injection solutions should include monitoring for colour, reconstitution time and water content. Specific parameters to be examined at appropriate intervals throughout the maximum intended use period of the reconstituted drug product stored under condition(s) recommended in labelling should include clarity, colour, pH, sterility, pyrogen/endotoxin and particulate matter. The stability studies for suspensions for injections should include particle size distribution, redispersibility and rheological properties. The stability studies for emulsion for injections should include phase separation, viscosity, mean size and distribution of dispersed phase globules.
- Large volume parenterals (LVPs): Colour, clarity, particulate matter, pH, sterility, pyrogen/endotoxin and volume.
- Transdermal patches: In vitro release rates, leakage, level of microbial contamination/ sterility and peel and adhesive forces.

Key Messages

- Stability testing is a routine procedure performed on drug substances and products, and it is involved at various stages of product development.
- The shelf life of a drug is the time it is known to stay within acceptable specifications for potency and other important parameters.
- Data from stability studies should be provided on at least three primary batches of the drug substances.
- Testing should be conducted using the containers and closures proposed for storage and distribution.
- A detailed knowledge of the stability requirements, their impact on other areas such as container closure and the process changes required to properly design and evaluate stability studies are necessary to ensure minimal delays and minimise the costs in developing a new drug product.

QUESTIONS

1. Define stability study.
2. What are the objectives and factors affecting stability?
3. What are the storage conditions for the different climatic zones based on worldwide temperature and humidity?
4. Give a brief note on the protocol for conducting stability studies.
5. What are the parameters to be evaluated during stability studies for various dosage forms?

25

Regulatory Aspects of Cosmetics

Shobha Rani R Hiremath and Amit Kumar Das

Learning Objectives

At the end of this chapter, you will be able to:

- Explain the regulatory aspects of cosmetics in different countries
- List the prohibited ingredients and other hazardous substances included in cosmetics
- Explain the labelling and packaging of cosmetics
- State the regulatory requirements and explain the health hazard issues relating to specific cosmetic products

Introduction

The Food, Drug and Cosmetic Act defines cosmetics by their intended use, as 'articles intended to be rubbed, poured, sprinkled or sprayed on, introduced into or otherwise applied to the human body for cleansing, beautifying, promoting attractiveness or altering the appearance'. Among the products included in this definition are skin moisturisers, perfumes, lipsticks, nail polishes, eye and facial makeup preparations, shampoos, permanent waves, hair colours, toothpastes and deodorants, as well as any material intended for use as a component of a cosmetic product.

The pharmaceutical industry is the most regulated of all industrial segments. The Regulatory Affairs department is responsible for the regulatory and safety compliance of cosmetic raw materials. This is primarily due to the fact that the industry provides products and services that have a huge impact on healthcare outcomes among the world's population.

Food and Drug Administration (FDA)

The US FDA has been accepted globally as the gold standard, model regulatory agency in terms of its standards and efficiency. It was created on the recommendations of the Kefauver–Harris Committee as a sequel to the thalidomide tragedy, which maimed over 10,000 babies after the mothers had taken the sedative marketed by Chemie Gruenthal. It was then that safety data and investigational new drug applications became mandatory. The FDA not only has the responsibility of approving new drugs, but also has to clear the use of generic versions of patented drugs. The legislation, which is an important component of this exercise, is the

Hatch–Waxman Act of 1984, which stipulates the conditions for approval of an abbreviated new drug application (ANDA). The Act provides for exclusivity in the market for the first generic manufacturer if it survives the so-called Para IV filing and has no infringement suit against it from the patent holder. Postmarketing surveillance of the drug is yet another responsibility of the FDA.

Cosmetic Ingredient Review (CIR)

In the US, the Cosmetic and Toiletry Manufacturers Association (CTMA) has funded a programme to systematically test the commonly used cosmetic ingredients. This programme was started in 1977 and is called the Cosmetic Ingredient Review (CIR). In this programme, the safety data is examined by a panel of independent experts. The CIR Panel currently has 7 experts, a representative of the Consumer Federation of America, a representative of the CTMA, a representative of the FDA and the Director and Scientific Coordinator of the CIR. To date they have examined over 450 ingredients. The results are published, mostly in the Journal of the American College of Toxicology. Furthermore, testing is carried out to internationally recognised standards. So they can be assured that the information on the safety of cosmetic ingredients is sound. The CIR is an ongoing process, and the testing priority for untested raw materials is determined partly by frequency of use and partly by an assessment of potential biological activity using a computer programme called TOPKAT®.

Regulatory Requirements for Marketing Cosmetics in the United States

The cosmetics marketed in the United States, whether manufactured locally or imported from abroad, must comply with the provisions of the Federal Food, Drug and Cosmetic Act (FD&C Act), the Fair Packaging and Labelling Act (FPLA) and the regulations published under the authority of these laws.

The regulations published by the FDA are all codified in Title 21, Code of Federal Regulations (21 CFR). The regulations applicable to cosmetics are stated in 21 CFR, parts 700–740.

Cosmetics that are Also Drugs

Products that are cosmetics but are also intended to treat or prevent disease, or otherwise affect the structure or functions of the human body, are also considered drugs and must comply with the drug and cosmetic provisions of the law. Examples of products that are drugs as well as cosmetics are: anti-caries toothpastes (for example, 'fluoride' toothpastes), hormone creams, sun tanning preparations intended to protect against sunburn, antiperspirants that are also deodorants and anti-dandruff shampoos. The regulatory requirements for drugs are more extensive than those applicable to cosmetics.

Adulterated or Misbranded Cosmetics

The FD&C Act prohibits the distribution of cosmetics that are adulterated or misbranded. A cosmetic is considered adulterated if it contains a substance that may make the product harmful to consumers under customary conditions of use; if it contains a filthy, putrid or decomposed substance; if its container is composed of a harmful substance; or if it is manufactured or held under insanitary conditions whereby it may have become contaminated with filth, or may have become harmful to consumers.

A cosmetic is misbranded if its labelling is false or misleading, if it does not bear the required labelling information or if the container is made or filled in a deceptive manner.

Cosmetic Safety

Although the FD&C Act does not require that cosmetic manufacturers or marketers test their products for safety, the FDA strongly urges manufacturers to conduct appropriate toxicological and other tests to substantiate the safety of their cosmetics.

The use of the following ingredients is either restricted or prohibited in cosmetics: bithionol, mercury compounds, vinyl chloride, halogenated salicylanilides, zirconium complexes in aerosol cosmetics, chloroform, methylene chloride, chlorofluorocarbon propellants and hexachlorophene.

Cosmetic Labelling

Cosmetics bearing false or misleading label statements or which are otherwise not labelled in accordance with the codified requirements may be considered misbranded and may be subject to regulatory action. The net quantity of contents statement of a solid, semi-solid or viscous cosmetic must be mentioned. The name and place of business of the firm marketing the product must be stated on an information panel of the label.

Label Warnings

Cosmetics that may be hazardous to consumers when misused must bear appropriate label warnings and adequate directions for safe use.

Tamper-resistant Packaging

All cosmetic products must be packaged in tamper-resistant packages when sold at retail. A package is considered tamper-resistant if it has an indicator or barrier to entry (for example, a shrink or tape seal, sealed carton, tube, pouch, or aerosol container) which, if breached or missing, alerts a consumer that tampering has occurred.

Law Enforcement Authority

For law enforcement, the FDA may conduct examinations and investigations of products, inspect establishments in which products are manufactured or held and seize adulterated (harmful) or misbranded (incorrectly or deceptively labelled or filled) cosmetics. The FDA may also initiate criminal action against persons violating the law.

Voluntary Registration

Although the FD&C Act does not require cosmetic firms to register manufacturing establishments or formulations with the FDA or make available safety data or other information before a product is marketed in the United States, manufacturers or distributors of cosmetics may submit this information to the agency voluntarily.

Cosmetic Product–related Regulatory Requirements and Health Hazard Issues

Cosmetics contain ingredients that may potentially be hazardous, causing various allergies, birth defects and sometimes even cancer. Whenever a cosmetic is applied to the skin, it is absorbed to some degree by the skin; this could be harmful to people who are sensitive to the same. Also, the discarded makeup, millions of plastic jars, tubes and other containers and packages that are thrown out each year can be a matter of concern as they may be harmful to the environment. In addition, many cosmetic companies test their products on animals.

A cosmetic product that has received a lot of attention lately is nail polish. Some brands contain dibutyl phthalate (DBP), a chemical linked to cancer in animals. Even lipstick is a cause for concern as it contains artificial oils, synthetic colours and petroleum-based waxes. Other chemicals commonly found in cosmetics include acrylamide, formaldehyde and ethylene oxide—all reported as carcinogens. The other products that are increasingly causing concern among the general public are hair colours and bleaches, hair relaxers and skin lighteners.

Some of the ingredients that can cause toxicity include mercury, lead acetate, formaldehyde, toluene, coal tar and petroleum distillates. Therefore, companies are required to declare the chemicals used in cosmetics and research the effects of the same.

Ingredient Labelling

Cosmetics produced or distributed for retail sale to consumers for their personal care are required to bear an ingredient declaration. Cosmetics not customarily distributed for retail sale, for example, hair preparations or makeup products used by professionals at their establishments and skin cleansing or emollient creams used at places of work, are exempt from this requirement provided these products are not also sold to consumers. The ingredient declaration must be conspicuous so that it is likely to be read at the time of purchase. Off-package ingredient labelling is permitted if the cosmetic is held in tightly compartmented trays or racks.

Cosmetics that are also drugs must first identify the drug ingredient(s) as 'active ingredient(s)' before listing the cosmetic ingredients.

Prohibited Ingredients and Other Hazardous Substances

- *Hexachlorophene (HCP):* Because of its neurotoxic effects and ability to penetrate human skin, HCP may be used only when an alternative preservative has not been shown to be as effective. The HCP concentration of the cosmetic may not exceed 0.1%, and it may not be used in cosmetics that in normal use may be applied to mucous membranes.
- *Mercury compounds:* The use of mercury compounds as cosmetic ingredients is limited to the cosmetics used for the eyes and surrounding areas at concentrations not exceeding 65 parts per million of mercury and provided no other effective and safe preservative is available for use.
- *Chlorofluorocarbon (CFC) propellants:* The use of CFC propellants in cosmetic aerosol products intended for domestic consumption is prohibited. CFC-containing cosmetic aerosol products may continue to be manufactured for export provided they are not in conflict with the laws of the country to which they are to be exported.
- *Other prohibited ingredients:* The following additional substances are prohibited as cosmetic ingredients, but not as unintentional contaminants of cosmetics manufactured in accordance with current good manufacturing practice (GMP):
  - Bithionol and halogenated salicylanilides, because of the likelihood of causing photocontact sensitisation
  - Chloroform, because of its animal carcinogenicity and likely hazard to human health
  - Vinyl chloride as an ingredient of aerosol products, because of its carcinogenic effect in humans and animals
  - Zirconium-containing complexes in aerosol cosmetic products, because of their toxic effect on the lungs, including granulomas

  - Methylene chloride, because of its animal carcinogenicity and likely hazard to human health
- *Acetylethyltetramethyltetralin (AETT):* AETT should not be used in fragrance formulations and finished cosmetic products. It was found to cause serious neurotoxic disorders, discolouration of internal organs and penetration of human skin.
- *Musk ambrette:* Various tests and clinical experiences have demonstrated that musk ambrette may cause photocontact sensitisation, that is, allergic reactions of the skin on exposure to musk ambrette and sunlight. Other studies have indicated that musk ambrette may also cause neurotoxic effects. The International Fragrance Association has recommended that musk ambrette not be used in products applied to the skin, particularly those products used on skin that is customarily exposed to sunlight.
- *6-Methylcoumarin (6-MC):* This fragrance ingredient is a potent photocontact sensitiser that may cause serious skin and systemic disorders in some consumers in the presence of sunlight.
- *Nitrosamines:* Cosmetics containing amines or amino derivatives, particularly di- or triethanolamine, may form nitrosamines if they also contain an ingredient that acts as a nitrosating agent. The nitrosation may also occur during manufacture or product storage. Many nitrosamines have been found to cause cancer and have also been shown to penetrate the skin.
- *Dioxane:* Cosmetics containing ethoxylated surface active agents may be contaminated with 1,4-dioxane. This was found to produce cancer of the liver and the nasal turbinates. Skin absorption studies demonstrated that dioxane readily penetrates animal and human skin from various types of vehicles. However, it was also determined that most of the dioxane applied to the skin in a vehicle evaporates into the environment and may not be available for skin absorption.

Adequacy of Preservation

Cosmetics need not be sterile; however, they must not be contaminated with microorganisms that may be pathogenic, and the density of non-pathogenic microorganisms should be low. In addition, cosmetics should remain in this condition when used by consumers.

Significant progress has been made by the cosmetics industry towards implementation of sanitary manufacturing practices, more rigorous microbiological control and the development of better-preserved cosmetic products. The problem of adequacy of preservation of cosmetics to prevent contamination during consumer use continues to be of concern, particularly with respect to cosmetics that come in contact with the eye.

Aerosol Products

CFC propellants, vinyl chloride and zirconium compounds are prohibited as ingredients of cosmetic aerosol products. Such products must bear the following label statement:

Caution - Avoid spraying in eyes. Contents under pressure. Do not puncture or incinerate. Do not store at temperatures above 48.88 °C (120 °F). Keep out of reach of children. Use only as directed. Intentional misuse by deliberately concentrating and inhaling the contents can be harmful or fatal.

Feminine Deodorant Sprays

Products whose labelling states or suggests that the product is for use in the female genital area or all over the body must bear the following label statement:

Caution - For external use only. Spray at least 8 inches from skin. Do not apply to broken, irritated or itching skin. Persistent, unusual odour or discharge may indicate conditions for which a physician should be consulted. Discontinue use immediately if rash, irritation or discomfort develops.

Bubble Bath Products

A bubble bath product is defined as any product intended to be added to the bath for the purpose of producing foam and containing a surface active agent serving as a detergent or foaming agent. The use of foaming detergent bath products, that is, bubble bath products, particularly on excessive or prolonged exposure, has been known to cause itching, rashes and urinary tract disorders. All bubble bath products not labelled as intended for use exclusively by adults must bear adequate directions for safe use and caution.

Hair Dye Products

All hair dye products should bear the following label statement:

Caution - This product contains ingredients that may cause skin irritation on certain individuals and a preliminary test according to accompanying directions should first be made. This product must not be used for dyeing the eyelashes or eyebrows; to do so may cause blindness.

If the label of a hair dye product that contains coal-tar colours does not bear the caution statement and patch testing directions, it may be subject to regulatory action if it is determined to be harmful under customary conditions of use.

Depilatories and Hair Straighteners

Chemical depilatories are highly alkaline pastes, creams or cream lotions that can cause degradation of hair keratin and deterioration of hair fibres. Hair straighteners are mostly creams or cream lotions.

Because improperly formulated or incorrectly used depilatories or hair straighteners may cause serious skin irritation, they should be thoroughly tested for safety, be subjected to careful quality control during manufacture and provide explicit warnings and directions for safe use.

Hair Shampoos, Rinses and Conditioners

Hair shampoos contain anionic or ampholytic detergents that serve as cleansing and foaming agents; rinses and conditioners may contain cationics (quaternary ammonium compounds) that serve as antistatic agents. When inadvertently introduced into the eye, these surface active agents may cause stinging, mucosal irritation or even corneal damage, and products contaminated with microorganisms may cause infection.

Hair care products, like all other cosmetics, should be tested thoroughly to determine the type and degree of irritation that may occur when they come in contact with the eye and to assure that marketed products are not contaminated and will not become contaminated during normal use. The labels of these products should bear appropriate warnings and directions for safe use.

Products Containing Estrogenic Hormones, Placental Extract or Vitamins

Products containing estrogen, estrone, estradiol,

progesterone, placental extract or vitamins may be considered as drugs, misbranded drugs or misbranded cosmetics, particularly if the label declaration is supplemented with standards implying prevention or treatment of disease or effect on the structure or any function of the human body. Cosmetics declaring ingredients as vitamins, for example, tocopherol as Vitamin E, convey the misleading impression that these ingredients and products offer a nutrient or health benefit and may therefore be deemed misbranded.

Nail Builders and Hardeners

Nail builders (elongators, extenders) have been involved in numerous reports of irritation, inflammation and infection of the nail bed and nail fold as well as in complaints of discolouration, splitting and loss of fingernails.

Nail hardeners often contain formaldehyde as the active ingredient. Although formaldehyde may be irritating to the skin or cause allergic reactions, the FDA does not object to its use as an ingredient of nail hardeners provided the product:

- Contains no more than 5% formaldehyde
- Provides the user with nail shields that restrict application to the tip (and not the nail bed or fold)
- Furnishes adequate directions for safe use
- Warns consumers about the consequences of misuse and potential for causing adverse reactions in sensitised users

Soap

Products that are deemed to be 'soap' are exempt from the provisions of the FD&C Act because soap is excluded from the definition of the term 'cosmetic' in the Act.

Products consisting of detergents or alkali salts of fatty acids and intended not only for cleansing but also for other cosmetic uses, such as beautifying, promoting attractiveness or altering the appearance, must comply with the regulatory requirements applicable to cosmetics. They may also be regulated as drugs if intended to cure, treat or prevent disease or if intended to affect the structure or any function of the human body.

Sun Tan Products

Sun tan products are generally sunscreen preparations that permit penetration of sufficient erythemal ultraviolet (UV) radiation to produce a perceptible erythema for best tanning results. When used as directed, consumers may remain in the sun for a predetermined time period without risking sunburn.

Sun tan products claiming to prevent sunburn are also regulated as drugs if:

- The labelling bears any direct or implied statement that the product screens out UV sunlight, prevents or treats sunburn, helps prevent wrinkles or premature ageing of the skin.
- The label bears a number representing the sun protection factor (SPF) value.
- The sunscreen ingredient is declared as an active drug ingredient and is listed before the cosmetic ingredients.

Products regulated as cosmetics should, and those regulated as drugs must, bear adequate directions for safe use.

Other 'sun tan' products of interest are capsules intended for ingestion and containing mostly beta carotene and canthaxanthin. These colour additives enter the bloodstream and are partially deposited in skin tissue, giving the skin a tan-like colour. Some reports of adverse reactions associated with 'tanning pills' are stomach cramps, hepatitis, nausea, diarrhea and deposition of the colour in the retina of the eye.

How to Obtain FDA Regulations

Regulations published by the FDA are codified under Title 21 Code of Federal Regulations. This is updated every year in April. It consists of eight volumes. Parts 600–799 contain regulations concerning biological products and cosmetics.

The website to access this information is http://www.cfsan.fda.gov/~dms/cos-cfr.html

Drug Regulatory System in the UK

In the UK, the authority responsible for approving new drugs and ensuring safety and efficacy of medicines and medical devices rests with the Medicines and Healthcare Products Regulatory Agency (MHRA). The committee on the safety of medicines established under the Medicines Act advises the UK licensing authority on all aspects of the new product including assessing its safety and efficacy profiles.

European System of Drug Regulation

The members of the European Union are given the facility to submit for approval of new drugs to a centralised agency that has two members from each of the member countries. The recommendations are then considered and approved or rejected by the regulatory agency of each member country.

EEC Cosmetic Directives

The Council of the European Communities has formulated the EEC Cosmetic Directives, which are designed to harmonise the cosmetic regulations of the various member states. The EEC Cosmetic Directives consist of a series of Articles, which state the principles and rules. Attached to this are several Annexes; Annexe I is an illustrative list of categories of cosmetic products. Annexes II–VII are lists of ingredients that cosmetics may or may not contain. The positive lists are concerned with colours, preservatives and sunscreens; in each case, limits have been placed on concentration and sometimes on conditions of use. There is also a list of materials that may only be used under certain conditions of use and concentration. There is a further list of ingredients that may not be used in cosmetics. The lists of colours, preservatives and sunscreens are initially subdivided into Allowed and Provisionally Allowed lists. In order to move an ingredient from the Provisionally Allowed to the Allowed list, it has to undergo a rigorous set of safety tests.

Japanese Drug Regulatory System

Japan follows the pattern of the FDA in matters relating to the approval of new drugs. Recently, Japan has adopted ICH-GCP guidelines and made the Japanese guidelines consistent with the former's provisions. Some countries have classes of products that fall between the two categories of cosmetics and drugs: for example, Japan has 'quasi-drugs'; Thailand has 'controlled cosmetics' and Hong Kong has 'cosmetic-type drugs'. The regulation of cosmeceuticals has not been harmonised among the American, European, Asian and other regions.

Regulatory Mechanism in India

India has a well-defined Drugs and Cosmetics (D&C) Act, 1940 (and Rules, 1945) on which the regulatory mechanism for all activities of the Indian pharmaceutical and cosmetics industry is based.

Requirements of factory premises for manufacture of cosmetics such as the location and surroundings, buildings, water supply, disposal of waste, health, clothing and sanitation requirements of the staff and medical services are in accordance with Schedule M II of D&C Rules, 1945. The equipment area and other requirements for the manufacture of powders, nail polishes and nail lacquers, lipsticks and lip-gloss, depilatories, preparations used for eyes such as eye liners, kajal and surma, aerosols, alcoholic fragrance solutions, hair dyes, tooth powder and toothpaste and toilet soaps are discussed in the same. There are other cosmetics such as attars and perfumes that are not covered in Schedule M II; the licensing authority has the discretion to examine the adequacy of factory premises and other requisites with regard to manufacturing operations involved and direct the licensee to carry on necessary modifications.

Cosmetics shall not contain dyes, colours and pigments other than those specified by the Bureau of Indian Standards and Schedule Q of the D&C Act. The permitted synthetic and natural organic colours used in the cosmetic shall not contain more than:

- 2 parts per million of arsenic calculated as arsenic trioxide
- 20 parts per million of lead
- 100 parts per million of heavy metals other than lead calculated as the total of the respective metals

For the manufacture of cosmetics for sale or distribution, a separate application for each such premise shall be made and a separate license obtained for each such premise. Application for grant or renewal of license for sale or distribution shall be made up to ten items to the Licensing Authority and should be accompanied by the prescribed fee. Application for grant of loan license shall also be made up to ten items and with the prescribed fee to the same authority. An original or renewed license is valid for a duration of five years from the date on which it is granted or renewed.

For importing cosmetics to India, all consignments sought to be imported shall be accompanied by an invoice or statement showing the name and quantities of each article of cosmetics included in the consignment and the name and address of the manufacturer. A declaration signed by or on behalf of the manufacturer or by or on behalf of the importer is required to be supplied to the Collector of Customs.

The labelling of the cosmetics should be appropriate and in accordance with the D&C Act.

Key Messages

- The Food, Drug and Cosmetic (FD&C) Act defines cosmetics by their intended use, as 'articles intended to be rubbed, poured, sprinkled or sprayed on, introduced into or otherwise applied to the human body for cleansing, beautifying, promoting attractiveness or altering the appearance'.
- Cosmetics marketed in the United States, whether manufactured or imported from abroad, must be in compliance with the provisions of the FD&C Act, the Fair Packaging and Labelling Act (FPLA) and the regulations published under the authority of these laws.
- The regulations applicable to cosmetics are stated in 21 CFR, parts 700–740.
- The Council of the European Communities has formulated the EEC Cosmetic Directives, which are designed to harmonise the cosmetic regulations of the various member states.
- Japan follows the pattern of the FDA in matters relating to approval of new drugs and cosmetics.
- The licensing, manufacturing, import and export of cosmetics in India are governed by Schedule M II of the D&C Rules, 1945.

Questions

1. Write briefly about the regulatory requirements for marketing of cosmetics in the United States.
2. Give a list of ingredients and other hazardous substances prohibited from use in cosmetics.
3. Write a note on the regulatory system followed in the UK and in European countries.
4. Explain the regulation of cosmetics followed in India.

Section III: Herbal Drug Technology

26

Natural Products and Drug Discovery—A Perspective

Mueen Ahmed KK

Learning Objectives

At the end of this chapter, you will be able to:

- Define pharmacognosy and related terms
- Explain the significance of Nature as a source of drugs
- Narrate the history of pharmacognosy and phytotherapy
- Explain the role of phytomedicines as future drugs
- Explain the past and present scenarios of the global herbal drug market
- Explain the traditional system of medicines (Ayurveda, Siddha, Unani, Chinese)
- Describe the research being carried out in phytopharmacology
- Describe the steps followed to perform a literature search in phytopharmacology
- Describe the research challenges, hurdles, pitfalls and key issues of natural products

Introduction

For centuries, developing countries have relied on the locally available and time-tested products of Nature as they, unlike the rich nations of the world, could not afford scientifically tested pharmaceutical products. Natural products have played an important role throughout the world in the treatment and prevention of human illness. Experience with medicinal plants as therapeutic tools, gathered over the course of hundreds of years, has helped introduce single chemical entities in modern medicine. Plants, especially those with ethnopharmacological uses, have been the primary sources of medicines for early drug discovery. Today many new drugs from plants have been approved for the treatment of immunological, inflammatory and related diseases, genetic disorders, cancer, neurological diseases, infectious diseases and cardiovascular and metabolic diseases.

This chapter provides an overview and explains the importance of Nature and its utilisation as a source of drugs. The exploration of natural products for hidden therapeutic properties is at the forefront of the development of future drugs.

The traditional system of medicine and its successful application in the treatment of disorders has been dealt with. This chapter also gives a concise and comprehensive note on starting research with natural products and a brief protocol about the same followed by detailed literature search for existing information to avoid repetition of previously conducted work or research. It is a myth that all herbs are safe and are used without any contraindications. Some of the herbal toxicities and herb–drug interactions are also discussed.

Definition of Terms

The WHO definitions of the terms used in natural products are given below:

Herbal drugs: Herbal materials including, in addition to herbs, fresh juices, gums, fixed oils, essential oils, resins and dry powders of herbs. In some countries, these materials may be processed by various local procedures such as steaming, roasting or stir-baking with honey, alcoholic beverages or other materials.

Herbal formulations: Finished herbal products consisting of herbal preparations made from one or more herbs. If more than one herb is used, the term mixture herbal product can be used. Finished herbal products and mixture herbal products may contain excipients in addition to the active ingredients. However, finished or mixture products to which chemically defined active substances have been added, including synthetic compounds and/or isolated constituents from herbal materials, are not considered to be herbal.

Herbal preparations: The basis for finished herbal products, and may include comminuted or powdered herbal materials or extracts, tinctures and fatty oils of herbal materials. They are produced by extraction, fractionation, purification, concentration or other physical or biological processes. They also include preparations made by steeping or heating herbal materials in alcoholic beverages and/or honey, or in other materials.

Herbal remedies: Over-the-counter (OTC) products, not subject to close regulation and obtainable from pharmacies and health food stores without specific diagnosis or prescription from a health professional. Millions of people all over the world use these products regularly.

Herbalism/Herbal Medicine: An alternative medical therapy, defined as the use of plants or substances derived from them in treating disease, usually by medical herbalists without an orthodox medical qualification. Before the relatively recent application of scientific method in diagnosis and therapeutics, traditional medicines were mostly herbal.

Herbs: Crude plant material such as leaves, flowers, fruit, seeds, stems, wood, bark, roots, rhizomes or other plant parts that may be entire, fragmented or powdered.

Natural products: Naturally occurring organic compounds that maintain life by regulating biological reactions. Natural products possess a variety of biological activities.

Pharmacognosy: A thorough study or knowledge of the history, distribution, cultivation, collection, selection, preparation, commerce, identification, evaluation, preservation and use of drugs obtained from plants, animals and other sources.

Phytochemicals: Materials extracted from plant tissue.

Phytochemistry: The study of substances/ chemicals found in plants.

Phytomedicines: Phytotherapeutic agents that are standardised herbal preparations consisting of complex mixtures of one or more plants which are used in most countries for the management of various diseases. According to the WHO, herbal drugs contain plant parts or plant materials in the crude or processed state plus certain excipients, that is, solvents, diluents or preservatives as active ingredients.

In other words, phytomedicines, or herbal medicinal products, are medicinal products containing as active ingredients only plants, parts of plants or plant materials, or combinations thereof, whether in the crude or processed state.

Phytopharmacology: The study of compounds that are found in plants that have medicinal uses; the related terms phytochemical and phytonutrient are used interchangeably to describe plant compounds that are thought to have medicinal properties.

Nature as a Source of Drugs

Despite modern scientific advances, approximately 60% of the world's population still relies entirely on plants for medicines, and plants supply the active ingredients of most traditional medical products. Plants have also served as the starting point for countless drugs in the market today. Researchers generally agree that natural products from plants and other organisms have been the most consistent, successful sources for ideas for new drugs.

Very few species of living creatures on earth have actually been seen and named by scientists. Many of these unidentified organisms may not necessarily live in uninhabited places. Scientists estimate that the earth is home to at least 250,000 different species of plants and that up to 30 million species of insects crawl or fly in this world. Equal numbers of species of fungi, algae and bacteria probably also exist. Despite these vast numbers, chemists have tested only a few of these organisms to find out whether they harbour a medically useful substance.

Searching Nature's treasure trove for potential medicines is often only the first step. Having tapped natural resources for new medicines, pharmaceutical scientists then need to determine ways to cultivate natural products or to make them from scratch in the laboratory. Chemists play an essential role in turning marine and other natural products, which are often found in minute quantities, into useful medicines..

Introduction to Natural Products

Chemical substances derived from animals, plants and microbes have been used to treat human diseases since the beginning of medicinal utilisation. Natural products play an important role in the research and development of new drugs, but it was not until the nineteenth century that humans began to isolate the active principles of medicinal plants. The landmark discovery of quinine from the *Cinchona* bark was made by the French scientists Caventou and Pelletier. Traditionally, natural products have been an important source of pharmaceuticals. Although synthetic chemistry has also produced many new bioactive substances and combinatorial techniques have considerably expanded the number of compounds available for tests, there are still a relatively high number of natural products and their derivatives among the best-selling drugs, and there has been renewed interest in natural products as a source of pharmaceuticals. Natural products and their derivatives have historically been invaluable as a source of therapeutic agents. However, the use of products extracted from plants for medicinal purposes can be traced to the beginning of civilisation. In fact, up until the end of the nineteenth century, natural products were the principal sources of medicines.

History

The use of plants as medicine goes back to prehistory; evidences of this early association have been found in the grave of a Neanderthal man buried 60,000 years ago. Pollen analysis indicated that the numerous plants buried with the corpse were all of medicinal value. The earliest known medical document is a 4000-year-old Sumerian clay tablet that recorded plant remedies for various illnesses. By the time of the ancient Egyptian civilisation, a great wealth of information already existed on medicinal plants. Among the many remedies prescribed were plants for pain relief and for the treatment of heart and circulatory disorders. This information, along with hundreds of other remedies, was preserved in the Ebers papyrus about 3,500 years ago.

Ancient China is also a source of information about the early medicinal uses of plants. The Pun Tsao, a pharmacopeia that was actually published around 1600, contained thousands of herbal cures that are attributed to the works of Shen Nung, China's legendary emperor who lived over 4,500 years ago. In India, herbal medicine dates back several thousand years to the Rig Veda, the collection of Hindu sacred verses. This has led to a system of healthcare known as Ayurvedic medicine. One useful plant from this body of knowledge is the snakeroot, *Rauwolfia serpentina*, used for centuries for its sedative effects. Today, the active components of snakeroot are widely used in Western medicine to treat high blood pressure.

In all parts of the world, indigenous people discovered and developed the medicinal uses of native plants, but it is from the herbal medicine of ancient Greece that the foundations of Western medicine were established. Western medicine can be traced back to the Greek physician Hippocrates (460–377 BC), known as the Father of Medicine. Hippocrates believed that a disease had a natural cause and used various herbal remedies in his treatments. Early Roman writing also influenced the development of Western medicine, especially the works of Dioscorides (1st century AD). Although Greek by birth, Dioscorides was a Roman military physician whose travels with the army brought him in contact with many useful plants. He compiled this information in *De Materia Medica,* which contained an account of over 600 species of plants with medicinal value. It included descriptions and illustrations of the plants, along with directions on the preparation, uses and side effects of the drugs.

After the arrival of Columbus, many New World plants became available to Europeans, and by the time of Henry VIII in England (1491-1547), an entire European or Western medical system that blended plant use and astrology had developed. For centuries, medicine in the West meant herbal medicine. In the other parts of the world, medicinal plants were also an important element of indigenous medical systems. For example, in the Northwestern

Amazon, indigenous people still use at least 1,300 plant species to create *drogas do certão* or 'wildness drugs'.

In Southeast Asia, traditional healers use 6,500 different plants to treat malaria, stomach ulcers, syphilis and other disorders. During the eighteenth century, as scientific knowledge progressed, a dichotomy in medicine developed between practitioners of herbal medicine and regular physicians. At about the same time, a similar split occurred between herbalism and scientific botany, the study of plants above and beyond their medical application.

While Western medicine strayed away from herbalism, 75– 90% of the rural population in the rest of the world still relies on herbal medicine as their only healthcare. The long tradition of herbal medicine continues to the present day in China, India and many countries in Africa and South America. In many village marketplaces, medicinal herbs are sold alongside vegetables and other wares. Practitioners of herbal medicine often undergo a rigorous and extended training to learn the names, uses and preparation of native plants.

Nature exhibits unique structure–activity relationships and has a proven ability to produce diverse and novel chemical prototypes with drug potential. There is also an accelerated interest in the areas of herbal drugs and functional foods. However, in drug discovery the application of traditional medicines and combinatorial chemistry together with high-throughput screening is an obvious challenge to research aimed at the discovery of new bioactive molecules from natural sources.

Phytomedicines as Future Drugs

Phytomedicine, medicinal products obtained from natural resources, has been used in healthcare practice for many years. Although traditional phytomedicine has been sidelined by modern medicine based on chemical entities since the beginning of the twentieth century, remainders of medical practice based on natural resources can be seen all over the world. There is a growing interest from both consumers and the industry for the development of food products with 'functional' properties, or those which promote good health. These products may take the form of dietary supplements or of foods. Health is promoted by particular ingredients and, in many cases, these are derived from botanicals. The variety of plants providing these functions is large, ranging from staple food sources such as cereals, fruits and vegetables, to herbs used in traditional medicine. The food or ingredients conferring health properties may comprise the plants themselves, extracts thereof or more purified components.

Despite the diversity of these traditional medical practices, it is interesting to observe that many plants were used for similar indications in different parts of the world, suggesting that the herb may indeed contain certain compounds with a particular pharmacological action. Unfortunately, modern education has driven a wedge between the extensive knowledge that has been built by many traditional pharmacognosists over thousands of years and the modern view of human physiology and pharmacotherapy. Today, the power of phytomedicine and the contributions that it has made to modern pharmacotherapy have not been given much prominence. It is, however, possible to study the pharmacotherapeutic action of herbal preparations using traditional knowledge and the experience of a pharmacognosist, but based on the modern scientific understanding of human physiology and using modern pharmacological tools.

It is important for the modern pharmacologist to realise that phytomedicine has certain particularities that are different from regular drugs. Most important is the complexity of herbal preparations. Whereas most common drugs are single-chemical entities, herbal medicinal products usually contain hundreds of compounds. The composition of this mixture depends on the botanical origin, part of the plant used, season and time of the day of harvest, method of extraction and presence of chemical or biological contaminants. The pharmacological action may depend on one single substance or on a combination of two or more compounds. The active compound, mode of action and molecular target are usually only partially known or sometimes completely unknown.

Another special property of phytomedicines is that they do not directly interfere in the pathology of the disease, but stimulate normal physiological and immunological function, resulting in enhanced homeostasis. This indirect pharmacological activity impedes the demonstration of effectiveness in simple assay systems.

Since the efficacy of phytomedicines is based on experiences in phytotherapeutic clinical practice, the contribution of digestion, absorption and metabolism to the activity of the product is usually unknown. The lack of efficacy in a molecular or cell-based assay may be due to lack of molecular activation by digestion or metabolism.

Finally, the public often believes that the natural origin of a medicine guarantees its safety. Needless to say, this belief is completely unfounded: there are many examples of natural toxins that can be highly toxic or fatal even in small quantities. It is important to prove the safety of the phytomedicine adequately, both in healthy humans as well as in patients with the indication concerned.

Global Herbal Drug Market: An Overview

Over 80% of the approximately 30,000 known natural products are of plant origin. The number of known chemical structures is estimated to be nearly four times greater than that of microbes. Of the 877 small-molecule, new chemical entities (NCEs) introduced between 1981 and 2002, roughly half (49%) were natural products, semi-synthetic natural product analogues or synthetic compounds based on natural-product pharmacophores. Despite this success, pharmaceutical research into natural products has experienced a slow decline during the past two decades. Although these trends seemed obvious to investigators working in the field, their downstream effects are somewhat difficult to measure precisely, given the long product development cycles encountered in the pharmaceutical industry. The lengthy delay—usually ten years or more—between the initial discovery of a potential therapeutic agent and the subsequent market launch of a new molecular entity (NME) means that agents reaching the market today are typically the products of discovery research programmes initiated at least a decade ago.

In 1985, of the 3,500 new chemical structures identified, 2,600 were from the higher plants. Worldwide, 121 clinically useful prescription drugs are derived from plants. The surveys of plant medicinal usage by the American public have shown an increase from just about 3% of the population in 1991 to over 37% in 1998. The US market sales of plant medicinals have climbed to about US$3 billion per year. Even today, 75% of the world's population relies on plants for traditional medicine. In the US, where chemical synthesis dominates the pharmaceutical industry, 25% of the pharmaceuticals are based on plant-derived chemicals. Plants will continue to provide novel products as well as chemical models for new drugs in the coming centuries, because the chemistry of the majority of plant species is yet to be characterised.

The use of herbal remedies is commonly referred to as 'unconventional' or 'alternative' medicine. The prevalence of alternative medicine in several United States surveys ranges from 10–40% and herbal supplements are a multi-billion-dollar industry that is growing rapidly. There is a growing movement towards the consumption of natural therapies out of a desire by people to take more control over their health. Historically, herbs have been found in cosmetics, food and medicinals. However, in recent years, herbs have been increasingly used as drugs. In 1997, an estimated 33% of adults in the United States used herbal remedies, spending over $3 billion.

The market for phytomedicines is estimated at US$ 400 million a year and is expected to grow at a rate of 12%. The rapid development of a more sophisticated market for herbal remedies and nutritional supplements has led to growing pressure for regulation and testing. Many small projects involving services provided by academic groups to the producers of phytomedicines have developed from quality control into more ambitious investigations of chemical composition and active constituents of existing products.

There has been a general impression that Ayurvedic drugs are already very popular in the global markets.

Much attention in the last two decades has focussed on tropical plants as sources of new natural products for potential pharmaceutical and agrochemical use. Recently, however, temperate plants have provided most of the commercially interesting plant compounds that have been identified. These include: etoposide (anti-cancer agent) from the *Podophyllum* species, artemisinin (anti-malarial agent) from *Artemisia annua* (Annual Mugwort) and taxol from *Taxus* spp. (Yew trees). Taxol, as a treatment for ovarian cancer, is now among the top 30 best-selling drugs.

If natural products are to conintue to play an important role in the discovery of potential and innovative leads in drug discovery and in the development of high quality herbal drugs with proven efficacy, improvements and development of new research strategies and in-depth studies are required. The selection of plants for improving diversity and increasing de-replication to avoid known molecules, and the development of faster and more efficient isolation procedures are thus routine challenges for a natural product scientist. Moreover, broad knowledge and experience is needed to avoid the pitfalls in dealing with a complex biomass and to reach the objective of discovering novel bioactive molecules. The discovery of new drugs, agrochemicals or other biologically active compounds is dependent on the ability to rapidly identify and characterise active chemicals for commercial development.

Biotechnology and Natural Products

Biotechnology offers an opportunity to exploit a cell, tissue, organ or organism by growing them in vitro and to genetically manipulate them to get the desired compounds. Since the human population in the world is increasing rapidly, there is extreme pressure on the available cultivable land to produce food and fulfill human needs. Therefore, for other uses such as production of pharmaceuticals and chemicals from plants, the available land should be used effectively. Hence, it is appropriate to develop modern technologies that lead to plant improvement for better utilisation of the land to meet the requirements. The development and adoption of plant cell and organ culture methods have led to the production of plant products on a large scale.

Using Drugs from Traditional Systems – An Overview

There is a growing focus on the importance of medicinal plants and traditional health systems in solving the healthcare problems of the world. Because of this awareness, the international trade in plants of medical importance is growing phenomenally, often to the detriment of natural habitats and mother populations in the countries of origin. Most developing countries have viewed traditional medical practice as an integral part of their culture. Despite this attitude, traditional healthcare systems suffered a setback during colonial times and lost patronage, particularly in urban areas.

According to the WHO, *'Traditional medicines are defined as the sum total of the knowledge, skills and practices based on the theories, beliefs and experiences indigenous to different cultures, whether explicable or not, used in the maintenance of health as well as in the prevention, diagnosis, improvement or treatment of physical and mental illness'.*

Ever since modern chemotherapy emerged, there have been two major approaches to sourcing chemicals for testing: the synthetic route and the natural route. Both these approaches have been successfully employed and continue to be relevant for the future of new drug discovery and advances in medicine. The problem of cost of new drug development is related to the very high cost of failures in this area. Recent efforts by big R&D-based companies have been directed to minimising the high costs and risks associated with drug research. A more meaningful approach would be to avail of the knowledge base and heritage available in traditional systems of medicine in India and other countries.

Some of these systems of medicine are now discussed in detail.

Homeopathic System of Medicine

Homeopathy is an alternative system of medicine that was founded in the early nineteenth century by a German physician, Dr. Hahnemann. It enjoyed great popularity in the late nineteenth century. Homeopathy is a complementary therapy that treats illnesses with very dilute preparations, called remedies, made from plant, mineral, metal and insect sources.

Classical homeopathy is based on three principles:

- The law of similars
- The single medicine
- The minimum dose

The law of similars states that a disease is cured by a medicine that in a healthy person creates symptoms similar to those the patient is experiencing. Hence, an important part of the prescription of a homeopathic medicine is a lengthy interview to determine all the symptoms the patient is experiencing. The homeopathic physician then determines which medicine best matches the symptoms the patient is experiencing and prescribes it.

The principle of the single remedy states that a single medicine should cover all the symptoms the patient is experiencing: mental, emotional and physical.

The principle of the minimum dose has two parts. First, the homeopathic physician only prescribes a small number of doses of the homeopathic medicine and waits to see what effect the medicine has. Second, the medicine is given in an infinitesimal dose. Homeopaths have discovered that the effect of homeopathic medicines is strengthened upon successive dilutions as long as the medicine is violently shaken between each dilution. Medicines are typically used in very high dilutions (1 part in 10^-60) or (1 part in 10^-400).

Homeopathy appears to be safe, probably because the active ingredients of homeopathic remedies are present in such low concentrations. However, some homeopaths report that after a remedy has been taken, the symptoms sometimes get worse for a short period of time before getting better.

Chinese System of Medicine

For thousands of years, traditional medicines and remedies have been practised and used in China. They have proved to be invaluable sources of historical experience. The Chinese people believe that their traditional medicine is consistent with their own culture and it continues to play a crucial role in helping China flourish. Traditional Chinese medicine is at least 2,500 years old.

There are four major sections in Chinese medicine:

- Traditional Chinese medicines
- Chinese folk medicines
- Western medicinal plants
- Traditional compound prescriptions

Traditional medicines are those that have been prescribed by the traditional medical doctors in China and recorded in the ancient medical classics and pharmacopeias. Folk medicines including materials taken by the Chinese minorities are usually adopted by traditional healers as well as some traditional physicians. Generally, folk medicines do not enjoy nationwide popularity, and are used mainly for the treatment of endemic diseases. They have not yet been described in Chinese medical classics.

The Chinese definition of herbs can include various parts of plants as well as minerals and animal parts. These herbs can come in several forms:

- ***'Loose' or 'raw' herbs***: Various dried pieces of roots, bark, leaves, seeds, powders and other items are usually boiled and the 'tea' is considered as the most potent form for herbs.
- ***Powdered herbs***: Dried herbs are ground into a powder and the powder might be mixed with water to drink, or is taken in a capsule.
- ***Tinctures***: Dried herbs are prepared in a mixture of water and alcohol and administered as a dose of the tincture.
- ***Patent medicines***: Some of the most common combinations of herbs are available in prepared form as pills, capsules, creams or other forms. There is usually very little or no labelling on these medicines except in Chinese.

The Chinese healing art of acupuncture dates back thousands of years. Though its exact age is uncertain, up until the twentieth century, much of the population of the world was uninformed about acupuncture, its origins and its capacity to promote and maintain good health. Today, in most Western cultures, it is considered as an alternative medicine. Used for over 3,500 years in China on both animals and humans, acupuncture is not only safe, but is also the favoured treatment method for a quarter of the world's population. Acupuncture acts by stimulating specific spots in the body with needles, lasers, heat and massage to balance energy and promote healing.

In acupuncture, doctors insert thin, flexible, sterile, stainless steel needles at precise points on the body to stimulate the nervous system and to help promote natural healing abilities. Studies show that acupuncture causes the release of hormones, cortisones and natural painkillers such as endorphins, which accounts for its extraordinary effects.

Ayurvedic System of Medicine

Ayurveda is a holistic system of medicine that originated in India. It was placed in writing over 5,000 years ago and it was said to be a world medicine dealing with both the body and the spirit. Its aim is to provide guidance regarding food and lifestyle so that healthy people can stay healthy and people with health challenges can improve their health.

In Ayurveda, each person is viewed as a unique individual made up of five primary elements. The elements are ether (space), air, fire, water and earth. When any of these elements are present in the environment, they will influence the individual. Food and weather are just two examples of the presence of these elements. While a composite of these five primary elements exists in earch person, certain elements are seen to have an ability to combine to create various physiological functions. In Ayurveda, ether and air combine to form the Vata dosha. Vata governs the principle of movement and therefore can be seen as the force which directs nerve impulses, circulation, respiration and elimination. Fire and water are the elements that combine to form the Pitta dosha, which is the process of transformation or metabolism.

The transformation of foods into nutrients that our bodies can assimilate is an example of a Pitta function. Pitta is also responsible for metabolism in organ and tissue systems as well as cellular metabolism. Finally, it is predominantly the water and earth elements that combine to form the Kapha dosha. Kapha is what is responsible for growth, adding structure unit by unit. Another function of the Kapha dosha is to offer protection. Cerebrospinal fluid protects the brain and spinal column and is a type of Kapha found in the body. The mucosal lining of the stomach is another example of the Kapha dosha protecting the tissues. We are all made up of unique proportions of Vata, Pitta and Kapha. These ratios vary in each individual, and because of this, Ayurveda sees each person as a special mixture that accounts for the diversity of human life.

Ayurveda provides a model using which the unique combination of these three doshas that make up an individual are assessed. This enables the Ayurvedic physician to design treatment protocols that specifically address a person's health challenges. When any of the doshas become accumulated, Ayurveda will suggest specific lifestyle and nutritional changes or guidelines to assist in the reduction of the dosha that has become excessive. Certain herbal supplements are also suggested to hasten the healing process. If the body has abundant toxins, a cleansing process known as Pancha Karma is recommended to eliminate the unwanted toxins.

Unani System of Medicine

Unani is the Arabic spelling of Ionian, meaning Greek. It is also known as Greco-Arabic medicine or Islamic medicine. It originated in Greece and was founded by Hippocrates (Buqrat 460–377 BC). In this system of medicine, the physiological functions of the human body are considered to be based on of the following seven factors, known as '*Umoor-e-Taba'ya*':

I. *Elements (Arkan):* There are four basic elements: fire, air, water and earth. These elements actually symbolise the four states of matter.

II. *Temperament (Mizaj):* The interaction of the elements produces a new state of admixture, which determines the temperament of an individual.

III. *Humours (Akhlat):* These are the secondary body fluids, synthesised in the liver from the nutrient components of the ingested food and beverages. Hippocrates presented the concept of existence of four humours in the body, namely, blood (*dam*), phlegm (*balgham*), bile (*safra*) and black bile (*sauda*).

IV. *Organs (Azaa):* The organs of the body are derived primarily from the humours, just as the humours are derived primarily from the ailments, which are composed of the elements.

V. *Vital Forces (Arwah):* These are considered to be a life force and are therefore given importance in the diagnosis and treatment of diseases. These are present in organs such as brain, liver, heart, ovaries and testicles.

VI. *Faculties (Quwa):* Faculty is a potential power.

VII. *Functions (Af'al):* This represents actualised potentiality.

Unani physicians use four methods of treatment: diet-o-therapy (*Ilaj-bil-Ghiza*), pharamacotherapy (*Ilaj-bil-Dawa*), regimental therapy (*Ilaj-bil-Tadbeer*) and surgery. (*Ilaj-bil-Yad*).

Siddha System of Medicine*

Siddha medicine is practised in Southern India. The origin of the Tamil language is attributed to the sage Agasthya, as is the origin of Siddha medicine. Before the Aryan occupation of the Sind region and the Gangetic plain, there existed in southern India, on the banks of the rivers Kavery and Tamirapani, a civilisation that was highly organised.

According to Siddha medical science, the universe consists of five elements: earth, water, fire, air and ether, which correspond to the five senses of the human body. Humans consume water and food, breathe the air and then maintain heat in the body. Humans are alive because of the life force given by ether. The earth is the first element that gives shape to the body, including the bones, tissues, muscles, skin, hair, etc. Water is the second element and it represents blood, secretions of the glands, vital fluids, etc. Fire, the third element, is responsible for emotions, vigour and vitality. It also helps digestion, circulation and stimulation besides respiration and the nervous system.

* Adapted from Dr.V. Shanmugavelan. Siddhar's Science of Longevity and Kalpa Medicine of India. Part I. Antiquity of Siddha system. (Madras: Pub: by Sakthi Nilayam, Umayal St. Alagappa Nagar,1963), pp.17-19, 23, 28, 31-32.

Above all others is the characteristic of the mental and spiritual faculties of humans. A suitable proportion of these five elements produces a healthy person. These elements are classified as physical and subtle and the subtle class is further subdivided into two equal parts, of which one is retained as such and the other part is again subdivided into four equal parts. This is what is known in the Siddha system of medicine as the theory of Panchikarnam (fivefold combination).

Other Alternative Therapies

Chiropractic – Physical manipulation of the spinal joints in order to return a normal range of motion to the spinal column. Chiropractic is a unique form of healthcare which stresses overall body wellness. The focus of chiropractic is to locate and help correct spinal problems that disrupt the controlling nerve impulses between the brain and every cell, tissue, organ and system of the body. Spinal bones that have lost their normal motion are restored by a series of carefully directed adjustments. Because these adjustments help to restore the function of the nervous system, they can have a profound effect on overall health without recourse to drugs or surgery.

Laser Therapy – Low level, 'cold' lasers are used therapeutically. They are most effectively used to stimulate acupuncture or trigger points and therefore require accuracy. When used correctly, they can be effective for pain relief.

Magnetotherapy – It is a gentle and natural treatment for the human body. The action of a pulsative magnetic field (PMF) favourably affects tissues of the body. PMF is known to work at the cellular level. This treatment may lead to the suppression or complete elimination of some health problems. This safe, non-invasive therapy can be successfully applied for the treatment of different diseases, both acute, and chronic, and often provides fast removal of pain and edemas, which arisc from physical trauma. Magnets have been shown to be helpful in the treatment of a number of conditions including arthritis, back pain, pain in joints, sporting injuries, poor circulation, lack of energy and stamina, etc. This form of therapy has not been substantiated with scientific research. However, magnets are reported to increase blood flow and/or influence cell membranes to speed healing. Magnetic fields generated by electricity (pulse magnetic field therapy) appear to achieve a more consistent benefit.

Plants used in Phytomedicines

In this section, the following topics are discussed:

- Concepts of phytopharmacological research
- Steps involved in the development of a phytomedicine
- How to perform a literature search for medicinal plants

Concepts of Phytopharmacological Research

The rationalisation of new concepts and strategies requires scientific evidence. This enormous task, however, can be mastered only through concerted cooperation among phytochemists, molecular biologists, pharmacologists and clinicians. The efforts should focus on three research areas:

- Application of all available modern, high-tech methods to standardise phytopreparations before conducting systematic pharmacological and clinical investigations

- Integration of new molecular biological assays into the screening of extracts and plant constituents to evaluate their exact pharmacological profiles and elucidate the synergistic effects of the constituents of an extract to gain a better understanding of the various mechanisms underlying these pharmacological effects
- Controlled clinical studies paralleled or followed by pharmacokinetic and bioavailability studies

Steps in Phytopharmacological Research (Fig. 26.1)

Identification of Phytoconstituents

The choice of the test system is obviously highly dependent on the herbal preparation and its presumed activity. The quality of herbal medicinal products is usually tested by fingerprinting on thin layer chromatography and analysis of active and/or marker compounds by high pressure liquid chromatography (HPLC) or similar chromatographic techniques. Analysis of the product for impurities and certain specified contaminants such as insecticides are performed based on general guidelines for drug products.

Optimisation of the preparative method may result in superior products by higher levels of active compounds or reduced levels of contaminants. Preparative method development and possible isolation of the active compound(s) is achieved by research in the extraction method, separation procedures and affinity testing. Optimisation should always be based on an appropriate biological activity assay system.

Expert reports, based on phytotherapeutic experience and scientific literature, should be prepared for marketing authorisation purposes or as a basis for further research to prove the product's activity. It is important to have access to many phytomedicine research journals and have extensive experience in the evaluation of biological literature. Biological activity is analysed by in vitro functional assays, or if

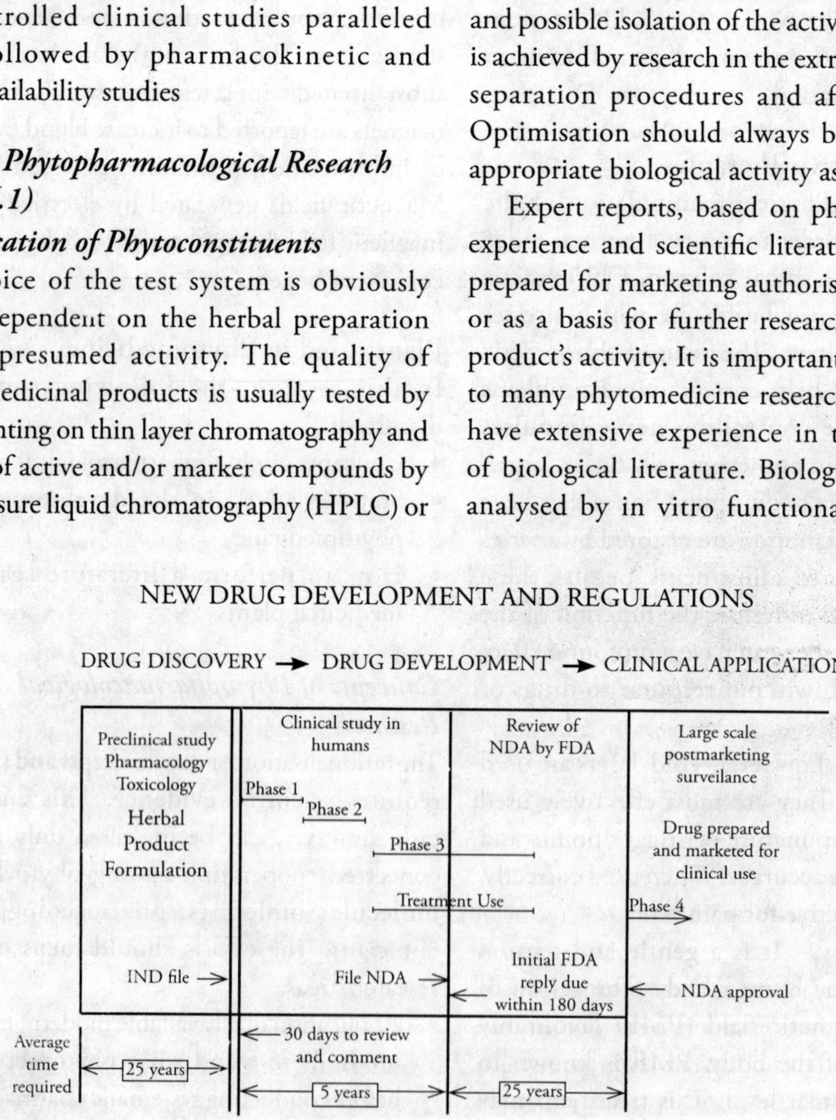

NEW DRUG DEVELOPMENT AND REGULATIONS

DRUG DISCOVERY → DRUG DEVELOPMENT → CLINICAL APPLICATIONS

Figure 26.1: New drug development and regulations

necessary in isolated organ assays or an in vivo animal model. The development of an assay for phytomedicinal activity will be based on a comprehensive literature review of the product or related products, and on the known molecular targets for the indicated activity. The approach for phytomedicine will not differ largely from the test systems described in research area–specific brochures.

Difficulties may exist in finding an appropriate control if the active compound of a phytomedicine is not known. In in vivo experiments, the proper control should have comparable nutritional properties or should preferably be prepared from a non-active plant in a manner similar to that used in the medicinal product. In in vitro experiments, care should be taken to ensure that the absorbance spectrum of the product does not interfere with detection systems or that the product acts non-specifically by changing buffer pH or isotonicity. Combinations of phytomedicinal preparations may result in altered activity. The addition of another phytomedicine may enhance, inhibit or abolish biological action, alter pharmacodynamics or result in toxicity. The enhancement of biological action may be the result of simultaneous action on a different or the same molecular target. If the same molecular target is involved, the effect may simply be additive or synergistic. Interactions of phytomedicines can be studied in any pharmacological assay system as they have been used for proving efficacy.

Clinical trials are conducted in three phases (I, II and III), with each phase providing the answer to a different fundamental question about a potential new drug: Is it safe? Does it work? Is it better than the standard treatment? Typically, researchers do years of basic work in the laboratory and then use animal models before they even consider testing an experimental drug on people. Importantly, scientists who wish to conduct human drug tests must follow strict rules that are designed to protect those who volunteer to participate in clinical trials.

Phase I study tests a drug's safety in a few dozen to a hundred people and is designed to determine what happens to a drug in the body—how it is absorbed, metabolised and excreted. Phase I studies usually take several months.

Phase II trials test whether or not a drug produces a desired effect. These studies take longer—from several months to a few years—and can involve up to several hundred patients.

A phase III study further examines the effectiveness of a drug as well as whether the drug is better than current treatments. Phase III studies involve hundreds to thousands of patients, and these advanced trials typically last several years. Many phase II and phase III studies are randomised, meaning that one group of patients gets the experimental drug being tested while a second control group gets either a standard treatment or a placebo (that is, no treatment, often masked as a 'dummy' pill or injection). Also, phase II and phase III studies are usually 'blinded'—the patients and the researchers do not know who is getting the experimental drug. Finally, once a new drug has completed phase III testing, a pharmaceutical company can request approval from the Food and Drug Administration (FDA) to market the drug.

Medicinal Plant Research Projects

These projects are always customised to the present needs and are optimised for each individual product. The steps involved in these projects are discussed below:

1. Optimisation of preparative method and/ or isolation and identification of the active constituents

Based on the biological activity, the extraction and separation method can be optimised to obtain superior products with higher therapeutic efficacy. The isolation and identification of the active compound can be useful for drug registration and patenting, and possibly further development of the drug.

Phytopharmacological Research Timelines

Literature research and preparation of research program	2–6 weeks
Development of validated assay systems and chemical analysis	4–8 weeks
Biological activity	4–8 weeks
Extraction method development	8–12 weeks
Separation method development	8–12 weeks
Isolation of active compound(s)	4–6 weeks
Identification of active compound	8–12 weeks
Report	2–4 weeks
Total period	Approximately 1 year

2. Pharmacological profiling

This programme is designed to define pharmacological activity in relation to other active compounds. In addition, interaction with other therapeutics may be useful for combination preparations or use of herbal products in combination with regular drugs.

Pharmacological Profiling Timelines

Literature research and preparation of research program	2–6 weeks
Concentration dependent activity on selected target organs/cells compared to known extract(s)	4–8 weeks
Define molecular target(s) by selective inhibition assays	4–8 weeks
Pharmacodynamics	12–24 weeks
Interaction with food/other therapeutics	6–12 weeks
Report	2–4 weeks
Total period	Approximately 1 year

3. Safety profiling

This program is designed to detect any toxicological effects and to quantify the safety margin of the herbal medicinal product.

Safety Profiling Timelines

Literature research and preparation of research program	2–6 weeks
Effect on vital body function	8–12 weeks
Single dose and multiple dose toxicity	12 weeks
Mutagenicity tests	8 weeks
Report	2–4 weeks
Total period	Approximately 0.5 years

Typical information required for preparation of a study protocol:

- Aim of the study
- Aim for marketing authorisation: country and authorisation level
- Therapeutic indication
- Administration route and dosage
- Any available information of pharmacological action and pharmacokinetics /pharmacodynamics
- The number of compounds
- The preferred starting date

Literature Search in Phytopharmacological Research

Why perform a literature search?

Any investigation will involve reading and reviewing what other experts have written about the area of interest under consideration. This is done for a number of reasons: to find evidence to support and justify the work undertaken and to ensure that there is no repetition of past research. It can also aid in finding helpful ideas and enable comparison with prior research.

As part of the written report, the literature review will ground the reader in the area and explain why the research undertaken fills a gap. It usually forms at least one chapter of the report. To review the literature, a search should be made for the papers and research published in the field of interest, and this is where literature search comes into play.

A literature search needs to be systematic and focussed—only what is relevant to the current research should be considered. A literature search must also be evaluative— each reference must be critically assessed to determine if it is worth pursuing. Searching for and reviewing literature is a skill that can be learnt, but it takes a little practice.

Steps

Conducting a literature search is a ten-step process. It is very important to accurately record everything that is performed and found at the time. This will demonstrate the progress of literature search and save much time and effort for accessing the information later on.

The ten steps are as follows:

1. Plan the search strategy.
2. Carry out the search on relevant bibliographic indexing databases.
3. Refine the search strategy until it produces relevant results.
4. Evaluate the search results.
5. Save the useful results.
6. Record what has been done.
7. Repeat the process using different databases.
8. Evaluate all the saved literature references.
9. Find the required literature.
10. Read it thoroughly.

The Internet as an Information Search Tool

The Internet is a global computer network that enables communication among millions of computer users and access to resources from around the world. No matter what type of computer is used for connecting to the Internet, a virtually limitless wealth of resources is available for everyday use.

Natural products have been a source of drugs for centuries. With major advances in biotechnological and phytochemical techniques, academic and industrial interest in discovering and developing bioactive natural products has been a growing trend. Medicinal plants are treated as a subject of serious study and intense research all over the world. The immense surge in scientific interest in natural products as a potential source of drugs has contributed to the development of phytopharmacology research. However, the almost intimidating volume of this scientific information presented in various forms such as databases, virtual libraries and journal sites, may often tend to confuse the prospective researcher. Many of the published articles from India are but minor variations of work already done elsewhere and the reason for this unfortunate 'reinvention of the wheel' is that a thorough literature search would not have been done before planning the experiments. Ironically, the presence of vast information may itself make scientific research elusive. Most academicians and researchers agree that rational drug discovery can be initiated if the review of existing information can be conducted in a systematic and objective manner. Today, the Internet presents the researcher with more effective tools for systematic literature search.

Simple as it may seem, acquiring information on the World Wide Web is like seeking a selective fish in the ocean. When beginners search the Internet, they often restrict themselves only to search engines such as Google, Yahoo, Infoseek and MSN, which results in a narrow range of search results. This compilation was done with a view to addressing the difficulties often faced by beginners (Fig. 26.2 and Table 26.1).

Planning a search

Before starting a search, define the search criteria.

Step 1: Write out the search criteria as a statement. For example, 'The role of Azadirachta indica in the treatment of Diabetes mellitus'

Step 2: Identify the important words/concepts. The sentences should be translated into keywords by thinking of all possible synonyms and variant spellings, so that relevant articles are not missed. Some keyword examples are Azadirachta indica, Diabetes mellitus, apocynacea, hypoglycemic etc.

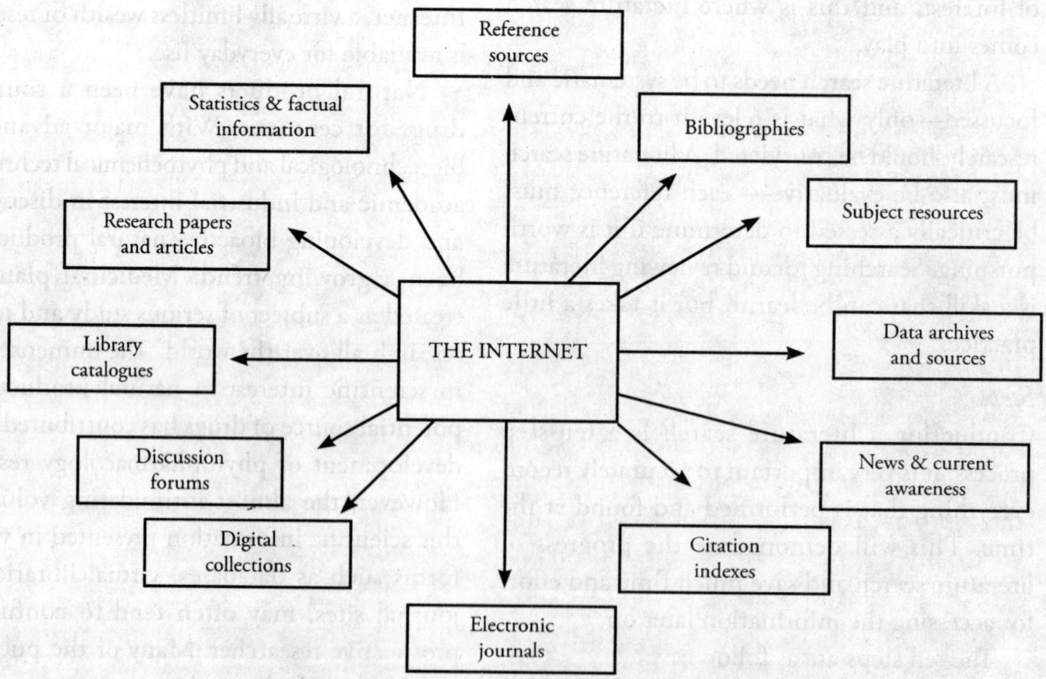

Figure 26.2: Different sources of scientific literature

Reference: Mueen Ahmed KK., AC Rana, VK Dixit and BG Shivananda. 2003. Internet - Implications for future phytopharmacological research, *Indian Journal of Experimental Biology;* 41:11, 1233–1238.

Table 26.1: Classification of sources for literature search		
Primary	*Secondary*	*Tertiary*
• Reports • Dissertations • Conference reports • Annual reports • Market research • Some public reports • Unpublished manuscripts	• Newspapers • Books • Journals • Magazines • Some public reports	• Indices • Abstracts • Catalogues • Encyclopedia • Dictionaries • Bibliographies • Quotation indices • Computerised search programmes

Redundant words

Some words in sentences will be redundant because they are another way of expressing the same concept, or they can be determined from reading the actual material. For example, in the case of 'novel methods', search for every type of method and then decide which are novel by reading the articles.

Spelling

Proper spelling of search terms is essential. For example, Azadrachta – Azadirachta (correct)

Phrases

If there is a particular group of words that are always used to describe a particular concept, treat them as a phrase; this means that results where the words are used together in the given order are required. For example, 'sugar reducing'.

Truncation

Use truncation to use a single term for related words that express the same concept. The truncation symbol is usually * or $—the Help software available for each database should provide this information. For example, 'optim*' will find optimise, optimised, optimising, optimal and optimum. It will also find the American and British spellings of these words. For more related words and synonyms, the Merriam Webster website (www.m-w.com) is useful. The following example shows how a sentence has been broken down into keywords and grouped by concept. It also shows how they relate to one another.

'Antihyperglycemic activity of Neem'

Keywords: Azadirachta indica, neem, Diabetes mellitus, medicinal plants, blood glucose lowering activity, hypoglycemic activity

Step 3: Think about ways of limiting the search. In some subjects, there will be more published information than can be handled. To deal with this, the search can be limited in other ways:

- Date – restrict the search to items published only in the last few years?
- Language – restrict the search to references only in English?
- Geography – restrict the search to specific places or countries?
- Medicinal plants – restrict the search to a specific genus or species of a plant

- Type of publication – restrict the search to references in journal articles, books or theses?

What are electronic databases?

Databases are the collection of citations published in indexed journal articles using storage devices such as online servers, hard disks and compact discs. Online databases enables a precise query and retrieves a particular set of items by matching words to words from the field of citations.

Some of the libraries subscribe to a range of bibliographic databases, some cover all subject areas (for example, web of knowledge), some cover particular types of publication (for example, index to theses) and some cover specific subject areas (for example, Embase, PsycINFO).

Bibliographic indexing databases are used for literature searches. These databases hold records containing details of publications including books, journal articles, conference papers and proceedings, theses, etc. These databases can be used to find useful references on specific subjects. Another type of electronic database is a full-text collection. This refers to databases that hold the full-text of all the articles from specific journals.

Searching Techniques

There are a number of important methods you need to use to make sure you search efficiently and effectively to ensure that you find only relevant references and that you find all of them:

- Truncation/Wild card symbols
- Search operators
- Phrase searching
- Searching using indexes

Truncation/Wild Card Symbols

Most databases will only retrieve records that match exactly what is typed. Truncation and wild card symbols can help overcome this limitation. These symbols can be substituted for letters to retrieve variant spellings and word endings.

A wild card symbol replaces a single letter, which is useful for retrieving alternative spellings and simple plurals. For example, wom?n will find woman or women.

A truncation symbol retrieves any number of letters and is useful for finding different word endings based on the root of a word. For example, Africa* will find Africa, African, Africans, Africaans; Agricultur* will find agriculture, agricultural, agriculturalist.

Check the online Help screens for details of the symbols recognised by the database being searched—not all databases use the ? and * symbols.

Search Operators

Search operators (also known as Boolean operators) are used to combine search words. The records retrieved are indicated by the shaded areas on the diagrams. For example, 'AND' retrieves records containing both words. It also narrows the search. Some databases automatically connect words typed with AND. 'OR' retrieves records containing either word. It can also be used to broaden the search. For example, it can be used to include synonyms in the search.

'NOT' retrieves the first word but excludes the second. When this operator is used, relevant records may be excluded because those records that include both words will be lost.

Phrase Searching

Phrase searching is a useful technique that can increase the relevance of the search results. Sometimes, the search may be made up of common words which, when combined in an 'AND' search, retrieve too many irrelevant records. Databases use different techniques to specify phrase searching, so checking the online Help would be useful. Examples of phrase searching:

In web search engines, a phrase may be specified using inverted commas. For example, 'agricultural development'; 'foot and mouth'. In some databases, 'adj' may be specified between search words to indicate that these words are adjacent to each other. For example, agricultural adj development. Some databases automatically perform a phrase search if search operators are not used.

Searching Using Indexes

It is possible to search some databases using indexes. These are usually alphabetical lists of authors or subjects. Indexes are particularly useful for searching for authors: there may be inconsistencies in the way an author has been cited. By browsing the index, all possible variant forms of the name can be selected to ensure that relevant references are not excluded.

Saving Search Results

Databases usually provide several ways of saving search results:

- Email records—the most common option
- Save on floppy disks or another directory on the PC or the network directory
- Print out
- Export into bibliographic management software, for example, RefWorks, Endnote, Papyrus

Hurdles and Pitfalls in Herbal Drug Development

Herbal drugs comprise a large share of the healthcare system and thus it plays a major role in the healthcare programmes throughout the world. In India, their use is very high, because of their easy accessibility, economic value, unrequired expert consultation and also due to the popular belief that herbal medicines are safe without any adverse side effects.

However, the common belief that "anything natural is safe is incorrect". The fact that herbal medicines contain ingredients to maintain health and to cure ailments is well known. Nonetheless, the fact that they may contain toxic substances which are harmful or even dangerous to health is least known. A study to assess bioactivity of commonly used herbal drugs is the need of the time.

Many commonly used herbal medicines in their irregular high doses or with other medications are toxic in the long term. Toxic effects of herbal medicines range from allergic reactions to cardiovascular, hepatic, renal, neurological and dermatological toxic effects. Some of the examples are *Kaempferia galanga*, *Revernia spectabilis*, *Wedebra calendulacea*, *S.occidemtalis* etc.

Botanical Quality, Quality Control and Product Standards

Natural product quality, and herb quality in particular, has stood out as one of the most frequently cited critical issues. For as long as humans have been using medicinal plants, they have also been assessing the quality of these medicines. It is probably safe to assume that as soon as people began to trade in herbal medicines, detecting adulterations was an important aspect of these quality evaluations.

Standardisation of botanicals or active ingredients can solve a number of problems in herbal drug development. 'Standardisation refers to the information and controls necessary to produce material of reasonable consistency. This is achieved through minimising the inherent variation of natural product composition through quality assurance practices applied, to agricultural and manufacturing processes'. The purpose of standardisation includes:

- Batch-to-batch consistency
- Confirmation of the correct amount of extract per dosage unit
- Positive control to indicate possible loss or degradation during manufacturing

Some of the essential components for production of quality products include:

- High quality herbs
- Knowledgeable and experienced staff
- Proper formulation
- Excellent manufacturing process
- Adequate finished product testing throughout the intended shelf life

For the vast majority of botanicals, it is impossible to determine the potency using chemical analytical methods since the quantity of active principles can neither be conclusively identified nor measured. Even in the few cases where 'actives' have been identified, relevant biological activity assays are required to obtain meaningful measurements of potency.

Herbal Toxicity and Herb–Drug Interactions

Herbal remedies have been commonplace in various cultures throughout recorded history and still serve as the main means of therapeutic medical treatment in some countries. Some herbal products actually have the potential for significant adverse reactions. An allergic reaction calls for lowering the dose or stopping intake of the herb altogether. Taking larger-than-recommended dosages can cause side effects or be fatal in some cases. Patients/Consumers should also beware of interactions. Many herbal reference books neglect to mention these factors. Herbal therapies can interact with each other if taken in combination with certain foods, synthetic prescription and on-prescription drugs. One example of an interaction is wintergreen tea and aspirin, possibly leading to excessive anti-clotting action, and thus bleeding. Another example is St. John's wort and a synthetic mono amine oxidase (MAO) inhibitor for alleviating depression, leading to serotonin syndrome. It is commonly believed that all herbal medicines and natural substances used as remedies must be inherently safe. Brief references, however, to the toxicity of some plants show this to be a fallacy. Interactions with other drugs can also be harmful: 78 herbal products may react with heart medication, 58 with anti-coagulants, 35 with diabetic medication and 9 with oral contraceptives. Some products interfere with the accuracy of diagnostic tests and 64 drugs and food supplements require therapeutic monitoring, generally unavailable to non-medically qualified herbalists.

Some of the herbs are relatively harmless, but the highly reactive state of pregnancy and the fact that fetal growth is a template that can manifest pharmacokinetics should be considered.

Some of the well known herbs possess marked pharmacological activity, for example,

Teratogenic/Mutagenic activity – *Podophyllum, Baptisia*

Uterine Vasoconstrictors – *Arctostaphylos, Ephedra vulgaris, Ustilago, Vinca, Viscum album, Xanthium*
Uterine Vasodilators – *Actea rubra, Aloe (Aloes Socrotine, etc.), Angelica sinensis, Apocynum cannabinum, Aristolochia serpentaria, Aristolochia watsonii, Arnica (A. montana, A. cordifolia, A. latiflora, etc.), Artemisia absinthium, Artemisia tridentate, Artemisia vulgaris, Asclepias asperula, Asclepias tuberose, Cacalia decomposita Chamaelirium Chenopodium ambrosioides Cimicifuga racemosa, Corynanthe, Crocus, Daucus carota, Podophyllum, Polygala senega, Ruta graveolens, Xanthoxylum*
Cathartics/Sacral Irritants – *Aloe (Aloes Socrotine. etc.), Cassia marilandica (American Senna), Chenopodium ambrosioides, Podophyllum, Rhamnus californica Rhamnus Frangula, Rhamnus purshiana, Rheum, Senna (Cassia angustifolia,)*
Oxytocin Synergists – *Asclepias asperula, Capsella bursa-pastoris, Caulophyllum, Gossypium, Root Bark Leonurus cardiaca, Lophophora, Scoparius (Cytisus Scoparius,), Ustilago (Corn Smut)*
Drugs Present in Milk – *Acorus calamus (Calamus. Sweet Flag), Ailanthus altissima, Allium sativum (Garlic), Aloe (Aloes Socrotine, etc.), Aristolochia serpentaria, Aristolochia watsonii, Artemisia absinthium, Artemisia tridentate, Artemisia vulgaris, Cacalia decomposita, Cannabis sativa (Marijuana, Hemp), Cassia marilandica, Chenopodium ambrosioides, Commiphora (Myrrh Gum), Daucus carota (Carrot, Wild Carrot) Ginkgo biloba, Juniperus, Ligusticum porteri, Pilocarpus, Rheum, Sanguinaria, Senna (Cassia angustifolia), Ruta graveolens, Tanacetum, Xanthoxylum*
Sympathomimetics - *Aconitum carmichaeli, Acorus calamus- ASARONE, Caffea arabica (Coffee) caffeine, Corynanthe –yohimbine, Ephedra vulgaris -ephedrine Gelsemium, gelsemine lophophora mescaline, peganum harmala (syrian rue) harmines Paullinia (guarana) caffeine, hypoxanthines scoparius (cytisus scoparius, broom) cytisine, sparteine*
Parasympathomimetics - *Aesculus (all), Anemone hirsutissima, Apocynum cannabinum, Arnica (A. montana, A. cordifolia. A. latiflora. etc.) Asclepias asperula, Asclepias tuberose, Bryonia, Corynanthe (Pausinystalia Johimbe, Yohimbe) Euonymus, I. missouriensis, Leptandra (Veronicastrum) Lobelia inflata (Lobelia, Indian Tobacco), Pilocarpus (Jaborandi) Piscidia, Polygala senega (Senega Snakeroot) Sanguinaria, Solanum dulcamara, Spigelia, Veratrum*
Anticholinergic - *Datura, Garrya, Hyocyamus niger, Solanum dulcamar*
Vasopressomimetic - *Corynanthe, Lophophora, Tribulus terrestris*
Pituitary/Limbic 'Potentiating'- *Centella asiatica, Oplopanax horridum, Panax ginseng, Panax quinquefolium*
Thyroid Stimulating - *Aconitum carmichaeli, Centella asiatica, Corynanthe, Ephedra vulgaris.*
Thyroid Depressing - *Chlorophyllin, Leonurus cardiaca, Lycopus*
Aldosterone Synergists - *Glycyrrhiza glabra (Licorice) Marrubium*
Metabolic: 'anabolic' - *Angelica sinensis, Oplopanax horridum, Panax ginseng (Asian Ginseng), Panax quinquefolium (American Ginseng), Ptychopetalum, Smilax (Sarsaparilla).*
Anticoagulant - *Chrysanthemum parthenium (Feverfew), Ginkgo biloba, Leucanthemum (Chrysanthemum leucanthemum), Populus tremulioides.*
Cyanogenic Potential- *Amygdalis persica, Prunus species.*

Allergic/Atopic Potential - *Allium sativum (Garlic), Asafetida (Ferula asafetida, Devil's Dung), Aspidium (Male Fern) Caffea arabica (Coffee) Linum (Flaxseed), Panax ginseng (Asian Ginseng) Propolis (Beehive scrapings, gathered from trees), Solanum dulcamara.*

Hypo-Hyperglycemic (Reactive) - *Aconitum carmichaeli (CURED), Berberis (Barberry), Corynanthe (Pausinystalia Johimbe, Yohimbe), Mahonia (Oregon Grape, Berberis aquifolium) Peganum harmala (Syrian Rue).*

Cardioglycoside Potentiating - *Apocynum cannabinum, Asclepias asperula, Aspidosperma (Quebracho Bark), Convallaria, Scoparius, Veratrum.*

Bradycardic/Hypotensive - *Aconitum columbianum, Actea rubra, Anemone hirsutissima, Arnica (A. montana, A. cordifolia, A. latiflora. etc.) Asclepias asperula, Asclepias tuberose, Capsella bursa-pastoris, Cereus grandiflorus, Cimicifuga racemosa, Crataegus (Hawthorn), Lobelia inflate (Lobelia, Indian Tobacco), Pilocarpus (Jaborandi), Prunus (Wild Cherry, Choke Cherry) Veratrum (Green, False or American Hellebore), Vinca major (Periwinkle) Viscum album.*

Tachycardic - *Aconitum carmichaeli, Corynanthe, Ephedra vulgaris, Lophophora, Nicotiana, Panax ginseng, Scoparius.*

Hypertensive Potential - *Aconitum carmichaeli, Aspidosperma, Cinchona, Corynanthe (Pausinystalia Johimbe. Yohimbe) Ephedra vulgaris (Ma Huang, Chinese Ephedra), Glycyrrhiza glabra (Licorice), Nicotiana, Ptychopetalum, Scoparius*

Herbs Altering Liver Drug Metabolism - *Aristolochia serpentaria, Aristolochia watsonii, Artemisia tridentate, Berberis vulgaris Cephalanthus, Mahonia, Podophyllum.*

Herbs that can alter GI Absorption - *Aesculus (all) Aloe (Aloes Socrotine, etc.) Arctostaphylos, Capsicum, Chlorophyllin, Ephedra viridis, Frangula, Mirabilis multiflorum, Rhamnus californica, Rhamnus Frangula, Rhamnus purshiana, Senna*

Immunostimulants that can raise WBC Count - *Aristolochia serpentaria (Virginia Snakeroot), Aristolochia watsonii (Indian Root) Baptisia, Commiphora (Myrrh Gum) Guaiacum officinale, Polymnia uvedalia*

Hepatic: Herbs that may alter SGOT/SGPT Readings - *Silybum marianum*

Future Trends

Worldwide, there has been a resurgence in the use of traditional herbal drugs and, similarly, a growing interest in scientific investigations of their clinical efficacy and safety.

Table 26.2: Herb–Drug interactions

Name of the Herb	Name of the Drug	Uses of Herbs	Adverse Effects
CAYENNE (Capsicum spp.)	ASPIRIN ACE INHIBITOR *(Antihypertensive)* MANY DRUGS	• Herb protects against stomach irritation • Increases side effects • Reduces drug action • Increases bioavailability	• Excessive doses may be required for effect • Aggravates cough, may affect blood pressure • Cayenne enhances gut absorption

Name of the Herb	Name of the Drug	Uses of Herbs	Adverse Effects
EPHEDRA (Ma Huang)	CAFFEINE MAOI's *(Antidepressant, antihypertensive)* BETA BLOCKERS *(Anti-anginal, anti-arrhythmic)* EPHEDRINE *(Bronchodilator)* STEROIDS *(Anti - inflammatory)*	• Additive effect on neurotransmitter levels • Reduces drug performance • Additive effect increases drug toxicity • Increases steroid drug clearance	• Increases thermogenesis (metabolism) • Elevation of blood pressure (Ephedra alone can cause this) • May cause arrhythmias or BP elevation • May reduce steroid therapy effectiveness
GARLIC (Allium sativum)	WARFARIN *(Anticoagulant)* GENERAL ANESTHETIC	• Additive blood thinning effects • Blood thinning action of garlic	• Spontaneous bleeding • Advise prescribing physician • Risk of excess bleeding post operatively • Advise surgical team
GINGER (Zingiber officinale)	CHEMOTHERAPY GENERAL ANESTHETIC WARFARIN *(Anticoagulant)* MANY DRUGS	• Reduces side effects (nausea) • Herb reduces after effects of anesthesia • Synergy, possible increased coagulation • May increase drug bioavailability	• Probable, trials inconclusive • Nausea and vomiting reduced • Probable but studies inconclusive • Ginger increases gut absorption
GINKGO (Ginkgo biloba)	ASPIRIN WARFARIN *(Anticoagulant)* Acetaminphen caffeine & ergotamine GENERAL ANESTHETIC	• Increases anti-coagulation • Increases anti-coagulation • Unknown blood thinning action of herbs	• Spontaneous bleeding • Brain hemorrhage (intracerebral,subdural) • Risk of excess bleeding post operation • Advise surgical team pre-operatively
GINSENG (Panax ginseng)	WARFARIN *(Anticoagulant)* ALCOHOL INFLUENZA VACCINE INSULIN	• Potentiation • Increases alcohol clearance • Synergy, enhances resistance • Synergy, antidiabetic actions of herb	• Spontaneous bleeding • Stimulates alcohol metabolism • Reduces flu symptoms frequency & severity • Improves blood sugar and diabetes

Name of the Herb	Name of the Drug	Uses of Herbs	Adverse Effects
KAVA KAVA (Piper methysticum)	ALCOHOL BENZODIAZEPINES *(Sedative)* MAOI's *(Antidepressant, antihypertensive)* GENERAL ANESTHETICS	• May reduce alcohol toxicity • Possible additive effects	• One trial supports interaction • Combination not recommended • No clinical evidence
LICORICE ROOT (Glycyrrhiza glabra)	STEROIDS *(Anti - inflammatory)* ORAL CONTRACEPTIVES ASPIRIN ANTIBIOTICS	• Potentiates drug levels/activity • May increase side effects • Reduces drug-induced stomach bleeding • Drugs reduce herb activity	• Herb can help steroid drug withdrawal • May cause water retention and raise blood pressure • Licorice also helps heal gastric ulcer
	DIURETICS (loop/thiazide) DIGOXIN *(Cardiac glycoside)*	• Increased drug toxicity due to possible increased potassium loss	• Caution in cardiac cases & Digoxin for potassium loss toxicity • Herb needs gut flora for bioavailability
MILK THISTLE (Silybum marianum)	MANY DRUGS (Acetaminophen, alcohol etc.) CHEMOTHERAPY	• Herb reduces drug toxicity to liver • Herb reduces toxic side effects of chemo	• Herb increases liver detox capacity & protects liver from drug damage • Herb does not reduce anti-cancer action of cisplatin • Obtain qualified professional advice
	GENERAL ANESTHETICS CYCLOSPORINE *(Immunosuppressive)*	• Herb helps reduce liver toxicity of anesthetics • Herb reduces drug blood levels	• Take 3 weeks preoperatively • Advise surgical team • Potentially dangerous for transplant patients
ST JOHN' S WORT (Hypericum perforatum)	SSRI's *(Antidepressant)* BENZODIAZEPINES *(Sedative)* MAOI's *(Antidepressant, antihypertensive)*	• Potentiation drug effects • Herb reduces blood level drug, lowers drug effect • Herb reduces blood level drug, reduces drug effect	• No clinical evidence • Risk of transplant rejection. Notify prescribing physician • May cause arrhythmias. Notify prescribing physician

Name of the Herb	Name of the Drug	Uses of Herbs	Adverse Effects
ST JOHN' S WORT (Hypericum perforatum) (continued)	CYCLOSPORINE *(Immunosuppressive)* DIGOXIN *(Cardiac glycoside)* INDINAVIR *(Protease inhibitor)* MANY DRUGS (exact number & significance not known)	• Herb reduces blood level drug, reduces drug effect • Herb activates liver clearance, reduces drug levels or effects	• May cause failure of therapy in AIDS • Notify prescribing physician of SJW use
VALERIAN (Valeriana officinalis)	ALCOHOL BARBITURATES *(Anticonvulsant, sedative)* BENZODIAZEPINES *(Sedative)*	• Herb reduces drug hypnotic effects • Herb amplifies drug effects • Additive effect	• Clinical studies and lab studies conflict • No clinical studies • Interaction used to wean off drugs • Valerian/SJW combo more effective than diazepam
YOHIMBE (Pausinystalia yohimbine)	TRICYCLICS (TCA's) *(Antidepressant)*	• Hypertension risk increases	• Yohimbe may cause raised BP • Use with psychotropic drug not recommended

However, pursuing the goal of popularising the ancient Indian system of Ayurveda, which is primarily based on medicinal plants, by promoting and marketing classical Ayurvedic products and practices in the global markets is an uphill task. On the other hand, there is ample opportunity for developing products based on the proven therapeutic utility of medicinal plants used in Ayurvedic medicines and getting them approved as prescription drugs, over-the-counter (OTC) preparations or even as nutraceuticals. Pharmacognosy, with all of its tools and expertise, plays an integral role in this process, by ensuring the authenticity, purity and consistency of the materials being used and investigated.

Key Messages

- Despite modern scientific advances, approximately 60% of the world's population still relies on plants for medicines, and plants supply the active ingredients of most traditional medical products.
- The exploration of natural products for hidden therapeutic properties is at the forefront of the development of future drugs.

- Over 80% of the approximately 30,000 known natural products are of plant origin. The number of known chemical structures is estimated to be nearly four times greater than that of microbes.
- India has a rich and ancient history of traditional plant medicines, such as those used in Ayurveda, Siddha, Unani and Homeopathy.
- The rationalisation of new concepts and strategies requires scientific evidence. This enormous task, however, can be mastered only through concerted cooperation among phytochemists, molecular biologists, pharmacologists and clinicians.
- The common belief that 'anything natural is safe' is incorrect. A study to assess the bioactivity of commonly used herbal drugs is the need of the hour.
- Some herbal products may produce significant adverse reactions. An allergic reaction calls for lowering the dose or stopping intake of the herb altogether.

Questions

1. Define pharmacognosy, phytomedicines and herbal formulations.
2. Explain the significance of Nature as a source of drugs.
3. Narrate the history of pharmacognosy and phytotherapy.
4. Explain the traditional systems of medicines (Ayurveda, Siddha, Unani, Chinese)
5. Describe the research being carried out using medicinal plants.
6. Describe the steps to be followed to perform a literature search in phytopharmacology.
7. Describe the research challenges, hurdles, pitfalls and key issues of natural products.

27

Introduction to Isolation, Identification and Estimation of Lead Compounds from Natural Products

MUEEN AHMED KK

Learning Objectives

At the end of this chapter, you will be able to:

- List the different extraction methods for natural products
- Describe the basic techniques involved in the separation and isolation of phytoconstituents
- Explain the fundamentals of chromatography
- Describe the methods used to isolate active constituents from the crude extract
- Explain the fundamentals of high performance thin layer chromatography (HPTLC), nuclear magnetic resonance (NMR) and mass spectrophotometry

EXTRACTION OF HERBAL DRUGS

Extraction can be defined as the removal of soluble materials from an insoluble residue, either liquid or solid, by treatment with a liquid solvent. The different methods used to extract materials are as follows:

- Infusion
- Decoction
- Maceration
- Percolation

Infusion

The weighed quantity of drug is kept in contact with a known quantity of solvent for a specified period of time, and at the end of the period, the supernatant liquid is collected and poured into the receiver. Hence, the menstrum may be either cold or hot depending on the drug material. For example, fresh quassia infusion.

Decoction

This is not an official preparation in pharmacopeia. In this method, a known quantity of a drug is boiled with the menstrum for a specified period of time (15 minutes), at the end of which the supernatant liquid is collected. For example, coffee or tea decoction.

Maceration

It is defined as the phase in which the solid materials are mixed with the whole of the menstrum in a closed vessel and allowed to stand for 7 days, while being shaken occasionally. The marc (residue) is then strained and pressed, and the liquid obtained is mixed with the mother liquor and clarified by filtration. This method may be used for a number of purposes such as for preparing tinctures from organised drugs.

Percolation

Percolation is of three types:

- Percolation for tinctures
- Percolation for concentrated preparations
- Continuous hot percolation or soxhelation

The percolation process has three main stages:

1. *Imbibition*: The powdered drug is moistened with some of the menstrum and allowed to stand for 4 hours. During this time, the drug swells and the menstrum penetrates the cell walls.
2. *Maceration*: The moistened drug is left in contact with the menstrum for 24 hours. During this time, the menstrum is saturated with the soluble constituents of the drug.
3. *Percolation*: This consists of the downward displacement of the saturated solution formed from maceration and extraction of the remaining soluble matter by slow passage of the menstrum through the column of drug.

Liquid/Liquid Extraction

This method will be familiar from the purification procedures used in alkaloidal assays, and large-scale processes are based on similar principles. A solution of the substance that must be extracted is brought into contact with another solvent for the substance that is immiscible with the first solvent. A concentration gradient is set up between the phases and mass transfer occurs until equilibrium is established and the solute is distributed depending on the distribution coefficient.

Solid/Liquid Extraction

The extraction of a soluble constituent from a solid by means of a solvent is commonly referred to as leaching. The general term extraction is also frequently used. Certain operations involve the extraction of a soluble substance from an insoluble mineral material. However, this is subject to control by the usual factors affecting the solution and will not be considered further.

Extraction of Plant Materials (Fig. 27.1)

All plant materials used should be properly authenticated. The choice of extraction procedure depends on the nature of the plant material and the components to be isolated. Dried materials are usually powdered before extraction, whereas fresh plants (leaves, etc) can be homogenised or macerated with a solvent such as alcohol. The latter is also particularly useful for stabilising fresh leaves by dropping them in the boiling solvent.

Alcohol is a general solvent for many plant constituents (most fixed oils expected) and as such may cause problems in the subsequent elimination of pigments, resins, etc. Water and immiscible solvents are widely used. Light petroleum (essential and fixed oils, steroids) ether and chloroform (alkaloids, quinones) are also used. The extraction of organic bases,

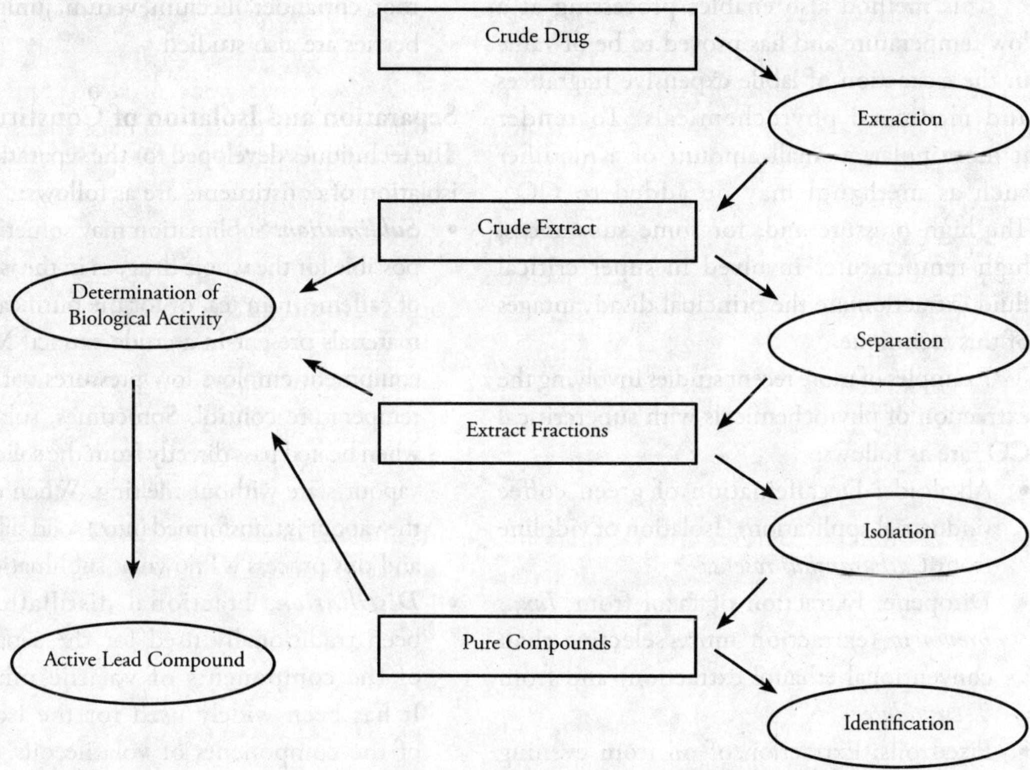

Figure 27.1: Steps involved in plant research

for example, alkaloids, usually necessitates basification of the plant material if a water immiscible solvent is to be used for aromatic acids and phenols acidification may be required.

Ultrasound may enhance the extraction process for some plant materials and the British Pharmacopeia uses this in the preparation of a 50% ethanolic solution of opium for the assay of alkaloids.

The general methods of plant extractions are now discussed.

Super Critical Fluid Extraction

Plants produce a flavouring odour that is of cosmetic interest. In 1822, Charles Cagniard de la Tour reported that above a certain temperature and pressure, single substances do not condense or evaporate but exist as fluids. Under these conditions, the gas and liquid phases possess the same density, and no division exists between the two phases. This is called the **critical state.**

For water, the critical conditions for temperature (tc) and pressure (pc) are 374 °C and 220 atm, respectively, and for carbon dioxide, tc = 31°C and pc = 74 atm. In practice, conditions somewhat above the critical temperature and pressure for a particular substance are usually used, and these super critical fluids exhibit properties intermediate between those of the liquid and gaseous phases.

This method also enables processing at a low temperature and has proved to be of value in the extraction of labile expensive fragrances and medicinal phytochemicals. To render it more polar, a small amount of a modifier such as methanol may be added to CO_2. The high pressure and, for some substances, high temperatures involved in super critical fluid extraction are the principal disadvantages of this technique.

Examples of more recent studies involving the extraction of phytochemicals with supercritical CO_2 are as follows:

- Alkaloids: Decaffeination of green coffee (industrial application). Isolation of vidoline from *Catharanthus roseus.*
- Ditopene: Extraction of taxol from *Taxus brevtocia* (extraction more selective than conventional ethanol extraction) and from *T. cuspidate.*
- Fixed oils: Extraction of oil from evening primrose (shift in triglyceride composition oxidation of γ-linolenic acid during extraction reduced).
- Pigments: Extraction of annatto seeds.
- Sesquiterpene lactones: In conjunction with gas chromatography (GC) for the isolation of parthenolide from fever few (extracts contain significant amounts of camphor and chrysanthenol acetate); addition of methanol or methyl cyanide as CO_2 modifiers produce higher yields but also co-extractives.
- Volatile oils and resins: Hops (commercial application), transkinase and myrrh piper nigram muntok (superior aroma of oil: yield 2.8% volatile oil compared with 0.6% steam distillation). Rose petals richer in relevant fragrance compounds (compared with steam distillation) rosemary, angelica root, coriander, illecium, verum, juniper and berries are also studied.

Separation and Isolation of Constituents

The techniques developed for the separation and isolation of constituents are as follows:

- ***Sublimation:*** Sublimation may sometimes be possible for the whole drug, as in the isolation of caffeine from tea, or for the purification of materials present in a crude extract. Modern equipment employs low pressures with strict temperature control. Sometimes, substances when heated pass directly from the solid to the vapour state without melting. When cooled, the vapour is transformed into a solid substance and this process is known as sublimation.
- ***Distillation:*** Fractional distillation has been traditionally used for the separation of the components of volatile mixtures. It has been widely used for the isolation of the components of volatile oils. Steam distillation is used to isolate volatile oils and hydrocyanic acid from plant materials.
- ***Fractional Liberation:*** Some groups of compounds present in plants lend themselves to fractional liberation from the mixture of compounds. For example, a mixture of alkaloid salts in aqueous solution treated with aliquots of alkali first produces the weakest base in the free state, followed by base liberation in the ascending order of basicity. If the mixture is shaken with an organic solvent after each addition, a fractionated series of tests will be obtained. A similar scheme can be used for organic acids soluble in water immiscible solvents; in this case, starting with a mixture of acid salts. It is possible to fractionally liberate the acids by adding mineral acids.

Extraction

The commonly employed technique for removing active substances from the crude drug is called **extraction.** The choice of plant material for extraction depends on its nature and the components to be isolated. The dried, powdered plant parts are homogenised and material is extracted with a solvent such as alcohol, which is a general solvent for many plant constituents. A water immiscible solvent such as light petroleum is used for the extraction of fixed and essential oils. Steroids and aglycons, chloroform and ether are used for separation of alkaloids and quinines. Water soluble compounds such as tannins and glycosides can be extracted by using methanol. Extraction may be performed by repeated maceration with agitation and percolation by continuous soxhlet extraction.

Fractional Crystallisation

This is one of the traditional isolation methods and is still used for the resolution of otherwise intractable mixtures. This method exploits the differences in solubility of the components of a mixture in particular solvent. Frequently, derivatives of particular constituents are employed (picrates of alkaloids, osazones of sugars).

Adsorption Chromatography

Of the various methods of separation and isolation of plant constituents, the chromatographic procedure developed by Tswett is one of the most useful techniques of general application.

The use of charcoal for decolourising and clarifying solutions is well-known. Coloured impurities are adsorbed by charcoal and a colourless solution results on filtration. The phenomenon of selective adsorption is the fundamental principle of chromatography, the general process of which may be described with reference to one of Tswett's original experiments.

A light petroleum extract of green leaves is allowed to percolate slowly through a column of powdered calcium carbonate contained in a vertical glass tube. The pigmented contents of the solution are adsorbed on the substance of the column and undergo separation as percolation proceeds. The more strongly adsorbed pigments xanthophylls and chlorophylls accumulate in distinct, characteristically coloured bands near the top of columns, while the less strongly adsorbed pigments accumulate lower down. Frequently, complete separation of all the constituents into distinct bands does not take place during the first adsorption stage. However, the bands remain crowded together near the top of the column. Such a column may be developed by allowing more of the pure solvent to percolate through the menstrum, when the adsorbed materials pass slowly downwards and the separate bands become wider.

In many cases, the process may be rendered more efficient by the use of a different solvent, one from which the substance is less strongly adsorbed. Light petroleum containing a little alcohol is percolated through the chromatogram obtained in the experiment described above. The bands become wider and pass down the column more rapidly than when pure light petroleum is used. As percolation continues, the lower bands reach the bottom of the column and disappear. The pigment is then obtained in the solution leaving the bottom of the column. This process of desorption is termed elution and the solution obtained is called the elute.

Substances are more rapidly adsorbed from

nonpolar solvents such as light petroleum and benzene while polar solvents alcohol, water and pyridine are useful eluting media. Many substances are adsorbed at one pH and eluted at another. Various substances may be used as adsorbing materials. Alumina is the most common adsorbing material and other materials include kaolin, MgO, $CaCO_3$, charcoal and sugar. Powdered sucrose was used by Tswett for separating chlorophylls A and B.

When colourless substances are chromatographed, the zones of adsorbed material are not visible to the eye although they may in some cases be rendered as fluorescent zones when the column is examined under ultraviolet (UV) light. Thus it becomes necessary to divide the chromatogram into discrete portions and elute an extract with each portion separately. Sometimes, it is more convenient to collect the elute from the whole column in fractions for individual examination.

The apparatus required comprises a vertical glass tube into which the adsorbent has been packed and a small plug of glass wool or a sintered glass disc at the base of the tube that supports the column. With volatile developing solvents, it is preferable to use positive pressure at the head of the column. Adsorption chromatography has proved particularly valuable in the isolation and purification of vitamins and hormones. Many alkaloids such as cardiac glycosides and anthraquinones were isolated by chromatographic methods with adsorbents such as silica and alumina.

Counter Current Extraction (CCE)

This is a liquid–liquid extraction process and the principles involved are similar to those of droplet counter current chromatography and partition chromatography. A lower stationary phase is combined in a series of tubes and the upper moving immiscible liquids are shaken and allowed to separate between each transference. The mixture to be fractionated is placed in the first tube containing the immiscible liquids, the apparatus is agitated and the layers are allowed to separate. The compounds of the mixture are distributed between the two layers according to their partition coefficient.

The upper phase is moved to the second tube containing the lower phase and more moving phases are brought into contact with the lower phase of the first tube. Shaking and transference again takes place and continues along a sufficient number of tubes to produce fractionation of the mixture. If a mixture of unit quantities of three substances A, B and C, whose partition coefficients between two immiscible liquids are 0.111, 1.0 and 9.0 respectively, is subjected to counter current extraction, the distributes for the first two transfers and first three mixings are as shown in Fig. 27.2. In this example, a small number of transfers would suffice to produce a good separation of the three compounds.

The distribution of each substance over a given number of tubes can be ascertained by the terms of the binomial expansion if, for the substance after an equilibrium, a fraction p appears in the upper phase and a fraction q, that is, (1-p), in the lower. Then, after three equilibriums, the distribution in the upper and the lower phases will be

pq2 2p2q3 p3
q3 2pq2 p2q

If the buffer solutions are used as the stationary phase, the differences in ionisation constants of various solutes are exploited. In some instances, the effectiveness of the

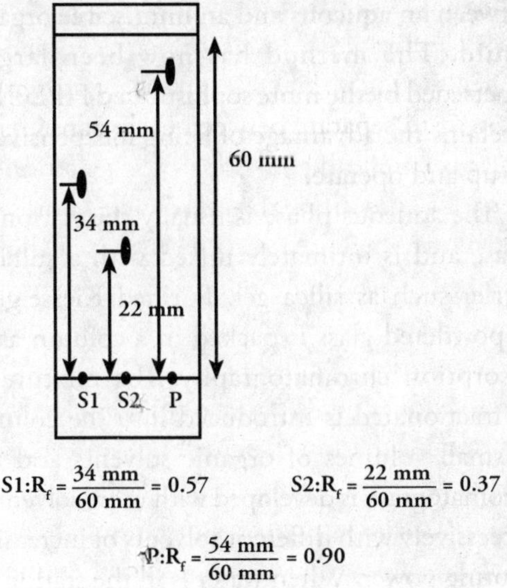

$S1{:}R_f = \frac{34\ mm}{60\ mm} = 0.57$ $S2{:}R_f = \frac{22\ mm}{60\ mm} = 0.37$

$P{:}R_f = \frac{54\ mm}{60\ mm} = 0.90$

Figure 27.2: Counter current extraction

separation can be improved by using a series of buffer solutions of acids and alkalis.

The larger machines have tubes of varying capacity, commonly consisting of 100 units, and are fully automatic. The mixture to be fractionated is fed continuously into the centre of the column and, according to the solvents, the solutes may move in either direction. This machine allows the concentration of minor components from a mixture and the continuous fractionation of mixtures.

Counter current extraction may be used in many fields of plant chemistry including alkaloids, aminoacids, antibiotics, phenols including anthraquinone derivatives, cardiac glycosides, essential oils, fatty acids, prostaglandins, steroids and vitamins.

Advantages

- Saponins do not produce troublesome foams, and unwanted oxidation changes are avoided.
- Little preliminary purification of the plant extract is required.
- The apparatus is simple to operate and clean.

Disadvantages

- Relatively long separation times—up to several days—during which the unstable compounds may decompose and produce a solution that does not compare with HPLC.
- This method has been used for the satisfactory separation of many groups of compounds including saponins, triterpenoid, spirostanol, cardioactive ginsenoside bupleureum or saiko saponins, iridoid, secoiridoid glycosides and polyphenols including anthraquinone glycosides, alkaloids and sugars.

High Speed Counter Current Chromatography (CCC) or Plane Oil Centrifuges

This is a method in which a spool wound with polytetraflouroethylene (PTFE) tubing is rotated at about 800 rpm in a planetary motion around a central axis. In such a system, heavier and lighter immiscible solvents move in different directions and one phase remains stationary while, the other passes through the column. Coils of tubing with an internal diameter of 1.6–2.6 mm and volumes of 300–380 ml have been used to good effect. Mixtures of the endoperoxides, arteminirin and artemistine, not separable by partition chromatography or fractional crystallisation, have been efficiently separated by this method as crude tannins and a commercial extract of *Ginko biloba.*

Droplet Counter Current Chromatography (DCCC)

This technique, first described by Tanimura and colleagues in 1970, is an extension of

CCE and utilises the passage of droplets of the mobile phase through an immiscible liquid to achieve fractionation. The stationary phase is held in two narrow bore columns. In practice, 200–600 internally silanised glass columns (1.5–2.0 mm internal diameter, 20–60 cm long) are connected in series by capillary Teflon tubes. The system, filled with a stationary phase and discrete droplets of a lighter mobile phase are pumped into the bottom end of the first column and then transported and introduced into the bottom of the next column through the capillary tubing. After the sample is inserted, the process continues by the flow of a more mobile solvent. The droplets that emerge from the end of the apparatus run in the opposite direction, with the mobile phase being introduced again droplet-wise at the head of each column.

Conditions that must be fulfilled for the satisfactory operation of the process include the retention of discrete droplets during their passage through the columns and the non-movement of the stationary phase into the capillaries. Critical after this are the internal bore of the columns and the correct choice of solvent systems.

Some of the solvents commonly used in CCE may cause problems. A few good solvents are $CHCl_3$/methanol/water and CH_2Cl_2/methanol/water.

Partition Chromatography

Partition chromatography was introduced by Martin and Synge in 1941 for the separation of acetylated amino acids. It was first applied for the separation of alkaloids by Evans and Partridge in 1948. The process used to separate the components of a mixture is the same as that of CCE. This method is dependent on differences in the partition coefficient of the components between an aqueous and an immiscible organic liquid. The method has now been largely superseded by the more sophisticated HPLC but it retains the advantage of being inexpensive to set up and operate.

The aqueous phase is usually the stationary phase and is intimately mixed with a suitable carrier such as silica gel. Purified Kieselguhr or powdered glass is packed in a column as in adsorption chromatography. The mixture to be fractionated is introduced into the column in small volumes of organic solvents and the chromatogram is developed with more solvent or successively with different solvents of increasing diluting power. When water is in the stationary phase, the solutes undergoing separation travel down the column at different speeds depending on the partition coefficient between the two liquid phases. The use of a buffer solution as an aqueous phase widens the scope of the technique as ionisation constants and partition coefficients are used to effect the separation.

The separated zones may be located by methods similar to those employed in adsorption chromatography, with water as the aqueous phase. The position of separated zones of acids or alkalis may be shown by employing a suitable indicator dissolved in water. This method is not clearly applicable to the buffer, acids, bases and loaded columns and in these cases, complete elution of the separated zones is necessary. The elute is collected in aqueous portions and estimated chemically or physically for the dissolved solute.

The fractions obtained in partition chromatography are influenced to a considerable degree by the displacement effect of one solute. Another advantage is in displacement development, in which the chromatogram is developed with a solution of acid or base that is stronger than any mixture to be separated. This results in the stronger acids or bases displacing the weaker ones, leading to the rapid cut separation of the constituents for the elution development of these separated zones. It is essential that there is no distortion of the zones.

Partition Chromatography on Paper

The solution of components to be separated is applied as a spot near one end of a prepared filter paper strip. The paper is then supported in an air-tight chamber that has an atmosphere saturated with solvent and water and a supply of the water-saturated solvent. The most satisfactory solvents are partially miscible with water, for example, phenols, n-butanol and amylalcohol. Either paper may be dipped in the solvent mixture so that the solvent front travels up the paper (ascending technique), or the trough of solvent may be supported at the top of the chamber, in which case the solvent travels down the paper (descending technique).

As the solvent moves, the components also move along the paper at varying rates, depending on the difference in the partition coefficient between the aqueous (hydration shell of cellulose fibres) and organic phases. After the filter paper strips have been dried, the positions of the separated components can be revealed by the use of suitable developing agents: ninhydrin solution for aminoacids, iodine solution or vapour or a modified Dragendroff reagent for alkaloids, ferric chloride solution for phenols, alkali for anthraquinone derivatives, antimony trichloride in chloroform for steroids and some components of volatile oils and aniline hydrogen phthalate reagent for sugars. The relative positions of the components and the size of the spots depend on the solvent and this should be selected to ensure good separation of the components with well-defined compact spots. Improved separation of mixtures can often be obtained by adjusting the acidity of the solvent with ammonia, acetic acid or HCl or by impregnating the paper with a buffer solution or a formamide solution.

For the separation of some substances, it may be necessary to use a two-dimensional chromatogram: first, one solvent is run in one direction, then, after drying the paper, a second solvent is run in a direction at right angles to the first. This is particularly applicable to mixtures of aminoacids. The ratio between the distance travelled on the paper by a component of the test solution and the distance travelled by the solvent is termed the RF value and, under standard conditions, this is a constant for the particular compound. However, in practice, variations of RF often occur, and it is desirable to run reference compounds alongside the unknown mixtures. The quantity of substance present determines the size of the spot with any one solvent and can be made the basis of quantitative evaluation. Also, the separated components of the original mixture can be separately eluted from the chromatogram by treating the cut out spots with a suitable solvent and then determined by some suitable method, for example, fluorescence analysis colourimetry or UV adsorption. Drugs evaluated in this way include aloes, digitalis, ergot, hemlock, lobellea, nux-vomice, opium, Rauwalfia, rhubarb, solanaceous herbs and volatile oils.

Thin Layer Chromatography (TLC)

In 1985, Stahl demonstrated the various applications of TLC. In outline, the method consists of preparing, on a suitable glass plate, a thin layer of material and the solvent which may be an adsorbent as used in column adsorption chromatography. The mixtures to be resolved are dissolved in a suitable solvent and placed as spots on the film towards one end of the plate; this end is then dipped in a suitable solvent mixture and the whole enclosed in an air-tight container. The solvent front travels up the film and, after a suitable time, the plate is removed. The solvent front is marked. The solvent is allowed to evaporate and the positions of the separated compounds are determined by suitable methods.

- *Tradionations* can effect more rapidly with smaller quantities of the mixture.
- The separated spots are usually more clearly demarcated from one another and the nature of the film is such that drastic agents, such as concentrated H_2SO_4 which would destroy a paper chromatogram, can be used.
- With adsorption TLC, various substances exhibit different adsorptive capacities and any one material may vary in its activity according to the pre-treatment.
- The method of detection does not place any restriction on the choice of eluent (solvent used in chromatography) which is easily inspected.
- Neutral, basic, acidic or purely aqueous eluents may be employed. The whole chromatographic system is flexible.
- TLC can be used for the investigation and cultivation of medicinal plants; it is possible to run many samples of extracts that have a different chemical nature simultaneously with authentic standards, and high performance individuals can be recognised, selected and bred.

High Performance Thin Layer Chromatography (HPTLC)

HPTLC is a major advancement of the TLC principle, requiring less time and producing better resolution. The basic difference between conventional TLC and HPTLC is in the particle and pore size of the sorbents. The use of smaller particles helps produce greater resolution and sensitivity. Solvent front migration of about 3–6 cm is sufficient for effecting proper separation. Whaman HPTLC plates are produced from 4–5 μm of silica gel with an inert binder to form a 200-μm layer. A development distance of about 7 cm is achieved in about 4 minutes.

Sample preparations in HPTLC require highly concentrated solutions, as only a small amount of the sample is applied. The size of the sample must not exceed 1 mm in diameter. Different techniques are used for the spotting of samples. One of them is self-loading capillaries, in which a small volume of the sample may be applied to the HPTLC plate surface using platinum iridium tubing fused into the end of a length of glass tubing. Contact spotting, pre-adsorbent or concentration zones, chemicals focussing and programmed multiple developments are the other methods of spotting samples.

The linear development method is the most familiar technique in HPTLC. Here, the plate is placed vertically in a solvent system in a suitable container. The solvent is usually fed by capillary action and chromatograms can be developed from both sides. Circular development, anti-circular device and multiple developments are some of the other methods used to develop plates.

The analytical profiles for cardenolides, tropane alkaloids, flavanoids, steroidal compounds, antracene glycosides and lipids have been developed using the HPTLC technique.

The TLC and HPTLC techniques are conveniently applied for the completion of profiles pertaining to a varied range of bioconstituents such as berberine, quinine and related alkaloids, opium alkaloids, coclchicine, chelidonine, sanguinarine, serpentine, raubasine, asarone, elemicin, eugenol, thymol, coumarin, pulegon sarsapogenin lanatosides digitoxigenin, purpurea glycoside A, flavones, diosgenin, silymarin, silybin, glycyrrhizin, robinin aesallitin, polygallic acid, ginsenosides, catechin, antraqunone derivatives, valtrate, rotenone, aristolchic acids, gebberlins antibiotics and number of other compounds of natural origin.

Gas Liquid Chromatography (GLC)

It was introduced by James and Martin in 1952, based on the suggestion of Martin and Synge. GC separates volatile substances by percolating a gas stream over a stationary phase. The basis of separation in GLC is partitioning of the sample in and out of the film of liquid spread over an inert solid. A wide range of liquid phases usable up to 450 °C exists. In pharmaceutical analysis, GLC is applied to three types of problems:

- Assay of the starting materials and drug substances
- Quantification of drugs in formulations
- Assay of impurities and/or solvents in raw materials or in drug substances

Applications

- Examination of many volatile oils, plant acids, alkaloids of opium, tobacco, conium and belladonna resins of cannaba steroidal compounds, cardioactive glycosides and aglycons, sugars and aminoacids, etc.
- The technique has strong separation power and even complex mixtures can be resolved into constituents.
- The sensitivity of the method is quite high. It is a micro method where only a few mg of the sample is sufficient for analysis.
- It gives good precision and accuracy.
- The analysis is completed in a short time.

Principle

When gas or vapour comes in contact with an adsorbent, a certain amount of it gets adsorbed on the solid surface. This phenomenon takes place according to the laws of Freundlich, that is,

$$x/m = K_1C+K_2C$$

where x is the mass of the gas or vapour sorbed in mass m or the sorbent, C is the vapour concentration in the gas phase and K, K_2 and K_1 are constants.

Instrumentation

GC separation is carried out in a tubular column made of glass metal or Teflon. In this column, a sorbent is filled as the stationary phase. The adsorbent is re-packed in the form of a fine, graded powder whereas the liquids are coated as fine film on the column wall over an inert, size-graded porous support such as fire brick powder followed by packing in the column.

A gas serving as the mobile phase flows continuously through the column. This is known as the carrier gas and it transports sample components in the column. The sample is introduced in the vapour form at the carrier gas entrance end of the column. Different components of the sample are sorbed on the stationary phase to different extents depending on their distribution coefficients. The portion of each component in the gas phase is swept further immediately by the carrier gas. As a result, a fraction of the sorbed amount also desorbs out to maintain the K-value. At the same time, out of the swept amount, some will go into the sorbent at the next point in the column to maintain the K-value. This goes on successively and continuously and as a whole, the band for each component moves further in the column and produces a more or less Gaussian distribution. It should be noted that the gas is the driving force for the movement of zones through the column and the solid provides the selective retarding force. The detector can be regarded as the brain of the chromatograph and the column as it heart.

High Performance Liquid Chromatography (HPLC)

In this method, the separations take place with a packed column. The material is the stationary phase and it may be a solid or a liquid coated over an inert material. A liquid mobile phase is used as eluent in HPLC. The mobile phase is forced through the column under high pressure either with autocratic elution or gradient elution.

It has become the most versatile, most dependable, safest, fastest and most sensitive chromatographic technique for the quality control of drug components. Drugs such as morphine, papaverine, codeine, emetine, antibiotics, steroids, ergot alkaloids, cardiac glycosides, sennosides, capsaicin, vitamins, rhubarb constituents, etc. are analysed by HPLC. Digoxin and gitoxin are analysed using reverse phase (RP) column 65% methanol. The reverse phase packing material (spherisorb ODS) is produced by the bonding of the ocladecylsilyl groups ($C_{18}H_{37}Si$) to the silica gel.

To reduce the tailing effects that may be caused by the remaining free hydroxyl groups, the latter can be masked by treatment with a short chain silane. Usually, trimethylchlorosilane silica-based columns are restricted to use in the pH range of 3–8 and to overcome this, polymers phase operation at pH 1–13.

Column Chromatography

This is a type of liquid chromatography in which the mobile phase in the form of liquid passes through (over) the stationary phase packed in a column. Column chromatography has been derivatised into other forms such as gel permeation, ion exchange and column partition (affinity).

In column chromatography, a fairly large number of adsorbents such as starch $CaCO_3$, magnesia lime, silica gel, alumina and charcoal are used. To optimise the resolution, the various mobile phases used whether singly or in combination, are petroleum ether, cyclohexane, chloroform, acetone, water, pyridine and organic acids. For better separation, it is essential to consider the polarity of the sample, adsorbent and the mobile phase.

Gel Permeation Chromatography (Gel Filtration, Molecular Sieves)

This is also called size exclusion chromatography. Separation occurs not on the basis of adsorption of partition but on the effective size of solutes present in the solution. For separation purposes, the stationary phases used are cross-linked polymers that produce an open network with a large number of pores of fairly uniform size during the flow of the mobile phase through the stationary phase.

Very large molecules cannot enter the pores

and hence are 'excluded' and continue to travel further along with the mobile phase but small molecules enter freely into different pores and hence find a longer path through the column. During the elution, the largest molecules in the mobile phase elute first followed by the molecules in decreasing order of size. This phenomenon is observed because the extent to which the molecules are retained depends on the size of the included molecules relative to the size of the pores.

The various types of gels used as stationary phases are soft, semi-rigid or rigid. Soft gels such as Agarose (sepharose), Dextran (sephadex) and polyacrylamide (bio-gel) are used.

Examples of semi-rigid and rigid gels are alkylated dextran, polystyrene and glass beads.

Soft gels are used with primarily aqueous mobile phases and this process is called gel filtration. If the other gels mentioned are used along with a non-aqueous mobile phase such as acetone, pyridine and chloroform, the process is called gel permeation. Gel filtration is used to separate large biomolecules such as proteins and polypeptides.

Chromatography – A Separation Tool in Natural Products: A Practical Approach

A sample that requires analysis is often a mixture of many components in a complex matrix. For samples containing unknown compounds, the components must be separated from each other so that each individual component can be identified by other analytical methods.

The different separation procedures used are as follows:

- Chromatography
- Centrifugation
- Crystallisation
- Distillation
- Extraction
- Electrophoresis
- Ultrafiltration

1. Chromatography

Chromatography is one of the best separation methods. It uses the differences in the partitioning and adsorption co-efficient between a flowing mobile phase and a stationary phase to separate the components in a mixture. Chromatography encompasses a range of techniques in which mixtures of compounds present in natural products are separated into individual constituents by using a mobile phase (usually a liquid or gas) to push the mixture along a stationary phase (usually a solid or liquid coated on a solid). Because, the individual substances have different molecular structures, they interact differently with both the stationary and mobile phases, and consequently are 'pushed' at different rates by the mobile phase.

In other words, chromatography is a technique that can be used to separate and identify a wide range of compounds found in higher plants. The separation of the components of a mixture is a function of their different affinities for a stationary phase, such as a solid, and their differential affinity for a mobile phase, such as a liquid or gas. The separation of compounds is controlled by their tendency to associate with the mobile (usually hydrophobic) liquid phase or to adsorb onto the solid (usually hydrophilic) surface. The solid phase is often made up of paper (cellulose), starch or silica gel.

A number of chromatographic techniques are summarised below.

Specific Chromatographic Methods

Thin Layer Chromatography (TLC) is a simple and rapid method used to identify the mixture or check the purity of natural products. The mobile phase is a solvent and the stationary phase is a solid adsorbent on a flat support.

High Performance Liquid Chromatography (HPLC) is a variation of liquid chromatography that utilises high pressure pumps to increase the efficiency of the separation.

Gas Chromatography (GC) is used to identify volatile oils/compounds. The mobile phase is a gas and the stationary phase is usually a liquid on a solid support or a solid adsorbent.

Liquid Chromatography (LC) is used to separate compounds in a crude extract. The mobile phase is a solvent and the stationary phase is a liquid on a solid support, a solid or an ion-exchange resin.

Size-exclusion Chromatography (SEC), also called gel permeation chromatography (GPC), is a technique in which the mobile phase is a solvent and the stationary phase is a packing of porous particles (sephedex gel).

Introduction to TLC

TLC is a simple and inexpensive technique used to identify the number of compounds present in a crude extract. In this technique, a small quantity of the extract to be analysed is placed as a small spot on a TLC plate, which consists of a thin layer of silica gel (SiO_2) or alumina (Al_2O_3) coated on a glass or plastic sheet. The plate is then placed in a TLC chamber containing a suitable solvent, which is the mobile phase. The solvent gradually moves up the plate by capillary action and separates the compounds. The compounds are moved to different distances up the plate by the solvent. The components then appear as a series of spots at different locations on the plate.

Substances can be identified by calculating R_f values. The R_f value of a substance is the ratio of the distance that the substance moves, to the distance that the solvent moves up the plate; it is also known as the solvent front. For example, an R_f value of 0.5 means that the spot corresponding to the substance travels exactly half as far as the solvent travels along the plate.

Preparation of TLC Plates

Stationary Phase

In the stationary phase, a special, finely ground matrix (silica gel, alumina or similar material) is coated on a glass plate, metal or plastic film as a thin layer (~0.25 mm). In addition, a binder such as gypsum is mixed into the stationary phase to make it stick better to the slide. In many cases, a fluorescent powder is mixed into the stationary phase to simplify the visualisation later on (for example, bright green when it is exposed to 254 nm UV light).

- **Silica Gel GF254**
  1. Weigh 25 g of Merck silica gel GF254 powder and suspend in 50 ml of de-ionised water.
  2. Shake vigorously for 45 seconds in an Erlenmeyer flask (with a rubber-stopper) of about 500 ml volume.
  3. Pour the thickened slurry into the trough of the spreader.
  4. Pull the spreader with a 0.25 mm trailing edge to prepare 21.5 x 20 cm plates.
  5. Allow the plates to air-dry (until they turn white) for about 30–45 minutes.

6. Activate the plates by heating in an oven at 120 °C for 30 minutes prior to use. Such plates are approximately Activity Grade II.

Readymade precoated plates provide better results. However, they remain costly.

- **Aluminium oxide GF254**
  1. Weigh 40 g of aluminum oxide GF254 Merck and suspend the powder in 65 ml of tap de-ionised water.
- **Other sorbents**
  - Aluminium oxide 60, 150
  - Cellulose
  - PEI-Cellulose
  - LiChrospher® Si 60
  - LiChrospher® RP-18
  - Silica gel 40, 60
  - Silica gel 60 caffeine impregnated
  - Silica gel 60 silanised (RP-2)
  - Silica gel 60/Kieselguhr
  - Kieselguhr

Preparative TLC Plates

To separate the compounds in bulk quantity, preparative TLC plates are used. To prepare 1.0 mm preparative layers, silica gel and alumina are mixed with a suitable solvent. This is then poured and the preparative layer prepared by pulling the spreader. The plates are allowed to stand for several hours at room temperature and are then activated at 120 °C in a hot air oven.

The TLC plate should not be disturbed. To obtain a baseline, make two marks on each side by using a sharp needle on the TLC plate. Draw a thin line with a pencil. The start line should be 0.5–1 cm from the bottom of the plate.

Capillary Spotters

Place a melting point capillary in the dark blue part of the Bunsen burner flame. Hold it there until it softens and starts to sag. Quickly remove the capillary from the flame and pull on both ends till it is about 2–3 times its original length. Allow the capillary to cool down, and then break it in the middle. Make sure that you break off the closed end on one of them.

Spotting the Plate

The thin end of the spotter is placed in the dilute solution; the solution will rise up in the capillary (capillary forces). Allow the solvent to evaporate and spot at the same place again. This way a concentrated and small spot can be obtained. Try to avoid spotting too much of the sample as this will result in a deterioration of the quality of the separation ('tailing'). The spots should be far enough away from the edges and from each other as well. If possible, spot the compound or a mixture together with the starting materials and possible intermediates on the plate.

Developing a Plate

A TLC plate can be developed in a beaker or a TLC chamber.

1. Place a small amount of solvent (mobile phase) in the container. The solvent level has to be below the baseline marked on the TLC, otherwise the samples spotted on the baseline will dissolve.
2. Dip the lower edge of the plate in a solvent. The solvent (eluent) travels up the matrix by capillarity, moving the components of the samples at various rates because of their different degrees of interaction with the stationary phase and solubility in the developing solvent. Nonpolar solvents will force nonpolar compounds to the top of the plate, because the compounds dissolve well

and do not interact with the polar stationary phase.
3. Allow the solvent to travel up the plate until ~1 cm from the top.
4. Take the plate out and mark the solvent front immediately. Do not allow the solvent to run over the edge of the plate.
5. Allow the solvent to evaporate completely.

Visualisation

Visualisation is used to identify the colourless separated compounds. Identification of compounds can be done by:

- Chromatographic properties
- Physical properties
- Chemical properties
- Biological properties

Various techniques are used to visualise the compounds:

- Physical method
- Chemical method
- Microbiological method
- Enzymatical method

Physical Method

Non-destructive methods such as absorption of light (UV, VIS, IR) and emission of radiation (fluorescence, radioactivity) can be used.

Chemical Method

A simple chemical reagent can be sprayed to identify the colourless compounds as coloured complex compounds. Pre- or post-chromatographic derivatisation of compounds also yields coloured, fluorescent or UV-active derivatives.

Derivatisation of compounds that are not visible without absorption of UV or VIS light improves the sensitivity (lower detection limits), specificity and/or selectivity and also improves substance stability.

The techniques of derivatisation reagents are as follows:

- Spraying (manual or instrumental)
- Dipping (manual or instrumental)
- Reagent in eluent
- Reagent in sorbent
- Application by overspotting
- Application through gas phase

Examples such as ninhydrin (nitrogen-containing compounds) and 2,4-Dinitrophenylhydrazine (aldehydes, ketones) are used.

Reagents Used in Visualisation of Spots

Various chemical reagents can be used to visualise TLCs:

- Sulfuric acid reagent/heat: Destructive, leaves charred blots behind.
- Ceric stain: Destructive, leaves a dark blue blot behind for polar compounds.
- Iodine vapours: Semi-destructive, iodine absorbs onto the spots, not permanent. The plate can be stained with iodine. This can be achieved rapidly by shaking the plate in a bottle containing silica and a few crystals of iodine. The iodine will stain any compound that reacts with it and so is especially good for visualising unsaturated compounds. Most spots show up within a few seconds, but the stain is not usually permanent.
- UV light: Non-destructive, long wavelength (background green, spots dark), short wavelength (plate dark, compounds glow).

Circle the spots on the TLC plate to have a permanent record of the compounds separated on the plate. Also draw a sketch of the developed plate by placing a tracing sheet on the TLC plate.

Analysis

The components, visible as separated spots, are identified by comparing the distances travelled with those of the known reference compounds. Measure the distance of the baseline to the solvent front (= d). Then measure the distance from the centre of the spot to the start line (= a). Divide the distance the solvent moved by the distance the individual spot moved. The resulting ratio is called the R_f-value. This value should be between 0.0 (spot did not move from the starting line) and 1.0 (spot moved with solvent front).

The R_f (= retardation factor) depends on the following parameters:

- Solvent system
- Absorbent (grain size, water content, thickness)
- Amount of material spotted
- Temperature

p-Anisaldehyde Reagent

Preparation: Anisaldehyde (15 g) in ethanol (250 ml) + concentrated sulfuric acid (2.5 ml). Good general reagent, gives a range of colours.

p-Anisaldehyde (Modified) Reagent

Preparation: Anisaldehyde:$HClO_4$:acetone:water (1:10:20:80). Spray plates and heat with heat gun until spots appear. For example, terpenes, cineoles, withanolides, acronycine, etc.

Bromocresol Green

Preparation: 0.3% in 1:4 water-methanol. Add 8 drops of 30% NaOH/100 mL carboxylic acids; stain yellow-green on a blue background.

For compounds containing carboxylic acids as functional groups.

Ceric Ammonium Sulfate Spray

Preparation: 1% cerium (IV) ammonium sulfate (CAS) in 50% phosphoric acid. For example, vinca alkaloids.

Ceric Sulfate Reagent

Preparation: 15% aqueous sulfuric acid saturated with ceric sulfate. It gives a range of colours with different compounds.

Distilled Water Spray

Spots turn translucent or opaque while background of plates turns clear.

DNP (Dinitrophenyl hydrazine) Reagent

Preparation: 2, 4-dinitrophenylhydrazine (12 g) + concentrated sulfuric acid (60 ml) + water (80 ml) + ethanol (200 ml). Mainly for aldehydes and ketones, gives orange spots.

Dragendorff Reagent

Preparation: Solution A: 1.7 g basic bismuth nitrate in 100 ml water/acetic acid (4:1). Solution B: 40 g potassium iodide in 100 ml of water. Mix reagents together as follows: 5 ml A + 5 ml B + 20 ml acetic acid + 70 ml water. Spray plates, orange spots develop. Spots intensify if sprayed later with HCl, or 50% water-phosphoric acid. It is ideal reagent for alkaloids.

Ferric Chloride Spray

Preparation: 1% Ferric (III) chloride in methanol/water (1:1). Good for phenols.

Ninhydrin Reagent

Preparation: 200 mg ninhydrin, 95 ml butanol and 5 ml 10% AcOH. Aminoacids.

PDAB-NaNO$_2$ Reagent - Ehrlichs, Van Urks Reagent

Preparation: Solution A: 0.1%p-dimethylamino-benzaldehyde (PDAB) in conc. HCl.

Solution B: 0.1% $NaNO_2$ (nitrite) in water. Spray plates with PDAB (solution A), then warm using a heat gun and finally spray with $NaNO_2$.

Indole alkaloids give blue colours if the 2nd position of the indole ring is not substituted.

Potassium Permanganate Solution

Preparation: Potassium permanganate (3 g) + potassium carbonate (20 g) + 5% aqueous, NaOH (5 ml) + water (300 ml). Mainly for unsaturated compounds and alcohols, gives yellow spots.

PMA (Phosphomolybdic Acid)

Preparation: Phosphomolybdic acid (12 g) in ethanol (250 ml). General reagent, gives blue-green spots.

Sulfanilic Acid Reagent (Diazotized), Pauly's Reagent

Preparation: Solution A: 0.5% sulfanilic acid in 2% HCl; Solution B: 0.5% $NaNO_2$ (nitrite) in water; Solution C: 0.5% NaOH in 50% ethanol. To prepare, mix equal volumes of A and B and spray TLC plates. Warm the sprayed plate in an oven if necessary. Spray plates with solution C. Phenolic compounds turn orange or yellow with this reagent.

Sulfuric Acid

Preparation: 5% sulfuric acid in methanol. This reagent is usually sprayed on the TLC and is ideal for compounds that are organic in nature.

Vanillin reagent

Preparation: Vanillin (15 g) in ethanol (250 ml) + concentrated sulfuric acid (2.5 ml). Good general reagent, gives a range of colours for different compounds.

FeCl$_3$ Reagent

Saturated solution of ferric chloride reagent gives bluish-black colour with tannins and phenolic compounds.

Other reagents include

- Ceric ammonium nitrate
- Vanadium oxinate
- Silver iodine
- Formaldehyde–Phosphoric Acid
- Alizarine
- Ferric chloride–Potassium ferrocyanide
- Vanillin–KOH
- p-nitrophenyl diazonium fluoroborate
- p-aminobenzoic acid
- 2,3,5-triphenyltetrazolium
- p-anisidine–phthalic acid
- Naphthoresorcinol
- Cupric acetate–Potassium ferrocyanide
- Sodium nitroprussiate–Sodium hydroxide
- Ferric hydroxamate
- Antimonium chloride solution
- Libermann–Burchard's reagent
- Ammonia solution
- Ferric chloride solution
- Benedict's reagent
- Cobal chloride reagent
- Lead tetracetate solution
- N,N-dimethyl-p-phenyldiamine solution
- Ferrous sulfocyanate solution
- Diphenylamine–Zinc chloride
- 3,5-dinitrobenzoic Acid
- Kedde's reagent
- Magnesium acetate

Factors affectingTLC

- Stationary phase
- Mobile phase
- Type of chamber
- Preloading with solvents (conditioning)
- Relative humidity
- Activity of the stationary phase
- Saturation of chamber and layers with eluent vapours
- Particle size and distribution of the sorbent
- Extension of the start zone
- Distance between start zone and level of eluent in the chamber
- Gradient formation
- Quality fluctuations of the layer
- Velocity of the mobile phase
- Size of the Rf value
- Temperature
- Volume of the sample
- Binder in stationary phase
- Deviations of the layer thickness
- Production mode of the stationary phase
- Layer thickness
- Convection currents in the vapour space of the separation chamber
- Kind of development
- Impurities in the eluent
- Migration distance
- pH value of the layer
- Solvent for the sample

Separation of Plant Pigments by Thin Layer Chromatography (TLC) (Fig. 27.3)

Chemicals and materials:

- Solvents
- Fresh/Dried crude drug

Apparatus and glass wares:

- Rotary evaporator
- TLC chamber 22 × 22 × 10
- TLC silica gel plate (Kieselgel 60 / Kieselgur F254, Merck)
- Paint brush
- Mortar and pestle
- Separating funnel 100 mL
- Measuring cylinder 100 mL
- 5 measuring cylinders 25 mL
- Erlenmeyer flask 100 mL
- Round-bottomed flask 100 mL

Preparation

Developing the solvent (mobile phase):

The solvent, previously established with TLC, or a combination of different solvents such as petrol ether, acetone and distilled water may be used. Different solvent mixtures based on their polarity indices can also be established for use in compounds of unknown nature.

Solvents used in TLC

Different solvents with an increasing degree of polarity are used in liquid–solid or adsorption chromatography. The solvents listed in elutropic series are selected:

- n-hexane
- Cyclohexene
- Toluene
- Benzene
- Diethylether
- Chloroform
- Dichloromethane
- 1,2-dichloroethane
- Acetone
- Etlylacetate
- Acetonitrile
- Propanol
- Ethanol
- Methanol
- Acetic acid
- Water

Increasing polarity ↓

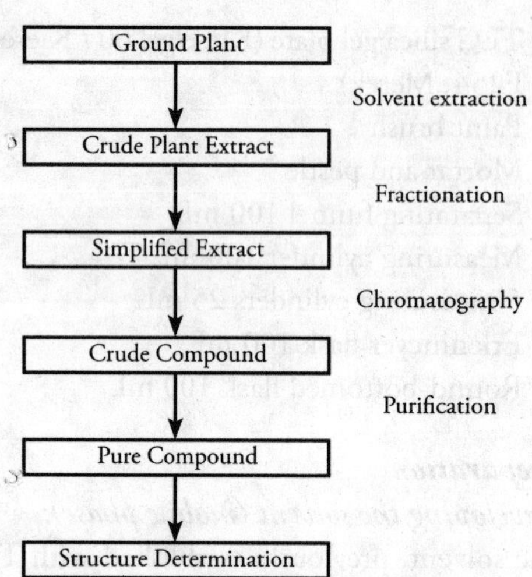

Figure 27.3: Steps involved in determining the structure of compounds

Preparation of the TLC chamber

The developing solvent is placed into a TLC chamber. The solvent should completely cover the bottom of the chamber to a depth of approximately 0.5 cm. The chamber is closed and shaken to saturate it completely. It is kept covered so that evaporation does not change the composition of the solvent. After 15 minutes, the chamber will be saturated with the solvent vapour.

Extraction of the phytoconstituents

Using a pestle/grinder, grind fresh/dried leaves or any other part of the plant in a mortar containing solvents. Filter the extract. Place the filtrate into a separating funnel and mix with petrol ether/$CHCl_3$ along with Na_2SO_4. Shake the separating funnel carefully. When the layers have separated, allow the lower layer to drain into a beaker and throw away the phase. Wash the upper layer 3-4 times with 5 mL of distilled water. Afterwards, place the extract in an Erlenmeyer flask and dry with about 4 spatula tips of Na_2SO_4. Decant the liquid carefully into a round-bottomed flask. Using a rotary evaporator, concentrate the crude extract to a final volume of about 3 mL.

Application of the extract to the TLC plate

1. With a pencil, draw a line approximately 1.5 cm from the bottom of the plate. The coating of the plate should not be scraped.
2. Using a capillary or a Pasteur pipette, apply the extract as a band on the TLC plate.
3. Repeat the procedure until the line is dark green.
4. Allow the transferred extract to dry thoroughly after each addition. The line is kept as thin and straight as possible.

Experimental procedure

1. Carefully place the loaded TLC plate in the TLC chamber with the sample line towards the bottom.
2. Keep the plate intact with the solvent with an angle of 45° (solvent surface must be below the extract line).
3. Cover the TLC chamber.
4. Allow the TLC plate to remain undisturbed for two hours.
5. When the solvent front has reached three-quarters of the length of the plate, remove the plate from the developing chamber and mark the position of the solvent front immediately.

As the solvent rises by capillary action up through the TLC plate, the components of the extract are partitioned/adsorbed between the mobile phase (solvent) and the stationary phase (silica gel) due to their different adsorption and solubility strengths. The more strongly a given component is adsorbed to the stationary phase, the less easily it is removed by the mobile phase. The more weakly a component is adsorbed, the faster it will migrate up the TLC plate. On the other hand, the running distance depends on the solubility of the pigment in the solvent.

Examples – TLC of Natural Products

TLC method for analysis of flavonoid glycones in plant exudates

Sample: Air-dried (but not ground) plants (2 g) were rinsed with 20 mL acetone for 2 minutes. After evaporation of the acetone, the dry extracts were dissolved in 250 µL methanol.

Stationary Phase: Silica gel GF 254

Mobile Phase: Toluene–dioxane–acetic acid, 95:25:4

The fluorescence emission of apigenin (R_F = 0.34) and quercetin (R_F = 0.37) was recorded under UV radiation at 336 nm.

Analysis of glycosides

Sample: The dried leaves are soaked in distilled water for a night. 20 mL from each sample is applied to the plate.

Mobile Phase: The samples are developed in ethyl-acetate–methanol–water (75:10:7,5).

After the treatment at 120 °C for 10 minutes, the plate is observed at 366 nm UV light. The samples are compared based on the standards. At 366 nm UV light, digitoxin fluoresced yellow, gitoxin light blue and digoxin purple.

Analysis of flavanoids

Sample: Sample and standard solutions (10 µL), the plates are developed.

Stationary Phase: TLC performed on 20 x 20 cm TLC plates coated with 0.25 mm layers of silica gel 60 F254.

Mobile Phase: Two chromatography solvents are used:

- Ethyl acetate/formic acid/acetic acid/water, 100:11:11:26 (V/V)
- Ethyl acetate/formic acid/water, 8:1:1 (V/V)

Phenolic acids are visualised by spraying the sheets with natural products–polyethylene glycol reagent (NP/PEG), which results in typical intense fluorescence in UV light at 365 nm. On spraying, flavonoids appear as orange-yellow bands, whereas phenolic acids form blue fluorescent zones.

Analysis of Carbohydrates

Stationary Phase: Silica gel 60 plates (5.0 x 5.0 cm; 0.2 mm thickness) are spotted with 5 µL of the carbohydrate at a position of approximately 5 mm above one edge of the plate.

Elutions of the plate (in two-dimensions) are carried out in an appropriate TLC chamber, pre-equilibrated with solvent.

Mobile Phase: n-butanol:formic acid:water (4:6:1); ethyl acetate:methanol:acetic acid (8:2:0.2); 2-propanol:water (8:2); 95% ethanol; ethyl acetate: methanol: water: acetic acid (7:1:1:1).

Detection of the resulting bands can be made using an ultraviolet light source with excitation at 365 nm (long-wavelength). Comparison of the resultant bands with those obtained from standards, produced under the same conditions and developed on the same plate, will enable identification of the unknown carbohydrates.

Solvent Systems Used for TLC of Some Natural Compounds

1) Steroids:

a. Benzene or benzene-ethyl acetate (9:1 or 8:2)

b. Chloroform-ethanol (96:4), alumina
c. Ethyl acetate-cyclohexane (x:y)
d. Benzene-isopropanol
e. Methanol-water (95:5)
f. Cyclohexane-heptane (1:1)
g. Cyclohexane-ethyl acetate (9:1)
h. Benzene-chloroform (9:1)
i. Benzene-methanol

2) Terpenoids:
a. Hexane or hexane-ethyl acetate (85:15)
b. Benzene or benzene-petroleum ether or benzene-ethanol
c. Isopropylic ether or isopropylic ether-acetone (5:2 or 19:1)

3) Essential Oils:
a. Benzene-chloroform
b. Petroleum ether

4) Cardenolids:
a. Chloroform-pyridine (6:1)

5) Fat Acids:
a. Petroleum ether-isopropylic ether-acetic acid (70:30:1)
b. Chloroform-petroleum ether

6) Vitamins:
a. Methanol-carbon tetrachloride-xylene, chloroform (alumina)
b. Chloroform-petroleum ether
c. Methanol, propanol or chloroform
d. Acetone-hexane (9:1)

7) Alkaloids:
a. Chloroform or ethanol or hexane-chloroform (3:7) + 0.05% diethylamine (alumina)
b. Benzene-ethanol (9:1)
c. Chloroform-acetone-diethylamine (5:4:1)

8) Flavonoids and Coumarins:
a. Petroleum ether-ethyl acetate (2:1)
b. Methanol-water (8:2 or 6:4) (polycaprolactam)
c. Toluene-ethyl formate-formic acid (5:4:1)

Column Chromatography

Column chromatography (CC) is an extremely valuable technique used for the purification of synthetic or natural products. Compounds are separated by CC through the same mechanism as in TLC: by distribution between two phases, one of which is stationary and one of which is moving. A variety of adsorbents can be used as the stationary phase; silica gel (which is very polar) is most commonly used in natural product chemistry.

Factors Affecting the Success of Column Chromatography

- Choice of adsorbent (silica gel or alumina are most common); activity grade (amount of water); pH
- Size of the column (height and diameter)
- Amount of adsorbent versus sample
- Packing of adsorbent (even, free of gaps or air bubbles)
- Polarity of the solvent
- Elution rate neither too fast (no separation) nor too slow (diffusion)

General Steps in Column Chromatography

1. Preparation of column
2. Development of column
3. Construction of column
4. Loading of column
5. Eluting of column
6. Collection of fractions
7. Analysis of fractions

1. Preparation of column

Efficiency of separation depends on how the column is prepared and the sample applied. A glass column is uniformly packed with slurry of silica gel in the mobile phase solvent system; it must contain no holes or bubbles and the surface must be even. The sample (dissolved in the mobile phase) is gently applied with a pipette as a concentrated band to the top of the column (after the mobile phase has been drained until the top is free of liquid).

2. Development of column

The mobile phase is applied to the top of the column, again taking care not to disturb the top. The column is developed by allowing the mobile phase to pass through the column at a flow rate of 1–3 mL/minute. As compounds of interest elute through the column, they are collected in test tubes for TLC analysis. Fractions containing pure compounds are combined and concentrated for HPLC analysis.

3. Construction of column

Add a few mL of selected solvent system to the column and mix SiO_2 gel in a beaker to form a slurry. Quickly pour this into your column, lightly tapping the side of the column to pack the SiO_2 gel. Use less than 1–2 mL of solvent to rinse excess silica from the sides of the beaker and column. Once the SiO_2 gel has settled, open the stopcock and allow excess solvent to elute into a 50 mL Erlenmeyer flask until the top of the silica bed is almost dry, then close the stopcock.

4. Loading of column

With a glass pipette, carefully apply 1 mL of the sample solution to the top of the column. Open the stopcock and allow the sample to flow into the column, then close the stopcock. Rinse the sample remaining on the sides of the column down with ~1–2 mL of the solvent used. Further, open the stopcock and allow the solvent to flow into the column. Close the stopcock and add another 2 mL of solvent. Finally, open the stopcock, and allow ~1 mL to elute into the column. Close the stopcock.

5. Eluting of column and collection of fractions

Carefully add 10 mL of the second solvent system (for example, ethyl acetate) to the top of the column. Begin collecting the 4 x 2 mL fractions in the test tubes. When this second solvent system has eluted to ~1 inch from the top of the silica surface, start adding 20 mL of the third solvent system (for example, 15:85 methanol/ethyl acetate). Finally, collect (4) 6 mL of fractions.

6. TLC analysis of fractions

About 1 cm above the bottom of a 2–3-cm-wide TLC sheet, make marks (with a pencil) for 5 spots. Apply a spot of the sample solution in the middle lane and then spot fractions 1 through 4 on either side. Repeat with fractions 5–8. Develop in suitable solvent and circle spots with a pencil. Draw a diagram of the TLC plate on the final report.

- Once fractions have been identified, determine which fractions contain the most pure compounds.
- Combine the fractions containing pure compounds of similar Rf values into a pre-weighed container containing boiling chips and evaporate the solvent on a hotplate.
- Once the solvent has evaporated, re-weigh the sample containers to determine the percentage

of recovery of each active fraction.
- Perform TLC and store in small containers for further study on structural interpretation.
  1. Place a small amount of crystals of each purified sample into a small auto analyzer vial.
  2. Add 1 mL of HPLC solvent and perform HPLC analysis.

Example for CC

Separation of Plant Phytoconstituents by CC

Chemicals and materials:
- Silica gel 60 (Merck)
- Solvents

Apparatus and equipment:
- Glass chromatography column with a porous membrane at the bottom and a stopcock at the outlet
- Separation funnel 500 mL, 100 ml
- Funnel
- 5 measuring cylinder 25 mL
- Beaker 100 mL, 500 ml
- 9 Erlenmeyer flasks
- Mortar and pestle
- Glass rod
- Cork ring
- Fractions collector
- Test tubes (different volumes)

Preparation

Extraction of the phytoconstituents

Using a pestle, fresh leaves are ground in a mortar containing acetone, petrol ether and $CaCO_3$. The obtained extract is filtered. The filtrate is poured into a separation funnel and mixed with petroleum ether and 10% aqueous NaCl solution. The separating funnel is shaken carefully.

When the layers have separated, the lower layer is allowed to drain into a beaker. The aqueous phase is thrown away. The upper layer is washed 3–4 times with 5 mL of water. Afterwards the extract is placed in an Erlenmeyer flask and dried with about 4 spatula tips of Na_2SO_4. The liquid is carefully decanted into an Erlenmeyer flask.

Eluting solvent (mobile phase): The solvent to be used in CC should be a single solvent or a mixture of different solvents.

Silica gel slurry

A slurry of silica gel and the eluting solvent is made using a beaker.

Packing of the column

A uniform well-consolidated packing of the column is critical to the success of this chromatographic separation. A clean, dry column is aligned in a vertical position. A beaker is placed under the column outlet. The column is slowly and evenly filled about two-thirds full with silica gel slurry. The stopcock is opened to allow the liquid to drain into the beaker. Pouring the slurry down a glass rod held against the wall of the column will minimise bubbling and turbulence.

The side of the chromatographic tube is gently tapped with a cork ring during the packing process, to make the silica gel compact. Meanwhile the stopcock is opened to allow the excess eluting solvent to run out. Using a powder funnel, a small amount of sand is carefully added to the top of the silica gel column to prevent it from being disturbed when fresh solvent eluent is added. The solvent level is allowed to drop to 1 cm above the sand. The bottom outlet of the separation column is closed. It is very important not to allow the column to run dry.

Experimental procedure

Using a volumetric pipette, the required quantity of the extract (which is previously adsorbed with silica gel) is added directly (or carefully down the side of the column) to the sand layer. The mobile phase is then drained continuously to the top of the column with the aid of a separation funnel. The bottom outlet of the column is opened. The eluent flows down through the column.

The column, with the adsorbent and the sample, is 'developed'. As the eluent passes down the column, the components of the mixture begin to move down the column. The separated zones 'flow out' of the column, where the eluates are collected in Erlenmeyer flasks. The flasks are changed as the eluent changes colour.

The mobile phase slowly flows down through the silica gel column by gravity leaving behind zones of colour—the chromatogram. The theory of CC is analogous to that of thin layer chromatography. The different components in the sample mixture pass through the column at different rates due to differences in the partitioning behaviour between the mobile liquid phase and the stationary phase.

High Performance Liquid Chromatography (HPLC)

This is a form of liquate chromatography that is used to separate and analyse natural products dissolved in solvents. HPLC instruments consist of

- a reservoir of mobile phase,
- a pump,
- an injector,
- a separation column and
- a detector.

Compounds can also be separated/detected by injecting a plug of the sample mixture onto the column of GC. It is applied to volatile organic/natural compounds. The mobile phase is a gas and the stationary phase is usually a liquid on a solid support or sometimes a solid adsorbent.

Planar Chromatography

Planar chromatography (PC), like any other chromatographic technique, is a multistage distribution process. It is a form of liquid chromatography in which the stationary phase is supported on a planar surface rather than a column. Separations in PC occur because of differential migration velocities through the sorbent layer in a fixed separation time.

Applications

- Pharmaceutical industry: Quality control, content uniformity test (CUT), identity/ purity check, phytopharmaceuticals
- Food analysis: Quality control, additives, pesticides, stability testing
- Clinical applications: Lipids, metabolism studies, drug screening, stability testing
- Industrial applications: Process development and optimisation, in-process control, cleaning validation
- Forensic: Detection of document falsifications, poisoning investigations, dye stuff analysis

High Performance Thin Layer Chromatography (HPTLC)

HPTLC is a modern separation technique that is accepted worldwide as an extremely flexible, reliable and cost efficient method. Planar chromatography is operated in off-line mode and, therefore, features:

- Enormous flexibility
- Parallel analysis of many samples

- Unsurpassed clarity through simultaneous visual
- Evaluation of all samples and sample components
- Simplified sample preparation because of the single use of the stationary phase
- Possibility of multiple evaluation of the plate with different parameters because all fractions of the sample are stored on the plate

Basic Steps

The four basic steps in HPTLC analysis are as follows

- Sample application
- Chromatogram development
- Derivatisation
- Chromatogram evaluation

1. Sample application

The samples are applied onto the separation layer, either as spots through contact transfer or as narrow bands using the spray-on technique. Precision of applied volume, small size of application zone and exact positioning are essential for the quality of the analysis. Band-wise sample application as is available with Linomat 5 or Automatic TLC Sampler offers the best separation results and highest flexibility regarding sample solvents and application volumes.

With the spray-on technique, the applied volume can be easily adjusted to match the required detection limit of the analytical task. With the Linomat 5, samples are sprayed onto the chromatographic layer in the form of narrow bands. This technique allows larger sample volumes to be applied than by contact transfer (spotting). While the solvent is almost completely evaporated in the process, the sample is concentrated on the layer surface into a narrow band of selectable lengths. Even samples dissolved in rather polar solvents such as methanol or water form compact and narrow zones. Starting zones sprayed on as narrow bands ensure the highest resolution attainable with any given planar chromatographic system

2. Chromatogram development

The chromatogram is drawn by capillary forces. The developing solvent (mobile phase) migrates through the layer (stationary phase) over a defined distance. During this process, the sample is separated into fractions (components). After evaporation of the mobile phase, all fractions are stored on the layer. An almost unlimited choice of mobile phases and a large selection of stationary phases are the special features of this technique.

3. Derivatisation

It is an inherent advantage of planar chromatography that fractions are stored on the plate and can be derivatised after chromatography. By derivatisation, substances that do not respond to visible or UV light can be rendered detectable. In many cases, substances or classes of substances can be identified by specific reagents.

4. Chromatogram evaluation

The chromatogram is evaluated under ultraviolet or white light. Options range from visual inspection, electronic image processing, video densitometry and documentation to quantitative determination by means of monochromatic light in a classical densitometer, which additionally facilitates measurement of spectral information.

This information is available through the densitometer. Special features include multiple evaluation of the chromatogram with different parameters and detection methods.

Automated Development (CAMAG)

The HPTLC plate is developed repeatedly in the same direction. Each successive run extends over a longer solvent migration distance than the one before and between runs, the solvent is completely removed from the developing chamber and the layer is dried under vacuum. Each successive run uses a solvent of lower elution strength than that of the one used before. In this way, a stepwise elution gradient is formed. The combination of focussing effect and gradient elution results in extremely narrow bands. Their typical peak width is about 1 mm. This means that, with the available separation distance of 80 mm, up to 40 components can be completely resolved, with base line separation.

Twin Trough Chambers

The Twin Trough Chambers offer several ways to improve the results of TLC/HPTLC, developing techniques that enable low solvent consumption. This not only saves solvent but also reduces the waste disposal problem as there is almost no solvent left when the run is completed.

Reproducible pre-equilibration with solvent vapour is done by placing the empty trough opposite the trough that contains the preconditioning solvent.

TLC Scanner

The CAMAG TLC scanner comprises two continuum lamps, a deuterium and a tungsten halogen lamp, in combination with a monochromator that generates light of 254/300 nm bandwidths in the spectral range of 190—800 nm. A third, high pressure mercury vapour lamp provides high energy for scanning by fluorescence.

The lamps are selected and positioned automatically. Plates up to 20 cm x 20 cm are placed on a stage that is mechanically operated in the *x*- and *y*-directions. The scanning speed is variable to a maximum of 100 mm s^{-1}. All functions of the scanner as well as generation and processing of data are controlled by a personal computer using WinCATS software.

A typical sequence of quantitative evaluation of a chromatogram includes raw data acquisition, data integration, calibration and calculation of results and generation of the analysis report. Peak data of unknowns are related to those of the calibration standards. From several calibration functions, including single or multilevel with linear or polynomial regression, the most suitable for the task is chosen. Multiwavelength scanning that initially acquires raw data of up to ten different wavelengths can be separately processed post-run in the integration and calibration routine. Therefore, each substance can be quantified at the wavelength of its maximum absorbance

In the CAMAG scanner, both deuterium and halogen tungsten lamps remain powered the whole time and are therefore well-stabilised. The spectral data can be processed post-run for various purposes:

- To determine the optimum wavelength(s) for quantitative scanning
- To identify individual fractions by comparison with spectra of authentic standards co-chromatographed on the same plate or stored in a spectrum library
- To check identity by superimposing the spectra of all fractions within the same *R*F window

- To check the purity of fractions by superimposing the spectra from different positions within a spot

Future developments of instrumentation are likely to focus on improvements to the speed and flexibility of all automated individual steps. The future will see systems that combine the automated steps in sample applications, chromatogram development and evaluation by video technology.

Examples: HPTLC Identification of Schisandra Berries

Sample: 5.0 g + 150 ml methanol; filtered, concentrated; 10 ml (make up the volume to 15 ml with methanol). 1 ml of this solution is the test solution.

Standard (optional): 1 mg stigmasterol in 1 ml chloroform

Anisaldehyde reagent: In an ice bath, 9 mL 98% H2SO4 + 85 ml methanol + 10 ml acetic acid and 0.5 ml anisaldehyde.

Stationary Phase: HPTLC plates 10 x 10 cm silica gel 60 F254 (Merck)

Mobile Phase: Toluene:ethyl acetate:acetic acid (70:33:3)

With Linomat 4 or Automatic TLC Sampler III, 3 ml volumes of test solution are applied as an 8 mm bands, 6 mm apart and 10 mm from lower edge of plate. A 10 x 10 cm twin trough chamber, saturated for 10 minutes, with 5 ml developing solvent per trough, is placed at a developing distance of 55 mm from lower edge of plate. Dry the plate with warm air for 5 minutes. For detection:

a) UV 254 nm
b) UV 366 nm
c) Anisaldehyde reagent: Immerse plate in reagent for 1 second, dry in stream of cold air, heat to 110 °C for 5 minutes. Examine plate in visible light

Track 1:	2 µl of Schisandra chinensis.
Track 2:	3 µl of Schisandra chinensis.
Track 3:	5 µl of Schisandra chinensis.
Track 4:	5 µl of Schisandra sphenanthera
Track 5:	3 µl of Schisandra sphenanthera
Track 6:	2 µl of Schisandra sphenanthera

Top: UV 254

Middle: UV 366

Bottom: Anisaldehyde

Example: HPTLC Identification of Chaste Tree Fruits (Vitex agnus-castus)

(Courtesy: CAMAG TLC Identification of Chaste Tree)

Sample for Identification: Hydrophilic flavonoids

Sample: 0.75 g of powdered drug + 30 mL methanol in a turbo-extractor. After centrifuging, the sediment + 30 mL methanol is further centrifuged.

The combined supernatants are reconstituted with 5 mL methanol. This is the test solution.

Standards (optional) preparation: 1 mg chlorogenic acid and 2 mg of iso-orientin are dissolved in 5 mL methanol.

Derivatisation reagents: *Natural Products reagent (NP reagent):* 1 g of diphenylborinic acid aminoethylester is dissolved in 200 mL ethyl acetate. *Macrogol reagent*: 10 g of polyethylene glycol 400 (macrogol) are dissolved in 200 mL dichloromethane.

Stationary Phase: HPTLC plates silica gel 60 F254 (Merck), 10 x 10 cm or 20 x 10 cm.

Mobile Phase: Tetrahydrofurane, toluene, formic acid, water (8:4:1:0.5)

Sample application: 2 µL test solution and

standard are applied as 8 mm bands, min. 2 mm apart, 8 mm from lower edge of plate. CAMAG 10x10 cm or 20x10 cm Horizontal Developing Chamber (HDC), unsaturated, 2 mL (respectively 5 mL) developing solvent. Developing distance 60 mm from lower edge of plate. The plate is then dried with a dryer (warm air) for 5 minutes. For detection:

a) UV 254 nm
b) NP/Macrogol reagent: The plate is heated at 100°C for 3 minutes, then dipped while still hot in NP reagent, dried in a stream of cold air, then dipped in Macrogol reagent. Examination is done under UV 366 nm.

Example: HPTLC Determination of Caffeine in Stimulant Herbal Products and Power Drinks

Caffeine, 1,3,7-trimethylxanthine, is the major alkaloid in about 60 herbs, including *Thea sinensis* (tea leaves), *Coffea arabica* (coffee beans), *Theobroma cacao,Paulinea coppana* (guarana seeds) and *Cola nitida* (kola nuts),to which their CNS stimulant is attributed

Materials: Pure caffeine can be obtained from Merck (Darmstadt, Germany). Three herbal products and six energy drinks from the local market.

HPTLC plates: Silica gel 60 F254, 20X10 cm, Merck (Darmstadt, Germany) used as supplied.

TLC development system: EtOAc–MeOH (85:15, v/v).

Standard stock solution I (SS1): Caffeine (10.7 mg/100 mL) in MeOH.

Standard stock solution II (SS2): Caffeine (21.4 mg/100 mL) in MeOH.

The HPTLC system (Camag, Muttanz, Switzerland) consists of:

- TLC scanner connected to a PC running WinCATS software under MS Windows NT
- Linomat IV sample applicator using 100 µ L syringes and connected to a nitrogen tank.

Each plate accommodates 20 tracks of samples and standards to be applied according to the following settings: band width 6 mm; distance between bands 3 mm; application volume 2–12 µL; gas flow 10 s/L.

The scanner is optimised for maximum light with the following settings: slit dimension, 4.00 mm X 0.30 mm, micro; scanning speed, 20 mm/s; high data resolution. All remaining measurement parameters are left at default settings. Regression analyses and statistical data are generated by the WinCATS software.

Specificity (selectivity): UV – 254 nm

Calibration curve: Four concentrations of SS1 are applied in triplicates (2, 4, 8 and 12 µl equivalent to 214, 428, 856 and 1284 ng/spot, respectively.

Precision: Repeatability is determined by running a minimum of four analyses per sample and evaluating the coefficient of variability (CV%) for each sample. Repeatability is further confirmed from the CV% values of the standard addition at three concentration levels (Table 27.1).

Recovery: On the same plate, 4 and 5 µL of SS2 are applied in quadruplicates. Their tracks are scanned simultaneously with (A).

Applications of Planar Chromatography

- Qualitative analysis of phytochemicals
- Quantitative analysis of isolated pure compounds and phytochemicals
  - Analyses based on peak height
  - Analyses based on peak areas

Table 27.1: Caffeine levels in herbal products and power drinks

Product	*Product code*	*Found (ng/spot ± SD, n=4)*	*CV (%)*	*Concentration (%w/w)*	*Caffeine/ serving*
Kola Extract	HP1	762.72 ± 10.61	1.39	4.76	33.32
Mega Ripped	HP2	1013.89 ± 9.66	0.95	12.68	198.06
Guarana Power	HP3	681.76 ±19.48	2.86	13.29	70.60
Magic Energy Kick	ED1	393.42 ± 1.78	0.45	0.013	32.78
Power Horse	ED2	638.77 ± 7.34	1.15	0.032	79.85
Shadow	ED3	435.26 ± 6.59	1.51	0.022	54.4
Red Bull	ED4	608.00 ± 14.29	2.35	0.030	76.00
PepsiX Energy Cola	ED5	411.30 ± 6.61	1.61	0.021	52.50
Pepsi Cola	ED6	323.15 ± 9.34	2.89	0.011	26.93

Ehab and Mossa, Journal of Pharmaceutical and Biomedical Analysis 36 (2004) 617–620

- Calibration and standards
- The internal standard method
- The area normalisation method

Nuclear Magnetic Resonance (NMR) – An Introduction

Nuclear magnetic resonance (NMR) is a non-destructive technique for mapping molecular structures and learning how molecules function and relate to each other. This is important for many applications, including:

- Discovering effective new drugs
- Evaluating new synthetic material
- Exploring realms of the proteomics

NMR is based on the principle that the nuclei of many atoms found in nature act as little magnets. When these little magnets are placed inside a bigger magnet, their south poles line up with the north pole of the big magnet. They absorb some energy in doing so and behave in a way that has been described as 'flip', 'spin' or 'wobble', as a result. This action is called resonance and can be physically mapped, showing which atoms are present in the molecule and where they are located in relation to each other, hence the term nuclear magnetic resonance.

Each molecule has a different internal structure, depending upon the atoms it contains, and these varying structures paint a unique profile, or spectrum, when exposed to magnetic energy. Not only does this technology allow researchers to understand the three-dimensional structure and relationship of atoms in molecules, it also explains how they relate to other atoms in the molecule over time. This characteristic is important in the study of proteins, carbohydrates and genetic material, such as DNA and RNA.

Working of NMR Spectrometer

The NMR spectrometer consists of several parts or components, each of which is critical to its operation. Depending on the specific experiment, the process can take weeks and even months, but this will provide an understanding of how the components work together:

The test sample is placed in a long slender glass tube with 1" of liquid. Samples can be less than 1/1000 cubic inch of the gas, liquid, or solid.

The sample is lowered into the bore, a hollow tube at the centre of the magnet. The sample tube is spun with an air jet, to produce a more uniform sample for scanning.

The computer workstation and software directs the experiment from start to finish. The experiment begins with the computer sending directions to the spectrometer console. The NMR console triggers split-second bursts, or pulses, of radio frequency (RF) energy that are precisely sequenced to excite the sample in the probe and cause the atomic nuclei to resonate. The high-power RF energy pulses are sent to the NMR probe, the 'antenna' that provides the RF link between the sample and the instrument electronics.

The superconducting magnet provides a strong, homogeneous magnetic field that can be as much as 200,000 times stronger than the earth's magnetic field. The natural magnets in the nuclei line up with the powerful NMR magnet, similar to iron filings aligning with the magnetic field of a toy magnet. The RF pulses from the NMR console excite the atoms in the sample, making the nuclei resonate.

As soon as the RF signal stops, the nuclei return to their natural state. As the nuclei relax, the NMR probe receives a very weak RF resonance response back from the sample and transmits it to the NMR console for amplification. The NMR console amplifies the faint returning signals over 1,000,000 times before sending them to the computer workstation for analysis.

The computer workstation stores and processes the NMR data using complex software and creates a unique 'spectrum' for the sample, showing the atomic structure of each molecule as well as the dynamics of its chemical environment for interpretation by the scientist.

Key Components

The NMR spectrometer is a complex system integrating several technologies into an analytically powerful, information-rich system. Key parts of the system are the computer workstation and control software, the NMR console with its advanced radio frequency (RF) electronics, the superconducting magnet and the NMR probe.

The Computer Workstation and Control Software

The computer workstation and control software is perhaps the 'brains' of the operation; it directs the NMR experiment. NMR spectrometers make heavy use of computers and software, both for the control of the various RF pulses, as well as for storing and processing the NMR data. NMR signals are subjected to complex digital signal processing algorithms, including the Fourier transform, to convert the NMR information into a form that is easily interpreted by the end user. The signals are displayed as a series of peaks, or spectra, on the workstation's monitor.

NMR Console

The NMR console's job is multi-faceted and includes acting as transmitter, receiver and amplifier. Its sophisticated RF electronics send split-second pulses that are precisely delivered to excite the sample in the probe. The NMR console also receives the faint return signals from the sample and then amplifies them one million times so they can be read by the computer workstation.

NMR Probe

The NMR probe provides the RF link between the sample and the instrument electronics. Inserted in the magnet, the probe holds the sample at the centre of the magnetic field. It bombards the sample with RF energy and then receives the very weak RF responses from the sample, which it sends on to the console. In recent years, engineers have developed a unique NMR probe where the internal electronics of the probe are chilled to approximately –250 °C (comparable to temperatures on the surface of Pluto).

NMR Magnet

The superconducting magnet provides a strong, extremely homogeneous magnetic field into which the sample (liquid or solid) is placed. Depending on the magnet, the field strength can range from 200 MHz to 900 MHz. This strength is typically specified in terms of the resonance frequency for the hydrogen atom expressed in megahertz (MHz). The 900 MHz NMR magnet is 10 times stronger than the most powerful magnetic resonance imaging (MRI) system used in hospitals and 200,000 times stronger than the earth's magnetic field.

Applications of NMR

Pharmaceutical laboratories focus mainly on studying small chemical samples that were synthesised in-house or isolated as a natural product. These studies take advantage of NMR's capability to determine complete molecular structure, which now combined with the high sensitivity, makes NMR a very powerful and an essential tool. Metabolomics research has also greatly benefited from the improved sensitivity of Cold Probes.

Academic research laboratories mainly focus on demanding and relevant biological problems, including AIDS and cancer research and structural proteomics.

Mass Spectrometry

Mass spectrometry is a powerful analytical technique that is used to identify unknown compounds, to quantify known compounds and to elucidate the structure and chemical properties of phytochemicals. Detection of compounds can be accomplished with very minute quantities (as little as 10–12 g, 10–15 moles for a compound of mass 1000 Daltons). This means that compounds can be identified at very low concentrations (one part in 1012) in chemically complex mixtures. Mass spectrometry provides valuable information to a wide range of professionals: physicians, astonomers and biologists, to name a few.

Uses

- Detect and identify the use of steroids in athletes
- Monitor the respiration of patients during surgery
- Determine the composition of molecular species found in space
- Determine whether honey is adulterated with corn syrup
- Locate oil deposits by measuring petroleum precursors in rock
- Monitor fermentation processes in the biotechnology industry
- Detect dioxins in contaminated fish
- Determine gene damage from environmental causes
- Establish the elemental composition of semiconductor materials

Mass Spectrometers

Mass spectrometers are analytical tools used to determine the molecular weight (MW) of a sample. They can be divided into three fundamental parts, namely, the ionisation source, the analyser and the detector.

The sample under investigation has to be introduced into the ionisation source of the instrument. Once inside the ionisation source, the sample molecules are ionised, because ions are easier to manipulate than neutral molecules. These ions are extracted into the analyser region of the mass spectrometer where they are separated according to their mass (m)-to-charge (z) ratios (m/z). The separated ions are detected and this signal is sent to a data system where the m/z ratios are stored together with their relative abundance for presentation in the format of m/z spectrum.

The analyser and detector of the mass spectrometer, and often the ionisation source as well, are maintained under high vacuum to give the ions a reasonable chance of travelling from one end of the instrument to the other without any hindrance from air molecules. The entire operation of the mass spectrometer, and often the sample introduction process, is under complete data system control on modern mass spectrometers.

Sample Introduction

The method of sample introduction to the ionisation source often depends on the ionisation method used, as well as the type and complexity of the sample. The sample can be inserted directly into the ionisation source or can undergo some type of chromatography en route to the ionisation source. This latter method usually involves the mass spectrometer being coupled directly to a HPLC, GC or capillary electrophoresis (CE) separation column, and hence the sample is separated into a series of components which then enter the mass spectrometer sequentially for individual analysis.

Methods of Sample Ionisation

The ionisation method to be used depends on the type of sample under investigation and the mass spectrometer available. Ionisation methods include atmospheric pressure chemical ionisation (APCI), chemical ionisation (CI), electron impact (EI), electrospray ionisation (ESI), fast atom bombardment (FAB), field desorption/field ionisation (FD/FI), matrix-assisted laser desorption ionisation (MALDI) and thermospray ionisation (TSP). With most ionisation methods there is the possibility of creating both positively and negatively charged sample ions, depending on the proton affinity of the sample. Before embarking on an analysis the user must decide whether to detect the positively or negatively charged ions.

Analysis and Separation of Sample Ions

The main function of the mass analyser is to separate, or resolve, the ions formed in the ionisation source of the mass spectrometer according to their mass-to-charge (m/z) ratios.

The detector monitors the ion current, amplifies it and transmits the signal to the data system where it is recorded in the form of mass spectra. The m/z values of the ions are plotted against their intensities to show the number of components in the sample, the molecular weight of each component and the relative abundance of the various components in the sample.

Mass spectrometry is a particularly powerful detector for separation techniques such as GC,

LC, CE and supercritical fluid chromatography because of its great sensitivity and ability to identify chemical compounds positively. The challenge in interfacing a mass spectrometer to a separation system such as a gas or liquid chromatograph is maintaining the required vacuum in the mass spectrometer while introducing flow from the chromatograph. Interfaces that restrict or reduce the gas flow into the mass spectrometer (flow splitters or devices that differentially remove carrier gas from the GC effluent) have made the combination of GC and MS (GC/MS) a widely used technique for years. To generate this information, the mass spectrometer scans the mass range (for example, m/z 30–500) repetitively during the chromatographic run of 30 minutes, An average of 1800 spectra can be recorded. Information is displayed in several ways:

- The intensities of all the ions in each spectrum can be summed, and this sum can be plotted as a function of chromatographic retention time to give a total ion chromatogram (TIC).
- Each peak in TIC represents an eluting compound that can be identified by TIC interpretation of the mass spectra recorded for the peak.
- The intensity at a single m/z ratio over the course of a chromatographic run can be displayed to yield a selected ion current profile or mass chromatogram.

Tandem or Multistage Mass Spectrometry (MS/MS)

An ion produced by fast atom bombardment (FAB) will indicate the molecular weight of the sample but often may not fragment much, if at all, thus giving little structural information. By coupling together two analysers, separated by a collision cell, further information can be obtained. The first analyser is used to select the ion of interest. This ion is then passed into the collision cell, which usually will have been pressurised with an inert gas such as argon. Collision of the ion with the atoms in the cell can induce dissociation of the ion. This is known as collision induced dissociation (CID)—the original ion is referred to as the 'precursor' ion and the dissociated ions are known as 'product' ions. These product ions are then analysed in the second mass spectrometer thus generating a product ion mass spectrum of the original precursor ion.

To confirm the presence of specific substances and its quantification, the mass spectrometer is set to monitor only m/z values of ions representative of molecule of interest, thereby saving time. In some cases, form of ionisation is chosen to produce a single type of ion, thus maximising the sensitivity by keeping the ion signal in an m/z value.

Future Trends

Contrary to affordability of scientifically tested natural products by rich nations, many in developing and underdeveloped nations have relied on the naturally available and time-tested products of nature. However, the scientific rationale for such benefits observed remains unanswered and the lack of proper documentations and scientific evaluations have often led to some adverse affects due to their improper use. When appropriately tested using different instruments and documented, these herbal/natural products will prove to be of immense aid in improving the general health status of the population in the less privileged nations of the world.

Key Messages

- Extraction can be defined as the removal of soluble materials from an insoluble residue, either liquid or solid, by treatment with a liquid solvent.
- The different methods used to extract materials are infusion, decoction, maceration and percolation.
- All plant materials used should be properly authenticated. The choice of extraction procedure depends on the nature of the plant material and the components to be isolated.
- Sublimation, distillation and fractional liberation are the techniques used to separate and isolate plant constituents.
- Chromatography is a technique that can be used to separate and identify a wide range of compounds found in higher plants.
- Planar chromatography (PC) is a form of liquid chromatography in which the stationary phase is supported on a planar surface rather than a column.
- Mass spectrometry is a powerful analytical technique that is used to identify unknown compounds, to quantify known compounds and to elucidate the structure and chemical properties of phytochemicals.

QUESTIONS

1. What are herbal drugs? Explain extraction of herbal drugs in detail.
2. What are the different methods of identification and isolation of natural products?
3. Write a note on the chromatographic applications of natural products.
4. Explain the different procedures involved in isolating pure compounds from the crude extract using column chromatography.
5. What is meant by planar chromatography? Write a note on HPTLC.
6. What is mass spectrometry? Write a note on instrumentation of MS.
7. Explain different components of the NMR spectrophotometer.

28

Quality Control and Standardisation of Herbal Drugs—An Overview

MUEEN AHMED KK

Learning Objectives

At the end of this chapter, you will be able to:

- Describe the global market scenario for herbal medicines
- List the important areas of usage of herbal medicines
- Describe herbal drugs and the quality control measures used in herbal drugs
- Describe the process of standardisation of raw materials

Introduction

Healthcare policies are largely driven by the pharmaceutical industry diverting attention away from health preservation and towards the cure, prevention and eradication of diseases. This has undermined the economic basis of this industry. No satisfactory drugs are available for the degenerative disorders characteristic of the ageing population and for re-emerging resistant infections. Many modern drugs do not have proven clinical utility.

The twenty-first century is the century of biology powered and propelled by scientific knowledge and technological expertise. The three major technologies, namely, biotechnology, herbal technology and information technology (bioinformatics) are expected to be the most powerful elements crucial for the prosperity and welfare of people. About 2 million plants have been taxonomically named and identified. Only 5–15% of these plants, however, have been screened for their biological activity while it has been estimated that 1 in 125 plant species contains therapeutically useful phytoconstituents.

The turnover of herbal medicines in India as over-the-counter (OTC) products, ethical and classical formulations and home remedies of the Ayurveda, Unani and Siddha systems of medicine is about $1 billion with exports worth about $80 million.

Psyllium seeds and husk, castor oil and opium extract together account for 60% of the exports. About 80% of the exports to developed countries comprise crude drugs and unfinished formulations, leading to low revenue for the country. So, ideally, India should export herbal medicines as well as knowledge about the same.

Three of the ten best-selling herbal medicines in developed countries, namely preparations of *Allium sativum*, *Aloe barbadensis* and the *Panax* species, are available in India. India is the largest grower of the Psyllium (*Plantago ovata*) and Senna (*Cassia senna*) plants and is one of the largest growers of the Castor (*Ricinus communis*) plant. These are also exported in large amounts and yet our market share is dismal because of export of crude extracts/drugs. Twenty other plants are commonly exported as crude drugs worth $8 million.

Terms and Defintitions

According to the WHO, **herbal medicines** are plant-derived materials and preparations with therapeutic or other human health benefits, which contain either raw or processed ingredients from one or more plants, inorganic materials or animals. Herbal medicine preparations are developed and created as drugs by the modern pharmaceutical industry.

Phytotherapeutic agents or **phytomedicines** are standardised herbal preparations consisting of complex mixtures of one or more plants that are used in most countries for the management of various diseases. Usually, the active principles responsible for their pharmacological action are unknown.

Herbal drugs are best suited for:

- Primary healthcare
- Infectious diseases such as AIDS and other viral infections, opportunistic infections, multidrug resistant (MDR) infections (for example, tuberculosis and malaria)
- Degenerative and gerontological conditions such as osteoporosis, chronic ailments such as osteoarthritis and rheumatoid arthritis, neurological conditions such as Alzheimer's disease and Parkinsonism
- Anti-ageing treatment
- Metabolic disorders
- Diabetes
- Dyslipidemias
- Other conditions such as microcirculatory disorders, liver diseases, and as immunostimulants, anti-cancer drugs and drugs affecting the male libido

Herbal drugs are officially included in various pharmacopeias:

- *Chinese Pharmacopeia;* the 1997 edition has 647 traditional drugs
- *European Pharmacopeia;* the 2000 edition contains monographs on 152 crude drugs
- *Indian Pharmacopeia;* the 1996 edition contains information about 57 drugs including only 12 crude drugs

Herbal Drugs: An Overview

The WHO compiled an inventory of 21,000 plants used for medicinal purposes in 91 countries. Less than 10,000 species have been investigated. Over 17,500 species are native and indigenous to different countries. Traditional systems of medicine use about 2,000 species of plants; Ayurvedic medicines alone need 800 while folklore medicine uses 8,000 plants.

In contrast to modern medicines, herbal medicines are frequently used to treat chronic diseases. Phytotherapeutic agents are normally marketed as standardised preparations in the form of liquid, solid (powdered extract) or viscous preparations. They are prepared by maceration, percolation or distillation (volatile oils). Ethanol and water or mixtures of both are used for the production of fluid extracts. Solid or powdered extracts are prepared by evaporation of the solvents used in the process of extraction of the raw material. Some phytotherapeutic agents are greatly concentrated in order to improve their therapeutic efficacy. As the industry has developed and demand has grown in industrialised countries, consumer awareness of these products and the issues associated with them has also grown. Concerns over safety, efficacy, purity and product origins (that is, country of origin and whether cultivated or wild harvested) have entered public consciousness.

Quality Control of Herbal Drugs

Quality control monitoring ensures the safety, efficacy and quality of herbal medicines and their preparations. Quality control consists of a regular check of the quality of herbal medicines and is performed according to the specifications of the product which provides details about the requirements for identity, purity and content of characterising compounds. The test methods for quality control involve sensory inspection (macroscopic and microscopic examinations) as the first step towards establishing the identity and degree of purity of herbal medicines. They also involve analytical inspection using instrumental techniques such as thin layer chromatography, high-performance liquid chromatography (HPLC), gas chromatography (GC)/MS, liquid chromatography coupled with mass spectrometry (LC/MS), nuclear magnetic resonance (NMR) and ultraviolet (UV) spectrophotometry.

Sensory inspection, according to the specified description of the monographs of any of the pharmacopeias, provides the simplest and quickest means of establishing the identity and purity of herbal medicines. Since herbal medicines originate from natural products and macroscopic inspection is based on the odour, colour, taste, shape, size and surface of characteristics, microscopic inspection is more essential for the identification of powdered or cut herbal medicine for quality control than physicochemical testing methods.

The quality control procedures used for herbal medicines include the determination of foreign matter including tests for hazardous contaminants such as pesticide residues, arsenic and heavy metals, microorganisms including aflatoxins, and sulfur dioxide residue. However, there is a lack of data about the following:

- Active constituents; metabolites
- Pharmacokinetics
- Pharmacology
- Toxicology
- Adverse effects and their frequencies; effects of long-term use
- Drug–herb interactions; interactions with food and alcohol
- Use in specific patient groups; children, elderly, individuals with renal or hepatic disease, gender effects, individuals with different genetic profiles
- Contraindications and warnings; use in pregnancy and lactation

Regional linguistic nomenclature for plant collectors often creates confusion regarding the exact botanical identity of the plant material. Ecotypic (Eclipta alba), genotypic (Acorus calamus) or chemotypic (Withania somnifera) variability may also exist. The harvesting time, period and stage influence the quality of the raw material. Postharvesting practices such as the method of drying, garbling, packing and storage conditions influence the quality of raw material. Good gathering practices (GGP), good agricultural practices (GAP), good harvesting practices (GHP) and good processing practices (GPP) can reduce the level of inconsistencies in the quality of raw materials.

Standardisation of Raw Material

Quality, efficacy and safety are parameters that are required for all medicines. These are particularly important in herbal preparations as they gain popularity. The past decade has witnessed significant worldwide growth in the use of herbal medicines. Due to the increasing knowledge of traditional and scientifically documented benefits of herbs, consumers are now more likely to consider herbal remedies as a viable alternative to conventional medicines. Hence, standardisation of raw materials has become essential to maintain and ensure the quality of these herbs.

Plant Identification

Pharmacognostic identification tests of botanicals are performed by trained analysts in histology and taxonomy. Earlier, morphological, histological and taxonomical identification were considered sufficient for positive identification of a botanical. However, with the spectacular advances made in analytical technology during the last four decades and the ready availability of a number of spectrophotometric and chromatographic techniques, which provide a wealth of information, a better and more positive identification can be achieved with these techniques.

The quality of the raw materials can be tested according to the following format:

- Name of the drug (English, regional names, exact botanical nomenclature)
- Part of the plant used
- Area of collection
- Distribution details
- Season of crop
- Time and year of collection
- Pesticide and insecticides
- Condition of the drug (fresh or dry)
- Form of the drug (powdered, intact or cuttings)

Testing techniques include:

1. ***Macroscopic/Organoleptic:*** This test comprises the unaided senses of sight, smell and taste. However, the inclusion of a hand lens with 4–20x magnification would be useful for visual identification. These methods are typically used for a herbal or botanical ingredient in whole or uncut form.
   a. Analysis is based on attributes such as:
      1) Defined morphological and/or anatomical characteristics of the whole plant or individual plant parts (for example, leaf, flower, fruit, seed, root, rhizome, bark)
      2) Characteristic colour, fracture, smell or taste
   b. Identification is achieved by positive comparison of morphological characteristics with authenticated or in-house plant reference material or an authoritative technical reference description or test that can assure the identity of the botanical ingredient.
   c. Herbs and plant parts that have been cut or ground to the point where morphological characteristics are no longer observable to the unaided eye are best analysed by microscopic and/or chemical means.
2. ***Microscopic Analysis:*** This involves the use of higher magnification (than provided by a hand lens) and special light or staining

techniques to examine powdered or chopped representative sample material. Analysis is based on observation of specific microscopic characteristics that have been established for the specific dietary supplement ingredient. This analysis also is used to identify some adulterants.

a. Identification is based on microscopic observation of cell and tissue structures of plants and animals:
   1) Defined histological characteristics of plant parts (for example, stems, roots, rhizomes, bark, leaves, flowers, seeds, wood)
   2) Defined histological characteristics of animal tissues and cells
   3) Defined staining or microscopic chemical reactions
b. Identification is achieved by using a validated method, comparison of a representative sample from the commercial batch with authenticated or in-house working plant reference material or authoritative technical descriptions of established microscopic characteristic(s).

Table 28.1 lists the microbial contamination limits for different types of microorganisms.

Thin Layer Chromatography (TLC)

Among the various chromatographic techniques, TLC offers the best hope because it is inexpensive, provides a wealth of information on the nature and possible number of compounds present in the herbal raw material and is readily available in all laboratories around the globe. Unlike synthetic, organic, medicinal compounds that exhibit predictable pharmacological activity at a given dosage, the world of botanicals is quite different in the sense that it is not always known with certainty what constitutes the active ingredient(s). It is generally believed that the reported pharmacological action of a botanical is a result of multiple constituents acting synergistically with other constituents.

From the pharmacopeial perspective, better quality control of raw material can be achieved by specifying a quantitative test procedure for the determination of the range or a minimum content of the marker substance or the 'active' ingredient. In chemical identification of the raw material, a marker substance is identified which may be defined as the substance that is characteristic of the botanical raw material and is quantifiable. Since chromatographic conditions may vary, this can be achieved unequivocally with the help of an authentic reference standard of the marker substance. Other chromatographic techniques such as GC and HPLC are powerful tools and could be easily employed in the identification of botanical raw material.

A chromatographic fingerprint profile represents the qualitative/quantitative determination of various components present

Table 28.1: Limits for microbial contamination

Microorganism	*Finished Product (Microbial Count)*	*Raw Materials (Microbial Count)*
E. coli	10^1	10^4
Salmonella	-	-
Aerobic bacteria	10^5	-
Enterobacteria	10^3	-

in a complex plant extract irrespective of whether or not their exact identity is known. In view of the enormous progress made during the past four decades, standardisation of botanical raw material with respect to the active ingredient or marker substance poses no problem. The advances made in separation science have given a clear advantage to chromatographic methods over conventional titrimetric and spectrophotometric methods. Thin layer chromatographic technique, the simplest and least expensive, is thus the technique of choice for the positive identification of raw material.

In view of the TLC's limitations in quantitative analysis, liquid chromatography, which provides simultaneous separation and detection, is the technique of choice for the quantitative determination of active ingredients or marker substances. The HPLC technique combines selectivity and sensitivity, thus providing stability-indicating features. In recent years, the liquid chromatography-mass spectrometry (LC-MS) technique has found increasing application in the analysis of medicinal plant material. It is an expensive technique but the cost may be justified by the wealth of information it provides. The information generated by the LC-MS technique can be productively used in the development of public standards for plant drugs.

DNA-based techniques have been widely used for authentication of plant species of medicinal importance. This is especially useful in case of those plant species that are frequently substituted or adulterated with other species or varieties that are morphologically and/or phytochemically indistinguishable. A fully traceable crop production protocol is essential for a quality product. Before the plant is sown in the field, properties of the plant should be identified and measured against the target profile of the ultimate product. Plant breeding can help to create different strains of a species that have more suitable characteristics, both in terms of chemical profile and agronomically, and these strains can increase yield and reduce cost.

Limits for Impurities

A test requirement for foreign organic matter would ensure the extent of contamination of extraneous matters such as dirt, as other parts of botanicals not covered by the definition of the herbal drug. As sand and soil are predicable contaminants of botanicals, test requirements for total ash, water-soluble ash, acid-insoluble ash, residue on ignition and sulphated ash would be expected to limit such contaminants.

Test requirements for heavy metals in botanical raw material are probably more relevant for the parts of plants that grow below the ground than above. However, to ensure that processing operations such as grinding or milling of the material have not contaminated the material, a limit test for heavy metals should always be done.

Thus, the following tests are performed to check for impurities:

- Foreign matter
- Total ash
- Ash insoluble in hydrochloric acid
- Water-soluble extractive
- Extractable matter

Particle Size

For some herbal materials intended for use in herbal teas or solid herbal medicinal products, particle size can have a significant effect on dissolution rates, bioavailability and/or stability.

In such instances, testing for particle size distribution should be carried out using an appropriate procedure, and limit criteria should be provided.

Water Content

This test is important when the herbal materials are known to be hygroscopic. For non-pharmacopeial herbal materials, the criteria should be justified by data on the effects of moisture absorption. A 'loss on drying' procedure may be adequate; however, in some cases (essential oil–containing plants), a detection procedure that is specific for water is required.

Incidental Metals and Non-metals

The need for tests and acceptance criteria for incidental metals and non-metals should be studied during development and, based on the knowledge of the plant species, during its cultivation and the manufacturing process. Acceptance criteria will ultimately depend on safety considerations. Where relevant, procedures and acceptance criteria for sulfated ash/residue on ignition should follow pharmacopeial precedents. Other impurities may be determined by appropriate procedures, for example, atomic absorption spectroscopy.

Microbial Limits

If the plant material reaches the consumer directly without any reduction in bio-burden, unless the material is expected to be boiled in water prior to consumption, restrictive limits on microbial contaminants are in order. A more permissive standard for microbial limits would be required where the bio-burden of the material reaching the consumer has been subjected to extensive processing such as boiling with water or solvent extraction. Pathogens such as Salmonella should be absent and more restrictive limits placed on Enterobacteriaceae and E. coli in material to be taken internally. A lower level of yeasts and moulds and a limit on total aerobes are considered appropriate in plant material for topical use. The presence of aflatoxins detected by chemical means is generally independent of the number of viable moulds that are detected using microbiological methods. However, a screening test based on the serological response to Aspergillus antigen as a first tier, followed, if positive, by an aflatoxin test would be appropriate.

Pesticide Limit

A limit for pesticides is one of the major issues in standardisation of medicinal plants and products in view of the worldwide use of pesticides in cultivated plants. The challenge here is the enormous and uncontrolled use of a wide variety of organochlorine and organophosphorus pesticides. Well-validated analytical methods for the quantitative determination of pesticides by GC coupled with MS are in day-to-day use; however, these methods call for specially trained analysts. Harmonised methods of analysis of pesticides as part of public standards are not difficult to achieve although the question of which pesticides should be tested remains unanswered. While industrialised countries have taken the necessary actions to limit the number of pesticides that are allowed in cultivation, a different situation exists in developing nations. The complexity of the situation is compounded by the fact that the list of banned and permitted pesticides varies from country to country. In view of this, the WHO has declared that the label of the medicinal plant material should indicate the country of origin. This enables the importing country to test the plant material imported for those pesticides that are allowed for use in the country of origin. While this may sound easy, it requires the preparation of standards of enormous number of pesticides for quantitative determination. This is what has perhaps led the WHO to suggest testing of a minimum number of pesticides in medicinal plant material. The best solution for this problem, as WHO experts suggest, appears to be in developing and establishing lists of pesticides that would be permitted for worldwide use in the cultivation of botanicals and those that are not desirable.

The plant material should also be tested for toxicity, for example, of heavy metals such as cadmium, lead, arsenic, mercury, etc. and pesticide residues, which can be calculated as follows:In the

$$\text{Maximum residue limits} = \frac{\text{Acceptable daily index} \times \text{Body weight} \times \text{Extraction factor}}{\text{Mean daily intake of drug} \times \text{Safety factor} \times 100} \times \text{Therapeutic doses}$$

case of radioactive contamination, microbial growth in herbals is usually prevented by irradiation. This process may sterilise the plant material but the radioactivity hazard should be taken into account. The radioactivity of the plant samples should be checked according to the guidelines of International Atomic Energy (IAE) in Vienna and that of WHO.

Assay

In the case of herbal materials with constituents of known therapeutic activity, the content of the constituents should be assayed. Where possible, a specific, stability-indicating procedure should be used to determine the content of the active constituent in the herbal material. In cases where a non-specific assay is used, other supporting analytical procedures should also be used to achieve overall specificity. For example, where determination of essential oils is adopted to assay the herbal material, the combination of the assay and a suitable test for identification (for example, chromatographic profile) can be used. In the case of herbal materials where the constituents responsible for the therapeutic activity are unknown, appropriate marker substances may be assayed.

Pharmacopeial Monographs

Herbal monographs are now entering and re-entering various pharmacopeias; this is likely to result in the introduction of more herbal medicines during this century. Herbal monographs appear in various pharmacopeias of the world, for example, the United States Pharmacopeia (USP), European Pharmacopeia, American Herbal Pharmacopeia (AHP), British Herbal Pharmacopeia (BHP), Japanese standards for herbal medicines, Pharmacopeia of the People's Republic of China and Ayurvedic Pharmacopeia of India.

Basic Requirements of Quality Control of Herbal Production

Adequate facilities, trained personnel and approved procedures should be available for sampling, inspecting and testing of packaging materials and intermediate, bulk and finished products. These samples are taken by personnel using methods approved by quality control:

- Test methods are validated.
- Records, made manually and/or using recording instruments, demonstrate that all the required sampling, inspecting and testing procedures were actually done and any deviations are fully recorded and investigated.
- The finished products contain active ingredients that comply with the qualitative and quantitative composition of the marketing authorisation, are of the purity required and are enclosed within proper containers and correctly labelled.
- Records of results from inspection, material testing and intermediate, bulk and finished products are formally assessed against specifications, including a review and evaluation of relevant production documentation and an assessment of deviations from specified procedures. No batch of product is released for sale or supply unless certified by a qualified person that all material is in accordance with the requirements of the marketing authorisation.
- Sufficient reference samples of starting materials and products are retained to permit future examination of the product if necessary, and the product is retained in the final pack unless exceptionally large packs are produced (www.pharmacos.eudra.org).

Need for Quality Control

In spite of the availability of modern chemical analytical procedures, only rarely do phytochemical investigations succeed in isolating and characterising all secondary metabolites present in the plant extract. Apart from this, plant constituents vary considerably depending on several factors that impair the quality control of phytotherapeutic agents.

Quality control and standardisation of herbal medicines involve several steps. However, the source and quality of raw materials play a pivotal role in guaranteeing the quality and stability of herbal preparations. Other factors such as the use of fresh plants, temperature, light exposure, water availability, nutrients, period and time of collection, method of collecting, drying, packing, storage and transportation of raw material, age and part of the plant collected, etc., can greatly affect the quality and consequently the therapeutic value of herbal medicines. Some plant constituents are heat labile and the plants containing them need to be dried at low temperatures. Also, other active principles are destroyed by enzymatic processes that continue for long periods of time after plant collection. This explains why the composition of herbal-based drugs is frequently quite variable. Thus, proper standardisation and quality control of raw materials and also the herbal preparations should always have permanency in their application.

In cases where the active principles are unknown, marker substance(s) should be established for analytical purposes. However, in most cases, these markers have never been tested to see whether they really account for the therapeutic action reported for the herbal drugs. As pointed out before, apart from these variable factors, others such as the method of extraction and contamination with microorganisms, heavy metals, pesticides, etc., can also interfere with the quality, safety and efficacy of herbal drugs. For these reasons, pharmaceutical companies prefer using cultivated plants instead of wild-harvested plants because they show smaller variation in their constituents. Furthermore, and certainly more relevantly, when medicinal plants are produced by cultivation, the main secondary metabolites can be monitored and this permits definition of the best period for harvesting.

Among others, thin layer chromatography, GC, HPLC, MS, infrared-spectrometry and ultraviolet/visible spectrometry, can be successfully used alone or in combination to standardise and control the quality of both the raw material and the finished herbal drugs.

Analysis is done at each of the following steps,

Seed Cultivation > Harvesting > Drying > Storage > Extraction > Formulation > Storage

A sufficient number of tests should be performed on representative samples as necessary to establish ingredient identity. An integral quality control (IQC) system has many benefits, such as providing insight into company management, improvement in the efficiency and effectiveness of the production process, provision of products with constant quality, economic methods for production and demonstrable activities. Moreover, quality control provides a guarantee for the customer, results in cost reduction for the supplier and, perhaps most importantly, leads to identification and traceability of errors.

Key Messages

- Herbal medicines are plant-derived materials that contain either raw or processed ingredients from one or more plants, inorganic materials or animals.
- Quality control monitoring ensures the safety, efficacy and quality of herbal medicines and their preparations.
- Quality control consists of a regular check of the quality of herbal medicines, which provides details about the requirements for identity, purity and content of compounds.
- Standardisation of raw materials has become essential to maintain and ensure the quality of herbal drugs as with any other medicine.
- Quality of raw materials can be tested by both macroscopic/organoleptic and microscopic analysis.
- Source and quality of raw materials play a pivotal role in guaranteeing the quality and stability of herbal preparations.
- Factors such as the use of fresh plants, temperature, light exposure, water availability, nutrients, period and time of collection, method of collecting, drying, packing, storage and transportation of raw material, age and part of the plant collected, etc., can greatly affect the quality, and consequently the therapeutic value, of herbal medicines.
- Thin layer chromatography, GC, HPLC, MS, infrared-spectrometry and ultraviolet/visible spectrometry can be successfully used alone or in combination to standardise and control the quality of both the raw material and the finished herbal drugs.

Questions

1. Discuss the herbal medicine global market scenario.
2. Define herbal drugs and quality control.
3. Describe the quality control measures used in herbal drugs.
4. Describe the process of standardisation of raw materials.
5. Discuss the need for quality control of herbal drugs.

29

Phytopharmacological Screening of Natural Products

Mueen Ahmed KK and Arun Kumar HS

Learning Objectives

At the end of this chapter, you will be able to:

- Initiate basic research on plant extracts
- Plan the research protocol by selecting suitable methods for pharmacological screening
- Select the right method for the extraction of drugs
- Perform the preliminary screening of extracts for their pharmacological activity

Introduction

Over the past decade, herbal medicine has become a topic of increasing global importance, with both medical and economic implications. In developing countries, as much as 80% of the indigenous population relies on traditional systems of medicine and medicinal plants as their primary source of healthcare.

The use of products extracted from plants for medicinal purposes can be traced from the beginnings of civilisation, and up until the end of the nineteenth century, natural products were the principal sources of medicines. India has a great range of medicinal plants. Traditional herbal medicines and their preparations have been used widely in India as well as in Western countries for thousands of years. Phytotherapeutic agents are standardised herbal preparations that consist of complex mixtures of one or more plants that contain active ingredients, either as plant parts or plant material in the crude or processed state. A marked growth in the worldwide phytotherapeutic market has taken place over the past 15 years.

There is a widely held belief that herbal preparations, being 'natural', are intrinsically harmless. Their effects are generally not attributed to their natural origin but rather to the pharmacological characteristics and dose levels of their active constituents. The pharmacological assessment of these constituents is the most important part of drugs based on herbs. However, herbal medicines can potentially be toxic if used incorrectly or as substitutes for conventional medicines. A variety of interactions between the active components of herbal medicines may occur. In addition, the components of these herbal medicines are not rigorously substantiated. Thus, instances of efficacy and toxicity have recently surfaced with several commercially available herbal medicines. This chapter highlights current advances in the knowledge of the efficacy and safety assessment of their biological activities as an essential part of phytopharmacological research.

Natural Products Drug Discovery–An Overview

The use of natural products with therapeutic properties is as ancient as human civilisation, and, for a long time, minerals and plant and animal products were the main sources of drugs. Research on natural products continues to provide a tremendous variety of lead structures, which are used as templates for the development of new drugs by the pharmaceutical industry. The main thrust of research in large pharmaceutical corporations is directed towards the discovery and development of new drugs (Fig. 29.1).

Natural product research is a part, albeit a small one, of the discovery process. The screening of natural products is one of the earliest steps in drug discovery, namely 'lead' identification. A lead compound, the term currently used, is a compound with many of the characteristics of a desired drug, which will be used as a model for chemical modification. It must be potent, but need not possess potency at the nanomolar or picomolar levels expected of a product candidate. It must be specific to the desired target, but does not need to possess the exquisite biochemical specificity required of a new drug. Finally, it must be available in sufficient quantities to support the early stages of development, such as biological characterisation and toxicity studies, while total synthesis of the product candidate

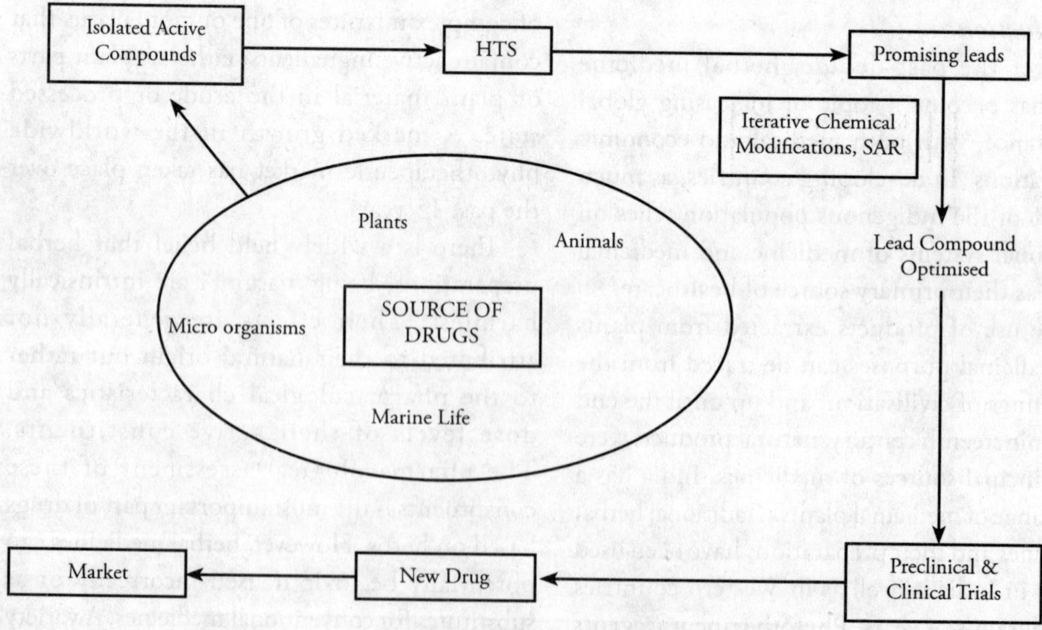

Figure 29.1: Natural product drugs

is being completed. It is relatively easy to find a lead compound than a product candidate. New assays that can selectively and effectively detect biologically active molecules at very low levels, and advanced chemical techniques that enable the chemist to isolate and identify minute amounts of active compounds have together lead to the current interest in natural product drug discovery.

Isolation of suspected new compounds from extracts that show activity in screening involves close collaboration between the chemist performing the isolation and the biologist or biochemist performing the assay. Experience suggests that plant extracts are usually more complex than extracts from fermentation broths, but modern isolation methodologies routinely allow the purification of the active constituent in an acceptable timeframe.

Once a pure, active phytochemical is in hand, the research activities surrounding it are essentially the same as those for a microbial or synthetic product. The compound is identified and, along with a range of related compounds, is biologically characterised. The best member of the group is taken forward through pharmacological evaluation and safety assessment and into clinical trials. If all goes extraordinarily well, after 8–12 years and with substantial investment (100–500 million USD), a new drug based on this lead may reach the market. Advances in bioassay techniques and chemical methodologies have combined to make natural products a cost-effective source of new leads.

Biological Assays in Evaluating Natural Products

Herbal products are heterogeneous in nature and contain complex mixtures of different constituents; therefore, analytical methods such as titrimetry, chromatography or spectroscopy are not of much use for the purpose of evaluation. Bioassays offer a special advantage in the standardisation and purity assessment of heterogeneous mixtures of extracts. Extracts with high therapeutic value are always assessed for their bioactivity; furthermore, an active extract is selected and fractionation is performed using different solvents to obtain pure compounds. In natural product drug discovery, researchers systematically evaluate the product by isolating, characterising the chemical structures and evaluating their therapeutic value by performing simpler cell-based assays, isolated organ studies or in vivo studies using various animal models (Fig. 29.2).

Phytopharmacological Evaluation of Natural Products

Pharmacological researchers are presently focussing attention on the most promising area of development of alternatives to animal methods (Fig. 29.3). The alternative method in pharmacological research has several advantages:

- Reduction in the number of animals used
- Reduction in animal pain, suffering and experimental insult
- Reduction in the time spent; quicker results

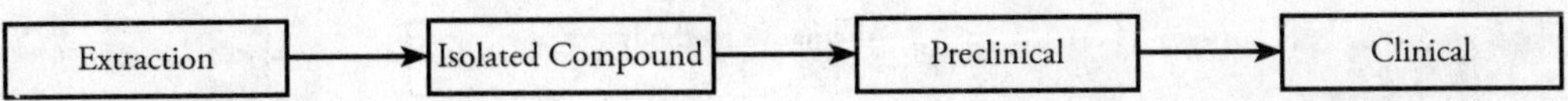

Figure 29.2: Schematic diagram showing the process of natural product development

- Reduction in cost
- Ease in changing conditions and variables

At the same time, alternative methods have some disadvantages, pertaining to the reduced ability to:

- Study integrated biochemical and metabolic pathways
- Study the recovery of damaged tissue
- Study interactions between the organism and its environment
- Study idiosyncratic or species-specific responses
- Study sea-specific phenomena

Globally, pharmacological studies are under the purview of mandatory ethical considerations and the emphasis is on the three Rs—refine, reduce and replace.

Toxicity Studies

In the drug discovery process, assessment of toxic potential is always used to prioritise compounds for further evaluation, and natural products are no exception to this rule. This is done by assessing a probable safe dose for administration during preclinical development and evaluating the risk caused by prolonged exposure.

Almost one half of all failures in investigational drug development phases are because of unacceptable efficacy and approximately one-third (27–40%) because of safety issues. The failure rate of drugs in the early and late stages remains alarmingly high. A high proportion of early and late pipeline dropouts occur because of undesired human toxicity. Drug toxicity is traditionally determined in animals by examining observable changes, serum biochemistry and histopathology. Based on these studies, risk assessment to humans is extrapolated.

Toxicity studies in animals (or in vitro systems) must be carefully observed to avoid errors in estimating the potential risk to humans. However, including new technologies that involve in vitro screens with biomarkers for

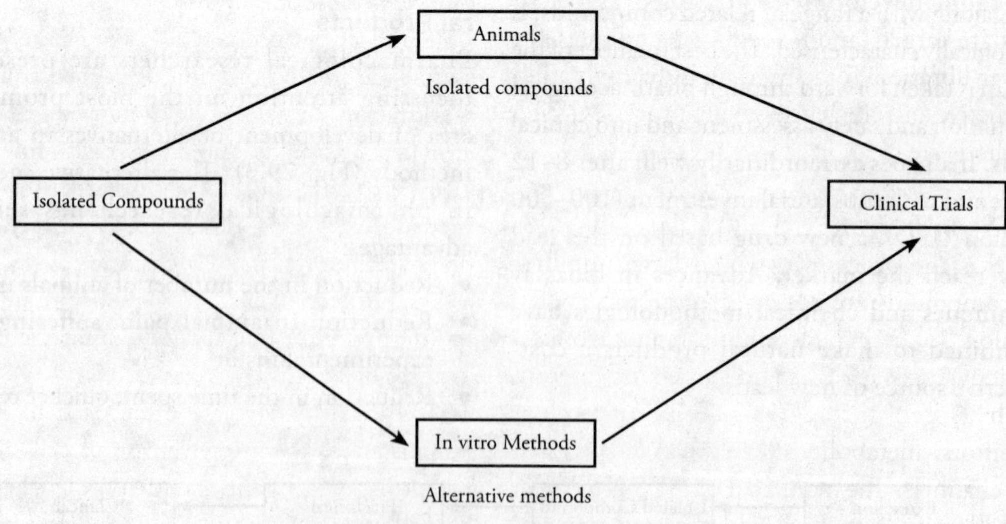

Figure 29.3: Diagram showing phytopharmacological evaluation of isolated compounds

toxicity in high throughput screening (HTS) systems, in addition to the animal studies, will greatly enhance the predictability and relevance of such studies to human safety assessment.

HTS and Drug Evaluation

Biomedical research allows dissection of the basis of multifunctional diseases and determines the most suitable point of targeting for future therapeutics. In recent years, technological advances have caused tremendous changes in the drug evaluation process. Concurrently, new approaches have increased the number of compounds that can be tested for various activities. This stimulated the adoption of HTS as a primary tool for drug evaluation. HTS has been increasingly used in the lead identification and selection process for the next step—the so-called 'lead optimisation'.

However, only a small portion of drug molecules advance, and approximately 80% of these fail to become drugs. In spite of these obstacles, there has always been a high demand for rapid development of drugs, assays to validate targets and screening techniques for newer libraries. To achieve high quality, rapid, predictive and efficient assaying processes, HTS methods are used.

HTS–An Insight

HTS is the process by which large numbers of compounds are screened in an automated fashion, for activity as inhibitors (antagonists) or activators (agonists) on targets of interest, such as cell surface/intracellular/nuclear receptors, metabolic/biochemical enzymes or ion channels. The main goal of HTS is to select and identify 'hits' or 'leads' that are active at a low concentration with high specificity and supply directions that eventually become drugs. A well-designed HTS in addition to providing information about the potency and specificity of compounds can significantly boost the drug discovery process. In addition, the spectrum of compounds scoring positive signals in HTS helps in understanding the structural features/basis of molecular activity.

HTS requires four elements:

- Suitably arrayed compound libraries
- A configured assay method
- A robotic work station
- A computerised system for handling data

The 96-well plate or higher is the standard format for automated assays. The synthesis of combinatorial libraries accomplished in microtitre plates provides information about particular compounds generated by a given subset of reactions, thus identifying compounds. Concentrates of fermented broths, natural product extracts and chemicals can be dispensed in 96/384/1284-well plates, either singly (simple array) or as a mixture of 10–20 compounds in one well (multiplex arrays).

Robotic systems for HTS range from simple automated dilution devices to complex workstations in which one or more mechanical arms perform multiple functions. Full automation allows round-the-clock operation, which increases the screening speed. Bioinformatics plays an important and increasing role in HTS assays. Different data handling software are used to interpret HTS output and to use data for the next set of screens.

Cell-based assays are often used in HTS. For instance, agonist activation of cell surface receptors or a ligand gated ion channel can be followed by monitoring coupled cellular response. Cell-based assays have some advantages over in vitro assays, as they provide an insight into the bioavailability and cytotoxicity studies of leads. However, mammalian cells are expensive to maintain and culture and difficult to propagate in the automated HTS system.

The advent of DNA sequencing, microarrays, combinatorial chemistry, cell-based assays and HTS has enabled the pharmaceutical industry to build lead molecules at a faster rate. With improvements, especially in the area of lead identification and optimisation, HTS assays are very useful tools in the drug discovery process. Further developments in HTS will provide new avenues for the diagnosis, treatment and prevention of diseases.

Extraction of Herbal Drugs

Extraction can be defined as the removal of soluble materials from an insoluble residue, either liquid or solid, by treatment with a liquid solvent. The commonly employed technique for removal of the active substance from the crude drug is called extraction. The choice of the plant material for extraction depends on its nature and the components to be isolated.

The commonly employed technique for removing active substances from the crude drug is called extraction. The choice of plant material for extraction depends on its nature and the components to be isolated. The dried, powdered plant parts are homogenised (mixed) with a solvent such as alcohol, which is a general solvent for many plant constituents. A water immiscible solvent such as light petroleum is used for the extraction of fixed and essential oils. Steroids and aglycons, chloroform and ether are used for separation of alkaloids and quinines. Water-soluble compounds such as tannins and glycosides are extracted with methanol. Extraction may be performed by repeated maceration with agitation and percolation by continuous soxhlet extraction.

The different methods used to extract materials are as follows:

- Infusion
- Decoction
- Maceration
- Percolation

Infusion

The weighed quantity of drug is kept in contact with a known quantity of menstrum (solvent for extraction) for a specified period of time, and at the end of the period, the supernatant liquid is collected and poured into the receiver. Hence, the menstrum may be either cold or hot depending on the drug material. For example, fresh quassia infusion.

Decoction

This is not an official preparation in pharmacopeia. In this method, a known quantity of a drug is boiled with the menstrum for a specified period of time (15 minutes), at the end of which the supernatant liquid is collected. For example, coffee or tea decoction.

Maceration

It is defined as the phase in which the solid materials are mixed with the whole of the menstrum in a closed vessel and allowed to stand for 7 days, while being shaken occasionally. The marc (residue left behind) is then strained and pressed, the liquid obtained is mixed with the mother liquor and is clarified by filtration. This method may be used for a number of purposes such as for preparing tinctures from organised drugs.

Percolation

Percolation is of three types:

- Percolation for tinctures
- Percolation for concentrated preparations
- Continuous hot percolation or soxhelation

The percolation process has three main stages:

1. Imbibition: The powdered drug is moistened with some of the menstrum and allowed to stand for 4 hours. During this time, the drug swells and the menstrum penetrates the cell walls.
2. Maceration: The moistened drug is left in contact with the menstrum for 24 hours. During this time, the menstrum is saturated with the soluble constituents of the drug.
3. Percolation: This consists of the downward displacement of the saturated solution formed from maceration and extraction of the remaining soluble matter by slow passage of the menstrum through the column of drug.

Liquid/Liquid Extraction

This method will be familiar as it is the same as the purification procedures used in alkaloidal assays, and large-scale processes are based on similar principles.

A solution of the substance that must be extracted is brought into contact with another solvent for the substance that is immiscible with the first solvent. A concentration gradient is set up between the phases and mass transfer occurs until an equilibrium is established and the solute is distributed depending on the distribution coefficient.

Solid/Liquid Extraction

The extraction of a soluble constituent from a solid by means of a solvent is commonly referred to as leaching. The general term extraction is also frequently used. Certain operations involve the extraction of a soluble substance from an insoluble mineral material. However, this is subject to control by the usual factors affecting the solution.

Extraction of Plant Materials

All plant materials used should be properly authenticated. The choice of extraction procedure depends on the nature of the plant material and the components to be isolated. Dried materials are usually powdered before extraction, whereas fresh plants (leaves, etc) can be homogenised or macerated with a solvent such as alcohol. The latter is also particularly useful for stabilising fresh leaves by dropping them in the boiling solvent. Alcohol is a general solvent for many plant constituents (most fixed oils expected) and as such may cause problems in the subsequent elimination of pigments, resins, etc. Water and immiscible solvents are widely used. Light petroleum (essential and fixed oils, steroids), ether and chloroform (alkaloids, quinones) are also used. The extraction of organic bases, for example, alkaloids, usually necessitates basification of the plant material if a water immiscible solvent is to be used for aromatic acids and for phenols acidification may be required.

Ultrasound may enhance the extraction process for some plant materials and the British Pharmacopia (BP) uses this in the preparation of a 50% ethanolic solution of opium for the assay of alkaloids.

The general methods of plant extractions are now discussed.

Super Critical Fluid Extraction

In 1822, Charles Cagniard de la Tour reported that above a certain temperature and pressure, single substances do not condense or evaporate but exist as fluids. Under these conditions, the gas and liquid phases possess the same density, and no division exists between the two phases. This is called the critical state.

For water, the critical conditions for temperature (tc) and pressure (pc) are 374 °C and 220 atm, respectively, and for carbon dioxide, tc = 31°C and pc = 74 atm. In practice, conditions somewhat above the critical temperatures and pressure for a particular substance are usually used and these super critical fluids exhibit properties intermediate between those of the liquid and gaseous phases.

It also enables processing at a low temperature and has proved to be of value in the extraction of labile expensive fragrances and medicinal phytochemicals. To render it more polar, a small amount of a modifier such as methanol may be added to CO2. The high pressure and, for some substances, high temperature involved in super critical fluid extraction are the principal disadvantages of this technique.

Examples of more recent studies involving the extraction of phytochemicals with supercritical CO_2 are as follows:

- Alkaloids: Decaffeination of green coffee (industrial application). Isolation of vidoline from *Catharanthus roseus.*
- Ditopene: Extraction of taxol from *Taxus brevtocia* (extraction more selective than conventional ethanol extraction) and from *T. cuspidate.*
- Fixed oils: Extraction of oil from evening primrose (shift in triglyceride composition oxidation of γ-linolenic acid during extraction reduced).
- Pigments: Extraction of annatto seeds.
- Sesquiterpene lactones: In conjunction with gas chromatography for the isolation of parthenolide from fever few (extracts contained significant amounts of camphor and chrysanthenol acetate); addition of methanol or methyl cyanide as CO_2 modifiers gave higher yields but produced co-extractives.
- Volatile oils and resins: Hops (commercial application), transkinase and myrrh piper nigram muntok (superior aroma of oil: yield 2.8% volatile oil compared with 0.6% steam distillation). Rose petals richer in relevant fragrance compounds (compared with steam distillation) Rosemary, angelica root, coriander, illecium, verum, juniper and berries were also studied.

Separation and Isolation of Constituents

The techniques developed for the separation and isolation of constituents are as follows:

- *Sublimation:* Sublimation may sometimes be possible for the whole drug, as in the isolation of caffeine from tea, or for the purification of materials present in a crude extract. Modern equipment employs low pressures with strict temperature control. Sometimes, substances when heated pass directly from the solid to the vapour state without melting. When cooled, the vapour is transformed into a solid substance and this process is known as sublimation.
- *Distillation:* Fractional distillation has been traditionally used for the separation of the components of volatile mixtures. It has been widely used for the isolation of the components of volatile oils. Steam distillation is used to isolate volatile oils and hydrocyanic acid from plant materials.

- *Fractional Liberation:* Some groups of compounds lend themselves to fractional liberation from mixtures. For example, a mixture of alkaloid salts in aqueous solution treated with aliquots of alkali first produces the weakest base in the free state followed by base liberation in the ascending order of basicity. If the mixture is shaken with an organic solvent after each addition, a fractionated series of tests will be obtained. A similar scheme can be used for organic acids soluble in water immiscible solvents; in this case, starting with a mixture of acid salts. It is possible to fractionally liberate the acids by adding mineral acids.
- *Chromatography:* Many types of chromatography such as thin-layer chromatography and HPLC have been discussed previously.

Preparation of Extracts

Processing of Plant Drugs

The first step involves the removal of extraneous matter such as dirt and adulterants from the plant part intended to be studied. This is performed after collecting but before drying and processing the plants and their parts. The drying operation is carried out at room temperature without exposure to sunlight.

Extract Preparation

Fresh Plants: Fresh plants or parts are collected randomly from different regions. Fresh plant materials are washed under running water, air-dried and then homogenised to a fine powder before being stored in air-tight bottles.

Dried Plant Materials: Air-dried plant materials (measured in grams) are powdered and extracted with 50% ethanol under reflux. After the removal of ethanol *in vacuo,* the aqueous residue is consecutively treated with chloroform and ethyl acetate. Ethyl acetate extract is evaporated to produce a solid residue measured in grams.

Flower Parts: The powder of the stigma or petals of flowers of medicinal plants are extracted by maceration with ethanol or water (80% v/v) for a period of 3 days and, subsequently, the mixture is filtered and concentrated under reduced pressure at 40 °C. The yields (w/w) of aqueous and ethanolic extracts of stigma are calculated and expressed as percentage weight.

Method II

The aerial part of the plant is cleaned with water and dried in the shade until a constant weight is obtained. Extraction is carried out with 95% ethanol (total alcoholic extract = TAE) and then with double distilled water (total aqueous extract = TAQ). The extracts are then concentrated over a water bath maintained at 55 °C until a semisolid concentrate mass is obtained. The yields for TAE and TAQ of the plant material are calculated.

Aqueous Extraction

For aqueous extraction, 10 g of air-dried powder is placed in distilled water and boiled for 6 hours. At intervals of 2 hours, it is filtered through 8 layers of muslin cloth and centrifuged at 5000 x g for 15 minutes. The supernatant is collected. After 6 hours, the supernatant is concentrated to make the final volume about one-fourth of the original volume. Finally, 10 g of the material is extracted in 25 ml of distilled water, producing a concentration of 40 mg/0.1 ml. It is then autoclaved at 121 °C and 760 mm Hg pressure and stored at 4 °C.

Rhizome Drugs

The dried rhizome is powdered mechanically and extracted by cold percolation with 95% ethanol for 24 hours. The extract is recovered and 95% ethanol is added to the plant material and the extraction continued. The process is repeated three times. The three extracts are pooled together and the combined extract is concentrated under reduced pressure (22–26 mmHg) at 45–60 °C. Solvent-free extract (30 g) equivalent to 1 kg of dried powder of rhizome (w/w) is obtained.

Method II

Air-dried and powdered roots of plants (in grams) are extracted by percolation at room temperature using methanol. The methanolic extract is concentrated under a vacuum in a rotary evaporator to yield a dark brown, semisolid mass which is further dried in a vacuum oven drier (at approximately 25 °C for 3 days) and expressed as a percentage of solid residue of dried, powdered plant materials.

Method III

Crushed leaves and flowers measured in grams are extracted with a series of solvents such as double distilled water, acetone, methanol, ethanol and methylene dichloride. Aqueous extracts are prepared by leaching the crushed plant material in 100–200 ml double distilled water in a flask in the dark at 4 °C. Leaching is performed for 4 days and each day the extract is filtered using Whatman Grade No. 1 filter paper. The combined filtrates are freeze-dried by lyophilisation. Extracts from the organic solvents are prepared in a similar manner but acetone, methanol and ethanol extracts are left at room temperature to soak. All organic extracts are dried using rotary evaporation by maintaining the temperature at not more than 60 °C.

Method IV

Extraction and Isolation of Compounds: The stem bark of plants is shade-dried and ground to a powder; 2.5 kg of powdered bark is extracted with methanol. The obtained filtrate is concentrated under reduced pressure which yields a dark brown, semisolid mass. This mass is washed with petroleum ether (40–60 °C) to remove the fatty portion. The fat-free part is dried and the final mass subjected to silica gel (60–120 mesh) column chromatography. The column is eluted with various solvents in increasing order of their polarity.

Method V

Fresh roots measured in grams are macerated at room temperature in $CHCl_3$ for 24 hours. The solvent is then evaporated in vacuum to obtain a crude chloroform residue in grams. The leaves are washed, air-dried and pulverised and then extracted with ethanol by the same method. Approximately 5 g of dark brown, sticky extract is obtained from 100 g of dried, pulverised leaves. The extract is dissolved in distilled water, centrifuged at 10,000 rpm (9410 × g) at 4 °C for 20 minutes and passed through a 0.2 µm filter. The filtrate is used as the starting material for subsequent studies.

Method VI

The air-dried and powdered plant materials are extracted successively by shaking with chloroform ($CHCl_3$) three to five times at room temperature, with 90% methanol in a water bath at 50 °C and finely with water in a water bath at 70 °C. The obtained extracts are filtered and evaporated using vacuum evaporator or freeze dryer, which yields the crude dried extract.

Method VII

The powdered roots (in grams) of plants are extracted with ethanol (96%, v/v) using a soxhlet apparatus to remove low molecular weight compounds. When no more coloured material is observed in the ethanol extract, the procedure is stopped. The residue is extracted twice with water at 50 °C for 2 hours, filtered through gauze and Whatman GF/A glass fibre filter, concentrated at 40 °C in vacuum and dialysed at cut off 3500 Da to yield a 50 °C crude extract (%). The extract is stored at –18 °C or lyophilised.

Solvent Extraction

About 10 g of air-dried powder is placed in 100 ml of organic solvent (methanol) in a conical flask, plugged with cotton and then kept on a rotary shaker at 190–220 rpm for 24 hours. After 24 hours, it is filtered through 8 layers of muslin cloth and centrifuged at 5000 x g for 15 minutes. The supernatant is collected and the solvent is evaporated to make the final volume one-fourth of the original volume, giving a concentration of 40 mg/0.1 ml. It is stored at 4 °C in air-tight bottles for further study.

Additional Procedures

Removal of Sulphated Polysaccharides: Sulphated polysaccharides have consistently shown activity in anti-HIV assays and are believed to function by destabilising the glycoprotein complex and/or inhibiting reverse transcriptase. Many compounds from this class have already been described extensively in the literature as having anti-HIV activity. To determine if any potential anti-HIV activity seen in the aqueous extracts is due to sulphated polysaccharides, a portion of the aqueous extract from each of the drugs is subjected to 50% ethanol precipitation. After ethanol addition, extracts are stirred at 4 °C for 30 minutes and then filtered and dried.

Tannin Removal: Tannins are widely found in plants, and most HIV inhibitory effects attributed to plant materials are caused by tannins. Tannins have been shown to inhibit HIV reverse transcriptase (HIVRT) but are non-specific and inhibit a large range of enzymatic pathways. Although tannins show antiviral effects, they are also known to cause liver damage and have carcinogenic potential and anti-nutritional activity. Drugs are added to assay buffers to a final assay concentration of 0.2% (w/v) to adsorb possible tannins from crude extracts that show a 50% or more inhibitory effect in the anti-HIV assays.

Drug Preparation

The extract obtained is reconstituted in distilled water if it is soluble in water to get the desired concentration for all pharmacological tests. It can be suspended in 5% dimethyl sulfoxide (DMSO) in water for pharmacological experiments. Some of the extracts are directly dissolved in normal saline. For subsequent pharmacological and biochemical studies, 1% of extract is suspended in 5% gum acacia, if insoluble in water, and extracts, which are water soluble. Hence, an aqueous solution is used. The concentrate is weighed and an equivalent dose of the crude drug:kg of body weight (w/w) is calculated and stored in the dark at 4 °C. The drug doses containing petroleum ether (mg/kg), chloroform (mg/kg), ethanol (mg/kg) and distilled water (mg/kg) extracts can also be prepared in 1% Tween-80 as suspension.

Toxicity Studies

Acute Toxicity Studies

Acute toxicity (LD_{50}) can be estimated orally in

rats. Dose levels used have a range of 200–2000 mg/kg. Clinical signs and the number of deaths in each group of rats (within 72 hours) are monitored.

Method I: Subacute Toxicity Studies

Twenty-four male rats are selected by stratified randomisation and divided into four groups of six each. The first group serves as a control (only water is given) while the remaining three groups orally receive 125, 250 and 500 mg/kg, respectively, of extract for 21 days. The first day of dosing is taken as D0 (Day 0), and the day of sacrifice is designated as D21 (Day 21).

Weekly Body Weight

The body weight of each rat is assessed using a sensitive balance during the acclimatisation period, once before commencement of dosing, once every 5 days during the dosing period and once on the day of sacrifice.

Feed and Water Consumption

The amount of feed and water consumed are measured daily from the quantity of feed and water supplied and the amount remaining after 24 hours.

Mortality and Clinical Signs

During the four-week dosing period, all the animals are observed daily for clinical signs and mortality patterns once before dosing, during dosing and up to 4 hours after dosing.

Relative Organ Weight

On D21 of the dosing period, all the animals are euthanised by exsanguinations under chloroform anesthesia. Different organs such as the heart, liver, lungs, spleen, kidneys and testes are surgically dissected out and weighed in grams (absolute organ weight). The relative organ weight (ROW) of each animal is then calculated as follows:

$$\text{ROW} = \frac{\text{Absolute organ weight x 100}}{\text{Body weight of rat on the day of sacrifice (g)}}$$

Gross Pathology and Microscopic Examination

Dead animals are weighed and necropsied soon after death (or as soon as possible if death occurs overnight) and macroscopic examination of vital organs carried out. Tissue biopsies from the heart, liver, kidneys, lungs, spleen and testes are fixed in 10% normal saline. These are processed with an automatic tissue processor. Following dehydration and embedding, sections are cut at 4–5 microns with the rotary microtone, stained with hematoxylin and eosin and examined microscopically. Additional thin sections of the kidneys are cut at 3 microns and stained for the periodic acid Schiff (PAS) reaction.

Hematology

The packed cell volume (PCV) and hemoglobin (Hb) estimation are carried out using the microhematocrit and cyanmethanemoglobin methods and the total leucocytes counts (TLC) are also performed.

Preparation of Sera Samples

On D21 of the dosing period, all the animals are exsanguinated under chloroform anesthesia and blood samples are drawn from the heart of each sacrificed animal. The samples are collected in plastic test tubes and allowed to stand for 3 hours to ensure complete clotting. The clotted blood samples are centrifuged at 3000 rpm for 10 minutes and clear serum samples are aspirated and stored frozen.

Serum Biochemistry

The following parameters can be determined colourimetrically by employing the standard ready-to-use kits and methods of human glutamate oxaloacetate transaminase (GOT), glutamate pyruvate transaminase (GPT), alkaline phosphatase (ALP), total proteins, albumin, total bilirubin, creatinine kinase (CK), calcium, urea, blood urea nitrogen (BUN), uric acid, total cholesterol and triglycerides.

Statistical Analysis

The results are expressed as mean ± standard error of the mean (SEM). The data is analysed as a completely randomised design using one-way analysis of variance (ANOVA). Sometimes, two-way ANOVA is applicable. Significant difference between means is assessed by both the Student's t-test and Dunnett's post-hoc test. About 95% level of significance ($P < 0.05$) is used for statistical analysis.

Method II: Acute Toxicity (TD_{50} and LD_{50})

Mice are selected for this study. They are divided into five groups of six animals each. One group is treated with a physiological solution and the remaining groups with increasing doses (4, 8, 10, 12, 14, 16, 32, 64, 128, 256, 512, 2048 and 4096 mg/kg) of aqueous extract IP in the requisite volume of 0.1 ml/kg. Animal behaviour is observed at 10, 30, 60 and 90 minutes after treatment.

A time–effect curve is built for all extract doses assayed for the purpose of estimating the time of the peak effect (TPE), this being the time at which most animals present a particular toxic effect. LD_{50} and DT_{50}, and their 95% confidence intervals, are obtained.

Method III: Determination of Oral LD_{50}

The study is conducted on Swiss albino mice (25–30 g body weight). The animals are divided into four groups, each containing 10 mice of both sexes (five males, five females). The extract is administered by the intragastric route starting from smaller to higher doses in 1 ml of vehicle. Records of mortality and manifestation of toxicity are made during 24 hours. Based on the mortality rate and probit values, the oral LD_{50} dose is determined.

Maximum Non-fatal Dose (MNFD) and Acute Toxicity

Different doses of the extract are injected into different groups of five animals. After 48 hours, the highest dose that did not induce any mortality is considered as the maximum non-fatal dose. The number of deaths is counted 48 hours after treatment. LD_{50} values and the corresponding confidence limits (CL, 95%) are determined by the Litchfield and Wilcoxon method. Doses of 10, 40 (50), 70 and 100% MNFD are chosen for most tests.

Brine Shrimp Lethality Assay

Brine shrimp eggs (*Artemia salina,* leach) are hatched in artificial sea water (33 g/l of sea salt) and then incubated at room temperature for 48 hours. With the help of a light source, the larvae (nauplii) are attracted to one side of the vessel and easily collected for the assay. The extract and fractions are dissolved in DMSO at a maximum concentration not exceeding 0.05% and then diluted with sea water to be tested at final concentrations of 10, 100 and 1000 μg/ml. Each dose is tested in triplicate.

Ten nauplii are used to test each dose of extract. Nauplii are counted under a magnifying glass after 24 hours of incubation. The number of dead nauplii is recorded and used to calculate LC_{50} concentration by the Finney probit analysis programme.

General Pharmacological Screening

Effect of Extracts on General Behaviour

Studies on general behaviour in mice injected with the extracts are determined using albino mice of either sex weighing 20–35 g and divided into different groups (n = 6). The extracts are administered at a dose of 1 g/kg body weight orally. After administration of test compounds, the animals are observed for gross behavioural effects for the first four hours and then at every 10 hours up to 72 hours. The gross behavioural, neurological, autonomic and toxic effects are observed.

Selection of Doses: About one-tenth of a well-tolerated dose that showed no mortality is selected for detailed pharmacological screening and phyotpharmacological screening of extracts.

Effect of Extracts on Pentobarbitone-induced Sleep

Albino mice of either sex weighing 20–35 g are divided into different groups (n = 6). Group I receives 1% v/v Tween-80 solution as control and Groups II, III, IV and V receive extracts at a dose of 100 mg/kg of body weight, PO. After 20 minutes of drug treatment, all groups receive pentobarbitone sodium at 35 mg/kg of body weight IP. The effect of the drugs on the duration of sleep is assessed as the time between loss and gain of righting reflex.

Effects of Extracts on Barbituric Sleeping

After oral administration of distilled water, haloperidol and extracts, pentobarbital (50 mg/kg G1) is injected intraperitoneally. The threshold and duration of sleep are determined as described previously.

Effects of Extracts on Rectal Temperature

Sixty minutes after administration of extracts, rectal temperature is determined.

Effects on Apomorphin Stereotypes

Sixty minutes after administration of extracts, intensity of stereotypes induced by subcutaneous injection of apomorphin (1 mg/kg G1) is evaluated during 60 minutes.

Effects on Apomorphin Hypothermia

Six groups of rats are orally given distilled water, clomipramin (16 mg/ kg; G1) and extracts (400 and 800 mg/kg; G1). Sixty minutes after administration of drugs, apomorphin (16 mg/kg; G1) is injected subcutaneously and the rectal temperature is measured during 4 hours.

Effect on Catalepsy and Ptosis Induced by Haloperidol

Sixty minutes after drug administration, catalepsy and ptosis are evaluated. The reaction time on the horizontal metallic bar and ptosis intensity is determined 4 hours after IP injection of haloperidol (5 mg/kg; G1).

Effect on Immobility Induced by Forced Swimming

Sixty minutes after oral administration of distilled water, clomipramin (16 mg/kg; G1), leaves and extracts (mg/kg; G1), animals are submitted to forced swimming and the duration of immobility is determined for 3 minutes.

Study of an Eventual Tolerance on Analgesic Effect

Three groups of mice receive distilled water and extracts (mg/kg; G1) for 21 days. On the 7th,

14th and 21st days, acetic acid (0, 6%, 10 ml/kg; G1) is injected IP and the writhing syndrome is studied.

Effect on Water Consumption

Six groups of rats orally receive distilled water, scopolamine (0.5 mg kg; G1) and extracts (mg/kg; G1). Sixty minutes after drug administration, a feeding-bottle containing 200 ml of water is placed in the animal cage and the water consumption is determined for 30 minutes.

Anti-inflammatory Studies

Carrageenan–induced Paw Edema in Rats

Pedal inflammation in rats is induced essentially by injecting 0.1 ml of 1% Carrageenan suspension into the right hind foot of each rat under the subplantar aponeurosis. The test groups of rats are treated intraperitoneally with the extract (mg/kg) 1 hour before the Carrageenan injection. The control group receives only the vehicle (0.2 ml normal saline) and the reference group 150 mg/kg aspirin (IP). The paw volume is measured by wrapping a piece of cotton thread around the paw of each rat and measuring the circumference with a meter rule. This procedure is done prior to irritant injection and 1, 2 and 3 hours later. The percentage of edema inhibition in drug-treated rats versus control rats is calculated using the following formula:

$$\% \text{ Inhibition} = 100 \times \frac{(C_t - C_0) \text{ Control} - (C_t - C_0)}{\text{Treated } (C_t - C_0) \text{ Control}}$$

where C_t is the paw size 1, 2 or 3 hours after the Carrageenan injection and C_0 is the paw size before the injection.

Statistical Analysis

Data is expressed as mean ± SE. The results are statistically analysed by the Student's t-test; $P < 0.05$ versus respective control is taken as significant.

Xylene-induced Ear Edema

Mice are divided into groups of seven. Thirty minutes after IP injection of the extract, diclofenac and dexamethasone, 0.03 ml of xylene is applied to the anterior and posterior surfaces of the right ear. The left ear is considered as control. Two hours after xylene application, the mice are killed and both ears are removed.

Circular sections are taken, using a cork borer with a diameter of 7 mm, and weighed. The increase in weight caused by the irritant is measured by subtracting the weight of the untreated left ear section from that of the treated right ear section. The formula for computing percent inhibition is average writhes in the control group (normal saline) minus writhes in the drug group divided by writhes in the control group times 100%. Control receives normal saline (10 ml/kg, IP). Diclofenac (10 mg/kg, IP) and dexamethasone (15 mg/kg, IP) are used as reference drugs.

Formalin-induced Inflammation

Rats are divided into groups of six. The inflammation is produced by subaponeurotic injection of 0.1 ml of 2% formaldehyde in the right hind paw of the rats on the first and third day. The animals are treated daily with the extracts or diclofenac intraperitoneally for 10 days. The daily changes in paw size are measured by wrapping a piece of cotton thread around the paw and measuring the circumference with a meter rule.

Statistical Analysis

The data is expressed as mean values ± SEM and tested with analysis of variance followed by the multiple comparison test of Tukey–Kramer.

Antinociceptive Study

Hot-plate Test: The hot-plate test is assessed on groups of 8 mice. The temperature of a metal surface is maintained at 55 ± 0.2 °C. Latency to a discomfort reaction (licking of paws or jumping) is determined before and after drug administration. The cut-off time is 20 seconds. The latency is recorded before and 30, 60, 120, 150 and 240 minutes following intraperitoneal administration of the agents. The prolongation of the latency times compared with the values of the control is used for statistical comparison. Control receives normal saline (10 ml/kg, IP), and morphine (10 mg/kg, IP) is used as the reference drug.

Acetic acid–induced Writhing in Mice

Swiss mice are divided into various treatment and control groups of five mice per group. Writhings are induced and the test groups are administered with the extract (mg/kg) IP, while the control group receives 0.2 ml normal saline. The reference group receives 150 mg/kg aspirin, IP. The animals are made to fast for 16 hours prior to treatment.

One hour after treatment, the mice are injected with 0.2 ml of 3% acetic acid solution IP to induce writhing. The number of abdominal constrictions (writhing) and stretching with a jerk of the hind limb is counted between 5 and 15 minutes after acetic acid injection. The response of the extract and aspirin-treated groups are compared with those of the animals in the control group (0.2 ml saline). Percentage protection against writhing movement (% inhibition of writhing) is taken as an index of analgesia and is calculated as follows:

$$\% \text{ Inhibition} = \frac{W_r \text{ (Control)} - W_r \text{ (test group)}}{W_r \text{ (Control)}}$$

where W_r = Mean number of writhing

Test Microorganisms

The microbial strains are identified and obtained from the standard laboratories. The bacterial strains studied are *Pseudomonas testosteroni NCIM 5098, Staphylococcus epidermidis ATCC 12228, Proteus morganii NCIM 2040, Bacillus subtilis ATCC 6633, Micrococcus flavus ATCC 10240* and *Klebsiella pneumoniae NCIM 2719.*

Antibacterial Assay

A loop full of the strain is inoculated in 30 ml of nutrient broth in a conical flask and incubated on a rotary shaker for 24 hours to activate the strain. Mueller–Hinton Agar No. 2 is prepared for the study. The assay is performed using two methods: Agar disk diffusion for aqueous extract and Agar ditch diffusion for solvent extract.

The media and the test bacterial cultures are poured into petri dishes. The test strain (0.2 ml) is inoculated into the media (inoculum size 108 cells/ml) when the temperature reaches 40–42 °C. Care is taken to ensure proper homogenisation. The experiment is performed under strict aseptic conditions.

For the Agar disk diffusion method, the test compound (0.1 ml) is introduced onto the disk (0.7 cm) and then allowed to dry. Thus the disk is completely saturated with the test compound. Then the disk is introduced onto the upper layer of the medium with the bacteria. The plates are incubated overnight at 37 °C.

For the Agar ditch diffusion method, after the medium is solidified, a ditch is made in the plates with the help of a cup-borer (0.85 cm). The test compound is introduced into the well and the plates are incubated overnight at 37 °C.

Microbial growth is determined by measuring the diameter of the zone of inhibition. Methanol and distilled water are used as the control.

The control activity is deducted from the test and the result obtained is plotted.

Cardiac Stimulant Activity

Frog Heart In Situ Preparation

Frogs are pithed and the heart exposed. The inferior vena cava is cannulated to enable perfusion of the heart with Ringer's solution (the composition of frog Ringer's solution in millimoles: NaCl–110; KCl–1.9; $CaCl_2$–1.1; $NaHCO_3$–2.4; NaH_2PO_4–0.06; Glucose–11.1). The basal cardiac contraction is recorded on a smoked kymographic drum after the administration of frog Ringer's solution and gum acacia (5%), which is given to ensure that it does not contribute to the effects of the extracts. The drugs and extracts are administered through the cannula.

The average basal heart rate and the contraction amplitude are 70 beats/minute and 18 mm, respectively. The effects obtained with the drugs and extracts are transposed to the respective percentage of the basal values. Graded dose response is recorded for each extract (0.5, 1 and 1.5 mg) and the dose that caused the maximum effect is chosen as the experimental dose.

The frog's heart is washed with the Ringer's solution after each administration of extracts and drugs, till it is brought back to the normal state. The frog's heart is perfused with propranolol, a ß-adrenergic blocker at 3×10^{-5} M concentration in frog Ringer's solution for 60 seconds, followed by the administration of extracts. The recordings are then noted.

Nifedipine, a calcium channel blocker at 2.88×10^{-5} M concentration in frog Ringer's solution is administered for 60 seconds followed by extracts, and the recordings are noted.

Biochemical Studies

Wistar albino rats are divided into three groups of 6 animals each. Group I receives extracts with 5% gum acacia suspension; this serves as the control. Group II and Group III are treated with extracts at a suitable dose in mg/kg (approximately one-tenth of the LD_{50}) body weight IP for 7 days. On the eighth day, the animals are sacrificed, the blood and heart tissue are collected and the serum is separated from the blood. The heart is washed in ice-cold saline and about 100 mg of tissue is weighed and homogenised in chilled 0.1 M Tris-HCl buffer in a Potter–Elvehjem teflon homogeniser. The serum and homogenised samples are assayed for clinical marker enzymes such as creatine phosphokinase (CPK) and lactate dehydrogenase (LDH) and the transaminases AST and ALT. Heart homogenate samples are also assayed for $Na^+ K^+$ATPase, Ca^{2+}ATPase and Mg^{2+}ATPase.

Statistical Analysis

The in situ frog's heart experiment and biochemical parameters obtained are subjected to one-way ANOVA followed by Tukey's multiple comparison test. A P value of <0.05 is considered significant.

Cardiotonic Activity

Cardiovascular disease continues to be one of the major causes of human morbidity and mortality, and is growing at an exponential rate worldwide. The various cardiovascular screening techniques employed are patch clamp technique, isolated cardiac myocyte, isolated arteries, etc. Among these, the isolated rat heart method is one of the most efficient ways of determining the effects of drugs on the heart in vitro. In the present study, the isolated perfused heart method is used to study the effects of extracts.

Preparation of Krebs–Henseleit Solution

Freshly prepared Krebs–Henseleit solution is used. Ingredients with their respective weights in gm/L are outlined in Table 29.1.

Requisite quantities of NaCl, KCl, KH_2PO_4, $MgSO_4$ and glucose are dissolved thoroughly in half of the volume of distilled water. A diluted solution of $CaCl_2$ and $NaHCO_3$ is prepared separately in distilled water. Initially, a $CaCl_2$ solution is added slowly to the stock solution and is followed by a diluted solution of $NaHCO_3$, while mixing the contents thoroughly (to avoid turbidity). After complete dissolution, the volume is finally made up to a sufficient quantity. The solution is thoroughly filtered by using Whatman filter paper.

Isolated Rat Heart Studies

A modified Langendoıff's set up for the isolated perfused heart is used for cardiovascular screening of extracts. The system consists of a water jacket coil, 14 x 3.2 cm with 10 spirals, with a three-way piece inlet and a three-way outlet. The lower limb of the outlet passes through the stopper for cannulation of the aorta.

Table 29.1: Ingredients of the Krebs–Henseleit solution with their weights

Ingredients	*Quantity*
NaCl	6.90 gm/L
KCl	0.35 gm/L
$NaHCO_3$	2.10 gm/L
KH_2PO_4	0.16 gm/L
$MgSO_4 .7H_2O$	11.28 gm/L
$CaCl_2$	0.37 gm/L
Glucose	1–2 gm/L

A latex injecting port is provided between the stopper and the outlet for administration of drugs. The upper limb of the outlet traps the air bubbles produced while injecting. The stopper fits into a hollow, water-jacketed, thermostatically controlled chamber, and a monobasic water pump (1/4 hp) circulates the water at 37 °C from a water bath to the water-jacketed apparatus and back. The Krebs–Henseleit solution passes through the lower limb of the outlet before entering the aorta. The upper limb of the inlet also traps air bubbles.

Isolation and Mounting of Rat Heart

Albino rats of either sex weighing 150–200 gm are deeply anesthetised with a combination of ketamine hydrochloride (65 mg/kg) and xylaxine (8 mg/kg). Heparin (100 units total) is injected IP ten minutes before anesthesia. The rat is anesthetised and the heart with at least 1 cm of aorta attached is removed and placed in the Krebs–Henseleit solution at room temperature and gassed with carbogen (95% O_2 + CO_2).

The heart preparation is squeezed several times to remove blood from it. The aorta is located and dissected free and other vessels connected to the heart are trimmed. The aorta is cut just below the point where it divides, the heart is mounted on perfusion apparatus and the aorta is tied to the cannula using a cotton thread. The heart is then perfused through the aorta with a flow rate of 5 ml/minute at 37 °C by means of a roller pump. A fine thread is tied to the apex of the heart and passed through a thermostatically controlled, water-jacketed, moist chamber and then through a pulley to the transducer (Fig. 29.4).

The chamber is easy to position at the bottom of the system once the isolated heart is

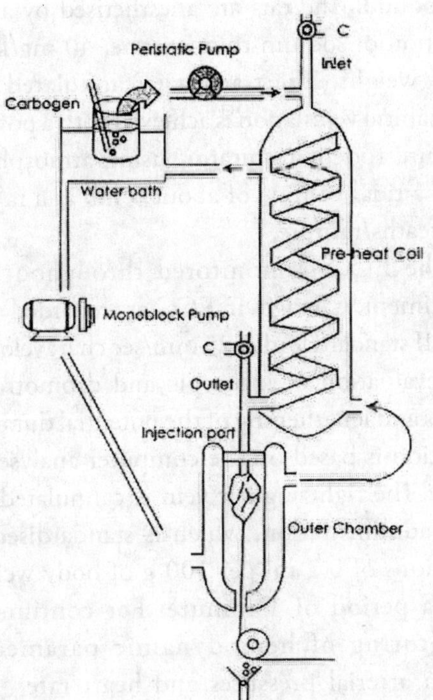

Figure 29.4: Langendorff's heart apparatus

cannulated. In the thermostatic chamber, the heart is allowed to equilibrate for 10 minutes and the regular recording is taken for a control period of 15 minutes followed by test readings. Care is taken to avoid air bubbles entering through the aorta. The perfusion fluid is a carbogenated Krebs–Henseleit solution, which is pumped at constant pressure from the reservoir and warmed to 37 °C by water circulated from the water bath and controlled by the thermostat.

A funnel is placed beneath the lower chamber and the perfusate is collected. The rate of the flow (5 ml/minute) is measured after each dose of extracts. The physiograph is run continuously and a reading of the heart rate and flow is simultaneously measured using Niviqure software for physiology experiments. Doses of the different extracts are adm[illegible] once the heart rate and flow rate return to normal.

Experimental Design

The animals are divided into different groups, each group containing 6 animals.

Group I: Normal (Tween-20) followed by adrenaline tartarate (2 µg), acetyl choline (0.1 mM)

Group II: Standard digoxin (10 µg, 20 µg)

Group III: Extract 1 (Serial dilutions starting from lowest to highest)

Group IV: Extract 2 (Serial dilutions starting from lowest to highest)

Group V: Extract 3 (Serial dilutions starting from lowest to highest)

Group VI: Extract 4 (Serial dilutions starting from lowest to highest)

Each experiment is performed after 10–15 initial stabilisations of the heart.

Measurements: The following parameters are studied:

- Developed tension
- Heart rate/minute
- Ion content (Na^+, K^+, Ca^{2+}in heart perfusate in selected groups)

Resting Tension

The resting tension (2 g) is the basal tension required for recording the contractions of the heart. For 2 g of resting tension, the physiograph is calibrated to 14 mm, that is, each gram corresponds to 7 mm. However, after calibration, the baseline is moved down in the graph to record the developed tension in the middle portion of each channel recording. The increase in resting tension is the difference between the resting tension recorded at any given point and the original resting tension at the beginning of the experiment.

Developed Tension

Developed tension is the tension in grams developed during contraction at the optimum resting tension of the heart and is a function of the work done by the isolated heart. Total developed tension is calculated by measuring the contractions recorded in mm above the resting tension, converting them (each gram corresponds to 7 mm) into a gram unit and adding to it the 2 g of resting tension maintained. Percentage changes in developed tension are calculated by considering the normal response as 100% and hence, the percentage decrease/increase from the contractile process in the presence of extracts gives the percentage change in developed tension, and the results are tabulated.

Heart Rate

The heart rate can be calculated from the RR intervals of these recordings. The base line heart rate is calculated from the RR interval in the ECG just before sample application. The subsequent heart rates at any instant during and following sampling are calculated from the RR intervals in the continuous ECG record. From the data thus generated, the peak heart rate and time to peak heart rate are obtained. Percentage change in heart rate in comparison to the normal is calculated.

Ion Content (Na^+, K^+, Ca^{2+} in heart perfusate in selected groups)

To study the mechanism of action, the heart perfusate collected from different groups that showed cardiotonic activity are subjected to measurement of Na^+, K^+ and Ca^{2+}.

Hemodynamic Screening in Rats

To assess the effect of purified test compounds on the blood pressure and heart rate of anesthetised animals, six rats are used for each compound. The rats are anesthetised by an IP injection of sodium thiopentone, 40 mg/kg of body weight. The trachea is cannulated and mechanical ventilation is achieved with a positive pressure rodent respirator, using atmospheric air at a tidal volume of about 5 ml, at a rate of 25 breaths/minute.

The ECG is monitored throughout the experiment. Changes in ECG are recorded only from II standard lead at 25 mm/sec chart velocity. The evaluation of inotropic and dromotropic effects and lengthening of the potential duration of action is based on the computer analyses of ECG. The right jugular vein is cannulated for drug administration, which is standardised to injections of 0.2 ml per 100 g of body weight over a period of 1 minute. For continuous monitoring of hemodynamic parameters (mean arterial pressures and heart rate), the left common carotid artery is cannulated and the catheter is connected to a pressure transducer. After obtaining control values for 15 minutes, isoproterenol (1 μg/kg) is administered intravenously, followed by the test substance. To check for beta-receptor blocking activity, isoproterenol administration is repeated 20 minutes after injection of the test compound. In some experiments, a beta-blocker (propranolol, 2 mg/kg, IV) is used as a positive control.

Anti-dysrhythmic Effects

The effects are evaluated on chemical and ischemia reperfusion models of arrhythmia. $CaCl_2$-induced arrhythmia is used to evaluate possible anti-arrhythmic calcium antagonistic effect. The arrhythmia is produced by an IV injection of a 2.5% $CaCl_2$ solution (140 mg/kg). A model of adrenaline-induced arrhythmia is produced by IV injection of adrenaline

(10 μg/kg) for evaluating β-blocking activity.

Regional myocardial ischemia and reperfusion are both powerful arrhythmogenic stimuli with different underlying mechanisms of arrhythmogenesis. In anesthetised and artificially ventilated rats, the chest is opened using a left thoracotomy, followed by sectioning of ribs 4 and 5, approximately 2 mm to the left sternum. After incising the pericardium, the heart is exposed out of the chest. A 6.0 silk non-traumatic suture is passed through the epicardial layer around the major branch of the left coronary artery, about 2 mm of its origin. A small plastic button (diameter about 5 mm) is threaded through the ligature and placed in contact with the heart. The end is passed through a small vinyl tube and exteriorised. The heart is replaced in the chest and the chest is closed after removing the residual air to avoid pneumothorax.

Any animal in which the abovementioned surgery produces arrhythmia or a sustained fall in blood pressure to less than 70 mm Hg is discarded from the experiment. The animals are left to recover for 15 minutes. Occlusion of the artery is produced by applying tension to the ligature, and reperfusion is achieved by releasing the tension. The rat heart is used for ischemia-reperfusion arrhythmias because its lack of functioning collaterals leads to reproducible zones of severe ischemia upon ligation of a coronary artery, and because rat atria receive blood supply almost exclusively from extracoronary vessels. Therefore, the resulting arrhythmias are of the ventricular type.

The main experimental protocol comprises 30 minutes of occlusion (ischemia), followed by a 20-minute reperfusion. In some experiments, drug pre-treatment is replaced by ischemic preconditioning, produced by three 3-minute occlusion periods, interspaced with a 3-minute reperfusion. This is followed by a 30-minute occlusion and 20-minute reperfusion. To confirm that reperfusion is taking place, 0.1 ml/100 g of a 10% solution of fluorescein is administered through IV immediately before sacrificing the animals.

The heart is rapidly removed from the chest and placed in ice-cold 10% KCI solution for 1 minute to stop it beating. A gross examination of the heart is made under UV light to determine if areas of non-perfused myocardium are present. These appear as dark blue areas under UV light whereas perfused areas are stained green. The control non-ischemic and 30-minute ischemic, non-reperfused hearts are treated in the same way. The guidelines of the Lambeth Conventions are used for classifying, quantifying and analysing arrhythmias in ischemia, infarction and reperfusion.

Statistical Analysis

All results are evaluated originally as mean ± SEM and, after statistical analysis, are presented, where indicated, as a percentage of the baseline value. For all analyses, the INSTAT V2.04 program is used, including one-way and two-way ANOVA, t-test and Chi-Square test. p values of less than 0.05 are considered to be statistically significant.

Hypotensive Activity

Animals Used: Experiments are performed in WKY and SHR male rats (Le Genest Saint Isle, France), weighing between 210 and 260 g, housed at 23 ±1 °C in a 12 hour light/12 hour darkness photoperiod, and food (standard rat diet) and water provided *ad libitum*. The animals are assigned to three different groups of five rats each (n = 5) and treated as follows.

The first group, serving as the control group, receives distilled water, the second receives the extract at a dose of 20 mg/kg while the third is treated with irbesartan as a reference drug (20 mg/kg). The rats are dosed orally with the drug solutions (extract or irbesartan) or vehicle (distilled water) at a volume of 10 ml/kg once daily for 3 weeks. The influence of circadian rhythms is avoided by starting all experiments at 10:00 am. Immediately after gavage, the rats are individually housed in metabolic cages and provided *ad libitum* access to water and food throughout the experiment period.

The animals are maintained on a 12 hour light–dark cycle during this study. Urine is collected in graduated cylinders on Days 0, 7, 14 and 21 after daily oral administration, and its volume and electrolyte content are measured. Arterial blood pressure and heart rate of the conscious animals are measured using a blood pressure recorder. The systolic blood pressure and heart rate are measured before starting the experiments on Days 0, 7, 14 and 21 after oral administration. The mean bloodless pressure recording is avoided at the same time to discard the influence of circadian rhythms. Blood samples for plasma electrolytes, creatinine and urea levels are obtained from all animals under anesthesia from the retro-orbital sinus on Days 0, 7, 14 and 21 after oral administration. Blood samples are centrifuged and the plasma is then recovered.

Determination of Parameters: Sodium, potassium, chloride, creatinine and urea levels are determined in plasma and urine samples using an autoanalyser; pH, sodium and potassium content of the extract are also determined.

Statistical Analysis: All data is analysed and expressed as mean ± SEM. Mean values are considered significantly different if $p < 0.05$. The experiment design allows application of a factorial ANOVA (time, treatment and interaction) for comparison. The Fisher post-test is used to perform group-by-group comparison.

Anti-arrhythmic Activity

The plant alkaloid aconitine, obtained from the Aconiticum species, persistently activates sodium channels and induces arrhythmia, ventricular extrasytoles, ventricular tachycardia and ventricular fibrillation. Infusion of aconitine in anesthetised rats causes abnormal changes in rhythm, as observed using ECG. Increased doses of aconitine to induce arrhythmia in the treated group are an indication of anti-arrhythmic activity. Aconitine antagonism in vivo has been proven as a valuable screening model for anti-arrhythmic activity.

Method

Studies on Anti-arrhythmic Activity

Adult albino rats of either sex weighing 200–250 g are used for the study and fed with standard commercial diet with water *ad libitum* and maintained in clean polypropylene cages at 25 °C with relative humidity. Rats of either sex are divided into different groups (n = 6) as follows:

Group I receives 1% v/v Tween-80 and serves as the control group

Group II receives lignocaine (50 mg/kg, IP) and serves as the standard

Group III receives extract I in mg/kg of body weight

Group IV receives extract II in mg/kg of body weight

Group V receives extract III in mg/kg of body weight

All drugs are administered orally one hour before aconitine is given.

Induction of Arrhythmia

An hour after drug administration, the rats are anesthetised using urethane (1.25 g/kg, IP). Arrhythmia is induced in animals by constant infusion of aconitine at the dose of 5 μg/ml using a constant infusion pump at a rate of 0.5 ml/minute (1 mg/ml) into the femoral vein of the animal. ECG is recorded in lead II by subcutaneous needle electrodes using a Student's physiograph throughout the experiment.

Statistical Analysis

All results are expressed as mean ± SEM. Differences are analysed by one-way ANOVA followed by Dunnett's test and Student's t-test with the criterion set for statistical significance at $P < 0.05$. Prism® (GraphPad) software can be used for data analysis.

Anti-myocardial Infarction Activity

Isoproterenol-induced Myocardial Necrosis in Rats

Isoproterenol [L-β (3-4–dihydroxy phenyl) - ∝ - isopropyl amino–ethanol hydrochloride], a β-adrenergic agonist, has been reported to cause oxidative stress in the myocardium, resulting in infarct-like necrosis of the heart muscle. The pathophysiological changes following isoproterenol (ISO) administration are comparable to those that occur in human myocardial infarction. Large doses of ISO cause oxygen insufficiency and blood supply imbalance in the myocardium, resulting in myocardial hypoxia. Furthermore, an increase in the level of marker enzymes in the serum could be caused by a leakage of enzymes from the heart, because of necrosis induced by isoproterenol. The marker enzymes are used to diagnose myocardial infarction (MI).

Free radicals are of increasing importance and acceptance in a large number of diseases and are reported to have a deleterious effect on heart function. During ISO-induced MI, enhanced free radical formation and lipid peroxide accumulation have been proposed as one of the possible mechanisms for myocardial damage.' Due to increased lipid peroxidation, glutathione levels are lowered. Significant changes in marker enzyme levels in animals treated with drugs are suggestive of myocardial protection.

Adult albino rats of either sex weighing 200–250 g are used for the study and fed with standard commercial diet with water *ad libitum,* and maintained in clean polypropylene cages at 25 °C with relative humidity. Rats of either sex are divided into different groups (n = 6) as follows: Group I receives 1% v/v Tween-80 and serves as the normal group

Group II receives distilled water (1 ml)

Group III receives extract I mg/kg of body weight

Group IV receives extract II mg/kg of body weight

All drugs are administered orally twice a day for a period of 30 days.

Induction of Myocardial Necrosis

At the end of the treatment period, myocardial necrosis is induced in animals by administering isoproterenol twice at an interval of 24 hours, at a dose of 20 mg/100 g of body weight, subcutaneously.

Blood Collection

After 24 hours of final ISO administration,

the animals are anesthetised with ether and blood is collected from the retro-orbital sinus. The blood is allowed to coagulate for two hours and centrifuged at 3000 rpm for 5 minutes, and the supernatant serum is separated and used for enzyme estimations.

The separated serum can be used to estimate the following marker enzymes:

- Creatine kinase–Isoenzyme (CK-MB)
- Lactate dehydrogenase (LDH)
- Serum glutamate oxaloacetate transferase (SGOT)
- Serum glutamate pyruvate transferase (SGPT)

Estimation of CK-MB

Creatine phosphokinase (CPK) or creatine kinase (CK) is present in various tissues such as striated muscle, brain and heart. When tissue is damaged, CK-MB, an isoenzyme present in the heart, leaks into the blood. An increase in serum CK-MB levels is a good diagnostic tool for myocardial necrosis. In MI, the CK-MB isoenzyme level usually exceeds 6% of total activity and increased CK levels are also found in tachyarrhythmias and congestive heart failure.

Principle

The serum is added to a creatine kinase reagent that contains goat serum to M sub units of CK isoenzymes. During incubation, antigen–antibody reaction and enzyme reactivation by N-acetyl cysteine take place. AMP and fluoride together reduce adenylate kinase interference at low levels which can be measured. The ATP formed reacts with glucose in the presence of hexokinase to yield glucose-6-phosphate (G-6-P). In the presence of G-6-P, it is converted to 6-phosphogluconate and nicotinamide adenine dinucleotide phosphate (NADP) is reduced to nicotinamide adenine dinucleotide phosphate (NADPH). The rate of $NADP^+$ reduction at 340 nm is proportional to the CK-MB activity.

$$\text{Creatine phosphate} + \text{ADP} \xrightarrow{\text{CK-MB}} \text{Creatine} + \text{ATP}$$

$$\text{ATP} + \text{Glucose} \xrightarrow{\text{CK-MB}} \text{ADP} + \text{G-6- P}$$

$$\text{G-6- P} + \text{NADP}^+ \xrightarrow{\text{CK-MB}} \text{6-phosphogluconate} + \text{NADPH} + \text{H}^+$$

A commercially available diagnostic kit contains the following:

Solution 1: ADP (0.2 mmol/L), AMP (5.0 mmol/L), diadenosine pentaphosphate (10 mmol/L), NADP (2.0 mmol/L), creatine phosphate (30 mmol/L), hexokinase (2.5 U/ml), G-6-PD (1.5 U/ml) and N-acetyl cysteine (20 mmol/L).

Solution 2: Imidazole buffer (0.1 mol/L, pH: 6.7), glucose (20 mmol/L), Mg-acetate (10 mmol/L) and EDTA (2 mmol/L).

Parameters: The enzyme activity is determined at 340 nm in a cuvette of 1 cm path light. The linear reaction time is 0–8 minutes and delay time is 60–90 seconds at a temperature of 30 °C. The initial absorbance is taken after the lag phase and readings are repeated after 1, 2 and 3 minutes. The mean absorbance change per minute (ΔA/min) is calculated.

Calculations: CPK activity (IU) = 4127 x Δ A/min (30 °C)

Estimation of LDH

The liver, heart and skeletal muscles are rich in LDH. In MI, serum LDH levels peak within 48–72 hours and return to normal after one or two weeks. Elevated serum LDH levels are also found in cirrhosis, hepatitis, hepatic metastases, hepatoma, pulmonary embolism, megaloblastic anemia, progressive muscular dystrophy and destructive renal diseases. There are 5 isoenzymes, namely, LD_1, LD_2, LD_3, LD_4 and LD_5. The first three types are heart-specific while others are liver-specific.

Principle: Lactate dehydrogenase (LDH) is a hydrogen transfer enzyme that catalyses oxidation of lactate to pyruvate with the mediation of NAD as hydrogen receptor.

$$\text{L- Lactate + NAD} \xrightarrow{\text{LDH}} \text{Pyruvate + NADH}$$

Estimation of AST (SGOT) (Reitman and Frankel, 1957)

SGOT or aspartate aminotransferase (AST) belongs to the transaminases, which catalyse the inter-conversion of amino acids and α-keto acids by transferring the amino group. Although the heart muscle is found to have the most activity of the enzyme, significant activity has also been seen in the liver, brain, gastric mucosa, adipose tissue, skeletal muscle and kidneys. AST is present in both the cytoplasm and the mitochondria of cells and released into the serum on cell damage and destruction. The rise in SGOT levels is related both to the rate and the extent of myocardial necrosis. Elevated levels of transaminases can signal myocardial infarction, hepatic diseases, muscular dystrophy and organ damage. A span diagnostics reagent kit is used to determine the enzyme.

Principle: SGOT catalyses the following reaction:

$$\alpha\text{-ketoglutarate + L-aspartate} \xrightarrow{\text{SGOT}} \text{L-glutamate + Oxaloacetate}$$

The oxaloacetate so formed is coupled with 2, 4 dinitro phenyl hydrazine to yield the corresponding hydrazone, which produces a brown colour in the alkaline medium. This can be measured colourimetrically at 505 nm.

Test Procedure

1. Incubate 0.5 ml of buffered aspartate substrate at 37 °C for 5 minutes.
2. Add 100 µl of serum to it and further incubate at 37 °C for 60 minutes.
3. Add 0.5 ml of DNPH colour reagent to the mixture and allow it to stand for 20 minutes at room temperature.
4. To this mixture, add 5 ml of solution 1, mix well and allow it to stand for 10 minutes at room temperature.
5. Measure the absorbance at 505 nm.

The enzyme activity is determined by extrapolating the optical density on a standard graph and is expressed as units/ml. All the serum samples are treated in a similar manner and the results taken up for statistical analysis.

Estimation of ALT (SGPT)

SGPT or alanine aminotransferase (ALT) also belongs to the transaminases. The heart muscle is found to have the most activity of the enzyme. Significant activity has also been seen in other organs such as the brain, liver, gastric mucosa, adipose tissue, skeletal muscle and kidneys. ALT is a cytosol enzyme released into the serum on cell damage and destruction of AST. A rise in transaminase levels is also related to the rate and extent of cardiac cell necrosis. The increase in ALT is observed to be greater in myocardial infarction than in AST.

Principle: SGPT catalyses the following reaction:

$$\alpha\text{-ketoglutarate + L-alanine} \xrightarrow{\text{SGPT}} \text{L-glutamate + pyruvate}$$

The pyruvate thus formed is coupled with 2, 4 dinitro phenyl hydrazine (DNPH) to yield the corresponding hydrazone, which produces a brown colour in the alkaline medium and can be measured colourimetrically at 505 nm.

Procedure

1. Incubate buffered alanine substrate at 37 °C for 5 minutes and add serum to it and further incubate at 37 °C for 30 minutes.
2. Add DNPH colour reagent to the mixture and allow it to stand for 20 minutes at room temperature.
3. To this mixture, add 5 ml of solution 1, mix well and allow it to stand for 10 minutes at room temperature
4. Measure the absorbance at 505 nm.

The enzyme activity is determined by extrapolating the optical density on a standard graph and is expressed as units/ml. All the serum samples are treated in a similar manner and the results taken up for statistical analysis.

Estimation of Enzymes in Heart Homogenates

Rats are dissected under light anesthesia (ether) to isolate the heart from all the abovementioned groups, and the ventricular part of the isolated myocardial tissue from each group is used to determine antioxidant enzyme levels. Lipid peroxide, glutathione and protein content are estimated.

Preparation of Heart Homogenate

Method

- 5% heart homogenates are prepared in 0.15 M KCl and centrifuged at 3000 rpm for 10 minutes. The supernatant obtained is collected and used to estimate proteins, catalase and peroxidase.
- 5% heart homogenates are prepared in 0.25% sucrose in phosphate buffer pH 7.4 and centrifuged at 3000 rpm for 10 minutes. The supernatant is used to estimate superoxide dismutase and glutathione.

Estimation of Proteins

Proteins are estimated based on the formation of a coloured complex of proteins with Folin–Ciocalteu reagent, which can be measured colourimetrically at 610 nm using bovine albumin as a standard.

Method

1. To 0.1 ml of 5% heart homogenate preparation in 0.15 M KCl, add 0.9 ml of 90% alcohol and centrifuge at 3000 rpm for 10 minutes. Discard the supernatant and dissolve the precipitate in 1 ml of 0.1 N NaOH.
2. Take 0.05 ml of this solution in a test tube, and add 4 ml of freshly prepared alkaline mixture to it, and allow it to stand for 10 minutes.
3. To this mixture, add 0.4 ml of phenol reagent and allow it to stand for a further 10 minutes for the reaction to complete.
4. Measure the absorbance at 610 nm using distilled water as a blank.
5. Take 0.1 ml of the standard in a test tube and process it as mentioned in Steps 2 and 3.

The protein content is calculated using the formula:

Proteins (mg/ml) = OD of sample × final volume × dilution factor × concentration of standard ÷ OD of standard

Estimation of Catalase

Catalase is present in virtually all mammalian cells and may play a dual role in scavenging hydrogen peroxide. Catalase catalyses the following reactions:

a) $2H_2O_2 \xrightarrow{CAT} 2H_2O + O_2$

b) $ROOH + AH_2 \xrightarrow{CAT} H_2O + ROH + A$

Catalase activity can be measured either by decomposition of H_2O_2 or liberation of O_2.

Catalase activity is estimated by determining the decomposition of H_2O_2 at 240 nm in an assay mixture containing phosphate buffer.

Method

1. Add 100 μl of 5% heart homogenate in 0.15 M KCl buffer to 1.9 ml of phosphate buffer (pH 7) and measure the absorbance at 240 nm.
2. To this mixture, add 1 ml of hydrogen peroxide solution and measure the absorbance after allowing it to stand for one minute at 240 nm, using the phosphate buffer as a blank solution.

One international unit of catalase utilised is the amount that catalyses the decomposition of 1 mM hydrogen peroxide per minute at 37 °C and is expressed in terms of units/mg of protein.

Estimation of Superoxide Dismutase (SOD)

SOD catalyses the following reaction:

$$O_2^- + O_2^- + 2H^+ \xrightarrow{SOD} H_2O_2 + O_2$$

Estimation of SOD is based on detection of O_2^- by oxidation of hydroxylamine hydrochloride yielding nitrite, which is measured colourimetrically. O_2^- can also be generated during autoxidation of hydroxylamine. Accompanying the autoxidation of hydroxylamine at a pH of 10.2, nitroblue tetrazolium (NBT) is reduced and nitrite is produced in the presence of EDTA, which can be detected colourimetrically.

Procedure

1. Take 100 μl of 5% heart homogenate in 0.2 M sucrose in phosphate buffer (pH 7.4) in a test tube.
2. To this, add a mixture containing 1 ml of sodium carbonate, 0.4 ml of NBT and 0.2 ml of EDTA and take a zero-minute reading at 560 nm.
3. Initiate the reaction by adding 0.4 ml of 1 mM hydroxylamine hydrochloride to the test tube and incubate at 25 °C for 5 minutes; measure the reduction of NBT at 560 nm.

A parallel control without heart homogenate is also treated in a similar manner. One enzymatic unit of SOD is the amount in the form of proteins present in 100 μl of 5% heart homogenate required to inhibit the reduction of 24 mM NBT by 50% and is expressed as units/mg of protein.

Estimation of Peroxidase

Peroxidase catalyses the formation of I_2 as follows:

$$2KI + H_2O_2 \longrightarrow I_2 + 2KOH$$

$$I_2 + KI \rightleftharpoons KI_3$$

Periodide formation is instantaneous when there is an excess of iodide substrate. The enzymatically generated I_2 is bound as I_3 because of the equilibrium constant. Periodide can be determined spectrophotometrically at 353 nm, which is directly proportional to the peroxidase concentration in the reaction mixture containing approximate amounts of H_2O_2 and enzyme.

Procedure

1. To 0.5 ml of heart homogenate in 0.1 M KCl, add 1 ml of potassium iodide solution (fc: 10 mM) and 1 ml of sodium acetate solution at a pH of 5.25 (fc: 37.5 mM) and read the extinction at 353 nm.
2. To this solution, add 200 μl of hydrogen peroxide and note the change in absorbance after letting it stand for 5 minutes.

One unit of peroxidase activity is defined as a change in one OD per minute and expressed in terms of units/mg of protein.

Estimation of Glutathione

Glutathione is estimated using Ellman's reagent (DTNB). The sulfhdryl group present in glutathione forms a coloured complex with DTNB, which is measured colourimetrically at 412 nm.

Procedure

1. To 1 ml of 5% heart homogenate in 0.25 M sucrose in phosphate buffer, add 1.8 ml of water and 2 ml of phosphate buffer at a pH of 7 and measure the absorbance at 412 nm to deduct the sample blank.
2. To this mixture, add 200 μl of DTNB reagent and measure the absorbance at 412 nm after 5 minutes.

A parallel blank without heart homogenate is also done. The amount of glutathione is determined using its molar extinction coefficient of 13,600/m/cm and expressed in terms of μg/mg of proteins.

Estimation of Lipid Peroxidation (TBARS Method)

In radical-mediated cardiac damage, the free radicals attack polyunsaturated fatty acids. This results in the formation of lipid radicals that readily react with molecular oxygen to produce a peroxy radical initiating lipid peroxidation. This is considered as the major factor influencing the breakdown and turnover of biomembranes. Thus an elevated level of lipid peroxidation is observed in ISO intoxication. Inhibition of lipid peroxidation implies cardioprotection.

The chief secondary product of lipid peroxidation reactions is malondialdehyde (MDA). This reacts with thiobarbituric acid to form a chromogen, which is measured at 535 nm.

Procedure

1. To 0.5 ml of heart homogenate in 0.15 M KCl, add 1 ml of KCl and 2 ml of chilled 0.25 N HCl containing 15% trichloroacetic acid, 0.38% thiobarbituric acid and 0.05% of butylated hydroxy toluene.
2. Incubate the reaction mixture at 80 °C for 1 hour. Then cool and centrifuge the mixture and collect the supernatant.
3. Measure the absorbance of the supernatant at 532 nm against the blank.

The amount of lipid peroxidation is determined using the molar extinction coefficient of 1.56 x 10^{-5} M/cm and expressed as units of thiobarbituric acid reactive substance (TBARS) per mg of protein.

Histopathological Studies

The ventricular parts of myocardial tissues from all groups are subjected to histopathological studies.

a) Processing of Isolated Heart

The ventricular part is rinsed with saline and sliced into 3 mm pieces and fixed in neutral formalin (10% solution) for 3 days. The pieces are then washed under running water for about 12 hours. This is followed by dehydration with alcohol of increasing strength (70%, 80% and 90%) for 12 hours each. Final dehydration is carried out using absolute alcohol with 3 changes at 12-hour intervals. Cleansing is done using xylene with 2 changes at 20-minute intervals. After cleansing, the organ pieces are subjected to paraffin infiltration.

b) Embedding in Paraffin

Melted hard paraffin is poured into L-shaped blocks and the heart pieces are dropped into the liquid paraffin quickly and allowed to cool.

c) Sectioning

The blocks are cut using a microtome to obtain sections of 5 μm thickness. The sections are placed on a microslide to which egg albumin is added. The sections are dried completely and taken up for staining.

d) Staining

Staining is done using eosin and hematoxylin. Eosin is used to stain the basic components red (cytoplasm). Hematoxylin is used to stain all the acidic components blue (DNA, RNA in nucleus).

e) Experimental Procedure

1. De-paraffinise the sections by washing with xylene for about 15 minutes.
2. Dehydrate the sections by washing in alcohol of decreasing strengths (100%, 90%, 80% and 70%).
3. Wash the sections with water.
4. Stain the sections with hematoxylin for 15 minutes and rinse in tap water.
5. Differentiate acid alcohol by 3–10 quick dips. Differentiation with a microscope shows nuclei as distinct and a very light or colourless background.
6. Wash the slide in tap water very briefly and dip in ammonia water with lithium carbonate until the sections become bright blue.
7. Wash the slide section in running tap water for 10–20 minutes (complete washing is ensured as eosin does not stain even otherwisc).
8. Stain the slide with eosin for 2 minutes to obtain an even stain.
9. Re-dehydrate the slides in 95% alcohol and absolute alcohol until excess eosin is removed. Perform two changes at 2-minute intervals of different treatments such as 95% alcohol, absolute alcohol and xylene.
10. Mount the section in diphenyl xylene (DPX). The staining results show a blue-coloured nucleus and cytoplasm with various shades of pink with changes in different tissue components.

All the samples are stained in a similar manner and photographed.

Effect of Extracts on Blood Clotting Time

The capillary tube model, which is the classic method, is a reliable way of testing blood clotting time. It is based on the principle of time taken for the formation of fibrin threads in the capillary tubcs filled with the blood of treated animals and compared with that of the untreated groups.

Method

Animals: Adult albino rats of either sex weighing 200–250 g are used for the study and fed with standard commercial diet with water *ad libitum,* and maintained in clean polypropylene cages at 25 °C with relative humidity.

Procedure

Rats of either sex are divided into six groups of six animals each and treated orally with extracts as follows:

Group I receives 1% v/v Tween-80 and serves as the control group

Group II receives standard aspirin (50 mg/kg of body weight)

Group III receives extract 1 in mg/kg of body weight

Group IV receives extract 2 in mg/kg of body weight

Group V receives extract 3 in mg/kg of body weight

Group VI receives extract 4 in mg/kg of body weight

After 1 hour of drug administration, blood is withdrawn into capillary tubes from the retro-orbital sinus. After withdrawing the blood in capillary tubes, they are broken from one end at regular intervals of 30 seconds, till fibrin threads of blood appear between the broken ends of the capillary tube, and the time taken to form fibrin threads is noted.

Statistical Analysis: All results are expressed as mean ± SEM. Differences are analysed by one-way ANOVA followed by post-test with the criterion set for statistical significance at $p < 0.05$. Prism® (GraphPad) software can be used for data analysis.

Antioxidant Activity of Extracts

Reactive oxygen species (ROS) and oxygen free radicals exert a beneficial and detrimental effect on aerobic life. Excess ROS have been implicated in a variety of pathophysiological phenomena, such as inflammation, ageing, cardiovascular diseases, cancer and atherosclerosis. Considering the importance of this area, extracts obtained from *medicinal plants* should be tested for antioxidant activity. In vitro antioxidant activity can be performed by DPPH free radical activity, superoxide radical scavenging activity and hydroxyl radical scavenging activity.

Chemically Stable Radical Scavenging Activity using DPPH as Stable Free Radical

Scavenging free radical potentialities are evaluated against a methanolic solution of 1,1-di phenyl-2-picryl hydrazyl (DPPH), a stable free radical. Antioxidants react with DPPH and convert it to diphenyl-2-picryl hydrazine and the degree of discolouration indicates the scavenging activity of the drugs. The change in absorbance produced at 517 nm has been used as a measure of antioxidant activity.

Procedure

1. Take 100 μL of 1% extract solution and standard in different test tubes.
2. To this, add 5 ml of methanolic solution of DPPH, shake well and allow the mixture to stand at room temperature for 20 minutes.
3. Prepare a blank in a similar manner and measure the absorbance at 517 nm. The change in sample absorbance is calculated with blank absorbance as a percentage of scavenging activity.

Scavenging activity is expressed as the inhibition percentage calculated using the following formula:

$$\% \text{ Antiradical activity} = \frac{\text{Control}_{\text{Abs}} - \text{Sample}_{\text{Abs}}}{\text{Control}_{\text{Abs}}} \times 100$$

Superoxide Scavenging Activity of Extracts

Superoxide radicals are the most important ROS and produced at relatively high rates by cells during normal metabolism. Auto oxidation of hydroxyl amine at a pH of 10.2 generates superoxide anions that reduce the yellow dye nitroblue tetrazolium to blue-coloured formazon. Drugs possessing superoxide scavenging activity thereby reduce NBT to blue formazon, which is a measure of such activity.

Procedure

1. Take 100 microlitres of 1% alcoholic solution of the extracts in different test tubes and evaporate in a water bath.
2. Add 1 ml of 50 mM sodium carbonate, 0.4 ml of 24 mM NBT and 0.2 ml of 0.1 mM EDTA and take a zero-minute reading at 560 nm.

3. Imitate the reaction by adding 0.4 ml of 1 mM hydroxyl amine hydrochloride to the reaction mixtures.
4. After incubating for 15 minutes at 25 °C, measure the reduction of NBT at 560 nm.

Percentage scavenging of superoxide anions is calculated by comparing the results of test compounds with the blank. The necessary corrections are made for absorbance of test compounds. Superoxide scavenging activity is calculated using the formula:

% Superoxide scavenging activity

$$= 1 - \frac{\text{Difference in sample absorbance} \times 100}{\text{Difference in blank absorbance}}$$

Hydroxyl Radical Scavenging Activity

Hydroxyl radicals have been implicated as highly damaging species in free radical pathology. These radicals are capable of attacking nucleotides in DNA, causing strand breakage, which contributes to carcinogenesis, mutagenesis and cytotoxicity. In addition, this species is considered to be one of the initiators of the lipid peroxidation process. The hydroxyl radical scavenging activity of the selected plants can be assessed by generating hydroxyl radicals using the ascorbic acid–iron EDTA model.

The hydroxyl radicals formed by oxidation react with dimethyl sulphoxide (DMSO) to yield formaldehyde. The formaldehyde production from DMSO provides a convenient way of detecting hydroxyl radicals formed during the oxidation of DMSO using Fe^{3+}/ascorbic acid.

Procedure

1. Take 100 μL of 1% alcoholic solution in different test tubes and evaporate in a water bath.
2. To this, add 1 ml of iron–EDTA solution, 0.5 ml of EDTA and 1 ml of DMSO and initiate the reaction by adding 0.5 ml of ascorbic acid to each of the test tubes.
3. Cap the test tubes tightly and heat in a water bath at 80–90 °C for 15 minutes.
4. Terminate the reaction by adding 1 ml of ice-cold TCA (17.5% w/v) to all test tubes.
5. Allow all test tubes to stand for 2 minutes and determine the formaldehyde formed by adding 2 ml of Nash reagent and leave undisturbed for 15 minutes for colour development.
6. Measure the intensity of yellow colour formed spectrophotometrically at 412 nm against a reagent blank.

The percentage scavenging of hydroxyl radicals is calculated by comparing the results of test compounds with that of the blank. The necessary corrections are made for the absorbance of the test compounds.

The percentage hydroxyl radical scavenging activity is calculated using the following formula:

% Hydroxyl radical scavenging activity

$$= 1 - \frac{\text{Difference in sample absorbance} \times 100}{\text{Difference in blank absorbance}}$$

Other Methods

Measurement of Antioxidant Activity of Plant Extracts

The water phase antioxidant activity of plant extracts could be determined by the ABTS (2, 2-azinobis (3-ethylbenzothiazoline-6-sulfonic acid)) radical decolourisation assay (Re et al, 1999). The technique for the generation of ABTS radical (ABTS•+) involves the direct production of the blue/green ABTS•+ chromophore through the reaction between potassium persulfate and ABTS.

Addition of antioxidants to the pre-formed

radical reduces it to ABTS. The extent of decolourisation as a percentage inhibition of the ABTS•+ radical cation is proportional to the concentration of antioxidants and calculated relative to the reactivity of Trolox (registered trade-mark of Hoffman–LaRoche, 6-hydroxy-2,5,7,8-tetramethychroman-2-carboxylic acid) as a standard (Trolox equivalent antioxidant capacity, TEAC).

Results are presented as mean ± SD (*n*, number of independent experiments = 3–6). Differences between the variants are analysed by Student's t-test and referred to as significant at $p < 0.05$.

NBT/XO (Superoxide Scavenging) Assay

The scavenging potential of the extract for superoxide radicals is also analysed using a hypoxanthine/xanthine oxidase generating system coupled with NBT reduction, with a slight modification involving the use of 96-well plates. Briefly, the reaction mixture contains buffer (50 mM KH_2PO_4/KOH, pH 7.4), 100 mM Na_2EDTA, 3 mM hypoxanthine, 10 mM NBT and the extract. The microplates are read 2.5 minutes after adding xanthine oxidase (1 unit per 10 ml buffer) at 540 nm using an ELISA reader. The superoxide scavenging activity is expressed as a percentage of the inhibition when compared to the blank (buffer instead of extract). L-ascorbic acid is used as a positive control.

DCF/AAPH Assay

An azo initiator, AAPH, is used to produce peroxyl radicals, and the scavenging activity of the mushroom extracts is monitored through spectrophotometric analysis of 2,7-dichlorofluorescin-diacetate. DCF is activated by mixing DCF and NaOH and allowing the mixture to stand for 20 minutes before adding a sodium phosphate buffer (25 mM, pH 7.2). The reaction mixture contains the extract (diluted to final concentrations of 50, 10 and 5 µg/ml), activated DCF solution and 600 mM AAPH (adjusted to a final concentration of 60 mM). The reaction is initiated by adding the AAPH (**2,2-azobis**(2-aminopropane) dihydrochloride) solution. After 10 minutes, the absorbance is read at 490 nm using an ELISA reader. The inhibition rate versus l-ascorbic acid is determined.

Protective Effects of Extract after Treatment with Hydrogen Peroxide

Human HaCaT cells are seeded in 96-well plates at a density of 6000 cells/well. The cells are grown to near 70–80% confluence, and then synchronised by incubation in DMEM containing 0.5% FBS for 8 hours. Extracts are added at concentrations of 10 and 50 ng/ml, respectively. After 16 hours, the cells are washed and 1 mM of hydrogen peroxide is added. The cell viability is measured by means of the MTT assay. To compare the data, the cytotoxic effects of extracts are also evaluated. l-ascorbic acid and catalase are used as positive controls. The significance of the differences between the results is assessed using the Student's t-test, and significance is accepted for *p* values <0.01.

Anti-fertility Testing

Preliminary Screening for Anti-fertility Activity

Five groups of mature female rats (5–6 rats per group) are selected for this experiment. One group serves as a control and receives the vehicle intragastrically for 7 days. The other four groups receive 2.2, 2.5, 2.8 and 3.0 g/kg of body weight of the crude extract daily by the same route of administration for the same period. All the animals are then allowed to mate with mature male rats of proven fertility (one male for two females) and vehicle and extract administration is continued for 21 days. The number of litters is determined after completion of one gestation period in the control and test groups. The litters of the extract-treated rats are then allowed to grow to check for postnatal growth and congenital anomalies.

In a study, four rats are treated with the extract at 2.2 g/kg of body weight for 21 days. After another 21-day, drug-free period, the animals are allowed to mate with males of proven fertility in the ratio of 1 male to 2 females. After the completion of one gestation period (21 days), the number of litters is determined.

Effect of the Extract on the Estrous Cycle

Five mature female Wistar albino rats (200–210 g) are used. A vaginal smear from each animal is examined under a microscope every morning for 21 days (about 5 cycles). The smears are evaluated. The duration of the estrous cycle together with that of the various phases is determined for 21 days. All rats then receive g/kg of body weight of the extract every day by the intragastric route for another 21 days and the same parameters are determined. The vaginal smears from all rats are examined under a microscope for another 21 days after administration of the extract is stopped.

Effect of the Extract on the Weight of Genital Organs and Body Weight

Ten mature colony-bred Wistar strain female albino rats are used. The animals are divided in two groups (five each). The first group receives the extract in g/kg of body weight for 10 days by the intragastric route. The second group receives the vehicle for the same number of days by the same route. On the 11th day, all the animals in both groups are weighed and sacrificed using diethyl ether anesthesia. The ovaries and uteri are dissected out, freed from surrounding tissues, blotted on filter paper and weighed quickly on a balance sensitive to 0.0001 g. The ovary and uterine ratios are then calculated by dividing the ovary and uterine weight in milligrams by body weight in grams.

Effect of Extracts on Kidney Renal Dysfunction

Wistar albino rats of either sex, weighing 120–200 g are divided into three groups of six rats each randomly. Animals in Group I receive only 1% CMC in distilled water (10 ml/kg) and serve as the control group, while animals of Groups II and III receive extracts (mg/kg) suspended in 1% CMC in distilled water. These treatments are given orally daily through the stomach tube in equal volume (10 ml/kg) for 7 days. On the next day, blood samples are collected from the retro-orbital plexus with the help of a glass capillary under light anesthesia. Blood samples are kept at room temperature for 2 hours so that the coagulation processes are completed. The blood samples are centrifuged and the serum thus separated is analysed to determine the concentration of urea and creatinine.

Effect of Extracts in $CdCl_2$-induced Kidney Damage in Rats

The rats are divided into four groups of six animals each. Groups I and II are given vehicle, 1% CMC in distilled water (10 ml/kg/d, PO), while Groups III and IV are given extracts (mg/kg/d) for eight days. In addition, the animals in Groups II, III and IV are co-administered with cadmium chloride from Day 4 to Day 8. Cadmium chloride (mg/kg/d) is injected subcutaneously in the neck region at a volume of 1 ml/kg. Group I receives normal saline instead of cadmium chloride. On the next day, blood samples are collected from the retro-orbital plexus. The serum is separated to measure the concentration of urea nitrogen and creatinine.

Effect of Extracts in Potassium Dichromate-induced Kidney Damage in Rats

The rats are divided into four groups of 10 animals each. Drugs are administered in the form of a suspension using 1% CMC as a suspending agent in distilled water. Animals from Group I (control) receive 1% CMC in distilled water (10 ml/kg/d) for 5 days. Animals from Group II (toxic) receive 1% CMC in distilled water (10 mg/kg/d) for 5 days. Animals from Group III receive extracts (mg/kg/d) suspended in the vehicle (10 ml/kg) for 5 days. Animals from Group IV receive extracts of higher dose suspended in the vehicle (10 ml/kg) for 5 days.

A single dose of potassium dichromate (20 mg/kg) is administered subcutaneously in the neck region at a volume of 1 ml/kg on the fourth day to all the animals except those that belong to Group I. Group I receives only normal saline. On the sixth day, blood samples are withdrawn from the retro-orbital venous plexus and the serum is separated for the estimation for urea nitrogen and creatinine concentrations.

Effect of Extracts on Mercuric Chloride–induced Kidney Damage in Rats

The protocol adopted in the potassium dichromate–induced nephrotoxicity model is followed in this study. Mercuric chloride (1.5 mg/kg/d) is used as reno-toxin instead of potassium dichromate, and injected subcutaneously in the neck region at a volume of 1 ml/kg. The blood samples withdrawn from the retro-orbital venous plexus are centrifuged and the sera thus obtained investigated to determine the concentrations of urea nitrogen and creatinine.

Effect of Extracts in Gentamicin-induced Kidney Damage in Rats

The rats are divided into four groups of six each. Groups I and II are given the vehicle (1% CMC) in distilled water (10 ml/kg/d, PO), while Groups III and IV are given extracts (mg/kg/d) suspended in the vehicle (10 ml/kg) for eight days. In addition, the animals in Groups II, III and IV are co-administered subcutaneously daily with gentamicin at a dose of 100 mg/kg, in the neck region at a volume of 1 ml/kg for the last 5 days.

Animals from Group I are given normal saline (SC) instead of gentamicin. On the next day, blood samples are collected from the retro-orbital venous plexus. The serum is separated to measure concentration of urea nitrogen and creatinine. Blood urea nitrogen and serum creatinine are estimated by the standard methods.

Vasorelaxant Assay

Male Wistar rats (250 ± 20 g) are used for this assay. Isolated aortic rings, deprived of the endothelium layer, are prepared. After an equilibration period of 60 minutes, endothelium removal is confirmed by acetylcholine (ACh, 10μM)-induced relaxation on norepinephrine (NE, 3 μM) pre-contracted tissues. A relaxation of ≤10% indicates satisfactory removal of endothelium and only such tissues are used for experiments. After a wash-out and an equilibration period of 60 minutes, three different experimental protocols are applied.

Primary Protocol: The aortic preparations are pre-contracted by a single concentration of NE (3 μM) and three-fold increasing concentrations of crude extract (10–5 to 10–3 g/ml) are added cumulatively to the organ bath. When required by the experimental protocol, the medication of saline with indomethacin, nifedipine (1 mM) and cyclopiazonic acid (20mM) is performed 30 minutes before the administration of NE 3 mM.

Secondary Protocol: The aortic rings are contracted with increasing cumulative concentrations of NE (0.1 nM–0.1 mM). Subsequently pre-treatment with the extract (10–4 g/ml) is performed 30 minutes before the administration of NE. This experimental protocol is performed either in standard Tyrode solution or in Ca2+-free Tyrode solution.

Tertiary Protocol: The aortic rings are contracted by a single maximal concentration of caffeine (5 mM). After washing with Tyrode solution, the preparations are incubated with three different concentrations of the plant extract (10^{-4}, 3×10^{-4}, 10^{-3} g/ml) 30 minutes before the new administration of caffeine (5 mM). For each experimental protocol, the relaxing effect on preparations pre-contracted with NE and the inhibitory activity on the caffeine response of the standard reference papaverine (3×10^{-7} to 10^{-4} M) are evaluated as positive controls.

Data Analysis

Primary Protocol: The vasorelaxing efficacy and potency of the extract are expressed, respectively, as *E*max = maximal vasorelaxing response, evaluated as percentage relaxation of the NE-induced contraction, and pIC50 =–log10 IC50, calculated as the concentration (gram of extract/ml of organ bath solution) required to produce a half-reduction of the NE-induced contracting tone.

Secondary Protocol: When cumulative curves to NE are performed, the levels of responses to the first and the second curves are expressed as percentage contractions of the maximal response of the first one. The effect of the crude extract is expressed as efficacy and potency of NE after the incubation period with the extract itself. *E*max = maximal contracting response, evaluated as a percentage of the maximal contraction of the first curve, and pEC_{50} =$-\log_{10}$ EC_{50}, calculated as the molar concentration required to produce a half-effect in the second NE concentration–response curve.

Tertiary Protocol: When caffeine is used as a contracting agent, changes to caffeine-induced contractions obtained in the presence of the extract (10^{-4}, 3×10^{-4}, 10^{-3} g/ml), expressed as a percentage of the control caffeine-induced contraction (*E*), are evaluated. All analyses are performed by sigmoidal non-linear regression of concentration–response curves (computer program: GraphPad Prism® 3.00). All data is expressed as mean ± SEM of six experiments. The significance of differences is evaluated by means of ANOVA and Student's t-test for unpaired data. $P \leq 0.05$ is considered significant.

Hepatoprotective Activity

CCl_4-induced Hepatocyte Injury In Vitro

Hepatocytes are isolated from rats (male Wistar rats weighing 150–200 g). After a preculture (30 minutes), the cells are exposed to fresh culture medium (RPMI-1640 medium supplemented with 10% inactivated fetal bovine serum, penicillin 100 IU/ml, streptomycin 100 μg/ml, dexamethasone 10 mM and insulin 1 mM) containing 10 mM CCl_4 with or without test samples in DMSO (0.01 ml). The final concentration of DMSO must not exceed 0.05%.

For the test, the aqueous extract is added to the vials to produce a final concentration of 10, 100 or 1000 μg/ml. The ethyl ether fraction is added to give a final concentration corresponding to 10, 100 or 1000 μg/ml of aqueous extract. Silymarin is tested as a positive control at doses of 10, 100 and 1000 μg/ml. Each dose is tested in triplicate. Control cultures should contain the same amount of DMSO.

Assessment of Hepatotoxic Activity In Vitro

AST and LDH activities in the medium are measured 60 minutes after the CCl_4 challenge. After incubation, the culture medium from each vial is collected and centrifuged at 50 × *g* at 4 °C for 2 minutes. The supernatant is used to measure the AST and LDH levels using AST/UV-Autom and LDH/UV Liquid test kits with a bioanalyser. It is generally accepted that experiments are valid only if the background activity of control cells is ≤25% of total available intercellular activity. So, for control cells, the total intracellular enzyme content is determined after treatment of cells with Triton X-100 detergent to induce 100% lysis.

MTT Reduction Assay

The cell survival rate is assessed by the 3-(4,5-dimethylthiazole-2-yl)-2,5-diphenyl tetrazolium bromide (MTT) reduction assay. MTT (0.3 mg/ml) is dissolved in phosphate buffered saline (PBS) at a pH of 7.4 and a MTT solution (200 μl/ml) is added to each vial and incubated for 2 hours at 37 °C with 5% CO2. After incubation, the cell suspension with formazan crystals is transferred into Eppendorf tubes and centrifuged at 5000 × *g* for 3 minutes. The supernatant is discarded and 1 ml of a lysis-solubilisation solution (10% Triton X-100 in isopropanol, pH 2) is added to each tube. The pellet is dissolved by sonication and cell debris is collected by brief centrifugation. The absorbance of the purple solution is measured at 565 nm with a spectrophotometer (Shimadzu UV-1601). The cell survival rate is expressed as a percentage of formazan production by treating samples compared with control samples.

Hepatoprotective Activity of Extracts using CCl_4-induced In Vivo Model

Male albino rats weighing between 150 and 175 g are used as animal models. The rats are divided into four groups, each group consisting of six animals. The hepatoprotective activity of the extracts is evaluated using the CCl_4-induced model. Group I is kept on a normal diet and serves as the control, Group II receives CCl_4 (1.25 ml/kg) by the oral route, while Groups III and IV receive silymarin (100 mg/kg; PO) and extracts in (mg/kg; PO), respectively, once daily for seven days.

On the seventh day, CCl_4 is given orally 30 minutes after the administration of silymarin and the test drug. After 36 hours of CCl_4 administration, blood is collected and the serum separated is analysed for various biochemical parameters, such as SGOT, SGPT, alkaline phosphatase, total bilirubin and gamma glutamate transpeptidase (GGTP). The liver is examined grossly, weighed and stored in 10% formalin and processed for paraffin embedding using the standard microtechnique. A section of the liver (5 mm) stained with alum hemotoxylin and eosin is observed microscopically for histopathological studies.

Paracetamol-induced Liver Damage in Rats

Rats are divided into control (normal), control (paracetamol) and test (plant suspension + paracetamol) groups, each comprising 6 animals in all set of experiments. Paracetamol is suspended in 40% (w/v) aqueous sucrose solution and administered orally at a dose of 2 g/kg. Control (normal) rats receive daily doses of 2% gum acacia for four days and a single dose of sucrose solution (1 ml/rat) on Day 3. The control (paracetamol) group receives 2% gum acacia, daily for four days and a single dose of paracetamol (2 g/kg) on Day 3. The experimental groups receive indicated doses of the drug daily for 4 days and a single dose of paracetamol on Day 3. Animals are killed under mild ether anesthesia 48 hours after paracetamol administration. Blood samples are collected and the serum is separated. The liver is observed morphologically for visible changes. SGPT and SGOT are assayed according to the method of Reitman and Frankel, and an alkaline phosphatase assay is carried out.

Anti-hypercholesterolemic Activity

Method I

Choleretic Activity: To study the choleretic activity of the plant drugs, an independent set of normal male rats are made to fast overnight and divided into three groups of 6 rats each. These rats are anesthetised with an IP injection of sodium pentobarbitone.The common bile duct is surgically exposed by middle line caprotomy and cannulated with polyethylene tubing (No. 48) The body temperature is maintained by a heating lamp.

Bile collected for the first 10 minutes is discarded and then collected in pre-weighed graduated tubes. Bile is collected for 1 hour and 1 ml of 2% gum acacia is administered intraduodenally to control rats (Group I). Rats from Groups II and III receive extract suspension intraduodenally (500 mg/kg, fresh weight). The bile volume collected for 4 hours following drug administration is divided with the volume of the bile collected in the first hour to obtain a ratio. An increase in the bile flow in the treated animals compared to control (2% gum acacia treated) is taken as the criterion for choleretic activity.

Method II

A total of 40 male adult albino rabbits (1.5–2 kg) are used. They are acclimatised in an air-conditioned room at 22±2 °C for 7 days and provided with free access to food and water. The rabbits are divided into four groups: Group I, normal healthy control; Group II, pathogenic hypercholesterolemic diet (HCD) control; Group III, HCD extract treated; Group IV, HCD gemfibrozil treated, 10 rabbits in one group (n = 10).

Treatment Schedule

Hypercholesterolemia is induced by oral force feeding of an atherogenic diet containing 0.5 g cholesterol in 5 ml hydrogenated vegetable oil for 10 weeks along with normal rabbit feed in Groups II–IV. The extracts (mg:kg in 2% gum acacia) and gemfibrozil (60 mg:ml per kg body weight) are administered orally daily for 10 weeks to Group III and Group IV animals, respectively. Group II serves as a pathogenic HCD control and receives 2% gum acacia for 10 weeks while Group I is kept as a normal healthy control.

Blood Collection

The fasting blood samples are collected from the marginal ear vein of all rabbits on Day 0 (before treatment) and after 15, 35 and 70 days for estimation of serum total cholesterol, serum triglycerides and serum phospholipids. On the 70th day, blood samples withdrawn from animals that were made to fast are also tested for serum lipoproteins, serum total proteins and albumin fraction. On the 71st day, all the groups of animals are sacrificed for tissues (liver and aorta) cholesterol estimation and for gross grading of atherosclerosis in the aorta (on a scale of 0 to 5).

Anti-ulcer Activity

Animals: Male Wistar rats (180–200 g) are maintained under standardised environmental conditions (22–28 °C, 60–70% relative humidity, 12 hour dark/light cycle) and fed with standard rat feed and water *ad libitum.*

Ethanol (80%) induction of gastric ulcer in rats and its prevention by the extracts

The animals are divided into five groups of six each. Group I is kept normal without any treatment and all other groups are made to fast for 36 hours and administered 80% ethanol. Group II animals receive 1 ml of 80% ethanol. Groups III, IV and V are treated with ranitidine (50 mg/kg) and extracts of 3 different doses (mg/kg) respectively, 1 hour prior to the administration of 80% ethanol. The animals are sacrificed 4 hours after administration of ethanol.

Effect of 70% methanolic extract on gastric ulcer induced by aspirin

The animals are divided into five groups of six each. Group I is kept normal without any treatment and all other animals are administered with aspirin (400 mg/kg); Groups III, IV and V are pretreated with ranitidine (50 mg/kg) and extract (250 mg/kg, 500 mg/kg), respectively. After 4 hours, the animals are sacrificed and the stomach from each animal is removed and opened along the greater curvature to determine the ulcer index.

Determination of ulcer index (UI)

The ulcerative index is calculated by the severity of gastric mucosal lesions and graded as follows:

Erosions Score:

1 mm or less = 1; 1–2 mm = 2; More than 2 mm = 3

The UI is then calculated by using the formula:

UI = 1× (number of lesions of grade 1) + 2 × (number of lesions of grade 2) + 3 × (number of lesions of grade 3).

The overall score is then divided by a factor of 10, which is designated as the ulcer index (Main and Whittle, 1975).

Biochemical Analysis

After the measurement of gastric lesions, the mucosa of the glandular stomach is removed by scraping with a blunt knife, and a 10% homogenate is prepared and subjected to biochemical analysis by the following methods.

Superoxide dismutase (SOD) is estimated by the riboflavin photoreduction method and catalase by measuring the rate of decomposition of H_2O_2 at 240 nm. Tissue lipid peroxidation is estimated by the thiobarbituric acid (TBA) method, glutathione (GSH) by measuring its reduction with DTNB and glutathione peroxidase (GPx) by the degradation of H_2O_2 in the presence of GSH. The protein content of the enzyme is determined by Lowry's method.

Histopathology

After the experiments are terminated, the animals are sacrificed, the stomach is excised and cut open through the ventral suture and a small portion is fixed in 10% formalin solution immediately after sacrifice. This is then passed through ascending grades of alcohol, cleared in xylene and impregnated and embedded in paraffin-dehydrated specimens. Three-to-four–micrometer sections are made using a microtome and after staining with hematoxylene and eosine, the sections are moulded in DPX and observed under light microscope.

Statistical Analysis: The values are expressed as mean ± SD. Statistical significance for ulcerogenic and in vivo antioxidant activities is calculated using the Student's t-test.

Subacute Inflammation Study

Cotton Pellet Granuloma in Rats

Under light ether anesthesia, sterile cotton pellets (10 mg) are implanted subcutaneously in the axilla and groin regions of rats. The animals are treated intraperitoneally with different extracts (50 mg/kg) daily for 7 consecutive days. Animals in the control group receive either normal saline or the vehicle gum acacia. Phenyl butazone (100 mg/kg, IP) is given to animals in the reference group. They are sacrificed on Day 8, the cotton pellet removed, freed from extraneous tissue and dried overnight at 60 °C and weighed. The percentage inhibition of the dry weight of the granuloma is calculated and compared.

Antipyretic Activity

Hyperpyrexia is induced in rats by subcutaneous injection of 10 ml/kg of 20% aqueous suspension of dried yeast in the back below the nape of the rat. The animals are then made to fast for the duration of the experiment, water being made available *ad libitum.* Control temperatures are taken 24 hours after the yeast injection to determine the pyretic response to yeast. Temperatures taken 1 hour prior to drug administration in fevered animals serve as the pre-drug control. Extract (50 mg/kg) is given intraperitoneally 24 hours after yeast injection. Paracetamol (150 mg/kg) serves as the reference drug. The temperatures are recorded and compared.

Statistical Analysis: Values are expressed as mean ± SEM. Statistical significance is determined using the Student's t-test. Values with $P < 0.05$ are considered significant.

Anti-cancer Activity

Anti-cancer Activity In Vitro Cell Line and Culture: HeLa cells procured from standard research centres are grown in Eagle's minimum essential medium (MEM), supplemented with 10% fetal calf serum, 1% l-glutamine and 50 μg/ml gentamicin sulfate. The cells are routinely grown in flasks with loosened caps, and incubated at 37 °C in a humidified atmosphere of 5% CO_2 in air.

Pratt and Willis Test: The cytotoxic effect of different fractions of extracts is evaluated in HeLa cells. Briefly, a fixed number of exponentially growing cells (1:105) are inoculated into several individual culture dishes and allowed to grow for 24 hours. Thereafter, the different cell cultures are treated with various fractions of extracts for a specified time period. After the lapse of the stipulated time, the extracts containing media from each culture is replaced with the fresh extract-free medium, taking care to avoid disturbing the attached cells. About 72 hours after initiation of the cultures, the cells are dislodged by trypsin–EDTA treatment and the viability of the cells is determined by trypan blue dye exclusion test using a hemocytometer under an inverted transmitted light microscope.

Anti-diabetic Activity

Animal Study: Eighty male Wistar rats (200–300 g) are housed in individual plastic cages with stainless steel covers and kept at room temperature (24–28 °C) under 12 hour dark/light cycles. The rats are allowed free access to their respective diets and water. The experiment is carried out over 4 weeks, and body weight, food intake and blood glucose levels are recorded weekly.

The rats are divided into four groups: normal rats + normal diets (Group A); normal rats + extract (Group B); diabetic-induced rats + normal diets (Group C); diabetic-induced rats + extract (Group D). Diets containing the extract are given in three different dosages (1, 2 and 3%) before and after the rats are diabetically induced with streptozotocin (STZ). Groups C and D are injected intraperitoneally with 60 mg/kg body weight of STZ (STZ is prepared in 0.05 M citrate buffer, pH 4.5). Three days after the STZ injection, blood is collected from the tail vein and the level of plasma glucose is checked to ensure that the rats had diabetes.

Determination of Glucose Levels and Lipid Profiles: At 0 and 4 weeks of the experiment, 5 ml blood is collected from the intracardiac cavity and placed into a vacutainer tube. The samples are then centrifuged for 10 minutes at 1000 x *g* at room temperature (25 °C). The supernatant is collected and kept at –20 °C for further analysis. Serum glucose and cholesterol levels are measured using a chemistry analyser.

Statistical Analysis: Data is expressed as mean ± SEM. One-way ANOVA is applied to find the difference between the groups. Duncan's multiple range test is used to find the significant difference among means. Results are considered significantly different at the level of $p < 0.05$.

Pharmacokinetic Studies of Herbal Extracts

Design: Studies can be organised for a single dose as an open, uncontrolled pharmacokinetic trial on 12 healthy male volunteers, with a one week pre-drug wash-out period.

Subjects: Healthy male volunteers between 18 and 50 years of age, free from significant physical or psychiatric disorders as determined by medical history, physical examination, clinical chemistry, hematology and urine analysis are included for the study. Volunteers are excluded from the study if they have any significant abnormal test results or have received any drugs during the previous three months. They are also excluded if they have a history suggestive of allergy or blood donation in the previous one month.

The written, witnessed and informed consent in vernacular language from the volunteers should be obtained prior to participating and they are free to withdraw at any time during the study and one week after withdrawal of the last blood sample. Occurrence of any adverse events is recorded. Oral temperature, pulse rate and blood pressure are monitored before drug administration and at intervals in the post-dosing period. Adequate arrangements for entertainment are made for volunteers so that they feel relaxed during the trial. Standard diet such as breakfast, lunch, snacks, tea and dinner is allowed, as is water *ad libitum*.

Study Protocol

On the day of the trial, volunteers are given a standardised breakfast after briefing, documentation and acclimatisation. Then, an indwelling venous catheter (Vasofix No. 20) is fixed in the forearm while taking aseptic precautions. One capsule of the extract is then administered orally with 100 ml of water, under supervision. Volunteers remain inside the CPU until the last blood sample is taken, and during this time, they receive the same meals. Concomitant medication, tobacco or other intoxicants are not permitted during the study. Venous blood samples (5 ml each) are drawn from each volunteer prior to drug administration and at 30, 60, 120, 150, 180, 210, 240, 300, 360, 480, 600, 720 and 840 minutes after drug administration. Blood samples are collected in an EDTA Vacutainer and centrifuged (1500 rpm for 20 minutes) immediately to separate the plasma. The collected plasma is refrigerated till analysis. The concentration of active constituents in plasma is determined by HPLC.

PK Analysis

Non-compartmental pharmacokinetic analysis of concentration time data is performed by using actual blood collection times and could be used for all calculations. Maximum observed plasma concentration (Cmax) and the time to Cmax (tmax) are determined by visual inspection of individual concentration versus time curves. The area under the concentration versus time curve through Clast, the last measurable concentration (AUClast) is calculated by the linear trapezoidal method. The area under the concentration versus time curve, extrapolated to infinity (AUC0–∞), is calculated according to the following equation:

$$AUC0\text{–}\infty = AUClast + Clast / Kel.$$

The elimination rate constant (Kel) and elimination half life (t 1/2) are determined by log linear regress based on data from the terminal monoexponential phase of the concentration versus time profiles, while for calculating absorption rate constant (Ka) and absorption half life (t 1/2 a), the method of residuals is used.

Assuming complete absorption, clearance (Cl) and apparent volume of distribution (V_d) are calculated

as $Vd\ (L) = Dose / Kel\ .\ AUC0\text{–}\infty$

$Cl\ (ml/min) = Kel.\ V_d /60$

Key Messages

- In developing countries, as much as 80% of the indigenous population relies on traditional systems of medicine and medicinal plants as their primary source of healthcare.
- Research on natural products continues to provide a tremendous variety of lead structures, which are used as templates for the development of new drugs by the pharmaceutical industry.
- A lead compound is a compound with many of the characteristics of a desired drug, which will be used as a model for chemical modification.

- Isolation of suspected new compounds from extracts that show activity in screening involves close collaboration between the chemist performing the isolation and the biologist or biochemist performing the assay.
- Bioassays offer a special advantage in the standardisation and purity assessment of heterogeneous mixtures of extracts.
- In the drug discovery process, assessment of toxic potential is always used to prioritise compounds for further evaluation, and natural products are no exception to this rule.
- Biomedical research allows dissection of the basis of multifunctional diseases and determines the most suitable point of targeting for future therapeutics.
- HTS is the process by which large numbers of compounds are screened in an automated fashion, for activity as inhibitors (antagonists) or activators (agonists) on targets of interest, such as cell surface/intracellular/nuclear receptors, metabolic/biochemical enzymes or ion channels.
- Extraction can be defined as the removal of soluble materials from an insoluble residue, either liquid or solid, by treatment with a liquid solvent.
- Modern drug discovery research often requires a continual application of newer, simpler and more efficient techniques to assure therapeutic activity and safety of isolated compounds from natural sources.
- New chemical entities are rigorously screened for efficacy and safety in animal models followed by an evaluation of their therapeutic merit in human subjects, before being approved by the regulatory body to launch them as new drugs. Despite such rigorous scrutiny, many compounds have been withdrawn from the market due to their potential adverse effects.
- Novel high throughput methods to evaluate the efficacy and safety of new chemicals are required to simplify and speed up the drug discovery process. The availability of improved *in vitro and in vivo* methods and newer technologies has greatly helped the drug discovery process but much refinement is still required.

Questions

1. Describe the natural product drug discovery process.
2. Explain the different methods of extraction of plant materials in detail.
3. What are bioassays? How can plant material or extracts be screened by bioassays?
4. Discuss the general methods involved in the pharmacological screening of plant extracts.
5. Write a note on assessment of anti-cancer activity for plant extracts.
6. Discuss pharmacokinetic profiling of plant extracts.

30

Patents and Intellectual Property on Natural Products—An Overview

MUEEN AHMED KK AND ARUN KUMAR HS

Learning Objectives

At the end of this chapter, you will be able to:

- Define patents and intellectual properties
- Explain the importance of patents on medicinal plants
- Explain the patentability of natural products
- List some of the patents on medicinal plants
- List some online resources of patent-related information

Introduction

Phytomedicines—medicinal products from natural resources—have been used in health practice for many centuries. Phytomedicines, simply defined, are a special category of plant drugs. They are standardised, which means that certain compounds in the plant material are quantified and elucidated so as to have a replicable final product, batch after batch. Among the various parts of the world, India, the United States and Europe are considered to be the largest markets for phytomedicines. Over the last five years, it has been estimated that the American medicinal herb industry has grown at a rate exceeding 20% per year and this trend continues till date.

Global Healthcare Requirements

About ten years ago, the World Health Organization (WHO) launched its programme of 'Health for all by the year 2000.' Right from the outset, WHO realised that any programme adopted in any of the minimally industrialised countries would have no impact if it did not take into consideration the development and integration of traditional medicine into the primary health care programmes of these countries.

WHO had estimated conservatively that between 60% and 90% of the population of non-industrialised countries rely on medicinal plants to meet their healthcare needs, either totally or partially. With the scarcity of doctors and paucity of hospitals and clinics in some countries, the majority of the population has to rely on sources other than allopathic medicines for their healthcare. For example, in Ghana (Africa) there is one traditional doctor for approximately every 400 people, while the ratio of allopathic doctors to patients is 1:12,000.

Various reports from the United Nations (UNCTAD and GATT) have indicated that 33% of drug products in the highly industrialised countries are derived directly from higher plants (seed plants, including gymnosperms, in which the seed is 'naked', and angiosperms or flowering plants, in which the seed is contained in an ovary; most of these are tropical plants that grow in equatorial countries). Lower plants is a collective term for the three main groups of plants: mosses, liverworts and lichens, which do not have roots and which produce spores to reproduce, rather than flowers. Mosses and liverworts have stems and leaves and attach themselves to rocks, soil or trees using modified stems called rhizoids. This group of plants produce another 27% of drugs found on the market. Indeed, more than 67% of the world's plant species—at least 35,000 of which have potential medicinal value—originate in non-industrialised countries of the southern hemisphere. The market for plant-based drugs is growing every year throughout the world. These drugs account for over $50 billion of the total worldwide drug market, now worth over $173 billion.

The estimated manufacturer's price value of medicinal materials derived from plants obtained from developing countries is expected to have reached between $35 and $47 billion in 2000. In fact, the highly industrialised countries—which constitute only 20% of the total world population of over 5 billion—consume 80% of all pharmaceuticals produced in the world. Overall, only 15% of worldwide pharmaceutical purchasing takes place in developing countries. The international community has a clear duty to ensure the full conservation of whatever alternative sources of healthcare are currently available to the remaining 80% of the world's population.

Invention

To invent means to find out something, to discover something not found or discovered by anyone before. It is the production or introduction of a new thing for the first time by exercising one's own mind, skill and labour.

An intellectual property right is intended to provide rights to the creator of products of intellectual labour to exclude others from using the products. The patent system confers monopoly rights on the inventor for a limited period of time. The conferment of intellectual property rights in the form of patents is justified both from the perspective of the inventor as well as that of the general public. Patent is a form of individual property conferring monopoly rights, for a predetermined period of time, on a person who invents a product or a process. It is a reward given by the government to the inventor for the input of his/her intellectual labour to produce something that is useful to the public.

Patents

According to the US Patent Office, "A patent for an invention is a grant of a property right by the Government to the inventor (or his heirs or assignees), acting through the Patent and Trademark Office. The term of the patent is 17 years from the date the patent is granted, subject to the payment of maintenance fees".

The right conferred by the patent grant is, in the language of the statute and of the grant itself, 'the right to exclude others from making, using or selling' the invention. What is granted is not the right to make, use or sell, but the right to exclude others from making, using or selling the invention. Some people occasionally confuse patents, copyrights and trademarks. Although there may be some resemblance in the rights of these three types of intellectual property, they are different and serve different purposes.

Copyrights

A copyright protects the writings of an author against copying. Literary, dramatic, musical and artistic works, architectural works, works of artistic craftsmanship, films, entrepreneurial copyrights and computer programs are included within the protection of the copyright law, which in some instances also confers performing and recording rights. The copyright goes to the form of expression rather than to the subject matter of the writing.

Trademarks

A trademark relates to any word, name, symbol or device used in trade with goods to indicate the source or origin of the goods and to distinguish them from the goods of others. Trademark rights may be used to prevent others from using a confusingly similar mark but not to prevent others from making the same goods or from selling them under a non-confusing mark. Similar rights may be acquired in marks used in the sale or advertising of services (service marks).

Criteria of Patentability

Under Section 1 of the Patent Act, 1977, in the UK, a patent may be granted only for an invention which is new, which involves an inventive step and is capable of industrial application.

Every legal system insists upon certain conditions for an invention to be patented. Although the requirements vary in different legal systems, certain basic common features exist. They are novelty, utility and non-obviousness/ inventive step.

Novelty

An invention is novel, if it has not been a part of any state of the art, that is, it should not have been made available to the public before the date of filing the application. Prior use and prior publication can be obstacles in the way of granting the patent.

Utility

One of the requirements that the purported invention must process before it can be patented by the applicant is that it must be capable of industrial application, that is, it must perform some function of positive benefit to society.

Inventive step/Non-obviousness

This measures the technical accomplishment reflected in an invention. It attempts to measure whether an invention is an adequate technical advancement to merit the award of a patent. Even if an invention is new and useful, it does not deserve a patent if it represents merely a small step forward in the art.

Patents comprise a specification and claims. The specification is a written description of the invention. It must describe the invention so that those skilled in the art related to the invention, for example, one typically involved in that area of endeavour can make and use the invention. The claims describe what is to be protected by the patent. Thus, patents are negative rights, not positive privileges. A patent provides its owner with the right to prevent the manufacture, sale, use, importation or offer for sale of the patented product, process or composition.

Claims

The claims of a complete specification define the monopoly or protection that the patentee claims as his or her exclusive right. The function of the claim is to show with conciseness, precision and accuracy what the invention in respect of which monopoly is sought to show how much of what is described in the specification constitutes the invention and to show what is not claimed and therefore open to public use.

In every country, there are certain legal requirements that govern all prescription drugs—their manufacture, wholesale and retail distribution, dispensing procedures and usage. In European Union (EU) countries, all phytopharmaceuticals are subject to general drug regulations. Like synthetic drugs, all phytopharmaceuticals must comply with specific criteria pertaining to quality, safety and efficacy. Their pharmacological, toxicological and clinical profiles have to be scientifically established through standardised tests and deposited with the appropriate licensing committee before permission can be granted for the drug's distribution and sale.

Article 1 (2) of European Council Directive 65/65/EEC defines a medicinal product as follows:

'Any substance or combination of substances presented for treating or preventing disease in human beings or animals. Any substance or combination of substances which may be administered to human beings or animals with a view to making a medical diagnosis or to restoring, correcting or modifying physiological functions in human beings or in animals is likewise considered a medicinal product'.

A herbal drug will therefore be considered as a medicinal product if it is:

- Presented for treating or preventing disease in human beings or animals
- Administered with a view to restoring, correcting or modifying physiological functions in human beings or animals

Hence, for use as drugs, herbal preparations are legally required to be tested for contamination by foreign materials, pesticides, foreign plants, parasites and bacteria. To get a license for marketing in the EC, a drug must meet the basic standards of quality, safety and efficacy.

One of the difficulties bedevilling any attempt at integrating traditional medicine into primary healthcare has been the secrecy with which each herbalist guards his or her own preparations for any particular ailment. New drugs that are developed from a plant source originate initially from the folkloric knowledge of the local herbalist. This was the case for aspirin, quinine, vincristine, physostigmine, pilocarpine, morphine, codeine, atropine and other essential drugs. The existing problem is that there are no patent laws regarding such knowledge. Normally, one cannot patent a plant. One can only patent a particular formulation or a substance isolated from a plant.

If a herbalist identifies a plant used for the treatment of a disease or disorder, and if the scientist is then able to isolate the active ingredient or to formulate even a crude herbal preparation that is thoroughly tested and accepted, then the scientist can patent the drug or the preparation. However, the herbalist cannot patent the plant material, because this is considered to be 'God's universal property'. Moreover, that same plant may exist in so many different countries and may have been used for years for the same purpose by many people independently. So the herbalist has no other alternative but to keep his or her knowledge private; this has, however, led to serious implications.

The norm in Europe and America and increasingly in African countries is to compel the herbalist to subject every preparation to scientific quality control—to test it for efficacy, toxicity and so on. Then the herbalist will be compelled by law to reveal the name of the plant, source, mode of preparation and so on, to the licensing authority. The protocol of secrecy exists even in highly industrialised countries, but only during the time that a drug is being developed by a pharmaceutical firm. Once patenting is completed and legal protection secured, all the information about a drug can become public knowledge and can even be published in professional journals without threatening the credit and benefit due to its discoverer.

Patentability of Products of Nature

Products of nature as they are found in their natural environment are generally not patentable. *'An inventor who wishes to patent a chemical product obtained from nature must avoid the natural products exception'.* One way to avoid this exception is to synthesise the natural compound with a molecular structure that is somewhat different from the molecular structure of the natural product while retaining the benefits of the natural product. A second way of avoiding the natural product exception is to purify the naturally occurring substance. However, mere purification is usually not enough to make the natural compound patentable, the purified product must produce 'unexpected results'.

Table 30.1: Natural product patents in various countries

Country	*Number of Patents*	*Percentage*
Belgium	2	0.8
Brazil	1	0.4
China	14	5.6
Czechoslovakia	2	0.8
European Union	26	10.5
France	5	2.0
Germany	12	4.8
Hungary	1	0.4
Japan	148	59.6
Poland	2	0.8
United Kingdom	2	0.8
United States	13	5.2
Soviet Union	7	2.8

With American drug firms moving away from natural products, the Japanese are increasing their share of the world's natural product patents. Surveys (Duke 1990) over the last four years have shown that the Japanese percentage of the world's natural product patents surged from 40% to 60%. In 1990, at least among those natural product patents reported in Phytotherapy Research, Japan obtained more than five times the number of patents that the United States did (Table 30.1). As American consumer demand for the *natural* increases, the pharmaceutical dissatisfaction for the *natural* ironically also increases.

Indian Scenario on Patents

There was a strategic shift from the liberal features of the Indian Patents and Designs Act 1911 (Act II of 1911) to the new regime, which introduced restrictive changes related to patenting of inventions, especially in the areas of chemicals, pharmaceuticals, agrochemicals and foods. The granting of patents for inventions claiming substances intended for use or capable of being used as food, medicine or drugs, or all substances resulting from chemical processes, was withdrawn. However, the claims for methods or processes of manufacture remained patentable.

The Ministry of Commerce has already initiated a Patent Office infrastructure modernisation programme for the electronic submission of patent applications, prosecution, and publication of the Gazette of India and electronic databases of patents, designs and trademarks. There is no official electronic database of patents published by the Patent Office as of now. However, the Department of Science and Technology, under the Technology Information and Forecasting Council (TIFAC), has published a CD of the titles of the filed and granted patents in India. This has also been made available, by subscription, on TIFAC's website. The creation of a Traditional Knowledge Digital Library (an essentially Indian initiative) on traditional medicinal plants and systems in India and linking it to the International Patent Classification System (IPC) through a Traditional Knowledge Resource Classification System (TKRC) is an important conceptual step taken in the last few years. In summary, India has come a long way and is now on the threshold of a new patent paradigm and is preparing to set up world-class patents and patents information systems.

Patents on Medicinal Plants

A few examples of patents on medicinal plants are given below (Source: US patents, Herbal gram)

- Council for Scientific and Industrial Research (CSIR): India's successful challenging of a US patent (No. 5,401,504) on the use of turmeric (Curcuma longa L., Zingiberaceae) for healing has been an encouraging victory for Indian activists campaigning to protect indigenous wisdom.
- Uses of aloe products: Inventors Bill H McAnalley and others assigned to Carrington Laboratories, Inc., Irving, TX. US Patent 5,308,838, issued May 3, 1994.
- Extracts of ginkgo biloba and their methods of preparation: Invented by Ezio Bombardelli, Giuseppe Mustich and Marco Bertani, all from Milan, Italy. US Patent 5,700,468. Assigned to Indena, SpA, Milan, Italy. Issued December 23, 1997.
- Anxiolytic ginger/ginkgo combination: Invented by Rudiger Hacker (Herrsching, Germany) and Claudia Mattern (Starnberg, Germany). US Patent 5,622,704. Assigned to Arrowdean Limited., Dublin, Ireland. Issued April 22, 1997.
- Medication for impotence containing lyophilised roe and a powdered extract of ginkgo biloba: Invented by Lotfy Ismail Omar (Kew Gardens, NY). US Patent 5,730,987. No assignee. Issued March 24, 1998.
- Process for the formation, isolation and purification of comestible xanthophyll crystals from plants: Invented by

Rodney L Ausich and David J Sanders (Des Moines, IA) and assigned to Kemin Industries, Inc. (Des Moines, IA). US Patent 5,648,564. Issued July 15, 1997.

- Neem oil as a male contraceptive, invented by Gursaran P Talwar, Shakti N Upadhyay and Suman Dhawan (JNU Complex, Shahid Jeet Singh Marg, New Delhi 110 067, IN), no assignee. US Patent 5,501,855, issued March 26, 1996.
- Mistletoe: Pharmaceutical preparations derived from European mistletoe, and pharmaceutical preparations derived from Korean mistletoe. Invented by Tasneem A Khwaja (Newport Beach, CA), and assigned to University of Southern California (Los Angeles, Aug. 20, 1996, and 5,565,200, issued October 15, 1996.)
- Ashwagandha, Sallai Guggul, Turmeric, Ginger combination: Method of treating musculoskeletal disease and a novel composition, invented by Bhushan Patwardhan (1471 Shukarwar Peth, Bhaumaharaj Bol, Poona 411 002, IN), no assignee. US Patent 5,494,668, issued February 27, 1996.
- Tobacco: Tobacco extract composition and method, invented by Joseph A. von Fraunhofer (Baltimore, MD), and assigned to University of Louisville (Louisville, KY). US Patent 5,435,941, issued July 25, 1995.
- Method of extracting a physiologically active substance from the husks of pine nuts and anticontagion medicine made of said extract as principal raw material: Invented by Masazumi Yoshihara et al., and assigned to Masazumi Yoshihara, Hiroshima, Japan. US Patent 5,241,091 issued August 31, 1993.
- Pycnanthus Angolensis; Terpenoid-type quinones for treatment of diabetes. Invented by Rosa P Ubillas, Jolad D Shivanand, Christopher D Mendez, Diana M Fort, Joseph L Evans, and Jian Luo; all of California. Assigned to Shaman Pharmaceuticals, Inc., South San Francisco, CA. US Patent 5,674,900, issued October 7, 1997.
- Cryptolepis: Hypoglycemic agent from Cryptolepis. Invented by Jian Luo, Diana M Fort, Donald E Bierer and Reimar C Bruening, all of California. Assigned to Shaman Pharmaceuticals, Inc., South San Francisco, CA. US Patent 5,629,319, issued May 13, 1997.
- Cryptolepine Analogs: Cryptolepine analogs with hypoglycemic activity. Invented by Donald E Bierer of Daly City, CA. Assigned to Shaman Pharmaceuticals, Inc., South San Francisco, CA. US Patent 5,681,958, issued October 28, 1997.
- Treatment of skin diseases using ginkgolide PAF antagonists: Invented by Ruth Korth, D-80639, Munich, Federal Republic of Germany. Assigned to Ruth Korth, Munich, Federal Republic of Germany. US Patent 5,605,927, issued February 25, 1997.
- Cinnamon: Method for inhibiting growth of Helicobacter priori. Invented by Itzhak Neeman, Mina Tabak and Robert Armon. Assigned to Technion Research & Development Foundation Ltd., Technion City, Israel. US Patent 5,560,912 issued October 1, 1996.
- Piperine: Use of piperine to increase the bioavailability of nutritional compounds. Invented by Muhammed Majeed, Vladimir Badmaev and R Rajendran. Assigned to Sabinsa Corporation, Piscataway, NJ. US Patent 5,536,506 issued July 16, 1996.

- Ciwujla: Method to improve performance during exercise using the ciwujia plant. Invented by Robert Portman. Assigned to PacificHealth Laboratories, Inc., Woodbridge, NJ. US Patent 5,585,101 issued December 17, 1996.
- Polygonum: Composition and method for treating hyperglycemia utilising an extract of Polygonum multiflorum. Invented by Nan-Zheng Cheng and Barbara Stoecker. Assigned The Board of Regents of Oklahoma State University, Stillwater, OK. US Patent 5,531,991 issued July 2, 1996.
- Herbal cancer treatment: Natural composition extracted from plants used in the treatment of cancer. Invented by Howard David Kass, Valley Village, CA; Arnold I. Freeman, Azor Modiin, Israel; and Albert Leyva, Lenexa, KS. Applicant: Howard David Kass, Valley Village, CA. US Patent 5,876,728. Issued March 2, 1999.
- Hemorrhoid treatment: Herbal composition for hemorrhoid treatment. invented by Mercedes Flores Garza, Houston, TX. Assigned to Mon's Tea Partnership, Houston, TX. US Patent 5,869,059. Issued Feb. 9, 1999.
- Weight loss compound: Herbal appetite suppressant and weight loss composition. Invented by Brian Haveson, Yardley, PA. Assigned to HPF, L.L.C., Horsham, PA. US Patent 5,798,101. Issued Aug. 25, 1998.
- Method of reducing blood glucose by administering Harunganin or Vismin: Invented by Wayne DeWald Inman (Belmont, CA) and Jian Luo (Brisbane, CA) and assigned to Shaman Pharmaceuticals, Inc., South San Francisco, CA. US Patent 5,837,255. Issued Nov. 17, 1998.
- Plant patents: Process for preparing grape seed extracts enriched in procyanidol oligomers. Invented by Enrico Frangi and others, and assigned to Tecnofarmaci S.p.A. (Pomezia, Italy) and Indena S.p.A. (Milan, Italy). US Patent 5,484,594 issued January 15, 1996.

Intellectual Property Web Resources

INDIA

- Patents Act 1970
  Patents (Amendment) Act, 1999
  Patents (Amendment) Act, 2002
  http://patentoffice.nic.in
- Design Act 2000
  http://patentoffice.nic.in

Trademark Acts

- http://www.tmrindia.com

Copyright

- http://www.education.nic.in

General information

- http://www.iprlawindia.org
- www.indiainfoline.com
- www.indiaip.com
- www.nrdcindia.com
- www.lawguru.com
- www.laws4india.com

INTERNATIONAL

- Australia
  http://www.aipo.gov.au
- Austria
  http://www.ping.at/patent/index.htm
- Brazil
  http://www.bdt.org.br/bdt/inpi
- Canada
  http://strategic.ic.gc.ca

- China, People's Republic of
  http://www.cpo.cn.net/
- Croatia
  http://pubwww.srce.hr/patent
- Denmark
  http://www.dkpto.dk/
- European Patent Office
  http://www.european-patent-office.org
- Trilateral Offices' (EPO, JPO, USPTO) Trilateral Statistics Report, 1995 Edition, http://www.epo.co.at/epo/tritab.htm (2 Jan97)
- Finland
  http://www.prh.fi/
- France
  http://www.evariste.anvar.fr/inpi/
- Germany
  http://www.deutsches-Patentamt.de/
- Greece
  http://www.epo.co.at/epo/patlib/country/greece/
- Hong Kong
  http://www.houston.com.hk/hkgipd
- Hungary
  http://www.hpo.hu
- Patent Facilitating Cell,India
  http://www.indianpatents.org.in
- TIFAC
  http://www.tifac.org.in
- Italy
  http://www.epo.co.at/epo/patlib/country/um_noit.htm
- Japan
  http://www.jpo-miti.go.jp
- Korea
  http://www.ik.co.kr/kopatent/work.htm
- Lithuania
  http://vytautas.is.lt/vpb/engl/
- Luxembourg
  http://www.etat.lu/EC/
- Malaysia
  http://kpdnhq.gov.my/ip/
- Monaco
  http://www.epo.co.at/epo/patlib/country/monaco/
- New Zealand
  http://www.govt.nz/ps/min/com/patent/
- Peru
  http://www.rcp.net.pe/INDECOPI/indecopi.htm
- Poland
  http://www.ibspan.waw.pl/
- Portugal
  http://www.inpi.pt/
- Romania
  http://www.osim.ro/
- Slovenia
  http://www.sipo.mzt.si
- Spain
  http://www.eunet.es/InterStand/patentes/index.html
- Sweden
  http://www.prv.se
- United Kingdom
  http://www.patent.gov.uk/
- World Intellectual Property Organization (WIPO)
  http://www.wipo.org

Key Messages

- Herbal medicines play an important role in foreign trade; hence the patenting of the process of cultivation and methods of production reserves and protects the traditional knowledge of individual countries.
- Although products from nature, such as plants, cannot be patented, a genetically modified variety can be patented.
- Patents are essential, as they indicate the purity and originality of individual herbs.
- Various researchers have procured their patent on the method of isolation/extraction, process, cultivation and packaging of herbs to reserve their interest in the same.
- Patents have become one of the essential elements in the present era of natural product drug discovery.

Questions

1. What are patents? Write short notes on copyrights and trademarks.
2. Discuss the criteria for the patentability of a product.
3. Describe in detail the patentability of natural products.
4. Write a note on the Indian scenario on patents.
5. Give five examples of patent-related medicinal plants.
6. List out websites related to patents in different countries.

Index